D1306144

Public Management Information Systems

Bruce Rocheleau
Northern Illinois University, USA

IDEA GROUP PUBLISHING

Hershey • London • Melbourne • Singapore

Acquisitions Editor:	Michelle Potter
Development Editor:	Kristin Roth
Senior Managing Editor:	Amanda Appicello
Managing Editor:	Jennifer Neidig
Copy Editor:	Bernard J. Kieklak, Jr.
Typesetter:	Cindy Consonery
Cover Design:	Lisa Tosheff
Printed at:	Integrated Book Technology

Published in the United States of America by
Idea Group Publishing (an imprint of Idea Group Inc.)
701 E. Chocolate Avenue
Hershey PA 17033
Tel: 717-533-8845
Fax: 717-533-8661
E-mail: cust@idea-group.com
Web site: http://www.idea-group.com

and in the United Kingdom by
Idea Group Publishing (an imprint of Idea Group Inc.)
3 Henrietta Street
Covent Garden
London WC2E 8LU
Tel: 44 20 7240 0856
Fax: 44 20 7379 0609
Web site: http://www.eurospanonline.com

Copyright © 2006 by Idea Group Inc. All rights reserved. No part of this book may be reproduced, stored or distributed in any form or by any means, electronic or mechanical, including photocopying, without written permission from the publisher.

Product or company names used in this book are for identification purposes only. Inclusion of the names of the products or companies does not indicate a claim of ownership by IGI of the trademark or registered trademark.

Library of Congress Cataloging-in-Publication Data

Rocheleau, Bruce A.
  Public management information systems / Bruce Rocheleau.
      p. cm.
  Includes bibliographical references and index.
  Summary: "This book focuses on the key processes faced by managers in governmental organizations, including planning, purchasing, training and learning, politics, accountability, ethics, best practices, and evaluation"--provided by publisher.
    ISBN 1-59140-807-5 (hardcover) -- ISBN 1-59140-808-3 (softcover) -- ISBN 1-59140-809-1 (ebook)
  1. Public administration--Data processing. 2. Management information systems. I. Title.
  JF1525.A8R62 2005
   352.3'8'011--dc22
                            2005022458

British Cataloguing in Publication Data
A Cataloguing in Publication record for this book is available from the British Library.

All work contributed to this book is new, previously-unpublished material. The views expressed in this book are those of the authors, but not necessarily of the publisher.

Public Management Information Systems

Table of Contents

Preface vi
Framework for Governmental Information Management ix
The External Environment xi
The Organizational Environment xiii
Plan of the Book xxi
References xxiii
Additional Reading xxv
Key Concepts xxvi
Discussion Questions xxvi
Exercises xxvii

**Chapter I. Public and Private Information Systems: How Are They Similar?
How Are They Different?** 1
Introduction 1
Previous Research 2
Competition and Perceived Importance of Information Systems 5
Methodology 11
Findings 12
Implications 15
References 18
Additional Reading 21
Key Concepts 21
Discussion Questions 22
Exercise 22

Chapter II. Planning for Information Technology in the Public Sector 23
Introduction: Why Plan? 23
Components of Information Technology Plans 26
Conclusion 50
References 50
Further Reading 52
Key Concepts 53
Discussion Questions 54
Exercises 54

Chapter III. Procuring Information Technology for Government **56**
Introduction 56
The Needs Assessment Process in Purchasing 57
The Contracting Process 75
Project Management Issues 87
Conclusion 91
References.. 92
Further Reading.. 96
Key Concepts 97
Discussion Questions 98
Exercises 99

Chapter IV. Prescriptions for IT in Government: How Do We Know What Works Best? **100**
Introduction 100
Prescription Sources 101
Best Practices 102
Traditional Survey and Other Quantitative Analyses of Information
    Management 114
Benchmarks and Benchmarking 116
The Problem and Disaster Literature 118
Conclusion 121
References.. 122
Additional Reading 126
Key Concepts 126
Discussion Questions 126
Exercises 127

Chapter V. Electronic Government **128**
Introduction 128
Financing E-Government 134
Planning for E-Government 140
E-Government Planning and Enterprise Architectures 145
Web Site Design and Evaluation Issues 157
References.. 168
Additional Reading 173
Key Concepts 173
Discussion Questions 174
Exercises 175

Chapter VI. Politics, Leadership, and Information Technology **177**
Introduction 177
Information Systems and Internal Organizational Politics 181
The External Politics of Information Management 194
Conclusion 207
References.. 207
Additional Reading 213

Key Concepts 214
Discussion Questions 214
Exercises 215

Chapter VII. Information Technology, Training, and Organizational Learning **216**
Introduction 216
Planning for Learning: Needs Assessment 221
Sources for IT Training 223
E-Learning and Online Communication 226
Informal Learning 226
References 231
Additional Reading 233
Key Concepts 234
Discussion Questions 234
Exercises 235

Chapter VIII. Information Management and Ethical Issues in Government **236**
Introduction 236
Factors That Influence Ethical Behavior 237
Ethical and Legal Issues Concerning Computer-Mediated Communication .. 238
The Difference Between Digital and Non-Digital Communication 239
Organizational Computer-Mediated Communication Policies 241
Freedom of Information Acts and Electronic Records 255
Privacy and Ownership of Data 258
Ethical and Legal Policies for E-Government 260
Accuracy of Government Data and Legal Liability 260
Web Site Advertising and Links to Government Web Sites 261
Computer-Matching and Privacy Laws 262
Purchasing and Legal Issues 264
Conclusion 264
References 265
Additional Reading 271
Key Concepts 272
Discussion Questions 272
Exercises 273

Chapter IX. Evaluation and Information Technology **274**
Introduction 274
Questions to Ask in Planning for Evaluation of IT 277
Evaluation Approaches and Models 288
Examples of Governmental Evaluation Measures 294
Conclusion 302
References 302
Additional Reading 306
Key Concepts 306

Discussion Questions 307
Exercises 307

Chapter X. Governments and IT Sharing **308**
Introduction 308
Previous Research 310
Sources 312
Sharing Among Local Governments 312
Criminal Justice Sharing Efforts: Local-Local and State-Local Efforts 315
State-Local (Including Private Provider) Systems 317
State-to-State and Interdepartmental Sharing Within States 318
Federal-State Intergovernmental Sharing 319
Informal Sharing 324
Framework for Studying Sharing Relationships 324
Conclusion 327
References 329
Key Concepts 333
Discussion Questions 334
Exercises 334

**Chapter XI. Information Technology, Accountability, and Information
Stewardship** **335**
Introduction 335
E-Reporting 336
Accountability and Empirical Studies of Performance Measurement 345
Conclusion and Implications 367
References 369
Key Concepts 375
Discussion Questions 376
Exercises 376

About the Author **378**

Index **379**

Preface

Over the past two decades, governmental information systems have changed from being a relatively unimportant "back office" function to a crucial element in making governmental organizations more accountable, efficient, and effective. Prior to the revolutions brought on by personal computers and the Internet, most government employees, including top managers, gave little attention to computerized information systems. Information systems were primarily used for routine reports and transactions such as payroll and utility billing. Now information technology is viewed as a major asset that needs to be actively managed. Information technology (IT) has become integral to the jobs of most employees and now is used by citizens through e-government. Consequently, it is incumbent on governmental managers to understand how to build and maintain information systems that are responsive to their users — both internal and external. It is my thesis that generalist managers and end users must play an active role in the planning and implementation of these systems for these systems to be responsive. They must not leave IT to the technicians.

There is a substantial literature on information management aimed at managers in the private sector. There are very few such books that concentrate on public sector information systems. Why not just have managers apply the same principles as employed in the private sector? Why is it necessary to develop a book for governmental managers? Although public and private organizations use much the same hardware and software, there are important differences concerning the goals and purposes of these systems that influence every aspect of computing, from planning to evaluation. Consequently, we need a book devoted to governmental information system management. This book will help provide generalist managers with an overview of governmental information management. It will also assist IT managers who have strong technical backgrounds but need to better understand the governmental context.

I have built upon several bodies of knowledge in this book. First, I synthesize from the extensive bodies of research about information management in public and private sectors. Although there are important differences in information management between the public and private sectors, I also agree that the two sectors perform many of the same functions, face many similar dilemmas, and that the two sectors can learn from each other. Indeed, for the last decade, most public sector agencies have been engaged in attempting to emulate private sector practices concerning their purchasing methods. Thus the private sector literature provides relevant guidance, although they often need to be adjusted to the governmental context. Moreover, the empirical literature on governmental information systems is limited (e.g., Kraemer & Dedrick, 1997), although there is a newly emerging body of research on certain topics, such as e-government activities. In short, we attempt to ground our observations as much as possible in information management research conducted in both the public and private sectors.

Second, I have searched for detailed examples of governmental information management in practitioner-oriented magazines, as well as online sources, provided by public IT managers themselves. The speed of IT innovation and implementation leads to a situation where academic research often lags far behind the existing practices of management. Consequently, I have employed these other sources because they provide information on emerging technologies that have not been systematically studied by researchers. However, it is important to note the limitations and potential bias of these sources. The limitations include the fact that the information from these sources is often not very systematic or detailed in nature and is generally presented by someone involved in the implementation, not an independent outsider. I have found valuable sources from the Internet, resulting from the fact that many governments are now putting their plans, RFPs (Request for Proposals), and other relevant documents online. Many of these provide excellent, and often candid, insights into how they manage IT.

Thirdly, I employ my own experiences of more than 20 years of studying information management in governmental organizations. I have conducted information management research at the federal, state, and local governmental levels. Several of my research projects involved case studies and interviews with a wide variety of governmental staff concerning information systems. I also employ information I have gained from listservs comprised of IT officials in government, as well as my experiences in organizations composed primarily of governmental IT directors. I have had many students who work in the governmental IT field and I make use of their experiences and insights.

To supplement and update this information, I conducted case studies of 14 governmental organizations during 2003. In these case studies, I interviewed the IT director and other IT staff, one or more members of "generalist management," and one or more end users. In addition, I conducted interviews with others, such as consultants and vendors, who have worked extensively with governmental organizations. The total number of interviews was 51. These interviews were taped and transcribed and I have included many passages from them in this book. The interviews covered a wide range of topics. To ensure candor, the interviewees were promised complete confidentiality, and the benefits of this candor are evident in the openness of the responses that I employ, such as admitting problems and limitations they have experienced. These interviews were conducted in the Midwest but I believe that experiences in the IT field are generic. The commonality of the problems of governmental information management is reflected in the discussions I have observed in the listservs of national organizations (e.g., Government Management Information Sciences organization) — the same problems and issues appear regardless of location. In my view, qualitative research such as comparative case studies offers important insights into crucial issues. The interviews included a range of organizations in size but included many organizations that are small (averaging about 50,000 employees) in population and an IT staff of six. Smaller governments represent a large portion of public sector agencies but they are grossly underrepresented in books and articles on governmental information systems and thus this book will be an important resource for them. Despite their small size, these organizations have to implement many of the same technologies that large organizations with large IT staffs do. Consequently, researchers need to pay more attention to organizations with limited IT staff and resources and this book fills a significant gap.

Reliance on my experiences, interviews, and qualitative case studies is necessary due to the limitations of research on governmental information systems. Although there is a growing body of literature on governmental information systems that I draw upon, this research has been focused primarily on a few areas, such as e-government and Web-related technologies. Although this research has furnished some important insights, it does not address many of the issues which I have found to be central to understanding the governments and IT, such as the critical importance of the informal system. Consequently, my interviews focus on these areas that have been lightly researched and that require "rich" information, such as observation and open-ended interviews because of their sensitive and complex nature.

Any book on information technology will quickly become dated in terms of the technical aspects that are covered. For example, just a decade ago, the use of e-mail and Web sites was rare for most organizations, and now their use is universal. By focusing on underlying management processes and issues, the information I present here will remain relevant despite changes in the specific hardware and software employed. I welcome feedback and suggestions from readers.

Research in information management tends to be prescriptive in nature. Works, including this one, tend to focus on developing insights into what can improve the responsiveness of governmental systems. Prescriptive advice is common in works in the IT field. Although I also do develop prescriptions in this book, I try to be cautious in doing so by basing them on more than one source of information, while at the same time making readers aware of the tentativeness of these conclusions. When I feel that there is strong evidence concerning prescriptions, I state these prescriptions. However, when there is disagreement, or I feel that the there is no strong evidence for a particular approach, I prefer to state the various alternatives and not to endorse particular prescriptions. In this respect, this is not a traditional textbook in which clear sets of steps or prescriptions are given to be followed. I do not believe that the knowledge base justifies such an approach in many of the areas that are covered.

Framework for Governmental Information Management

As I have studied information systems for more than 20 years, I have continually looked for relevant frameworks and theories that will help guide my understanding of information systems. There are numerous conceptual frameworks for studying IT and they cover a myriad of variables and often are aimed at the perspective of researchers in the IT field (e.g., Ives, Hamilton, & Davis, 1980). I have borrowed from this previous work in developing my framework, but my focus is different. In the past, the interest of governmental managers in IT has been sporadic and not focused on the most important issues. Kraemer and King (1976) argue that public executives spend too much of their time on decisions concerning the purchase of equipment and too little on other important information management issues, such as the goals of computing. Frameworks need to simplify reality and draw attention to factors that are most critical to success. Most of these frameworks have been academic in nature, as their purpose has been to guide researchers (Ives, Hamilton, & Davis, 1980). My goal here is practical, not academic. The purpose of my framework (see Figure 1) is to make generalist managers aware of the major forces, actors, processes, and managerial skills that determine how responsive information systems will be to the needs of political executives and legislators, citizens, internal staff, business and other groups. The framework distinguishes between external and internal forces. The external forces have become much more important over the last decade as governmental systems now directly serve them. In each environment, my framework alerts generalist managers to underlying factors which they need to understand if they are to identify good, achievable goals for their organization. It also identifies key actors whose interests need to be considered in making governmental IT policy. Next it identifies key IT processes in which managers need to participate if these processes are to be successful. The model depicts critical managerial skills that need to be exercised if the desired services and outcomes are to be achieved. Overall, I believe that managers can use this framework as a "roadmap" to focus their efforts on making their IT systems as responsive as possible to the full range of users. Although I have organized this book so that I focus on certain processes (e.g., purchasing, planning, training and evaluation) in particular chapters, in practice it is impossible to separate these processes — they are integrally related to one another and to various issues such as politics, leadership, and ethical issues that will appear in several of the chapters.

Figure 1. A framework for understanding governmental information management

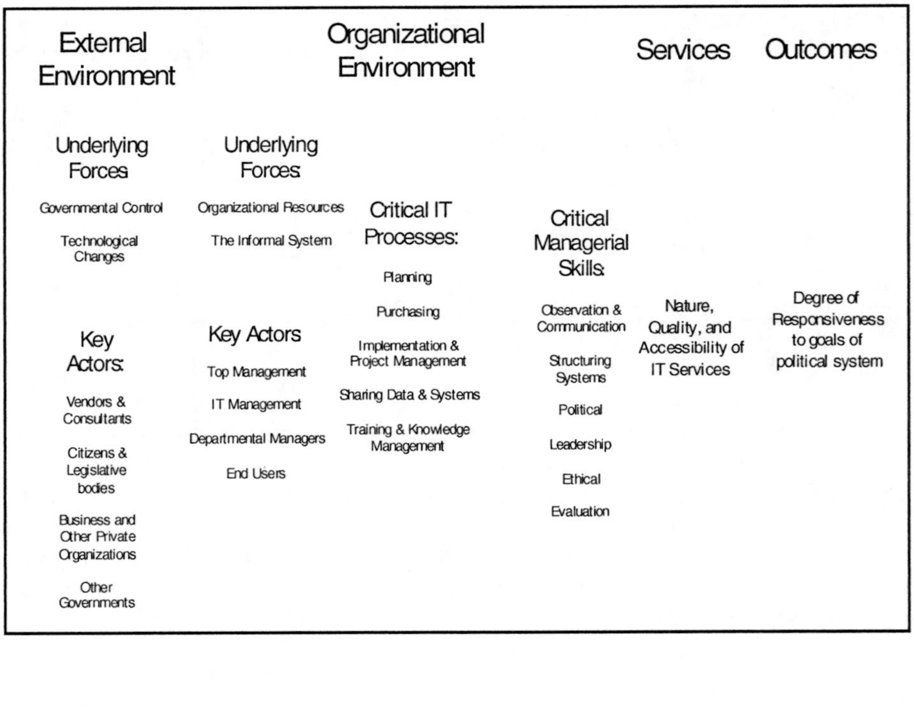

The External Environment

The Impact of Sector: Governmental Control

In my model, I use the term "underlying factors" to refer to those forces that exert a pervasive influence over IT policy and outcomes but over which generalist managers exert little if any control. In my view, the role of sector is important. Governmental information systems have some important differences in their computing from the private for-profit sector. In particular, the goals of computing in the government sector are more complex and thus not easily translatable into hard business cases that emphasize financial outcomes and competitive advantage (Bozeman & Bretschneider, 1986; Center for Technology in Government, 1996). For example, governmental computing is subject to more stringent laws concerning access and privacy than most private data. The "customers" of governmental computing are a much broader constituency since, theoretically, all citizens have a direct investment in the systems. Although there are some forms of mild competition among general-purpose governments, such as in the area of economic development, competition is not the driving force for IT investment that it is in the private sector. Governmental IT investments are often made for service reasons. Indeed, governmental organizations tend to be externally oriented and generally freely share their "secrets" of IT success, while private sector companies will guard them if they believe they contribute to competitive advantage. Thus planning and evaluation of governmental IT systems will be quite different because non-economic goals will be more important. It is important for governmental managers not to simply assume that they can blindly copy processes and techniques taken from the private sector and expect to be successful. We will devote a chapter to a detailed comparison of public and private computing.

Technological Change

Organizations have to continually adapt to rapidly changing hardware and software. As technologies such as the use of intranets, e-mail, and the World Wide Web have become integral to everyday management, organizations have to ensure that they provide the infrastructure to ensure these crucial applications work in a timely and reliable manner. Networks become much more complex not only due to the increased number of important applications, but also due to the fact that organizations are demanding that their data be integrated. Organizations are faced with decisions as to whether they should purchase and implement new technologies such as geographic information systems (GIS), mobile computing, enterprise resource planning (ERP) systems, customer resource management (CRM), among many. As a consequence, the complexity of organizational systems today is far greater than it was two decades ago, so that even small organizations often have a complex array of servers, routers, databases, and many different and complex software technologies. Given the relatively small IT staffs that most governmental organizations have, I have wondered how these organizations cope with this rapidly changing technology. Given the fact that governments cannot make profits, they need to be able to develop a process to make reasoned decisions about IT investments. When is it worthwhile to invest in expensive new systems or even upgrades? Managers must be engaged in understanding the potential of new technologies so they can make informed decisions. In my chapters on planning and purchasing of information technology, I will examine the processes by which organizations make decisions about new technologies.

Key Actors in the External Environment

Governmental staff must learn how to make effective use of vendors and consultants because they are major vehicles for dealing with this rapidly changing and complex technology. It is virtually impossible for internal staff to master all of the new hardware and software that governmental organizations will need to adopt. Negotiating contracts with vendors and consultants is a major challenge, but the relationship does not stop there. Vendors and consultants are essential components of the maintenance and support of governmental IT systems. Indeed, in some organizations, vendors and consultants are present so often that they become part of the organization's IT staff. Yet there is little research in the public sector on the role and impact of vendors and consultants on information management. I will give in-depth consideration to vendors and consultants in the chapter on purchasing.

The customers of governmental IT used to be primarily internal managers and employees, but the development of e-government has provided a means for governments, businesses, and citizens to conduct many operations online and consequently their influence over governmental IT has grown (Stowers, 2001). Many governments are using computer technology to provide information and services to citizens (G2C). For example, many governments use IT to automate the process of sending notices to property-owners who live near a proposed development. Likewise, citizens may now use computers to provide input to government (C2G) on rules and regulations (e.g., Mahler, 2002). Legislative bodies have always exerted control over IT projects of any size, but until recent years IT projects have tended to have low salience for them. In several chapters, including those on planning, purchasing, and politics, I will discuss the role that legislative bodies and citizens have played in information management.

Governmental organizations generally have particular groups that have a major investment in their policies and actions. For example, many governments are concerned with economic development and have created "extranets" to allow businesses (such as developers) to be served on a 24/7 basis for obtaining permits for new projects. These extranets allow governments to provide information to businesses (G2B) and to receive information from the businesses (B2G).

Many e-government services are directed at other governments (G2G), including interactions related to funding and regulations. There are many intergovernmental programs such as human services and criminal justice programs that involve federal, state and local governments. Sharing of information among governments in some cases is legally required, while in others is optional and voluntary. Many governments, particularly smaller governments, have developed shared efforts concerning technologies such as GIS that are too costly for them to undertake individually. Consequently, other governments are also "end users" and their interests need to be taken into consideration. Therefore, I have included a chapter devoted to intergovernmental information systems.

The Organizational Environment

Organizational Size and Resources

It would seem obvious that organizational size and resources have a tremendous impact on how computing is to be managed in government, but there has been little research (Note: Brudney & Selden, 1995, is one exception) devoted to studying smaller governments in empirical research or management literature on government computing. The literature that does exist concerning computing has tended to focus on large organizations such as states and major cities (e.g., Barrett & Greene, 2001). But many government agencies are small with minimal, and sometimes no, full-time professional IT staff. Yet they are faced with dealing with many of the same demands as large governmental organizations such as e-government, need for data integration, and networking. Small organizations have notable successes and have been leaders in some aspects of IT. But size and resources do influence IT administration. In these small organizations, generalist managers will need to play a substantial role not only for leadership but also for dealing with vendors and consultants and making decisions about whether to adopt expensive new technologies such as GIS. Therefore, this book will also give consideration to the dilemmas of smaller governments.

The Informal System and Non-Digital Data

A major theme of this book is that computerized and formal information system components provide only a portion of the knowledge required by decision-makers in government. A manager's information can be divided into two categories of sources: (1) Formal sources that are digitized; and (2) Informal sources that are communicated by (unrecorded) conversations and/or observations. Generalist managers need to be aware of the need to cultivate informal sources and to integrate that information with the formal, digitized system. It is clear that the role of digitized information has significantly increased over the last two decades vis-à-vis informal information. The presence of end-user tools such as spreadsheets and easy-to-use data base systems has made formal tools far more useful for everyday tasks than the data present from the mainframe days characterized by routine reports. Even more importantly, e-mail and related communication technologies allow workers to quickly share valuable information and insights with a wide range of people in similar positions.

But IT research has downplayed or ignored the role of information gathered outside the digitized system, through participant observations and other qualitative sources. Research has found that executives favor face-to-face meetings, both scheduled and unscheduled, over written media when dealing with entrepreneurial tasks and handling disturbances (McLeod & Jones, 1987). Indeed, executives rate many of the formal reports they receive as having little or no value and rated oral media (e.g., information from meetings) as the most valuable (McLeod & Jones, 1987). Part of this preference for these sources has been ascribed to the need for *"rich" data*. Daft (e.g., Daft & Wiginton, 1979) has defined richness of information as "the capacity for multiple cues and rapid feedback such as that obtained in face-to-face oral communication." Daft and other researchers have found that managers favor the use of rich information when dealing with situations of *equivocality*. These are situations involving messages that are "ambivalent and open to multiple meanings" (Jones, Saunders, & McLeod, Jr., 1988-89; Weick, 1979), such as negotiating, bargaining, and persuasion.

An even more important issue than the concern with richness is that non-digital data can be private and this privacy is crucial to conducting many important tasks. Although tele-conferencing and other digital communication systems provide the possibility of digitizing rich data (e.g., tele-conferencing can reveal body language, inflection of voice, etc.), the fact that they are recorded makes them fundamentally different from confidential face-to-face exchanges. Participants who are aware that the information is being recorded are likely to act differently than if it were not.

The implications are important for information management because the more sensitive the topic, the more likely that informal data will play a large role. For example, we know that politics influences many governmental decisions. Yet public bureaucracies need to avoid the appearance of making decisions on the basis of politics. Consequently, it is dangerous to put politically-relevant information in print form, much less into computer systems. It is important for public officials to be able to deny that political considerations played a role in decisions even though we know that politics does influence policy. Thus much of the information used to make sensitive decisions will be gathered and discussed outside the formal, digital information system.

Such findings do not mean that computerized information is irrelevant or unused by executives. Many of those reporting to executives are heavy users of information technology and thus executives often are heavy indirect users of information technology (McLeod & Jones, 1987). Informal and formal information systems complement each other. Many of the rich data sources are cultivated by executives in order to corroborate information received from formal information sources. As managers ascend the ladder, they tend to use computers less. In summary, McKinnon and Bruns (1992) recently concluded that personal interactions remain the main vehicle for exchange of information:

"...formal reports serving mainly to reinforce orally exchanged information. There are three major modes of interpersonal communications: meetings, one-to-one interactions, and unfocused walking through the business, known as management by walking around." (p. 124)

Preference for rich information is not restricted to executives. Although police have sophisticated information technology, the most important information to solve cases often does not reside in information systems but requires that police concentrate more on "people issues" (Laudon, 1986). Wilson has pointed out that the most valuable information is gained by talking with suspects and their associates and visiting places where they are likely to be found but there are few incentives to do this (Wilson, 1984, p. 8). The centrality of the informal system has long been recognized by public administration researchers and is prominent in Simon, Smithburg and Thompson's (1961) text on how public organizations work. Classic studies such as Roethlisberger and Dickson's (1939) Hawthorne Study and Blau's The Dynamics of Bureaucracy showed how workers made use of the informal system (e.g., set up informal norms about quotas) to resist unwelcome threats from the formal system. Despite its significance, IT researchers have given it little emphasis in their research (Orlikowski & Barley, 2001). A complicat-

Figure 2. Manager's personal information system

Manager's Informal Information System:	*Interaction between Formal and Informal System:*	Formal Organizational Information System:
Methods: Non-digital data gathered through qualitative sources such as: 1. Participant Observation 2. Private, face-to-face discussions with persons Advantages: Gets at information that formal system doesn't and is used to protect employees from formal system. Disadvantage: May be biased, based on a partial perspective, atypical and unreliable. Some typical functions: Develop and maintain friendships and networks to provide information to protect and foster career. Conduct bargaining and other sensitive tasks that have a high degree of equivocality.	*Compare information from both sources. If they agree, confidence is bolstered. If they disagree, seek additional information and/or put faith in one with higher credibility.*	Written reports and digitized data from memos, letters, reports, data bases, and other formal sources. Advantages: Ability to cover entire organization and thus be more comprehensive than data from informal sources. Also, the fact that it is formal allows it to be checked for validity and reliability. Disadvantages: Often does not address most important and sensitive issues. Some typical functions: Accountability to Internal and External sources.

ing factor is the "merger" of the two types of data. As I will discuss in my chapter on communication, many employees share sensitive and personal information via e-mail that formerly would only have been communicated through informal, non-digitized communications. However, there can be adverse consequences to the use of e-mail for sensitive purposes because these e-mails may be subject to open disclosure.

The two types of data, digital and non-digital, can help to make up for the other's gaps and distortions. I will show how knowledge gained from the informal system often helps to throw light on the biases and limitations in digital systems aimed at providing accountability, such as performance measurement systems. The challenge for managers is to gather critical information not included in the formal systems and synthesize it with that available from formal sources (while being aware of the limitations and biases present in all sources of information). Thus, in my framework (see Figure 2), a manager's overall personal information system will be a combination of digital and non-digital inputs. The challenge for managers is to ensure that they integrate information from both sources. I will explore issues related to the informal system in all of my chapters, but particular emphasis will be given in the chapter on accountability and quality of data.

Key Actors: Whose Interest is Served?

Kraemer et al. (1989) developed a model of computing in organizations based on whose interest was served as well as which group controlled IT decision-making. Although their model was developed in the era of mainframe computing, tensions remain among the same three groups on which they focused: top management, IT management, and departmental management.

In the Kraemer model, top management is viewed as the one group who looked at the organization from an enterprise-wide perspective. Thus Kraemer et al. refer to the situation where top management's interests dominate as the "strategic state." Of course, these top managers, both political and non-political, also have career interests, and many managers have found that innovation in IT is one of the best ways to achieve positive recognition and career advancement. In other cases, top managers are disengaged from computing. I will study the role of top management in IT decision-making in several of the chapters.

In the manner in which Kraemer et al. use the term, the IT managers are distinct from the top management because they have their own department or sub-unit of a department (e.g., finance department). In the Kraemer model, the interests of IT tend to be technical with emphasis given to keeping up with state-of-the-art technology (Kraemer et al., 1989, p. 115). In some small governments that I have studied, there is no professional IT manager or any IT staff, and a generalist manager handles the IT function with the assistance of vendors and consultants.

The third category (Kraemer et al., 1989) includes the managers of the "line" departments. This group is seen as focusing on how their substantive, departmental interests are served and are therefore narrower than those of the top management.

In my own interviews, I found that differences in perspectives and goals among these three categories of leaders are still important. However, there have been changes with governmental IT staff. The governmental IT staff I encountered are not as concerned about maintaining state-of-the-art technology as they are about standardization and centralization of decision-making concerning IT hardware and software because they want to minimize the difficulty of maintaining networks and supporting systems. Thus IT managers often need to seek the support of top management in setting strategic objectives and adopting enterprise-wide standards.

A related but complementary point is made by Huxhold's (1991) model of computing in which information systems are viewed as pyramids, with three different levels of information management:

1. **Policy Level**: This level involves top policy-makers and deals with organization-wide concerns such as providing support for making new ordinances.

2. **Managerial Level**: This level involves middle- and upper-level administrators in their management of departmental level issues such as management of personnel and performance monitoring.

3. **Operational Level**: This level involves daily work done at the "street level."

The *operational level* (Huxhold, 1991, pp. 17-20) would include tasks such as identifying information about work to be done at a specific address for the public works department in a city or for a particular client in a human services system. This raw operational data is then aggregated to the *managerial level* so it can be analyzed by departmental and "middle managers" who make decisions, such as to how to improve allocation of personnel, conduct personnel evaluations, and other managerial issues. Finally, the data may be further passed up to the *policy level*, where political and professional administrators at the top of the hierarchy use it to make changes in policy, create new legislation, statutes and laws, and locate new services. Huxhold's point is that in order to be truly effective, an information system needs to be effective on all three levels.

In recent years, much attention has been given to the need to involve top management in making IT policy. Caudle (1996) argued that the most important element of best practices in IT is the involvement of senior management. In the past, senior managers often ignored IT, so the emphasis on the necessity of top management involvement has helped to rectify this neglect. Both the Kraemer et al. and Huxhold models support the importance of having an enterprise-wide perspective.

However, I argue that it is the end users, usually those who are the low ends of the organizational hierarchy, who know the most about the functionality of hardware and software and are the best source of information on the effectiveness of information systems. Moreover, since they usually are the source of the data input into the system, they are crucial to its validity. Their reaction is critical to the success of new systems. They can render systems ineffective by overt or passive resistance, as will be seen in my chapter on the politics of information management. If end users sabotage systems so the systems, or the data emanating from them, are not valid or reliable, then the systems cannot be effective, regardless of the degree of senior level involvement. Often, the membership of IT decision-making bodies emphasizes departmental and top management. This approach may work well if departmental managers represent the views of end users. But for planning and purchasing activities, failure to understand the end users point of view is a deadly mistake. To summarize, generalist managers need to ensure that balanced attention is given to the needs of all of the major groups and remember that the end users form the basis of the IT system.

Critical IT Processes

In this book, I concentrate on critical IT processes in which generalist managers must play an important role in order for the information system to be effective. Some areas, such as security, are extremely important but primarily technical and do not require direct involvement of generalist managers, whose role is to provide the resources needed by IT managers. But the areas outlined in the following sections, although they have major technical aspects, also depend in a major way on judgments and activities of generalist managers if they are to be effective.

Planning

There is a consensus among researchers and experts that strategic planning for IT must be performed and that generalist managers need to be heavily involved in this process. I found discrepancies between these prescriptions and the actual practices of governmental organizations, and I present an in-depth analysis of planning for IT, both as prescribed and as practiced.

Purchasing

Purchasing choices shape the nature of the system and help to determine how successful it will be. Purchasing has many technical aspects that IT staff and other technical experts, such as consultants, will dominate. However, there are many important decisions that generalist managers should participate in, such as establishing the goals of purchases, how much should be spent on IT projects, choices between doing projects in-house versus outsourcing, among others. This book will cover the purchasing process in depth.

Implementation and Project Management

Much of the implementation of systems and project management requires technical knowledge and skills. But generalist managers will by necessity take part in certain crucial aspects that require their authority. Indeed, I will review several examples involving project management where non-technical issues dominated. I will provide additional examples of how generalist managers contribute to both the successes and failures of projects in the chapters on purchasing and politics.

Sharing Data and Systems

One of the strongest movements in IT today is towards enterprise-wide access to data and systems so that any legitimate user can access data from any department. The basic premise is that information should only have to be entered once into an organization's system and should then be available to any department and user who can make effective use of it. Many information needs (e.g., those involving financial and economic development) require the integration of information from several different departments and even other governments. Thus interoperability of systems has become a crucial issue. Also, in government, shared systems between organizations and levels of government are common. Sharing data and systems generally requires strong action on the part of generalist managers because there is often strong resistance to sharing among line departments and among agencies.

Training and other HR Needs Related to Technology

Because of its technical complexity and rapidity of change, training is especially important in the IT area, but both public and private organizations often have difficulty in implementing and sustaining IT training. It tends to be given low priority, especially when budgets are tight. Research shows that most personnel only make use of a fraction of the power of software applications, though organizations devote large amounts on upgrading that software. The chapter on training will discuss alternative approaches to training. More generally, organizations must establish ways for their personnel to take advantage of IT for knowledge-acquisition and this creates demands for cooperative action among generalist managers and the HR and IT departments.

Communication

IT has affected the nature of communication in governmental organizations as a larger portion of information is exchanged via e-mail, and this communication often has important ethical and legal consequences. As I pointed out earlier, managers cannot rely on only digital sources of information. They must gain much of their critical information from observation and qualitative data-gathering methods. Another communication is-sue is that a fairly substantial portion of IT managers come from technical backgrounds and often are not strong communicators. Yet communication is a critical factor in deter-mining how successful they will be in dealing with other departments and with general-ist managers. I will discuss these communication issues throughout the book.

Structuring Systems, Politics, and Leadership

There are many internal and external decisions that involve conflict among different constituencies, such as how to structure the IT decision-making process. For example, what IT decisions should be centralized? Generalist managers need to be engaged with these issues. IT managers lack the formal authority and often the political and negoti-ating skills to solve these conflicts. Thus generalist managers will have to employ political and negotiating skills as well as their formal authority to provide the leader-ship to settle these disputes.

Ethical-Legal

Many ethical and legal issues have arisen concerning computing that require the par-ticipation of generalist managers to resolve. What rules should be imposed concerning the use of governmental computing resources? What penalties should be imposed if they are violated? Should governments raise revenue on their Web sites by advertis-ing? Should government unions be authorized to use organizational systems to com-municate their points? Although a lawyer or consultant knowledgeable about legal aspects of computing may have to be consulted about such issues, many of these necessitate value judgments in which generalist managers will have to be engaged. New technologies are constantly raising new legal and ethical issues. For example, do police have the right to place GPS (Global Positioning System) units on cars of sus-pects without obtaining court authorization (McCullaugh, 2005)? States such as Cali-fornia (Holmes, 2005) have passed several privacy protection laws that can have impli-cations for governmental as well as business organizations. These are examples to illustrate the fact that new technologies and legislation may lead to decisions in which generalist administrators will have to be involved. I will discuss ethical and legal issues in several chapters, including those on communication and purchasing.

Evaluation

Assessing the value of IT in the private sector is difficult and the challenge in the public sector is much greater. There is much dispute on how to measure the effective-ness of governmental information systems due to the complexity of their goals. Despite this difficulty, it is important to evaluate IT because it competes for funding with other investments. Organizations are often dissatisfied with traditional measures used in IT such as the percent downtime or cost indicators, such as the cost per workstation. I discuss the dilemma of evaluation and alternative solutions in the chapter on evalua-tion.

IT as Infrastructure

Internally IT now serves as the infrastructure which organizations employ to deliver services. Ideally, IT will contribute to making these services more accessible and cost effective. Regardless of the government, there is no question that IT has become recognized as the major infrastructure that underlines all other key government functions. Its importance is shown in Figure 3 developed by the Governmental Performance Project of The Maxwell School at Syracuse University in its study of state and local governments. I would like to emphasize again that the "information" includes both non-digital as well as digital information. The range of services provided by the IT staff can vary considerably. Some governmental IT organizations have already invested in systems that can be very expensive, such as geographic information systems (GIS) and enterprise resource planning software, while others find it impossible to afford such systems. Externally, some governments have sought to become major broadband providers in their community, while others are still considering the extent to which they should become involved in e-government. In short, the range of services and functions of the IT leadership can vary greatly depending on the organization, and it is generalist managers who ultimately determine the nature and extent of these services.

IT, Accountability and Data Stewardship Issues

Ultimately, IT will be judged by the political systems and key external users concerning the degree to which it is responsive to their values and goals. Indeed, the distinguishing characteristics of governmental organizations include their focus on openness and accountability. Consequently, an emerging use of governmental IT is to provide greater accountability for public services, such as through online report cards on various

Figure 3. Information as infrastructure

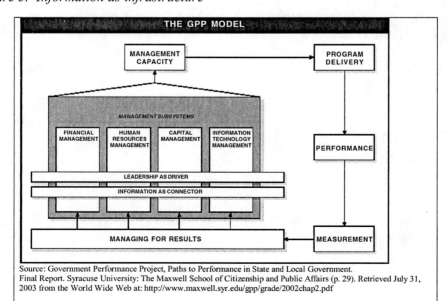

Source: Government Performance Project, Paths to Performance in State and Local Government.
Final Report. Syracuse University: The Maxwell School of Citizenship and Public Affairs (p. 29). Retrieved July 31, 2003 from the World Wide Web at: http://www.maxwell.syr.edu/gpp/grade/2002chap2.pdf

governmental agencies. These report cards represent important and sensitive data concerning organizational performance and there can be strong factors aimed at manipulation of this information. Thus the issues of accountability and quality of data are important but these are issues that have been largely neglected in the literature on governmental IT management. An entire chapter will be devoted to them.

Best Practices and IT

The pace of change in IT is rapid and has become more rapid in recent years. It is difficult for IT researchers to keep up with the fast pace of change. Consequently, practitioners frequently have to make their own decisions without much guidance as to what is the best course of action for their organizations. One of the most common approaches in this situation has been to adopt so-called "best practices." I will explore the meaning of best practices in depth in one chapter, but basically it means that managers attempt to identify organizations that are consensually viewed as doing an excellent job, and it assumed that the practices and procedures of these high performing organizations are the cause of their excellence. I will also attempt to take advantage of areas where IT researchers have developed and tested hypotheses through comparative empirical studies. Accepted wisdoms such as best practices, if they are to be employed in a wide variety of contexts, must be tested formally because they may not work in all contexts or different best practices may conflict with one another.

Theory and Research

In terms of theory, the basic point upon which all IT researchers agree is that information technology brings about changes in governments and thus is an independent variable. But technology is in turn influenced by organizational factors and that can block or alter the intended goals of IT. Thus IT can also be viewed as a dependent variable. This insight was made long ago by IT researchers. For example, in 1983 in an article entitled "Power, Politics, and MIS Implementation," Markus identified the need to look at the interaction between technological and "people" factors to understand why implementation of IT systems resulted in a success or failure. She (Markus, 1983, p. 441) goes on to state that resistance to change should not be viewed just as "a problem but a clue" and that technology itself cannot "accomplish the task of organizational change." She details how some parts of an organization continued to employ their old accounting methods after having implemented a new IS system, even though it required twice the effort.

More recently, Fountain (2001) has developed a theory of *"enacted technology"* in which the results of IT changes are influenced by a variety of bureaucratic and institutional forces who are often interested in preserving certain routines and patterns, so that the outcomes resulting from new technologies are often unintended and disappointing compared to the aspirations of those initiating the changes. Fountain provides three detailed case studies in which the attempt to implement new IT (including e-government) technologies ran into strong resistance that limited the success of the projects. Markus's interaction theory and Fountain's theory of enacted technology are both useful antidotes to the simplistic assumption, often referred to as the *technological imperative* that implementing a new technology is only a technical process and IT is primarily an independent variable. As Kraemer et al. (1989) demonstrate, "management matters" and the same technology introduced into two different organizations may have drastically different results depending on how skillful the managers are in dealing with IT. In this book, I will analyze technology as an independent variable, such as its use in e-government, to bring about transformation to better processes, and as a dependent variable influenced by factors such as politics and informal communication.

Plan of the Book

Chapter I: Public and Private Information Systems: How Are They Similar? How Are They Different? This chapter will explore in detail how systems from the two sectors both resemble one another and are different. I view governmental information management as having some important differences in that competition is less prevalent and the willingness to share is more common in the public sector.

Chapter II: Planning for Information Technology in the Public Sector: This chapter looks at the prescriptions concerning the need to do planning and the reality that many organizations do not do long-term planning. It outlines the key steps of a comprehensive planning process and illustrates these with samples drawn from actual plans.

Chapter III: Procuring Information Technology for Government: This chapter outlines and provides details concerning the key steps that experts recommend for purchasing IT. It provides in-depth discussion of methods used to procure IT. It describes the challenges of project management that follow the purchase. The chapter employs examples of Request for Proposals and purchases done by governmental organizations to illustrate the points.

Chapter IV: Prescriptions for IT in Government: How Do We Know What Works Best? Governmental managers often need to make decisions about how to manage IT. The most common approach to making these decisions is to identify best practices used by other organizations, public and private. This chapter critically examines the concept of best practices and other approaches to managing IT.

Chapter V: Electronic Government: The development of e-government represents the tremendous growth in importance of IT to government. I will show how e-government is not only making government more accessible, but that e-government is being employed to transform government to make it more integrated and hence more effective and efficient.

Chapter VI: Politics, Leadership, and Information Technology: This chapter will analyze how internal and external politics play an integral role in determining the success of information management. It will use numerous examples concerning struggles over "turf" and other political concerns. It will also discuss how leadership by generalist managers is necessary to overcome the centrifugal forces that are common in governmental information management.

Chapter VII: Information Technology, Training, and Organizational Learning: Both researchers and practitioners acknowledge the centrality of training and learning in the IT field. Most end users employ only a fraction of the power of the software. The hardware and software change so rapidly that generalist managers need to ensure that adequate training is provided. This chapter will show that managers must take on innovative approaches including the use of informal as well as formal training. Other HR issues are also explored.

Chapter VIII: Information Management and Ethical Issues in Government: Information technology can lead to ethical dilemmas for managers. Indeed, IT technologies change so rapidly that managers are often forced to make ethical, and sometimes legal, judgments about technology before there have been any clear legal or ethical guidelines set. This chapter will examine emerging ethical issues caused by new technologies and outline steps and approaches that managers can use to get a handle on how to deal with these new dilemmas. It will give particular emphasis to computer-mediated communications, such as e-mail, because they are the most heavily used technologies and are often associated with the most difficult dilemmas.

Chapter IX: Evaluation and Information Technology: There is a consensus that it is important to evaluate information management, but it is not an easy task. Easy-to-measure metrics such as percent of downtime are unsatisfactory. I discuss alternative approaches to evaluating information systems.

Chapter X: Governments and IT Sharing: Governmental IT has one major advantage over private sector IT—there is no competition to inhibit sharing of information with other governments. Some of the most important information systems involve exchanges between different levels of government. Sometimes these shared information systems are voluntary and viewed as mutually beneficial. Sometimes they are mandated and one party often is less than enthusiastic about its participation, and this situation can lead to problems. The basic point is that these shared systems are extremely important but have received little attention.

Chapter XI: Information Technology, Accountability and Information Stewardship: The ultimate goal of public information systems is to be responsive to the citizenry and the political system. This chapter will study the use of governmental IT systems to achieve greater accountability of government through various performance measurement and report card systems. It will focus on the problems of quality of data and the ability of the informal system to resist the formal system.

References

Andersen, D. F., & Dawes, S. S. (1991). *Government information management: A primer and casebook*. Englewood Cliffs, NJ: Prentice Hall.

Anderson, R., Bikson, T. K., Lewis, R., Moini, J., & Strauss, S. (2003). *Effective use of information technology: Lessons about state governance structures and processes*. Santa Monica, CA: The Rand Corporation. Online materials related to the book are available at http://www.rand.org/publications/MR/MR1704/index.html

Barrett, K., & Greene, R. (2001). *Powering up: How public managers can take control of information technology*. Washington, DC: CQ Press.

Blau, P. M. (1955). *The dynamics of bureaucracy*. Chicago: University of Chicago Press.

Brudney, J. L., & Selden, S. C. (1995). The adoption of innovation by smaller local governments: The case of computer technology. *American Review of Public Administration*, *25*(1), 71-86.

California (State of). (n.d.) *Prescription for change: A report of the California performance* review. Retrieved August 19, 2004, from http://www.report.cpr.ca.gov/cprrpt/preschg/pdf/prescriptionforchange.pdf

Carr, N.G. (2003, May). IT doesn't matter. *Harvard Business Review,* 41-49.

Caudle, S. L., & Marchand, D. A. (1989). *Managing information resources: New directions in state government.* Syracuse, NY: Syracuse University, School of Information Studies.

Center for Technology in Government. (1996). *Making smart IT choices.* Retrieved August 28, 2002, from, http://www.ctg.albany.edu/resources/smartin.html

Daft, R. L., & Wiginton, J. C. (1979). Language and organization. *Academy of Management Review, 4*(2), 179-191.

Fletcher, P. T., Bretschneider, S. I., & Marchand, D. A. (1992). *Managing information technology: Transforming county governments in the 1990s.* Syracuse, NY: Syracuse University: School of Information Studies.

Fountain, J. E. (2001). *Building the virtual state.* Washington, DC: Brookings Institution Press.

Government Performance Project (GPP). (n.d.). *Paths to performance in state and local government.* Final Report (p.29). Syracuse, NY: Syracuse University: The Maxwell School of Citizenship and Public Affairs. Retrieved July 31, 2003, from http://www.maxwell.syr.edu/gpp/grade/2002chap2.pdf

Holmes, A. (2005, January 15). Riding the California privacy wave. *CIO magazine.* Retrieved January 21, 2005, from http://www.cio.com/archive/011505/california.html?printversion=yes

Huxhold, W. E. (1991). *An introduction to geographic information systems.* London: Oxford University Press.

Jones, J. W., Saunders, C., & McLeod, R., Jr. (1988-89). Information media and source patterns across management levels: A pilot study. *Journal of Management Information Systems, 5*(3), 71-84.

Kraemer, K. L. (1989). *Managing information systems.* San Francisco: Jossey-Bass.

Kraemer, K. L., & Dedrick, J. (1997). Computing and public organizations. *Journal of Public Administration Research, 7*(1), 89-112.

Kraemer, K. L., Dutton, W. H., & Northrop, A. (1981). *The management of information systems.* New York: Columbia University Press.

Kraemer, K. L., & King, J. L. (1976). *Computers, power, and urban management: What every local executive should know.* Beverly Hills, CA: Sage.

Kraemer, K. L., Mitchel, W. H., Weiner, M. E.. & Dial, O. E. (1974). *Integrated municipal information systems: The use of the computer in local government.* New York: Praeger.

Mahler, J., & Regan, P. M. (2002, September). Learning to govern online: Federal agency internet use. *American Review of Public Administration, 32*(3), 326-349.

Markus, M. L. (1983). Power, politics, and MIS implementation. *Communications of the ACM, 26*(6), 430-444.

McCullagh, D. (2005, January 12). *CNET News.com.* Retrieved January 20, 2005, from http://news.com.com/Snooping+by+satellite/2100-1028_3-5533560.html?tag=st.num

McKinnon, S. M., & Bruns Jr., W. J. (1992). *The information mosaic*. Boston: Harvard Business School.

McLeod, R., Jr., & Jones, J. W. (1987, March). A framework for office automation. *MIS Quarterly, 11*, 87-104.

Orlikowski, W. J., & Barley, S.R. (2001, June). Technology and institutions: What can research on information technology and research on organizations learn from each other? *MIS Quarterly, 25*(2), 145-166.

Peterson, S. (2002, October). End of the line. *Government Technology*, 18-24.

Roethlisberger, F. J., & Dickson, W. J. (1947). *Management and the worker*. Cambridge, MA: Harvard University Press.

Simon, H. A., Smithburg, D. W., & Thompson, V. A. (1961). *Public administration*. New York: Alfred A. Knopf.

Stowers, G. L. (2001). Commerce comes to government on the desktop: E-Commerce applications in the public sector. In M.A. Abramson & G.E. Means (Eds.), *E-government* (pp. 44-84). Lanham: Rowman & Littlefield Publishers.

Weick, K. E. (1979). *The social psychology of organizing*. Reading, MA: Addison-Wesley.

West, D. M. (2001). *State and federal e-government in the United States*. Retrieved October 10, 2002, from www.insidepolitics.org

Additional Reading

Governments began using computing decades ago. Kenneth Kraemer and his various associates conducted major studies of information systems for decades and their works form the foundation of research on governmental management information systems. They studied the issue of integration of urban information systems in the 1970s and clearly anticipated Enterprise Resource Planning and the emphasis on enterprise-wide systems (Kraemer et al., 1974). They employed a variety of data sources including quantitative performance measures, structured surveys, and qualitative case study interviews (e.g., Kraemer et al., 1981, 1989). Any serious student of governmental management information systems will review their work. The idea that governmental information systems might be significantly different from private information systems was initiated by a seminal article by Bozeman and Bretschneider (1986). Syracuse University researchers have produced some important empirical volumes such as studies of information management in states (Caudle & Marchand, 1989) and counties (Fletcher et al., 1992). There is a growing body of empirical literature on e-government and governmental Web sites. The Andersen and Dawes (1991) book on Government Information Management continues to be worthwhile for its succinct "lenses" approach to IT management in government. Barrett and Greene's book (2001) is valuable in providing some detailed case studies of information management in governments. Overall, there are serious limitations of the work on governmental information systems and the Kraemer and Dedrick (1997) article identifies some of these problems.

Key Concepts

- B2G
- C2G
- Equivocality
- G2C
- G2B
- Managerial level
- Operational level
- Policy level
- Rich data
- Technological Imperative
- Theory of enacted technology

Discussion Questions

1. I have listed what I believe to be key actors, processes, and factors that influence information management. Can you think of any other actors, processes, and forces? Which forces are most important in organizations with which you are familiar?

2. Can you think of any cases where new technologies introduced into the organization did not work as intended? In what situations are information technologies most likely to be successful? Unsuccessful?

3. Identify an organization with which you are familiar and discuss how good you think it operates at the three levels that Huxhold identifies.

4. I have argued that generalist managers must be actively involved in these critical processes if information systems are to be effective. Do you agree or disagree?

5. Discuss with people in your organizations about the role of qualitative, non-digital data versus formal data residing in the digital information system. Discuss the role each kind of data (qualitative, non-digital and formal-digital) plays in making important decisions. Do any qualitative types of data have important influences on these decisions?

6. After reading the Carr article and those arguing against his position, reflect on your knowledge of organizations. Do you agree or disagree with Carr concerning the role and importance of IT?

7. Read the following case chapters and article and prepare an analysis of what are the key actors and forces at work in the case of the termination of the California Department of Information Technology. Based on these readings, the Anderson et al. chapters, and Peterson article on California, who are the key actors and what are the forces that played a significant role in the outcome of this particular incident? Discuss what this analysis tells about the role of IT policymakers.

What recommendations for change would you make if you were in charge of reorganizing the State of California's IT structure? Finally, read the recent report on California's "Prescription for Change" put out by the Schwarzenegger administration in California and identify its recommendations for changes in the IT structure. Do you agree with the report's recommendations?

Exercises

1. Analyze the structure of decision-making concerning information management in an organization with which you are familiar. Who has formal authority to make decisions? Create a schematic (e.g., using drawing tools in Microsoft Word) showing the formal structure of your organization with respect to IT decision-making. Discuss if there are any persons who have important influence even though they do not have formal authority.

2. Describe the major hardware and software systems that are used in an organization with which you are familiar. If the organization is large, you may focus on a sub-unit. Does the organization have an inventory of all major hardware and software? The organization may have a systems diagram that provides an overview of the system components and how they relate. Obtain this diagram if possible and bring to class to hand in. (Note, however, that IT staff sometimes may be reluctant to share these diagrams and some of the hardware and software information for security reasons.)

Acknowledgments

This book represents a synthesis of the research I have conducted about governments and information management for the past 25 years. Over these years, I have been the beneficiary of assistance from many people who have made the book possible. In particular, this book builds on the knowledge that I have gained from many practitioners in the information technology area, including numerous individuals affiliated with the Government Management Information Science and Innovation Groups organizations. The members of the Illinois Government Management Information Science organization have been especially instrumental in aiding my research efforts.

I also wish to acknowledge that the title and inspiration for this study evolved from the important research of Professors Barry Bozeman and Stuart Bretschneider in their article "Public Management Information Systems: Theory and Prescription", which appeared in 1986 in the *Public Administrative Review*.

I am also indebted to insights from students in my information management classes at Northern Illinois University. The staff of the Division of Public Administration has provided invaluable assistance, and I would like to especially thank Ellen Cabrera for her hard work done with speed, quality, and graciousness.

I would also like to thank all of those associated with Idea Group Inc., who took an interest in the book and provided the support necessary to bring it to a successful conclusion, including Jan Travers, Kristin Roth, and Amanda Phillips.

Finally, I would like to thank my wife, Georgette, who has provided me support when I needed it most. Any problems and limitations of the book are the results of purely my own efforts.

Chapter I

Public and Private Information Systems:
How Are They Similar?
How Are They Different?

Introduction

Information managers need to be aware of the fact that managing IT in the public sector presents different challenges than those faced in the private sector. However, there has been little systematic attention given to these differences by IT researchers. The purpose of this chapter is to review these differences and to present some empirical information concerning the differences between IT management between the two sectors. I conclude by discussing the implications of these differences for managers involved in public sector IT.

Citizens and policymakers have long made assumptions about differences between public and private organizations. Researchers have tested a variety of propositions concerning differences in public and private organizations (Rainey et al., 1976). These differences include environmental factors (e.g., higher degree of market exposure for private organizations), greater legal constraints and political influences in public organizations, greater scrutiny of public organizations, and greater complexity of objectives and fewer incentives for high performance in public organizations. For example, due to their openness and the demands for accountability, public organizations are expected to be more cautious and more involved in red tape while private organizations are expected to be willing to take on added risks (Bozeman & Kingsley, 1998; Rainey, Pandey, & Bozeman, 1995). Several studies have focused on hypothesized differences in workers in the two sectors such as concerning job satisfaction, motivation, and commitment (e.g., Buchanan, 1974; Rainey, 1983). Recently, Nutt (1999) found differences in their approaches to decision making.

Copyright © 2006, Idea Group Inc. Copying or distributing in print or electronic forms without written permission of Idea Group Inc. is prohibited.

In 1986, Bozeman and Bretschneider synthesized this literature to propose a framework for public management information systems (PMIS) that argued that there were important underlying differences between public and private information systems. In particular, the public sector systems necessarily give much more attention to concerns such as accountability, openness, and representativeness than private sector systems. Also, they state that a PMIS will have a greater focus on external and vertical linkages than private sector organizations. Consequently, they develop a number of prescriptions that argue that a PMIS often needs to be structured and managed in different ways than a private sector system. For example, Bozeman and Bretschneider argue that a PMIS head should not function at the top of the executive structure in order to insulate information technology (IT) from political interference. They argue that planning for a PMIS should be incremental rather than holistic. They point out that budgeting and other constraints on purchasing make it impossible for more comprehensive approaches to work well. They also state that, while private sector organizations often have to act quickly, PMIS errors can affect a much larger body of people in deleterious ways (e.g., cutting off of Social Security or welfare benefits) and thus public systems need more deliberate development and more extensive testing.

Bozeman and Bretschneider do not dispute the fact that there are many similarities between information systems in public and private agencies, but they argue that most of the research ignored these important differences and thus they developed a framework for studying PMIS. Despite the importance of the topic and the wide attention given to the Bozeman-Bretschneider article, there have been few studies that have researched differences between public and private information systems. An update is important because the nature of computing has changed radically from the situation in 1986, the year that Bozeman-Bretschneider article was published. In 1986, mainframe computers were dominant and the development of the Internet was still in its infancy. In this chapter, I review the few studies that have compared public and private systems and then present some data concerning public vs. private differences. I also outline future lines of research that could contribute to a better understanding of public management information systems.

Previous Research

There is some consensus about certain aspects of public-private differences related to information management. The Center for Technology in Government (1996) summarized this consensus about public information systems as follows: (1) Extreme risk aversion makes PMIS less likely to invest in risky technologies that have not been tried out; (2) Divided authority over IT decisions due to legal, civil service, and political constraints makes it difficult to manage IT projects; (3) Multiple stakeholders with competing goals characterize governmental systems; (4) One-year budgets make it difficult to plan long term and adopt IT innovations; (5) Highly regulated procurement using a competitive RFP process makes it difficult to learn from experience; and (6) Many other factors such as inter-agency linkages through budgets, legal requirements, and other connections that make it difficult to undertake changes without affecting other agencies.

Copyright © 2006, Idea Group Inc. Copying or distributing in print or electronic forms without written permission of Idea Group Inc. is prohibited.

Many people would probably agree with these some if not all of these assumptions about the special problems of PMIS but they need to be empirically tested. First of all, as Bozeman (1987) has articulated, private organizations can have a degree of "publicness." For example, some private organizations (e.g., defense contractors) have only the government as a client and thus may face the same kinds of constraints as public agencies. Bozeman (1987) argues that the degree of publicness of organizations is a variable and that differences between public and private organizations are not absolute but a matter of degree. Certain specialized governmental agencies may have the missions and resources to undertake risky IT projects and be leading innovators. Good examples are the founding of the Internet based on the efforts of the DARPA (Defense Applied Research Projects Agency) and the key role of the National Science Foundation in encouraging its early spread (see, e.g., Norberg, O'Neill, & Freedman, 1996). These organizations generally want and need to be on the cutting edge in order to fulfill their missions. Consequently, these assumptions are more likely to hold if generalizations about PMIS are limited to general purpose governments compared with private organizations that do not have governmental organizations as their primary clients.

Secondly, the nature, extent, and importance of computing in public and private sector organizations have undergone fundamental changes since their 1986 article was written. Indeed, there are some key changes in the nature of the public sector computing that are likely to alter its practices to be more similar to those of the private. One major change is that governments at many different levels are attempting to implement "best practices" which are often modeled after those of the private sector. Best practices now include giving governmental agencies much more control over purchasing decisions (Rocheleau, 2000). Also, one of Bozeman and Bretschneider's prescriptions is that the information leader should not be at the top of the organization. But many federal, state, and some local organizations have now followed the practices of private sector organizations by creating the position of the Chief Information Officer (CIO) who is supposed to be at the top level of the agency. For example, a study by Lee (2001) found that 42 of the 50 states have a formal CIO. These changes in purchasing and leadership structure suggest that there may be a growing convergence between public and private information systems. In short, both public and private information management are rapidly changing, so it is necessary to revisit comparisons of computing in the two sectors periodically.

I found few studies that empirically examined differences between public and private information management practices and the findings have not been very consistent. Bretschneider (1990) surveyed top computer executives in the public and private sectors. Bretschneider's survey responses confirmed the hypothesis that there is greater organizational interdependence in public sector, especially in the personnel and procurement areas. His study also found that government data processing tends to be placed lower in the hierarchy than it is in similar private organizations. This lower placement is in agreement with the prescription that the head of a PMIS should be insulated from politics. He also confirmed that economic factors are less dominant in public sector procurement decisions. Bretschneider concludes by arguing that his study proves the importance of environmental factors. He notes that their model does not argue that public or private systems are better but that awareness of these differences will enable both public and private managers to be more effective in their own environments.

Copyright © 2006, Idea Group Inc. Copying or distributing in print or electronic forms without written permission of Idea Group Inc. is prohibited.

Caudle, Gor & Newcomer (1991) conducted a survey of key information systems issues for the public sector that contained a set of questions about priorities for computing that were similar to those that had been asked of private sector officials in previous surveys. Some of their key findings are as follows (Caudle, Gor, & Newcomer, 1991): (1) Middle managers were critical for public systems while top managers dominated in private systems; (2) There were differences between local governments that were focused on transaction processing computing and federal and state governments that were more interested in oversight missions; (3) Public agencies were interested in technology transfer that shared applications while this is not a priority issue at all for private sector agencies. Caudle, Gor and Newcomer (1991) conclude that none of the top ten public sector issues identified as the top priorities by public sector officials are uniquely "public" in nature. Nevertheless, there were distinct differences in priorities because technology transfer, the top rated issue as ranked by the public sector officials, was ranked only 14th by the private sector. They also note that the issues rated at the top by the public sector such as "end user computing" tended to be issues that had already peaked in the private sector and were on the decline in regard to their ranking in the private sector surveys which may suggest that public sector information management priorities tend to lag those of private sector management. Another finding was that different levels of government varied in importance assigned to issues. Overall, Caudle, Gor and Newcomer's (1991) study suggests more similarities than differences but it also emphasizes the difficulty of making generalizations concerning differences between public and private sector systems. Their results show that there is great variation in priorities within governmental organizations based on the level of government and the level of management being studied. Consequently, statements about public vs. private differences may have to be stated contingently based on key variables such as level of management and government.

Bretschneider and Wittmer's (1993) study found that governmental organizations had adopted greater numbers of microcomputers per employee than private sector organizations. They conclude that the size of the public sector investments were most likely due to the information intensive nature of government as well as use of microcomputers as a "side payment" to compensate personnel for low salaries. Bretschneider and Wittmer's study also found differences among sub-areas of the public and private sectors with, for example, criminal justice and manufacturing areas consistently scoring high and low on numbers of computers per FTE respectively.

Aggarwal and Mirani (1999) studied the use of decision support system models in public and private sectors. They sent surveys out to decision makers such as the top three or four people of federal agencies and also asked them to distribute the survey to other decision makers in their agencies. Private sector users were selected from a corporate directory listing businesses in Maryland, Washington, D.C. and Virginia. Their study concluded that the private sector DSS use was greater. They also found that middle managers were the primary users of the models for public agencies while top managers were more likely to be users in private agencies.

Elliot and Tevabichulada (1999) compared "computer literacy" in the public and private sector. They sent questionnaires to human resource professionals in public and private sector. Their study was aimed at comparing computer literacy among human resource administrators in public and private agencies. Overall, they found that the government

Copyright © 2006, Idea Group Inc. Copying or distributing in print or electronic forms without written permission of Idea Group Inc. is prohibited.

and private sector agencies were similar in their use of programs. They argue that the "lack of differences" could be explained because of the ubiquitous nature of applications that are now used for the same personnel purposes. They found that governments gave more computing training (95% vs. 82%) but that the frequency of "regular training" was higher in the private (40%) than public (30%) sectors. They also note that most organizations, both public and private, waited for training to be specifically requested rather than provide it proactively.

There is one area where differences between the private and public sector quite clearly are reflected in computer software: budgeting in the private sector does not have to deal with the same demands as the public sector according to Metzgar and Miranda (2001, p. 143). Metzgar and Miranda go on to state that budgeting modules are the weak spot in ERP systems and that most governments do not use them and often don't even purchase them because they are so weak.

David Coursey (forthcoming) has made the point more recently that politics has influenced how governments have approached planning for investments in e-government. He cites examples of how the desire to take advantage of positive publicity can influence investment decisions. Likewise, the political cycle of elections can, Coursey argues, lead to "rush innovations and projects." Of course, politics can influence investment decisions in private organizations too as Markus (1983) has shown but the politics that Coursey describes is external in nature, aimed at the citizenry. In my chapter on politics, I explore in more detail how politics influences IT decisions in the public sector.

Competition and Perceived Importance of Information Systems

Based on my analysis of these other studies, although there are many similarities between public and private agencies, there are some important differences that can distinguish governmental from private management information systems. In particular, I believe that while both types of organizations want to provide good services to their customers, competition makes it more likely that private organizations will consider IT to be crucial to their survival and thus be willing to invest more resources in it. The degree of competition faced by organizations was not emphasized by Bozeman & Bretschneider (1986) in their model but I believe it is a crucial factor.

Although I am not aware of any empirical studies that show IT is viewed as more crucial in the private sector, there is much anecdotal evidence available. As noted earlier, one of the defining aspects of public organizations concerns their openness and this openness has fostered a willingness to share information about their computer systems. Indeed, borrowing of government computer systems is often encouraged and sometimes even mandated. For example, the State of Florida was directed to use a modified version of the Ohio welfare system (Miller, 1994). Another example is the sharing of programs financed by the Medicaid system (National Electronic Commerce Coordinating Council, 2001):

Copyright © 2006, Idea Group Inc. Copying or distributing in print or electronic forms without written permission of Idea Group Inc. is prohibited.

However, when public funding is used to develop software companies responded that the resulting product should be made available in the public domain regardless of the author. In these instances, they feel that any plug-ins utilized in these applications should be developed under open systems standards and should be replaceable if not already available for licensing. A good example of this publicly funded situation was cited in the area of Medicaid Management Information Systems or MMIS, where the Federal government funds 90% of the cost of systems design, development and implementation, and systems are routinely transferred from one state to another with a high level (60-80%) of component sharing and code re-use. While the customization required for each state is extensive and expensive, companies feel that without this sharing, the costs would be several times as great to the States. (p. 45)

Public officials are often willing to share the most intimate details of their systems about which they feel pride. As noted earlier, governments are much more interested in technology transfer than businesses. Indeed, state governments have created an online facility for sharing reusable software (Douglas, 2001). Public sector officials can gain prestige and professional opportunities by sharing such information. Such willingness to share is unlikely in the private sector if the information to be shared has the slightest possibility of giving away a competitive advantage.

Indeed, since the mid-1980's, the theory (e.g., the work of Michael Porter & Millar, 1985) has arisen that information systems can be strategic assets to businesses and allow them to gain competitive advantage. Although the importance of IT as a competitive asset varies by industry, in many cases it has become a central element, as the following article in a recent article noted (Morgan, 1998):

Companies that have developed Web-based businesses are understandably nervous about revealing how these are put together or how they integrate with traditional transactional systems. After all, with a Web business, the e-commerce architecture **is** *the business—it is the company's competitive advantage.* (p. 40)

Morgan (1998, p. 40) goes on to illustrate this point by noting that his requests to Amazon.com for basic information about the nature of their computer system were met with a refusal stating that, "Amazon.com absolutely will not discuss the specifics of its Web computer architecture." Likewise, Yahoo has taken a similar position on refusing to provide any information concerning its databases (Whiting, 2000):

Ralston [Vice President and general manager of Yahoo's communications groups] calls the central database that supports Yahoo's ability to provide universal logon for all of its services a 'crown jewel', though he refuses to talk about it, or any of the multitudes of databases the company employs, in any detail. 'They're not only mission-critical,' Ralston says, 'in many cases, they're a competitive advantage. (p. 50)

Stowers' (2001) review of e-commerce applications brings out the point that the potential market for businesses is worldwide and thus can justify investment in sophisticated

Copyright © 2006, Idea Group Inc. Copying or distributing in print or electronic forms without written permission of Idea Group Inc. is prohibited.

staffing and the latest software if there is an expectation of expanding their market share and profit. By way of contrast, government's "market" is limited to its assigned geographical area and for small governments, this is a very limited area and less supportive of heavy investments (Stowers, 2001):

While one of the benefits of private sector e-commerce is the ability to stretch beyond geographical boundaries (to reach globally), by definition public sector jurisdictions are confined to their own geographical boundaries. With a potential worldwide market from which to benefit, private sector firms are able to take advantage of the newest technologies. They can be staffed to maintain their Web sites with the absolutely newest information, designs, security, and transaction methodologies. Governments, however, serve only their own citizens— a limited number — and a limited geographic area, not a worldwide market. Except when jurisdictions are large enough (states), this makes e-commerce less efficient than for private sector firms. It is more difficult to earn benefits over a broader scale and scope of customers. (p. 15)

These observations support the argument that generalist governments will lag private sector organizations and, in the case of those with limited resources, will wait for the cost of new technologies to drop before investing. Therefore, it is very logical for governments to be more risk averse. The business cases for expensive governmental purchases of IT would be different. For-profit businesses would likely include as key factors the impact of the system on helping to expand market share and improve profits. Stowers' point also brings out the fact that there are thousands of small- and medium-sized local governments that face particular difficulties in trying to keep up with the practices of large governments and private sector organizations.

Another important difference between the public and private sector concerns their use of information systems concerning their citizens or customers. In some cases, businesses such as banks are using IT as a way of deciding whether they want you as a customer depending on the amount of profit that the bank makes off of you. Banks sometimes use fees to discourage use by customers they view as drags on their profits (Wahl, 1998). Public organizations are not free to use IT to get rid of unprofitable citizens. This is a potentially important difference between the purposes for which the systems are used. By allowing private organizations to achieve competitive advantage and to focus on the most productive customers, IT can contribute to profits and may even drive their competitors out of business. By way of contrast, programs such as Medicaid are aimed at many citizens who cannot pay for the full cost of their services received. Thus, the strategy of using information technology to identify and get rid of unprofitable customers is not possible.

There are other features that most likely distinguish public and private systems such as the complexity of the goals for which they are used. Certainly, the importance attached to accountability, openness, and equity issues appears to distinguish the two types of systems. Nutt (1999) points out that sunshine laws make all discussions about governmental strategic decision subject to disclosure:

Copyright © 2006, Idea Group Inc. Copying or distributing in print or electronic forms without written permission of Idea Group Inc. is prohibited.

Most public organizations do not have the luxury of keeping strategic decisions secret. Sunshine laws often force the conduct of business into the open.... Even when sunshine laws do not apply, mechanisms of accountability and oversight make all actions in public organizations, even contingency plans or hypothetical scenarios, subject to review and interpretation by outsiders. (p. 312)

As is pointed out in the chapter on accountability, private organizations gather much performance data but generally keep it internal. By way of contrast, e-reporting puts government data on the Internet for everyone to see. Moreover, in gathering materials to write this book, the author was able to access the detailed strategic technology plans of many major governmental bodies posted on their Web sites. I doubt that this information would be made available by most private sector companies. Likewise, the e-rulemaking activities such as e-dockets also force governments to be more transparent than private sector organizations. Consequently those engaged in designing public information systems need to employ accountability and openness as major organizing principles for their systems. In contrast, private sector organizations would be expected to use them primarily for internal purposes that enhance their competitive position in their market sector.

The emergence of IT as a method to gain competitive advantage makes IT likely to be viewed as much more important to private sector organizations. If IT means the difference between thriving versus going out of business, then it can be hypothesized that private agencies will be willing to invest many more resources in IT. For many private sector agencies, investments in IT to improve services to clients are not just desirable (as they are in the public sector), but absolutely necessary.

This is not to deny that many public organizations are now beginning to view IT as a major asset. Bajjaly (1998) found a considerable amount of attention to strategic information system concepts in state agencies. But Bajjaly (1998, p. 76) also notes that public agencies use their strategic systems for the purpose of "cooperative advantage." There are some forms of mild competition. For example, many public agencies are attempting to use Web pages and other information system devices to attract business to their localities, according to articles in computer magazines such as Government Technology (e.g., Newcombe, 1998). Many of the Web-based approaches to attracting businesses are low cost and low risk for public agencies and consequently governments are happy to engage in these activities. Indeed, Coursey & Kilingsworth (2000) recently noted that government Web site development was very innovative in the early years of the Web, while business Web innovation did not occur much until substantial profit opportunities opened up.

However, I believe that competition is much less important in the public sector and that consequently public sector organizations will be much less willing to invest large amounts of money in IT to gain competitive advantage. Nutt (1999) summarizes the literature on public-private differences by stating the following:

Competition for customers can be cumbersome or even prohibited for public and third-sector organizations. Public organizations often are expected to collaborate with each other when offering similar services. (p. 312)

Copyright © 2006, Idea Group Inc. Copying or distributing in print or electronic forms without written permission of Idea Group Inc. is prohibited.

IT is more often a cost-cutting device for the public sector, a way of doing more with the same number of staff, and many public IT projects are aimed at providing access and are not crucial to the organization's existence. To illustrate, Mohan, Holstein, and Adams (1990) noted that if a private consumer goods corporation overspends their budget but that the overspending results in the doubling of profit, they will be likely to be rewarded. But such overspending would not even be allowed in the public sector. Thus they note that governments are less likely to invest in projects like Executive Information Systems (EIS) (Mohan, Holstein, & Adams, 1990):

Public sector organizations operate with fixed budgets and have little leeway to shift dollars from one category to another. In these circumstances, a risky project with an EIS...is not likely to show up high on the MIS priority list. (p. 435)

Another example of the compelling force for private sector IT spending is provided by the following observation of Ken Lacy, the CIO of United Parcel Service (UPS):

A lot of CIOs do feel that if they don't spend the money on leading-edge technology, they're going to be left behind. We've spent a lot of money just because we need to stay in the game. (Whiting & Davis, 1999, p. 37)

Lacy supported this statement with the example of how UPS is investing in voice recognition technology in order to explore the possibility of having customers speak phone numbers into a telephone headset that could reduce time for customer requests. If technology is affordable, many public managers are glad to use it to improve services to their customers too, but it is not mandatory for their survival and it would be hard to justify investment in expensive or risky technologies unless their central mission necessitates their use.

There is a contrarian argument recently advanced by Nicholas Carr (2003) in a Harvard Business Review article that IT has become a commodity for private sector organizations—that gains reaped from IT innovation cannot be sustained. Thus Carr (2003) argues that IT investments should be treated like a utility in that they provide crucial infrastructure that must be secure but that the smartest approach is to minimize costs while maintaining the integrity of the system. He goes on to argue that the biggest threat in the current environment is "overinvestment" due to vendors pushing acquisitions that are not necessary. The title to an article that serves as a follow-up on Carr's position summarizes his position well: "Follow, Don't Lead" (Carr, 2004). However, most experts disagree with Carr (see, e.g., Computerworld, 2003). They acknowledge that hardware quickly becomes a commodity but that advantages gained through smart uses of software and knowledge management have clearly produced important competitive advantages to corporations like Wal-Mart and Dell. Although Carr's "utility" approach to IT investment seems to be rejected by a majority of private sector companies, this low-risk, follow-don't-lead approach resonates well with most of the governmental IT staff that I interviewed.

Copyright © 2006, Idea Group Inc. Copying or distributing in print or electronic forms without written permission of Idea Group Inc. is prohibited.

I acknowledge that the degree of competition is a variable in both public and private sector systems. For example, prior to the development of prospective reimbursement systems, private as well as public hospitals had little incentive to use their information systems as strategic weapons (Lindberg, 1979). But when prospective reimbursement systems and managed care developed, IT became a much more important management tool for both public and private medical information systems (e.g., Traska, 1988). It is clear that for some special purpose organizations, such as public universities, investment in high technology is a strategic factor that is necessary for them to compete successfully for professors and students. Overall, I believe that there has been a secular trend among all organizations, both public and private, to view their information systems as strategic tools. However, I believe that IT is less crucial to general-purpose governments than private sector corporations.

Consequently, I hypothesize that the most striking differences between public and private agencies would involve those areas that are characterized by high cost and high risk. In general, I expect that private sector organizations will perceive IT as more important to their success than public organizations such as general-purpose local governments. Likewise, I would also expect private sector organizations to invest a higher level of resources in IT.

In order to test these hypotheses, the area of training for information technology is employed to compare the two sectors. Why use training as a focus of interest? First, there has been little systematic research generally on IT training but there is a general consensus that training can be crucial to the effective use of IT (e.g., see George and Theis, 1991; Steen, 1998). Coursey and Bozeman (1990) point out that little attention in public-private literature has focused on organizational behaviors—most of the research has focused on issues such as job satisfaction, motivation, identification and commitment. Thus IT training represents a significant new area in which to compare public and private organizational behaviors. The little work that exists suggests that agencies may under-invest in this area (Fletcher, Bretschneider, & Marchand, 1992). But Fletcher's study looked at only governmental organizations. Provision of formal training can be expensive both in terms of the cost of training and the lost time off from their jobs that must be incurred by the training participants. The payoff of training efforts is often in the future, as the enhanced efficiency of the use of computing may result in increased profits in the private sector. But the public sector may obtain less financial benefit from such training. Thus, if private organizations view their information systems as a competitive weapon, it is expected that they will be more willing to invest in training despite the cost and the delay in benefits.

To summarize, my arguments earlier lead to the following hypotheses that are tested:

#1:   Private sector organizations perceive information systems as more important to their success than do public organizations.

#2:   Private sector organizations invest more resources in information technology than do public organizations.

#3:   Private sector organizations perceive training for information technology as more important than do public organizations.

Copyright © 2006, Idea Group Inc. Copying or distributing in print or electronic forms without written permission of Idea Group Inc. is prohibited.

#4:   Private sector organizations invest more resources in training for IT than do public organizations.

Methodology

A survey was employed to test these hypotheses on a group of comparable public and private organizations. The survey was conducted in the late fall of 1994 through the first quarter of 1995. As a preliminary step to conducting a survey of training, two case studies of training were carried out in a private and public organization respectively (Wu, 1999). Qualitative data based on open-ended interviews with end-users and IS managers were employed to assist in developing the survey instrument. Based on these revisions, the following steps were used to implement the survey:

1.   A list of 144 municipalities was gathered in a nine-county area of Illinois. Only municipalities that had at least 50—but not more than 500—employees were included, which resulted in a sampling frame of 97 municipalities.

2.   Since municipal governments are service-oriented organizations that do not, for example, become involved in manufacturing, the Illinois Services Directory (1993-1994) was employed in determining the sampling frame for business organizations. There is some evidence that manufacturing organizations use of IT is different from and more complex than that of service-oriented private sector organizations (see Culpan, 1995; Caudle, Gor, & Newcomer, 1991, p. 179). Thus, by using only service-oriented organizations as the private sector comparison group, there is a fairer comparison with the public sector. Then a systematic sample with a random start was employed to obtain a list of 137 private service-oriented organizations that were located in the same nine-county area with the same requirements in terms of numbers of employees.

3.   The initial survey was sent to the IS manager in both the public and private organizations. Forty-five (45) responses were obtained from private organizations (27 surveys to private organizations were returned due to no forwarding address) and thus the private IS manager survey obtained a 41 percent response rate of those who could be located. Seventy-four (74) responses from the IS managers of the municipalities were received for a 76 percent response rate.

Wave analyses (Bozeman, Reed, & Scott, 1992) were done to compare early vs. late users (e.g., in terms of size and answers to various questions in the survey) in order to give an indication if there was bias in the results, but no major differences were found. The characteristics of the responding private sector organizations were compared with the characteristics of the original sampling frame of private businesses in terms of organizational size and there were no significant differences between responding and non-responding organizations.

Copyright © 2006, Idea Group Inc. Copying or distributing in print or electronic forms without written permission of Idea Group Inc. is prohibited.

The IS manager survey's response rate for the private organizations (41 percent) is good compared to the rate reported for most published studies of private sector which are often in the 20 to 30 percent rage. Follow-up phone calls were placed to a random sub-sample of private organizations that did not respond to the survey and most of their reasons were among the following: (1) They were too busy to participate; (2) They did not feel they had the information to respond to the survey; or (3) They did not want to reveal that type of information. The low response rates obtained by most surveys on private sector information systems support the argument that they view information on their systems as crucial and don't want to share it. Unfortunately, this phenomenon also undoubtedly results in some biases, since those who refuse to share may be different from those willing to answer.

The perceived importance of information technology was determined by asking IT managers two questions: (1) Evaluate the importance of the information system to the decision making process of their organization (on a 1 to 5 point scale); and (2) Assess on a scale of 0 to 100 the degree to which the organization is dependent on its computer system. The study measured the amount of resources spent on information technology overall by the total amount reported spending on their information system per FTE and by the number of Information System professionals employed per FTE (in effect, controlling for the size of the organizations).

The perceived importance of end-user training was assessed by responses to two questions from the IS manager: (1) How important do they (i.e., the Information System mangers) think end user training is? and (2) How important does the CEO of their organization perceive training to be to the organization?

The amount of resources devoted to training was measured in two ways: (1) Respondents were asked to report the total number of IS staff devoted to training and then this number was to calculate the ratio of IS staff to FTEs of the organization; and (2) Respondents were then asked to estimate the amount of money spent on IS training and this figure was employed to calculate this amount spent per FTE. Questions were also asked about the extent and nature of training offered, including the following: What different types of formal training does your organization do with a list of nine different types (information center, interactive videos, print guides, classes offered by internal staff, classes offered by external trainers, end user support groups, technology labs, training provided with systems, and other types of training which they could specify)? It was expected that if private sector organizations invest more in training that they would be likely to offer a wider variety of types of training.

Findings

Figure 1 shows the results of the analysis. T-tests were conducted to compare the means of the public and private sector variables. This analysis revealed that the average number of IS professionals in private sector organizations exceeded that of public sector agencies by 4.40 to 1.38. Since the mean size of the public organizations in the sample was larger (199) than that of the private (154) sector, the ratio of IS staff to FTEs was even

Copyright © 2006, Idea Group Inc. Copying or distributing in print or electronic forms without written permission of Idea Group Inc. is prohibited.

more disparate (.04 to .01) and was statistically significant (p < .01). The average number of IS trainers was larger in the private sector (1.11) than the public (.66), but did not quite reach the level of statistical significance (.089). However, when the ratios of IS trainers per FTE are compared, the private sector ratio was higher and statistically significant (p< .05).

When total spending on information technology is compared for the two sectors, the mean of the private sector was larger than that of the public ($644,930 vs. $182,119). When the amount of spending is compared per FTE the difference ($4,436 vs. $676) is statistically significant (p < .05). Finally, when the amounts spent on information technology training are compared, the amount spent by the private sector is reported to be more than twice that of the public sector ($17,436 vs. $7,550) and calculated on a per FTE basis ($147 vs. $37), this difference is again statistically significant (p < .01) and suggests that the private sector spends nearly four times as much as the public sector.

Figure 1. Comparison of public and private sector organizations

Variables	Mean (Public)	Mean (Private)	Degrees of Freedom	Sig. Level (1 tail)
Resource-Oriented Variables				
Number of IT professionals	1.38	4.40	117	0.011
Ratio of IT staff to FTEs	0.01	0.04	114	0.004
Total spending on IT	$182,119	$644,930	105	0.017
IT spending per FTE	$676	$4,546	105	0.021
Number of IT trainers	0.66	1.11*	64	0.089
Ratio of IT trainers to FTEs	0.005	0.012	104	0.041
Total Spending on IT per FTE	$37	$147	105	0.008
Number of training methods	3.07	2.80	117	0.197
Perception-based Variables				
Importance of IT in decision-making**	3.88	3.75	116	0.258
Importance of end-user training***	8.16	7.89	116	0.206
CEO's attitude toward training****	6.77	7.00	114	0.319
Importance of IT training*****	4.46	4.20*	71	0.077
* Unequal variance t-test was used.				
** 1-to-5 scale: 1= Unimportant; 5=Crucial				
*** 1-to-10 scale: 1=Not at all; 10=Crucial				
**** 1-to-10 scale: 1=Not al all; 10-Extremely important				
***** 1-to-5 scale: 1=Not at all; 5=Very important				
Adapted from Rocheleau, B., & Wu, L. (2002). Public vs. private information systems: Do they differ in important ways: A review and empirical test. *American Review of Public Administration*, 32(4), 379-397.				

Copyright © 2006, Idea Group Inc. Copying or distributing in print or electronic forms without written permission of Idea Group Inc. is prohibited.

However, the total number of different types of training methods did not differ significantly—indeed, the mean number of methods for the public sector (3.07) exceeded by a slight amount the number (2.80) used by private sector organizations. In retrospect, I suspect the number of different training methods is not a good indicator of overall investment in training. An organization might use different methods, but spend very little on any of them while another organization might focus on only one method but spend a good deal on it.

Overall, these results confirm Hypotheses 2 and 4 that private agencies spend more on IT and IT training. However, it should be noted that the amounts spent on training in absolute terms are not large even for private organizations. This finding suggests that training is not given a high priority even in the private sector, though they did support it much more than the public sector. This study's results appear to conflict somewhat with those of Bretschneider & Witmer's (1993) study that found that public sector organizations provided more microcomputers per employee than their private sector sample. However, this study's sample of private organizations included only service-oriented private businesses, thus excluding some of the low-scoring private sectors in their sample such as manufacturing organizations. This study's public sample consisted only of general-purpose local governments rather than the state agencies that they studied. Likewise, this study focused on spending on technology in general which includes software and training while the Bretschneider & Witmer study focused on the number of computers per FTE.

This study found no statistically significant differences between public and private sector perceptions of the importance of IT. Indeed, public sector IS managers actually rated the importance of training slightly higher than those of the private sector (3.88 vs. 3.75 on a 1 to 5 scale of importance where 5 is very important), although the difference is not statistically significant. Information system managers perceived that chief executive officers would have similar attitudes concerning the importance of IS (6.77 vs. 7.00 on a 1 to 10 scale of importance), but the difference was not statistically significant. IS managers in the public sector rated the importance of IS training slightly higher (4.46 vs. 4.20 on a 1 to 5 scale of importance) than those of the private sector, although the difference was not statistically significant.

To summarize, the data show that IS managers and CEOs (as reported by their IS managers) perceived their information and training just as important as managers in the private sector. However, private sector organizations do invest more resources in both information systems in general and training in particular, so some important differences remain.

The study findings identify an apparent inconsistency: both public and private sector managers believe that information system training is important but both, especially public organizations, fail to invest many resources in absolute terms in it. How can this discrepancy be explained? I suspect that it may be due to the fact that training is often aimed at improving general ability and cannot be linked to specific, pressing demands made on organizations. Immediate needs are likely to override long-term investments like training in both public and private organizations. It is quite common for differences to exist between perceptual and objective measures (e.g., Fletcher and Lorenz, 1985; Hougland, 1987). People may say that they believe training is important but, "when push

Copyright © 2006, Idea Group Inc. Copying or distributing in print or electronic forms without written permission of Idea Group Inc. is prohibited.

comes to shove," fail to support this view with the financial investment required. Thus, both types of organizations, but especially public agencies, may give lip service to training but in reality sacrifice training to other priorities when it comes time to make budget decisions. Unlike private organizations, public organizations will not obtain higher profits due to these training expenditures and thus they are likely to have an even greater discordance between their ratings of importance versus actual expenditures. Indeed, most public organizations will not be able to demonstrate a close relationship between training and achievement of their goals in general because of the complexity and often conflicting nature of their goals.

Implications

In studying differences in public-private information systems, I emphasize the importance of the degree of competition to make it likely that private sector organizations will invest more in training and other aspects of information technology. This study found that private sector organizations were willing to invest more resources in training their workers for information technology even though they rated it as no more important to the success of their organization than the public sector did. Yet, it is important to note that these data were collected in the 1994-1995 period. The technology sector has grown even more rapidly in importance since those years with the huge increase in the importance of the Internet and e-commerce. I suspect that both the ratings of importance attached to information technology and the amounts invested in training are likely to be much higher in both types of organizations now and that our own study results need to be retested. Governments clearly view the Internet and technology as a key mechanism for saving on personnel costs and they make substantial investments for this reason, rather than because of competition. While this study focused on public-private differences, future studies should also study what the characteristics are of organizations that invest high amounts of resources in IT regardless of sector. As I noted previously, there are public organizations that do consider information technology to be a strategic weapon important to their success and they are likely to invest in IT and IT training at a high rate. The enormous changes that have occurred in technology since this study began and the importance of the issues deserve replication of the analysis conducted here.

Comparisons between public and private organizations cannot be viewed as unchanging. As I noted earlier in this chapter, public organizations over the last decade have been, in many cases, seeking to emulate the private sector on many characteristics that have distinguished them in the past including the purchasing process and positioning of top IT leadership. I suspect that the differences between the two sectors have been narrowed on these dimensions since the data was gathered. Indeed, there are other changes that may have also moved the two sectors closer together. For example, in several prominent cases, outsourcing of many public sector functions including information technology to the private sector has become a possibility which could possibly instill a greater sense of competition to IT workers in the public sector or even result in the fact that a good deal

Copyright © 2006, Idea Group Inc. Copying or distributing in print or electronic forms without written permission of Idea Group Inc. is prohibited.

of public sector computing is actually done by private sector organizations. There is some evidence that IT is used as a mild form of a strategic weapon in such public entities as municipalities employing GIS-based online maps to advertise their "wares" on the Internet and, according to an official with a GIS consulting firm (Perlman, 2004), there is a growing expectation that local governments will offer an online visual presentation of property and related information. Thus there have been some additional competitive forces among governments to lure businesses via easily accessible and relevant information on their Web sites.

There is another potentially important aspect that I have not addressed in this chapter: the importance of career ambitions on the part of IT staff and generalist managers. The IT area, especially with respect to e-government but also other areas, is one method for establishing a reputation for innovation. This is particularly the case because there are several rating systems by organizations like the Center for Digital Government and individual researchers like West that can provide independent verification of excellence and such awards quite naturally emphasized by those organizations do very well. This recognition can possibly lead to career advancement. Career ambitions can provide some impetus towards innovation and possibly risk-taking, though I doubt that it is strong enough to overcome most government's aversion to risk.

But I believe that there remain key differences between information management in the two sectors that revolve around the fact that information technology is now viewed as a key factor to achieve competitive advantage in the private sector. Based on this analysis, I believe that there are certain areas that are most likely to be different between the two sectors such as the following: (1) Public sector organizations will be willing to share information about their systems to a much greater degree than private sector organizations; and (2) Attention to access and equity issues will be perceived as much more important in public than private sector organizations and these differences will be reflected in the amount of attention and resources devoted to these aspects of their systems. In my view, the competitive use of IT is more the exception than the rule. Generally governments are oriented to cooperation and sharing in the IT area. Given the constraints on public budgets at all levels of government, sharing and cooperation can lead to significant savings. This free and easy culture of sharing is the distinguishing feature of governmental IT. I have an entire chapter devoted to sharing in which I detail the wide variety of IT sharing that exists.

Most of the previous work comparing public and private sector information systems (including the hypotheses studied in this chapter) tend to implicitly assume that public information systems are inferior compared with the private sector's. While this may be true concerning technological sophistication, I argue that the public sector model of sharing information about key systems has important advantages. For example, public organizations involved in implementing new technologies such as geographic informa-tion systems can benefit from each other's experiences while private sector organizations are likely to keep secret any information that they feel gives them competitive advantage. Consequently, the public sector is likely to be better able to take advantage of other organization's experiences and avoid many problems—if they seek out this information. Sharing could encourage more cost effective solutions to the adoption of new technolo-gies in the public, rather than private, sector and this sharing could provide advantages to public sector computing such as rapid dissemination of innovations. Comparison of

Copyright © 2006, Idea Group Inc. Copying or distributing in print or electronic forms without written permission of Idea Group Inc. is prohibited.

information sharing in public and private sectors appears to offer a fruitful area for comparison and research.

On the other hand, I believe that private organizations are much more likely to invest substantial amounts of money in expensive and potentially risky technology ventures if they believe that these could lead to advantage and ultimately profits. I have emphasized that generalizations about public vs. private sector differences may be contingent on their nature (general purpose vs. special purpose governmental agencies). General-purpose government does not normally have the incentive to undertake such risk. When there is little chance for profit from technology, the public sector may lead but when profit becomes a possibility, I expect the private sector to lead in innovation. As discussed in the chapters on planning and purchasing, general purpose public sector organizations do not want to be on the "bleeding edge." They will wait until a technology and/or company has proven itself before they will invest major resources in it. In short, I believe that comparisons of public and private sectors that involve risky IT investments may be most likely to show interesting differences.

As I have noted previously, there has been a dearth of serious research comparing public and private organizations. There seems to be an assumption that management models developed for the private sector can be directly applied to public sector organizations without significant alteration. In some areas, there may be little or no differences. For example, due to the desire to improve the efficiency of public management information systems by copying the practices of the private sector, it is likely that the approaches to purchasing of information technology have narrowed between the two sectors over the last 15 years. Many public organizations have also followed private organizations in terms of structure such as hiring a CIO and thus structural differences may have narrowed too. But this study points out the need to test such assumptions.

The differences in competitiveness and profit incentive have broad-reaching implications that may affect every area of the organization. Governmental agencies have trouble recruiting IT personnel due to low salary structures and lack of stock options to compete with the private sector (Varon, 2000). This study shows that private sector organizations invest more resources in IT than comparably sized governmental organizations. If government cannot obtain technical staff with requisite skills, they may have to outsource more of their computing than the private sector does. As I have shown, for many private sector organizations, the information system is a core competency because it provides the company with its competitive edge and thus should not be outsourced according to some experts (e.g., Venkatraman, 1997). There is disagreement as to whether IT is a core competency in the public sector. Bretschneider and Wittmer's article (1993) explains more use of microcomputer technology in the public sector by noting that the public sector is information intensive. But, when Connecticut planned to outsource its entire IT and telecommunication functions, the head of the outsourcing effort justified it by stating that IT was not a core competency for the state (McGee, 1997, p. 22). Others argue that core functions of government are based on information processing and thus IT is a core function (Singer, 1995b). Research has been done in England on outsourcing of IT by local authorities and found that some government organizations there also had outsourced their entire IT activity (Cronk & Sharp, 1998). But Cronk and Sharp (1998) go on to argue that government too needs to preserve a "cadre of competence" in order to effectively manage their IT contracts and infrastructure.

Copyright © 2006, Idea Group Inc. Copying or distributing in print or electronic forms without written permission of Idea Group Inc. is prohibited.

In short, if governments and private sector organizations differ in their views of whether IT is an area of core competency, it may have important impacts on their willingness to outsource the entire function. Likewise, if it is true that private information systems are designed with a primary emphasis on competition while public sector managers are structured primarily around accountability and openness themes, then there may be important sector differences with respect to a wide-range of aspects including the degree and amount of investments on expensive and risky new technology, the degree of sharing, and investments in training. As one example of a potentially important difference, Reed (2001) studied strategic information system planning in U.S. state governments and found that there was a much more diverse set of stakeholders present than is the case in private organizations. He speculates that this diversity could be an obstacle to effective strategic IT planning because political considerations may dominate technical considerations. West (2001) recently found that e-government has made limited use of interactivity in Web sites and that its early impacts are incremental in nature. This finding appears to contrast with much of the online business sites that have a good deal of interactivity. I hope that the study encourages new research on public-private differences in managing IT.

References

Aggarwal, A.K., & Mirani, R. (1999). DSS model usage in public and private sectors: Differences and implications. *Journal of End User Computing, 11*(3), 20-28.

Bajjaly, S.T. (1998). Strategic information systems planning in the public sector. *American Review of Public Administration, 28*(1), 76-86.

Bozeman, B. (1987). *All organizations are public.* San Francisco: Jossey Bass.

Bozeman, B., & Bretschneider, S. (1986). Public management information systems: Theory and prescription. *Public Administration Review, 46*(Special Issue), 475-487.

Bozeman, B., Reed, P.N., & Scott, P. (1992). Red tape and task delays in public and private organizations. *Administration & Society, 24*(93), 290-322.

Bretschneider, S. (1990). Management information systems in public and private organizations: An empirical test. *Public Administration Review, 50*(5), 536-545.

Bretschneider, S. (2001). Organizational adoption of microcomputer technology: The role of sector. *Information Systems Research, 4*(1), 88-108.

Buchanan, B. (1974). Government managers, business executives, and organizational commitment. *Public Administration Review, 34*(4), 339-347.

Carr, N. G. (2003, May). IT doesn't matter. *Harvard Business Review,* 41-49.

Carr, N. G. (2004, May 17). Follow, don't lead. *Computerworld, 38*(20), 31-32.

Caudle, S.L., Gor, W.L., & Newcomer, K.E. (1991). Key information systems management issues for the public sector. *MIS Quarterly,* 171-188.

Copyright © 2006, Idea Group Inc. Copying or distributing in print or electronic forms without written permission of Idea Group Inc. is prohibited.

Center for Technology in Government. (1996). *Making smart IT choices.*

Computerworld. (2003, July 7). IT does so matter! *Computerworld, 37*(27), 36.

Coursey, D. (forthcoming). Strategically managing information technology: Challenges in the e-gov era. In J. Rabin (Ed.), *Handbook of public administration* (3rd ed.). New York: Marcel Dekker.

Coursey, D., & Bozeman, B. (1990). Decision making in public and private organizations: A test of alternative concepts of publicness. *Public Administration Review, 50*(5), 525-535.

Coursey, D., & Killingsworth, J. (2000). Managing government Web services in Florida: Issues and lessons. In G. David Garson (Ed.), *Handbook of public management information systems* (pp. 331-343). New York: Marcel Dekker.

Cronk, J., & Sharp, J. (1998). A framework for IS outsourcing strategy in private and public sector contexts. In L. P. Willcocks, & M. C. Lacity (Eds.), *Strategic sourcing of information systems* (pp. 163-185). New York: John Wiley.

Culpan, O. (1995). Attitudes of end-users towards information technology in manufacturing and service industries. *Information & Management, 28*, 167-176.

Douglas, M. (2001, September). Building blocks. *Government Technology*, 24-25.

Elliot, R.H., & Tevavichulada, S. (1999). Computer literacy and human resource management: A public/private sector comparison. *Public Personnel Management, 28*(2), 259-274.

Fletcher, C.N., & Lorenz, F.O. (1985, April). Structural influences on the relationship between objective and subjective indicators of well-being. *Social Indicators Research, 16*, 333-345.

Fletcher, P.T., Bretschneider, S.I., & Marchand, D.A. (1992). *Managing information technology: Transforming county governments in the 1990s.* Syracuse, NY: Syracuse University, School of Information Studies.

George, J.F., & Theis, J.W. (1991). Microcomputer training: Do trained users differ from non-trained users? *Data Base, 22*, 1-10.

Hougland, J. G. (1987). Criteria for client evaluation of public programs: A comparison of objective and perceptual measures. *Social Science Quarterly, 68*, 386-394.

Lee, M. (2001, May). *The missing link: State profiles of the chief information officer.* The Maxwell School, Syracuse University, Governmental Performance Project, Learning Paper Series. Retrieved from http://www.maxwell.syr.edu/gpp/Publications/Working_papers/CIO%20Learning%20Paper.pdf

Lindberg, D. A. B. (1979). *The growth of medical information systems in the United States.* Lexington, KY: Lexington Books.

Markus, M. L. (1983, June). Power, politics, and mis implementation. *Communications of the ACM, 26*, 430-444.

McGee, M.K. (1997, March 17). Connecticut proposes outsourcing. *InformationWeek, 22.*

Copyright © 2006, Idea Group Inc. Copying or distributing in print or electronic forms without written permission of Idea Group Inc. is prohibited.

Metzgar, J., & Miranda, R. A. (2001). Ch.12: Technology for financial planning and forecasting. In R. A. Miranda (Ed.), *ERP and financial management systems: The backbone of digital government* (pp.135-146). Chicago: Government Finance Officers Association.

Miller, B. (1994). Lessons from Florida's public assistance automation. *Government Technology*, *7*(1), 1, 42.

Mohan, L., Holstein, W. K., & Adams, R. B. (1990, December). EIS: It can work in the public sector. *MIS Quarterly*, 435-448.

Morgan, T.P. (1998, September). Ecommerce options. *Global Technology Business*, 40-42.

National Electronic Commerce Coordinating Council. (2001, December 11). *Sharing: Best practices and lessons learned*. Retrieved August 1, 2004, from http://www.ec3.org/Downloads/2001/App_Sharing_ED.pdf

Newcombe, T. (1996, June). Web makes economic sense. *Government Technology*. Retrieved from http://www.govtech.net/publications/gt/1996/June/trends2june.shtm

Norberg, A., O'Neill, J. E., & Freedman, K. (1996). *Transforming computer technology: Information processing for the pentagon, 1962-1986*. Baltimore: Johns Hopkins University Press.

Nutt, P. C. (1999). Public-private differences and the assessment of alternatives for decision making. *Journal of Public Administration Theory and Research*, *9*(2), 305-350.

Perlman, E. (2004, October). Graphic details. *Governing Magazine*. Retrieved November 5, 2004, from http://www.governing.com/articles/10gis.htm

Porter, M., & Millar, V. E. (1985). How information gives you competitive advantage. *Harvard Business Review*, *63*(4), 149-160.

Rainey, H. G. (1976). Comparing public and private organizations. *Public Administration Review*, *36*(2), 233-244.

Rainey, H. G. (1983). Public agencies and private firms: Incentives, goals, and individual roles. *Administration & Society*, *15*(2), 207-242.

Rainey, H. G., & Kingsley, G. (1998). Risk culture in public and private organizations. *Public Administration Review*, *58*(2), 109-118.

Rainey, H. G., Pandey, S. K., & Bozeman, B. (1995). Public and private mangers' perceptions of red tape. *Public Administration Review*, *55*(6), 567-574.

Reed, B. J. (2001). *Strategic information systems planning in U.S. state governments: States and prospects indicated by quantitative analysis of year 2000 government performance project data*. The Maxwell School, Syracuse University, Governmental Performance Project, Learning Paper Series, August. Retrieved January 10, 2002, from http://www.maxwell.syr.edu/gpp/Publications/Working_papers/Strategic_Info_Systems.pdf

Rocheleau, B. (2000). Guidelines for public-sector systems acquisition. In G. D. Garson (Ed.), *Handbook of public sector information systems* (pp. 377-390). New York: Marcel Dekker.

Copyright © 2006, Idea Group Inc. Copying or distributing in print or electronic forms without written permission of Idea Group Inc. is prohibited.

Rocheleau, B., & Wu, L. (2002). Public vs. private information systems: Do they differ in important ways: A review and empirical test. *American Review of Public Administration, 32*(4), 379-397.

Singer, L. (1995, December). IT outsourcing: Wisconsin and Indiana compared. *Government Technology,* 104-105.

Steen, M. (1998, June 22). The training imperative. *Infoworld,* 78-82.

Traska, M. R. (1988). Managed care: Whoever has the data wins the game. *Hospitals, 62*(5), 50-56.

Varon, E. (2000, August 1). Uncle Sam wants you. *CIO,* 132-144.

Venkatraman, N. (1997, Spring). Beyond outsourcing: Managing IT resources as a value center. *Sloan Management Review, 38,* 51-64.

Wahl, M. (1998, November 8). Sizing up customers: Are you happy with our bank? More and more, that may depend on how happy your bank is with you. *Chicago Tribune,* Business Section, 1.

West, D. (2001, August 30-September 2). *E-government and the transformation of public sector service delivery.* Paper prepared for delivery at the annual meeting of the American Political Science Association, San Francisco.

Whiting, R. (2000, May 8). Web data piles up. *Informationweek,* 50-64.

Whiting, R., & Davis, B. (1999, August 23). More on the edge. *Informationweek,* 36-48.

Wu, L. (1999). *A comparative study: End-user training in public and private organizations.* Ph.D. Dissertation. DeKalb, IL: Northern Illinois University.

Additional Reading

The Bozeman and Bretschneider article is a classic and still one of the very few to discuss systematically the differences between public and private systems. The Center for Technology publication (1996) expands on these issues. The Carr article and the rebuttals to his position provide a stimulating thought material concerning what the appropriate level of investment should be in organizations. As I point out earlier, though Carr initially aimed his argument at private sector IT, it is even more relevant to governmental organizations and is worth reading.

Key Concepts

- Public Management Information Systems
- Market share
- Strategic weapon

Copyright © 2006, Idea Group Inc. Copying or distributing in print or electronic forms without written permission of Idea Group Inc. is prohibited.

Discussion Questions

1. Do you agree with Carr's position that the IT investments should be treated like a utility, minimizing costs subject to maintaining the integrity and security of the system? Is this approach appropriate for government? Under what conditions should government try to undertake risky investments in IT? Do you think that the differences between public and private information systems make any difference in the willingness of governmental organizations to make investments in expensive systems such as Enterprise Resource Planning (ERP), Data Warehousing, Customer Relations Management, and Geographic Information Systems? What, if any, would be the major differences between the business cases that governments would make for adoption of these programs compared with for-profit organizations?

2. Have you come across any examples of competition among governmental organizations that would make it reasonable if not necessary to invest heavily in IT? Do you know of any governmental or nonprofit organizations that view IT as a crucial aspect to competing effectively, for example, in attracting economic development or (for human services agencies) customers? What role, if any, does competition play in governmental organizations with which you are familiar?

3. How central to government is the IT function? How important is it to have a strong IT system? Would you characterize IT as a core function and, if so, should IT be heavily outsourced?

Exercise

Conduct a study to test for the differences between public and private sector organizations. There are several possibilities for comparison. For example, compare the structure and nature of the Web sites of pubic and private organizations. Are there any systematic differences? A second option would be to interview executives and/or IT managers in the two sectors and assess their attitudes towards IT. To what extent do you think that managers in the public sector view IT as a competitive weapon?

Copyright © 2006, Idea Group Inc. Copying or distributing in print or electronic forms without written permission of Idea Group Inc. is prohibited.

Chapter II

Planning for Information Technology in the Public Sector

Introduction: Why Plan?

Experts agree that formal strategic IT plans should not only be done, but they should also be revised regularly at least on a yearly basis (Barrett & Greene, 2001). Reed (2003) cites data from the Government Performance Project that high-performing governments tend to update their plans one or more times during a year. Raumer (2001) points out that with the cutbacks in governmental budgets, IT projects are no longer rubber stamped but must make their *business case* and argues that the strategic planning process is needed to set sound priorities. The term business case refers to a case based on solid business reasons such as increased revenues and/or decreased costs that are expected to improve the effectiveness and efficiency of the organization and may be contrasted with changes for non-business reasons such as for prestige and "keeping up with technology." Failure to plan adequately has led to serious problems. For example, Ward (2003) has argued that organizations must plan their intranets or the intranets will die. He cites examples of intranets that have failed and have to be restructured frequently because they were done "on a whim" of management with no clear direction and became political "footballs."

In this chapter, I discuss the key issues and problems encountered in planning for information technology. In particular, I will focus on the logic behind prescriptions to do planning and the challenges and complexities that occur in planning for IT. I also seek to explain why planning is often not done at all or not done according to the recommendations laid out by experts.

Copyright © 2006, Idea Group Inc. Copying or distributing in print or electronic forms without written permission of Idea Group Inc. is prohibited.

Despite general agreement that planning for IT is important, many governments do not have formal IT plans. Moulder (2001) found that only about 6% (41 out of 691) reported that they had a "current" plan concerning IT. Another study (Schulz, 2001, p. 18) found that about 29% of cities had technology plans and that the existence of plans correlated strongly with city size. In my own case studies of local governments, fewer than half of the small to moderate-size municipalities that I visited had formal IT plans. Even those departments that did have IT plans generally did not revise them on an annual basis. Often they would do a 3- to 5-year plan and did not revise it until the period ended and often not even then.

Why do so many governments lack formal IT plans or not keep their plans updated? First, many IT heads are skeptical about the utility of IT plans because they believe that IT changes so quickly that spending a great deal of time on formal planning is futile. Steve Steinbrecher (2000), head of Contra Costa, California's IT department was asked how IT will change over the next five years and replied that he had "no idea" and that he could not plan or "strategize further than 18 months out." One head of a small local government IT department also felt that a formal plan would not be very useful because of the rapidity of change:

I have an IT vision. I don't have a formal plan. I have no clue where we are going to be in a year. I know that we will continue with a more secure system. I will know that we will continue to try to improve on minimizing downtime.... So we don't really have a plan because I can't foresee the future. Technology changes so quickly and I also believe we are fairly ahead of the curve right now.... We are on the leading edge of the curve...that is my perception. I don't have a clue as to what is going to happen next. I think we are going to have to hold for a while...changes are very hard to find right now.

Beaumaster (1999, pp. 81-82) conducted a study of IT planning in small and medium-sized governments in the state of Virginia and likewise found that 66% did not employ a strategic technology planning process and only 25% said they did any kind of formal IT planning. At the same time, she (Beaumaster, p. 84) found that a majority (57%) admitted that they did not think that their planning process was effective.

Other IT directors take the position that a very general plan outlining broad objectives is okay, but generally they only had a one-year working plan required as part of their budgetary process, not a long-term strategic plan, and did not feel that detailed planning for the future would be useful as the following director put it:

We plan every year based on what our budget is, we meet every quarter to see where we are with that annual plan, what we don't have and what is requested with us is to develop that strategic plan. And I think that that strategic plan needs to be done with generalities like, "What are you doing with wireless? With your hard-wired infrastructure? What are you doing with your plans for disaster recovery? Where are you going to go with your efforts to get into those departments and review those processes...if you are going to create a plan with all of the checkmarks of here is what I am going to do in year 1, year 2, etc.,.... It is too much a moving target....

Copyright © 2006, Idea Group Inc. Copying or distributing in print or electronic forms without written permission of Idea Group Inc. is prohibited.

Another reason is that many small governments have few if any full IT staff. In some cases, a generalist administrator (e.g., assistant to the city manager) performs the role of the IT director as well as other duties. The pressures on their time to meet demands of day-to-day services makes long-term planning seem like a luxury to these administrators. However, the lack of a formal plan does not mean that municipalities without such plans are devoid of IT planning. Many of them say they have a plan "in their head," as the IT director said. Indeed, the policies of the non-plan cities that I interviewed appeared to be similar to those that did have formal plans such as standardizing software and setting hardware standards aimed at minimizing support costs for IT. It should be remembered that planning is a process, not a document, and if organizations take actions aimed at improving long-term computing (e.g., implementation of standards and increased sharing of information), then it can be argued that planning is taking place even if there is no formal plan.

One major problem raised by several IT directors about planning is that the legislative and political leaders of these governments have not set strategic goals or made clear their priorities, making it impossible to construct an IT plan in the manner envisioned by experts, as the following IT director noted:

I have not been able to do that [develop a strategic plan] because...they [council] have not put together a strategic plan with their goals. So I tell them that I cannot do my own strategic plan unless you have an overall one for the city. I tell them if they set up a plan and say they want to spend more dollars on IT for some purpose, then I can do my own strategic plan or if you want to be conservative in spending on IT, then I can come up with my plan to agree with that approach.

Some cities required departmental "business plans" in conjunction with the budget process and, in some cases, these plans can cover several years and may accomplish some of the functions of a strategic plan, though these plans tend to focus on specific projects and often do not include elements common to strategic plans such as an analysis of existing systems and statements of guidelines concerning information architecture. In the following, an IT director discusses the nature of their IT business plan:

Each department puts together a business plan for the next four years and basically presents it to other departments and council. The focus of that business plan is to align ourselves with city-wide goals. And the justification for each line of the business plan is to link it to one of the city-wide goals. And then we talk about what our strategies are for attaining those goals. Each department does that. Before they do it, we [the IS Department] meet with each department and...ask what kinds of things do you want to achieve for the next four years? We do so in order that we ensure that we have the resources (equipment and personnel) and skills necessary to support the proposed applications.

To summarize, formal strategic plans are often not done or updated regularly in many organizations due to limits of time and staff as well as the perception that IT changes too

Copyright © 2006, Idea Group Inc. Copying or distributing in print or electronic forms without written permission of Idea Group Inc. is prohibited.

quickly to make a detailed long-range plan. Schulz (2001, p. 20) says that if an organization lacks many resources to plan, it is best to create a "one- or two-page working project list." Many governments, often small but also larger organizations, rely on informal planning and/or short "vision statements."

Components of Information Technology Plans

There are many different kinds of IT plans. Some IT plans now focus in on one area of IT such as an "e-government plan" (e.g., Washtenaw County's E-Government Strategic Plan) or a Geographic Information System Plan (e.g., City of Santa Barbara's GIS Master Plan). As IT expands to cover new technologies, it becomes difficult to cover everything in a single plan. However, due to the close inter-relationships, it is useful to have a comprehensive plan that looks across technologies. For example, GIS is now being used to provide e-government access to information on parcels available for sale and both GIS and e-government now often interact with the government's other applications such as finance and permitting. Consequently, it is useful to have a document that views all of the information technologies of governments in a comprehensive manner. Strategic technology plans differ greatly as to how comprehensive and detailed they are. Some plans are limited to short vision statements. Others are large volumes providing detailed analyses of the past, present, as well as the future IT activities. In the following, I list the major components that may be included in comprehensive strategic plans:

1. **Aligning IT with the organizational goals:** Plans identify the goals and priorities of the government and outline an IT vision and discuss how IT will help to achieve these goals. Methods used to identify goals and priorities including use of focus groups for "visioning" and stakeholder analyses that are described next.

2. **Identification of IT policies and architectural standards:** Most government plans specify IT policies concerning issues such as the role and functions of the IT department including the degree of authority the IT unit will exercise in purchasing and other key IT decisions. They also specify technical "architectural" standards such as standard hardware and software platforms.

3. **Analysis of the current IT system including identification of gaps and the need for projects:** Many plans provide a detailed analysis of the current system. In several cases, the plans include a history of IT in the organization, showing how IT has evolved through time. This analysis of the existing system may also identify the strengths, weaknesses and limitations of the current system. This information is based on various sources such as interviews, surveys, and analysis of government documents. Some plans may include a thorough analysis of business processes. The end result of this component would be a list of areas that need to be improved.

4. **Analysis of best practices and industry standards:** Some plans review the various software and hardware currently being used or planned for by the organization and

Copyright © 2006, Idea Group Inc. Copying or distributing in print or electronic forms without written permission of Idea Group Inc. is prohibited.

compare it with prevailing industry standards. They may also examine the practices of organizations that are recognized to be in the forefront of IT and/or they report on the practices of other similar, often nearby, organizations that they believe to be realistic comparison organizations as well as being worthy of emulation.

5. **Identification of new projects and project planning:** The gaps identified in the analysis of the current systems combined with the best practices analysis provide the basis for identifying specific IT projects that need to be accomplished in order to achieve better alignment of IT with the government's goals. In some cases, the strategic plan includes detailed specification of priorities among the projects, projected budgets, timelines for the projects, and how these projects will affect other departments and the overall organization. The timeline, including a Gantt chart and estimates of budgets and personnel requirements for each project, may be included. "Dependencies" may be identified in which a project's success may be contingent on certain other steps that have to occur. For example, this was one of the key steps in KPMG's e-government plan for Houston, Texas. Likewise, the plans may identify interdepartmental effects of specific projects.

Thus the length of time devoted to IT planning varies tremendously. Plans that cover most if not all of these components require the use of many workdays and staff to complete. In my review, the most comprehensive plans tended to be conducted by outside consulting firms. Some internal plans were fairly extensive though not comprehensive. For example, Norfolk, Virginia did an extensive IT plan based on the methodology of Deloitte and Touche consultants but did not attempt to do a business process analysis despite its desirability due to time constraints (ICMA, 1998, p. 99). The costs in terms of resources of these extensive plans can be large. However, if the plan is well-done, the planning process may make other tasks, such as creating RFPs for purchasing projects, easier as many parts of the plan need to be incorporated into good RFPs (such as a discussion of current business practices and a detailed history and context of the IT system). Next, I analyze some of the key issues that need to be addressed in planning.

Obtaining Input for Strategic Plans

The development of a formal plan involves many steps that may be missed out if planning is kept informal. For example, formal plans usually involve a systematic attempt at obtaining input from end users such as through surveys and systematic discussions with various departmental staff. By putting the plan into draft format and submitting it to end users and others, they may obtain more feedback than is likely with informal planning alone. Some municipalities hired consultants to do their plans including gathering input but these were usually relatively larger municipalities with more resources.

As I noted previously, one of the most difficult problems is that those at the very top of the hierarchy—the executive, legislative, and generalist managerial leaders of the organization—have not made clear their goals for technology. Some governments (e.g., see Rockville, Maryland) use focus group studies of key actors to attain this information. One of the steps put forth by the GFOA (Government Finance Officers Association) is

Copyright © 2006, Idea Group Inc. Copying or distributing in print or electronic forms without written permission of Idea Group Inc. is prohibited.

aimed at achieving this input by conducting what they call a *"visioning analysis"* (Miranda, 2002a). As described by Miranda (2002b), the exercise would be somewhat similar to that employed to define a mission and would be aimed at getting the leadership to state what "long term functionality" they would like to obtain—what would the ideal system look like? In the example that Miranda et al. (2002b) employ, they had the Technology Steering Committee of a mid-size county government identify the strengths and weaknesses of the existing systems and then asked them to develop "a vision of an improved system for five years into the future."

One of the areas that visioning could well delve into concerns the information needs of decision-makers at various levels of the organization. Are they being met? For example, a Center for Technology and Government (2000) study aimed at developing a homeless information system discovered through its interviews that the funding agency (Bureau of Shelter Services) was not obtaining evaluative data that would allow them to determine how successful their contracts were. On the opposite side of the coin, an inventory of data currently being collected can be useful in identifying information that is not being used by any actor in which case serious consideration can be given to dropping its collection as long it is not legally required.

Today, IT planning requires obtaining input from a wide range of sources. Strategic IT plans require in-depth discussions with IT staff about planning for the future. These discussions should also include end users as well as employees who are performing IT jobs but who are not part of the IT department. Taken together, the process of seeking out the full range (not just the leadership's) assessment of the needs of users of the existing and/or planned system is referred to as a *stakeholder analysis*. Typically these involve meetings with individuals and groups (Miranda, 2002a), although formal surveys may also be employed. A full range of departments should be covered for a comprehensive technology plan. Failing to obtain input from actors who are expected to react negatively is likely to lead to the failure of a project according to a study done by the Center for Technology in Government (2000, p. 14) of the building of a data mart for organizations serving the homeless. In many governments, certain employees (e.g., they may be police, fire, or public works departments in local government) perform jobs that entirely or primarily involve IT tasks such as supporting departmental servers, developing GIS systems, etc. In effect, they are part of the IT staff of the organization even if they do not formally belong to that unit. Likewise, today many employees' jobs may necessitate them becoming expert in a particular area of technology. For example, finance officers with whom I talked had learned to create sophisticated revenue projection spreadsheets. Also, external vendors/consultants generally play major roles in providing ongoing or periodic support of governmental IT systems. Often these consultants have provided long-term service to the government and, in effect, they too form a significant part of the government's IT staff. Consequently, they too should be included in the data-gathering process. Thus gathering information from internal and external sources can be an extended process with several steps. Figure 1 is a flow chart of the process used by the City of Rockville (Maryland) to develop its 2001 Strategic IT Plan which is a four-phase process taking nearly a year to do.

Planners need to consult with the IT department's internal customers including generalist managers, department heads, and end users. In some cases, governments tend to

Copyright © 2006, Idea Group Inc. Copying or distributing in print or electronic forms without written permission of Idea Group Inc. is prohibited.

Figure 1. Outline of the City of Rockville's IT strategic planning process

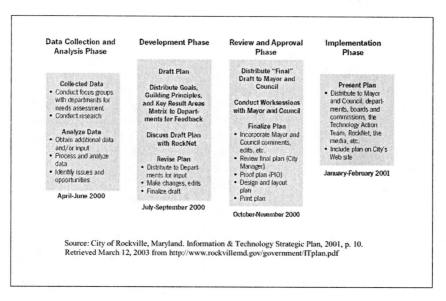

Source: City of Rockville, Maryland. Information & Technology Strategic Plan, 2001, p. 10.
Retrieved March 12, 2003 from http://www.rockvillemd.gov/government/ITplan.pdf

rely on IT committees for this input but it is important to obtain input from the full range of internal customers. It is dangerous to focus only on the leadership of departments and not directly communicate with end users who often are most knowledgeable about the functionality of applications (Rocheleau, 2000). It is best to *triangulate* by obtaining different types of information (qualitative and quantitative) from different sources (all levels of the hierarchy in all departments). It is also questionable to rely on formal documents because these documents do not throw light on the crucial informal system of the organization and information involving politics and personalities that can influence IT policy. It is best to use multiple sources to obtain a more comprehensive and stronger understanding. For example, KPMG in studying the technology of the City of Houston employed both formal departmental surveys and informal interviews with departmental staff. Informal interviews enable gathering of much richer information as to the reasons *why* users like or dislike systems. Structured surveys are useful in preventing a few very vocal persons from dominating input. For example, in one case study that I did, one end user department was unhappy with the IT department and their unhappiness tended to affect the views of others such as the top management concerning IT. But when consumer satisfaction surveys were done of all end users, the results were much more positive for the IT department.

With the development of e-government, it is now necessary for plans to seek out extensive external feedback too. Legislative bodies (e.g., councils and boards for local government) provide input and formally approve plans but the value of the input varies greatly depending on the degree of expertise and interest their members have in IT. Many governments seek input from community-based organizations in constructing their IT

Copyright © 2006, Idea Group Inc. Copying or distributing in print or electronic forms without written permission of Idea Group Inc. is prohibited.

plans. Some conduct community surveys to gauge the unmet need for e-government services as the following IT director noted:

(Did you have any customer demand for that [developing online interactive e-government services] or did you just go ahead with it?)

We did have some demand based on a survey that [name of survey organization] did. It is a fairly large survey done for the entire city. We did ask some e-government and e-commerce type of questions, something like 'if you had electronic billing, would you use it?' That kind of stuff. ...we had some data that drove it [their decision to develop e-government applications on their Web site].

Many of the people on the councils and boards often do not get very involved in IT projects because they may lack expertise or time required to understand and critique complex IT projects. However, some cities form IT committees made up of professionals from the community who have expertise in IT (but who don't sit on the board or council). These committees review both proposed purchases and IT plans of the IT department. These committees can have a big impact on decision-making as the following IT director noted:

We have a technology commission made up of community members who are in the IT business selected by the Mayor. They do not review day-to-day activities but they do review major IT purchases and projects. They give... advice and counsel about the proposals.

(Do they ever come to different conclusions than you?)

If they did, we would work it out [i.e., differences] because we know that if the commission does not agree, the council will never approve the...project.

Another set of data used to plan involves the review of *best practices* and/or industry standards. I will discuss best practices in detail in another chapter but for our purposes here, best practices may be loosely defined as those that are employed by organizations that are widely accepted as having achieved excellence and thus are worthy of emulating (Rocheleau, 2000). Assessments of best practice organizations may be based on quantitative ratings by groups such as Syracuse University's Government Performance Project (http://www.govexec.com/gpp/about.htm) and other rating systems. Or it may be based on informal reputation in the region. The systems of these "leading" organizations are reviewed and may be used as the model by other governments. Copying other organizations' successful projects is widely accepted by governmental organizations as the following IT director noted:

Copyright © 2006, Idea Group Inc. Copying or distributing in print or electronic forms without written permission of Idea Group Inc. is prohibited.

Well, I will be the first to admit that I borrow from my peers as much as I can borrow. Borrow ruthlessly. [Name of IT organization with many governments as members] is an organization that I have taken a lot away from..... You go to people who are doing things successfully and try to see how they are doing them. And if it fits for your organization, see if you can do the same thing.

This director went on to argue that best practices may be specific to a particular functional area because there was no case in which a single organization was excelling in all areas. Likewise, differences in resources (staff and financial) may make borrowing impossible and, even when similar, adjustments may have to be made due to differences in the organizations.

Strategic plans often include an analysis of the industry standards in major hardware and applications in which the government is involved. For example, the Naperville (Illinois) plan looked at the status of applications in various areas such as electronic and mobile government, enterprise resource planning, geographic information systems, human resource information systems, and so forth. In each case, an assessment may be made as to whether there is an industry standard and a discussion of what leading governmental organizations with similar resources are employing. The latter issue can be important since limited resources may prevent a municipality from adopting the "best of breed" application in some areas. In particular, certain applications employed by leading organizations such as Enterprise Resource Planning (ERP) systems tend to be very expensive and may not be affordable by smaller governments.

Planning and Alignment of Technology with Governmental Goals

It is the accepted wisdom of IT experts that the very first step in building an effective IT system is that the organization must ensure that their technology is aligned with its strategic goals. In this view, the IT system should be viewed as a tool to achieve organizational purposes—IT should not be the "tail wagging the dog." There should be consistency between the true goals of the government and its information technology. What does *alignment* mean in practical terms? For example, if the top goal of the city is to provide easy access to governmental services, then the organization should already have or be investing in a robust e-government infrastructure. There is empirical evidence in the private sector to show that alignment of IT with organizational goals matters. Chan (2002) and Cragg (2002) both found that private sector organizations with closer alignment between technology and organizational goals tend to be more successful and this was true for small as well as large organizations. But, evidence shows that close alignment between IT is often lacking even in private sector organizations. According to a study by Jahnke (2004), 44% of Chief Financial Officers said that alignment was weak and 4% said it did not exist. According to Sauer and Burn (1997), there are *two kinds of alignment: external and internal*. In the external fit, the organization's top leadership must set strategic goals so there is a fit between the organization's strategy and its market. Sauer and Burn (1997, p. 91) define internal fit as that between technology and

Copyright © 2006, Idea Group Inc. Copying or distributing in print or electronic forms without written permission of Idea Group Inc. is prohibited.

this external strategy by structuring their IT department and its practices in a way that will allow the organization to compete successfully. For example, if an organization exists in a highly competitive industry in which new products are introduced regularly, its internal IT structure would need to be structured to allow quick development of these new products. Thus internal processes that slow the introduction of these new products and services would have to be modified or they are likely to suffer market loss.

How relevant are the concepts of alignment of technology and business goals with technology to the public sector? Burn (1997, p. 64, 74) believes that most governments fall into the category of "*defender*" organizations that tend to have "narrow product domains and a narrow management focus." Generalist governments (e.g., municipalities) tend to focus on providing the same set of services through time (e.g., snowplowing, meter reading, police patrols, etc.) and they are not forced to continually develop new services and products as many private sector organizations do in order to maintain or expand market share. Governments do innovate but much of the innovation over the past decade involves changes in the access to these traditional services by making them available over the Internet (e.g., paying parking tickets and water bills) but these e-government functions do not usually involve the creation of new products and services. This difference between public and private sectors may help to explain why Burn finds that governments tend to employ "bottom-up short-term planning."

However, governments do find the idea of alignment relevant to IT planning. The City of Irvine (California) put it this way in their Year 2000 Strategic Technology Plan:

In 1996 the computing environment at the City of Irvine was outdated and did not support the City's vision of a responsive, efficient, and cost-effective government. The

Figure 2. City of Irvine's (California) longer term vision

✓ Users will have access to data directly,
✓ Information will be stored in an integrated database, which is accessible to all needing it,
✓ Individual users of information will be able to access, analyze and develop reports on the City's database without programmer intervention being required,
✓ Information will be shared between all departments,
✓ The "islands of data" will be replaced with an integrated database that allows key data to be input only once,
✓ The integrated database will be linked to the spatial (map) database when appropriate, forming a true Geographic Information System (GIS),
✓ The public will have access to public information without having a staff person retrieve it for them,
✓ The public will have the tools to get public information from the City twenty-four hours a day, seven days a week,
✓ The new systems will facilitate a two-way communication with the City and the public (i.e., the public will be able to send information in the form of applications, electronic mail, police reports, business license information and permits to the City for processing),
✓ Decision-makers will be able to make better-informed decisions because data is readily available,
✓ Council members could be in contact with their constituents through electronic mail through the Internet,
✓ Public opinion may be more easily shared thus promoting more community involvement,
✓ A City bulletin board will convey City issues to the public through the Internet

Source: City of Irvine, California. Strategic Technology Plan, 2000-2005 (April 2000 Update), p. 12.
   Retrieved July 9, 2003 from http://www.misac.org/state_library/irvine_tp2000.doc

---

Copyright © 2006, Idea Group Inc. Copying or distributing in print or electronic forms without written permission of Idea Group Inc. is prohibited.

City of Irvine recognized that the quality of information systems is key to organizational effectiveness and to the ability to serve the citizens of the City.

The Irvine plan goes on to develop a goal of becoming a "smart city" that will meet the City's goals and its longer term vision is shown in Figure 2. Note that six of the 13 goals involve the public. The increasingly external orientation of government IT plans shows the tremendous change from the internal focus that used to dominate IT planning.

The types of goals present in the Irvine long-term vision are typical of goals in many other IT strategic plans and, indeed, do not differ much from the goals held by communities that do not have formal IT plans. A more difficult test is whether the organization is able to develop a good system of prioritization based on goals stated by leadership.

What should IT managers do if top leadership does not set strategic goals thus making alignment more difficult? If the leadership of the organization does not clearly identify their strategic goals, then IT leadership has to set its own strategies for IT, albeit with caution. Many of the IT directors with whom I spoke did not feel they got clear guidance from their councils, boards, or generalist managers as the following director noted:

I read a lot about that [necessity to align technology with the business goals] too…from the other side, you have to try to get them to tell you (from the political end) 'Where do you want to go?' and that is the biggest problem of all, you try to get that from the manager but if he is not getting that from the board, you are reacting as opposed to planning. So if your board has a well defined 'here is where we would like to take the organization' and it is the manager's job to get them there, then I think you can align.… But without knowing those, it is a crapshoot.

Lacking a clear vision from political leadership, many IT managers pursue their own vision of how IT can best serve the organization and community. For example, most of the IT and generalist managers I spoke with reported little pressure from the community to innovate with e-government. These IT directors initiated e-government projects and were ahead of the political system in this respect. As one IT director said, "I am always ahead of them [the council]."   Holley, Dufner and Reed's (2002) study of strategic information systems planning at the state level also found that top the leadership was generally not actively involved.

A similar set of general goals appear in several different plans. For example, the so-called "*any-any-any-any*" goal was used or mentioned by several governments. The City of Phoenix (2002, Information Technology Architecture, p.4) describes this goal as follows:

The overarching IT strategy is summarized in the any-any-any-any model *[italics added] (any authorized individual accessing any information from any location using any device). A corollary of the any-any-any-any is that the right data should be available at the right place at the right time.*

Copyright © 2006, Idea Group Inc. Copying or distributing in print or electronic forms without written permission of Idea Group Inc. is prohibited.

Other organizations echo this goal and they often undertake projects such as mobile computing to achieve it. The similarity of goals and language in many of these IT strategic plans suggests that IT professionals are playing a proactive role in articulating goals that IT professionals have come to accept and share widely among themselves regardless of whether their boards or generalist managers define their goals. This helps to explain why the general policies and goals of many local governments appear to be very similar whether their plans are formal or informal, extensive or skimpy.

The lack of strategic planning can create difficulties in setting priorities. There are limited IT funds and governments must choose from an array of projects that different departments view as deserving. For example, how much of IT money should be spent on e-government projects that will provide better access to community services via the Internet versus other IT priorities such as improving servers and other infrastructure? Due to limited staff and money, aligning goals means making tough choices among desirable alternatives and systematic planning should aid this process. Due to cutbacks in funding resulting from the poor economy, hard choices are common for state and local governments (McKay, 2003).

One major purpose of strategic planning is to make sure that there is a strong business case made for a project. Peterson and DiCarco (1998) report many examples of "*technophilia*" in which organizations purchase costly software even if there is no strong business case for it. For example, this author has seen some governments invest in geographic information systems because "everyone is doing it" despite the fact that they lacked a plan for building applications to justify the enormous costs. End user staff may be eager to purchase the best and most expensive software system available and some consultants may encourage this approach. However, in the current climate of budget cutbacks, this author sees increased emphasis on projects that promise to save money or increase revenues. However, government exists to provide services and not make profits so their business plan and priorities do not rely simply on financial concerns.

In the private sector, Peterson and DiCarco (1998) find that technophiles are common. By way of contrast, most IT directors of the public organizations I have visited are cautious in purchasing expensive software. Indeed, they often resist upgrading many of their software systems until they were forced to (e.g., due to the system no longer being supported). Although the plans of these municipalities state the desirability of purchasing industry standard hardware and software, most confined their purchases to affordable packages that had the functionality desired but were easily affordable by the organization.

One of the implications of the "alignment" prescription is that the technology should not determine what goals and activities should be pursued but rather organizational priorities should drive IT projects. Thus public and private organizations now emphasize the importance of using "business process reengineering" (BPR) to find the best way to achieve goals and then use IT as a tool to facilitate these processes.

However, at the same time, there is also a strong trend in software purchasing by governmental (and private) sector organizations to employ "*commercial-off-the-shelf*" *(COTS)* software in order to save money. The logic of the COTS strategy is that it saves a great deal of money for the vendor and government since the software does not have to be customized. This COTS strategy is one of several guidelines common to several IT

Copyright © 2006, Idea Group Inc. Copying or distributing in print or electronic forms without written permission of Idea Group Inc. is prohibited.

plans that I have examined. For example, the Strategic Plan of the City of Sunnyvale (1999, p. 15), California states as one of its principles that "commercially developed software applications will be used whenever available" in order to reduce costs of software development. The City of Honolulu (Hawaii) makes an even stronger statement of its intention to use the COTS approach in its 2000 Information Technology plan:

Adapt business processes to applications (implement "vanilla"). Applications, wherever possible, should be purchased rather than developed. Customization should be kept to a minimum in order to enable upgrades by the vendor and business practices should adapt to applications to avoid customization.

If organizations pursue this COTS approach, they generally need to limit customized modifications of the software not only due to increased costs but also because changes can create problems with software code. Consequently, rather than using the software as a tool to do things the way the organizations believes is best, the COTS approach may force the organization to adopt to the procedures of the software. Many software developers would claim that the processes forced by the COTS version are based on best practices of leading organizations and thus the changes forced by COTS are beneficial over the long term. This is the argument of major producers of Enterprise Resource Planning software (Miranda, 2001). However, it is possible that adhering to a strict COTS approach may force changes in the nature of the services offered. A good example occurred at Indiana University where the faculty council (Olsen, 2002) cancelled a popular "four-years-and-out" graduation policy because the university's new PeopleSoft system could not support the program except with very expensive, customized program-ming. This is a case where changes are made to policies to accommodate the limitations of the software and shows how the COTS IT policy can dictate organizational goals. Some would view this as an example of the "tail wagging the dog" and opposite to the philosophy of making computing a tool to improve functionality. However, budget scarcity can make cost efficiency the top priority and organizations are often willing to sacrifice some functions to save money.

Similarly, in several of my interviews with local governmental staff, they emphasized how departmental staff would have to make changes in their practices to accommodate major new software packages to avoid the heavy costs of customized programming. These changes may not always be bad because it is possible that the new procedures are superior to the ones they are replacing. IT directors like the one in the following emphasize to end user staff purchasing new software that they had better not promise anything other than the "vanilla" version:

So expectation-setting is huge. [The director discusses new system they are in process of purchasing].... The city clerk is our project manager and she says that the departments keep telling her 'these are the things that we want' and she keeps telling them that we will be able to do it. I kept focusing her, saying 'but the base product won't do it.' [She says] 'Well, I know that but down the road it will.' But what is the expectation that you are giving them? That out of the box they are going to get this stuff and they are going

Copyright © 2006, Idea Group Inc. Copying or distributing in print or electronic forms without written permission of Idea Group Inc. is prohibited.

to get it next month…that's what they think. [She says] 'Well, I don't want the conflict.'
[The IT director] says, 'You are going to get the conflict if you continue to leave the
expectation out there'.

In short, adhering to principles such as buying COTS products can lead to conflict. One could argue that in these cases, there is ultimately an alignment of goals and technology because the goal of cost containment is dominant over the desire to carry on existing programs or conduct activities not supported by the vanilla version. The point is that the statement of general goals in an IT plan often does not give clear direction to IT staff on what to do in case of conflict between service and cost containment goals.

Most goals in IT plans are non-controversial such as to improve customer services by developing e-government functions or to improve the efficiency of government by deploying applications such as document management systems and geographic infor-mation systems. In some cases, goals can be controversial. For example, in order to facilitate their economic development goals, some states such as Virginia (Patterson, 2003) and several municipalities are developing their own broadband pipes and making this broadband available to businesses and citizens. These steps are often taken because either (e.g., in rural areas) the cable systems still do not exist or they have been slow to offer high-speed broadband services and the local cable services have been viewed as inadequate. The governor of Virginia (Patterson, 2003, p. 24) puts the rationale for governmental involvement in providing broadband as follows:

An analogy that I often use is that 100 years ago it was the railroad, and if you missed
the railroad, your town didn't prosper. Fifty years ago it was the interstate highway,
and you can see which cities were along the interstate highway and which ones
weren't,' Warner said. 'A town that misses both the railroad and the interstate highway
doesn't have the luxury of missing broadband. Three strikes and you're out'.

But controversial issues are subject to challenge and change. Cable companies combat local government initiatives with advertising and mailing campaigns as recently occurred in St. Charles, Illinois (e.g., Groark, 2003). Such projects also may be the first to be cutback and eliminated in times of fiscal stress. For example, the State of Iowa (Carnevale, 2003) is considering selling the state-owned high-speed network used by its colleges and schools in order to save money. Faced with a deficit, many of the state leaders don't believe they can afford to run the network which provides high-speed Internet connec-tions including full-motion-video links. Thus while many if not most goals pursued by IT are non-controversial, some are and they are open to change and reversal and will require the exercise of political will to incorporate into plans.

These illustrations highlight the importance of having extensive *community input* as part of the strategic planning process for IT. Just a decade ago, IT was almost entirely oriented to internal issues and constituencies. But the development of e-government and the issue of broadband have made their information technology plans much more commu-nity-oriented. Many communities employ structured surveys to obtain community input, sometimes as part of an overall survey of community services and sometimes the survey

Copyright © 2006, Idea Group Inc. Copying or distributing in print or electronic forms without written permission of Idea Group Inc. is prohibited.

is dedicated to assessing demand for e-government and other IT services. Some communities use focus groups, both internal and external, in their planning efforts. The City of St. Charles (IL) employs its Web site to recruit members of the community as volunteers for focus groups including planning efforts.

In some IT plans, priorities are clearly specified. In others, a list of desirable goals and projects is provided but no prioritization is done. Those plans that do set priorities tend to use a similar set of criteria. One major criterion is to give priority to projects that involve "mission critical" activities such as payroll, billing for utilities, and dispatch systems for emergencies as did Hickory, North Carolina (ICMA, 1998, p. 34).

In many cases, there may appear to be a logical relationship among projects such that one project needs to antedate another. For example, Keene (New Hampshire) found that their VAX system would not support some of the information needs of the Code Enforcement unit. But rather than address this need immediately, Keene used a "a workaround" to meet the immediate needs of code enforcement and supported the development of a GIS system that would provide much of the information needed by Code Enforcement, albeit 18 to 24 months later. The latter option would save money in the long-term and provide greater functionality. Gantt charts are often used in IT plans to show the timing sequences of among projects and/or activities. Figure 3 provides an example of a Gantt chart that shows the relationship among projects proposed by Visalia (California) 2002 Information Systems Plan.

Figure 3. Example of Gantt chart used in IT plan

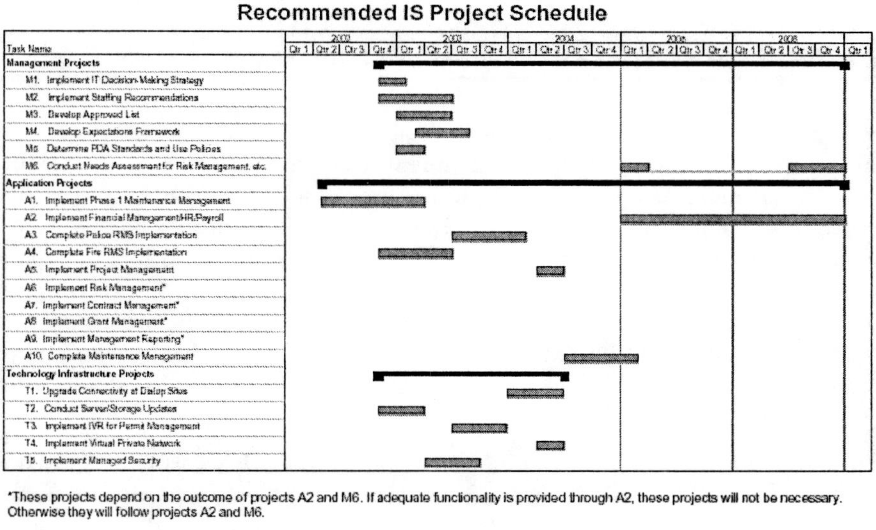

Recommended IS Project Schedule

*These projects depend on the outcome of projects A2 and M6. If adequate functionality is provided through A2, these projects will not be necessary. Otherwise they will follow projects A2 and M6.

Source: City of Visalia (California). (2002, June 28). Information Systems and Geographic Information Systems Plan.), p. 1-10. Prepared by Pacific Technologies Inc. Retrieved July 8, 2003 from http://www.misac.org/state_library/visalia-final_is_plan.pdf

Copyright © 2006, Idea Group Inc. Copying or distributing in print or electronic forms without written permission of Idea Group Inc. is prohibited.

Gantt and Pert charts can provide a great deal more useful information for planning and management such as comparisons of planned versus actual comparisons and a variety of cost and personnel analyses (Friedrichsen & Bunin, 2000). They allow organizations to identify bottlenecks such as those caused by staff who are overcommitted to a variety of tasks during the same period of time.

Some organizations develop systems to assist in assigning priorities to projects. One common trend is to give high priority to projects that will affect several departments such as infrastructure projects and applications that are enterprise-wide in their scope. One municipality had an automated system for setting priorities based on a set of questions including the following: (1) Is it beneficial for all citizens?; (2) Is it beneficial for all of the municipality?; and (3) Is it beneficial for more than one department? However, organizational staff including top management often find it difficult to adhere to structured criteria. For example, the following IT director reported that the city manager often called him in order to reorder the priorities that had been set by their automated system so as to give higher preference to the projects that he (i.e., the city manager) favored:

(IT Director) We have ranked these based on a set of criteria that have been approved by the manager for development. And he gets caught by his own system? Because sometimes the ones he wants done have a low priority....

Consequently, although there are objective criteria that can be used to set priorities, other criteria including politics and power issues may override them. In cases where strategic plans do not set priorities, they will have to be worked out in the annual budget process in which political and cost factors will often dominate.

Guidelines: Architectural and Managerial

Although there are major variations in the format of IT plans, the majority of these plans enunciate certain general IT guidelines that the entire organization is expected to conform to. Many if not most of these general guidelines are now referred to as part of the organization's "technology architecture." Raumer (2001) defines *architecture* as "the set of values and preferences used to guide decisions in the selection, acquisition, deployment and management of information technology." These architectural guidelines cover both technical and managerial issues. There are several common managerial principles and goals that affect the architecture of their systems that appear in several plans:

1.   Investments in technology should be supported by evidence of benefits that will be accomplished such as Return on Investment (ROI) projections. Thus a clear business case must be made to justify investments—they should not be done due to technophilia. Plans such as those of Honolulu and Fairfax County, Virginia emphasize the business case approach. It should be noted that ROI is often difficult if not impossible to calculate in numeric form—we will discuss this more fully in the chapter on evaluating information systems performance.

Copyright © 2006, Idea Group Inc. Copying or distributing in print or electronic forms without written permission of Idea Group Inc. is prohibited.

2. Increase sharing of information—capture data once, share it, and reduce or eliminate "data islands" and information silos (e.g., the plans of Fairfax County, Virginia and Hillsborough County, Florida).

3. Reduce the number of stand alone databases (e.g., the plans of Houston, Texas and Naperville, Illinois). Most governments are attempting to integrate their information so that databases are available to anyone (subject to legal and other privacy constraints) who needs them.

4. Emphasize total costs of ownership (TCO) in making decisions. The initial cost of the software must be adjusted to calculate total costs so that it includes costs such as training, support, maintenance, and the cost of making modifications (e.g., the plans of Honolulu and Hillsborough County, Florida). For example, an expensive but easy-to-use package will save money on training costs and consulting help from the vendor and may be cheaper in TCO terms.

5. Specification of interdepartmental (often with community participation) committees to establish and enforce IT policies such as computer policy committees (e.g., Keene, New Hampshire).

6. Computer replacement policies such as establishment of replacement funds and setting of cycles for replacement: most governmental units now have a replacement period, though the length of it may vary according to factors such as the budgetary resources.

Other architectural guidelines concern technical standards and issues such as the following:

1. Emphasize *Open Standards* in purchasing hardware and software (e.g., the plans of Fairfax County, Virginia; Keene, New Hampshire). Open standards are non-proprietary such that programmers can access and modify the source code (Peterson, May 2003). Peterson describes open software as a "hybrid of freeware and shareware" because, although those with the programming skills can download and modify the software for free, nevertheless companies such as Red Hat Linux and IBM sell commercial versions with enhanced features. Still such software tends to be much cheaper than proprietary options. By emphasizing open standards, the governmental organization makes data exchange easier and avoids being entrapped by a proprietary vendor and thus makes for more competition among vendors and lower costs, and makes it easier to change systems.

2. Emphasize *industry standard* hardware and software (e.g., the plans of Keene, New Hampshire and Naperville, Illinois). By adhering to industry standards set by the dominant company or companies, governments hope to avoid being stuck with hardware or software vendors whose market share is small or declining with the possible consequence that the organization is stuck with a dying platform that can be costly and difficult to replace.

3. Use Commercial-off-the-shelf (COTS) software to the maximum extent possible. Plans that emphasize the use of COTS software generally include prescriptions to

Copyright © 2006, Idea Group Inc. Copying or distributing in print or electronic forms without written permission of Idea Group Inc. is prohibited.

use process-reengineering of tasks to avoid customization if necessary. The purpose is to reduce software costs and also problems that may occur due to revising original code of programs (See Honolulu, Keene (Hew Hampshire), Fairfax County (Virginia), Sunnyvale California, Hillsborough County Florida plans).

4.   Emphasize adherence to centralized standards set by the IT department. In particular, organizations demand that any new software be compatible with the organization's network. Compatibility must also be achieved for any major applications and databases that it will have to interact with. Most organizations and their plans stress centralized purchasing process along with centralized standards for shared applications. However, in practice, the degree of control of the IT department can have significant limitations due to a number of factors that I discuss in Chapter 3 (Procuring Information Technology for Government).

These guidelines generally make good sense but they may sometimes conflict with one another or need to be adjusted to deal with the specific situations of the organizations involved. The guideline to pursue open systems may conflict with the guideline to use industry standard software and hardware. Most of the cities that advocated adherence to open standards also employed proprietary software such as Microsoft Office as their standard because of its status as the industry standard. For example, Hickory's (North Carolina) 1996-2001 information technology plan stated its intention to move from WordPerfect to Office because of external reporting requirements of state and Federal agencies that employed Office as the standard application suite (ICMA, 1998). The City of Phoenix's (2002, p. 18) Information Technology Architecture Plan noted the attractiveness of the Apache Web server and Linux operating systems. Both are open and free but the City of Phoenix also pointed out that "there is no vendor responsibility for the product's integrity and standards compliance." Consequently Phoenix decided to wait until industry-wide standards have been set before committing to these open platforms because they did not want to build "dependence upon a product set that may not have long-term viability." In short, the guidelines are useful but planners will still face tough decisions due to resource constraints and conflicting goals.

Analysis of Existing Systems: Strengths, Weaknesses, and Priority-Setting

Some plans include a major section on analysis of existing systems in which they study the strengths and weaknesses of current systems and *gaps* between expectations and performance as the basis for recommending future changes. This analysis is often valuable as a starting point for concrete planning, although the findings may not lead to the changes originally recommended. For example, a consultant organization developed an IT plan for a municipality and, as part of their analysis of existing systems, the consultants found that many end users were unhappy with their major financial program and the consultant recommended that they replace it with a top-line Enterprise Resource Planning (ERP) program that would cost a great deal more than their current system. The municipality was experiencing budget stress and the director inquired further into the

Copyright © 2006, Idea Group Inc. Copying or distributing in print or electronic forms without written permission of Idea Group Inc. is prohibited.

reasons behind the staff's dissatisfaction with the financial system and discovered that it was primarily due to unhappiness with the old "DOS" style interface that made it difficult to use, especially for those users who did not employ the system on a daily basis. The users were generally satisfied with the functionality of the system but disliked its interface. Thus they found that the major complaints could be solved by obtaining an update of their current system with a browser-based interface and they avoided the huge capital expenditure to purchase the more expensive system.

Thus analyses of existing problems form the basis of much of the priority-setting. The 1998 Information Technology Strategic plan of Prince Williams County (Virginia) was put together by Coopers and Lybrand and provides a good example of a plan that is candid about weaknesses. The plan's approach is to identify an issue and discuss the County's current practices concerning this issue. Then they proceed to identify the industry trends and the gap between the county practices and the industry standard, thus providing a goal for the organization to improve. The plan identifies positive accomplishments of the Prince Williams County's IT Department such as its achievement of better customer service and more feedback from end users via its agency IT representatives and establishment of a citizen advisory group. The consultants surveyed its internal customers and found the following assessments of IT services: (1) Outstanding: 4%; (2) Good: 29%; (3) Average: 25%; (4) Fair: 31%; (5) Poor: 0%; (6) Unknown: 11%. The analysis found that the county does not align all of its IT projects with the county's business goals. It also reports that the county suffers from many "stove pipe" applications and has many services dedicated to specific agency functions and the report calls for the IT department to exercise greater leadership in encouraging sharing and integration of data across departments. The report found that some end users relied on their "personal relationship" with IT staff to obtain services rather than adhere to the standard help desk and thus there was not a consistent means of communications with end user agencies. In each of these cases, the plan identifies the issue, how the government is responding to the issue, the industry trend, and a gap. For example, the County found that the department had not been proactive in identifying opportunities for sharing of data resulting in "stove pipe" applications and servers that were specific to individual agencies. The report then contrasts this situation with industry trends that view information from a corporate-wide perspective that encourages broad, interdepartmental sharing. The gap in this case was determined to be a "need for leadership." The conclusion that the report reached was that this was a non-technical problem that can only by solved by active leadership.

Boulder (Colorado's) 2002 Strategic Plan also identifies strengths and weaknesses of its IT department. The 2002 plan was based on an updating of the previous strategic technology plan done in 1998. The updating process included the following activities: (1) A debriefing of the IT department's "management team" concerning the previous planning effort; (2) An online survey of city employees about the strengths and weaknesses of the city's IT environment; (3) A SWOT (Strengths, Weaknesses, Opportunities, and Threats) analysis done by the management of the IT department; (4) Interviews with the city's managers and the city council's Technology Group, and input from staff responsible for individual departments; (5) The results of a 2001 citizen survey; and (6) Comparisons with other cities that had received recognition as "digital cities."

Copyright © 2006, Idea Group Inc. Copying or distributing in print or electronic forms without written permission of Idea Group Inc. is prohibited.

The plan reported that one of the major strengths of the Boulder's system was its "robust infrastructure" including an extensive fiber network and servers that support organization-wide connectivity and a "powerful intranet." The plan praised the IT department for employing project management methodology that has improved its success rate in implementing new projects. It praised the workforce for its broad knowledge and willingness to "try new things." Concerns are expressed in the plan about the amount of downtime and the fact that the IT department is seen as not being responsive to requests for "small business" needs in the 40 to 60 hour range. The plan also found that the commitment to projects was done on an individual departmental basis and there had been no priority system established based on contributions to the city as a whole. Some departments felt that they deserved more help and that there were "have" and "have not" departments.

The City of Rancho Mirage's 2000 Strategic Technology Plan was put together by an outside consulting firm and shows how the city's analysis of its existing system led to

Figure 4. List of areas needing improvements in the City of Rancho Mirage's 2000 strategic technology plan

- Although most users felt comfortable that business processes were reasonably effective and efficient in meeting the needs of their internal and external customers, there were some identified shortcomings in business service processes primarily in records management and in the tools utilized for office automation activities.

- The use of computers for inter-office and Internet communication does not support the City's operations, as lack of consistent use by all employees makes the tool less valuable.

- Business processes and active records are almost entirely paper-based rather than electronic and information sharing is primarily accomplished orally and through memos rather than through online access to an inter-departmental database and online document retrieval.

- Many of the computer applications currently in place are adequately addressing the City's needs although enhancements would increase the effectiveness of these systems.

- The City does not have an integrated database that can be commonly accessed by all departments. Currently, people only ask for very basic information, which does not require a sophisticated reporting environment. As information requests become more elaborate or increase in volume, the City will need to create an online reporting environment drawing from various sources including the Pentamation and Sierra Permits databases.

- A geographic information system (GIS) is a potential addition to the City's application software portfolio that would greatly enhance service delivery to external and internal customers. However, GIS tends to be costly, including costs for implementation, training, workflow redesign, interface development, system administration, and data acquisition. Also, GIS can be bandwidth-intensive, and may accelerate the need for a network upgrade.

- The technical infrastructure in place adequately meets the city's current day-to-day needs. However it is very likely that network bandwidth will soon need to be increased (a) between City Hall and the library, public works yard, and fire stations, and (b) between City facilities and the Internet. In addition, the City's business software and data may also be vulnerable to hackers because library public access terminals, employee desktop PC's and application servers are all connected to the same network, without firewalls.

- Like other cities in the Coachella Valley, Rancho Mirage is currently using "display only" technology ("online brochures") on its web site. The City has not acquired "electronic commerce" technology to use its web site to transact business. Full electronic commerce applications typically require (a) a capability for web-entered credit card transactions, and (b) web interfaces to financial and other application software. The City's technical infrastructure does not have these capabilities. However, there is no apparent demand for electronic commerce at this time.

- Like many cities, Information Services tends to be reactive in developing the information technology environment. A more proactive role will be needed in order for the City to stay current and optimize its investment in information technology. Current staff does a good job of responding to user requests. However, many users feel that additional staff may be needed to meet continued demands for system maintenance. AEF concurs with this assessment.

- Governance over Information Technology purchases and future direction is reactive in nature. Overall decisions for scoping and prioritizing information technology projects appears to be decentralized, resting with department heads individually, in concert with the City Manager. A more centralized approach will be required for the future projects to transition from paper-based processes to electronic workflows.

Source: City of Rancho Mirage, Information Systems Master Plan, Prepared by AEF Systems Inc., May 2000. Retrieved July 8, 2003 from www.misac.org

Copyright © 2006, Idea Group Inc. Copying or distributing in print or electronic forms without written permission of Idea Group Inc. is prohibited.

a specific set of priorities. In Figures 4 and 5, the weaknesses of the current system are discussed and a prioritized list of interrelated projects to address these weaknesses is presented. The list of challenges and solutions show the wide range of problems that IT staff must deal with including concerns about governance, infrastructure capacity, inadequate use of existing technology, and lack of an integrated database. The plan discusses the relevance of GIS but notes that it is a costly technology and the municipality should look to a shared system with other entities.

Figure 5. Recommended projects for the City of Rancho Mirage in order of priority

---

Overview of Projects

The City's IS Master Plan strategy to update its information technology has been designed to be executed in projects over two-three years, with our cost estimates for the initial 18 months. Once the initial recommendations are implemented, additional costs will be identified that will be expended during the remaining 18 months. The IS Internal Environment Assessment study found that while most of the core business systems were in decent shape and acceptable to the user population, integration between the applications is lacking and some key technical architecture components required further enhancement. AEF feels that the City should concentrate on the technical infrastructure, and implement a few projects that will directly impact how the user accesses data. AEF has identified the following projects as having priority for implementation. Each project is designed to be a building block for subsequent projects. These projects will lead to other projects that the City may choose to implement over the next 18 months.

1) Establish a governance process for system development and information technology acquisitions.

2) Hire an information systems application analyst.

3) Evaluate the City's network capacity. Install a firewall.

4) Establish a consistent standard on employee workstations and during the upgrade cycle ensure these standards are met. Develop a daily procedure to restore a standard software configuration on the public-use PC's in the library. Review each workstation to validate up-to-date virus protection mechanisms are installed and running. In concert with this activity, adopt a three-year PC replacement/refreshment strategy.

5) Standardize on Microsoft Office Professional including implementing Microsoft Outlook as the City's scheduling software.

6) Develop an online reporting environment for general use in querying and analyzing information.

7) Study the feasibility of developing interfaces between application software products, such as a feed from Sierra Permits into Pentamation's accounts receivable function and interfaces among Public Works' application software products. Also, develop a training plan to ensure that users have enough depth of knowledge of the software to carry out their assigned responsibilities.

8) Evaluate the future of its web site and create a vision of what message to present to the public as well as what additional services to offer. In addition, plan for the development of an Intranet. The City will need to evaluate the required server capacity, network communications, etc.

9) Develop a Task Force to work with other nearby cities and county government to plan a long-term cooperative strategy for GIS, to foster economies of scale for data acquisition, database maintenance, system administration, user training, and inter-agency information exchange.

10) Begin an ongoing project to analyze its current business processes to identify opportunities for transition from paper-based processes to electronic workflows and online information retrieval. Develop requirements regarding which departments would be candidates for digital imaging software and products and then evaluate potential products to meet these requirements.

Source: City of Rancho Mirage, Information Systems Master Plan, Prepared by AEF Systems Inc., May 2000. Retrieved July 8, 2003 from www.misac.org

---

Copyright © 2006, Idea Group Inc. Copying or distributing in print or electronic forms without written permission of Idea Group Inc. is prohibited.

Figure 6. Tradeoffs in IT investments

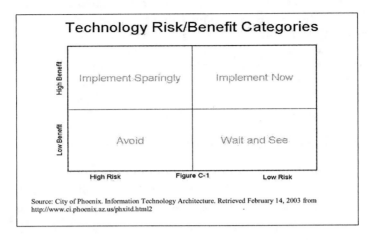

The Boulder and Rancho Mirage plans are good examples of the value of openly discussing areas that need improvement. An open and thorough analysis of the existing system is a prerequisite to improving IT services. Many governments would be reluctant to air any weaknesses but by putting this analysis into print form, the government is able to effect a clearer consensus on what needs to be changed than would be possible if such an analysis were not done.

Some plans include detailed priorities while others do not address priorities. The City of Phoenix's 2002 Information Technology Plan developed four categories of technologies: (1) Do Now; (2) Implement Sparingly; (3) Wait and See; (4) Avoid. These categories are based on rating these technologies by their degree of benefit (high versus low) and risk (high versus low) (See Figure 6). Projects to be done at the earliest opportunity included "browser access to business applications." Browser access was viewed as desirable because it eliminates conflicts between "client" software. Aspects that Phoenix planned to implement sparingly include streaming video which was seen as being able to help training efforts but that attention must be given concerning its demands on the organizational network bandwidth utilization. Projects to observe for future opportunities include Linux, an open-operating system, and Voice over IP VOIP). Both of these technologies are seen as having potential for the future but with too many risks and current limitations to commit fully to (at the time the plan was written in July of 2002). In short, the Phoenix plan provides a general framework to guide priority-setting for IT projects.

Case Study of Fairfax County IT Plan

Fairfax County (Virginia) has won a number of honors for their IT accomplishments so it is instructive to look at their 2005 plan which currently is available on their Web site at http://www.fairfaxcounty.gov/gov/dit/images/ITPlan05/2005ITPlan.pdf.

Copyright © 2006, Idea Group Inc. Copying or distributing in print or electronic forms without written permission of Idea Group Inc. is prohibited.

1. **General Principles:** After listing some general goals such as "Ensure effective technical and fiscal management of the department's operations, resources, technology projects and contracts" (Section 1, p. 4), the plan proceeds to list Ten Fundamental Principles of Information Technology that echo many of the standards that various organizations hold to whether they have a formal plan or not such as: (1) "Evaluate business processes for redesign opportunities before automating them" to make new business models a reality and exploit commonalities across departments; (2) Manage IT as an investment using tools such as multi-year budgeting, replacement funding of depreciated equipment and life-cycle planning; (3) Keep current with emerging technologies but test them out through pilot projects; (4) Both hardware and software should adhere to open standards and minimize proprietary standards; (5) Emphasize the purchase and integration of quality commercial-off-the-shelf (COTS) software requiring minimal customization as the first choice to speed the delivery of new business applications while realizing that this may require redesigning some existing work processes to be compatible with beneficial common practice capabilities; and (6) Capture data once and emphasize the use of common databases to the maximum extent possible.

    The plan discusses the logic of the organization of the IT function such as noting the fact that the CIO (of Fairfax County), who is one of the County's four Deputy County Executives, chairs and receives input from an internal advisory committee made up of high-level County management, including the County Executive, the three other Deputy County Executives, the County's CTO/Director of Department of Information Technology and the Director of the Department of Management and Budget, in order to tie IT investment directly to overall County goals and objectives. The CIO also receives input from an external advisory committee, which is appointed by the County's Board of Supervisors and made up of expert citizens. The CIO as Deputy County Executive has a broad strategic role for information and technology in the County through the departments for which he is responsible. Functions reporting to the CIO include the Department of Information Technology, Fairfax County Public Library, Department of Cable Communications and Consumer Protection (Cable Television, Document Services, and Consumer Protection), and County-wide Health Information Portability and Accountability Act (HIPAA) Compliance. The CIO also works closely with the Office of Public Affairs and the Fairfax County Economic Development Authority. The focus on both information and technology in a very strategic and enterprise-wide manner, always with an emphasis on understanding the customer and providing excellent customer service through information and technology, is a key element to the Fairfax County IT strategy and the role of the CIO.

2. **Major Strategic Directions:** The Fairfax County Plan proceeds to outline major strategic directions and initiatives they are pursuing including the following: (1) E-government: Fairfax has adopted an integrated multi-channel e-government delivery approach in which access to government is "without walls, doors, or clocks" including not just the County Web site but also interactive voice response, multi media Kiosks, mobile access, Access Fairfax (a staffed customer service center to assist citizens in the use of technology to do business with the County government) and cable TV integrated into a single strategy; (2) The development

Copyright © 2006, Idea Group Inc. Copying or distributing in print or electronic forms without written permission of Idea Group Inc. is prohibited.

of an Integrated Content and Document Management approach: The organization is developing an information architecture, an enterprise document management technology that makes it possible to view hard copy records with automated applications, and share information across departmental boundaries; (3) Development of a 311 Customer Relationship Management system that is to integrate the call taking aspects for "front office" functions that deal with citizens and compliment the County's existing "Contact/Complaint Management Systems" which are currently used by the Board of Supervisors' Offices, Clerk to the Board of Supervisors, Office of Public Affairs, Consumer Protection Division, Human Rights office, County Health Department, Department of Public Works and Environmental Services and the Office of the County Executive and other departments and functions; (4) The continued development of the county's GIS system whose GIS data warehouse enterprise available, include over 400 data layers and is integrated into the business of multiple departments and functions; (5) Telecommunications: Fairfax County is currently lighting a new fiber WAN institutional network (I-Net), which will combine voice, video and data over one network and serve over 400 County/Schools sites. The County is also beginning the process to replace its phone system. The County is considering a VoIP system albeit using a hybrid PBX/ IP technology; and (6) The development of an integrated inspection software system that will serve the not only The Department of Public Works and Environmental Services Inspections group, but will also be used by County Agencies such as The County Health Department, Fire and Rescue Department, Planning and Zoning, Public Works and the Department of Tax Administration. The inspections and permitting system is a perfect example of the movement to replace formerly separate systems with an integrated application—in Fairfax's case, the permit system would replace the following individual systems:

- Inspection Services Information System (ISIS)

- Building Code Services Online (ISISnet)

- ISIS Handheld Inspections System

- Permit Applicant Tracking System

- Fairfax County Contractor Licensing Database (live interface with Commonwealth of Virginia Licensing System)

- Plan Review Comments Web Application

- Elevators Inspections Database

- County Cross-connections Database

- HMIS system for Environmental Health Services

- HealthSpace system (an interface to the State HealthSpace system will remain)

- Residential Use Permits (RUPs) portion of the PAMS Application

Copyright © 2006, Idea Group Inc. Copying or distributing in print or electronic forms without written permission of Idea Group Inc. is prohibited.

- Non-Residential Use Permits (Non-RUPs) Application
- Multiple stand-alone Fire Prevention Services Databases
- Multiple stand-alone Environmental Health Services Databases
- Paradox Complaints Tracking System
- Wireless real-time interaction for inspectors via ruggedized laptop

3. **Discussion of Funding Issues**: The plan then proceeds to discuss and provide some basic analysis of its IT funding by categorizing its initiatives into the following categories: (1) Projects that are done in order to meet the mandated requirements of the County Board of Supervisors, the state, and Federal Governments: $0.3 million; (2) Completion of Prior Investments: $2.0 million; (3) Security Issues: $1.3 million; (4) Improved service and efficiency: $4.2 million; (5) Maintenance of Current Technology: $2.6 million.

4. **Project Management Approaches**: The plan then proceeds to discuss each of its new projects in more detail with the following categories of analysis: (a) description of the project and its goals; (b) a discussion of Return on Investment (ROI) that is primarily in non-financial terms (e.g., the justification for the improved Computer Aided Dispatch (CAD) system is to "save time" not money). It also outlines key milestones of development for the projects if these have been defined. All County IT Project Managers are also certified through a County certification program.

5. **Infrastructural Issues**: The plan then proceeds to discuss infrastructure developments such as the plan to implement a Windows 2003 server upgrade as a vehicle to developing their .NET framework to "seamlessly" tie together systems and devices as well as other infrastructure developments such as new radio and phone systems.

6. The next parts of the plan discuss its planning process, details on the architecture of its systems, a discussion of its adherence to Systems Development Life Cycle, and how people are trained for project management. The Appendix to the plan contains a detailed listing of its IT architecture standards.

    As one goes through the Fairfax County plan, the underlying theme is an intense drive to integrate all of the data and technologies and to make the data easily available to anyone with a legitimate need via a wide range of media at any time or location.

Technology Planning for Particular Areas

In this chapter, I have concentrated on the development of general strategic technology plans that cover the full range of IT technologies because technologies are so closely interrelated and, with the development of an enterprise approach to IT, governments want to have databases shared across the organization. However, many organizations will also conduct planning for particular areas such as financial systems or geographical information systems with an eye to replacing or upgrading these systems.

Copyright © 2006, Idea Group Inc. Copying or distributing in print or electronic forms without written permission of Idea Group Inc. is prohibited.

For example, the GFOA (Miranda, 2002b) outlines a needs assessment methodology to judge the various functions of a financial system. Their methodology has a checklist to determine if the software supports particular functions such as General Ledger (e.g., Does it support project accounting?), the staff who should be interviewed, information to collect (e.g., processes to create and maintain accounts), system requirements, and "things to look for" (e.g., document "handoffs"). This same framework is employed to study other ERP modules such as budget preparation, accounts receivable, purchasing, accounts payable, fixed assets/inventory, human resources, payroll, and system assessment modules (Miranda, 2002b). The next steps of the GFOA methodology are to study best practices and conduct market research to identify the vendor with the most appropriate software for the needs of the government.

Huxhold (1991, p. 240) outlines a detailed methodology for planning for a new GIS system. Among the steps that he recommends is a simple but very useful map "cross-reference" chart in which individual map applications (e.g., quarter section mapping, zoning, tax plats, election district, incident maps, etc.) are cross referenced by the user departments (e.g., city engineer, planning department, building inspector, traffic engineering, street and sewer maintenance, etc.) in terms of their frequency of use (used continually, frequently, or just "used"). This chart provides a good overview of the existing situation, a key step in the planning process.

Interagency and Intergovernmental Planning

Planning in an intergovernmental context has a great number of challenges of its own. There are few detailed accounts of such planning, so I am drawing on the Center for Technology in Government's (2000) case of planning for a homeless information system (HIMS) to illustrate some of the challenges of intergovernmental IT planning. The primary agency leading the effort was the New York State's Bureau of Shelter Services (BSS) but a wide array of other agencies were involved including: (1) New York State Office of Temporary and Disability Insurance (OTDA); (2) New York City's Department of Homeless Services; (3) The New York State Office of Children and Family Services; (4) The New York State Department of Health; (5) The New York State Department of Labor; (6) The Office of Alcohol and Substance Abuse Services; (7) The New York State Division of Parole; and (8) A wide array of private non-profit organizations like the Salvation Army that provide direct services to the homeless in shelters. The number and diversity of the organizations involved creates a huge challenge for planners. Because of the sensitivity of certain subgroups of homeless, in particular victims of domestic abuse, the immediate and overwhelming need was to develop a sense of trust among the key actors and this step required a large number of face-to-face meetings over an extended period of time.

The agencies first had to establish major goals for a new system which they identified as follows (Center for Technology in Government, 2000): (1) The development of an integrated database of information from a variety of sources; (2) The system would need to accurately track client information across several different systems; and (3) The system would necessitate that "effective partnerships" be established to ensure that the

Copyright © 2006, Idea Group Inc. Copying or distributing in print or electronic forms without written permission of Idea Group Inc. is prohibited.

necessary and accurate data would be obtained. They studied the existing system and identified as one of the key weaknesses the lack of adequate information on the effectiveness of services so the development of data to support "outcome-based assessments" became one of the key goals for the new system (Center for Technology in Government, 2000).

A prior plan had been developed to use a "canned commercial" system but many of the user agencies reacted negatively to this plan because, they said, it would not be useful to the case managers and also because they had concerns about the sensitivity of much of the information. Indeed, the reaction to the planned new system stimulated the creation of a "Technology Committee" to oppose the initial system. The BSS staff had to work hard to gain the trust, pointing out that confidentiality issues such as documenting the state rules, regulations, and statutes concerning client data. Thus, in such human services cases, the confidentiality of data is a crucial starting point. For the domestic violence clients, it was agreed that the "facility information" would have to be "masked" to protect the location of the client.

Another major issue concerned how the data were to be used. Shelter agencies were worried that the new evaluative data would be used to set goals that were too high for them and could be used against them. The system developers argued that the new system would provide valuable information to the shelter providers that would help them identify "best practices" that they could model to improve their own performance (Center for Technology in Government, 2000). Up until this point, the "evaluation" of the shelter providers relied primarily on a basic "headcount." Concerns about evaluation and reimbursement issues are almost certain to occur whenever funding and regulatory bodies propose to gather new information about the clients of agencies they fund. The regulatory and evaluative agencies may be able to calm fears about sudden changes in funding but the underlying tension between funder and funded agencies is inevitable.

These funding concerns carried over into the definitions of key concepts such as the "admit date" for clients. It turned out that there were several different operating procedures with some agencies using the date that clients entered the shelter as the admit date while other agencies used another date—the date when the facility made an assignment decision. Any issue that affects reimbursements received by agencies will be important. Agencies had to discuss how they could agree on a "unique identifier" that would allow them to track clients across agencies because agencies used different identifiers and many organizations are now reluctant to use Social Security numbers for this purpose. Levels of aggregation for identifying ethnicity were also an issue—one agency wanted to have twelve options due to Federal requirements in contrast to the eight used by others (Center for Technology in Government, 2000).

What tools are available to plan an intergovernmental system like this? The approach selected to plan a system with so many different users was to develop a prototype. Prototyping is useful because it provides end users with visible examples of how the new system would look and makes concrete issues that may have been fuzzy otherwise. This particular system was especially challenging because the underlying model of the new system changed from primarily an "online transactional processing" approach (Center for Technology in Government, 2000) for the current year to one that would emphasize a historical view of services and thus allow better analysis of the impacts of the system.

Copyright © 2006, Idea Group Inc. Copying or distributing in print or electronic forms without written permission of Idea Group Inc. is prohibited.

Lessons learned from the HMIS experience include the fact that planning for new systems requires in depth programmatic knowledge as much as technical expertise and that "soft" issue of building of trust was the primary challenge and had to be resolved first.

Conclusion

Every organization must plan in order to have an effective IT system. There is clear value to the information included in comprehensive detailed plans. A comprehensive plan discusses organizational and IT goals and how they relate to one another. It will identify goals and objectives of key actors and conduct an extensive stakeholder analysis of relevant users of individual systems. It will analyze the existing system of the organization including its strengths and weaknesses and derive a set of priorities for future investments. It will analyze options for these investments including an analysis of best practices and how feasible they are. However, the majority of governmental organizations appear to have similar policies and architectural guidelines regardless of the comprehensiveness of the plans. Many plans do not have detailed analyses of business practices and detailed plans for new projects. Some plans are based primarily on perceptions of the planners but most plans employ some attempts at systematic gathering of data from internal and external sources about the status of the existing systems. The IT systems in governments may thrive regardless of whether their plans are comprehensive and detailed or not. However, if this information is not gathered as part of the planning process, it is likely to be needed at other times such as when the organization needs to develop an RFP or make tough decisions among alternative IT investments.

References

Barrett, K., & Greene, R. (2001). *Powering up: How public managers can take control of information technology*. Washington, DC: Congressional Quarterly Press.

Beaumaster, S. (1999). *Information technology implementation issues: An analysis*. Ph.D. Dissertation. Blacksburg: Virginia Polytechnic Institute and State University.

Carnevale, D. (2003, May 6). Iowa legislature considers selling high-speed network used by colleges and schools. *The Chronicle*. Retrieved May 6, 2003, from http://chronicle.com/daily/2003/05/2003050601t.htm

Center for Technology in Government (CTG). (2000, February). *Putting information together*. Retrieved March 25, 2005, from http://www.ctg.albany.edu/publications/reports/putting_info

Chan, Y. E. (2002, June). Why haven't we mastered alignment? The importance of the informal organization structure. *MIS Quarterly Executive, 1*(2), 97-112.

Copyright © 2006, Idea Group Inc. Copying or distributing in print or electronic forms without written permission of Idea Group Inc. is prohibited.

City of Boulder. (2002, November). *Strategic technology plan.* Retrieved May 8, 2003, from http://www.ci.boulder.co.us/it/FinalDraftPlan.pdf

City of Phoenix. (2002, July 22). *City of Phoenix information technology architecture.* Retrieved February 14, 2003, from http://www.ci.phoenix.az.us/phxitd.html

City of Sunnyvale, California. (1999). *Information technology strategic plan.* Retrieved February 14, 2003, from http://www.ci.sunnyvale.ca.us/info-tech/strategic-plan/itdocume.pdf

Cragg, P., King, M., & Hussin, H. (2002). IT alignment and firm performance in small manufacturing firms. *Journal of Strategic Information Systems, 11,* 109-132.

Friedrichsen, L., & Bunin, R. B. (2000). *Microsoft project 2000.* Cambridge, MA: Course Technology, Thompson Learning.

Groak, V. (2003, March 26). Tri-cities broadband campaign gets intense. *Chicago Tribune.*

Holley, L. M., Dufner, D., & Reed, B.J. (2002, June). Got SISP? Strategic information systems planning in the U.S. state governments. *Public Performance & Management Review, 25*(4), 398-412.

Huxhold, W. E. (1991). *An introduction to geographic information systems.* London: Oxford University.

International City/County Management Association. (1998). *Long-range information technology plans: Strategies for the future.* Washington, DC: ICMA.

Jahnke, A. (2004, June 1). Why is business-IT alignment so difficult. *CIO Magazine.*

McKay, J. (2003, May). Dry spell. *Government Technology,* 16-21.

Miranda, R. (2002a, October). Needs assessments and business case Analysis for technology investment decisions. *Government Finance Review, 18*(5), 12-16.

Miranda, R., Kavanagh, S., & Roque, R. (2002b). *Technology needs assessments: Evaluating the business case for ERP and financial management systems.* Chicago: Government Finance Officers Association.

Miranda, R. A. (Ed.). (2001). *ERP and financial management systems: The backbone of digital government.* Chicago: GFOA.

Moulder, E. (2001, September). *E-government: If you build it, Will they come?* Washington, DC: International City/County Management Association. Retrieved October 7, 2002, from http://icma.org/docs/500628

O'Looney, J. (2000). *Local government on-line: Putting the internet to work.* Washington, DC: International City/County Management Association.

Olsen, F. (2002, December 5). Software-coding costs force Indiana U. at Bloomington to drop a popular graduation guarantee. *Chronicle of Higher Education.* Retrieved December 5, 2002, from http://chronicle.com/free/2002/12/2002120501t.htm

Patterson, D. (2003, January). Dynamic duo: Virginia governor and technology secretary savvy to government service. *Government and Technology.*

Peterson, B. L., & Carco, D. M. (1998). *The smart way to buy information technology.* New York: MACOM, American Management Association.

Copyright © 2006, Idea Group Inc. Copying or distributing in print or electronic forms without written permission of Idea Group Inc. is prohibited.

Peterson, S. (2003, May). Something for nothing? *Government Technology*, 27-66.

Prince Williams County, Virginia. (n.d.). *Information technology strategic plan*. Retrieved May 12, 2002, from http://www.pwcgov.org/oit/strategic_plan/default.htm

Raumer, R. J. (2001). Strategic planning for technology investments. *Government Finance Review, 17*(6), 32-35.

Reed, B.J. (2003). Chapter 6: Information technology management (pp. 133-150). In Syracuse University, Final Report, Government Performance Project. Retrieved April 17, 2003, from http://www.maxwell.syr.edu/gpp/grade/2002chap6.pdf

Rocheleau, B. (2000). Prescriptions for public sector information management: A review and critique. *American Review of Public Administration, 30*(4), 413-435.

Sauer, C., & Burn, J.M. 1997. The pathology of strategic alignment. In C. Sauer, & P. W. Yetton (Eds.), *Steps to the future: Fresh thinking on the management of IT-based organizational transformation* (pp. 89-111). San Francisco: Jossey-Bass.

Steinbrecher, S. (2000, September). CIO Profile: Steve Steinbrecher. *Government Technology*. Retrieved January 16, 2003, from http://www.govtech.net/gt/2000/sept/CIO/profile.phtml

Ward, T. (2003, January). Intranets: Plan or Die. *Darwin Magazine*. Retrieved April 30, 2003, from http://www.darwinmag.com/read/010103/intranet.html

Further Reading

There are several books that prescribe lists of planning steps for governments (Barrett & Greene, 2001; Schulz, 2001; and O'Looney, 2000). Works such as O'Looney's are able to provide more details because it focuses on one area of IT (the Internet). The GFOA has excellent guides to planning for ERP programs by Miranda (2001, 2002). An excellent guide to planning GIS is contained in Huxhold's (1991) volume. It is very useful to view actual plans done by government agencies. Many government plans are now available on the Internet via search engines as well as by visiting the information technology Web sites of various governmental organizations. The following URL's were collected during the months from the 2003-2004 period and provide examples of governmental IT plans, although many will undoubtedly be unavailable or have new plans by the time you attempt to access them.

Municipality-Related

- Boulder Colorado: http://www.ci.boulder.co.us/it/FinalDraftPlan.pdf
- Fontana, California: http://www.misac.org/state_library/fontana_strat_plan.pdf
- Honolulu, Hawaii: http://www.co.honolulu.hi.us/it/itplan.htm
- Houston, Texas: http://www.ci.houston.tx.us/it/strategics.htm

Copyright © 2006, Idea Group Inc. Copying or distributing in print or electronic forms without written permission of Idea Group Inc. is prohibited.

- Indio, California: http://www.misac.org/state_library/indio_strat_plan.doc
- Irvine, California: http://www.misac.org/state_library/irvine_tp2000.doc
- Keene, New Hampshire: http://www.ci.keene.nh.us/ims/itmasterplan.pdf
- Phoenix, Arizona: http://www.ci.phoenix.az.us/phxitd.html
- Santa Barbara, California: http://www.misac.org/state_library/sb_toc_rev.doc
- Sunnyvale, California: http://www.ci.sunnyvale.ca.us/info-tech/strategic-plan/itdocume.pdf
- Visalia, California: http://www.misac.org/state_library/visalia-final_is_plan.pdf
- Watsonville, California: http://www.misac.org/state_library/watsonville_it_plan.pdf

County-Related

- Fairfax County, Virginia: http://www.fairfaxcounty.gov/gov/dit/images/ITPlan05/2005ITPlan.pdf
- Prince William County, Virginia: http://www.pwcgov.org/oit/strategic_plan/default.htm

State-Related

- Arkansas: http://www.cio.state.ar.us/Dwnlds/StateITPlan.pdf
- Colorado:http://www.oit.state.co.us/resources/docs/
- Statewide_IT_FourYearPlan_FY03-06-02.pdf
- Idaho: http://www2.state.id.us/itrmc/plan&policies/IdahoITPlan.pdf
- Kansas: http://da.state.ks.us/itec/SIMPlan.htm
- Kentucky: http://www.state.ky.us/kirm/sitp/sitp.htm
- Mississippi: http://www.its.state.ms.us/its/itsweb.nsf/MasterPlan?OpenForm

Key Concepts

- Alignment
- Architecture
- Any-Any-Any-Any Model
- Best Practices
- Business Case

Copyright © 2006, Idea Group Inc. Copying or distributing in print or electronic forms without written permission of Idea Group Inc. is prohibited.

- Community Input
- Gap Analysis
- Industry Standard
- Open Standard
- Stakeholder Analysis
- Technophilia
- Triangulate
- Visioning Analysis

Discussion Questions

1. How meaningful does the concept of alignment of technology and goals for government seem to you? Can you find any examples of organizations whose technology practices conflict with their purported organizational goals? Discuss whether an organization with which you are familiar has a good alignment between its technology and goals.

2. How important do you think it is to produce a formal strategic plan and to update it each year as recommended by many experts? Do you think that reliance on "plans in heads" and/or short-term business plans in place of thorough strategic plans would have negative impacts?

3. IT plans vary greatly in their degree of comprehensiveness as pointed out in this chapter. What components of these plans do you think are most valuable? Least valuable? Why?

4. Some organizations have consultants develop, organize and do much of the work involved in constructing an IT plan. Discuss the advantages and disadvantages of each approach.

5. Many of the plans have similar architectural norms such as centralized networking standards, preference for COTS software and industry standards, and a preference for open standards. How useful do you find these standards? Do organizations with which you are familiar adhere strictly to these standards? Can you identify other standards that are (or should be) included in an organization's policy guidelines and architectural standards?

Exercises

1. Obtain copies of three different governmental IT plans. These may be local plans to which you have access or ones that you can obtain from sources such as the

Copyright © 2006, Idea Group Inc. Copying or distributing in print or electronic forms without written permission of Idea Group Inc. is prohibited.

Internet. Read and analyze these plans. Write a paper in which you critique the plans. Which parts of them do you find best? Which are least effective? Why? What components do you feel should be included in a strategic plan? Which are not necessary? Why? What are the strengths of each plan? The weaknesses and limitations? How does each compare in terms of value with the other plans you have reviewed? Finally, specify how you would go about improving each of the plans.

2.   Let's assume that you are the IT director of your organization or that you are responsible for IT in a subunit of the organization. Do the following: Write a paper in which you outline the processes that you will follow in order to develop a strategic plan for your organization or a subunit. Outline the major components you would include in the plan. If the organization already has a plan, you may write the memo to discuss the steps you would take to update or revise the organization's current plan if it has one. You may limit your plan to certain units and/or software or hardware systems of the IT organization and not try to be comprehensive if the organization's IT system is extremely large and complex. If you are revising an existing plan, please attach this plan to your memo. Discuss the logic and rationale for all of your steps.

Copyright © 2006, Idea Group Inc. Copying or distributing in print or electronic forms without written permission of Idea Group Inc. is prohibited.

Chapter III

Procuring Information Technology for Government

Introduction

Over the past 15 years, the nature of procurement of information technology has undergone radical change in government. These changes are due to the development of new technologies such as the Internet, changes in laws and rules concerning procurement, and a changed philosophy concerning government purchase of IT. Overall, the changes have moved purchasing from a slow, legalistic process emphasizing lowest cost to a more flexible process emphasizing best value (Rocheleau, 2000). At the Federal level, this change was marked by the replacement of the Brooks Act by the Federal Acquisitions Reform Act of 1996 that pushed streamlining of the procurement process. Similar changes have been widely implemented in state agencies too (National Association of State Purchasing Officers, 1996) including the following recommendations: (1) Simplify procurement to make it more effective and lower costs of purchasing; (2) Use electronic commerce to speed the process and improve prices and competition; (3) Emphasize best value rather than lowest cost; (4) Use a problem-oriented bid process to get the vendor community to help use its creativity and discretion to solve problems; and (5) Study and revise the processes linked to applications in order to make the process less costly and more effective. In this chapter, I will break our discussion of purchasing into four key issues that need to be performed well for it to be effective: (1) Needs assessment; (2) Sourcing issues; (3) The contracting process; and (4) Managing the project.

Copyright © 2006, Idea Group Inc. Copying or distributing in print or electronic forms without written permission of Idea Group Inc. is prohibited.

The Needs Assessment Process in Purchasing

Setting Goals and Priorities

During the early years in government, IT was used for a limited number of functions such as payroll and billing. Thus purchasing choices were limited and there were few problems of prioritization. Today, IT is omnipresent and potentially useful new hardware and software are constantly emerging and there are many possibilities that compete for funding. A government must be selective in how it invests its scarce resources and choose among IT projects. Research by an economist (Ariely, 2003) reveals that technology heads often make poor investments because they are overly concerned with sunk costs of previous investments and also because they tend to think in "silos," comparing investments within one category like databases when they should compare any purchase with all possible IT investments. Thus a truly broad needs assessment as outlined in the planning chapter should be a prerequisite to purchasing. The organization must prioritize requests to meet organizational goals. Critical applications such as those which generate payrolls or revenue will receive high priority as will those that influence the most departments and users in the organization such as infrastructural investments. Since the purchasing process is continuous and cyclical, the needs of all departments and users eventually should be served. If an organization lacks a well thought-out prioritization process, the purchase of software can and often is dominated by individualistic and political choices. In the chapter on planning, I discuss some criteria and methods that organizations have employed to prioritize investments. Next, I provide some additional approaches and examples.

Due to the current budget problems, organizations have had to make tough decisions about cutting IT spending. Overall, there appears to be a movement to rating as top priority those projects that provide the best promise of cost-cutting or revenue increases (Newcombe, 2003). Analysis of these decisions reveals that a variety of factors influence the priority-setting process. The State of Texas CIO focused cutbacks on administrative expenses as well as leaving positions vacant while retaining higher priority items such as their Texas Online e-government system that is supported by "convenience fees" (CIO Magazine, Texas, 2003). Kentucky cut planned server upgrades, enterprise reporting system, and a new human resources (HR) system among other items while giving high priority to new microwave towers for public safety (CIO Magazine, Deep Cuts in Bluegrass Country, 2003). California's CIO, J. Clark Kelso, initially concentrated cuts in the costs of consultants working on the state's portal system while retaining projects that save money such as collaborative IT efforts among state agencies (CIO Magazine, California, 2003). Michigan's CIO found that cutting was not "a smooth process" that could use abstract principles but involved working backwards to see how much had to be cut, estimating the costs of projects, and then prioritizing them (CIO, Michigan, 2003).

In many of these cases, the process appears to be ad hoc and informal but some states such as Iowa have developed a formal prioritization scheme to rank projects (Varon, 2003). Iowa has a "Pooled Technology Account" in which projects are assigned points

Copyright © 2006, Idea Group Inc. Copying or distributing in print or electronic forms without written permission of Idea Group Inc. is prohibited.

based on the following criteria: (1) Is the project statutorily required?; (2) How much does it improve customer service?; (3) How much does it affect citizens?; (4) Does it reengineer processes?; (5) How risky is it?; (6) Does the agency proposing the project have a good track record?; (7) At what stage is the investment?; (8) Is the agency willing to share costs with the IT department?; and (9) How much revenue will the project generate? (Varon, 2003). Such a rating scheme is useful in that it makes sure that attention is given to a full range of issues that management considers important but scoring leaves room for plenty of subjectivity and some politics (Varon, 2003).

In 2004, the State of Iowa criteria were modified somewhat to include how many agencies were involved (the broader the participation, the higher the score). Technical and programmatic risk were also added in with higher scores going to less risky projects. The project's ROI is calculated and then assigned points based on a set of ten categories ranging from project's whose ROI was 0% (0 points) to the top category with a ROI of 83% or higher (10 points). The scorecard allows for projects whose "benefits are not readily quantifiable." For example, the textual description for the benefits of an electronic tax modernization system included the following text describing the system's "hard to quantify elements" (State of Iowa, 2004):

Agency's infrastructure of applications and services is diverse and complex; failure to maintain and enhance this infrastructure will mean a reduction in services that can be offered to our customers. In addition, the agency staff will find that it will lose the chance to work in an agency which places a premium on technology, thereby affecting morale and employee satisfaction.

The State of Iowa has a Web site for what they call "Return On Investment Program" at http://das.ite.iowa.gov/roi/index.html that provides a full description of the criteria including detailed project descriptions.

Writing a Business Case

Most public organizations require that a strong *business case* be made for new investments. The Center for Technology in Government (Dawes et al., 2004) has proposed that the structure of a business case include the following elements. According to Dawes et al. (2004), there should be a brief but "compelling" business statement identifying the need for the IT-related project or service. Examples of worthwhile projects include those that deal with problems that affect services to the public—in other words, don't base the case just on technology issues (e.g., the current system is "old technology"). Dawes et al. (2004) state that the second component is a statement that outlines the project's "mission"—how the investment will affect the organization. Here you want to present a picture of how the new project will improve services and functioning of the organization. Dawes et al. go on to state that a discussion of the more specific objectives of the project will be needed along with a statement of how the success of the project in attaining these objectives can be determined. Another component is a discussion of the rationale for your particular approach to the business case and why it is preferable to other ap-

Copyright © 2006, Idea Group Inc. Copying or distributing in print or electronic forms without written permission of Idea Group Inc. is prohibited.

proaches that could be employed. Dawes et al. point out that a business case should contain an analysis of how the project will affect the various stakeholders that will be involved and also analyze risks—what are the major risks of the project and how can they be minimized? A complete business case (Dawes et al., 2004) will also contain an elementary outline of project management issues such as the key milestones that will need to be achieved for the project to be implemented successfully and what staff will need to work on the project. Dawes et al. (2004) state that another element of the business case concerns cost estimates and potential sources of funding for the project. They also believe that the business case should include arguments against your proposal and your responses to these objections since these objections are likely to come up anyway when you present the proposal to the decision-making body that will need to approve it.

The Office of Management and the Budget (OMB) at the Federal level now requires a business case for Defense Department investments and failure to develop such a case caused 21 out of 51 billion dollars of IT investments to not be approved because of the lack of this substantiation (Frank, 2003, p. 21). Basic needs assessment information needs to be gathered about each project. The OMB requirements for a business case include the following components: (1) Setting performance goals, metrics, and measurements; (2) Analyzing benefits of the entire investment for the agency and mission; (3) Identifying true alternatives to the original envisioned solution; and (4) Determining realistic life cycle costs (Frank, 2003, p. 21). OMB is also forcing agencies to demonstrate their "architecture" frameworks and show how they mesh with the Federal Enterprise Architecture (Miller, 2003). Setting goals and metrics allows the organization to "baseline" the IT investment. This *baselining* will provide the basic information needed to improve the system and also make it possible to determine the impact of the new system. Willcocks et al. (2002, pp. 74-76) outline the baselining process as follows:

1. Identify every software system including version number.

2. Describe the basic system and its uses, and identify its users, how it is run, and its role in the overall system.

3. Identify all system interfaces.

4. Identify the location of all of the data that feed into or out of the program and also backup and recovering information.

5. Include a discussion of any relevant privacy issues and documentation available for the program.

In addition to these steps, a thorough baselining would include calculation of cost and performance information concerning the function so that the impacts (positive or negative) of the new systems can be calculated and help determine the return on investment. The best decision sometimes may be to do nothing. Willcocks et al. (2002) point out that organizations often fail to exploit the full potential of existing software. Costly investments in new programs or updated versions may be avoided by simply exploiting the full potential of the current programs. On the other hand, organizations also may underestimate the cost of existing programs due to the failure to examine maintenance costs. Consequently, a major goal of the needs assessment is to determine these

Copyright © 2006, Idea Group Inc. Copying or distributing in print or electronic forms without written permission of Idea Group Inc. is prohibited.

costs so the organization will be able to make an informed choice among the options such as upgrades versus whole new systems.

Procurement and Business Process Reengineering

According to Frank (2003), identifying alternatives to the original solution is the most difficult step for most organizations. Thus implementing new software does not involve just technical issues but brings about changes in organizational procedures. Public administrators need to try to maximize improvements and minimize harm from such changes. *Business processing reengineering* (BPR) requires that the organization analyze and describe fully its current processes which will require talking with end users to ensure that the description covers how the process is carried out fully, not just how "it is supposed to work." Then organizational staff discuss how the process could be changed in order to make it more effective and efficient. Programs such as *Enterprise Resource Planning* (ERP) programs are likely to force new processes onto the organizations because they link together processes that used to be independent of one another in separate applications such as payroll, general ledger, and human resource functions. Thus ERP software increases interdependencies and inconsistencies in data are immediately brought to attention that would have been ignored by previously independent systems (Boyer, 2001). Some changes due to software may improve effectiveness but others may be done simply to conform to the software's capabilities. Harris (1999) found that the implementation of an ERP system in Alameda County (California) necessitated a number of changes including the following: (1) Employees had to submit forms via the Web rather than by paper; (2) They had to substitute some "vanilla" processes in place of customized ways they had used to deal with problems before; and (3) The new software required different job functions for some positions and these changes necessitated in turn changes in personnel and confidentiality policies as workers took on new responsibilities with access to new information. Some of these changes will ultimately improve the effectiveness of the organization though they require training and a short-term drop in productivity as the organization adapts. It also can change power relationships in organizations such as enabling greater centralization of information that can lead to resistance (Sia et al., 2002).

Organizations sometimes develop flow charts to describe existing processes and they may incorporate these into their Requests for Proposals (RFPs) to enhance the ability of vendors to provide more informed proposals. For example, Fairfax County (Virginia) included a diagram of the flow of information used to construct their performance measures in an RFP aimed at purchasing a Web-based COTS program to replace their existing system (see Figure 1). Whether or not a flow chart is used, the public organization needs to describe its current system and technological environment as well as weaknesses of the current system that they want corrected. For example (see Figure 2), Hillsboro County's (Florida) RFP described its existing Human Resource Information System (HRIS) as being maintained in a "fragmented and redundant" manner and wanted to replace it with a single database. The RFP goes onto specify environment in which the new HRIS will have to work. This material was placed in the background section of the RFP.

Copyright © 2006, Idea Group Inc. Copying or distributing in print or electronic forms without written permission of Idea Group Inc. is prohibited.

Figure 1. Goal of RFP is to acquire a commercial-off-the-shelf (COTS) software solution for a Web-based performance measurement database

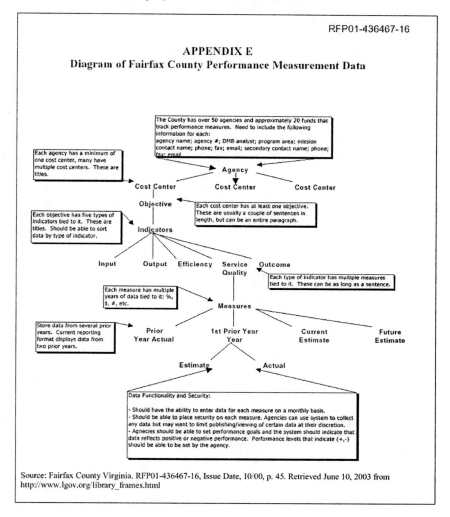

If organizations do not reengineer, they may miss out on major savings that could result from new systems. For example, Richter (1996, p. 9) gives an account of the acquisition of a benefits-processing system purchased by Los Angeles County that was designed to replicate all manual processing but the system suffered from numerous problems due partly to this requirement which resulted in a much more complex system than was necessary. The City of Chicago's Business & Information Services (BIS) Department helped to reengineer the purchasing function (Kustermann, n.d.) for a new ERP system. First they "mapped" how various processes worked by interviewing a cross-section of internal customers and external vendors involved with various categories of purchases such as commodities, construction, and professional services contracts. They identified

Copyright © 2006, Idea Group Inc. Copying or distributing in print or electronic forms without written permission of Idea Group Inc. is prohibited.

Figure 2. Hillsborough County RFP for HRIS system

---

2. BACKGROUND

The County maintains employee information in a fragmented and redundant manner. One objective of this project is to replace many independent databases with one central database – accessible by all.

Position information is also not centralized: vacancy information is kept in one system, funding information in another.

The Clerk of the Circuit Court provides financial accounting, requisition processing, fixed assets management, and payroll functions to the County. The HRIS will have to interface with a Genesys 5.5 and Genesys NT mainframe payroll system maintained by the Clerk of the Circuit Court to provide information sufficient to generate the biweekly payroll. This information includes hours worked, vacation time taken, and changes in payroll deductions. The HRIS must have an integrated payroll module; however, the functionality of such a payroll module will not be part of the criteria used to evaluate responses to this RFP. Moreover, the procurement of such a payroll module is not part of this RFP.

The HRIS will be used on an annual basis to populate the County's budget preparation application (KPMG FAMIS 4.2 BPREP) which is also maintained by the Clerk of Circuit Court.

The HRIS shall operate within the County's automation environment and maintain the established levels of security.

The County's automation environment consists of:

A. Intel-based Pentium II desktop personal computers with Windows 95 operating system; running GroupWise 5.x for electronic mail, calendars, and scheduling; running Netscape Navigator 4.x Web Browser, and connected to Local Area Networks and the Wide Area Network using TCP/IP protocol on Category 5 Ethernet wiring.

B. Compaq file servers with Novel 5.x operating system running office automation software (County standard is Microsoft Office 97 and Netscape 4.0) and other applications.

C. Compaq file servers with Windows NT 4.x operating system serving as application servers for specific applications.

D. Hewlett Packard 3000 minicomputers with MPE/ix 6.0 operating system running specific applications. Desktop personal computers access these applications using HP Windows 95 Reflections 7.0 for terminal emulation software.

E. Hewlett Packard 9000 minicomputers with HP Unix 10.20 operating system running specific applications. Desktop personal computers access these applications using HP Windows 95 Reflections 7.0 for terminal emulation software.

F. IBM RISC 6000 minicomputer with the IBM Unix operating system running one specific application. Desktop personal computers access these applications using the terminal emulation software wIntegrate 3.0.05.

G. Sun MicroSystems computers with the Solaris operating system serves as the County's Web Server and firewall. The County's Internet Service Provider requires that the County guarantee that the only access to the Internet be through County Managed facilities.

H. Current HP Printing services includes system printers and HP IV/V series laser printers. There are no wide carriage printers available for high-speed batch printing.

I. To accommodate Hillsborough County's accepted security standards, an automated procedure must be instituted to prompt for the changing of User Passwords every 30 days and to prevent re-use of the same password for one (1) year.

Source: Hillsborough County Purchasing Department, Request for Proposal S-778-99. Retrieved May 22, 2003 from LGOV.ORG

---

goals that the customers would like to achieve such as a single source for tracking contracts (Kustermann, n.d.) Next they studied best practices of organizations that had demonstrated high performance in this area. This included site visits by key employees to best practice sites. In the next step, BIS redesigned key processes. For example, their goal for high-volume orders was to "use fax server and e-mail technology" to eliminate most of the manual efforts that had led to lost documents. Likewise, they redesigned the contract process by putting the bidding process online including advertising, making RFPs and related information available over the Internet, and using work flow software to track the flow of documents to speed the awarding of contracts (Kustermann, n.d.).

In organizations that maintain up-to-date plans, some of this assessment information will be already available. In others, information can be gathered by surveys and discussions with key users. In most organizations, IT staff are not fully aware of what end users are

Copyright © 2006, Idea Group Inc. Copying or distributing in print or electronic forms without written permission of Idea Group Inc. is prohibited.

doing and it is important to talk with end users and learn about applications (e.g., end-user created spreadsheets and databases) and others processes that may affect a new application. For example, there are typically many databases stored in individual applications such as Microsoft Access or Excel that are unknown to IT managers and staff as the following IT consultant to local government related:

We [outside consultants] did a data inventory of all of the departments [of a moderately sized city] and...identified 1400 databases that are out there. And when we originally went out there, they [IT Staff] thought that 'we need to link probably into 40 or 50 databases' and we will migrate them over.... A lot of them are just piddly little things. But they [IT staff] were like, 'Oh my God, everyone and their brother is doing this.' And it is...why can't I [create a database], why should I wait for the IT...?

The inventory information will vary by the type of system that is being considered. Strock & Adkins (1993) have checklists for a variety of systems and Madden, Miranda & Roque (1999) have checklists for ERP system modules. It is important to indicate the size and complexity of the process, the number of end users, the number of interfaces, the size and frequency of data input, the reports and other documents created by the system, and the speed of growth in the system. The purpose of the assessment is to provide the information necessary to allow the system to handle current and future loads. For example, the builders of an accounts payable system will need to know the number of active vendors, purchase orders per month, and accounts payable checks issued monthly. For a water billing system, they would need to know information such as the number of parcels, number of bills per year, and collections per year would be necessary to estimate computer needs (Stock & Adkins, 1993, p. 39).

Part of the needs assessment process will be determining what functions and performance levels will be necessary. The initial assumption may be to assume that all existing reports and documents must continue to be produced by the organization. In many cases, organizations want expanded and refined reporting and other capacities and this information needs to be gathered through interviews and surveys. However, part of the needs assessment is to identify reports and other elements that may not be necessary, especially if they necessitate customized programming because the organization wants to restrict itself to functions that can be automatically produced by the COTS program. The difficult part of the decision is whether these customized functions are worthwhile and that is a determination that must be made by managers and other personnel who know the substantive value of the information. It is not a decision that can be made by IT staff alone. In some cases, governments specify that they will accept COTS programs and modify their procedures to the capabilities of the system selected. In other cases, governments retain an openness as to whether the software is to be customized or not as did Fairfax County (Virginia) in an RFP for an e-permitting system. The County stated that the "outcome of the RFP process will determine if the appropriate replacement...will be a custom-developed application, a commercial off-the-shelf solution, or a custom implementation of a COTS solution" (Fairfax County Virginia, Information Technology Plan, 2003). The possibility of a custom implementation of a COTS solution is made available by tools provided in some programs including ERP applications that are

Copyright © 2006, Idea Group Inc. Copying or distributing in print or electronic forms without written permission of Idea Group Inc. is prohibited.

sophisticated in the way they allow customizations to be done without endangering the source code as the following IT director notes:

Yes, we still do [customization of applications]. But the way we do it is that you are modifying base libraries that are temporary. So it doesn't affect the base code and doesn't affect our warranty.... It is unbelievable the way that customization can be done. It is almost a toolset that goes on top of the base.... The basic structure needs to stay the same. We will modify the program so they operate more like the flow of our business. We think that is important.

So purchasing of a COTS solution today does not necessarily mean that an organization is restricted to the built-in COTS functions. However, the customization described earlier was done by in-house programmers and many governments do not have that capacity.

In many cases, the purpose of acquiring a new program is to obtain functionality that is not previously available. However, there can be a tradeoff between flexibility and the potential for problems. A city manager wanted to purchase a new payroll system that would also provide human resource system functions too and produce a wider range of more sophisticated reports. So they purchased a generic program developed for all types and sizes of businesses to replace one that had been specifically geared towards the municipality but this manager found that the increased flexibility came at a price:

Because the new system provides so much flexibility, it can't provide all of the controls you need. Once you discover that you are having these problems, you can build in that control but you may not discover it for a while. I think we have caught them all and we haven't had any huge problems but it has been huge issue to manage it just because it is so complex. Whereas the system we had before was geared specifically to our [municipality's] needs, we knew how it worked and what it would do. If we had to make a change, it was sometimes difficult to make that change but it was very specific to our needs.

Indeed, there are a relatively limited number of applications that are directed towards the needs of governments for many important areas. Metzgar & Miranda (2001) have pointed out that even powerful and expensive ERP programs have weak budget modules that are not being used by governments due to the fact that the modules are primarily aimed at private sector organizations:

"The development cycle of most ERP systems is to take the commercial version of the product and to layer public sector functionality through templates and configurations. Budgeting in the commercial sector does not face the same demands as budgeting in the public sector. (p. 143)

An assistant village manager expressed frustration with the lack of good, affordable software that will provide the functionality required:

Copyright © 2006, Idea Group Inc. Copying or distributing in print or electronic forms without written permission of Idea Group Inc. is prohibited.

Interestingly enough, I have been through three...financial software transitions and the complexity of each one...gets worse each time.... The board gave us directions at our prompting that every time we go for financial software, they cap the amount of money related to modifications, which makes sense. Why buy a solution if you are going to spend twice as much for modifications? We don't disagree. It never works out that way. It always becomes an ongoing modification of a black hole. We just pour more money into these things each year because nothing ever seems to fit.... I keep going back and telling the people each time we go through this process, is that it is beyond my comprehension that you can't buy a package for a municipality without a huge modification investment. And I don't understand why that doesn't exist. I know that we are a little unique, each municipality has to be a little unique, but tell me why such a package doesn't exist or why haven't we found it. I challenge them each time we go through the process.... So far, nobody has been able to answer my question.

In the earlier-described village, the board decided to specify that if the software met their "minimal needs," then the government should change its operations to cope with the limitations of the software rather than making expensive modifications to the package.

The importance of the needs assessment phase is illustrated by the fact that one of the biggest causes of the failures of system implementations is *"scope creep"* in which the government agency expands the functions that it demands from software packages when it implements the system beyond that originally agreed to in the contract (e.g., Jacob & Wagner, 1999). Horowitz (1993) found that more than 45% of the effort to build software in the Defense Department was used to change the capabilities of a system after it had been installed. Thus it is important for each organization to decide what are the necessary functions that must be offered by the software and distinguish those from functions that are desirable but not absolutely necessary (Government Centre for Information Systems, 1995).

Cost and Funding Issues in Procurement

A key step in the needs assessment is to calculate the costs of the existing system. This cost assists in deciding the amount that should be budgeted for the purchase. The emphasis today is on calculating the *Total Cost of Ownership (TCO)* which includes capital costs (e.g., software, hardware, configuration, and training), operational and administrative support costs (e.g., administrative support costs and increased fees such as monthly fees for mobile services), and end user costs such as decreased productivity due to the learning curve (Pratt, 2002). Pratt cites a case where a company compared the use of completely wireless system vs. handheld devices that had to be plugged into phones and found that the handhelds would be much less expensive due to the increased cost of cellular packet transmissions. The ease of use of the software can make major differences in TCO that are missed by comparing capital costs only because training costs are expensive. The TCO is a widely accepted concept and mentioned in many strategic technology plans as a major criterion for purchasing in many strategic technology plans. But it is not easy to calculate. Wheatley (2000) reports that over 50% of TCO

Copyright © 2006, Idea Group Inc. Copying or distributing in print or electronic forms without written permission of Idea Group Inc. is prohibited.

lies in soft, difficult-to-calculate costs and cites some experts as saying that *time* may be a better measuring device for comparing systems. Thus, despite all the talk about TCO, it appears that most organizations focus on easily measurable costs in comparing options (Pratt, 2002). A related concern is to differentiate between recurring (or ongoing) costs and those costs which are one-time costs. Organizations need to know what the costs of maintenance and updates will be in order to compare packages fairly and budget accurately for them.

A crucial part of the needs assessment phase is to identify funding sources for IT expenditures. Voorhees (2002) identified the following sources: (1) General funds which he considers most appropriate for smaller systems with a short life span; (2) Enterprise funds based on user fees for systems that provide services such as utilities; (3) Long-Term Loans, bonds and other longer term investments are to be used for large, long-lived projects; (4) Commercial partnerships such as when a government becomes a testing site for a system that the vendor plans to market elsewhere once it is developed; (5) Philanthropy: many nonprofit agencies receive donations of software and IT equipment or resources to purchase it; (6) User Fees: some governments are employing user fees for providing certain services such as e-government functions; and (7) Non-commercial relationships with other governments in which resources are pooled among governments to purchase systems that individually they could not afford. The importance of this financial planning is emphasized by cases such as Houston (Texas) in which they were unable to finance a new application as described in the following in the City's strategic planning document:

The City of Houston issued an…RFP in November 1996 with the intent of replacing the City's existing Financial Management System…the systems in place at that time were not Y2K compliant…. The RFP effort included the development of a full set of system requirements and specifications for all core financial, human resource, and technical needs of the City. The resulting system would be fully integrated, eliminating the need for multiple entry of data…. The City did not issue an award because all proposals were beyond the funds available to the City for the procurement. Therefore…the City elected to upgrade its existing systems. (City of Houston, Strategic eGovernment Vision, p. 41)

User fees can be a source of IT funding for utilities but have provided less money for e-government functions. Some of the IT directors that I interviewed decided not to charge extra for online interactive services. They view these IT activities as providing a service to the community and they don't want to discourage adoption by the use of extra costs, though they may raise other fees to pay for the costs of e-government systems as the following IT director noted:

Well, some of that [costs of online payment by credit card] you eat because we didn't charge for the bank fee because we didn't want to put the onus on our residents. Just as we don't charge an extra fee for paying by credit cards. So we don't on the Web either. Breakeven on our utility bill is a numbers game. Same with parking tickets. You pay a flat transaction fee on the parking tickets so we are making money on that because

Copyright © 2006, Idea Group Inc. Copying or distributing in print or electronic forms without written permission of Idea Group Inc. is prohibited.

we upped the parking ticket penalty to pay for the transaction fees. And actually it pays for more than the transaction fee.

However, states such as Indiana are employing convenience fees for online services to business and these fees make-up the major revenue for the state portal system (Chen & Perry, 2003).

The use of enterprise funds can be a major source of income for hardware like fiber and software like geographic information systems and other programs that are used to manage utilities. Although these funds come from fees paid to the departments providing the utilities, the improvements in GIS and other hardware and software that result can be leveraged to improve services for other departments of the municipality. Another important source of funds concerns grants from federal and state governments for information technology related to law enforcement. These grants may help to lead to improvements in infrastructure (e.g., use of mobile computing) that can be leveraged for use by other departments.

I have come across several examples of non-commercial sharing such as several small municipalities sharing the services of a GIS consulting organization and another case where small municipalities wrote a joint RFP and shared the services of an IT consulting firm. Both took advantage of the economies of scale and these and other case studies will be further discussed in the chapter on Sharing IT. Special crises such as the Y2K crisis or 9/11 may lead to funding of systems that can support the entire organization. For example, it is notable how many governments used the Y2K crisis as a vehicle to achieve major upgrades of their systems. When such events occur, it is important for the government to look beyond the immediate problems in order to try to take advantage of these rare opportunities to make improvements in the overall infrastructure of IT.

Sourcing IT Projects

An organization should consider all possible options regarding system changes including the following: (1) Doing nothing; (2) Upgrade the existing system; (3) Use commercial off the shelf (COTS) software; (4) Purchase a customized system from a vendor to be run and supported by internal staff; and (5) Outsourcing the function entirely. Organizations may well decide to do little or nothing if they find there is no compelling business reason to make changes in a system. A system upgrade is often the cheapest solution over the short run if a change needs to be made since costs such as training of staff and users is less. As I pointed out previously, many organizations are now attempting to use COTS software and then adapt the system to their own needs via internal staff employing customizing tools or contracts with vendors to customize the COTS package. Some small governments are committing to a cooperative form of purchasing for very expensive systems such as telecommunication and geographic information systems (Harney, 1998).

There is no consensus on when it is best to outsource versus doing the work in-house. One basic theory put forth for private sector organizations is that it is best to outsource non-strategic activities but to keep core functions of strategic importance in-house (Venkatraman, 1997; Lacity, Willcocks, & Feeny, 1995) because these processes are key

Copyright © 2006, Idea Group Inc. Copying or distributing in print or electronic forms without written permission of Idea Group Inc. is prohibited.

to competitive success and too valuable to outsource. Outsourcing, in this view, is best done for processes that are low risk and low in importance (City of Houston, Strategic Technology Plan, 2001, p. 4). On the other hand, the head of a municipal finance and budgeting department was just as concerned about relying too heavily on in-house programming staff who may decide to leave as had occurred in a nearby school district that had trouble replacing the person. Thus he saw risk in becoming dependent on internal staff and believed that external vendors may be easier to replace. Lewis (2001) argues that the most strategic activities for businesses are those that affect customer relationships and that many of these activities such as sales, marketing, and service are commonly outsourced while non-strategic activities such as accounting are rarely outsourced. Moreover, the idea of gaining competitive advantage is less relevant to general purpose governments than to businesses. Indeed, a study of 150 government executives found that 90% had outsourced activities that were very important to them (Accenture, 2003). In short, there is no consensus as to what aspects of IT should be outsourced versus retained in house and this is an issue that generalist managers and IT staff will have to examine with respect to their particular situation.

Over the last decade, this debate has been highlighted by the attempts of governments such as the states of Connecticut and Indiana, and the County of San Diego to outsource their entire IT function. Former Indiana Governor Bayh (Lacity & Willcocks, 1997, p. 87) considered outsourcing the entire data processing function because he did not regard IT as one of the central missions of government. The head of the State of Connecticut's outsourcing effort justified it by stating that "IT is not a core competency for the state" (McGee, 1997, p. 22). Singer, however, argues that core functions of government are based on information processing whether they involve issuing licenses or doing human services and thus IT is a core function (Singer, 1995b). Strassman (1997, p. 197), a skeptic on outsourcing, sees outsourcing as being most useful if the organization is in turmoil, the new technology is very difficult or the organization can't retain talent for these technologies. There is conflicting evidence concerning to what extent cost savings will result from outsourcing. Lacity & Willcocks (2001) found cost reduction is a factor in 80% of outsourcing decisions. But there is little empirical validation that outsourcing saves money (Bartell, 1998; Mack, 2003). Michell & Fitzgerald (1997, p. 235) found that cost reductions were rarely mentioned as a factor in vendor selection and that organizations viewed it as "better" to allow the vendor to make a fair profit" in order to obtain quality service. Thai & Kim's (1998) study of 241 cities in Florida also found that generally cost saving was less important than other factors such as improving technology and freeing up management resources for the decision to outsource IT.

In my case studies, I found that outsourcing was more the result of affordability issues than strategic choice. Many small municipalities (e.g., less than 25,000 population) lack full-time IT staff and thus must outsource IT functions that require specialized expertise such as networking and telecommunications. They feel that they cannot afford a full-time IT person and could not keep them busy full-time if they did hire such a person. A study by a staff member of Gartner Consulting (Kumagai, 2002) likewise found that limitations of skills were the main drivers behind outsourcing decisions for both states and local governments. The survey found that 84% and 67% of state and local governments respectively stated that lack of available internal skills was a major factor in their decision to outsource (Kumagai, 2000). The next most important outsourcing reason for local

Copyright © 2006, Idea Group Inc. Copying or distributing in print or electronic forms without written permission of Idea Group Inc. is prohibited.

government was ability to focus on core competencies (44%), with "difficulty upgrading skills" and "cost factors" tied with 26% of local governments identifying them as a problem. For states, the second most important problem was "difficulty upgrading skills."

Larger organizations are willing to hire people but only when the tasks are done often enough that it makes economic sense as the following IT director put it:

It [when to outsource versus hire somebody to do it in-house] really goes back to what is determined to be heavy lifting or specialized. A Unix box upgrade system: We use a consultant for that because we don't have the skills on staff. And because we do it so infrequently that I have did it myself, I would lose the knowledge base. The configuring of a firewall: I will get a specialist because I want somebody who is up on it and does it a couple of times a week rather than once a year if that. So when a special knowledge base is needed.

(So if there is something you need frequently, you would consider hiring somebody?)

Yes. Which is what we did with our…application developer. We started using consultants heavily in developing databases [and so the IT director decided to hire a full-time staff person to do this programming].

In other cases, IT directors said that they would not want to outsource in cases where they would lose control over crucial financial data as they would if they adopted an *application server provider (ASP)* version of ERP software. The ASP model involves the renting of "applications via the Internet" from application service providers (ASPs) (Liang, Madden, and Roque, 2000). In this model, IT applications are viewed as a utility like electricity—something to be "pumped into" the organization in a routine manner from the outside. The term "*seat management*" is often used in conjunction with the utility model and has been defined as follows (Church, 2000):

The often-used, succinct definition of seat management is that it turns desktop computers into utilities—with per-seat payments, customers purchase the right to use the vendor's equipment and resources, and the vendor owns and is responsible for its upkeep. Rough analogs are cell phones, power lines, and television cables.

The ASP model has advantages because it allows fast and easy deployment of upgrades and more predictable costs of systems (Liang et al., 2000). However, ASP applications require a very fast connection and the ASP approach tends to limit customization. Avery (2001) says that two crucial issues in buying into ASPs are to have an exit strategy and make sure that you have rights to your data even if the assets of the ASP provider should become frozen. In the organizations I studied, the ASP model was most evident in e-government applications which often reside on the server of a vendor but the end users are rarely aware of this fact.

Copyright © 2006, Idea Group Inc. Copying or distributing in print or electronic forms without written permission of Idea Group Inc. is prohibited.

These governments did not mind outsourcing their e-government billing functions because they still had control over the billing data. Although most outsourcing appeared directed at technically complex tasks, in some cases personnel issues are cited for outsourcing less interesting activities and keeping some challenging tasks in house as the following IT director noted:

We try to outsource things that we don't want to do—that are mundane, repetitive or just so highly specialized we can't get people to do it...there are still things they [in house IT staff] need to do in order to keep current. And things that they like to do. We don't want to outsource things they are going to need to be current in their jobs and that are fun for them. That's why there are a certain number of projects you want to do in house. You want to keep these guys going. Otherwise, you might as well outsource everything.

The retention of IT staff has been a key concern during the IT boom years and thus managers had to bend over backward to keep them such as to allow them to use advanced hardware and software as the following assistant manager noted:

From the moment we decided to hire somebody in house, I went through four people in six years. I couldn't pay them enough, a bright guy with a good job, he has his eye on the want ads, his attention span is that of a flea, and if you don't have enough money to buy the fun toys, 'we're out.' ...and if you don't pay them enough, 'we are outta here because we can make twice as much in the next town'.

IT staff have an interest in keeping up with the latest hardware and software but governments in time of budget scarcity often deliberately avoid upgrades. Collins (1999) discusses how the decision to upgrade is an "art" based on weighing the additional costs versus the value of new functionality and threat of discontinuation of support. In most of the governments I interviewed, their policy was not to try to keep up with the latest applications of software such as the latest Microsoft Office version. The added functionality of new versions of such software was not viewed as important enough to update. It is easier to support software if everyone has the same version but this can be complicated to manage for purchases of equipment like personal computers.

To summarize, most organizations employ selective sourcing and the decision concerning what should be outsourced is based on a complex weighing of factors such as the resources and skills of the staff, potential impact on employees, risk factors, and satisfaction with the current situation.

In the planning chapter, I discussed the issue of open software standards and how many organizations subscribe to these standards in their strategic plans. Indeed, many IT managers look with interest at open source software such as Linux and MySQL that have been use widely, particularly, in the private sector. The reasons for the attraction are clear: the desire to save money and achieve independence from vendors (Yanosky & Zastrocky, 2004). But, according to Yanosky & Zastrocky (2004), analyses of the costs of switching from certain types of applications such as office suites have found that the

Copyright © 2006, Idea Group Inc. Copying or distributing in print or electronic forms without written permission of Idea Group Inc. is prohibited.

switch should not be based on financial considerations. Jackson (2004) notes that most open-source applications come without any support and thus a true cost comparison with vendor software must include the maintaining and supporting the open source program. Jackson notes that certain tasks that are very specific to institutions (e.g., academic library cataloguing) are excellent ones to share the costs of developing among organizations via an open source approach. But Yanosky & Zastrocky (2004, p. B21) state that complex programs such as ERP are "too intricate" for the open-source approach to make sense. The movement of the government sector to these open source standards has been slow according to Peterson (2003b). For example, none of the organizations that I interviewed used Linux and only one employed MySQL. Despite the lip service to open standards, governments like other organizations still choose market dominance and industry leadership over the open source standard in their purchasing decisions. Changing software is difficult as it requires a great amount of learning and effort on the part of end users.

Leasing is an option to consider in purchasing IT equipment. Leasing allows a smaller outlay and prevents an organization from being stuck with outmoded equipment. It may be the choice for certain kinds of expensive telecommunications devices and a careful "lease versus purchase" cost benefit analysis is relevant (Low, 2002). However, there used to be a debate concerning leasing for personal computers but these items have become so inexpensive that the organizations I have studied would rather purchase a new pc or printer than have one fixed if it breaks down after its warranty period.

Most organizations have pc *replacement funds* which they use to replace pcs when they reach a certain age (four years was the modal category in my case studies). This replacement funding approach has eliminated struggles among staff and departments about who gets what concerning IT that existed when pc purchases used to be ad hoc. The modal number of years for the replacement cycle that I found was four but organizations sometimes increased or decreased the cycle depending on finances. Updates in mission critical applications such as their financial software are viewed as more important but even in these cases, many organizations refrained from keeping up with the latest version. For many organizations, the mandatory time to upgrade is when the software vendor no longer will support the existing application as the following assistant manager described:

We made a policy decision initially that we were not going to chase the latest and greatest technology. We made the decision that we were going to stay one version behind what the most current one was. Because it was cheaper and more stable.... And what is driving our solution at this time is support time frames. With certain systems, they say they are no longer going to support stuff. That is basically moving up to the next step is...for example, we got away from Windows95 when we saw they going to stop support on that. So we progressed to the next operating system based on when those time frames started to occur. And it has been very successful for us—that strategy.

Some small, resource-scarce governments cannot afford to upgrade immediately even when vendors stop supporting applications which can lead to conflict with IT consultants as the following manager described:

Copyright © 2006, Idea Group Inc. Copying or distributing in print or electronic forms without written permission of Idea Group Inc. is prohibited.

...we don't have any budget [for IT] and we totally budget based on what we have to do. I don't want some hotshot consultant coming in and telling me that I can't survive without this, this, and this. That is important to me—[that the consultants] understand the constraints that we are working with. It is still a concern that we talk with our consultants about.... We had a consultant in last week...he was having a hissy fit [because the organization wanted him to reload a software program]...it was not under warranty anymore. [The consultant said] 'You want me to reload it? It is not under warranty and it can't be fixed....' And I said, 'Right, put it back on.' [The consultant said]. 'But they won't service it.' I said, 'Yeah, but we are still using it. We are not going to pay the $2,000 to keep it under warranty for six months and we're done with it.' And I thought he [the consultant] was going to start jumping up and down and stomping his feet....

Due to the current recession in the IT area, the job retention issue has lessened in importance. IT jobs are not as easily available and even relatively resource-wealthy governmental organizations are cautious in spending for IT. Thus IT staff are more cognizant of resource constraints.

Due to the frequency of costly updates, many see the long term future for software to be *"thin client"* platforms via the Internet or intranets in which applications are presented in a browser format that does not require end user machines to have a common and latest version of software. For example, this approach is used to display GIS maps on both intranets and the Internet for some municipalities.

There is considerable variation in how much outsourcing is done. Lacity & Willcocks (2001) found that the average company spent less than 10% of their IT budget on outsourcing and 76% of the companies spent less than 20%. Some strategic technology plans such as Keene New Hampshire's set an upper limit of 25% for outsourcing and noted a desire to keep a "balance" between in-house and outsourced IT processes. However, the percent of the IT budget spent by small and moderately sized municipalities for vendors and consultants that I visited easily exceeded 20%. Thus the degree of reliance on outsourcing is heavily influenced by the size of the budget and staff resources, but it is also clear that the philosophy of the generalist and IT management strongly influence the degree to which outsourcing is used.

As I noted earlier, there are many different forms of outsourcing relationships. There is a trend among governments to want to integrate their applications so that they can share a single database. However, vendors may have one strong module (e.g., for General Ledger) but have weak modules for other applications. Consequently, many organizations employ a *"best of breed"* approach (rather than an integrated system from a single vendor) in which they employ a variety of vendors depending on which has the best application for a particular function. Many public organizations use the best of breed approach because it maximizes the functionality of their software and they are not stuck with weak modules. Best of breed vendors also tend to be strong financially and thus there is little risk of them doing out of business. However, the best of breed approach increases the complexity and cost of support as noted by an IT director who employed a single data base application to construct most of the government's applications:

Copyright © 2006, Idea Group Inc. Copying or distributing in print or electronic forms without written permission of Idea Group Inc. is prohibited.

There are...municipalities that will buy best of breed. They will say this is the best payroll system and this is the best police report that the market has. My problem with that approach is that I would...need a specialist that can support that system. I would need an Oracle database person to support this system and I would need SQL database person to support that one. Which tends to lead to more staff.... For us, we put it all in one bucket and we need just one specialist to support those assorted platforms.

According to one expert I interviewed, there is a convergence recently of the quality of modules as those vendors competing for governmental business try to improve their weak modules so that the purchase of a single integrated ERP system may be more acceptable to end users in the future.

The most controversial approach is to outsource the entire IT function to a vendor or a group of vendors with one acting as the chief contractor. As I discussed earlier, complete outsourcing arrangements have been proposed but not actually been implemented. In the Connecticut case, opposition from public employee unions and Democrats in the State legislature thwarted the full outsourcing attempt and consequently Connecticut has adopted a selective sourcing approach with mixed results so far (Field, 2002a). The County of San Diego (California) outsourced its IT function based on the recommendation of Gartner consulting (Gartner Group, n.d.). The arrangement had positive impacts of quickly updating hardware but there have been a number of problems (Field, 2002b). The contractors have missed deadlines to implement a common e-mail program and have had to pay a performance penalty. There have been other problems such as a delay in an ERP implementation. The vendors found that costs of the project far outpaced their estimates. Key personnel changes of those managing the projects on the part of both the vendor and the County have led to problems (Field, 2002b).

These total outsourcing contracts described previously run counter to the current wisdom about managing contracts that it is best to break big projects into smaller components and have a short time frame with clear milestones set (Riper, 1999; Lacity & Willcocks, 2001; Perlman, 2002). Terminating outsourcing arrangements is difficult and Lacity & Willcocks' research generally found that renegotiation is better than termination because, even if the organization wins damages, they still lack the IT application they need. For example, in one local government case, the vendor did not have a working module they promised but the city revised the contract rather than terminating it since they did not have a good alternative.

Outsourcing requires that the vendor and government have a very complete and realistic scope of work statement for the contract with the vendor. In one city where I conducted interviews, the management had been interested in outsourcing the IT function and investigated the possibility. However, they decided against doing it in part because of the lack of a good scope. But, they are directing the IT director to gather and provide this information so that it would be possible to outsource in the future. In the private sector, outsourcing often leads to the elimination of jobs and thus can achieve major cost savings. For example, the Purina Mills Corporation reduced its head count by 43% in its accounting division through implementation of an ERP system (Wah, 2000). In public outsourcing arrangements, guarantees against job loss are generally made. Hurst (Texas) outsourced their accounting function but redeployed employees whose jobs were

Copyright © 2006, Idea Group Inc. Copying or distributing in print or electronic forms without written permission of Idea Group Inc. is prohibited.

replaced by the system. Similarly, Pennsylvania outsourced their data centers to Unisys but the managers worked with the American Federation of State, County and Municipal Employees (AFSCME) to ensure that nobody lost their job (Walsh, 2001). The displaced employees were retrained to perform Web and desktop functions. An Accenture (2003) study found that only 50% of the executives who outsourced in order to reduce costs felt that they had achieved this objective. Even when the decision is made to outsource, as in the San Diego case, IT employees are usually guaranteed jobs and benefits for a period of time with the vendor who wins the contract (Field, 2002).

Lacity, Willcocks, and Feeny's (1995) study found that *selective outsourcing* was a superior strategy to those that pursued keeping IT functions mostly in-house (less than 40% outsourced) or mostly outsourced (80% or more). In selective outsourcing, management identifies individual applications and functions that are best outsourced. Outsourcing does not relieve governments of the need to give careful attention to their contracts. Lacity et al. also note that it is useful to have in-house expertise in emerging technologies that you outsource or you may not be able to negotiate sound contracts. Someone has to monitor and manage the contracts and in large organizations with large contracts, this can be a substantial activity requiring many full-time in-house staff. Failure to have adequate monitoring of contracts can lead to disasters as happened to the United States Internal Revenue Service (IRS). GAO (Lacity & Willcocks, 1997) found that the IRS did not have the capacity to assess vendor capabilities nor to negotiate and monitor the contract.

Small organizations have an especially difficult time doing this monitoring. In my case studies, this task was often done on a part-time basis by a generalist manager such as an assistant to the city manager. Other solutions were to hire another consultant to check on the vendor. But lack of financial resources often forces heavy reliance on informal sources such as use of family and friends who are knowledgeable about IT. For example, two local government officials involved who worked for small organizations and were responsible for dealing with vendors described the difficulty of trying to monitor IT and their reliance on informal help:

(Official #1) "I have friends who work in IT and in particular, one who is a consultant in the IT area…. As we were trying to purchase a new server, I would call him for second opinions…we were talking every day for a while. You have to have people if you don't know what you are doing. Nobody knows everything."

(Official #2) "I get these reports and I look at them and I can't tell what they are talking about half the time…. I show them to my husband [spouse who works in IT area] and he says, 'Go back and tell them to be more specific because I can't understand what they did here…and if I can't understand it, nobody else can.' So I tell them [vendors] that I have had an independent consultant look at it and they can't understand it so you have to be more specific."

(And how does the vendor react to that?)

Copyright © 2006, Idea Group Inc. Copying or distributing in print or electronic forms without written permission of Idea Group Inc. is prohibited.

(Official #1) "They will say, 'You want more detail?' I say, 'Yes, we don't want to be charged for a guy to write up a report but I want have to be able to tell what they did during those eight hours and be able to account for their time and know that the customer was happy because the problem was fixed. We don't want to have someone else sent out and have a customer charged for 12 hours when it should have been done in eight'."

Saunders, Gebelt and Hu's (1997) study of outsourcing found that tight contracts are necessary for success. Assessments of the success of outsourcing vary greatly. While individual governmental agencies cite large expected savings, some studies (e.g., Caldwell, 1997) found no big savings resulted from outsourcing. The lack of savings could be due to the fact that personnel are usually not let go.

Outsourcing models tend to assume a *mechanistic, "machine model"* view of organizations in which external vendors can substitute for internal staff like replacing a motor in a car but this approach ignores the importance of the informal system. Some observers (e.g., Lewis, 2001, p. 68) point out that these informal relationships can be crucial to the success of IT:

What's lost are the minor services and untracked favors that lubricate the relationship between internal IT and the rest of the business. So whereas an end user might previously have called a buddy in internal IT for advice or help with some troubleshooting, now…requests for service are funneled through the formal prioritization process specified in the outsourcing agreement.

Crofts & Swatman (2001) found that outsourcing leads to the loss of tacit knowledge and also that experience-based knowledge gained through experience, observation, and knowledge of people are crucial to success of IT efforts. Often news releases concerning outsourcing emphasize successes and tend to gloss over resistance but detailed case studies and empirical research show that outsourcing inevitably creates tension and resistance. One of the few empirical studies of employee perceptions of outsourcing (Khosrowpour, Subramanian, Gunderman, and Saber, 1996) found that 81% of employees had negative or neutral feelings about outsourcing and 78% did not believe that the interests of employees had figured in the decision. In making decisions about outsourcing, these issues concerning employees and the informal system need major attention and appear to be more challenging than technical issues for IT managers. In short, managing outsourcing contracts is a major challenge for public managers, especially those in small organizations.

The Contracting Process

After the organization has done a thorough needs assessment and set priorities, they need to obtain a clear description of the process that will be used to implement new or

Copyright © 2006, Idea Group Inc. Copying or distributing in print or electronic forms without written permission of Idea Group Inc. is prohibited.

updated systems. If an organization decides to purchase from outside vendors, they need to use some form of solicitation such as an RFP or related mechanisms to obtain detailed bids. The responses to these RFPs will form the basis of the contract with these vendors, so developing a good RFP is important to the success of the project. If it is decided that the project will be done in-house, the IT department (or whoever is doing the project) will still need to go through a similar process in negotiating with management and end users what is to be done, although the process will be less formal and without the legalistic issues that weigh heavily in contracts with an external vendors.

There are a number of approaches to obtaining the services of vendors for contracts and I briefly describe them in the following based on works such as that of Caudle & Marchand, (1989, pp. 142-145):

1. **Invitation for Bids (IFB):** This bid process is generally awarded to the lowest cost bidder that complies with the requirements of the proposed contract.

2. **Request for Proposal (RFP):** It contains the functional and technical specifications but does not have to go to the lowest bid. The RFP allows the government to specify the performance requirements of the project, the environment that it will have to run in, and the evaluation criteria that will be used.

3. **Request for Information (RFI)** or Request for Expression of Interest (REI): An RFI is often used to determine the availability and potential costs of the services requested in the contract. An RFI is most likely to be used when the government is unsure about the availability of qualified vendors and also when the technology is relatively new and they are looking for ideas from the vendors on how to accomplish the task. In many cases, an RFI may be followed up by a full-fledged RFP, although in other cases the contract may be awarded on the basis of the RFI alone if the government receives what it considers to be an attractive response.

4. **Request for Qualifications (RFQ):** Government agencies wish to develop a small set of vendors qualified to do certain tasks for them so they can quickly obtain the services of vendor in whom they have confidence.

5. **Sole source** procurements which are non-competitive and thus often has stipulations attached to them such as a statement that the source proposed to be used for the task is the only one available for that service or product.

An IFB focusing on the lowest cost bid is most likely to be used when the product desired is regarded as a commodity (e.g., purchase of pcs, printers, toners, and computer supplies) with little variation in terms of quality and functionality. Sole source contracts are often viewed with distrust by councils and boards and they require substantial justification as to why they should be used. If a government agency believes that there is only a single vendor who can perform the task and they have trust in this vendor, they may wish to ensure that the bid goes to them and reduce the time and cost involved in the RFP process. However, in my case studies, even if an organization had a favorite vendor with whom they had a good relationship, they generally preferred to competitively bid projects in order to "check the market" and ensure they were getting a good price.

Copyright © 2006, Idea Group Inc. Copying or distributing in print or electronic forms without written permission of Idea Group Inc. is prohibited.

RFQs are often used to assure quick availability of capable vendors while at the same time reducing the cost of the bidding process. It is important that governments understand the perspective of the vendor if they are to obtain realistic bids from quality vendors who would be the best choices for the project. For example, the City of Seattle (RFQ, 2002) issued an RFQ to obtain a police Records Management System (RMS). The RFQ itself explained the purpose was to reduce RFP costs to the city and vendor alike:

The City recognizes the expense incurred by a vendor in preparing a quality response to an extensive RFP, as well as the expense to the City in reviewing and evaluating a large quantity of responses to the RFP. This RFQ is intended to elicit information from potential interested vendors that will be used by the City to determine a vendor's qualifications to supply a RMS that will meet the needs of the Seattle Police Department. This RFQ does not under any circumstance commit the City to pay any of the costs incurred by any vendor in the submission of a response. The purpose of issuing the RFQ is to condense the number of responses to the RFP to a manageable number of proposals.

Another example of an RFQ is from San Bernardino County (California) and part of it is displayed in Figure 3. The RFQ is aimed at getting vendors for a wide variety of

Figure 3. Example of request for qualifications (RFQ)

C. Program Description
  1. Program Objective:
    The purpose of this RFQ is to identify contractors that can provide the County with the necessary IT resources to meet the varied needs of County Departments. This will be accomplished by creating a list of contractors who have been qualified (through this RFQ) to provide County Departments with the appropriate technical and professional staff to assist in the development and implementation of its IT projects.
  2. Program Requirements:
  Service Types for Professional Services
  a. Application Development
    1) Mainframe (IBM S/390)
    2) Client/Server (Microsoft Visual Basic)
    3) Internet
    4) Specialized Skills (e.g. PeopleSoft, GIS, Graphics, FileNet)
  b. Project Management
  c. Business Consulting
  d. Database Design and Administration (e.g. DB2, Microsoft SQL Server, Oracle)
  e. Systems Programming
  Service Types for Technical Services
  f. LAN Support
  g. Desktop Support
  h. Network Server Support (e.g. Exchange, SQL, IIS)

Source: County of San Bernardino Information Services Dept. (2001, November 20). Information Technology Services RFQ ISD 01-01 Retrieved June 16, 2003 from http://www.co.san-bernadino.ca.us/isd/docs/ISDRFQ01-01ITServices%20_R12final.pdf

Copyright © 2006, Idea Group Inc. Copying or distributing in print or electronic forms without written permission of Idea Group Inc. is prohibited.

programming and other supportive services for their network, desktop, and server needs. The RFQ outlines the maximum amount per hour that they will pay for each service. Thus the RFQ is often used to determine a limited number of vendors capable of performing the job.

The RFP is the most commonly used mechanism and can be very expensive to construct. Vendors do not have to respond to RFPs and they may skip those that they feel are poorly-written and "fishing expeditions" (Porter-Roth, 2001). The development of a good RFP requires first that the organization have performed the needs assessment and prioritization processes that I described earlier. In many cases, organizations may reduce the cost of the process by obtaining copies of RFPs written for similar systems from other governments and use these as templates for their own. Nowadays, RFPs are available via the Internet and various groups provide online access to a variety of RFPs for various kinds of systems—I discuss some of these at the end of this chapter. But the agency "borrowing" the RFP will not only have to replace the substantive information in the RFP with their own but be sure that the structure and content of the RFP are fully adequate for their own needs.

Figure 4. County of Riverside California, request for proposals, software and implementation services for an enterprise financial system

Cross-Functional Teams. A team structure will be used to evaluate software and implementation services proposals. The teams are as follows:

End User Team. The End User Team is responsible for providing input on functionality of specific modules. The End User Team consists of staff from most County departments. These individuals are primarily mid-level managers and subject-matter-experts.

Evaluation Team. The Evaluation Team is responsible for the evaluation and rating of the proposals, vendor demonstrations, and site visits. The Team will evaluate software functionality, technology architecture, implementation capabilities, costs, and other business partnering criteria. The Team may consist of staff from the following areas:
General Accounting, Payroll, Human Resources, Information Technology, Purchasing, Executive Office, Sheriff, Health, Social Services, Mental Health, and a manager from the current financial system staff. The Team's objective is to make recommendations for vendor selection to the Executive Steering Committee. Most members of the Evaluation Team will participate consistently throughout the demonstrations.

Executive Steering Committee (ESC). The ESC will evaluate the recommendations of the Evaluation Team, input of the End User Team, and its own assessment of software demonstrations and other information, and make a final recommendation to the Board of Supervisors. The ESC will also be the main guidance mechanism for system selection and contract negotiations. The ESC is made up of the Auditor/Controller, CFO, CIO, Treasurer/Tax Collector, Sheriff, Director-Department of Social Services, Director-Human Resources, Director-Purchasing, and a User Committee Representative.

Source: County of Riverside California, Request for Proposals, Software and Implementation Services for an Enterprise Financial System, March 1999: RFP# 96995 Section 5.4, Page 36. Retrieved June 17, 2003 from http://www.lgov.org/document/RFPrvr000802.pdf

Copyright © 2006, Idea Group Inc. Copying or distributing in print or electronic forms without written permission of Idea Group Inc. is prohibited.

Organizations need to select staff to construct and evaluate RFPs. The development of an RFP for a program that is used by more than one department will need to have an interdepartmental committee. End users and subject matter experts are needed to provide knowledge of what functionality is needed as well as expertise in writing the substantive parts of the RFP. For making the decision, higher level decision-makers will be needed. Consequently, as in Riverside County (California), they may need to employ three separate teams (see Figure 4). One team consisted of end users who are most familiar with functionality issues of specific programs. A second group served as an evaluation team to rate the proposals. The description of this team specifies what departments the staff must come from but it does not determine exactly who from the department is to be on the team. The third team is an executive group that will make the final decision and consists of top officials as well as one representative from the end user team.

Despite all of the planning, outsourcing is a difficult process to manage. The fragility of the contracting process was brought home to me in my interviews by the fact that its success often depends on specific employees of the vendor. In several cases, governments found that when particular employees departed the vendor due to personal career decisions, the quality of work of the vendor declined. Thus forces beyond the control of the government such as personnel turnover in the vendor can affect the process.

Legal Aspects of the Contracting Process

The dominant approach to writing RFPs is a problem-oriented approach in which the government specifies the goals of the project but leaves many of the key specifics on how to achieve these objectives up to the vendor so they can use their own creativity to come up with the best solution. In the not too distant past, governmental RFPs often tried to specify the solution to be used, but Kelman (1990) relates cases where the vendors knew of a better solution than required by the RFP but the RFP often did not allow for such productive and innovative changes.

The RFP has several major tasks that need to be achieved: (1) It needs to protect the interests of the governmental organization; (2) It needs to describe fully the needs of the organization including the environment in which the system will run so that the vendor has enough information to construct an appropriate system; (3) It needs to identify the objectives of the project and measures to be used to determine whether the vendor has fulfilled the contract. RFP-writing can consume considerable amounts of time and money. For example, the huge San Diego project to outsource their IT system was tightly written but cost $3 million to put together (Perlman, 2000). Boards and managers may be reluctant to use consultants for RFP writing. In one case, an IT expert wished to hire a consultant to write a technical GIS-related RFP, but his board told him, "That's what we hired you for."

Much of the content of an RFP is legal in nature to protect the interests of the government. These legal issues are numerous and complex. Lacity & Willcocks (2001) have found that loosely written contracts are a "disaster." I will identify and illustrate some of the major issues but it is important that legal counsel review RFPs and other bidding instruments

Copyright © 2006, Idea Group Inc. Copying or distributing in print or electronic forms without written permission of Idea Group Inc. is prohibited.

before their release. According to Wyde (1997, p. 15), the buyer needs to know what *rights it has to the software* because the purchaser only has the "specific rights" listed in the license unless the contract states that the ownership rights have been given to the purchaser. Likewise, *ownership of the data* in the system needs to be specified. It is important for the purchasing organization to write *detailed specifications of the goals and performance requirements* including all functions, features, and outputs of the new system (Strock and Adkins, 1993) and withhold full payment until this *acceptance testing* has been done (Wyde, 1997, p. 16). Specific measurable outcomes with agreed-upon objective measures also need to be made clear. Performance standards such as response times should be incorporated. *Milestones* should be built into the RFP process to provide for the deliverables and *acceptance testing* of the new system such as response time and time to develop reports. Payment should only be given for deliverables that have been completed and work adequately (Wyde, 19097, p. 16). It is important to avoid what Peterson and Carco (1998, p. 31) refer to as *weasel words* such as "reasonable" and Wyde (1997) similarly cautions about the inclusion of the terms "substantially" or "materially" concerning performance or warranty standards. Even a term such as "update" may make it difficult to distinguish between an update and a totally new system, according to Peterson and Carco (1998, p. 31). Porter-Roth (2001) emphasizes the importance of identifying *continuing costs* such as maintenance and software licensing fees to determine the lifetime cost of the contract. In my case studies, some governmental organizations used vendors to teach them how to do technical processes and then they took over from them. In a time of huge budget shortfalls, California modified its contract for a Web portal to require that the consultants teach state employees the skills so they could take over from the contractors at the end of the project (Perlman, 2003, p. 54).

Many contractors view some of the information in their proposal as proprietary and that can be a problem because many governments have policies, rules, and even laws that make information in the bids public and thus the RFP needs to require that the contractor specify information that should be treated as confidential. In addition, some RFPs such as that of the City of Dubuque, Iowa RFP (2001) for a city government Web site specified that the "city reserves the right to...use any ideas submitted in a proposal regardless of whether that proposal is selected." Indeed, due to the current poor IT market, competition for contracts is so great that governmental organizations may be able to get a great deal of valuable information free through the RFP process as the following IT director learned from private IT officials who served on an advisory committee for his governmental agency:

They [the private advisory committee members] told me that the economy is so bad now with telecommunications companies that you can get them to come in and give you, in effect, free advice and consulting as part of the purchasing process. Tell them that you don't know what you want or what you have now. They told me that approach would not work if the economy were good. ...so we did that, we had people come in and study our usage and number of phones for free.

It is also customary for IT managers to make full use of free information sources from their peer organizations as well as from numerous online sources. For example, in local

Copyright © 2006, Idea Group Inc. Copying or distributing in print or electronic forms without written permission of Idea Group Inc. is prohibited.

government area, organizations such as the Government Management Information Science (GMIS) and Innovations Group have valuable listservs where queries often provide relevant information such as their experiences with purchasing similar systems. RFPs and other relevant documents are often shared. Recommendations about desirable contractors may be shared. This information is viewed as invaluable by governmental staff and would cost a large amount of money if it had to be obtained from consultants. It is safe to say that these online sources of information have greatly increased the capacity of IT and generalist managers to get a better handle on managing IT contracts.

The organization needs to specify what kinds of loads and demands the system must be capable of handling. Often during the purchase process, demonstration or prototype systems are only fed minimal data and the actual performance is far worse when the switch-over to full system begins. When the contract is signed and the organization begins receiving deliverables, it needs to monitor the contractor's performance, conduct acceptance testing, and write complaints to the contractor for failure to comply. Failure

Figure 5. Hillsborough County, Florida, RFP for a human resource information system

---

1 Deliverable 1: Project Initialization, Draft Project Architecture and Project Plan

Suggested due date of project plan: 2 weeks after Notice to Proceed.

1.1 Draft Project and Architecture Plan with a Work Breakdown Structure. The contractor will develop a summary level description of the contractor's approach to the project and a detailed work plan. The work plan shall include at least the following:

1.1.1 A summary of the project purpose, goals, scope, and the specific roles of the County and contractor staff.

1.1.2 A list of tasks, including subtasks as applicable, required for performance of the project. The list of tasks shall include for each task: start and end dates; contractor's staff who are responsible for the task's completion; the number of hours required; the number of County staff and hours required; and the order in which software modules and departments are implemented.

1.1.3 The timelines for tasks and subtasks.

1.1.4 Due dates for summaries, outlines, oral reports, drafts and final reports.

1.2 Project Plan Maintenance. The contractor's project manager shall maintain the work plan on Microsoft Project. The format shall allow for ongoing tracking of the percentage completion of each task and subtask. It shall allow a means of tracking any deviations from the planned timeline and adjusting the work plan to reflect those deviations. The contractor shall coordinate and advise its project team members and the County's project manager as to the status of each task on an on-going basis.

1.3 Training Plan. Provide training plan for primary users in the various functional areas, HRIS administration training for appropriate staff, systems support, and technical training. This plan must include optional additional training.

2 Deliverable 2: Final Project Architecture and Project Plan
Due date of final plan: two weeks after receipt of Draft Project Architecture and Project Plan. As the result of mutual review, the County and the contractor will produce a Final Project Architecture and Project Plan.

Source: Hillsborough County Purchasing Department, Request for Proposal S-778-99. p. MS-9. Retrieved
       May 22, 2003 from LGOV.ORG

Copyright © 2006, Idea Group Inc. Copying or distributing in print or electronic forms without written permission of Idea Group Inc. is prohibited.

to do this promptly can result in the vendor not being liable for contractual deficiencies due to "*waiver*" and "*estoppel*" rules (Peterson and Carco, 1998). Specifications about platforms that the system must run under or other systems that the proposed system must be able to interact with also need to be made clear. Although there is a general trend to open and common standards and thus theoretically most systems are potentially capable of interacting effectively, in reality the integration of different hardware and software can be very difficult. Part of the acceptance testing should be to determine if the system is effectively interacting with the organization's other systems. The size and complexity of today's governmental information systems means that these interfaces are likely to be numerous. For example, the City of Norfolk, Virginia issued an RFP for a comprehensive criminal justice information system (CJIS) and included requirements that the new system interface with internal city systems such as its CAD system, various State justice systems, the State Supreme Court system, the Department of Corrections system, and various regional information exchanges.

The contract needs to specify what the responsibilities of the government organization are as well as those of the contractor. It needs to define a reasonable schedule of planned activities and milestones. These timelines will likely need to be negotiated. Since the contractor knows more about the substance of the project than the governmental agency, one approach used is to require that the contractor develop a schedule of activities and timelines including specific tasks and personnel to be assigned to these tasks and the order in which tasks will be completed. For example, Hillsborough County's (Florida) RFQ for an HRIS requires that this project management information be provided as part of the vendor's response. Indeed, the RFQ even specifies the project management software (Microsoft Project) to track the progress of the work against the planned schedule (See Figure 5). The activities of the governmental employees that are needed as part of the project as well as those of subcontractors should also be incorporated into the project plan (Wyde, 1997, p. 18). If this project plan is accurate and comprehensive, it should allow project management people more capability in understanding and managing the projects. In short, project management information provided by the vendor can assist government staff in monitoring technical and complex projects even if they initially do not have thorough knowledge concerning them.

In many cases, project lags may be due to the fact that the governmental agency itself fails to commit the resources needed and is not the fault of the vendor. This failure occurs in internal projects as well as external. For example, a GIS manager noted that departments often want a new database incorporated into the GIS system but are not willing to commit the resources needed:

We really had an issue of whether the departments were devoting enough time to the projects. And that is an ongoing issue. It has gotten better over time. You first have to work and live without the resources and then show the departments that you would get this much faster if you devoted more people to it.... It has always been a continual problem getting enough resources to make things happen in app dev or conversion or a database design or whatever. People want it and think it is great but they don't realize how much time it is going to take. At a practical level, people want this but their management is not quite aware of how much time they are going to have to spend on it so their management may pull them off onto something else.

Copyright © 2006, Idea Group Inc. Copying or distributing in print or electronic forms without written permission of Idea Group Inc. is prohibited.

Projects inevitably disrupt organizations and getting commitment of resources from internal departments that will be affected by the new system is key to success.

Contracts need to specify what to do in various situations that may cause inability to complete the contract. This may include "*Acts of God*" (*force majeure*) in which neither party is held responsible due to disasters that were unpredictable. However, if there is an inability to perform on the part of the contractor, the contract needs to specify what is to be done. Possibilities include termination of the contract, performance penalties or payment of performance bonds. Compliance with laws and standards is another standard component of RFPs. The contractors are held responsible for confirming to federal, state and local laws. For example, Web site projects may specify compliance with disability rules for the disabled. The contract may specify that the contractor has the responsibility for updating the system to deal with changes in the law such as changed in federal/state

Figure 6. Criteria to assess responses to RFP at different stages of RFP process

---

D. WEIGHTING OF QUESTIONS
The scoring/weighting of responses is as follows:

THE COUNTY RESERVES THE RIGHT NOT TO BE LIMITED TO THE LOWEST COST BID.
PRELIMINARY SCORE
Topic Points
Methodology 15
Project Staff... 10
HRIS Application Experience of the Firm 10
Government Experience of the Firm.. 10
Functionality 30
Contract Cost 25
Total... 100
A maximum of 100 additional points may be awarded through post-preliminary investigation that may
include any or all of the following:

POST-PRELIMINARY SCORE
Topic Points
Oral Presentation.. 45
Site Visit(s)... 10
Detailed Contact Information from Investigation of Past Performance 45
Total... 100
The three proposers scoring the most points that is the sum of the Preliminary Score plus the Post-
Preliminary Score, if any, **MAY** be requested to submit a Best and Final Offer. The Best and Final Offer
score will include the following:

BEST and FINAL OFFER SCORE
Topic Points
Revised Methodology 30
Revised Project Staff... 20
Revised Contract Cost.. 50
Oral Presentation, if any .... 45＊
Site Visit(s), if any .... 10＊
Detailed Contact Information from Investigation of Past Performance, if any ..... 45＊
Total... 200

Source: Hillsborough County Purchasing Department, Request for Proposal S-778-99. p. MS-5. Retrieved May 22, 2003 from LGOV.ORG

Copyright © 2006, Idea Group Inc. Copying or distributing in print or electronic forms without written permission of Idea Group Inc. is prohibited.

deductions or accounting standards for financial systems. The contract should provide for *indemnification* from the contractor to protect the government from harm that is suffered as a result of the project. Some governments require performance bonds for projects to recover investments made in failed projects. A face-to-face vendor conference is usually a requirement for any complex project in which the government is able to answer questions concerning the project and communicate effectively what they are looking for. Wyde (1997) urges that the government's own model contract form be used, not the vendor's. There are many other legal issues concerning RFPs that are too numerous to fully describe here. Although much of the RFP will be dependent on the nature of the project, many of these legal issues have become fairly standard and they are the part of the RFP that can be largely copied from others. There are many RFP's available on the Internet at any point in time through search tools such as Google and some Internet sites (e.g., those of Innovations Group & LGOV.Gov) that provide examples of RFPs that governmental organizations have used in the past.

The RFP needs to specify the criteria that will be used to choose among vendors. Important criteria include cost, the substance of the bid and the proposed project including its functionality, the qualifications and experience of the vendor and its personnel. As I noted earlier, the emphasis now is on "*best value*" rather than lowest cost so the cost factors cannot be considered without relating them to performance. Some contracts include a "*not to exceed*" clause that ensures that the winning bid will be within their budget. The purchasing of a complex system usually goes through more than one stage and thus the criteria and their weighting may change from stage to stage. The top few bidders (typically four and no more than six) are invited to a second round in which they make an oral presentation and demonstrate their system. In this second stage, selected agency personnel will generally make site visits to installations where the vendor's system is already operating. Then there may be a third step where the top two are invited to make a final "best" offer. In Figure 7, we show the scoring criteria used by Hillsborough County (Florida) in their RFP for an HRIS system during these three phases. The weighting of criteria changes as the bidding process evolves. As can be seen, the proposal content weighs heavily in the initial phase but information derived from contacts weighs more heavily in the second round.

Michel argues that in most evaluations of RFPs that soft, unquantified factors such as "*cultural fit*" determine decisions. In my interviews with governmental officials, for example, it was clear that past experience with government and the ability to understand governmental needs was of primary importance. Porter-Roth (2001) says that some requirements may be "showstopper issues" and that these should be made clear. Many agencies now differentiate among the priorities for the functionality of the system into categories ranging from "must haves" to those which would be "nice but are not necessary." If the total contract bid of the highest rated vendor is unaffordable, then the government can negotiate down by eliminating some of the functionality that is a lower priority. An example of this approach is shown in Figures 7A and 7B where an RFP by Riverside County (California) for a budget system differentiated among "Existing Functionality," "Value Added" functions, and "Substantially Exceeds Basic Needs" functions.

Copyright © 2006, Idea Group Inc. Copying or distributing in print or electronic forms without written permission of Idea Group Inc. is prohibited.

Figure 7A. Example of RFP employing different levels of functionality: existing and value added levels

(Note: I have selected out a few examples of each of these levels)

2.5 Functional Requirements
Following are the County's functional requirements for a new budgeting system. They are divided into three groups:

A) Existing Functionality summarizes the capabilities of the present system that form the baseline for evaluation;
B) Value Added summarizes the minimum additional enhancements sought; and
C) Substantially Exceeds Basic Needs describes some of the distinguishing characteristics sought by the County from an ideal government budgeting system.

Examples of Existing Functionality:

Operates from relational database architecture.
Can stand alone or on three-tier client server.
Provides for entry of current year-end projections, departmental budget requests, CEO recommendations, and Board adopted final budget.
Provides columnar, side by side entry and comparison of budget data at the object (account) level by period/stage.
Projects salary and benefit data for each position by pay period, including pre-defined step increases, COLAs, benefit changes, etc.
Provides itemized listing of requested financed fixed assets, including unit cost, quantity, calculated total, beginning and ending dates of financing.

Examples of Value Added:

Fully GASB compliant (including GASB 34).
User environment uses fully object-oriented, Graphic User Interface.
Integrates fully with PeopleSoft Public Sector Human Resources Management (HRMS) and Financial Systems.
Shares/mirrors master tables and financial data live with both HRMS and Financial Systems; synchronization is automated or unnecessary.
Draws live data for beginning balances and existing reserves and designations from financial system.

Source: Adapted from County of Riverside, Request for Proposal #97379. pp. 27-29. Retrieved June 18, 2003 from http://www.lgov.org/library_frames.html

Governments employ a number of strategies in order to obtain a favorable price. One method (Peterson & Carco, 1998) is to insist on the "*most favored nation*" status (i.e., you get the same price as the one given the vendor's most favored customer) or benchmarking based on the price of some independent expert or index. Saunders, Gebelt, & Hu (1997) in their study of outsourcing contracts found that some businesses build renegotiation options into their contracts which means that fees are renegotiated if benchmark studies show that standard industry costs have dropped or other conditions occur (e.g., much greater loads than expected). This makes good sense due to the rapid decreases in prices in some technological areas—the best price at one time may be a poor price later. There are obvious advantages for multiple organizations to band together to bargain with a vendor.

Performance-based contracting has become common in some agencies such as the Transportation Safety Administration of the Federal Government (Hardy, 2003). It

Copyright © 2006, Idea Group Inc. Copying or distributing in print or electronic forms without written permission of Idea Group Inc. is prohibited.

Figure 7B. Example of RFP employing different levels of functionality: substantially exceeds basic needs level

---

(Note: I have selected out certain examples)

Examples of Substantially Exceeds Basic Needs:

Builds funding for salaries and benefits individually by position.
Allows allotment of salary and benefit data per pay period.
Allows allotment of expenses and revenues in monthly and quarterly increments, and across multi-year periods, with or without accruals.
Provides for annotation of individual data cells.
Enables forecasting expenses and revenues at the object level based on analytic trend analysis.
Enables construction and roll-up of budgets from lowest subdivision of budget unit.
Allows complete drill-down/drill-around to lowest levels of detail available.
Enables budgeting for grants across multiple years.
Enables budgeting for detailed project cost accounting across multiple years.
Enables program budgeting within budget units.
Tracks financed fixed assets and vehicles throughout life of financing period.
Calculates depreciation costs of each fixed asset and vehicle.
Pulls live cost per unit data for assets and commodities from PeopleSoft Purchasing Module.
Is browser-based.
Enables detailed "what if" analysis and scenario building.
Enables full scale bottom-up and top-down multi-year modeling by fund from the lowest subdivision within budget units on up, including expenditure rates, revenue forecasts, beginning and ending fund balance assumptions, debt service, depreciation & amortization, demographic impacts, etc.
Provides backstop which prohibits entry of appropriations above net cost allocated and revenues/fund balance available.
Enables entry of narrative, pictures, statistical information, etc., for reporting.
Draws statistical data from HRMS and Financials System.
Enables effective dating revenues and appropriations of short-term or one-time nature.
Supports multiple period fields: fiscal year, budget year, program year(s), calendar year.

Source: Adapted from County of Riverside, Request for Proposal #97379 Retrieved June 18, 2003
            from http://www.lgov.org/library_frames.html

---

requires that the government and the vendor first agree on objectives of the contract and then how to measure the degree of attainment of these objectives. The contractor is then reimbursed based on how well they achieve with "rewards for superior performance and penalties for sub-par work" (Hardy, 2003, p. 46). The model has a great deal of attraction but it is challenging to identify valid and useful performance measures. Easily available data such as network uptime (or downtime) usually are not adequate because the measures need to capture "the user experience" (Hardy, 2003, p. 47). Thus the government will have to gather and validate performance data information on a regular basis if they are to use the performance-based contracting model.

Generally, the governmental agency would like to have competition for its proposals to increase its leverage and obtain a better deal. Indeed, some governmental agencies conduct "parallel negotiations" with the final two vendors as Riverside County suggested it might do in its RFP for an enterprise financial system. If a proposal seems too vague or onerous, it may not attract many responses. So it is important that proposals are clearly written and appear reasonable from the vendor perspective to respond to them. Vendors must spend substantial resources replying to RFPs and they themselves

Copyright © 2006, Idea Group Inc. Copying or distributing in print or electronic forms without written permission of Idea Group Inc. is prohibited.

conduct their own "cost benefit" analysis to determine if it is worth devoting serious effort to making a response.

Project Management Issues

Substantial planning needs to be done for implementing IT projects whether internal or external. There are many potential causes of failure but three especially important ones are scope creep, complexity of large and extended projects, and failure to achieve adequate communication. I discussed earlier the importance of using the needs assessment to ensure a good original scope is written into the contract that will not have to be heavily revised. Jacob et al. (1999) found that they had to ignore the "bells and whistles" aspects in order to implement an ERP system rapidly including features that were the main reason for purchasing the new system such as paperless purchasing. After this minimalist implementation, these "value added" functions are implemented. I also have already noted that the consensus is to keep projects short. Willcocks et al. (2002, p. 221) suggest six to nine months maximum and to break large projects into smaller components if necessary.

Figure 8A. Examples of questions about various risk factors in the State of California Risk Assessment Model: strategic, financial, & project management risks

---

(Note: Below I have selected certain response categories to illustrate the nature of the choices in the tool).

Strategic Risk: To what degree is the project's purpose aligned with the agency's overall business strategy? This question assesses the degree of alignment between the project objectives and the agency's business objectives:

1. Project objectives have been clearly documented and can be linked to specific agency business objectives
2. The project direction is consistent with the business strategy but the relationship has not been clearly documented

Financial Risk: Are the cost/benefits clearly defined with a documented write-up?
This question will gauge the economic feasibility of the project. Without clear financial need for the proposed system, there is a risk that management will not see the need for the project.

1. Yes, a cost/benefit analysis has been performed by a qualified, experienced resource.
4. Cost/benefits have been informally derived but not clearly documented.
6. No cost/benefit analysis has been performed yet.

Project Management Risk: Does the project management team have relevant experience? This question determines the degree of experience in dealing with similar sized projects.

1. Members of the project management team have experience leading projects of similar size and complexity
4. Members of the project management team have had exposure to projects of similar size and complexity but not in lead roles

Source: Adapted from California Department of Information Technology. Retrieved January 10, 2000 from http://www.doit.ca.gov/SIMM/#RAM

Copyright © 2006, Idea Group Inc. Copying or distributing in print or electronic forms without written permission of Idea Group Inc. is prohibited.

Figure 8B. Examples of questions about various risk factors in the State of California Risk Assessment Model: technology, change management, & operational risks

(Note: Below we have selected certain response categories to illustrate
the nature of the choices in the tool).

Technology Risk: Is there a system load test or other measures to ensure good system performance(i.e. measures to test response time, system efficiency, etc.) This question measures system performance and the risk associated with failing to test for performance.

1. There is a load test for system performance in accordance with accepted industry standards.
2. There is a methodology for load testing but some phases are not complete.
5. The load testing plans have been discussed, but are not in place at this time.
9. There are no plans for load testing the system.

Change Management / Operational Risk

What will be the magnitude of change that the new system will impose upon the users?

This question will determine how much change the system will inflict upon the organization. The more change a project brings to the organization the less likely people are willing to accept it.

1. The new system will impose very little change, if any, upon the users.
2. The new system will change slightly the current daily operations of the users.
5. The new system will require significant changes by the users and will require training.
8. The new system will present an entirely new way for the users to complete daily operations.

Source: Adapted from California Department of Information Technology. Retrieved January 10, 2000
from http://www.doit.ca.gov/SIMM/#RAM

Part of the project management process is to deal with risks. According to Willcocks et al. (2002), there are six kinds of risks: strategic, cost, managerial, operational, contractual, and technical. Part of the challenge in technology is to select vendors who are fiscally strong and likely to remain involved in serving the governmental sector. Risks are unpredictable such as when another company takes over your vendor as happened to one city that I studied. The new vendor substituted their own utility package for the previous one and it was less focused on the needs of governmental organizations. In another case with which I am familiar, a municipality invested in a financial package only to have the vendor decide not longer afterwards that they were going to leave the municipal field. And many organizations have invested in platforms (e.g., Macintosh) that have not been successful in competing for market share. So part of the purchasing process involves soothsaying, picking a vendor that will be around for the indefinite future. The importance of picking a successful vendor is not new. There was an old adage during the mainframe era that "no one ever lost their job by buying IBM" that reflects the need for a stable vendor.

Some organizations use a systematic risk assessment management process in order to anticipate and avoid failures. For example, the State of California's former Department of Information Technology employed a formal Risk Assessment Model (RAM) model in recent years to cope with several failures of major systems (see Figures 8A and 8B). The model includes a rating scale to assess the likelihood of a project running into problems

Copyright © 2006, Idea Group Inc. Copying or distributing in print or electronic forms without written permission of Idea Group Inc. is prohibited.

and hence provide guidance on which projects to manage more closely. The strategic risk questions dealt with issues such as whether the project had been linked clearly to the organization's business strategy and how severe would be late delivery. Financial risk looks at issues such as the total cost of the project, its length and if a clear payback has been established. Project management risk focuses on matters such as the experience of the project management team, whether scope has changed in a major way, and whether clear milestones have been established. Technological risk factors include whether there are good system test measures for the technology while change management focuses on the extent of change required by the system and whether these changes would be viewed as threats by the staff. Tools such as California's RAM model are useful but failures of State of California projects such as a major Oracle database project subsequent to the implementation of the model show that no system guarantees success. California's procurement system had received a grade of B minus from Governing Magazine's rating of governmental IT systems and Richard Greene, a projects editor with Governing Magazine (Martin, 2002), stated that California's systems were good but that systems are "worthless" unless used by "capable people."

The project team will need technical knowledge, managerial, and political skills necessary to monitor a complex technical project. If internal skills are lacking, management may hire consulting firms not only to write RFPs, but also to monitor the success of the implementation of the project. This approach is common in large ERP implementations and can be costly. For example, in Toulumne County (California), the project team included seven employees from various departments plus a systems integration vendor with a core staff of three (Jacob & Wagner, 1999). Note that in Toulumne's case, the seven internal employees were still responsible for their regular jobs. The consulting group spent 7600 hours while the technical and functional internal staff were estimated to have spent 4600 and 5000 hours respectively. In an Alameda County (California) implementation, Harris reports that employees found it difficult to perform their dual roles and this conflict needed to be managed and sometimes consultants had to be brought in to alleviate their load. In a Des Moines (Iowa) implementation of an ERP system, consultant hours totaled 12,000 and the consultant cost was nearly $1 million (Riper & Duham, 1999). During this Des Moines project, the consultants warned that the project faced disaster unless additional governmental staff assistance were provided to the in-house project manager and unless an internal data base administrator were appointed (Riper & Dunham, 1999). The process of "backfilling" refers to the necessity to find staff to perform the tasks that were formerly performed by those assigned to major new projects. Although an ERP system with its necessity to integrate functions is exceptionally complex, many IT projects in government involve a wide range of departments and also are demanding—geographic information systems being one example. Indeed, good contract management can take up so much time that Sprehe (2003) has made the point that it can prevent government employees from doing "any real thinking about their 'inherently government' decisions" and thus they wind up letting contractors do their thinking for them. Thus part of the management of contracts is coping with the burden of managing contractors.

A key aspect of project management is communication. New technology inevitably creates anxiety in many personnel due to fear that it will threaten jobs. In my interviews with end users, some openly acknowledged their fear of losing their jobs when new

Copyright © 2006, Idea Group Inc. Copying or distributing in print or electronic forms without written permission of Idea Group Inc. is prohibited.

systems were first mentioned. Communication strategies are crucial and must be proactive as passive resistance can kill new systems because it is harder to detect than open rebellion. Organizations use all types of mechanisms for communicating including face-to-face brown bags, contests with prizes, and online sources (Boyer, 1999). Boyer used all of these techniques plus employee newsletters and still decided that the project would have benefited from earlier emphasis on communication and change management planning.

Short term steps to alleviate the burden of the implementation may have to be taken during the implementation. Boyer tells how they had to stop hiring people and cease making changes in the system to implement an ERP. The old and new systems often are run parallel for a period of time. As noted earlier, the initial implementation is often barebones with powerful features delayed to the future. Thus the implementation of complex projects like ERP can easily take several years.

Political support is necessary and projects need champions if they are to succeed (Lacity & Willcocks, 2001). The champion needs to come from outside the IT staff such as an end user or influential manager and it is part of the job of the project staff is to identify or stimulate supporters if not champions (Keen, 2003; Keen & Morton, 1978). Willcocks et al. (2002) recommend that project managers conduct a *"power audit"* in which they analyze existing political and cultural systems in order to identify feasible options. The problems experienced by the State of Arkansas in implementing an ERP system reflect the difficulties that can occur (Peterson, 2003a). A shift in project management from the State CIO Office to the Department of Information Technology led to infighting and the leakage of politically sensitive e-mails and aggravated a struggle between the governor and the State Legislature over the project. Politics and political negotiation are common components of major IT changes. However, at some point, changes may have to be forced, as Hall (2001) noted in her observations on the merging of financial systems between the City of Omaha (Nebraska) and Douglas County (Nebraska). She found that when "all else fails," the authority of the governing body must be exercised if the project is to succeed.

E-Procurement

Many organizations now do as much of their procurement of IT as possible over the Internet in order to save costs (Wood, 2000). The advantages of online procurement include reduced time and costs to disseminate the RFP (or whatever bidding process is being employed) as well as the reduced costs of printing the material. Online procurement also expands the number of vendors that can be reached and may foster greater competition. If the organization allows electronic submission of bids too, then the costs for the vendor are reduced.

There are different categories of purchases. In this chapter, I have focused on complex purchases of complex systems but the degree of automation for commodity like purchases such as pcs and printers can be much greater. For example, San Diego County uses a Web-based system (BUYNET) that automatically stores bids and puts them into an electronic "lockbox," puts them into a spreadsheet, and calculates the costs from least

Copyright © 2006, Idea Group Inc. Copying or distributing in print or electronic forms without written permission of Idea Group Inc. is prohibited.

to most expensive, and posts the results on the Web site (Wood, 2000). Although the issuing of RFP and much of the processing of RFPs may be done via the Internet, complex purchases cannot be as automated. Research about the impacts of e-procurement is scant but the existing research shows that actual benefits depend on factors such as user training (Subramanian & Shaw, 2002). Subramanian & Shaw found in their study of a manufacturer that 55% and 45% of the volume of their purchases were structured (i.e., commodity-like) and unstructured respectively.

Many states and other entities have put together cooperative online systems to leverage buying power of governments to get a better deal especially for commodity-type purchases. Many of these have been cooperative efforts such as the Western State Contracting Alliance (http://www.aboutwsca.org/). While these systems undoubtedly have achieved notable success, many have not achieved the level of use expected. Massachusetts was one of the first states to implement an online procurement system but it did not attract enough suppliers and sales to be successful and the private firm that provided the e-procurement system declared bankruptcy (Newcombe, 2002). Los Angeles County also developed an online procurement system but its procurement needs are complex with up to 700 purchasing agreements at one time and the online catalogs had not yet met their procurement needs (McKay, 2001). Many large online vendors have their own online systems and don't want them supplanted by a government-run system. Consequently, there are a myriad of online systems and the result is that none builds up the kind of leverage envisioned. Even in the private sector many companies have been disappointed with their level of use (Gilbert, 2000). In my case studies, I found that organizations often used an eclectic strategy of purchases, sometimes employing state or other procurements but they also often preferred buying from a low-cost vendor that was nearby. Also, I found that service remained a significant issue in their purchases even for commodity-like purchases and judgments about service are not easy to quantify and automate. In short, online procurement does save money but the procurement of IT remains complex and the online systems do not remove the necessity for judgment.

Conclusion

Purchasing is a difficult challenge for IT managers. Success requires the successful performance of needs assessment, contract development, and project monitoring tasks. The knowledge and skills required are complex including technical, managerial, interpersonal, and political. The combined talents of IT managers and staff, generalist managers and end users are necessary.

Copyright © 2006, Idea Group Inc. Copying or distributing in print or electronic forms without written permission of Idea Group Inc. is prohibited.

References

Accenture. (2003, May 15). *Vast majority of government executives reporting outsourcing 'important' or 'critical' Activities, Accenture report finds.* News Release. Retrieved May 21, 2003, from http://www.accenture.com/xd/xd.asp?it=enweb&xd=_dyn/dynamicpresslrease_609.xml

Ariely, D. (2003, May 1). Why good cios make bad decisions. *CIO Magazine.* Retrieved May 15, 2003, from http://www.cio.com/archive/05/0103/bad.html

Avery, S. (2001, April 19). Negotiating an ASP deal. *Purchasing, 130*(8), 59-60.

Bartell, S. M. (1998). Information systems outsourcing: A literature review and agenda for research. *International Journal of Organizational Theory & Behavior, 1*(1), 17-44.

Boyer, D. (2001). ERP implementation: managing the final preparation and go-live stages. *Government Finance Review, 17*(6), 41-44.

Caldwell, B. (1997, March 10). No big savings. *Information week,* 101.

California State Department of Information Technology. (1998). *California risk assessment model.* Retrieved January 10, 2000, from http://www.doit.ca.gov/SIMM/#RAM

Caudle, S.L., & Marchand, D.A. (1989). *Managing information resources: New directions for in state and local government.* Syracuse, NY: Syracuse University, School of Information Studies, Center for Science and Technology.

Chen, Y., & Perry, J. (2003, June). Outsourcing for e-government: Managing for success. *Public Performance & Management Review, 26*(4), 404-421.

Church, M. (2002, Fall). Plug IT in, Turn IT on: Seat management comes to the Commonwealth. *Virginia.edu, IV*(2). Retrieved June 18, 2003, from http://www.itc/virginia.edu/fall00/seats/home.html

CIO Magazine. (2003, June 1). California. Retrieved June 12, 2003, from http://www.cio.com/archive/060103/states_california

CIO Magazine. (2003, June 1). Deep cuts in bluegrass country. Retrieved June 12, 2003, from http://www.cio.com/archive/060103/states_kentucky.html

CIO Magazine. (2003, June 1). Michigan. Retrieved June 12, 2003, from http://www.cio.com/archive/060103/states_michigan.html

CIO Magazine. (2003, June 1). Texas. Retrieved June 12, 2003, from http://www.cio.com/archive/060103/states_texas.html

City of Houston. (n.d.) *Strategic e-government vision. Core system assessment.* Retrieved June 11, 2003, from http://www.ci.houston.tx.us/it/sip-3.pdf

City of Houston. (2001, July 20). *Strategic technology plan for the city of Houston.* Retrieved June 11, 2003, from http://www.ci.houston.tx.us/it/strategics.htm

Collins, K. (1999). Strategy and execution of ERP upgrades. *Government Finance Review, 15*(4), 43-47.

Copyright © 2006, Idea Group Inc. Copying or distributing in print or electronic forms without written permission of Idea Group Inc. is prohibited.

County of Riverside. (2000). Request for proposal #97379. Retrieved June 18, 2003, from http://www.co.riverside.ca.us/depts/gsa/purchase/97379.htm

Crofts, M., & Swatman, P. A. (2001, September 16). *The role of tacit organisational knowledge in IT-enabled organisational change.* Paper presented at the Program of the European CSCW 2001 Workshop on Managing Tacit Knowledge. Retrieved June 18, 2003, from http://www.unite-project.org/ecscw01-tkm/papers/crofts-ecscw01.pdf

Dawes et al. (2004). *Making smart IT choices: Understanding value and risk in government IT investments.* Retrieved October 5, 2004, from http://www.ctg.albany.edu/publications/guides/smartit2

Dean, J. (2000). Purchasing IT as a utility. *Government Executive, 32*(11), 88-80.

Field, T. (2002a, June 15). Connecticut: Rebuilding a dynasty or a dinosaur? *CIO Magazine.* Retrieved June 9, 2003 from http://www.cio.com/archive/061502/govt_connecticut.html

Field, T. (2002b, June 15). You can't outsource city hall. *CIO Magazine.* Retrieved June 9, 2003, from http://www.cio.com/archive/061502/govt.html

Frank, D. (2003, June 2). Making the case. *Federal Computer Week,* 20-23.

Gartner Group. (n.d.) *Case study: Largest local government technology outsourcing in history.* Retrieved June 9, 2003, from http://www.gartner.com/3_consulting_services/cs_SanDiego.jsp

Government Centre for Information Systems. (1995). *Managing information systems development and acquisition.* Cambridge, MA: Blackwell.

Hall, K.A. (2001, December). Intergovernmental cooperation on ERP Systems. *Government Finance Review,* 6-13.

Hardy, M. (2003, May 26). Performance-based contracting ascends. *Federal Computer Week,* 46-47.

Harney, D.F. (1998, June). Public purchasing: A checklist for the local government manager. *IQ Service Report, 30*(6). Washington, DC: International City Management Association.

Harris, J. (1999). Designing change management strategies for ERP systems: Observations from Alameda County, California. *Government Finance Review, 15*(4), 29-31.

Harris, S. (2003). The buying game. *Government Executive, 35*(3), 70-71.

Horowitz, B.M. (1993). *Strategic buying for the future: Opportunities for innovation in government electronics system acquisition.* Washington, DC: Libey.

Jackson, G. A. (2004, September 24). Open source is the answer: Now what was the question? *Chronicle of Higher Education,* B17-B18.

Jacob, G., & Wagner, T. (1999). Rapid ERP implementation: The Toulumne County, California experience. *Government Finance Review, 15*(4), 33-36.

Keen, J. (2003, May 15). Real value: Tough decisions. *CIO Magazine.* Retrieved June 12, 2003, from http://www.cio.com/archive/051503/value.html

Copyright © 2006, Idea Group Inc. Copying or distributing in print or electronic forms without written permission of Idea Group Inc. is prohibited.

Keen, P. G.W., & Morton, M. S. (1978). *Decision support systems: An organizational perspective.* Reading, MA: Addison-Wesley.

Kelman, S. (1990). *Procurement and public management.* Washington, DC: AEI.

Khosrowpour, M., Subramanian, G., Gunderman, H., & Saber, J. (1996). Managing information technology with outsourcing: An assessment of employee perceptions. *Journal of Applied Business Research, 12*(3), 85-96.

Kumagai, W. (2002, October). *Public sector challenges in 2002.* Gartner Consulting. Retrieved June 12, 2003, from http://www.misac.org/state_library/gartner_102902.pdf

Kustermann, K. M. (n.d.). *Reengineering the purchasing function: Identifying best practices for the city of Chicago.* Retrieved May 14, 2003, from http://www.cityofchicago.org/MgmntInfoSystems/Articles/Reengineering.html

Lacity, M. C., & Willcocks, L. (1997). Information systems sourcing: examining the privatization option in USA public administration. *Information Systems Journal, 7,* 85-108.

Lacity, M. C., & Willcocks, L. (2001). *Global information technology outsourcing.* Chichester, UK: John Wiley & Sons.

Lacity, M. C., Willcocks, L., & Feeny, D. (1995, May-June). IT Outsourcing: Maximize flexibility and control. *Harvard Business Review,* 84-93.

Levinson, M. (2003, June 1). Dire states. *CIO Magazine.* Retrieved June 12, 2003, from http://www.cio.com/archive/060103/states.html

Lewis, B. (2001, May 28). The o-word that IT fears. *Infoworld,* 68.

Liang, Y., Madden, M., & Roque, R. (2000). The ABCs of ASPs. *Governing Finance Review, 16*(6), 29-33.

Low, L. (2002, December 1). A lesson on leasing. *CIO Magazine.* Retrieved June 12, 2003, from http://www.cio.com/archive/120102/budget.html

Mack, R. (2003, May 23). A strategic approach will help IS organizations survive cost cuts. *CIO Magazine.* Retrieved June 12, 2003, from http://www2.cio.com/analyst/report1365.html

Madden, M., Miranda, R., & Roque, R. (1999). *A guide to preparing an RFP for enterprise financial systems.* Chicago: Government Finance Officers Administration.

Martin, J. (2002, May 30). The California mess: A chilling effect? *Governing Magazine,* Special Conference Report, Governing's Managing Technology. Retrieved June 6, 2002, from http://www.governing.com/

McKay, J. (2001, January). Getting through the maze. *Government Technology,* 46-48.

Metzgar, J., & Miranda, R. (2001). Bringing out the dead: Can information technology resurrect budget reform? *Government Finance Review, 17*(2), 9-13.

Michell, V., & Fitzgerald, G. (1997). The IT Outsourcing market-place: vendors and their selection. *Journal of Information Technology, 12,* 223-237.

Miller, J. (2003, June 2). OMB gets down to business for 2005. *Government Computer News,* 1 & 12.

Copyright © 2006, Idea Group Inc. Copying or distributing in print or electronic forms without written permission of Idea Group Inc. is prohibited.

National Association of State Purchasing Officers. (1996). *Buying smart: Blueprint for action*. Retrieved May 20, 2003, from www.naspo.org/reform/buyingsmart.html

Newcombe, T. (2002, January). Procurement hits some snags. Government Technology. Retrieved July 3, 2003, from http://www.govetech.net/magazine/story.php?id=8081&issue=1:2002

Newcombe, T. (2003, May). Changing gears. *Government Technology,* 24-25.

Perlman, E. (2000, May). Taking tech private. *Governing,* 20-25.

Perlman, E. (2002, December). Teaming up for IT. *Governing,* 32-34.

Perlman, E. (2003, July). The art of re-doing the deal. *Governing,* 50-54.

Peterson, B.L., & Carco, D.M. (1998). *The smart way to buy information technology.* New York: MACOM, American Management Association.

Peterson, S. (2003a, February). Lost signals. *Government Technology,* 28-34.

Peterson, S. (2003b, May). Something for nothing? *Government Technology,* 27-66.

Porter-Roth, B. (2001). Preparing an rfp. *Computer Technology Review, 21*(9), 28-29.

Pratt, M. K. (2002). *Computerworld, 36*(46), 48-49.

Richter, M.D. (1996, February). Technology acquisition and implementation: Learning the hard way. *Government Finance Review,* 7-11.

Riper, K., & Dunham, M. J. (1999). Phased implementation: The city of Des Moines (Iowa) experience. *Government Finance Review, 15*(4), 37-42.

Rocheleau, B. (2000). Guidelines for public sector system acquisition. In G. D. Garson (Ed.), *Handbook of public information systems* (pp. 377-390). New York: Marcel Dekker.

Sandlin, R. (1996). *Manager's guide to purchasing an information system.* Washington, DC: International City/County Management Association.

Saunders, C., Gebelt, M., & Hu, Q. (1997). Achieving success in information system outsourcing. *California Management Review, 39*(2),63-79.

Schulz, J. A. (2001). *Information technology in local government: A practical guide for managers.* Washington, DC: International City/County Management Association.

Sia, S. K., Tang, M., Soh, C., & Boh, W. F. (2002). Enterprise resource planning (ERP) systems as a technology of power empowerment or panoptic control? *Database, 33*(1), 23-37.

Singer, L.T. (1995, March). Systems integration risk reduction. *Government Technology.* Retrieved July 1, 2003, from http://govt-tech.govtech.net:80/1995/gt/mar/sirsk.shtm

Sprehe, J. T. (2003, March 31). Who manages contractors? *Federal Computer Week, 47.*

State of Iowa. (2004). Return on investment program. Project Summary for P-025-FY04-DRF (Electronics Tax Administration). Retrieved November 24, 2004, from http://das.ite.iowa.gove/roi/FY2004/58.htm

Strassmann, P.A. (1997). *The squandered computer: Evaluating the business alignment of information.* New Canaan, CT: Information Economics.

Strock, B., & Adkins, D. (1993). *The municipal computer systems handbook* (2nd ed.). Rensselaerville, NY: The Rensselaerville Systems Training Center.

Copyright © 2006, Idea Group Inc. Copying or distributing in print or electronic forms without written permission of Idea Group Inc. is prohibited.

Subramanian, C., & Shaw, M. J. (2002). A study of the value and impact of B2B e-commerce: The case of Web-based procurement. *International Journal of Electronic Commerce, 6*(4), 19-40.

Varon, E. (2003, June 1). R.O. Iowa. *CIO Magazine.* Retrieved June 12, 2003, from http://www.cio.com/060103/iowa.html

Venkatraman, N. (1997, Spring). Beyond outsourcing: Managing IT resources as a value center. *Sloan Management Review, 38,* 51-64.

Voorhees, W. (2002). How and why to strategically finance IT projects. *Government Finance Review, 18*(2), 42-43.

Wah, L. (2000). Give ERP a chance. *Management Review, 89*(3), 20-24.

Walsh, T. (2001, January). Outsourcing succeeds. *Government Computing News: State & Local,* 1 & 8.

Wheatley, M. (2000, November 15). Every last dime. *CIO Magazine*, 143-152.

Willcocks, L. P., Petherbridge, P., & Olson, N. (2002). *Making IT count: Strategy, delivery, infrastructure.* Oxford: Butterworth Heinemann.

Wood, L. E. (2000). The beginning of the end of paper procurement. *Government Finance Review, 16*(3), 38.

Wyde R. (1997, Summer). Managing the purchase of information systems technology: Guidelines for success. *Public Welfare, 55,* 14-20.

Yanosky, R., & Zastrocky, M. (2004, September 24). The questions you should ask. *The Chronicle of Higher Education,* B21.

Further Reading

IT purchasing is so complex and rapidly changing that online sources are most valuable. I found the online systems such as those of the Governmental Management Information Systems (www.gmis.org) and the Innovation Groups (www.ig.org) in the local government area are most valuable sources. They allow managers to get direct and very specific feedback from others who have done similar purchases as well as copies of RFPs and other relevant materials. Many organizations in specific substantive areas have posted Web sites that provide valuable information concerning IT purchasing in their particular area. Groups involved in purchasing such as the National Association of State Purchasing Officers (http://www.naspo.org/) have useful Web sites and links to others.

In terms of books, learning how to negotiate contracts with vendors is complex. The book by Peterson and DiCarco & Carco (1998) is most valuable in showing various strategies that can be used and all provides a great deal of information about legal issues. The ICMA books by Sandlin (2001) and Schulz (1996) both provide excellent overviews of purchasing issues for local government officials as does the volume by Strock & Adkins (1993). The legal articles are so complex that no one source can be adequate but the article by Wyde (1997) provides a good understandable overview of many of the key issues.

Copyright © 2006, Idea Group Inc. Copying or distributing in print or electronic forms without written permission of Idea Group Inc. is prohibited.

Articles in the Government Finance Review (the publication of the Govermental Finance Officers' Association) often contain some good case studies on purchasing of IT that will be useful for practitioners.

The Center for Technology (CTG) in Government has an excellent guide to purchasing issues in its publication entitled *Making Smart IT Choices: Understanding Value and Risk in Government IT Investments* is available at http://www.ctg.albany.edu/publications/guides/smartit2. Chapter 3 of this publication is an outline to use to develop a business case for IT and is located at: http://www.ctg.albany.edu/publications/guides/smartit2?chapter=5&PrintVersion=2. CTG has an example of a specific business case for building integrated justice IT systems at: http://www.ctg.albany.edu/projects/doj/doj_summary.pdf and a homeless information system at http://www.ctg.albany.edu/publications/reports/putting_info?chapter=4.

Key Concepts

- Acceptance Testing
- Act of God
- ASP model
- Backfilling
- Baselining
- Best of Breed
- Best value
- Business Case
- Business Process Reengineering
- Continuing costs
- Cultural fit
- Detailed specifications
- Enterprise Resource Planning
- Estoppel
- Force majeure
- IFB
- Indemnification
- "Machine model" and outsourcing
- Most favored nation
- Ongoing costs
- Ownership of data

Copyright © 2006, Idea Group Inc. Copying or distributing in print or electronic forms without written permission of Idea Group Inc. is prohibited.

- Performance-based contracting
- Replacement fund
- RFI
- RFP
- RFQ
- Rights to software
- Seat management
- Selective outsourcing
- Sole source
- Subject matter experts
- Sunk costs
- Thin client
- Waiver
- Weasel words

Discussion Questions

1. How thorough of a needs assessment (prior to its most recent purchase) for IT has been employed by the organizations with which you are familiar? What components of the needs assessment do you think are most crucial? Why? Did the information gathered in the needs assessment prove valid in view of the subsequent implementation of the system? What important points were missed?

2. What role does outsourcing of IT play in an organization with which you are familiar? Do you think the nature and level of outsourcing is appropriate? Why or why not? What are the major advantages of the outsourcing? The limitations and disadvantages?

3. How much of the RFP process can be borrowed from the RFPs of other entities for similar purchases? What parts would have to be customized? Under what conditions should an RFI or RFQ be used rather than an RFP?

4. Has any organization that you have worked with attempted to calculate the TCO of its IT systems? What costs are easiest to measure? Most difficult? How would you deal with these hard-to-measure costs if you tried to calculate the TCO of a system?

5. Who monitors contracts related to IT in your organization? What approaches do they use in dealing with vendors? What problems have they experienced?

6. How useful do you find BPR analyses? Has such an analysis been conducted during the procurement of any ICT that you are familiar with?

Copyright © 2006, Idea Group Inc. Copying or distributing in print or electronic forms without written permission of Idea Group Inc. is prohibited.

7.   Get a copy of an RFP (or related instrument such as an RFI) from an organization you know or off the Internet (or the accompanying disk) and critique it. What are its strength's from the governmental perspective? What are its weaknesses or limitations? If you were a contractor, what would be your concerns about the RFP? What questions do you think would be raised in the face-to-face conference that usually accompanies RFPs? Why? Explain.

Exercises

1.   Analyze the Information System of an organization with which you are familiar and develop a business case to purchase hardware/software/services that you believe the organization would benefit from.

2.   Develop an RFP or other instrument for a purchase (e.g., it could be an RFI or RFQ) that is relevant to an organization with which you are familiar. You may copy in pieces from existing RFPs and other instruments into your RFP. The RFP should be related to communications and information technology. In a paper to accompany the RFP, provide an explanation as to the reasons why you did the RFP the way you did. Be sure to let me know what parts you developed and/or modified yourself and what parts are borrowed (and, preferably, I would like to get copies of the RFP(s) that you borrow from, too). You should specify what process and criteria you would use to judge the responses to the RFP. Who would participate? What criteria did you use and why? What weights would you assign to the criteria? Why?

3.   Write a paper in which you identify and describe a process in an organization with which you are familiar. Analyze the process to determine if the current system could be improved and/or if a new system could help make the process more efficient. See if you can employ one or more ways to visually display processes used by those who do Business Process Reengineering (BRP) such as flow charts and/or Gantt & Pert charts, and other techniques you learn to aid in your analysis. Discuss whether there is any information or communication technologies that could improve the efficiency and effectiveness of this process.

Copyright © 2006, Idea Group Inc. Copying or distributing in print or electronic forms without written permission of Idea Group Inc. is prohibited.

Chapter IV

Prescriptions for IT in Government:
How Do We Know What Works Best?

Introduction

Information systems have become an important concern of generalist managers in governmental organizations and public managers need to learn how to manage IT. For generalist and IT managers, the current situation creates both difficulties and possibilities. It is the best of times because IT has become recognized as the major vehicle for achieving innovation in public organizations. At the same time, the number and speed of new technologies in the IT area can make it difficult for even the most highly-skilled IT professional staff to keep up with innovations in the field. What is a generalist manager to do who needs to attempt to not only comprehend, but manage these IT innovations? The situation facing these administrators (and IT staff themselves) is the sense of being on a "moving staircase" (Farbey, Land & Targett, 1999). The problem is that these managers must find a method for making rational choices in a field that changes so quickly.

Thus there is a strong demand for prescriptions on the part of public managers as to what practices, procedures, and approaches should be used to ensure that their information systems are successful and contribute to more effective performance and service. This is by no means a simple task. How does one know what is best to do? How can generalist

Copyright © 2006, Idea Group Inc. Copying or distributing in print or electronic forms without written permission of Idea Group Inc. is prohibited.

managers make reasoned judgments about emerging technologies? What sources of information can they employ? This chapter is an attempt to identify the sources of prescriptions that provide guidance to public managers on how to structure and implement successful information systems. In addition to identifying some of the key prescriptions, I also analyze the approaches used to develop prescriptions. How useful are they? Finally, in my view, each of them has limitations and it is important for manager to be aware of these limitations.

Prescription Sources

In attempting to identify prescriptions for public sector information management, I identified some major sources of prescriptions including those drawn from four different but related sources: (1) The so-called *best practices* for IT; (2) Prescriptions that evolve out of empirical research studies on IT; (3) Prescriptions derived from data and studies that *benchmark* IT performance and practices; and (4) Case studies of problems and disasters in the IT area that provide examples of "what not to do." In my view, each area has value for managers seeking prescriptions, but each also suffers from weaknesses that could lead a manager astray. I summarize some key characteristics of these four methods in Figure 1.

Figure 1. Characteristics, advantages and disadvantages of sources of prescriptions

Source of Prescription	Major Characteristics	Advantages	Disadvantages
Best Practices	Expert Opinion, Case Studies, Qualitative Data	Most directly focused on prescriptions of value to managers, Fairly up-to-date	Data is subjective and subject to questions of reliability and validity
Empirical research on IT	Includes quantitative measures, formal hypothesis-testing, attempts to control for threats to validity	Can be replicated and tested for validity and reliability	Empirical research trails practice. Often results in conflicting prescriptions
Benchmarking	Identifies and collects key performance measures over time	Focus on measurables, provides feedback to organizations, can facilitate cross-organizational comparisons	Can be subject to corruption, difficulty of cost comparisons
Disasters and Failures	Based on accounts of IT failures and disasters	Provides cautionary tales, complements best practices	Data not representative sample, data primarily qualitative and subject to differences in interpretation
Source: Adapted from Rocheleau, B. (2000). Prescriptions for public sector information management: A review, analysis, and critique. *American Review of Public Administration*, 30(4), pp. 414-435.			

Copyright © 2006, Idea Group Inc. Copying or distributing in print or electronic forms without written permission of Idea Group Inc. is prohibited.

Best Practices

The most notable source in terms of numbers and salience of IT prescriptions for the public sector is often referred to as "best practices." This literature is specifically directed at developing prescriptions for IT and has received the most attention from managers and thus I focus most of our attention on this source. Indeed, one of the established methods of organizations seeking to make decisions about IT is to consult the "best practices." The basic methodology is to identify practices used by leading organizations that are recognized as being excellent in the areas of information management of interest. Interest in best practices is visible at all levels of government. Organizations often research the practices of organizations themselves to identify best practices or hire consultants to do so. For example, Orange County (California) asked Gartner Consulting (Kriesman & Fraga, 2003) to investigate best practices on county e-government. The State of New York has established a Standing Committee on Best Practices. The National Governor's Association, the General Services Administration, and numerous other organizations have established awards for best practices involving IT systems and projects. To summarize, when managers are faced with the dilemma of making decisions about the rapidly changing IT area, their favorite method is to look for "best practices."

Defining Best Practices

What is a best practice? In a 1997 monograph by the Chief Information Officers Council entitled, "Best Practices in the Federal Government," *best practices* are defined as follows (DeSeve, Pesachowitz & Johnson, 1997):

We are not so presumptuous as to claim that these cases are the 'best' IT projects in the Federal Government. However, they are excellent examples of where and how IT has been applied successfully and in a cost-effective fashion to achieve a department or agency's goals and objectives. (p. iv)

More specifically, success in this study was defined as using IT (information technology) to do the following: (1) Solve problems; (2) Increase productivity or saving resources; (3) Improve quality, timeliness, or accuracy; and (4) Improve customer satisfaction. The directors of the CIO study add two additional principles to qualify as success. The system or project must be delivered on time and within budget and must demonstrate a positive *return on investment (ROI)* (DeSeve, Pesachowitz & Johnson, 1997, iv). So the DeSeve et al. (1997) study attempted to employ a high ROI as the major method to identify a best practice. However, they acknowledge that ROI was difficult or impossible to use in many cases because of the following reasons: (1) No ROI had been calculated at all for older projects; (2) There was great diversity in the definitions used to calculate ROI; (3) The prevailing practices did not account for all externalities, inputs and other costs. They also note that there were only a few instances in which a value had been developed for quantifying benefits or changes in business practices (DeSeve,

Copyright © 2006, Idea Group Inc. Copying or distributing in print or electronic forms without written permission of Idea Group Inc. is prohibited.

Pesachowitz & Johnson, 1997). For example, they note that in calculating ROI that the "prevailing practice" was to count work done directly by governmental staff as not costing anything and thus the real costs of these projects was significantly underestimated.

The General Accounting Office (Caudle, 1996) identified best practices in federal, state, and private sector organizations as those practices by organizations that were "better than the norm" and in which there was a "direct linkage" from their IRM practices to their competitive position or delivery of services" (Caudle, 1996, p. 84). Another distinguishing factor concerned projects with the most "customer-focused value" because they had reduced costs, improved quality, quantity and timeliness of customer services. Connelly and Pardo (1998) and the larger report on which their study is based (Dawes et al., 1997) looked at how best practices related to intergovernmental information systems. They state that their best practices should be thought of as "areas for continuous attention during the entire project" (Connelly & Pardo, 1998, p. 11). Cortada (1997) has written perhaps the most extensive work on the topic and defines best practices as follows:

Best practices are collections of activities within an organization that are done very, very well and ultimately are recognized as such by others. (p. 3)

Thus best practices depend upon perceptions by other organizations. Cortada goes on to say that best practices are ultimately those that give an organization the "capability to outperform its competitors" as well as to produce best "value to customers, employees, and shareholders" (Cortada, 1997, p. 79). There is clearly subjectivity in the definition of best practices. Miranda et al. (2001) point out that the term best practices is "loosely used" and that several different best practices can apply to a single process. To summarize, the term best practices is very commonly used in the IT field but it is not tightly defined and has plenty of room for subjectivity.

Methods to Identify Best Practices

There are similarities in the methods used to identify best practices. The GAO approach relied on expert opinion and a literature search (Caudle, 1996). Many of their best practices are based on private sector examples as well as those of state and federal organizations. Caudle (1996, p. 84) states that the Federal organizations were picked judgmentally based on "known effective management of their information resources," the importance of IT to their mission, and/or whether they had attempted to resolve IT problems. In-depth case studies were conducted of nominated agencies but were supplemented by information from three focus groups held with senior program and IRM officials. The Center for Technology in Government's (Connelly & Pardo, 1998; Dawes et al., 1997) best practices were identified and studied with the following steps: (1) A literature review was conducted and 11 projects were selected to participate in a study of state-local information systems; (2) A survey was done of both state and local participants in each of the 11 projects; and (3) Focus group interviews totaling about 150 participants were conducted by the project team. Cortada (1997) employed three sources

Copyright © 2006, Idea Group Inc. Copying or distributing in print or electronic forms without written permission of Idea Group Inc. is prohibited.

of information on best practices: (1) His work experience of more than 25 years as a manager, consultant and user of IT; (2) Information from colleagues at IBM and elsewhere who have studied IT; and (3) Secondary research concerning the management of computing. Miranda et al. (2002) state that good sources for best practices are industry and trade association magazines and well-known award systems such as those of Ford Foundation and GFOA. Kriesman & Fraga (2003) used award frequency as one of their major criteria to identify county governments to illustrate best practices in e-government.

Computer magazines often carry stories of successes of organizations but many of these are hard to assess because they rely heavily on self-reports. For example, the joint CIO/IAC study solicited nominations from council members for success stories, but they found that self-nominations were problematic because there was no consistent standard or definition of success and that the success stories were often long on hyperbole and short on narrative, objective, and context (DeSeve, Pescashowitz and Johnson, 1997, p. ii). Consequently, they formed a Task Force that included not only council members but also professionals drawn from private companies. The Task Force then conducted systematic interviews with the staff of 150 projects that had been nominated either by e-mail or through the council nominations. They note that they excluded projects that did not have enough documented performance data and also those that had not been in existence long enough to measure impact.

In short, expert judgment is the primary method that has been used to identify best practices. Given the complexity of the concept of success in IT, it is not surprising that qualitative judgment of experts has been the primary source. However, it is important that the methods and sources of data on these issues be expanded to include objective measures as much as possible. The perceptions of the effectiveness of IT can differ greatly depending on the nature of the job and level of those involved in systems. In particular, the end users, especially if they are in the low to middle ranks of organizations, often have very different assessments of systems from senior level managers and Information System (IS) professionals. For example, Lacity, Willcocks and Feeny (1995) found contradictory opinions concerning the success of outsourcing arrangements between end users and managers. In my own interviews, I have found that perceptions of success of systems can differ greatly depending not only on the level of users involved, but also their departments. Guaranteed confidentiality is essential to get an honest opinion. Clearly it is preferable to have quantitative measures of success including key outcome measures. The term "best practices" tends to assume that success is a nominal level, categorical variable. However, success may be viewed as a concept that can be measured on a continuum and there can be degrees of success–it is not really an "all or nothing" concept. Moreover, a variety of measures will likely be necessary to measure success as major systems usually have several goals and stakeholders. A system or project may do very well on one indicator such as cost savings, but do less well on others such as stakeholder satisfaction (Ammons, 1996, p. 283). Indeed, these two indicators can often be opposed. Finally, although information from participant observers in successful projects is crucial to bringing such projects to attention, we also need independent assessments of them by persons outside the organizations involved. It is clear that best practices literature also serves a public relations purpose and thus there is an incentive to emphasize the good and ignore limitations. Indeed, the joint CIO/IAC Task Force noted that one of the purposes of their study of best practices was to correct

Copyright © 2006, Idea Group Inc. Copying or distributing in print or electronic forms without written permission of Idea Group Inc. is prohibited.

false impressions that most federal IT systems have been failures. The correction of overemphasis in the media on failures is a legitimate purpose but such an emphasis can conflict with the goal of developing an objective set of empirically based prescriptions for public managers.

Figure 2. Selected best practices based on a 1994 study by the U.S. General Accounting Office

1) Senior managers should be "hands on" and take on actual leadership of IRM (Information Resources Management) projects including decision making, communications, and evaluation. IRM professionals should play a facilitating role. Senior executives should establish benchmarks and targets for change. Senior executives should use performance review and other incentives to reward good performance on IRM-related projects.

2) Start with customers in defining strategies but integrate new projects into a rigorous organization-wide strategic plan.

3) Rely on performance measures to assess progress. These measures are related to customer needs and perceptions such as quality and cycle time–not IT-oriented measures.

4) Senior executives view IRM with an investment-orientation and employ a disciplined process in decision-making including risk assessment and ROI analysis.

5) Identify vital core processes and determine if they need to be reengineered as part of the IRM project. Focus on a small number of processes at any one time.

6) Line managers take control of funding and direction of IRM projects while IRM professionals play a support role.

Sources: Adapted from Caudle, S. L. (1994). Strategic information resources management: Fundamental practices. *Government Information Quarterly*, 13(1), pp. 83-97, and U.S. General Accounting Office. 1994). Executive guide: Improving mission performance through strategic information management and technology. Washington, D.C.: U.S. General Accounting Office, GAO/AIMD-94-115, May.

Figure 3. Selected best practices based on Cortada's Best Practices in Information Technology

1) Align IT with business strategies so that it is a strategic enabler of the achievement of the company's objectives.

2) Senior management is involved in IT but also have a CIO who is end-user and customer-focused and acts like a business manger first.

3) Extraordinary emphasis is placed on skills with continuous upgrading supported by management.

4) Benchmarking is a major activity and all important objectives are benchmarked.

5) Invest in infrastructure including attention to the balancing legacy vs. new technologies.

6) Reward IT employees.

7) Assess the success of projects and systems continuously.

8) Communicate continually with stakeholders and make adjustments based on feedback.

Source: Adapted from Cortada, J.W. (1997). *Best practices in information technology: How corporations get the most value from exploiting their digital investments*. Upper Saddle River, N.J.: Prentice-Hall, Inc.

Copyright © 2006, Idea Group Inc. Copying or distributing in print or electronic forms without written permission of Idea Group Inc. is prohibited.

Figure 4. Selected best IT practices in the federal government based on a 1997 CIO/IAC study

1) Governmental IT investment should be viewed as an investment and may require spending more, not less.

2) You can't manage what you can't measure and thus it is important to include ROI and other measures of success.

3) In projects that involve certain kinds of activities such as automating manual processes and document management, there will be "pain" and resistance and thus the project has to be continually sold and resold.

4) In virtually every instance, a serious effort was made to identify customers and monitor customer satisfaction. Users have to embrace the system in order for it to be successful.

Adapted from DeSeve, E.; Pesachowitz, A. M.; Johnson, L. K. (1997). *Best IT practices in the federal government.* Washington, D.C.: Chief Information Officers/Industry Advisory Council

Figure 5. Best practices of leading companies that reengineered their approach to purchasing

1. Commitment: Secure Up Front Commitment from Top Leaders.

    A. Recognize and communicate the urgency to change service spending practices.
    B. Provide Good and clear executive leadership including goals and targets.

2. Knowledge: Obtain improved knowledge on service spending.

    A. Develop information system to identify how much is being spent with which service provider for what services.
    B. Analyze the data to identify opportunities to reduce costs, improve service levels, and provide better management of service providers.

3. Change: Create supporting structure, processes, and roles.

    A. Create or identify organizations responsible for coordinating or managing service purchases.
    B. Establish proactive business relationships between end users, purchasing units, and other stakeholders.
    C. Create commodity/service experts.

4. Obtain sustain support from senior leadership to facilitate change.

    A. Obtain sustain support from senior leadership to facilitate change.
    B. Establish clear lines of communication between all affected parties.
    C. Demonstrate value and credibility of new processes through use of metrics.

Source: U.S. General Accounting Office. (2002, January). *Best Practices: Taking a Strategic Approach Could Improve DOD's Acquisition of Services*. GAO-02-230. p7.

Examples and Discussion of Selected Best Practices.

Next, I have identified certain best practices from four studies. Note that I have selected only a few points from these works for illustrative purposes. Although "best practices" studies now number in the thousands, these studies serve to illustrate the nature of the

Copyright © 2006, Idea Group Inc. Copying or distributing in print or electronic forms without written permission of Idea Group Inc. is prohibited.

prescriptions offered by many of these studies. The first set of best practices is derived from a 1994 study by the U.S. General Accounting Office (Caudle, 1996; General Accounting Office, 1994) summarized in Figure 2.

The second set of best practices is derived from Cortada's (1997) book entitled, *Best Practices in Information Technology* (see Figure 3).

The third set of best practices was derived from the Federal CIO/IAC study (DeSeve et al., 1997) shown in Figure 4.

The fourth set of prescriptions are derived from a 2002 study by the U.S. General Accounting Office of the best practices of private sector companies for the Defense Department to emulate and included the following points listed in Figure 5.

There is quite a degree of consistency among these best practices. Common themes are the need to be customer-focused and to inform stakeholders. Emphasis is also given to measuring the success of the projects in three of the four examples. Although some best practices focus on end users (e.g., Figure 4, point 1), many of the best practices appear to be aimed primarily at senior managers (e.g., Figure 2, points 1, 4, and 6 and Figure 5, points 1 and 4) and senior management involvement in projects is proposed as one of the key best practices. This focus is appropriate due to the failure in the past of top management to give enough attention to IRM during the years when IT was just emerging as a strategic success factor.

However, end-user support is a necessary and sometimes even sufficient (e.g., for systems that don't require organization-wide cooperation) condition for system success and end-user resistance can undermine systems that even the highest-level executives support (e.g., Malvey, 1981). Often, it is the lower level managers and end users who are aware of problems with current systems and the knowledge required to improve matters. For example, Markus and Keil (1994) provide a detailed case study in which a technically improved system is implemented but end users failed to use it.

A major advantage of the general best practice literature principles is that they are potentially applicable to any IT projects and are relatively easy to conduct. However, as a result of their high level of generality, these best practices provide insufficient guidance in making specific choices on how to implement these best practices in a given situation. For example, one of the consensual points of the best practices literature (Figure 2, point 5) states that business processes should be studied for possible reengineering as part of the IRM project. As a general rule, few would disagree. Projects that simply copy processes that were part of manual or legacy systems may be ignoring major efficiencies that can be achieved with new technology. But the CIO-IAC study found that many projects became engaged in the use of overly long "total reengineering periods" prior to project implementation and thus reengineering led to dislocation and dissatisfaction with the project. Indeed, they argue that much of the detailed reengineering cannot be done until the project is implemented. They suggest that reengineering should be initiated with high-level business processes and then have more detailed reengineering done at the time of implementation (DeSeve, Peschowitz & Johnson, 1997, pp. 17-18). This agrees with the Miranda et al. (2002) study that finds the implementation of ERP systems can be so difficult and complex that attempts to conduct major BPR can overwhelm staff and in such cases should be delayed until after the ERP program has been fully installed. Most of the best practices focus on generic organizational and managerial issues that

Copyright © 2006, Idea Group Inc. Copying or distributing in print or electronic forms without written permission of Idea Group Inc. is prohibited.

are applicable to virtually any organization or information system project. Indeed, many of these best practices apply to most managerial areas—not just IT. The argument of Caudle (1988) and others involved in Information Resources Management (IRM) is that the crucial factors in determining success of IT are not technological, but involve how IT is integrated into the overall management processes (Kraemer & Dedrick, 1997, p. 95). The CIO/IAC (1997, p. 19) study reiterates the same point: the toughest issues are not technical but human.

Best Practices Specific to Technological, Functional, and Substantive Areas

These best practices tend to be stated as universal best practices potentially relevant to any organization. However, Cortada (1997, p. 76) asserts that the most important improvements "always come from industry-specific applications" and that IT architectures are becoming "increasingly industry-specific." The CIO/IAC (DeSeve, Pesachowitz & Johnson, 1997) study partially accomplishes this by organizing their case studies and analyses by certain software or functional categories including the following: (1) Automating Manual Processes; (2) Defining/Delivering New Services; (3) Document Management; (4) Efficient User/Allocation of Resources; (5) Executive Information Systems; (6) Fraud Detection; (7) Information Delivery/Sharing; (9) Infrastructure Upgrade; (10) Standardization; and (11) Training Delivery. By organizing their analysis

Figure 6. Client/server best practices

1) Senior Managers establish the business direction, align IT strategy with it, and make the client/server integral to strategy.

2) Encourage IS mangers to be more oriented to business and less systems-oriented and help business managers to conceptualize and integrate client/server applications.

3) Make IS management responsible for planning company's computing based on understanding of business functions and strategy.

4) Give functional mangers a role in developing IT and specification of requirements.

5) Form a project team of technically skilled people to create a migration plan.

6) Provide resources needed for hardware, software, and network requirements as well as education, training, operations, and product support.

7) Evaluate client/server projects for their strategic fit with business.

8) Allow users to participate in requirements specification, systems design, and testing activities.

9) Have the IS staff and users cooperate in developing and supporting client/server applications.

10) Encourage partnerships among IS professionals and users.

Sources: Adapted from Duchessi, P. & I. Chengular-Smith, I. (1998). Client/Server benefits, problems, best practices. *Communications of the ACM*, 41 (May), pp. 87-94.

Copyright © 2006, Idea Group Inc. Copying or distributing in print or electronic forms without written permission of Idea Group Inc. is prohibited.

this way, they were able to identify certain patterns of problems and solutions for certain categories. For example, they point out that some projects (e.g., automating manual processes) have solid return on investments while others, such as defining and delivering new services, have difficulty in identifying ROI with traditional accounting approaches. They also are able to identify certain characteristic problems that occur with certain kinds of projects such as document management (e.g., pressure to direct "pain" resulting from project impacts) and consequently the need to emphasize certain best practices such as internal selling for this category.

There also exist sources concerning best practices for specific categories of hardware and software in computing. For example, DuChessi & Chengalur-Smith (1998) recently published an article that relates to best practices and problems with client/server systems (see Figure 6). Several of these overlap those more general ones discussed earlier including aligning IT strategy and strategic issues in general, and business-focused planning. However, their best practices give more attention to the role of the end users, noting that "when end-users feel threatened and begin using old or alternative systems, companies have a tough go of it, experiencing serious management, organizational, and technical problems" (DuChessi & Chengular-Smith, 1998, p. 94). Consequently, three of their best practices are oriented to getting early and continuous involvement and support from end users.

Specific technologies such as geographic information systems (GIS) likewise can provide somewhat more detailed best practices applied to them. For example, Huxhold (1991) has described a "model urban GIS" project. His "model project" or best practices begins with three general steps: (1) Evaluating geographic information needs; (2) Gaining organizational support; and (3) Managing the GIS project. But Huxhold provides many more detailed specific measures that need to be taken to accomplish these three steps and also tools that can assist in successful implementation of these steps, such as a map inventory system and the use of a cross-reference chart showing the extent of map utilization among different users (Huxhold, 1991, p. 240). Like Connelly & Pardo (1998), Huxhold identifies specific roles that must be carried out if the project is to be successful, including manager, analyst, systems administrator, programmer, processor, database administrator, digitizer, drafter and others (Huxhold, 1991, pp. 262-263). Likewise, there is a large and diversified literature that discusses best practices for IT functions such as purchasing of systems that I discuss in some depth in the chapter on purchasing. The purchasing literature puts forth an array of prescriptions concerning activities such as the writing of requests for proposals, legal considerations, risk assessments of projects, among others that are too extensive to summarize here (see Strock & Adkins, 1993; and Wyde, 1997 for examples of such prescriptions pertaining to purchasing IT).

There have been developed some very detailed models to guide the software development process that many governmental and private organizations have bought into. The best known of these was originally known as the *Capability Maturity Model (CMM)*. As Koch (2004) relates, the CMM model grew out of the frustration of the Defense Department (specifically the Air Force) with their contracting for software. Carnegie Melon University's Software Engineering Institute (SEI) won a contract to develop a questionnaire to reflect best practices for software purchases. Their questionnaire evolved over the years into a complex assessment system and a group of persons were

Copyright © 2006, Idea Group Inc. Copying or distributing in print or electronic forms without written permission of Idea Group Inc. is prohibited.

Figure 7. Best practice standards used by selected states

Standard/Industry Best Practice	States Using
Software Engineering Institute, Software Capability Maturity Model	Kansas, Michigan, Minnesota, North Carolina, Ohio, Tennessee, Washington
Project Management Institute, "A Guide to the Project Management Body of Knowledge", and/or Project Management Professional certification	California, Missouri, North Carolina, North Dakota, Oregon, Tennessee
The Institute of Electrical and Electronics Engineers, software standards	California, Michigan, North Carolina, Tennessee, Washington
International Organization for Standardization ISO 9000-3:1997 "Quality Management and Quality Assurance Standards – Part 3: Guidelines for the Application of ISO 90001:1994 to the Development, Supply, Installation and Maintenance of Computer Software"	California, Washington
Adapted from Brotbeck, G.; Miller, T.; & Statz, Dr. J. (1999, November 23). A survey of current best practices and utilization of standards in the public and private sectors. Retrieved July 4, 2003 from http://www.dir.state.tx.us/eod/qa/bestprac.pdf	

trained to appraise organization's state of software development. This group studies the software processes of the organization in-depth and conducts interviews with key staff and they rate the organization on a 1 (status equals chaos) to 5 (status equals continuously improving) scale (Koch, 2004). In more recent years, the SEI has developed other models like a CMM (Capability Maturity Model) integration acquisition Model. One of the questions with all assessment systems like CMM is whether all of the documentation and standardization of practices actually pays off. There is some evidence that it does (Saiedian & Kuzara, 1995). It is useful to note that many states, when making purchasing decisions and implementing projects, look to the CMM and tools such as project management for guidance. For example, a study sponsored by the Texas Audit Authority (Brotbeck et al., 1999) of IT policies used by other states found that many states adhered to not only the CMM model but also those of the Project Management Institute, the Institute of Electrical and Electronic Engineers software standards, and the standards of the International Organization for Standardization (ISO) quality management practices (see Figure 7).

These models are primarily aimed at software development organizations. Most general purpose governmental organizations do not perform major software development projects themselves. But they would be interested nevertheless because they make crucial software purchases from vendors and they may be interested in whether these software vendors are adhering to the standards of these organizations and their models.

Best practices can be sought for a very specific process. For example, Xerox sent a team to L.L. Bean to discover their methods for filling orders because they were done so quickly (Harris, 1995). They found some desirable practices that they could adapt to their own organization. For example, Bean's computer software sorted incoming orders so that packers could combine trips for items shelved close together (Harris, 1995). In the local government sector, for example, the permit process for development projects is an

Copyright © 2006, Idea Group Inc. Copying or distributing in print or electronic forms without written permission of Idea Group Inc. is prohibited.

important and complex process and governments could seek to identify best practices for this particular function. Thus the technology-specific literature can provide decision support lacking in more general literature on best practices.

To summarize, future best practice development needs to focus more on specific functions and processes, software and hardware categories, rather than universal prescriptions that are characteristic of the current literature. This development will make for more useful prescriptions that can be applied to specific functional and structural issues. Universal prescriptions are useful, but provide only very general guidance. However, as prescriptions get more specific, managers need to be cautious because they are subject to quick change. For example, prescriptions concerning purchasing have changed substantially within the last 10 to 15 years. Not long ago, this literature tended to emphasize RFPs that specified the nature of the hardware and software to be used to accomplish the project, while the current approach is to give substantial leeway to the vendor as along as they meet the goals and expectations of the project (e.g., Kelman, 1990).

Best Practices and the Organization of Information Technology

The relationship between best practices and the overall organization of information management remains unclear. The generic best practices literature cited earlier (e.g., Caudle, 1996; Cortada, 1997) would appear to implicitly support a more centralized approach to organizing IT given their emphasis on senior management roles. However, Cortada (1997, p. 59) acknowledges that there is "no cookbook" and that the structures in best practice organizations can range from radical decentralization to centralization. He goes on to discuss how IT tasks and goals can differ significantly depending on the culture and nature of the organization (or sub-units within an organization) involved. Cortada identifies four types of cultures (craft, systematic production, continuous improvement, and systematic customization) and points out that their major IT needs differ. In recent years, there has been increased emphasis on enterprisewide standards and integration of functions among many of the organizations viewed as having best practices so the impact of using best practices is to support this more centralized organization of IT.

Do the Same Best Practices Apply to Public and Private Sectors?

The studies of best practices cited earlier and much of the other best practice literature draws heavily on practices from private sector organizations. The implicit assumption in this literature appears to be that best practices in the private sector are transferable to the public sector. For example, four of seven of the detailed examples Caudle (1996) uses in her article based on the GAO study are drawn from private sector examples. There certainly are great overlaps in the technology and management of IT in the two sectors

Copyright © 2006, Idea Group Inc. Copying or distributing in print or electronic forms without written permission of Idea Group Inc. is prohibited.

as Bozeman and Bretschneider (1986) acknowledged in their seminal article proposing the concept of a "public management information system" model. Thus I would expect that many of the generic prescriptions should be applicable to both sectors.

But there are important differences that could affect best practices and make them less transferable. For example, the primary motivation for investing in IT in the private sector concerns their ability to compete in the marketplace (Grover, Teng & Fiedler, 1998). Cortada (1997) makes this point:

In the final analysis, a best practice is what gives your company the capability to outperform its competitors, grow market and profits and provide compelling value to customers, employees, and shareholders. (p. 79)

Cortada (1997, p. 194) goes on to say that best practices can also be viewed as "me too" strategies because organizations are looking to copy practices of other organizations and that instead, they should try to come up with new practices that they can offer first so as to have a temporary advantage over their competitors, building up revenue and profits streams. Schrage (2003) likewise says that CIO's "should never let their IT investments be determined by someone else's best practices and that a best practice should never be a goal—it is a means to an end." Moreover, private sector organizations may be reluctant to share information they view as key to their success. Cortada (1997) notes that, although private sector organizations do a great deal of benchmarking, most of these data are not made public because they are afraid of giving their competitors valuable data (Cortada, 1997, p. 27). By way of contrast, public sector organizations are encouraged to copy the processes of others by the Harvard Policy Group on Network-Enabled Service and Government (2001a, p. 6): "Copy without embarrassment." Private sector organizations also emphasize the use of IT to reduce cycle-time, which is the time necessary to bring new products and services to market to improve their competitive position. These kinds of competitive forces driving investment in private sector IT are not as relevant to most general-purpose governments. In short, the public sector is generally is less concerned with using IT as a competitive weapon and more open to revealing its IT processes.

The development of business cases such as formal calculations of return on investment (ROI) is often viewed as being a best practice. However, as noted previously, many public agencies have ignored or misapplied the calculation of ROI to their projects and non-monetary benefits constitute a major part of many governmental projects. For some kinds of projects, increased revenue streams may result but in most there is no promise of revenue to cover the costs of new systems. Although IT is often seen as a way of cutting costs, research (e.g., Kraemer and King, 1986, p. 490) found that in the public sector, job creation and expansion offset and sometimes exceed job losses. Miranda et al. (2002) reaffirm the point with respect to ERP systems that hard monetary savings will take time to achieve through gradual workforce reductions. Public sector goals would appear to differ from private sector goals and thus methods of determining goals of projects may also have to vary from the private sector model. For example, a 2002 GAO study identified purchasing practices of leading private firms that could be helpful to the Defense Department. However, the GAO study also concedes that there are two important

Copyright © 2006, Idea Group Inc. Copying or distributing in print or electronic forms without written permission of Idea Group Inc. is prohibited.

differences in the Defense Department's situation. First, Defense procurement is huge compared to even large companies and the one-size-fits-all approach of the private sector companies might not work for the services (Army, Navy, and Air Force). Secondly, Defense Department procurement is constrained by purchasing rules such as competition and the need to contract with small businesses so that it would be hard to consolidate most of its small procurements into a large procurement—one of the recommended improvements based on the experience of the leading private firms.

In more recent years, many of the "best practices" revolve around the idea of integrated enterprise-wide view of investments and IT in general to replace fragmented, decentralized views. The Harvard Policy Group has developed many "imperatives" that encourage this perspective. For example, one of the Harvard Policy Group's imperatives is (2001b) is a call for governments to use a *"portfolio approach"* to IT investments in which a broad perspective would be taken in which risky investments can be balanced against more predictable, conservative investments:

Do not downplay costs or risks, but do not let the risks of individual projects discourage you unduly from investing in high-value IT. The risk of not spending on technology—and thus falling behind in productivity—is probably the larger risk for most governments today. (p. 7)

In another publication, the Harvard Policy Group (2001c, p. 9) argues for *"fast followership"* meaning that governments should aggressively seek out innovative IT practices once they have been proven by a "first mover."

These positions appear to imply that there is competitive environment pushing governmental organizations that will force them to take some chances on risky investments. Such a position might be appropriate for a special purpose organization like the Defense Department or NASA, but may not hold for general purpose governments. The organizations that I interviewed would have no interest in investing in risky technologies that have even a moderate chance of failure. They cannot justify them on the basis of increased market share.

Likewise, as Newcomer and Caudle (1991) have pointed out, the decision-making process for public sector organizations must be more externally focused with executives, legislatures, interest groups, and public playing a role. The influence of these outside interests has implications for many of the best practices which tend to assume that there is a clear hierarchy of decision-making over which the organization has control. By way of contrast, a review of major government purchases shows that projects need to secure the support and cooperation of semi-autonomous units of government and that the process of securing agreement is political and can go on for years. Federal, state, and local governments differ in the purposes for which they want to use systems. For example, California's Statewide Automated Child Support System was brought to a halt (Newcombe, 1998) in part due to struggles among the federal, state, and county governments over the structure of the system. The federal government mandated deadlines and requirements that state officials viewed as unrealistic and counter-productive (Newcombe, 1998). Likewise, many California counties preferred a decentralized multi-jurisdictional system

Copyright © 2006, Idea Group Inc. Copying or distributing in print or electronic forms without written permission of Idea Group Inc. is prohibited.

that would meet county needs, while the state preferred a single system (Newcombe, 1998). Governmental information managers must often resolve conflict among independent political bodies that have incompatible goals. The best practice approach tends to assume a centralized system with a clear set of goals and may not be helpful when you have different levels of government in conflict.

In the earlier discussion, I have assumed that private sector organizations are quick to adapt best practices in order to ensure their survival in a competitive environment. Changchit, Joshi and Lederer (1998) looked at prescriptive models of how investments were made in private sector organizations and then compared them with the actual process used by 15 private companies. They found that many of the techniques described in the prescriptive literature were not used at all in practice (e.g., competitive force analysis, value chain analysis, brainstorming, and other strategic planning approaches). Instead, they found that most of the analysis and "measurement" was qualitative, iterative, intuitive, based on past experience and judgment, and were subject to much uncertainty. Likewise, persuasion was used to achieve consensus with the system's intended users so they would feel as though they were part of the system. It is possible that these 15 organizations were mediocre in their IT operations and this explains the reason why their decision-making processes do not resemble that pictured as desirable by private (and public) sector organizations in the best practices literature. On the other hand, it may reflect the fact that the actual procedures used in private sector organizations, perhaps even those viewed as having best practices, may vary significantly from those presented in the best practices literature. One of the great values of empirical research is that it can challenge widely held assumptions based on subjective perceptions--and they are often wrong.

Traditional Survey and Other Quantitative Analyses of Information Management

I pointed out earlier that best practices tend to depend on expert judgment. In contrast, there does exist an extensive set of empirical studies disseminated in IT-related journals. Unfortunately, much of this literature is not very useful in developing prescriptions in assisting public managers concerning their IT decisions. First, IT empirical research tends to trail practice in both public and private sectors and thus managers have to make decisions concerning technologies before empirical research is available to help. Indeed, Kraemer and Dedrick (1997) note that it is hard to find in leading IS journals much less empirical literature at all on public management information systems, although this situation is changing in recent years with the rapid development of e-government. Even when rigorous empirical studies are implemented, they often result in findings that do not provide clear prescriptions for public managers. Rather the results are often unclear or tend to contradict assertions about best practices. For example, Kraemer and King (1986) summarized the results of research concerning the management of computing and

Copyright © 2006, Idea Group Inc. Copying or distributing in print or electronic forms without written permission of Idea Group Inc. is prohibited.

Figure 8. The implementation leadership matrix

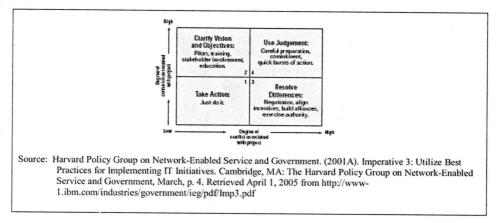

Source: Harvard Policy Group on Network-Enabled Service and Government. (2001A). Imperative 3: Utilize Best
         Practices for Implementing IT Initiatives. Cambridge, MA: The Harvard Policy Group on Network-Enabled
         Service and Government, March, p. 4. Retrieved April 1, 2005 from http://www-
         1.ibm.com/industries/government/ieg/pdf/Imp3.pdf

found that many of the dimensions of computing policy thought to be important had no consistent impact on the success of computing including end-user involvement in design of systems and the use of steering committees and policy boards to manage computing policy. Empirical studies can also result in contradictory results. Lacity and Willcocks (1998) developed five empirically-based best practices concerning outsourcing arrangements but they note that their findings disagree with other research and speculate that the reason may be that the contradictory studies focused on the different kind of deals. Practitioners may be frustrated by the lack of consensus in empirical literature and prefer the norms produced by the best practice approach.

Consequently, recent attempts often seek to reconcile these studies by moving toward a contingency approach in making recommendations. Success (and thus best practices) may be contingent upon key variables. For example, there is a fair amount of research to support the argument that there is no one best way to organize IT. Pinsonneault and Kraemer (1997) studied the impact of IT on downsizing of city governments and concluded that the organization of computing should be congruent with the general structure of the organization. If the organization is decentralized, its computing function should be, too. Even the best practice literature such as the Harvard Policy Group on Network-Enabled Service and Government (March 2001a, p. 4) points out that there are important parameters affecting decisions such as how much confusion and conflict surround a project. Thus the selection of a best strategy is contingent on the nature of the project and situation (see Figure 8).

The results of new technologies can be unpredictable and technologies that are perceived to be decentralizing can have opposite effects depending on the context in which they are implemented. For example, Duchessi and Chengalur-Smith (1998) reported that while client/server technology permits organizations to become more decentralized, management often uses the technology to retain control and centralize.

Most research is conducted in a small, subcategory of public organizations and additional research is needed to determine if the findings are valid beyond the original

Copyright © 2006, Idea Group Inc. Copying or distributing in print or electronic forms without written
permission of Idea Group Inc. is prohibited.

sample in which they are conducted. These findings may or may not be generalizable beyond the immediate type of organization upon which the study was conducted. In particular, there are thousands of very small governmental organizations and their resources tend to be much more limited than those of organizations that are studied in research, particularly those of the private sector. The advantage of empirical research lies in the fact that it can be replicated and tested for validity in other categories of departments and organizations. Recently, Kraemer and Dedrick (1997, p. 107) decry the shift from serious study of computing impacts and management to what they see as "promotion of computing" in all its forms. Certainly, we need more rigorous and varied approaches to the success of computing. In summary, the more traditional, academic empirical literature can reveal complexities and provide an important source of information that is more rigorous and objective than the other approaches.

Benchmarks and Benchmarking

Benchmarking is one of the recommended best practices according to the GAO (Caudle, 1996) and thus we could have discussed benchmarks in the best practices category earlier. Cortada (1997) and other best practice experts argue that anything important in IT needs to be measured. *Benchmarking* refers to the process of taking these measures, comparing your organization's performance with the highest-performing organizations, identifying reasons for the gap between your organization and the best, and then implementing changes to close the gap (Ammons, 1996, p. 6). So why put forth benchmarks as a separate category from best practices? Although the best practices literature emphasizes the importance of benchmarks, it has tended to be based primarily on qualitative methods of identifying best practices. Their prescriptions most often focus on process-oriented aspects of IT. Indeed, Strassmann (1995), a skeptic about the best practices literature, points out its lack of quality supporting data and its focus on processes. He argues that best practices award winners often subsequently do poorly in market competition and that the process-focus of much of the best practices literature is questionable (Strassman, 1995):

Typically, a consultant will parade an exhaustive catalogue of what are...the 'best practices,' which he is now ready to prescribe as a cure for the client's problems.... Invariably they use survey questionnaires to come up with a list of what people think is important.... The fundamental flaw with this approach is that none of the 'best practices' lists have ever been openly related to an objective measure of performance such as profitability. (p. 228)

The benchmarking movement, by encouraging organizations to systematically gather and share information concerning key measures of success, can help to create the possibility of more rigorous quantitative analyses of organizational performance which will complement the largely qualitative, case-study-oriented literature that currently exists.

Copyright © 2006, Idea Group Inc. Copying or distributing in print or electronic forms without written permission of Idea Group Inc. is prohibited.

Figure 9. Data processing benchmarks

Measure	Actual or Expected Level of Performance
System response time	Within 2 seconds
System downtime	2 percent or less
Response to Problems	Most (70-97) percent expected and/or accomplished in one day
Source: Adapted from Ammons, D. N. (1996). Municipal benchmarks: Assessing local performance and establishing community standards. Thousand Oaks, CA: Sage Publications, pp. 45-48.	

Cortada (1997) asserts that private organizations systematically gather and sometimes share benchmark data and there is just beginning to appear some online reports about performance indicators of governments related to IT and other areas as I discuss in the chapters on evaluation and accountability. This information is clearly subject to bias because, in some cases, organizations may be reluctant to share information that may reflect unfavorably on their performance and, if this information is to be relied on for making important decisions, it will need to be audited. Still, the growth of open public reporting of performance measures suggests that benchmarking will grow in importance in the future, especially if these data allow us to identify patterns in outcomes (e.g., those organizations with high performance on benchmarks tend to share a particular software or process).

There are a few publications with benchmark information for public sector IT. For example, in his account of the implementation of GIS in Milwaukee, Huxhold (1991, pp. 242-244) cites a variety of specific cost-per-parcel for digitizing information and other costs-per-square-mile that are key GIS activities. Another example concerns university computing officials who have banded together to share data on key costs of supporting networked systems. Leach and Smallen (1998) cite data based on 60 colleges and universities in the U.S. concerning measures such as network services annual costs (per active port and used port) and average costs-per-user at the 25th, median, and 75th percentiles.

David Ammons' *Municipal Benchmarks* (1996) is one of the few works to provide some generic IT benchmarks that apply across most organizations, although there are only a few measures reported even in this work. The benchmarks contained in his study are primarily drawn from municipalities who have been recipients of the Government Finance Officers Administration's Distinguished Budget Presentations Award. Thus this sample is self-selected and is likely to reflect organizations that tend to be better than average in their performance. The existence of such outcome measures provides empirical referents for organizations attempting to gauge the quality of their performance.

Figure 9 shows some of the key data processing measures and reflect a combination of actual performance measures and expected levels of performance (Ammons, 1996). In some cases such as response time for problems, certain municipalities broke out their data

Copyright © 2006, Idea Group Inc. Copying or distributing in print or electronic forms without written permission of Idea Group Inc. is prohibited.

according to the nature of the problem (e.g., networking, production, data, help desk queries) and many used other time standards (e.g., immediate response and within 4, 24, and 48 hours respectively). There are a few other measures indicated such as data entry accuracy, on-time production runs, and the accuracy of project cost estimates and timetables (Ammons, 1996, p. 48), but these measures only had one or two municipalities reporting them.

Ammons points out a number of problems and limitations of the benchmarks and the benchmarking literature. He sees cost data as very problematic due to accounting differences in how overhead, employee benefits, depreciation, and other aspects are measured as well as regional cost variations (Ammons, 1996, p. 5) and thus he avoids cost-based measures. Definitions of concepts can vary as well as how they are implemented which could render direct comparisons on quantitative measures invalid. Thus his book concentrates on measures that would be valid across many organizations. As he notes, the data are unaudited. There is evidence that if such measures were to become viewed as tied into important personnel functions and public relations (e.g., concerning evaluation of the department and its personnel), they could become corrupted and there is the possibility of goal displacement and a "white lie" effect (Ginsberg, 1984). Thus, if benchmarks were adopted by governmental agencies, it would be best if they were viewed as feedback mechanisms that should not be directly related to personnel or public relations functions. The development of truly useful prescriptions on IT in public organizations may have to await the establishment of a body of objective measures.

The Problem and Disaster Literature

The problem and disaster literature is the reverse face of the best practice literature. By studying known system problems and failures, we may be able to identify *critical failure factors (CFFs)*. Kraemer & Dedrick (1997) note that we need to study problems and failures such as those described in GAO and other governmental reports:

The U.S. General Accounting Office's audit reports on information technology in the federal government, and similar reports by state and local governments, provide ample evidence that these operational and management issues exist throughout the federal system. Moreover, the fact that these reports document the same kinds of management problems with the technology time after time indicates the need for serious research to address the underlying issues. (p. 109)

There have been several highly-disseminated disasters in the IT field including problems of developing and implementing new systems such as those of the Federal Aviation Administration (FAA) and Internal Revenue Service (IRS). There has emerged a literature that has used these and other examples of failures to identify CFFs and strategies for avoiding them. Although it is possible to do surveys of problems and disasters as McComb and Smith (1991) have done, most of the problem/disaster literature is based

Copyright © 2006, Idea Group Inc. Copying or distributing in print or electronic forms without written permission of Idea Group Inc. is prohibited.

primarily on case studies and often journalistic accounts of failures that happen to come to light and thus this literature is qualitative and open to challenge concerning the validity and reliability of its findings.

However, unlike the case with the best practices literature, organizations are reluctant to let us know of their failures and thus there is no problem of self-promotion. The problems and disasters reported in this literature are most likely atypical of the true problems and "disasters" which occur in public organizations (Rocheleau, 1997). It is likely that the smaller, more mundane failures are missed and only large disasters that affect the general public are likely to become known outside the organization. Still, while many want to take credit for the success stories that characterize the best practices literature, the analysis of failures can lead to a much harder, more critical assessment concerning the cause(s) of failure and thus offers valuable insight to both practitioners and researchers.

The problem/disaster and best practices literatures would seem to be complementary to one another but most best practice articles do not integrate material concerning failures. One exception is Cortada (1997, pp. 4-5) who identifies certain bad practices such as: (1) Copy systems from other organizations as is; (2) Adapt a best practice without validating it to see if it is a best practice and whether it has business value; (3) Don't keep the best practice up-to-date; and (4) Adopt best practices for fashion's sake rather than strategic reasons. Analysis of problems and disasters often leads to cautions about what not to do, rather than steps to positively pursue.

There are a fairly large number of failures that have been attributed to the purchasing and development processes of governmental (and private) information systems. Indeed, the Standish Group (1995) conducted a survey that shows that a majority of systems that are attempted to be developed ultimately fail. Cats-Baril and Thompson (1995) provide a detailed account of a flawed attempt to develop a new human resources management system in Vermont and conclude that the project managers failed to assess the risk of failure for the project. California's Department of Motor Vehicles (DMV) spent seven years and $50 million on a system that was never implemented (Towns, 1998). Analysis of this failure by state officials found that the project was so huge and complex that the state did not have adequate project management skills to handle it. Likewise, the failure of California's Statewide Automated Welfare System was ascribed to a "creaky procurement system" and "ineffective project management" as well as disagreements among federal, state, and local governments (Newcombe, 1997). In part due to these well-publicized failures, one of the best practices for IT management is to do risk assessment. Indeed, the California State Department of Information Technology (1998) developed an online risk assessment instrument that was intended to systematically guide one through the purchasing and development phases in order to identify problem projects early enough to take steps to solve problems or cut off funding. But, as I discuss in the chapter on procurement, the risk assessment tool did not prevent disasters and the department actually was terminated for both its failures as well as due to political reasons (Peterson, 2002).

One of the commonalities observed in many of the most spectacular IT failures is that the projects proved too huge to manage properly. In a Florida welfare system IT fiasco, the system was an ambitious effort involving three federal agencies and supporting 84

Copyright © 2006, Idea Group Inc. Copying or distributing in print or electronic forms without written permission of Idea Group Inc. is prohibited.

Figure 10. Examples of some IT problems and potential solutions

Functional Area/Problem	Description of problems	Potential Solutions
Purchasing process is slow and often fails to produce successful project.	Slow appeals-ridden, inflexible process with lack of skills on part of those involved	Make legal and rule changes that provide more flexible, faster processes. Provide training and assistance to those involved. Use risk management tools early to identify potential problems.
Development process is slow and often fails to produce successful project.	In addition to technical problems, poor project management and large projects involving overwhelming complexity.	Make sure that project managers have the experience, skills and resources available to do adequate job whether through use of training and/or outside resources. Break large projects up into smaller modules and use risk management to identify problems early. Senior managers should be involved in the process. Consider using tools such as software engineering.
Poor quality of data is common problem.	Inadequate oversight, lack of technical controls, organizational resistance and non-use spurs data quality problems.	Make technical checks, implement closer oversight, and use and provide feedback to data gatherers.
Obstacles prevent useful sharing of data.	Interoperability problems, database incompatibilities, legal, and organizational obstacles cause resistance to sharing	Legal changes and establishment of joint technical standards for organization(s) involved. Use political skills by managers to overcome organizational resistance.
Inadequate payoffs result from implemented projects.	New systems are not used as much as expected and don't have expected benefits due to resistance of end-users, poor implementation and training, and other reasons.	Use better implementation procedures including more training of end-users. Provide more realistic expectations of new systems.

Adapted from Rocheleau, B. (1997). Governmental information system problems and failures: A preliminary review. Public Administration and Management: An Interactive Journal, 12(3) http://brain.hbg.psu.edu/Faculty/jxr11/roche.html

databases. The project was so large that, according to some assessments (Miller, 1994; Kidd, 1995), it overwhelmed the public managers responsible for the contract and consequently they relinquished control to private developers (Kidd, 1995):

Unless the public manager has significant prior experience managing system development, the individual may defer leadership in the development and implementation effort to private sector project managers.... (p. 42)

Copyright © 2006, Idea Group Inc. Copying or distributing in print or electronic forms without written permission of Idea Group Inc. is prohibited.

Moreover, it is difficult to find and keep project managers capable of handling large-scale system development projects. If these public managers bring such projects to successful completion, they are often hired by the private sector (Kidd, 1995). Lessons learned from studying such failures evolves into a best practice for purchasing, which is to break large projects up into smaller, more manageable modules.

In Figure 10, I present a summary (based on Rocheleau, 1997) of certain types of problems and limitations that computer systems in governmental agencies have encountered. Many of the most prominent disasters have involved the purchasing process and, to a substantial extent, the problems involving the extreme delays, inflexibility, and legal challenges related to computing have been addressed as federal and state governments have passed new legislation and made new rules that allow more discretion to public officials to purchase systems. Governments are applying several approaches to solving problems with the development process including more training for project managers and/or the use of outside agencies for project overview, top executive involvement, software engineering, and risk analysis, among others.

Other problems and limitations have hindered the effective use of some systems even after they have been purchased and developed appropriately. Problems such as poor quality of data, inadequate payoffs, and obstacles to sharing can result from several causes and managers at all levels need to be aware of them. I discuss issues of data quality in the chapter on accountability and the resistance to sharing in the chapter on interorganizational and interdepartmental systems. Several of the prescriptions from the problem/disaster literature overlap those of the best practices literature, such as the need to provide training and do risk assessments of projects in the purchasing and development stages. By showing that such practices are not only used by best practice outfits, but also can avoid major problems and disasters, managers can make a stronger case for adopting these prescriptions.

Conclusion

The rapidity of change in the IT sector escalates each year, resulting in a gap between research and practice that grows ever larger. This situation is worse in the public sector because relatively little traditional empirical research has been done in the past, although that situation is now changing. Based on our analysis in this chapter, there is a dilemma. Managers must make decisions about IT with limited information available. How can they do this? I suggest that managers consider these possible alternatives:

1. Managers can institute the collection of benchmark data in their organizations. They can use both their own previous data and those drawn from other organizations to gauge their performance and as a method for determining how well their organization is performing and what impacts new projects have. The availability of online performance data is making this approach much more feasible.

Copyright © 2006, Idea Group Inc. Copying or distributing in print or electronic forms without written permission of Idea Group Inc. is prohibited.

2. Managers should conduct searches for traditional empirical research that pertains to their problems. Although academically oriented research is often reluctant to draw strong prescriptive conclusions, it can add to the depth of managerial understanding of their projects and there is some excellent research on issues such as outsourcing that are important to governmental IT.

3. Managers also should search for problems and disasters that have occurred (internally and externally) with respect to the kinds of projects they plan to implement. These findings may help them to avoid critical failure factors.

4. Managers should search for "best practices" literature, both generic and those that are applicable to specific functional and technological areas. Currently, this research tends to provide generic prescriptions that are aimed at applying to all cases and thus are limited in their utility. However, as studies of best practices evolve and begin to focus on specific technological, substantive, and functional areas, and use refined measures of quality, they may be able to provide more useful guidance.

5. Governments should seek information from other IT specialists, especially those from organizations similar to their own. The growth in listservs and online organizations such as the Innovations Group and Government Management Information Science Association make this approach perhaps the most valuable of all because it provides the most specificity and some of the organizations responding often are likely to have similar characteristics to those seeking assistance.

To summarize, all four major sources of prescriptions have serious weaknesses and limitations. Consequently, managers need to consult several different sources and even then their decisions will likely depend on other sources, such as intuition. I acknowledge that organizations may give lip service to such principles but deviate from them in practice. For example, Nelson and Cheney (1987) discovered that most organizations talk about the importance of IT training but fail to devote many resources to it.

We need more research concerning the validity of public sector prescriptions that will make a convincing case to public managers to adopt them. In the private sector, a substantial body of empirical research is aimed at developing answers to questions such as, "When it is best to outsource IT?" (e.g., Lacity, Willcocks and Feeny, 1995). Indeed, Bozeman and Bretschneider's (1986) classic article on public management information systems developed several prescriptions, but there has been little research that has analyzed or tested these or other prescriptions that have been proposed for public sector agencies.

References

Ammons, D.N. (1996). *Municipal benchmarks: Assessing local performance and establishing community standards*. Thousand Oaks, CA: Sage.

Copyright © 2006, Idea Group Inc. Copying or distributing in print or electronic forms without written permission of Idea Group Inc. is prohibited.

Bozeman, B., & Bretschneider, S. (1986). Public management information systems: Theory and prescription. *Public Administration Review, 46*, 475-487.

Brotbeck, G., Miller, T., & Statz, J. (1999, November 23). *A survey of current best practices and utilization of standards in the public and private sectors.* Retrieved August 11, 2004, from http://www.dir.state.tx.us/eod/qa/bestprac.pdf

California State Department of Information Technology. (1998). *California risk assessment model.* Retrieved January 10, 2000, from http://www.doit.ca.gov/SIMM/#RAM

Cats-Baril, W., & Thompson, R. (1995). Managing information technology projects in the public sector. *Public Administration Review, 66*(6), 559-566.

Caudle, S. L. (1996). Strategic information resources management: Fundamental practices. *Government Information Quarterly, 13*(1), 83-97.

Changchit, C., Joshi, K., & Lederer, A. L. (1998). Process and reality in information systems benefit analysis. *Information Systems Journal, 8*(2), 145-162.

Connelly, D. R., & Pardo, T. A. (1998). *Best practices in intergovernmental information systems.* Paper presented at the 1998 National Conference of the American Society for Public Administration, May, Seattle, Washington.

Cortada, J. W. (1997). *Best practices in information technology: How corporations get the most value from exploiting their digital investments.* Upper Saddle River, NJ: Prentice Hall.

Dawes, S. S., Pardo, T. A., Connelly, D. R., Green, D. F., & McInerney, C. R. (1997). *Partners in state-local information systems: Lessons from the field.* Albany, NY: Center for Technology in Government.

DeSeve, E., Pesachowitz, A. M., & Johnson, L. K. (1997). *Best IT practices in the federal government.* Washington, DC: Chief Information Officers/Industry Advisory Council.

DuChessi, P., & Chengalur-Smith, I. (1998). Client/server benefits, problems, best practices. *Communications of the ACM, 41*(5), 87-94.

Farbey, B., Land, F., & Targett, D. (1999). The moving staircase – Problems of appraisal and evaluation in a turbulent environment. *Information Technology & People, 2*(3), 238-252.

Ginsberg, P. S. (1984). The dysfunctional side effects of quantitative indicator production: Illustrations from mental health care (A message from Chicken Little). *Evaluation and Program Planning, 7*, 1-12.

Grover, V., Teng, J. T.C., & Fiedler, K. D. (1998). IS investment priorities in contemporary organizations. *Communications of the ACM, 41*(2), 40-48.

Harris, B. (1995, October). Best practices emerge from synergy of technology, processes and people. *Government Technology.* Retrieved April 10, 1997, from http://govt-tech.net:80/1995/gt/oct/best_pra.shtm

Harvard Policy Group on Network-Enabled Service and Government. (2001a, March). *Imperative 3: Utilize best practices for implementing IT initiatives.* Cambridge, MA: The Harvard Policy Group on Network-Enabled Service and Government. Retrieved from http://www-1.ibm.com/industries/government/ieg/pdf/Imp3.pdf

Copyright © 2006, Idea Group Inc. Copying or distributing in print or electronic forms without written permission of Idea Group Inc. is prohibited.

Harvard Policy Group on Network-Enabled Service and Government. (2001b). *Imperative number 4: Improving budgeting and financing for promising IT initiatives.* Cambridge, MA: The Harvard Policy Group on Network-Enabled Service and Government, April.

Harvard Policy Group on Network-Enabled Service and Government. (2001c, January). *Imperative 2: Use IT for Strategic Innovation, Not Simply Tactical Automation.* Cambridge, MA: The Harvard Policy Group on Network-Enabled Service and Government.

Huxhold, W. E. (1991). *An introduction to urban geographic information systems.* New York: Oxford University.

Kelman, S. (1990). *Procurement and public management.* Washington, DC: AEI.

Kidd, R. (1995, March). How vendors influence the quality of human services systems. *Government Technology, 8,* 42-43.

Koch, C. (2004, March 1). Bursting the CMM hype; U.S. CIOs want to do business with offshore companies with high CMM ratings. But some outsourcers exaggerate and even lie about their Capability Maturity Model scores. *CIO Magazine, 17*(10), 48-57.

Kraemer, K. L., & Dedrick, J. (1997). Computing and public organizations. *Journal of Public Administration Research and Theory, 7*(1), 89-112.

Kraemer, K. L., & King, J. L. (1976). *Computers, power, and urban management: What every local executive should know.* Beverly Hills, CA: Sage.

Kraemer, K. L., & King, J. L. (1986). Computing and public organizations. *Public Administration Review, 46*(special issue), 488-496.

Kreizman, G., & Fraga, E. (2003, February 13). Best practices in county e-government. Gartner consulting. Research Note. Tactical Guidelines. TG-19-3073. Retrieved March 26, 2005, from http://www.cira.state.tx.us/Docs/docs/bestpractices.pdf

Lacity, M. C., & Willcocks, L. P. (1998). An empirical investigation of information technology sourcing practices: Lessons from experience. *MIS Quarterly, 22*(3), 363-408.

Lacity, M. C., Willcocks, L. P., & Feeny, D.F. (1995). IT outsourcing: Maximize flexibility and control. *Harvard Business Review, 73*(3), 84-93.

Laudon, K. C., & Laudon, J. P. (1996). *Management information systems organization and technology* (4th ed.). Upper Saddle River, NJ: Prentice-Hall.

Leach, K., & Smallen, D. (1998). What do information technology support services really cost? *CAUSE/EFFECT, 21*(2). Retrieved April 4, 1999, from www.educause.edu/ir/library/html/cem9829.html

Lyytinen, K., & Hirschheim, R. (1987). Information systems failures—A survey and classification of the empirical literature. *Oxford Surveys in Information Technology, 4,* 257-309.

Malvey, M. (1981). *Simple systems, complex environments: Hospital financial information systems.* Beverly Hills, CA: Sage.

Copyright © 2006, Idea Group Inc. Copying or distributing in print or electronic forms without written permission of Idea Group Inc. is prohibited.

Markus, M. L., & Keil, M. (1994). If we build it, they will come: Designing information systems that people want to use. *Sloan Management Review, 35*(4), 11-25.

McComb, D., & Smith, J.Y. (1991). System project failures: The heuristics of risk. *Journal of Information Systems Management, 8*(1), 25-34.

Miller, B. (1994). Lessons from Florida's public assistance automation. *Government Technology, 7*(1), 1 & 42.

Miranda, R., Kavanagh, S., & Roque, R. (2002). *Technology needs assessments: Evaluating the business case for ERP and financial management systems.* Chicago: Government Finance Officers Association.

Nelson, R.R., & Cheney, P.H. (1987). Training end users: An exploratory study. *MIS Quarterly, 11*(4), 547-559.

Newcombe, T. (1997, December). Prodigal system: California's SAWS. *Government Technology.* Retrieved January 10, 1998, from http://www.govtech.net/publications/gt/1997/dec/coverb/coverb.shtm

Newcombe, T. (1998, February). Big project woes halt child support system. *Government Technology.* Retrieved February 14, 1998, from http://www.govtech.net/publications/gt/1998/feb/projectwoes/projectwoes.shtm

Newcomer, K. E., & Caudle, S. L. (1991). Evaluating public sector information systems: More than meets the eye. *Public Administration Review, 51*(5), 377-384.

Peterson, S. (2002, October). End of the line. *Government Technology,* 18-24.

Pinsonneault, A., & Kraemer, K. L. (1997). Middle management downsizing: An empirical investigation of the impact of the information technology. *Management Science, 43*(5), 659-679.

Rocheleau, B. (1997). Governmental information system problems and failures: A preliminary review. *Public Administration and Management: An Interactive Journal, 2*(3). Retrieved from http://brain.hbg.psu.edu/Faculty/jxr11/roche.html

Saiedian, H., & Kuzara, R. (1995). SEI capability maturity models impact on contractors. *Computer, 28*(1), 16-26.

Schrage, M.T. (2003, February 15). Making IT work worst practice: The practice of importing best practices is not a best practice. *CIO Magazine.* Retrieved August 10, 2004, from www.cio.com

Standish Group. (1995). *The CHAOS Report.* Retrieved April 10, 1996, from www.standishgroup.com/chaos.html

Strassmann, P. A. (1995). *The politics of information management.* New Canaan, CT: Information Economics.

Strock, B., & Adkins, D. (1993). *The municipal computer systems handbook* (2nd ed.). Rensselaerville, NY: Rensselaerville Systems Training Center.

Towns, S. (1998, March). Thinking big: CIO of California's dmv steers technology overhaul. *Government Technology.* Retrieved from http://www.govtech.net/publications/reseller/1998/march98/cio_spotlight/ciospotlight.shtm

United States House of Representatives. (1996). Subcommittee on Government Management, Information, and Technology of the Committee on Government Reform and

Copyright © 2006, Idea Group Inc. Copying or distributing in print or electronic forms without written permission of Idea Group Inc. is prohibited.

Oversight. 104th Congress, Second Session, February 26. *Using the best practices of information technology in government.* (Washington, DC: U.S. Government Printing Office: ISBN 0-16-055132-3, 1997).

U.S. General Accounting Office. (2002, January). *Best practices: Taking a strategic approach could improve DOD's acquisition of services.* GAO-02-230.

U.S. General Accounting Office. (2004, June). *Information technology training can be enhanced by greater use of leading practices.* GAO-04-791.

Wyde, R. (1997, Summer). Managing the purchase of information systems technology: Guidelines for success. *Public Welfare*, 14-20.

Additional Reading

The Cortada book provides the most in-depth discussion of best practices. The series of Harvard Policy Group on Network-Enabled Service and Government provide a variety of interesting useful "imperatives" which, in effect, constitute best practices. Ammon's books on benchmarking remain the major source for public sector benchmarking information. Lyytinen & Hirschheim's (1987) article on information system failures is a classic and a good place to start analyzing system failures. My 1997 article contains a number of detailed accounts of various limitations and failures of public sector information technology failures.

Key Concepts

*   Benchmarking
*   Best Practice(s)
*   Capability Maturity Model
*   Critical Failure Factors
*   Fast Followership

Discussion Questions

1. Which of the best practices discussed in this chapter or in other best practice literature do you find to be most useful? Why?

2. If you were instructed to find the best practices for a particular process (e.g., how to implement a new Customer Relations Management Program), what steps would you take to identify the best practices?

Copyright © 2006, Idea Group Inc. Copying or distributing in print or electronic forms without written permission of Idea Group Inc. is prohibited.

Exercises

1. Develop your own best practice(s) for a contemporary issue that governmental or non-profit organizations face. For example, it could pertain to the implementation of a new technology (e.g., wireless) or software package (e.g., Customer Relations Management) or process that is related to information and communication technologies. Write up a brief summary of the best practice(s) and how you obtained them.

2. Implement a benchmarking study in which you gather comparable information about the performance of IT departments for different governments. You may be able to find this information online or you may have to contact the governments directly to obtain it.

3. Pick some information technology issue that governmental and non-profit organizations must deal with. Then identify as many empirical studies as you can about this particular issue. How many empirical studies did you find? Are their findings relevant to the issue? Would they provide practical assistance to an organization?

Copyright © 2006, Idea Group Inc. Copying or distributing in print or electronic forms without written permission of Idea Group Inc. is prohibited.

Chapter V

Electronic Government

Introduction

Electronic government (e-government) has become a primary focus of information management for governmental officials as well as IT staff. In this chapter, I review the basic concepts of e-government and present information on its successes and limitations. I also outline key issues that need to be addressed in planning and implementing IT. Because governments are so active in the e-government area, the situation is changing rapidly so assessments that I make now will undoubtedly need to be revisited regularly.

E-Government: Definitions and Related Concepts

E-government has been defined in many ways. For example, some experts such as Marche (2003) define it as the provision of government information and transactions through electronic means and thus contrast it with other concepts such as *"e-governance,"* which she defines as "the use of technology to achieve civic communication and the expression of citizen will." Thus e-government activities are not restricted to Web-based services. I prefer to use e-government as the most general umbrella concept to cover all aspects of information technology used by government to serve the general citizenry and more specific categories of "customers." There are constantly evolving new terms added under the rubric of e-government (e.g., e-rulemaking and e-procurement) but for now, I prefer the categories employed by the Center for Technology in Government. They identified the following most common aspects of e-Government (Cook et al., 2002):

Copyright © 2006, Idea Group Inc. Copying or distributing in print or electronic forms without written permission of Idea Group Inc. is prohibited.

1.   **E-services** concern the delivery of information and services via the Internet.

2.   **E-management** is the use of information technology to improve the management of government such as through better communication and improved processes.

3.   **E-democracy** is the use of information and communication technologies (ICT) to increase "citizen participation in the decision-making process."

4.   **E-commerce** is the exchange of goods and services via the Internet.

Another basic way to view e-government is by the nature of the actors engaged in conducting business through e-government. These interactions are now characterized by well-known "acronyms" such as G2G (electronic exchanges among governments), G2B (exchanges between governments and businesses), G2C (exchanges between governments and citizens), and G2E (exchanges between the governments and their employees). Please take note that I am using the "2" in the above cases to potentially include 2-way, mutual exchanges.

The above definitions focus on the use of technology to serve citizens. However, over the last decade, the concept of e-government has also come to be strongly associated with an array of prescriptive principles that include internal management concerns such as the following (Garson, 2004; United Nations, 2002; Fountain, 2001a):

1.   E-government is viewed as allowing government to provide *"citizen-centric"* services that are focused on the needs of citizens such as through *"one-stop" Web portals* [emphasis added] and not dictated by bureaucratic boundaries. I would extend the concept to "customer-centric" since customers also include businesses and other organizations, other governments, and internal customers in other departments.

2.   E-government is viewed as a vehicle that governments should employ in conjunction with the use of *business process reengineering* (BPR) to improve the processes of government including the streamlining of processes and reduction of "transaction costs."

3.   E-government is aimed at achieving greater horizontal and vertical sharing among governmental organizations, both within the organization as well as with other governments.

4.   E-government is viewed as a mechanism to increase accountability and citizen participation.

5.   E-government is viewed as a way to achieve better knowledge management within the organization.

Thus the adoption of e-government is viewed as much more than simply the application of information technology to government. These prescriptive principles are currently accepted as goals that are being pursued vigorously by many governmental officials at all levels of government and political persuasions. For example, Mark Foreman, OMB's Associate Director for Information Technology and E-Government, stated that the Bush

Copyright © 2006, Idea Group Inc. Copying or distributing in print or electronic forms without written permission of Idea Group Inc. is prohibited.

Figure 1. Problems that e-government needs to avoid

1. Paving Cowpaths—Agencies that have automated existing outdated processes, instead of fixing underlying problems or simplifying agency procedures to take advantage of new e-business and e-government capabilities.

2. Redundant Buying—Agencies have made unnecessarily duplicative information technology investments.

3. Inadequate Program Management—Many major IT projects have not met cost schedule, and performance goals.

4. Poor Modernization Blueprints—Few agencies have had plans demonstrating and documenting the linkage between IT capabilities that are not inoperable with one another. Few IT investments improve mission performance.

5. Poor IT Security—Major gaps have existed in agency and government-wide information and IT-related security.

Source: Adapted from U.S. House of Representatives. (2003, March 13). Federal e-government initiatives: Are we headed in the right direction? Hearing before the Subcommittee on Technology, Information Policy, Intergovernmental Relations and the Census. 108 Congress, First Session, Serial 108-6, p. 17. Retrieved July 3, 2004 from http://www.gpo.gov/congres/house

Administration's e-government strategy includes several goals that overlap the pre-scriptive principles outlined below (U.S. House of Representatives, 2003, p. 17):

There is recognition that these highly ambitious goals cannot be achieved quickly and there have been many attempts to identify various stages and levels that governments pass through as they develop e-government efforts. Layne and Lee (2001) developed one of the most cited frameworks with four "states" of e-government: (1) Static information is presented on the Web site; (2) Transactions are conducted; (3) Vertical integration is achieved within one unit of government so that departments share information; and (4) Horizontal integration is achieved between levels of government. Others like Stowers (2004a) would insert "interactions" as an additional stage that can occur between the static and transactional states. The term *"transformational"* is often used to describe the integrative, reengineering, and other structural changes that technology can bring about to make government more responsive and effective for its customers. An example of a transformative goal for e-government occurs in Massachusetts's 2001 e-government plan developed by Accenture and the state's e-government team that views citizens as "deputized state employees" who devote effort in connecting to online services so as to complete their transactions more quickly and save both themselves and the state money.

The Status of E-Government Circa 2005

Over the past few years, there have been several national (and some international) surveys as well as more localized studies that have attempted to assess the status of e-government. Overall, the results of these various surveys have been fairly consistent in their substantive findings. A Pew Center Study (Horrigan, 2004) based on a 2003 survey found increasing use of the Internet to obtain information from government and to contact government. The trends show an impressive upward movement as 66% of

Copyright © 2006, Idea Group Inc. Copying or distributing in print or electronic forms without written permission of Idea Group Inc. is prohibited.

Internet users had looked online for governmental information in 2003 compared to only 56% in 2002. According to the same report, about the same percent (about 30% each of Internet users) employed the Internet as those who used a phone to conduct personal transactions with government.

The Pew Center does reveal the limitations of current use of the Internet. People considered some problems to be too complex for the Internet. There remains a substantial minority (around 36% in 2003) who do not use the Internet (Horrigan, 2004, p. 27). There is also evidence that those with greater education are more likely to use the Internet and that education is correlated with successful use—although these more educated people are also more successful in dealing with government regardless of the mode of interaction. As the Pew and other studies note (e.g., Thomas & Streib, 2003), people prefer to have *multiple channels* of accessing government and it is too soon to discourage these other avenues. But the assessment of the Internet and Web sites by citizens is quite positive—Thomas and Streib (2003) reported that 68% of the respondents rated governmental Web sites as excellent or good. There is also evidence of fairly good responsiveness in their dealings with Internet Web sites as 79% of those who e-mailed governmental Web sites reported that they received a response. The Pew study found that the most common problem (33%) was not finding the information they looked for at the Web site. The Pew study found that, although people who used the Internet more frequently were also more successful in their dealings with government, that technology was not the cause because differences in the rate of successful contacts disappeared when they controlled for socio-demographic variables. Today's phone systems bring many frustrations and often are not a friendly, personal alternative to the Internet as the following as the Pew (2004) study reports:

People who used the phone to contact government were confronted by the usual litany of voice mailboxes and automated touch systems. Nearly two-thirds (64%) of this group encountered automated menus, with one-third of this group finding this not helpful at all. A bit more than a third (36%) got to someone's voice mail where they could leave a message, and about a third found this not to be at all helpful. (p. 16)

Other phone medium problems such as not being able to stay on the phone long enough or being put on hold demonstrate the advantages of Web-based contacts, although many governments are still not prepared to deal with complex personal problems via the Internet. Still, for urgent and complex problems, in-person or phone contacts are preferred (Horrigan, 2004):

People's preferred means of contact also varies significantly by the nature of the problem at hand. For the 18% of government patrons who classify the reason they contact government as either very complicated or very urgent, 'real time' interaction is by far the preferred choice. The telephone or in-person visits are the most valued forms of contact for these kinds of problems, while the Web and e-mail fade in relative importance. The same is true for people who said that they sought out government help to solve a problem the last time they contacted government. For seeking information or executing a transaction, the Web and e-mail become more prominent. (p. 6)

Copyright © 2006, Idea Group Inc. Copying or distributing in print or electronic forms without written permission of Idea Group Inc. is prohibited.

Thus governments need to plan for *multi-modal* forms of contact including face-to-face meetings with their constituents.

Details about local governmental use of the Internet and e-government are revealed in a 2000 ICMA (International City & County Management Association) survey (Norris, Fletcher, & Holden, 2001). The survey, conducted found that only about 1 of 10 governments at that time had made financial transactions available online such as payment of taxes but that there was rapid change in progress with about 25% planning to offer some form of financial transactions on line. Reddick's (2004, p. 59) analysis of the 2002 ICMA survey points out that for many governments, the most common online applications are downloadable forms (present in 56% of municipalities), online requests for local government services such as pothole repair (32%), and online requests for government records (28%). Actual online delivery of records to the requestor was only done by about 18% of local governments. Reddick (2004, p. 58) points out that surveys of online services results can greatly depending on the nature of the sample—larger governments tend to have many more online services. The average size of the government responding to the 2002 ICMA survey ranged in population from 10,000 to 25,000. Coursey's (forthcoming) analysis of 2004 data collected by ICMA found that online tax payments were offered by 53% of governments with populations over 250,000 versus 7% of cities with populations less than 25,000. However, in some states such as Illinois, the state government has developed what they call the "Illinois E-Pay" program that involves a contract with a vendor to provide e-payment services that many small municipalities and county governments are using. Reddick (2004) did find substantial use of online purchases for equipment (about 46%) and office supplies (54%) among these governments. Analyses by Moon (2002) and West (2003) found that more than 80% of governments had Web sites in 2000. Outsourcing of Web-related functions is quite common—about 40% outsourced Web-hosting and around 25% Web design in 2000 (Norris et al., 2001, p. 6).

The most interesting (to me) findings of the Norris, Fletcher & Holden (2001) study concerned the impacts of e-government on these local governments: about 44% reported increased demands on staff versus 17% reporting decreased time demands on staff. About 36% said that e-government had resulted in re-engineering of government and 27% said that their business processes were more efficient. Only 10% reported reduced administrative costs and only 1.4% reported reductions in staff due to e-government. Coursey's (forthcoming) analysis of the 2004 ICMA data also found small percentage (11%) reporting reduced costs due to e-government. These findings raise questions for those who expect e-government to reduce burdens on government employees and save money in personnel expenditures, although it may simply reflect the fact that e-government is still in the very early stages of adoption and e-government has not yet affected most governmental processes. Cluff (2002) cites a Fresno (California) study that identified some 5,000 paper or human-driven processes (more than 3,000 on paper alone) and thus makes the point that current IT systems perform only a small fraction of municipal activities. However, the 2002 Status Report by Texas Online did one of the few studies of the impact of e-government on employee use of time and it does cite specific time savings due to some of its e-government applications. For example, processing time for some processes was reduced by 90% because the business or citizen is doing all of the data input and the applications have fewer problems as well as "no incomplete

Copyright © 2006, Idea Group Inc. Copying or distributing in print or electronic forms without written permission of Idea Group Inc. is prohibited.

applications" with online applications (e.g., for sales tax and TIFs) compared to the traditional service. Of course, even if e-government results in reduction of time for specific processes, the impact may not result in less work for governmental employees. For example, Gurwitt (2003) reported that when Denver put its jobs online, applications for jobs increased by 33% but that the rest of the process was still largely manual and the overall effect was to increase personnel loads. Likewise, when governments put property tax appraisal information online (Gurwitt, 2003), citizens are more likely to challenge the government's appraisals. This willingness to challenge may lead to better equity and accountability but it may also result in increased workloads. One of the major advantages of e-government is that it lowers transaction costs for its citizens but this advantage could lead to more demands on government employees. Coursey's (forthcoming) study also found that more local government respondents reported increased than decreased demands on staff due to e-government. O'Looney (2000, p. 24) makes the point that many citizens don't fill out forms such as police reports because of the burden—the cost in time of filling them out exceeds the amount of benefit from making the report. By lowering the cost of filling out such forms, more crimes may be entered into the system that the department will have to investigate.

The above findings contrast with West's 2000 study of state and federal chief information officers that found "remarkable optimism" about e-government with more than 80% stating that it had already improved efficiency and more than 60% reporting that it has resulted in lower governmental costs. The differences are likely due to the fact that West's 2003 survey focused on the Web sites of the 70 largest metropolitan areas. West found rapid growth in the provision of online services. He found that 48% of these sites offered services that were "fully executable online" compared to only 22% in his 2000 survey. These results emphasize the fluid nature of data pertaining to e-government and the gap between large and small governments.

Customer expectations are important when access to services is put online. The E-Government Plan (2002) of Irving, Texas notes that when customers submit service requests online by interactive voice response, e-mail, or online form, "they may expect instant response." Consequently, the Irving plan suggests that it is important for them to develop guidelines that will provide information to citizens about the kind of response times they can expect. The Irving Texas E-Government Plan also notes the importance of keeping the online policies completely up-to-date. For example, the plan asks, what if someone relies on online information as to how something is supposed to be done but that information is out-of-date?

Some aspects of government have been consistently targeted for early conversion to e-government by certain levels of government. For example, state governments have emphasized e-commerce capabilities in their approach to collecting taxes and revenues. Lassman's (2002) survey of states found that 20 states achieved a perfect score in their assessment of taxation and revenue services and that more than 60% of the states maintained online storage of records. Only four states in the survey did not have a fully functional online payment system. This finding contrasts with Reddick's (2004) survey of local governments where online payment of taxes was offered only by 2.4%.

A 2001 U.S. General Accounting Office (GAO) study analyzed federal e-government initiatives according to the following categories (see Chart 1): (1) Informational only; (2)

Copyright © 2006, Idea Group Inc. Copying or distributing in print or electronic forms without written permission of Idea Group Inc. is prohibited.

Forms-only; (3) Transactional; and (4) Transformational. They defined *transformational* as those cases where government takes a "global focus" so that citizens do not need to know what governmental agency is providing the service. At the time of the 2001 study, over half (57%) of the initiatives were classified as informational versus 4% transformational.

The *digital divide* between technological haves and have-nots, according to some experts, has been steadily declining. Research by Groper (2004) shows that education and income are the strongest predictors of Internet use but racial and ethnic gaps in access and usage have been decreasing and Internet use by African-Americans in California is similar to the population in general. Compaine (2001) argues even more strongly that most of the lack of access is not due to cost factors but to voluntary choices. However, Strover & Straubhaar's (2000, p. 9) survey does show some significant differences in Internet use. They found that 68% of Anglos used the Internet versus only about 45% of Hispanics and 33% of African-Americans. They also discovered that the patterns of use of minorities who were Internet users did not differ much from Anglos in terms of hours of usage except in one report respect: Anglos reported nearly 14 online transactions per year versus about 10 for Hispanics and 8 for African Americans. Strover & Straubhaar (2000, p. 13) also found that African-Americans and Hispanics both cited cost as an obstacle to Internet usage more frequently than Anglos. Sipior, Volonino & Marzec (2004) conducted an experiment to provide computer training and access in Chester, Pennsylvania, one of the most distressed communities in the U.S., and found that the combination of training and improved access to personal computers achieved many of their goals, though they noted that the task is not easy—the participants' happiness actually declined during the experiment, perhaps due to the fact that experimental participants compared their situation with the more advantaged trainers. Sipior & Ward (2004) also found that one-time use through a community training program was not sufficient to sustain intention for continued use of e-government Web sites. Thus, there remain substantial differences in Internet access and use based on income and there is a significant portion of the population who are not Internet users. The importance of overcoming the digital divide is supported by the fact that full access to information communication technologies such as the Internet are necessary in order to achieve full "inclusion in modern society" (Warschauer, 2003). Consequently governments need to address the digital divide issue in a variety of ways to provide public access points such as the placement of kiosks in places of easy and common availability and preserving multiple lines of access to government.

Financing E-Government

There are a wide variety of ways in which governments finance the development of e-government, especially e-commerce services. By far the most common method is traditional funding from general revenues (Robb, 2001). There is the hope and expectation that the impacts of technology from improved processes will help to save money so that the investments pay for themselves. For example, the State of Massachusetts's (2001)

Copyright © 2006, Idea Group Inc. Copying or distributing in print or electronic forms without written permission of Idea Group Inc. is prohibited.

E-Government plan reports savings due to its conversion of its tax system that enabled redeployment of personnel:

The Department of Revenue provides a good example of how this has been done in the past. In the early 1990's, the Department of Revenue was required to reduce headcount while still maintaining a high quality of customer service. DOR embraced the electronic filing of taxes, aggressively promoting this new application. As a result personal income tax returns filed electronically almost quadrupled in five years, rising from 222,000 in 1995 to a hefty 817,000 in 2000. By the year 2000, 26% of all returns were filed electronically, allowing significant redeployment of personnel who had been processing paper returns.

The Massachusetts plan provides a projection of benefits to grow larger over time and then to "level off in years four and five." Of course, all such projections are based on assumptions about factors such as usage levels and reductions in costs due to process reengineering savings. However, as noted above, these savings often do not occur at least in the short term and one study (Gant, Gant & Johnson, 2002) showed that only one state had employed a cost-benefit analysis before investing in Web portal development. Indeed, I found few attempts to analyze formally the costs versus the benefits of e-commerce applications among the local governmental officials that I interviewed either. Those who decide to proceed with e-commerce assume that eventually citizens will want to use electronic means for dealing with government and that in the long run, the switchover will payoff.

The Gant, Gant & Johnson (2002, p. 35) study found that governmental investments in Web portals were "viewed as operating rather than capital expenditures" and thus tended to be "underfinanced." One alternative to traditional financing are commercial partnerships with the private sector. One approach is to use government's control over right-of-ways to forge deals in which private enterprises provide expensive fiber infrastructure as occurred in Arizona (Robb, 2001). In cases where private companies develop the system with their own funds, they charge user fees for the convenience of using the system and for other value-added services (Gant, Gant & Johnson, 2002, p. 43). Bonds (sometimes called Information Technology or I-Bonds) have been used by states such as Massachusetts (Robb, 2001) to finance infrastructure projects. Coursey's (forthcoming) research (based on a 2004 ICMA survey of local governments) found that the vast majority of local e-government efforts are funded from general revenues. Some aspects of e-government may be able to pay for themselves. For example, Gant, Gant & Johnson's study found substantial revenue possibilities in Web portals for Indiana and Virginia with positive net incomes reported even in the early years of operation. Virginia's Department of Taxation (Richardson, 2004) worked out a deal with the American Management Association (AMA) to develop an online taxation system in which AMA is paid based on the difference between predicted revenues (based on traditional collection mechanisms) and the increased revenues achieved due to the establishment of the online system. Pennsylvania engaged in a partnership with Microsoft (Holmes, 2001):

Copyright © 2006, Idea Group Inc. Copying or distributing in print or electronic forms without written permission of Idea Group Inc. is prohibited.

...the state entered into a partnership deal with Microsoft, which provided at no cost to the government, a minimum of $100,000 worth of consulting services as well as value-added services so that citizens could check the weather, stock quotes, and news.... Microsoft hopes to recoup its investment through development work tied to the portal. (p. 47)

According to Holmes (2001, p. 47), the participating businesses and the local governments pay a subscription fee that asks for assistance with their Web sites. The 2002 E-Government Plan of Mecklenburg County proposed that a "E-government Strategic Investment fund" be created in which a small fraction (about 1%) of future funds are dedicated to strategic e-government investments. The logic behind this approach was dissatisfaction with a "pay-as-you-go" approach that has the following limitations (Mecklenburg County, 2002):

Under this [pay-as-you-go] approach each department requests funding on a project-by-project basis. This is the current model being used by the County with mixed results. This model encourages an entrepreneur approach within departments, which can be positive with regard to stimulating innovation. However, it also creates a system that does not establish priorities for the enterprise. It also encourages to a great degree a silo approach to designing and implementing applications, not necessarily taking into consideration a wider customer audience and the opportunity to enact economies of scale and customer service. (p.16)

Despite these successful outcomes noted above, there have been many disappointments with e-government ventures. Richardson (2004, p. 209) and Carr (2002) report that many e-government collaborations with vendors fail and that governments need to protect themselves by taking steps such as ensuring that ownership of the data in public/private partnerships is given to the public under the "stewardship of the government partners."

Charging *user fees* has been one of the most problematic issues for governments that engage in e-commerce. Logically, many believe that the charge for the extra convenience of using online services is equitable because the cost is borne by those who are using the service (Gant, Gant & Johnson, 2002, p. 44). It also can contribute in a major way to the financing of the e-government that otherwise would have to come out of the general pool of funds for IT. Norris et al. (2000) found that few governments were charging user fees for e-commerce services. McKay's review (2002) found a variety of approaches to service charges. For example, in Minnesota, the income tax director stated that he was "amazed at the number of people" willing to pay fees and has had no problem passing the fees onto the public while the Arkansas Office of Motor Vehicles absorbs the credit card fee itself based on the assumption that the end result will be a cost-effective business decision. The policy resulted in 75% of Arkansas vehicle registrations being done online (McKay, 2002, p. 25). DeKalb County (Georgia) decided not to offer online payment of taxes because the size of the credit-card fee on large transactions could "negate" the savings of paying online. Some local governments (e.g., Monroe County, New York) have been able to leverage their large account balances with banks to waive fees for e-commerce use of credit cards. Overall, West's 2003 survey showed that only

Copyright © 2006, Idea Group Inc. Copying or distributing in print or electronic forms without written permission of Idea Group Inc. is prohibited.

7% of the governments employ user fees. In some cases, state laws have to be amended in order to allow for charging online fees as was the case in Oakland County (Michigan) because Michigan's Freedom of Information Act law only allowed incremental fees—not fees that would pay for the capital and operational costs of setting up the new online system.

The North Carolina Information Resource Commission (2001) has emphasized the importance of developing a cohesive set of policies to govern the setting of fees for e-government. They developed a model that has a number of judgments that agencies need to consider including the following:

1. The initial usage rate for e-government and the rates of transition from traditional to e-government payment.

2. Impact of the fees on acceptance and use of e-government.

3. The availability of alternative sources of funding.

4. The degree of savings and additional value provided for by the online transaction.

5. The consistency of fees charged by agencies.

Rudolphy and Cullison (2002) discuss the attempt of the Motor Vehicles Division (MVD) of the state of Arizona to employ a "self-funding" model in which the third-party vendor (IBM) would recoup its costs via a convenience fee in return for providing the system. They began with vehicle registration because this is the type of activity that is perfect for online transactions. It requires little or no personal contact. However, they quickly discovered that users did not want to pay the additional user fee even though the fee represented only about 1.7% of transaction's cost. Thus the cost of the online system initially was high because the state had to maintain the costs of the "traditional over-the-counter business" service as well as the low-usage e-commerce application. Rudolphy & Cullison report that over the first year of operation, the registrations rarely exceeded 5,000 per month. Their solution was to replace the fee with a system that allows the vendor to retain a "portion" of the registration renewal fees and also be compensated for the credit card fees in return for renunciation of the convenience fee. Use of the online system (ServiceArizona) immediately more than doubled. The vendor (IBM) is responsible for managing credit card disputes. A study by the Arizona Department of Transportation found that online transaction costs were 65% lower than over-the-counter costs. The online system includes a customer feedback mechanism to gather information on the success of the system and any problems.

According to Franzel and Coursey (2004), Florida followed the opposite course of action. The state began by waiving fees for online services because they wanted to encourage usage of the lower cost online approach, but agencies were concerned about the lost revenues of the revenues from fees so they were reluctant to encourage online usage. Consequently, Florida now is charging fees (Franzel & Coursey, 2004, p. 69) and, in some cases, mandating that certain services must be done online.

Gant, Gant and Johnson (2002) suggest that some G2C costs should be subsidized either by G2B fees or from general revenues when the societal benefits of the online transactions are greater than the costs that can be recouped from the application. They don't

Copyright © 2006, Idea Group Inc. Copying or distributing in print or electronic forms without written permission of Idea Group Inc. is prohibited.

provide any examples but one could think of a possibility—for example, the development of applications for those who are disabled and homebound. Maryland (Perlman, 2000) created an Information Technology Investment fund from a combination of general revenues, phone commissions, and fees charged on telecommunication companies for rights-of-way access. Then it sets up a competitive grant process with state agencies bidding for the special monies.

The Texas OnLine (2002, p. 27) system (at least until their status report in 2002) was entirely self-funded with its private (e-government) partner investing some $20 million that it sought to recoup through a combination of user fees, subscription fees, and "premium service fees." The state of Texas (Texas Online, 2002, p. 27) will get 10% of the revenues generated by online applications until the partner recoups its costs when the state's share will then jump to 50% of revenues. Texas Online (2002), like other governments, has found that businesses are much more willing to pay additional fees for online services than general citizenry:

Who will be using the service? It is clear that businesses are more willing than citizens to pay fees for the convenience of electronic interaction with government. As a result, business applications such as driver records generate far more revenue than individual applications such as vehicle registration. Another important factor is users' ability to pay. People in lower income levels are less able and therefore less likely to pay such fees. Moreover, a certain segment of the population will resist paying any additional fee for service, believing that their tax dollars should cover any cost of service. (p. 28)

The Texas Online Report (2002) is also one of the few to provide some cost analyses comparing online and traditional transaction costs. They point out that there is a "natural cycle" in which initially the costs are higher for online than traditional services, but that they become lower through time as usage increases. In figure 2, I provide the chart from the Texas Comptroller of Public Accounts comparison between online and traditional costs.

The Texas OnLine Authority (2002b) argues that a government's Web portal should be viewed as an infrastructure investment, that some applications should be free, and that not every agency should be expected to be able to cover their costs. Consequently, it suggests that it may be appropriate for those services with paying customers to "bear the burden" for those without enough paying customers (Texas OnLine, 2002b, p. 28).

To summarize, e-government planners should look at the possibility of a wide range of funding mechanisms. The Massachusetts E-government (2001) plan provides a good example of the diversity of ideas that are considered for funding e-government initiatives including the following options listed in their plan:

1.   The reallocation of non-E-gov spending to E-gov spending.

2.   If there are budget surpluses, allocate the funds to E-gov development.

3.   Savings due to E-gov may allow funding of more E-gov initiatives.

4.   Public-Private partnerships as a vehicle for generating revenue.

Copyright © 2006, Idea Group Inc. Copying or distributing in print or electronic forms without written permission of Idea Group Inc. is prohibited.

Figure 2. Texas OnLine WebFile sales tax costs: online versus traditional costs compared

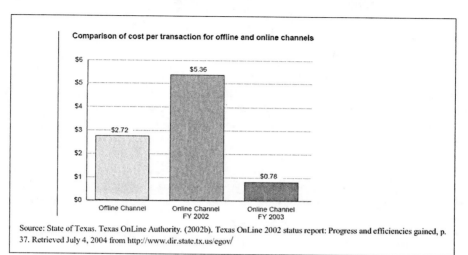

Source: State of Texas. Texas OnLine Authority. (2002b). Texas OnLine 2002 status report: Progress and efficiencies gained, p. 37. Retrieved July 4, 2004 from http://www.dir.state.tx.us/egov/

5. Maximization of Federal grants.

6. User fees for G2B and G2C services.

7. Consideration of the use of "self-funding" efforts such as the possibility of privatization of Web portal development.

8. Advertising on the Web.

9. The development of "split-funding" approaches between individual agencies and the central funding source.

10. Use of an I-Bond to fund Information technology.

11. A central E-gov fund that will include funds for cross-agency projects.

However, some sources are not seriously considered by most governments. For example, Norris et al. (2001) found that only a small fraction (1 to 2%) of governments were employing advertising as a source of revenue. The State of Texas's On-Line Authority (2002a) did a detailed analysis of the possibility of employing advertising as an e-gov revenue source. It notes several potential drawbacks to use of advertising including the following: (1) Possible problems due to legal challenges by organizations that are refused the chance to advertise; (2) Perception on the part of the public that the government is officially endorsing advertisers; and (3) Burden on the responsiveness of Web sites due to increased processing demands resulting from the advertising. The Texas Report (2002) states that all of these objections could be overcome but the major problem is that not enough revenue can be generated from advertising to justify its use. The Texas report notes that charges for banner ads, the most popular ads, are based on how many times

Copyright © 2006, Idea Group Inc. Copying or distributing in print or electronic forms without written permission of Idea Group Inc. is prohibited.

end users click these banners to access (referred to as "click-through rate) the ad material and that a charge of $15 for every thousand clicks is typical. The problem is that end users have been ignoring banner ads. The rate at which they have clicked on banner ads has declined from 1% to .025% since 1997. Thus the few public organizations that have used them (e.g., City of Honolulu, Nashville Metropolitan Transit Authority, and U.S. Postal Service) have derived significantly less income than they planned from this source.

To summarize, one of the top goals of the e-government movement is to create seamless government through breaking down stovepipe systems, but the funding of interagency applications remains one of the biggest challenges. One approach as proposed in the Massachusetts plan is to create special pots of money for these inter-agency projects.

Planning for E-Government

In addition to funding considerations, there are many other aspects that go into planning for e-government. The basic structure of planning for e-government is similar to the points that I discuss in the generic chapter on IT planning in this book. A first step is to prepare a business case for the e-government application. A GAO (2003a) study of 23 federal business plans for e-government initiatives found that all 23 included one of the best practices—a clear statement of expected benefits but fewer performed other recommended practices such as systematically studying customer needs (9 of 23) and analysis of collaborative opportunities with other agencies (only 8 of 23 business cases included this practice). The other best practices found by GAO include: (1) A clear statement of the problems and current conditions that are to be improved by the e-government application; (2) A description of the proposed "concept" (vision) for the future processes; (3) A clear statement of the assumptions of the project; (4) An indication that the project has assessed customer needs and that the project is driven by these needs; (5) The project is clearly linked to the organization's strategic objectives; (6) Steps have been taken to minimize risks of failure; and (7) Collaboration across agencies and governments has been given serious attention. The degree to which the federal e-government projects adhered to these best practices is shown in the Figure 3.

GAO considers the emphasis on selection of projects based on an accurate assessment of customer needs to be especially important because otherwise there is a great "risk" that the project will focus on "issues that customers do not consider important or disrupt processes that are already working well and accepted by users." In other words, planners should not just assume that new e-government applications are demanded by citizens. The same GAO (2003a) analysis looked at the plans for these projects and found that most had adopted certain best practices such as clear cost estimates, milestones and specified deliverables. But only 16 out of 24 of the plans contained information on how staffing commitments would be obtained and only 9 out of 24 had a strategy for obtaining funds for the project.

The National Electronic Commerce Coordinating Council (NEC3) developed an outline of a sound e-government business case (2001) and its analysis overlaps the GAO categories to a substantial extent. But it also includes the following additional factors:

Copyright © 2006, Idea Group Inc. Copying or distributing in print or electronic forms without written permission of Idea Group Inc. is prohibited.

Figure 3. GAO analysis of completeness of e-government business cases

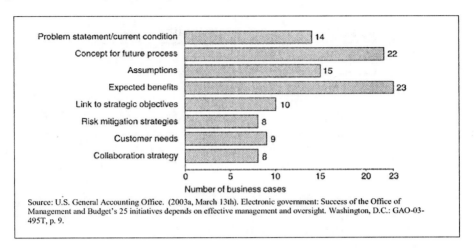

Source: U.S. General Accounting Office. (2003a, March 13th). Electronic government: Success of the Office of Management and Budget's 25 initiatives depends on effective management and oversight. Washington, D.C.: GAO-03-495T, p. 9.

(1) Estimated costs including both developmental and operational as well as their timing; (2) The extent of potential customer usage of the application; (3) Planned marketing efforts; and (4) Potential funding methods. They cite the difficulty of measuring benefits due to the fact that some of the benefits are intangible, such as the value of enhanced service delivery resulting from customers' savings of time. Often improved customer access also saves the government money as in the case (NEC3, 2004, p.6) of providing child care providers access to an Internet billing process because the project eliminated costs of mailing and data entry for some 90,000 child care providers in Michigan. They cite the importance of obtaining stakeholder support and recommend that customers be involved in all phases of the project and that a communications plan be developed to reach the multiple stakeholders. They also note the differences between public and private e-commerce business cases. Private sector organizations can justify expensive Customer Relations Management programs due to their expected impact on market advantages while the benefits of these applications for public sector organizations would involve intangibles such as more positive "images" of government (NEC3, 2001, p. 10).

I have not come across many specific business cases for local governments, although the elements of the business case for e-government are sometimes contained in their IT and e-government plans. One example is Oakland County's (Michigan) business case for the charging of fees (Pardee, 2000, p. 48-49) in which it identified the following benefits for citizens and the county government: (1) Greater access to government information; (2) Access to information on a 24/7 basis; and (3) Savings due to elimination of travel time and costs. The benefits for the government include: 1) Reduction in the over-the-counter requests for public records and thus decreased labor costs; 2) Less need for office space and records storage due to electronic imaging of documents; and 3) Funding for infrastructure (hardware, software, data preparation and programming) would be provided by user fees.

Copyright © 2006, Idea Group Inc. Copying or distributing in print or electronic forms without written permission of Idea Group Inc. is prohibited.

Figure 4. Massachusetts electronic government initiative take-up rate assumptions

Customer	Year 1	Year 2	Year 3	Year 4	Year 5
Individuals	10%	15%	20%	25%	35%
Businesses	15%	20%	30%	40%	50%

Source: Adapted from State of Massachusetts. (2001, January 9). Massachusetts Electronic Government Initiative. Organizational support and governance workshop. Final Report. Retrieved June 18, 2004 from http://www.mass.gov/itd/massgov/publications/strategicplan/table_contents.htm

The expected benefits of e-government projects are not easy to calculate because they depend heavily on assumptions such as the adoption or *"take-up"* rate—that is, how fast citizens and other customers will employ the e-government method. For example, the Massachusetts (2001) e-government plan employed the assumptions about take-up rates shown in Figure 4.

The themes of low usage rates and failures are prominent in early e-government literature. Low usage rates are not uncommon according to a report by Northrop (2004). For example, two municipalities that I know had online billing functions for water billing had low usage rates of less than 2%. The Council for Excellence in Government's survey (2003) found interest in using e-government transactions but up until now information-seeking dominated, even in so-called "best practice" areas:

Nearly two-thirds (63%) of e-government users report using government Web sites generally to find information such as an office address or a list of services provided by an agency, whereas only a quarter (23%) log on to conduct a transaction such as filing their taxes or renewing their driver's license. Even in best practice areas, where more transactional options are available, only one in four (28%) e-government users say that they tend to conduct transactions rather than just search for information. (p. 7)

How can governments improve take-up rates? Wang's (2002) analysis of use of online tax filing systems in Taiwan verified a model called the *"Technology Acceptance Model (TAM)"* that many IT researchers have employed to predict adoption rates of end-user technologies. The TAM model focuses on the perceived usefulness and ease of use as causal variables that affect usage. Wang revised the TAM model to include perceived credibility (i.e., concerning the confidence of the users in the privacy of information provided over the Internet) to help explain the use of e-government. Wang also found that an important underlying causal factor was the citizen's sense of computer self-efficacy. Although a high sense of efficacy made citizens somewhat more distrustful of government's handling of information, it nevertheless had an overall positive impact on usage due to its positive impacts on perceived usefulness and ease of use. As the general population becomes more computer proficient and as broadband usage expands, there should be steady increases in take-up rates.

The State of Texas's OnLine Authority (2002b) has provided some of the few detailed data about adoption rates of e-government applications. Overall, the Texas OnLine Authority (2002b, p. 10) states that visits to the state Web portal have increased "exponentially." E-payment transactions have also increased but not as fast as general visits to the Web site (see Texas OnLine Authority, 2000b, p. 11). Texas OnLine (2002b,

Copyright © 2006, Idea Group Inc. Copying or distributing in print or electronic forms without written permission of Idea Group Inc. is prohibited.

p. 16) has also provided data on the adoption rates of e-government registrations for licenses that have been put online—the adoption rate is defined as the ratio of online transactions to total "eligible transactions" (see Figure 5).

There are large differences in adoption rates. The Texas OnLine Report notes that one major reason for variation in rates is due to the aggressiveness with which the online systems are marketed. For example, the applications with the highest rates (Savings and Loan and Department of Public Safety) were very active in their marketing efforts. Among the market strategies employed by Texas were the following: (1) Radio and TV public service announcements; (2) Press conferences by the governor emphasizing the online services; (3) Securing media coverage statewide; (4) Joint funding (with American Express) advertising campaign; (5) Usage of posters; and (6) Development of a systematic communications plan. The term *"branding"* is used to describe efforts to make customers more aware and more likely to use e-commerce and other e-government services. Texas OnLine conducted some user surveys to discover how end users found out about the online transactions. The largest single group report that they found out about it from renewal notices. Other common sources cited were agency Web sites, search engines, libraries, and teachers. O'Looney (2000, p. 69) states that the e-government's Web site URL should be put on every printed communication from the government and also be advertised on government's cable, public access channels and even recommends the use of billboards.

One approach to increase usage is to make online services free but charge for in-person copies. For example, Conyers (Georgia) charges $3 for an accident report obtained in person at City Hall (Perlman, 2001) but provides the report free online. The logic for this approach is that the online report costs much less for the government to produce but most governments have been unwilling to take such steps to encourage online processing for

Figure 5. Texas OnLine Authority status report: estimated adoption rates (FY 2002)

Application	Adoption Rate
Nurses Board License Renewal	3.4%
Licensed Chemical Dependency Counselor Renewal	4.1%
Veterinary Board License Renewal	6.0%
Department of Insurance Agents License Renewal	9.3%
Real Estate Commission License Renewal	23.2%
Savings and Loan License Renewal	44.0%
Department of Public Safety Drive License Renewal	12.7%
Department of Public Safety Concealed Handgun License	27.3%
Department of Public Safety Driver Records	71.9%
Department of Transportation Vehicle Registration Renewal	1.0%
City of Mesquite Property Tax	0.1%
City of Mesquite Ticket Pay	0.2%
City of Dallas Water Bill Payment	0.2%
City of Houston Ticket Pay	0.6%
Travis County Property Tax	1.2%
Source: Adapted from State of Texas. Texas OnLine Authority. (2002b). Texas OnLine 2002 status report: Progress and efficiencies gained, p. 16. Retrieved July 4, 2004 from http://www.dir.state.tx.us/egov/	

Copyright © 2006, Idea Group Inc. Copying or distributing in print or electronic forms without written permission of Idea Group Inc. is prohibited.

e-commerce applications, though governments may charge for producing paper documents that are available online free. To summarize, the enthusiasm of many managers for the potential of e-government should not blind them to the need for careful planning and realistic estimates concerning usage rates. Likewise, governments need to do marketing and take other measures to increase take-up rates.

Governments also need to be aware that they have several options with respect to implementing e-commerce applications such as: (1) Governments may do the e-government function directly themselves; (2) They may contract with a third part to implement e-governmental transactions or they may contract to have a vendor develop the Web portal but take over administration once it is completed; (3) They may enter into a partnership with a third party in which they share revenues; (4) Governments may use services offered by other levels of government—for example, many states offer e-government transactions to local governments; and (5) Governments may enter into deals with electronic billing services offered by private organizations such as TransPoint (Newcombe, 1999) that offer bill-paying services for a variety of organizations, including governments. Governments with substantial IT resources may develop much if not all of their e-government infrastructure such as Fairfax County in Virginia did (Perlman, 2000). Those with few resources are likely to depend heavily on vendors like Conyers, Georgia (Perlman, 2001), a local government of 8,000 people that implemented an e-government system. This expansion in alternatives is important because it offers the potential for governments with very limited IT resources to engage in transaction services that were generally limited until recently to high-resource agencies.

The issues that I discuss in the purchasing chapter concerning contract issues are relevant here for e-government projects. For example, there have been cases of e-gov contractors going out of business or opting out of contracts if the e-gov venture does not work out financially for them. So the contract should be written to deal with such possibilities including ownership of data. Richardson (2004) cites studies that show the high risk of e-government failures are due to factors such as shaky relationships with e-government vendors. The State of Indiana's CIO (Perlman, 2001), Laura Larimer, also notes that multi-year contracts (the norm for e-government vendor contracts) should emphasize flexibility:

"If I were looking at outsourcing today," she says, "I would look at how to develop a contract such that I have room to move toward developments I can't even foresee today."

Some major e-government vendors have gone out of business (Perlman, 2001) and other vendors have made major policy changes (e.g., from a self-supporting to one based on maintenance and licensing fees) so the legal details of the contract are crucial to the success of e-gov applications.

These "free" deals in which partners take on the risk and provide funding for the e-government infrastructure are attractive to government which inherently tends to be risk averse. However, even those involved in such efforts would like to see some more rigorous analysis as to whether the deals make sense for government as the CIO of Maryland notes (Perlman, 2000):

Copyright © 2006, Idea Group Inc. Copying or distributing in print or electronic forms without written permission of Idea Group Inc. is prohibited.

Maryland's CIO Moore would like to see a thorough cost analysis done on the merits of a government [service] being set up for free by a company that then earns its money by helping the government do its business. 'I might want to spend $1 million if the return on my investment is really large,' she points out. 'I would rather put that back in the state than give it to private companies. As sites grow, transactions grow. It might be worth a million dollars.' (p. 32)

She goes on to note that these kinds of cost analyses have not been done. Many governments have limited IT staff and consequently outsourcing of e-government is viewed as a necessity. For example, Cobb County (Georgia) outsourced an online traffic ticket application that quickly obtained a 17% participation rate that helped to decrease lines at the county offices (Perlman, 2001). If the county had to wait for its IT staff to do the project, it would have been a "long wait" according to officials.

Conformance with state laws and politics may also be an issue in e-government planning. For example, the General Assembly of Virginia would not allow the state to enter into an "expensive partnership" with a private vendor, so the state had to come up with its innovative contract with AMS based on the assumption that both the vendor and state could make money due to increased revenue collections.

E-Government Planning and Enterprise Architectures

One of the major emphases of planning for e-government is the adoption of an *enterprise architecture*. An article in Federal Computer Week (Michael, 2004) characterized the Federal Enterprise Architecture as a "map" documenting the organization's technology investments. GAO's Director of Architecture Systems (Randolph Hite) argues that without an enterprise architecture, a government will have "stovepipe systems" and "disparate, non-integrated solutions." In the chapter on planning for IT, I employed Raumer's (2001) definition of enterprise architecture as "values and preferences" employed that guide information technology decisions. Goethals and Vandenbulcke (2005) point out that the concept necessarily implies restriction of choices:

If standards are not desirable or available, another form of coordination is needed. The discipline called enterprise architecture is gaining momentum in this context. Basically, an enterprise architecture fulfills the same role as a standard.... It restricts the choices of people (where needed) in order to make sure everything will fit together well once everything is implemented. (p. 12)

In many cases, architecture is thought of as the establishment of common hardware and software platforms, but it also can include policy and management prescriptions. North Carolina's enterprise architecture (Jenkins, 2003) includes three principles: (1) The

Copyright © 2006, Idea Group Inc. Copying or distributing in print or electronic forms without written permission of Idea Group Inc. is prohibited.

primary design point is to facilitate change; (2) Business processes should drive technical solutions; and (3) Data is a governmental asset that must be protected. North Carolina's enterprise architecture standards include: (1) TCP/IP, (2) Ethernet, (3) ANSI SQL, (4) Best Practices, and (5) 3/N Tier or Service Oriented Architectures and the general use of avoidance of the use of extensions that create vendor lock-in.

By establishing enterprise-wide standards, governments can more easily achieve some of the prescriptive goals of e-government such as sharing and integration of information. Since many e-government applications tend to be cross-agency in nature and involve secure transactions, it is important to have enterprise-wide standards in place before implementing specific e-government measures. There are also infrastructure standards that are especially important to many e-government applications such as online transactions including the establishment of credit card payment capability and associated policies, technologies to support secure transactions such as public key infrastructure, and the establishment of common software standards for e-government applications such as forms (North Carolina Information Resource Commission, 2001).

The Federal government began developing its *Federal Enterprise Architecture* (FEA) model in February of 2002. This effort is being led by part of OMB known as FEAPMO (Federal Enterprise Architecture Program Management Office). The purposes of the FEA is to create a "citizen-centered" and "results-oriented" government and it is aimed not just at technological issues but also at allowing cross-agency budget and performance-reporting systems to reduce duplicative investments and identify gaps and opportunities for collaboration among agencies. FEAPMO contends that "in contrast to many failed architecture efforts in the past that the FEA will be successful because it is entirely business-driven." The FEA consists of several interrelated "reference models" which together constitute a combination of business and technological analyses. For example, the Business Reference Model (BRM) identifies common *"lines of business"* of government; and the Performance Reference Model identifies standards measures of output (see www.feapmo.gov/fea.asp for more detailed descriptions). GAO (2004) has provided a capsule description of the components of the FEA in figure 6.

The core of the effort so far has been the *Business Reference model* which has gone through two versions (1.0 and 2.0). The basic logic of this model is to categorize all federal government activities into functions and more detailed "sub-functions" as FEAPMO points out in their discussion of the V2.0 model (FEAPMO, 2003):

One of the key features of the President's 2003 E-Government Strategy is the integration of IT investments across agencies around common users of government services and technologies (i.e., individuals, businesses, other governments or federal employees). The Business Reference Model provides the underlying foundation to support this cross-agency integration of IT investment and service delivery. The "functional" (as opposed to organizational) framework that characterizes the BRM provides a new way of thinking about the government's services and the functional commonalities that exist across organizations. (p. 24)

By analyzing all federal agencies by this common model, it is expected that they will be able to identify opportunities for technological savings by identifying agencies with

Copyright © 2006, Idea Group Inc. Copying or distributing in print or electronic forms without written permission of Idea Group Inc. is prohibited.

Figure 6. Federal enterprise architecture reference models

Reference model	Description	Status
Performance reference model	Provides a common set of general performance outputs and measures for agencies to use to achieve business goals and objectives.	Version 1.0 released in September 2000
Business reference model	Describes the hierarchy of federal business operations independent of the agencies that perform them including delivering the services provided to state & local governments	Version 2.0 released in June 2000
Service component model	Identifies and classifies IT service (i.e., application) components that support federal business operations and promotes the reuse of components across agencies.	Version 1.0 released in June 2000.
Data and information reference model	Is intended to describe, at an aggregate level, the data and information types that support program and business line operations and the hierarchical relationships among these types.	Release planned in 2004.
Technical reference model	Describes technology that is to support the delivery of service components including relevant standards for implementing the technology.	Version 1.1 released in August 2003.
Source: U.S. General Accounting Office. (2004a, May 19). Information Technology: The Federal Enterprise Architecture and Agencies' Enterprise Architectures Are Still Maturing. Washington, D.C.: GAO-04-798T, p. 7.		

similar functions that can share software. The agencies may save money on deals with vendors and on a common support staff. Likewise, these models may identify agencies that are serving the same clientele and thus support cross-agency technological collaborations such as to create "virtual agencies" that provide a unified Web site (e.g., a "one-stop portal") for these customers rather than have them contact agencies individually to obtain services. OMB requires each agency to analyze its operation using these reference models so that top management can identify such opportunities for saving and sharing on IT investments as pointed out in FEAPMO's BRM V2.0 (2003) analysis:

Each September, once agencies have submitted their budget requests, OMB analysts will map all IT investment business cases (Exhibit 300s) against the BRM to identify possible redundancies and additional opportunities for collaboration. OMB budget examiners will leverage these mappings during the fall review process in order to facilitate their own cross-agency analyses and to determine the best way to invest funds to achieve performance outcomes. The result will be the identification of opportunities to save money by taking advantage of the economies of scale offered by cross-

Copyright © 2006, Idea Group Inc. Copying or distributing in print or electronic forms without written permission of Idea Group Inc. is prohibited.

organizational collaboration and to improve and simplify the delivery of services to the citizen. (p. 25)

It is important to emphasize the point that the FEA and BRM are not primarily techno-logical in their focus, but constitute managerial tools emphasizing an enterprise-wide perspective. The assumption is that this approach will lead to more efficient and effective performance. GAO (2004a) has analyzed the FEA and its implementation by various federal departments and agencies. Its report argues that FEA is currently more akin to a "classification scheme" and is not sufficiently articulated and consistent to be an enterprise architecture. It also notes that departments have achieved varying levels of success with 50% attaining a "foundation for effective enterprise management." Among the criteria that GAO (GAO, 2004a, p. 26) uses to assess departmental and agency maturity with respect to FEA include criteria such as whether metrics exist for measuring enterprise architecture benefits and many departments lack such metrics.

Enterprise Architecture Examples Involving U.S. Department of Labor and Other agencies

The FEA and BRM are both fairly abstract documents and it is instructive to consider a substantive example to illustrate some of the potential issues and how they can assist in an e-government solution. One example of the potential application of the FEA and BRM concerns job training programs. There are a large number of such programs that are funded by several federal departments with the Department of Labor being considered the "lead" agency or "managing partner" (e.g., the Adult Work Program, Dislocated Worker Program, Job Corps, Senior Community Service Employment Program, and many others) for this function. But job training programs are also offered by the Department of Education (the Vocational Rehabilitation Program, Adult Education and Literacy, Perkins Vocational Education Program), the Department of Health and Human Services (its Community Service block grant program supports job training and employment as well as other activities), and Department of Housing and Urban Development (it offers employment and training programs for residents of assisted housing) (see below for full listing of programs). This wide array of programs can be confusing not only to potential customers but also to government workers serving this population. Consequently, the Workforce Investment Act (WIA) law requires that 17 of these programs (U.S. G.A.O., 2004, p. 9) cooperate in a "one-stop center" as shown in figure 7.

Thus an e-government goal would be to offer a "virtual agency" one-stop portal for citizens to access who want to find out about eligibility and other information concerning job training and employment programs. Likewise, there has been an effort to identify common performance measures that cut across programs and also how the same data source (e.g., unemployment insurance records) could provide many of the outcome measures needed to assess the success of the program (U.S.G.A.O., 2004, p. 8). Consequently data can be shared among agencies as shown in Figure 8 since many use the same measures and the data are often from the same sources.

Copyright © 2006, Idea Group Inc. Copying or distributing in print or electronic forms without written permission of Idea Group Inc. is prohibited.

Figure 7. Workforce Investment Act's One Stop Partner Program & related federal agencies

Federal Agency	Mandatory One Stop Partner Programs
Department of Labor	WIA Adult
	WIA Youth
	WIA Dislocated Workers
	Employment Services (Wagner-Peyser)
	Trade Adjustment Assistance Programs
	Veterans Employment & Training Programs
	Unemployment Insurance
	Job Corps
	Welfare-to-Work grant-funded Program
	Senior Community Service Employment Program
	Employment & Training for Migrant & Seasonal Farm Workers
	Employment & Training for Native Americans
Department of Education	Vocational Rehabilitation Program
	Adult Education & Literacy
	Vocational Education (Perkins Act)
Department of Health and Human Services	Community Services Block Grant
Department of Housing and Urban Development (HUD)	HUD-administered employment & training
Source: U.S. General Accounting Office. (2004, June). Workforce investment act: States and local areas have developed strategies to assess performance, but Labor could do more to help, Washington, D.C.: GAO-04-657, p. 10.	

It is important to note that, although these job training programs are primarily funded by the federal government, in most cases, state and local governments run the day-to-day administration of these programs so the complexity is great and represents a challenge for e-government efforts.

The U.S. Department of Labor has been placed in charge of all "benefit" programs and has been identified as the "managing partner" to construct a comprehensive Web site (GovBenefits.gov) that will allow citizens to access easily all governmental assistance programs, not just job training efforts. This Web site is instructive in showing what portals can (and cannot do). For example, when I visited the site and typed in "job training" into the keyword search option on the initial page (on July 1, 2004), I got a huge list of programs but they were not restricted to job training and thus the listing was not very useful. When I used another search option available on the GovBenefits.gov site, the "browse by category" option, I got more useful, selective information and I was forwarded to another search site (http://www.servicelocator.org/) that did allow me to access specific information on education and training effort programs available in my home community. Thus this Web portal currently functions as a "front-end" to other Web sites that have the required information. Labor's e-government plan states that its long-term "vision is to allow customers to apply for benefits online through a streamlined process."

Below, I have outlined some elements that it would be desirable to have in an e-government plan that emphasizes an Enterprise Architecture using the Labor Department's plan (and a few others) as examples:

Copyright © 2006, Idea Group Inc. Copying or distributing in print or electronic forms without written permission of Idea Group Inc. is prohibited.

Figure 8. Data sources for Workforce Investment Act-funded programs

Program	Performance measures	UI wage records	Supplemental data allowed	Other, such as educational data or survey
Adult	1.Entered employment rate	•	•	
	2.Employment retention rate at 6 months	•	•	
	3.Average earnings change in 6 months	•		
	4.Entered employment and credential rate	•	•	•
Dislocated worker	5.Entered employment rate	•	•	
	6.Employment retention rate at 6 months	•	•	
	7.Earnings replacement rate in 6 months	•		
	8.Entered employment and credential rate	•	•	•
Youth (age 19-21)	9.Entered employment rate	•	•	•
	10. Employment retention rate at 6 months	•	•	•
	11.Average earnings change in 6 months	•		•
	12.Entered employment/education/training and credential rate	•	•	•
Youth (age 14-18)	13.Skill attainment			•
	14.Diploma or equivalent			•
	15.Placement and retention rate	•	•	•
All programs	16.Customer satisfaction for participants			•
	17.Customer satisfaction for employers			•

Source: U.S. General Accounting Office. (2004, June). Workforce Investment Act: States and local areas have developed strategies to assess performance, but Labor could do more to help. Washington, D.C.: GAO-04-657, p. 8.

1. **Establish general goals and principles to guide the specific activities**: For example, the stated goals in Labor's e-government plan conform tightly with the prescriptive aspects of e-government that we discussed earlier: (a) "We are customer-centric, not organization-centric," (b) "We communicate with customers and know who they are and what they want," (c) "We seek transformation opportunities through innovation rather than automation," (d) "We simplify our business processes and reduce costs through integrating or eliminating redundant systems, thereby making it easier for our customers to do business with the Department," (e) "We integrate information technology investment decisions with business and program requirements, processes, and goals," (f) "We collect information from our customers only once, and reuse it appropriately," (g) "We provide a secure environment, with appropriate privacy protections, for our customers to conduct transactions with the Department," (h) "We leverage partnerships with customers, governments, and the private sector to improve the delivery of services to customers."

2. **Comprehensively identify all customers of the agency and conduct a systematic analysis of the needs of these stakeholders:** In attempting to become a "customer-centric agency," many e-government plans mention their intention to develop customer relationship management (CRM) programs. A first step to implement CRM is to fully identify all of the customers of the organization in order to recognize the diversity of their customers and how their needs vary. In the Labor Department's case, they make the following observations about customers:

A small business owner in Connecticut needs advice about retirement savings options; a Gulf War veteran in Oregon would like to know about Federal job preferences for veterans; a young man in New York seeks an opportunity for a new beginning and help in finding gainful employment; a doctor treating a patient in Michigan provides the

Copyright © 2006, Idea Group Inc. Copying or distributing in print or electronic forms without written permission of Idea Group Inc. is prohibited.

patient with a form to send to his insurance company to cover the cost of the procedure; a grape grower in California has a question about migrant worker housing and transportation requirements; an employer in Kansas wants to find out about potential hazards at her work site to improve occupational safety and health management systems; a new father in Maryland wants to know if he is eligible for family leave. All of these people rely on the Department of Labor (DOL or The Department) to help them meet a specific need or accomplish a particular objective: they are among DOL's customers.

Most agencies have a wide variety of customers—many of whose priorities and goals may be in conflict as the stakeholder analysis will reveal. For example, the U. S. Department of Energy's (DOE's) E-government Strategic Action (2003) Plan divides their customers into the following categories: (1) DOE employees including retirees and contractors; (2) The American public who they sub-categorize into the energy concerned (most concerned about price), energy efficient (those want to improve efficiency of their energy use), environmentally conscious, and transportation conscious, voting public, persons with limited access (to the Internet), disabled, low literacy individuals, local residents of DOE facilities, and indigenous communities; (3) Energy community; (4) Scientific community, (4) Environmental community; (5) Educational community; (6) News organizations; (7) Representatives of federal, state, and local governments; and (8) The international community with an interest in U.S. energy policy. This stakeholder analysis demonstrates the difficulty that an agency like DOE faces because some of their constituencies have conflicting priorities.

3. **Identify the lead and partner agencies in inter-agency projects but be aware that these designations could have political implications:** As noted above, the Department of Labor was recognized as "the managing partner" for the Gov.Benefits.com project. Based on organizational theory, we would expect agencies to want to have the leadership role as much as possible in programmatic activities that overlap other agency activities. Although the BRM currently is being used to create "virtual agencies" where their efforts are combined through Web portals, there is clearly the possibility that at some time, reorganization efforts may be made to formally integrate these shared activities under a single agency and thus the designation of lead agency (or managing partner) could have implications for who would be in charge of the reorganized system with implications for agency budgets and job security. The Labor Department plan notes that it was mandated to create the DisabilityInfo.gov Web site in 60 days in response to a memorandum by President Bush in August 2002. One can see how e-government activities can take on a high political and policy preference in such situations.

4. **Develop a plan for dealing with other levels of governments in intergovernmental projects:** As we noted above, Labor's programs are primarily implemented by local and state agencies. Thus Labor's e-government plan states that it is the first federal agency to try to implement its own "federated enterprise architecture" in a decentralized environment. Thus the Labor Department is developing its own architecture that distinguishes between "universal and unique functions" within the Labor Department's own array of programs and activities that it holds sway

Copyright © 2006, Idea Group Inc. Copying or distributing in print or electronic forms without written permission of Idea Group Inc. is prohibited.

over. The implication appears to be that universal functions appear to require cross-agency collaboration and integration while "unique" functions are totally "owned" by a single agency. The Labor Department can use its control over funding as an incentive to achieve its intergovernmental goals. In other e-government projects, the lack of funding or other incentives can be an obstacle. For example, the GAO (2003b, p. 28) reviewed the Department of Interior's initiative to create a "geo-spatial one-stop" and found that many state and local governments did not participate because they did not perceive any incentive to do so.

5. A general goal for all e-government projects is to **"minimize the burden on respondents and the cost of data collection for departmental agencies."** This goal may be achievable thanks to the help of the integrated management of data that we have talked about before and is effectively stated in the 2005 Fairfax County's (Virginia) Strategic Technology Plan that has as one of its fundamental principles: "Capture data once in order to avoid cost, duplication of effort and potential for error and share the data whenever possible. Establish and use common data and common databases to the fullest extent."

6. **Customer trust in security and privacy of transactions is crucial**: Most of the e-government plans I reviewed devoted significant attention to security and privacy issues. The Department of Labor's Plan makes the point that developing a credible security and privacy framework is a key to the success of e-government. I would expect high usage rates only if citizens and other customers have confidence to use security and privacy of the information they provide. Labor is attempting to demonstrate their credibility by showing their compliance with the National Institute of Standards Technology Self-Assessment Guide as well as conducting a vulnerability guide and the implementation of a computer security awareness program. They are also implementing a Public Key Infrastructure and smart cards as well as planning to use the Internal Revenue Service's (IRS's) privacy reference survey to see how well they are adhering to widely accepted privacy practices.

7. **Funding for interdepartmental and interagency projects need special attention.** Labor's plan briefly discusses funding issues and notes that it expected to obtain adequate funds from sources such as the "Presidential budget crosscut" and the "Enterprise Architecture Budget crosscut." Clearly funding sources that pertain specifically to interagency efforts are necessary to encourage the kind of prescriptive business process reengineering that is supposed to be at the heart of e-government. But, according to a recent report (Daft, 2004), $345 million was authorized for E-Gov Act projects, but the Administration asked only for $90 million and Congress appropriated only $8 million with the conclusion that Congress has trouble understanding the value of supporting "cross-agency initiatives."

8. Many important e-government projects can **improve internal processes** such as establishing intranets for better communication. Labor's plan outlines a number of other e-government efforts including those aimed at improving internal management processes. One is the plan to implement an integrated human resources and payroll system (They refer to it as the "Peoplepower" system employing Peoplesoft's Federal Human Resources System). Labor also has an "e-laws" system to provide information about Federal employment laws for its employees (http://www.dol.gov/elaws/

Copyright © 2006, Idea Group Inc. Copying or distributing in print or electronic forms without written permission of Idea Group Inc. is prohibited.

9. **E-government plans need to emphasize the need for multi-modal communication outlets to its customers including possible in-person communication.** For example, their call center vision is aimed at developing a "coordinated customer relationship management (CRM) approach using several media, or "channels," including phone, fax, Web, e-mail, regular mail, and in-person fieldwork. People with less income tend to use the Web and e-mail less and agencies with large numbers of working poor (like Labor) as customers need to pay particular attention to this issue.

10. **E-government can reduce transaction costs, eliminate "middlemen," and empower citizens with better information.** The 2001-2005 e-government plan of the U.S. Department of Housing and Urban Development (HUD) brings out other issues that e-government planners face. It argues that e-gov applications cut the costs of "middlemen" (transaction costs) and thus makes irrelevant physical barriers between buyers and sellers and cuts search costs such as for first-time homebuyers. Thus e-government in the housing area can lead to transformative effects such as reducing the need for real estate agents and brokers but replaces them with "integrators" from the private sector who try to provide a package of needs for HUD's (2001-2005 E-government Plan) customers:

As the traditional roles of middlemen shift, the industry is experiencing a rise in independent third-party players serving as 'aggregators' and 'integrators' of information and resources that bring suppliers, contractors, brokers, and lenders under one umbrella. Both savvy middle players in the housing market and completely new enterprises now offer comprehensive, end-to-end solutions for home buying, furnishings and home improvement, securing apartments, moving, construction and repairs, financial management, insurance, and processing consumer loans and commercial securities. (p. 10)

11. **Governmental organizations often must decide what should be the focus of their Web portals and how their portals should relate to private sector portals that contain potentially valuable information for citizens.** For example, HUD's plan included the short-term goal of setting up a Web portal for First Time Home Buyers but, one of the issues that HUD runs into is that the private sector has Web sites that provide a huge amount of relevant information and thus the issue is how government's Web portal should relate to these Web sites. The HUD Strategic E-Government plan refers to the strong "branding" that private sector companies had already achieved: (1) Consumers' trust in large brand names such as Homestore.com and Microsoft Home Advisor limits successful marketing by independent service providers; (2) The online housing industry relies on strategic partnerships with top-rated portals such as Excite, America Online, Netscape, Go Network, and Lycos to drive traffic to their sites. This issue can be difficult because government is generally reluctant to endorse particular private systems but in this case, the most popular housing-related market sites are in the private sector. It is an issue that other levels of government may face in dealing with issues such as economic development.

Copyright © 2006, Idea Group Inc. Copying or distributing in print or electronic forms without written permission of Idea Group Inc. is prohibited.

The e-government Presidential Priority Initiatives (PPI) of the Bush Administration include a wide array of cross-agency e-government efforts in which one department is the lead or "managing partner" and gives insight into the broad scope and ambitiousness of the goals of e-government. They illustrate the kinds of projects where e-government is aimed at achieving a more "customer-centric" approach to service delivery and also ones that are likely to have some "transformative effects" if they are successful. As the Harvard Policy Group has noted (2001), these interorganizational projects present special difficulties because agencies inherently tend to favor projects that they have full control over. Thus the development of interagency projects requires skills that I discuss in the chapters on politics and leadership. I have listed some of these initiatives in figure 9.

One strategy to deal with cross-agency projects is illustrated in the case (Harvard Policy Group, 2001, p. 15) of New Jersey's attempt to build a social services e-government project involving more 800 social service agencies called "One Ease E-Link" (http://www.oel.state.nj.us/framesetpublic.html). According to the Harvard Policy Group, the key to success was beginning with a small project that could be expanded later but even with a small version, the project nevertheless nearly "died" when it was discovered how much financial and human resources would be required. However, the Harvard Policy Group says, the establishment of a small pilot project's success was able to be leveraged to obtain critical support from the governor and other political leaders. Nevertheless, even after succeeding in obtaining leadership support, the project's leader said that an "overly aggressive rollout" still resulted in some difficulties. In short, one of the key dilemmas with e-government projects as with all IT projects is how ambitious the project should be in its various stages. By keeping projects small and aiming for low-hanging fruit in the early stages, success is more likely but the tradeoff for such projects is that it leaves intact many of the underlying stovepipe systems and thus are less transformational. The sensitivity of the balancing act is reflected in the Harvard Policy Group's (2001b, p. 3) advice to avoid "over-cautious incrementalism" but also don't undertake "impulsive innovations" either.

Is the kind of analysis performed by the federal government and its FEA relevant to other levels of e-government and particularly to smaller governments? Some large local governments have created their own enterprise architectures and business reference models. For example, Fairfax County's (Virginia) 2005 IT Plan identifies three major business areas (services to citizens, support delivery of services, and Internal Operations) that are further subdivided into 35 lines of business that cut across agencies for its Business Reference Model. However, many of the local governments I interviewed have few employees, departments, and programs and they are not likely to see the need for a formal enterprise architecture system similar to the FEA. However, there remain areas where various local governments including counties, municipalities, school systems, and other units (e.g., townships, independent parks and recreation departments) can make their operations more customer-centric through studying overlapping functions and perhaps creating unified, one-stop Web portals. Likewise, there are some internal processes that form the basis for common functions and vendor software. For example, Fairfax County plans to integrate several inspection systems that will cover the activities performed by the Health, Tax, Planning and Zoning, and Fire departments.

Copyright © 2006, Idea Group Inc. Copying or distributing in print or electronic forms without written permission of Idea Group Inc. is prohibited.

Figure 9. Selected cross-agency federal e-government projects

GovBenefits.gov Managing Partner: Department of Labor (DOL) Partners: SSA, VA, HUD, USDA, State, HHS, FEMA, DOE, & ED Description: Access to Information on government benefit programs and services through a common Internet Website.
One-Stop Business Compliance Managing Partner: Small Business Administration (SBA) Partners: DOL, EPA, IRS, DOT, EEOC, DOC, FERC, & SEC Description: Provides a common Internet site through which businesses can easily access information about laws and regulations.
USA Services Managing Partner: Government Services Administration (GSA) Partners: DOL, SSA, VA, HHS, ED, USDA, FEMA, and SBA Description: Provides citizens with more coordinated customer services across Federal agencies through different communications (Internet, e-mail, fax, etc.)
Online Rulemaking Managing Partner: Environmental Protection Administration Partners: DOL, DOT, USDA, GSA, HHS, and FCC Description: Creates a common Internet site for all Federal regulatory material, to help the public find and comment on proposed rules.
eGrants Managing Partner: Department of Health and Human Services (HHS) Partners: DOL, NSF, DOD/ONR, ED< HUD, DOT, & DOJ Description: Creates common Internet site through which customers access grant information and provides electronic application and processing of grants.
Integrated Acquisition Environment Managing Partner: Government Service Administration (GSA) Partners: DOL, DOT, DOD, & GSA Description: Creates a common Internet site to support electronic acquisition of goods and services by all Federal agencies.
eTraining Managing Partner: Office of Personnel Management (OPM) Partners: DOL, DOT, DOD, & GSA Description: Creates a common Internet site to consolidate training capabilities across the Federal government.
E-records Management Managing Partner: NARA Partners: GSA, DOE/NRC, DOC/NOAA, DOC/PTO, & VA Description: Helps Federal agencies better manage electronic records through common requirements and standards.
Source: Adapted from U.S. Department of Labor. E-Government Strategic Plan. Appendix B. Retrieved June 9, 2004 from http://www.dol.gov/_sec/e_government_plan/egov_stratplan_toc.htm

Implementation Issues

Organizational and political issues are likely to be especially important in e-government efforts that involve interdepartmental or intergovernmental projects. Fountain (2001a) provides detailed case studies of how organizations resisted e-government projects. For example, in the attempt to build a "seamless" International Trade Data System (ITDS), there needed to be "standardization of data definitions, practices, and information systems" across the three agencies involved: customs, transportation, and immigration (Fountain, 2001a, p. 141). However, the Department of Transportation desired to have a decentralized approach because they had different systems for the north and south borders of the U.S. Another finding of Fountain's case study is that the Customs Agency

Copyright © 2006, Idea Group Inc. Copying or distributing in print or electronic forms without written permission of Idea Group Inc. is prohibited.

emphasized the goals of its business customers while the Food and Drug Administration was more focused on citizens and this difference led to conflict in the e-government effort. The outcome was strongly influenced by the "iron triangle" formed by a coalition among Congressional committees, agencies, and interest groups (Fountain, 2001a, p. 145). Thus a primary step to successful implementation is to secure the needed political and organizational support. The continued importance of organizational and political factors is reflected in GAO's (2004a, p. 32) analysis of the obstacles that agencies encountered in trying to implement e-government—the percentage citing challenges increased from 2001 to 2003 as shown in Figure 10.

Fletcher (2004) is among those who cite the crucial importance of securing top management support for the success of any IT investments. Early e-government adopters generally have a champion among the top generalist managers. Stowers discusses how San Carlos (California) had an assistant manager (Brian Moura) who was the driving force behind the city's early entry into e-commerce that enabled them to establish an early Web presence in 1994. Cook et al. (2002) also cite the importance of learning from other projects, trying to get buy-in from those who can stop you, and the persistence and realization that complex projects will take a long time to implement.

Project management skills are an important component for any successful project as outlined in the chapter on procurement. The Massachusetts e-government plan is an example of one that calls for the development of project management skills to assist in the implementation of e-government projects. It cites the importance of establishing milestones and provides an example of a "roadmap" for implementation. Project management skills are important given the complexity of many e-government projects.

In planning implementation of e-government, it is important for governments to systematically analyze the need for e-government. Some governments conduct *SWOT* (Strengths-Weaknesses-Opportunities-Threats) analyses. For example, Mecklenburg County's 2002 (pp. 4-6) e-government plan contains a SWOT analysis that identifies several strengths including the following: (1) There was an identified e-government "champion;" (2) Employees had demonstrated initiative for exploring new and better ways of providing services; (3) The potential for expanding partnerships for city/county customer services; and (4) The foundation of employee knowledge, skills and abilities. Their listed weaknesses include: (1) The organization of service delivery is by department and not integrated for customer benefits and productivity; (2) Customers have found poor

Figure 10. Challenges to implementing federal enterprise architecture

Management Challenge	Percentage of Agencies that Frequently Identified Management Challenge	
	2001 Survey	2003 Survey
Fostering top management understanding	30	50
Overcoming Parochialism	30	47
Fostering Understanding	50	50
Obtaining Skilled Staff	32	49
Source: U.S. General Accounting Office. (2004, May 19). Information Technology: The Federal Enterprise Architecture and Agencies' Enterprise Architectures Are Still Maturing. Washington, D.C.: GAO-04-798T, p. 32.		

Copyright © 2006, Idea Group Inc. Copying or distributing in print or electronic forms without written permission of Idea Group Inc. is prohibited.

organization of Internet information and can't find what they are looking for; (3) Web, TV, and phone technologies are not integrated; (4) Lack of information in databases hampers efforts to provide timely information to customers; (5) There is a lack of customer self-service options; (6) There is limited marketing of county information sources; and (7) There is a lack of staff assigned to e-government initiatives. Their threats and barriers included the following: (1) Lack of funding and resources; (2) Continued departmental silos and "turf protection"; (3) Lack of dedicated staff in e-government; (4) Reluctance to change processes; (5) Lack of buy-in from the public board on investment in e-government; (6) Possible loss of e-government champion; (7) Paralysis by analysis; (8) Difficult relationship with the City of Charlotte; and (9) Neglecting relationship-building with other Mecklenburg municipalities.

How should e-government projects be implemented? Each organization has to decide how to organize its e-government effort. Complex projects require a variety of technical skills and knowledge but equally important are organizational and political skills and the will to exercise authority when necessary. According to Mecklenburg's 2002 e-government plan, the implementation is to be led by an executive assistant to the County Manager who will serve as the coordinator and "champion" of the plan. Other key actors will be the Communications and Information Management Group that controls Web content and an Applications Development Group as well as a stakeholder advisory group and the Information Services & Technology Department.

A key point that Stowers (2004b) makes in her case studies of San Carlos (Washington), and the State of Massachusetts's entry into e-commerce is the fact that these governments adopted an incremental approach, undertaking "small easy steps" first. She also demonstrates that smaller governments with limited resources like San Carlos can achieve innovative processes through use of shared resources. For example, San Carlos's initial e-commerce applications were on a server leased from the Association of Bay Area Governments and their efforts were also assisted by the help of a retired official from the City of Oakland recruited through a California League of Cities program that matches retired government officials with cities in need of advice (Stowers, 2004b, p. 21).

Web Site Design and Evaluation Issues

A tremendous amount has been written on the design of Web sites and portals and how to evaluate Web sites. Many if not most of e-government projects wind up on governmental Web sites (or internal Web sites known as intranets). My purpose here is to identify some of the key issues and ideas that practitioners and experts have evolved over the past decade since more governments have come to adopt Web sites. Web sites vary greatly in their design depending on the nature of their purposes and target groups. For example, sites that are aimed at doing training tend to be more linear in nature (Lynch & Horton, 2004), while those for general education would allow for more non-linear and flexible designs.

A basic step is to identify the intended users of a site. Most sites have multiple user groups and the identification of the full range of users is now crucial to the basic design

Copyright © 2006, Idea Group Inc. Copying or distributing in print or electronic forms without written permission of Idea Group Inc. is prohibited.

of the Web site. For example, many local governments now structure their Web sites so that there are links for categories such as for current residents, businesses, and visitors. The goal is to make it easy for each user to quickly find the content they are interested in. Sites have a variety of mechanisms to help users find their desired information such as search functions and indexes/maps of the Web site. The underlying premise of the e-government movement is that Web sites should be designed around the needs of customers and not by bureaucratic structures. On the other hand, it is useful to have multiple ways of finding material and a listing of departments and agencies will be desired by many users. It is instructive to look at Massachusetts' analysis of their own Web site into the categories based on the users that the pages are aimed at (Figure 11).

Some governmental Web pages also have political purposes as Franzel and Coursey (2004) have noted, and content favorable to the official heading the level of government may dominate the page. Some governmental sites (e.g., New Mexico) are beginning to allow citizens to *customize governmental Web sites* for the information that is most relevant to them and also have information follow users as they move from one page to another and thus avoid having to fill redundant information (Franzel & Coursey, 2004, p. 75).

Web site space is precious and organizations must decide how they shape the site. For example, some sites are now organized to be as *flat* as possible so that users have to perform a minimum number of clicks to get at the content they desire. For example, a "two-clicks" principle was employed in designing the www.geodata.gov Web site (Daukantas, 2003):

The portal was designed with the unofficial motto 'two clicks to content,' so that people can find data quickly, he said. 'We've really thought about the usability and worked very hard on it,' said Peter Bottenberg, a senior consultant with project contractor ESRI of Redlands, California.

A consistent and efficient interface and links to guide users around a Web site are important. One expert, Patrick Lynch, says that the top few inches on an organization's home page are the "most valuable real estate" of the Web site and deep thought needs

Figure 11. What groups are Web pages directed towards?

Customer Group	Percent of Pages Directed at Group
Residents	61%
Businesses	21%
Government	9%
State Employees	8%
Visitors	1%
Source: State of Massachusetts. (2001). Massachusetts Electronic Government Initiative. Organizational Support and Governance Workshop. Final Report. January 9. Retrieved 6/18/04 from http://www.mass.gov/itd/massgov/publications/strategicplan/table_contents.htm	

Copyright © 2006, Idea Group Inc. Copying or distributing in print or electronic forms without written permission of Idea Group Inc. is prohibited.

to be given to how to structure that area. There is disagreement over how "long" an individual Web page should be. The "Yale Guide" (Lynch and Forman, 2004) argues that less than 10% of novice users scroll below the top of Web pages and thus information needs to be provided in chunks with Web pages not consisting of more than 2 to 3 screensfull of information. Links to full length text (often in both PDF and HTML format) are provided with the size of the file indicated so that the end user can decide whether they want to download the file. Governments need to test the "usability" of Web pages such as through focus groups in which actual usage of the pages is studied and analyzed (Radosevich, 1997). Radosevich claims that such sessions reveal that users are willing to violate the rules that Web designers hold (e.g., she says that these sessions show that users are willing to go "below the fold of the page"). Designers cannot be sure how customers will use their sites based solely on assumptions. O'Looney (2000, p. 53) provides an example of a case where it was discovered that that applicants for services from a human services department were not completing an online application because some felt that they were being asked questions "that did not apply to them" or the application took too much time and interfered with their appointment. The agency increased usage by shortening the number of questions and also restructuring the online application so that it bypassed questions that did not apply.

In the early years, there was a great deal of variation in governmental Web sites with some Web site designers attempting to display their mastery of Web-design skills while others approached Web sites with minimalist designs. Over time, it seems to this author that variation has been reduced as Web-site designers recognize the need to be accessible to "the least common denominator"—i.e., a user with slow connections and little attraction for fancy graphics. The style of governmental Web pages tends to be understated with straightforward content. A minimum number of types of fonts and use of bolding is desirable according to the Yale Web Style Guide (Lynch and Horton, 2004):

The most effective designs for general Internet audiences use a careful balance of text and links with relatively small graphics. These pages load into browsers quickly, even when accessed from slow modems, yet still achieve substantial graphic impact."

However, individual Web sites or sub-pages of a Web site (e.g., aimed at a younger population) may have more high-powered graphics. As broadband connections become dominant, I would expect Web sites to employ more graphics and features such as video and audio-clips. Web-design issues tend to be issues involving philosophy about the content and purpose of Web sites combined with artistic sense of how to attractively implement this philosophy. Consequently, the control of Web pages varies greatly and is often not headed by the information technology department. Coursey's (forthcoming) study based on analysis of a 2004 ICMA e-government survey found that the IT department is in charge of the Web site in 31% of the cases and the manager's office in charge 20% of the time. I found a wide variety of arrangements. In some cases, the government's public information service department (if they have one) or the generalist manager's office will head up Web-design efforts, albeit with assistance from the IT department. As I cited earlier, many organizations outsource the initial Web design but retain in house control over maintenance efforts in house. Jakob Nielsen, an expert on

Copyright © 2006, Idea Group Inc. Copying or distributing in print or electronic forms without written permission of Idea Group Inc. is prohibited.

Web design, argues that Web design is a "core competency" and should not be outsourced (O'Looney, 2000, p. 66). If Web design is completely outsourced, including maintenance, then one of the great challenges will be keeping the Web site up-to-date and taking advantage of the knowledge and ideas that government employees have that might be useful for improving the Web site. Government e-commerce applications are also often outsourced and thus are likely to be on an entirely different server from the rest of the Web site. Indeed, the outsourcing creates problem for attempts to analyze Web site usage as the Massachusetts e-government plan points out:

Any conclusions about usage come with several caveats, however. Use of the site is actually higher because not all agencies are measured by ITD's [Information Technology Division's] Webtrends analysis tool. Like many states, Massachusetts does not measure usage in a consistent manner and it is almost impossible to get one coherent picture of usage for the entire Commonwealth site. The difficulty in tracking usage arises from the fact that not all sites are hosted on servers maintained by the Information Technology Division ("ITD"). In fact, ITD hosts only 52% of all agency Web sites. Thirty-three percent of agency sites are partially hosted by ITD and 15% have no connection to ITD whatsoever. Not surprisingly, many of the largest agencies are only partially hosted by ITD.

My experience with local governments is that some do not think to specify in their contracts with their e-commerce service providers what data they want to obtain concerning Web usage and thus it is often difficult to obtain detailed information from the vendors that is not included in the original contract.

One of the most challenging issues for governments concerns how to deal with persons with disabilities. There currently is a federal law that requires that Web sites make their sites accessible to the disabled and some states have similar laws. Clearly, as the Web sites and Web portals become the major form for obtaining information and conducting transactions with government, they must deal with the disability issue. The complexity of the issue is revealed in the fact that there are a variety of disability issues and it is challenging to meet them all. Brewer (2001) has outlined several disabilities along with possible methods for dealing with them: (1) An online color-blind shopper could use style sheets to assist her/him with shopping; (2) A worker with repetitive stress syndrome can use keyboard equivalents in place of the mouse-driven commands; (3) A deaf online student can be assisted by captions for the audio portion of the multimedia files; (4) A blind accountant can be assisted by synchronization of visual, speech and Braille displays; (5) A classroom student with dyslexia can be helped by the use of freezing of animated graphics and multiple search options; (6) A person with age-related conditions can be aided by magnification of text as well as the ability to stop scrolling text and avoidance of pop up windows; and (7) A person who is both deaf and blind can be assisted by device independent access mechanisms and user-controlled style sheets.

Many of the methods for dealing with disabilities depend upon the use of special assistive technologies (e.g., "user agents" that allow blind readers to easily read forms) and advances in browser software. However, many can be dealt with in terms of Web-site designers. In general, Web sites (Brewer, 2001) should use the "*universal design or*

Copyright © 2006, Idea Group Inc. Copying or distributing in print or electronic forms without written permission of Idea Group Inc. is prohibited.

design for all" principle to plan their Web site to be accessible when first developed. Brewer (2001) points out that many measures taken to aid the disabled may be assistive for most users—for example, captioning audio output to help the deaf also makes it easier for the general user to search for audio output online. Likewise, providing multimedia ways of accessing material can help those who are multi-tasking as well as those who have disabilities. In general, well-organized Web sites make it easier for someone (e.g., a blind person) to navigate through Web sites quickly to get to the material they want. Flexibility and the ability for the user to customize Web sites according to their needs is another principle, such as through the use of style sheets is desirable. According to Jeff Bennett (Patterson, 2002) who analyzes New York State Web sites for accessibility, Web sites can do well simply by keeping their Web sites simple such as to "label all links and graphics, make sure that all links can be accessed by the keyboard and don't require the mouse, and avoid using mouse-over links." Some are concerned (Patterson, 2002) that the accessibility standards will eliminate innovation and sophisticated graphics but proponents of accessibility standards argue that these features can still be offered but just have to be made accessible. This is much easier to do at the design stage than attempting to "retrofit" a site that has already been completed.

Figure 12. Selected high priority W3C standards

Provide text equivalents for each non-text element including images, symbols, animation, applets, and multi-media such as audio and video files and tracks.
Make sure that all information conveyed with color is also accessible without color such as from context or markup.
Organize documents so they can be ready without style sheets.
Make sure that equivalents for dynamic content are updated when the dynamic content changes.
Avoid screen-flickering.
Use the clearest and easiest-to-read language appropriate for the site.
If data tables are used, identify row and column headers.
If frames are used, title each from to make for easier identification and navigation.
If applets and scripts are used, make sure the page is still usable when these are turned off.
Provide an auditory description for important visual track of a multimedia presentation.
For any time-based multimedia presentation, synchronize the equivalent alternatives (e.g., auditory or captions) with the presentation.
If you cannot create an accessible web pages despite best efforts, then provide an alternative page that does meet @3C standards and be sure to update it as often as the inaccessible page.
Source: Adapted from Worldwide Web Consortium (W3C). Checklist of checkpoints for web content accessibility guidelines 1.0 http://www.w3.org/TR/WAI-WEBCONTENT/full-checklist Retrieved July 12, 2004. Copyright © 1999 W3C (MIT, INRIA, Keio) All Rights Reserved W3C. http://www.w3.org/Consortium/Legal/2002/copyright-documents-20021231

Copyright © 2006, Idea Group Inc. Copying or distributing in print or electronic forms without written permission of Idea Group Inc. is prohibited.

In 2001, the federal government released a regulation known as Section 508 that requires all federal agencies to purchase IT that is accessible to people with disabilities. New York State (Patterson, 2002) established guidelines that Web sites should conform to the World Wide Web Consortium (W3C) standards in 1999—the consortium is recognized as the "leading authority on Web accessibility standards." Jakob Nielsen (1999), an authority on Web-site design, points out that the W3C standards have three levels of priority (http://www.w3.org/TR/WAI-WEBCONTENT/full-checklist: (1) 17 high priority rules that, if not followed, may make it impossible for some disabled to use the site; (2) 33 medium priority rules that, if not followed, will make it difficult to use the site; (3) 16 lower priority rules that help improve Web-site accessibility. I have listed some of the W3C's Priority 1 points below. The Priority 1 guidelines include providing a text equivalent for every non-text element and conveying information in ways that do not require distinction of colors. If data tables are employed, provide headers for the rows and columns of the table. Web pages should be readable without the use of style sheets. The final priority 1 guideline states that if you cannot provide an accessible Web page despite your best efforts then you should provide an "alternative Web page" that adheres to W3C standards.

Organizations that have limited resources are advised by Nielsen to follow a rational plan in making sites more accessible such as to concentrate on high-volume pages and high priority rules for the short term and then addressing less traveled pages and lower priority items. More recently, Nielsen (2003) makes the point that that Web sites now have hundreds if not thousands of items on them that can make them difficult for the general user and even more so for users with visual and other disabilities so that the solution is to make it easier for users to "winnow items according to attributes of interest." Likewise, sites are now using "Alt(ernative) text" to assist blind users but some are employing too detailed ALT texts that make it tedious for such users to get through pages. Patterson (2002) found that states such as Washington have used templates to solve many of the digital access so that each department does not have to "reinvent the wheel."

Web sites that integrate a wide variety of information and e-commerce solutions as well as links to other related Web sites are now often referred to as "*Web portals*." There are many different definitions of the term Web portal. Fletcher (2004, p. 53) notes that at its "most basic" level, it is simply the "main doorway to access the Web." However, the term Web portal has come to take on additional connotations that conform to the prescriptive principles for Web design and e-government. Franzel & Coursey (2004) define Web portal as an "integrated gateway" that provides a "single point of entry" for the state's "e-services." The Massachusetts e-government plan identifies the following differences between a governmental portal and Web site (see Figure 13). One key change from old style Web sites is that a portal is designed to be customer-centric, attempting to make her/his use of the Web site as efficient and effective as possible.

Getting citizens and businesses to use Web portals can be challenging. One of the key issues is branding so that citizens automatically come to the Web portal to find material. However, Franzel & Coursey (2004, p. 66) point out that the move to integrated Web portals conflicts can conflict with the fact that it may be easier to give Web sites for specific services a special name "rather than make them sub-directory under a state Web portal." One of the interviewees in Fountain's (2001a) account of the development of a

Copyright © 2006, Idea Group Inc. Copying or distributing in print or electronic forms without written permission of Idea Group Inc. is prohibited.

Figure 13. Key differences between governmental Web sites and portals

Feature	Government Website	Government Portal
Organizing Principle	• Homepage is organized by structure of government	• Homepage is organized around the needs and interests of citizens
Home page	• Often contains a list of agencies	• Provides task options based on the intentions of citizens
Content	• Contains mainly static information • Offers few transactions	• Provides not only information, but also interactions, transactions • Continued roll-out of new transactions
Look & Feel	• Lack of a common look & feel from one agency web site to another	• Common look & feel across all agencies
Navigation	• Navigational systems for users may differ across agencies	• Offers a consistent portal navigation system throughout
Integration with IT Systems	• Treated as a standalone, with uneven integration with agency IT systems	• Robust and consistent integration with IT legacy systems
Customer Support	• Treated as a stand-alone offering with customer support to answer questions and provide human contact, when necessary	• Full system of Customer Relationship Management (CRM)

Source: State of Massachusetts. (2001, January 9). Massachusetts Electronic Government Initiative. Organizational Support and Governance Workshop. Final Report. Retrieved June 18, 2004 from http://www.mass.gov/itd/massgov/publications/strategicplan/table_contents.htm

virtual agency for small businesses points out how huge and complex integrated Web portals can be:

Our Web site is immense and complex. Now you've got somebody else's Web site that's immense and complex. How do you sit up here on high with the tech we have today and do anything to make that kind of a unity. (p. 156)

Thus having an easily understandable organization and good search functions for these huge Web sites is crucial.

Evaluation of Web Sites and Web Portals

Each year, different experts and organizations have done analyses and evaluations of Web sites of federal, state and local governments. These evaluations often differ significantly depending on the particular criteria used by the evaluator and also can change rapidly due to improvements in governmental Web sites and Web portals. For example, the State of Massachusetts plan (2001) notes the variation in ratings:

Copyright © 2006, Idea Group Inc. Copying or distributing in print or electronic forms without written permission of Idea Group Inc. is prohibited.

- The recent Governing Magazine "Ranking the States 2001" gave Massachusetts an average score of C+ and a specific IT grade of "C."
- Accenture's 2001 Benchmarking of the Web sites of the 50 states graded Massachusetts a "B." The 1999 Benchmarking of the Web sites of the 50 states also graded Massachusetts a "B."

Baker (2003) compared OMB Watch's assessment of "e-democracy" with West's rating of states Web sites and found only a .20 correlation. In short, measures of Web site quality and performance can vary greatly.

McClure, Sprehe & Eschenfeld (2000, p. e7) did an extensive review of performance indicators for federal agency Web sites. Their review yielded three major categories of indicators: (1) Legal and policy conditions; (2) Management and infrastructure issues; and (3) Performance measures in the "stricter" sense of the term. The legal and policy conditions pertain to whether the site conforms to legal and policy guidelines concerning issues such as privacy, accessibility, and security that are supposed to govern federal Web sites. Of course, these issues would vary depending on the nature of the level of government involved. In the Chapter on Ethics, I outline the major legal issues that need to be dealt with respect to setting up e-government and related systems.

The infrastructure and management issues deal with the following issues: (1) Does the Web site have adequate infrastructure and software to achieve its purposes, be responsive, and avoid errors (e.g., server and 404—pages not found—errors)?; and (2) Has the management adopted best practices, developed quality control mechanisms for Web pages, and adequate user support? Their third set of indicators examine performance goals such as the extent to which the site is used based on activity levels, efficiency measures such as the relationship of the site to decreased printing costs, effectiveness (e.g., extent to which Web site is expanding to new audiences), and service quality (e.g., number and handling of complaints by user help staff).

In West's (2003) recent rating of large city Web sites, one of the criteria that he employed was readability of the sites. He found that the average readability of large urban Web sites required 11th grade skills while half of the American population reads at the level of 8th grade or less. West assessed the disability access and one of his measures was the degree of conformance to W3C's "Priority One" compliance that I discussed above. The average score for large city sites was only 20% (compared to a 47% score for federal agencies.) The value of such evaluations is to draw attention to factors that had been neglected in earlier evaluations and meshes with well our discussion concerning accessibility in which multi-modal presentations may be needed to effectively communicate with some groups of citizens. West also found that only 16% of the city Web sites had "foreign language translation features." This feature could be important depending on the nature of the city's population. Denver and Orlando had a 100% rating on this indicator.

West also assessed more traditional evaluation measures such as the number of "fully executable, online services." He found a great deal of variation. About half offered at least one service while 33% had four or more services. Twenty-nine percent of the cities allowed credit card processing on their sites. Assessments were also made as to the presence of privacy and security policies. Accessibility to public information was judged

Copyright © 2006, Idea Group Inc. Copying or distributing in print or electronic forms without written permission of Idea Group Inc. is prohibited.

by whether the city site allowed for at least e-mail access to someone other than the Web master and over 70% met this criterion. West goes on to create an single index of e-government score based on 20 features of the Web site (including some that we noted above such as foreign language translation feature) that totaled 80 points and an additional 20 points based on the number of online executable services to form a scale of 0 to 100.

West (2003) critiques cities for putting too much information on individual pages and for not making it clear which department is responsible for particular information:

It is important to make Web sites clear and organized, with links to different departments clearly identified. Citizens should be able to access services without knowing the name of the sponsoring department (information that is beyond the knowledge level of many citizens). Some cities attempt to put too much material on one page, which could end up confusing citizens.

However, as I have pointed out above, the e-government movement encourages the integration of data from several different departments to create "virtual agencies" and following these rules could potentially conflict with West's assessment. West's point does raise the pertinent issue of accountability: how does a citizen determine who is at fault if (s)he is unhappy with a service based on a virtual agency site that is integrated composite of several different agencies?

The management of Web site content is becoming a significant managerial issue as Web sites grow and become very complex. One issue is whether to do the design in-house or through contracts. Even if design is outsourced, there remains the issue of how to get organizational personnel and citizens (and other customers) involved in assuring that the most relevant and up-to-date content and applications are on the Web site. Also, since one of the main aspects of Web site design is to have a "common look and feel," there is a need for centralization of design aspects and thus organizations must decide who will be involved in this decision? Complex Web sites with hundreds of pages and many departments involved may need a formal content management system. Friedlein (2000, p. 161) defines "middleware" as software "that sits between the Web front end and back office systems and processes." Many organizations now have documentation management systems to be able to digitally store and retrieve documents and some governments are looking to integrate these document management systems with Web content management systems as the Fairfax 2005 IT (section 2) Strategic plan discusses:

Content management intersects with document management. For business activities that also rely on a variety of documents, the initiative employs technology at the beginning of a document's life cycle, using the system to track the documents and enable automated workflow processes through the entire life cycle... Through research and analysis conducted in FY 2003, best in breed products for content management engines also incorporated document management needs. The integrated solution provides a seamless integration for use of information found in imaged documents and information in databases and other systems required for a complete business transaction. (p. 4)

Copyright © 2006, Idea Group Inc. Copying or distributing in print or electronic forms without written permission of Idea Group Inc. is prohibited.

As Web sites become the primary vehicle for governments to present information to the public, the merger of records and Web site management is likely to be a high priority. However, the most important Web content decisions are not technical but political questions such as whether to allow interactive discussions or put potentially controversial information (e.g., property assessments) on the Web site.

Stowers (2004b) analyzed Federal websites with the following criteria: (1) Number of services offered; (2) Usability and help features; (3) Accessibility; and (4) Legitimacy to assure users' confidence in content. It is instructive to look at the user help functions since they are not included in the West analysis. They include appropriate FAQ, help, e-mail, feedback, index, search, site map, and site map functions that have become common elements of most Web sites. There is a good deal of overlap between the criteria of various rating systems such as those of West and Stowers but there are also significant differences so that no single-rating scheme is adequate.

Stowers (2004b) provides a framework for the evaluation of states' e-commerce services. She lists a wide variety of output measures (e.g., number of user contact sessions, dollar amounts processed through the site, etc.) but most of these are raw data that mean little by themselves. Her "end or ultimate outcomes" are cost savings from e-government, staff time savings, and trust in government by citizens based on surveys. The cost and time savings are clearly important elements but they require a thorough and careful analysis that can require a good deal of time and the need to calculate overhead costs. Trust in government is affected by many factors other than e-government so I question whether it is a good measure of "ultimate outcomes." More useful as evaluative measures would appear to be what Stowers refers to as "intermediate outcomes" such as adoption rate (both overall and with specific groups) because unless e-commerce is used, it cannot be effective. The fact that many e-commerce projects have reportedly achieved low rates of usage increases the importance of this measure. As I noted earlier, low usage rates are affected by many factors including the nature of the audience, the perceived relative advantage of online over traditional commerce, Web site design features such as ease of use, and the degree to which the e-commerce site has been successfully marketed (or "branded").

A wide variety of Web site statistics are produced automatically by *Web server log analysis software* and can identify much useful information such as where the visitors are coming from, what pages they entered and left on, the most popular pages and most commonly downloaded pages. However, the implications of much of the analysis may be misleading. For example, Franzel & Coursey (2004, p. 71) point out that having a disorganized Web site can boost the number of hits. The criteria of success for governmental Web sites can be different from private sites. Private sector Web sites like to achieve "stickiness" (Davenport, 2000) in which customers are enticed into spending as much time as possible on a business Web site, but stickiness would not appear to be a legitimate goal of governmental Web sites—better to give citizens what they want and let them get out quickly.

Stowers (2004b) emphasizes customer satisfaction surveys gathered through both "pop up surveys" and through general citizen surveys. These pop-up surveys are useful for obtaining quick feedback from citizens who are already users while the general citizen survey could be important for learning why non-users have not adopted the system yet.

Copyright © 2006, Idea Group Inc. Copying or distributing in print or electronic forms without written permission of Idea Group Inc. is prohibited.

Satisfaction surveys can be useful especially for identifying problems but, as we pointed out in our chapter on evaluation, such measures tend to be limited in utility because of the uniformly high rates of satisfaction found and that satisfaction can be affected by other factors (e.g., general attitudes towards government) that have nothing to do with specific e-government performance factors. Stowers (2004b) cites data from the periodic American Customer Satisfaction surveys done by ForeSee Results to show that federal government Web sites actually surpassed private sector Web sites in overall satisfaction (during Year 2000) averaging over 73 with individual federal Web sites ranging from scores of 69 to 80. Stowers (2004b, p. 15) studied the frequency of usage of common e-government performance measures by various levels of government and found the following results for federal agencies (in order of frequency): (1) Amount of time saved; (2) Number of transactions or uses; (3) Number of participants; (4) Other (i.e., those not on Stower's list); (5) Cost savings; (6) Adoption rates; (7) Number of users, visitors, and site hits; (8) Reduction of error and redundancy; and (9) Customer satisfaction. Stowers distinguishes between measures that emphasize Web-based activity such as number of hits and downloads versus those that focus more on the services-based measures such as adoption rates and customer satisfaction. Some states (e.g., Texas, Virginia, and Mississippi) employ both types of measures. Her study of state and local e-government measures found that they tend to use less standardized measures with the "other category" being the most common. Use of non-standardized measures may be appropriate because, as Stowers (2004b, p. 7) recommends, evaluation should be tied into each "organization's strategic planning process and thus will tend to vary from organization to organization. She praises Texas' approach that employs a wide variety of performance measures including adoption rates (as we have seen above), customer satisfaction surveys, and cost benefit analyses.

Ultimately, governments may accept the measures that Stowers, West, and McClure et al. Propose. But the assessment of e-government should be related to the strategic goals of the government and the needs of its citizens and other customers. As I have noted earlier, most of the governments with whom I spoke did not perceive much of a demand currently for e-commerce services but e-commerce functions tend to be heavily emphasized by various evaluation scales to determine the quality of Web sites. The following assistant manager discussed their city's hesitancy to implement e-payment services illustrates the thinking of some of the local governments I visited as to why they were not implementing more e-commerce functions on their Web site:

(Assistant City Manager) "So again going back to that general premise, how can we help people avoid making a trip to city hall.... We did look at doing some e-payment things but the board decided that it was not really cost efficient. So we have not done that... What we found is that if a water bill is a 100 dollars, we need the 100 dollars and not have 10 dollars go to the processing company...so until that system was changed, they were not comfortable with charging residents extra...so we discussed that a couple of years ago and we haven't revisited it since."

(Interviewer) "So there is no demand among the citizenry for it yet—nobody calling and complaining?"

Copyright © 2006, Idea Group Inc. Copying or distributing in print or electronic forms without written permission of Idea Group Inc. is prohibited.

(Assistant City Manager) "No, that is correct."

In many cases, governments have acted proactively and are putting up e-commerce functions with the assumption that in the long-run citizens will demand and use these functions, thus saving money and time for both citizenry and governments. The main conclusion from all of this is that a strong business case should be made for major investments—that you cannot assume that e-government projects are necessary. Fountain (2001b) emphasizes the importance for generalist administrators to be involved because the primary issues are not technical. Faced with scarce resources and competing priorities, it is incumbent on governments that do spend a great deal of resources on e-commerce and other e-government functions to evaluate the effectiveness of these investments.

References

Baker, P. M.A. (2003, August 28-31). *Great expectations: The promise of digital government in the American states.* Paper prepared for delivery at the 2003 Annual Meeting of the American Political Science Association.

Brewer, J. (2001, January). *How people with disabilities use the web.* W3C Working Draft, 4. Retrieved July 9, 2004, from http://www.w3.org/WAI/EO/Drafts/PWD-Use-Web/20010104

Carr, J. (2002). Gartner exp says a majority of e-government initiatives fail or fall short of expectations. Retrieved June 18, 2004, from http://www4.gartner.com/5_about/press_releases/2002_04/pr20020430b.jsp

City of Irving Texas. (2002). E-government plan: Technology @ your fingertips. Prepared by The Project Team Spring. Retrieved October 6, 2004, from www.ci.irving.tx.us

Cluff, H. M. (2002). eGovernance: *A new organizational paradigm.* Retrieved June 6, 2004, from http://www.norfolk.va.us/egovernance/eGovernanceHCluff2002.pdf

Compaine, B. (2000). *Reexamining the digital divide.* Retrieved June 18, 2004, from http://itel.mit.edu/itel/docs/jun00/digdivide.pdf

Cook, M. E., LaVigne, M. F., Pagano, C. M., Dawes, S. S., & Pardo, T. A. (2002). *Making a case for local e-government.* Albany, NY: Center for Technology in Government.

Coursey, D. (2005, forthcoming). E-government: Trends, benefits, and challenges. In *The Municipal Yearbook 2004.* Washington, DC: International City/County Management Association.

Daft, T. (2004, July 1). Slow march toward online government. *CIO Magazine.* Retrieved July 10, 2004, from www.cio.com/archive/070104/tl_egov.html

Davenport, T. H. (2000, February 1). Sticky business. *CIO Magazine,* 58-60.

Daukantas, P. (2003). One site, two clicks. *Government Computer News, 22*(22), 8-11.

Copyright © 2006, Idea Group Inc. Copying or distributing in print or electronic forms without written permission of Idea Group Inc. is prohibited.

Federal Enterprise Architecture Program Management Office (FEAPMO). (2003, June). *The business reference model.* Version 2.0.

Fletcher, P. D. (2004). Chapter IV: Portals and policy: Implications of electronic access to U.S. Federal Government Information and Services. In A. Pavlichev & G.D. Garson (Eds.). *Digital government: Principles and best practices* (pp. 52-61). Hershey, PA: Idea Group Inc.

Fountain, J. E. (2001a). *Building the virtual state.* Washington, DC: Brookings Institution.

Fountain, J. E. (2001b, Fall). The virtual state: Transforming American government? *National Civic Review, 90*(3), 241-251.

Franzel, J. M., & Coursey, D. H. (2004). Chapter V. Government Web portals: Management issues and the approaches of five states. In A. Pavlichev & G. D. Garson (Eds.), *Digital government: Principles and best practices* (pp. 63-77). Hershey, PA: Idea Group Inc.

Friedlein, A. (2001). *Web project management.* San Francisco: Morgan Kaufmann.

Gant, D. B., Gant, J. P., & Johnson, C. L. (2002). *State web portals: Delivering and financing e-service.* The PriceWaterhouseCoopers Endowment for The Business of Government.

Garson, G. D. (2004). The promise of digital government. In A. Pavlichev & G. D. Garson (Eds.), *Digital government: Principles and best practices* (pp. 2-15). Hershey, PA: Idea Group Inc.

Goethals, F., & Vandenbulcke, J. (2005, January-March). Two basic types of business-to-business integration. *International Journal of E-Business Research, 1*(1), 1-15.

Gurwitt, R. (2001, August). Behind the portal. *Governing.* Retrieved June 30, 2003, from www.governing.com

Harvard Policy Group on Network-Enabled Services and Government. (2001a). *Eight imperatives for leaders in a networked world. Imperative 3: Utilize best practices in implementing IT initiatives.* Retrieved July 4, 2004, from http://www-1.ibm.com/industries/government/ieg/projects/projects.html

Harvard Policy Group on Network-Enabled Services and Government. (2001b). *Eight imperatives for leaders in a networked world. Imperative 2: Use IT for strategic innovation, not simply tactical automation.* Retrieved July 4, 2004, from http://www-1.ibm.com/industries/government/ieg/projects/projects.html

Holmes, D. (2001). *Egov, ebusiness strategies for government.* London: Nicholas Brealey.

Horrigan, J. (2004, May 24). Pew Research Center. *How americans get in touch with government internet users benefit from the efficiency of e-government, but multiple channels are still needed for citizens to reach agencies and solve problems.* Retrieved June 28, 2004, from http://www.pewinternet.org/pdfs/PIP_E-Gov_Report_0504.pdf

Jenkins, S. (2003). *Enterprise architecture and application development best practices.* Presented at 2003 North Carolina Conference-Information Systems. Retrieved June 7, 2004, from http://irmc.state.nc.us/

Copyright © 2006, Idea Group Inc. Copying or distributing in print or electronic forms without written permission of Idea Group Inc. is prohibited.

Lassman, K. (2002). *The digital state 2002: How states use digital technologies*. The Progress and Freedom Foundation. Retrieved June 18, 2004, from http://www.pff.org/publications/ecommerce/digitalstate2002.pdf

Lynch, P. J., & Horton, S. (2004). *Web Style Manual* (2nd ed.). Yale Center for Advanced Instructional Media. Retrieved July 9, 2004, from http://info.med.yale.edu/caim/manual/index.html

McClure, C. R., Sprehe, J. T., & Eschenfelder, K. (2000). *Performance measures for federal agency websites: Final report to sponsoring agencies*. Defense Technical Information Center, Energy Information Administration, Government Printing Office. Retrieved July 12, 2004, from http://fedbbs.access.gpo.gov/library/download/MEASURES/measures.pdf

McKay, J. (2002, September). Charge it? *Government Technology*, 24-25.

Mecklenburg County. (2002, July). *E-government strategic plan for Mecklenburg County*. Retrieved June 13, 2004, from http://www.charmeck.org/NR/rdonlyres/eotkyr7j54oiowteibgm53sy27cavozj7eyd7camitgkrvlezb6kvqxaj vstojdptmnwlf6gh6ajcdxqlski3tpo7yc/EGovernmentPlan03.pdf

Michael, S. (2004, September 6). Enterprise architecture: Frequently asked questions. *Federal Computer Week*. Retrieved June 19, 2004, from fcw.com

Moon, M.J. (2002). The evolution of e-government among municipalities: Rhetoric or reality? *Public Administration Review, 62*(4), 424-433.

National Electronic Commerce Coordinating Council. (2001, December 11). *Developing justification and support for e-government projects. Exposure Draft*. Retrieved August 1, 2004, from http://www.ec3.org/Downloads/2001/Dev_Justification_ED.pdf

Norris, D. F., Fletcher, P. D., & Holden, S. H. (2001). *Is your local government plugged in? Highlights of the 2000 electronic government survey*. Baltimore: University of Maryland, Baltimore County.

North Carolina Information Resource Management Commission. (2001). *E-government: Using technology to transform North Carolina's governmental services and operations in the digital age*. Retrieved June 18, 2004, from http://www.its.state.nc.us/News/EGovernment/_Docs/EGovernmentReport2001.pdf

Northrop, A. (2004, March). *E-government: What's on US cities' Web pages*. Paper prepared for delivery at the Western Political Science Association Annual Meeting, Portland, Oregon.

O'Looney, J. (2000). *Local government on-line: Putting the internet to work*. Washington, DC: International City/County Management Association.

Pardee, J. C. (2000, February). Charging a fee for e-government: Oakland county, Michigan's enhanced access project. *Government Finance Review, 16*(1), 48-49.

Patterson, D. (2002, March). Across the disability divide. *Government Technology*.

Pavlichev, A., & Garson, G. D. (Eds.). (2004). *Digital government: Principles and best practices*. Hershey, PA: Idea Group Inc.

Copyright © 2006, Idea Group Inc. Copying or distributing in print or electronic forms without written permission of Idea Group Inc. is prohibited.

Perlman, E. (2000, August). No free lunch online. *Governing,* 28-32.

Perlman, E. (2001. March). E-commerce: The outsourcing option. *Governing Magazine.* Retrieved June 30, 2003, from http://governing.com

Raumer, R. J. (2001). Strategic planning for technology investments. *Government Finance Review, 17*(6), 32-35.

Redick, C. G. (2004). A two-stage model of e-government growth: Theories and empirical evidence for U.S. cities. *Government Information Quarterly, 21,* 51-64.

Richardson, C. (2004). Chapter XIII. Digital government: Balancing risk and reward through public/private partnerships In A. Pavlichev, & G. D. Garson (Eds.), *Digital government: Principles and best practices* (pp. 200-217). Hershey, PA: Idea Group Inc.

Robb, D. (2001, May). Financing online government. *Government Technology.*

Rudolphy, C., & Cullison, J. (2002, June). ServiceArizona: Overcoming the obstacles to e-Government. *Government Finance Review, 18*(3), 44-46.

Sipior, J. C., Volonino, L., & Marzec, J. Z. (2004). A community initiative that diminished the digital divide. *Communications of the Association for Information Systems,* (13), 29-56.

Sipior, J. C., & Ward, B. T. (2004). E-government and the digital divide: Insights from a United States case study. *Proceedings of the 4th European Conference on E-Government,* Trinity College Dublin, Ireland (pp. 17-18).

State of Massachusetts. (2001). *Massachusetts electronic government initiative. Organizational support and governance workshop.* Final report. January 9. Retrieved June 18, 2004, from http://www.mass.gov/itd/massgov/publications/strategicplan/table_contents.htm

State of Texas. Texas OnLine Authority. (2002a, November 1). *A feasibility report on advertising on Texas OnLine.* Retrieved July 4, 2004, from http://www.dir.state.tx.us/pubs/txo/2002adfeasibility.pdf

State of Texas. Texas OnLine Authority. (2002b). *Texas online 2002 status Report: Progress and efficiencies gained.* Retrieved July 4, 2004, from http://www.dir.state.tx.us/egov/

Stowers, G. N.L. (2001, March). *Commerce comes to government on the desktop: E-Commerce applications in the public sector.* The PriceWaterhouseCooper Endowment Endowment for the Business of Government. Retrieved October 28, 2002, from www.businessofgovernment.org

Stowers, G. N.L. (2004a). Chapter XI. Issues in e-commerce and e-government service delivery. In A. Pavlichev, & G. D. Garson (Eds.), *Digital government: Principles and best practices* (pp. 169-185). Hershey, PA: Idea Group Inc.

Stowers, G. N. L. (2004b) *Measuring the performance of e-government.* IBM Series for the Business of Government. March. Retrieved July 8, 2004, from www.businessofgovernment.org

Copyright © 2006, Idea Group Inc. Copying or distributing in print or electronic forms without written permission of Idea Group Inc. is prohibited.

Strover, S., & Straubhaar, J. (2000, June). *E-government services and computer and internet use in Texas.* A Report from the Telecommunications and Information Policy Institute. Austin: University of Texas. Retrieved October 16, 2004, from www.utexas.edu/tipi

U.S. Department of Energy. (2003). *E-government strategic action plan: Following the road map-A Progress.* Report on Fiscal Year 2003 Activities. September.

U.S. Department of Labor. *E-government strategic plan.* Retrieved June 9, 2004, from http://www.dol.gov/_sec/e_government_plan/egov_stratplan_toc.htm

U.S. General Accounting Office. (2001, July 11). *Electronic government. 2001. Challenges must be addressed with effective leadership and management.* Washington, DC: U.S.GAO. GAO-01-959T.

U.S. General Accounting Office. (2003a, March 13). *Electronic government: Success of the office of management and budget's 25 initiatives depends on effective management and oversight.* GAO-03-495T.

U.S. General Accounting Office. (2003b, October). *Electronic government: Potential exists for enhancing collaboration on four initiatives.* GAO-04-6.

U.S. General Accounting Office. (2004a, May 19). *Information technology: The federal enterprise architecture and agencies' enterprise architectures are still maturing.* GAO-04-798T.

U.S. General Accounting Office. (2004b, June). *Workforce investment act: States and local areas have developed strategies to assess performance, but labor could do more to help.* GAO-04-657.

U.S. House of Representatives. (2003, March 13). *Federal e-government initiatives: Are we headed in the right direction?* Hearing before the Subcommittee on Technology, Information Policy, Intergovernmental Relations and the Census. 108 Congress, First Session, Serial 108-6. Retrieved July 3, 2004, from http://www.gpo.gov/congres/house

Wang, Y. (2002). The adoption of electronic tax filing systems: An empirical study. *Government Information Quarterly, 20,* 333-352.

Warschauer, M. (2003). *Technology and social inclusion: Rethinking the digital divide.* London; Cambridge, MA: MIT Press.

West, D. (2000, August 30-September 2). *E-government and the transformation of public sector service delivery.* Paper prepared for delivery at the meeting of the American Political Science Association, San Francisco.

West, D. (2003). *Urban e-government.* Retrieved January 30, 2004, from http://www.insidepolitics.org

Copyright © 2006, Idea Group Inc. Copying or distributing in print or electronic forms without written permission of Idea Group Inc. is prohibited.

Additional Reading

The Pavlichev & Garson (2004) book has a number of very useful chapters on e-government including an excellent overview of the e-government movement by Garson and the book as a whole, provides broad coverage of e-government issues. It is quite useful and important to look at governmental IT strategic plans (and specific plans for e-government if they should have one) such as the ones cited in this chapter to get a feel for how governments are attempting to implement e-government principles. Sources such as the Gant, Gant & Johnson book provide good overviews of Web funding issues. However, e-government is advancing so rapidly and the literature on it growing so quickly that readers should be on the lookout for new material.

Key Concepts

- Adoption rate
- Business Reference Model
- Citizen-centric
- Customize [Web site]
- Digital divide
- E-democracy
- E-government
- E-governance
- E-management
- E-services
- Federal Enterprise Architecture
- "flat" Web site
- G2B
- G2C
- G2E
- G2G
- I-Bond
- Lines of Business
- Managing (or lead) partner
- Multi-modal (and multi-channel)
- Private e-government partner
- Section 508

Copyright © 2006, Idea Group Inc. Copying or distributing in print or electronic forms without written permission of Idea Group Inc. is prohibited.

- Stakeholder analysis
- SWOT analysis
- Take-up Rate
- Technology Acceptance Model (TAM)
- Transformational
- Universal design
- User fees
- Web portal
- Web server log analysis software

Discussion Questions

1. What are the different aspects of e-government and which do you think are most important?

2. What are the normative principles that have become associated with e-government? Do you agree with all of these norms?

3. What factors can influence adoption rates of governmental ecommerce services? What can governments do to increase adoption rates in a manner that is cost effective?

4. What is the relationship between the FEA and BRM and e-government? Do you think the effort being devoted to the FEA and BRM makes sense? Do you think it has relevance to organizations with which you are familiar?

5. Is the digital divide relevant to the community and organization with which you are most familiar? If so, what can be done in your view to alleviate the digital divide?

6. List as many potential sources for funding of e-government efforts as possible. Which of would be highest for your organization (or your local government)? Why?

7. Do you see any chances for forming a "virtual" Web site that would integrate functions of different governmental (or non-profit) organizations that would be helpful to citizens?

8. Do the section 508 standards make sense to you and do you think governments should adhere rigorously to all of these standards?

9. After reading through the various evaluation criteria used to assess Web sites, which do you think are the most important?

10. What are the arguments for and against user fees? Are there any e-commerce services that you think should automatically be excluded from user fees?

11. What do you think are the major weaknesses of governmental Web sites that you have used? Why?

Copyright © 2006, Idea Group Inc. Copying or distributing in print or electronic forms without written permission of Idea Group Inc. is prohibited.

12. What do you think are the most important measures for assessing the success of governmental e-commerce services?

13. What do you think is the most effective way to increase funding for interagency e-government efforts?

14. What steps and strategies do you think are most important in planning for e-commerce and other e-government projects?

15. What is branding and how can it be employed to increase usage of e-government applications?

16. If you were in charge of designing your home Web site: what would be the key organizing and design principles that you would employ? Why?

Exercises

1. Develop a plan to determine the need for e-government services for some governmental or non-profit organization.

2. Develop a business case for some e-commerce (or other e-governmental) service that a government (or nonprofit) agency with which you are familiar does not provide. Then develop an implementation plan for how the organization should go about implementing this electronic service. Finally, develop a set of metrics that you would employ to judge the success of the service.

3. Write a report in which you analyze at least three similar governmental (or non-profit) Web sites (or Web portals) critically with respect to the following issues: (1) How would you assess their overall design? Develop your own set of criteria—you may borrow from West, Stowers et al., but you may also add in your own specific criteria; (2) Then do the assessment using the criteria you have adopted. What are their areas of strengths and weaknesses? Be sure to discuss the design aspects of the site. What are its organizing principles? Do they make sense? Would you classify any of the e-commerce or other e-government activities as being "transformational?" Does this Web site conform to the disability guidelines by the W3C organization?

4. Do an organizational analysis of some organization's e-government-e-commerce-Web site-Web-portal functions. Identify the organizational structure of some public or nonprofit organization with respect to these functions. What part of the organization is in charge of these functions? To what extent, if at all, have these functions been outsourced. Try to find out how these functions came to be performed as they are. Finally assess whether you think the current arrangements are working well or should be changed.

5. Study in depth one of the "business processes" in a public or non-profit organization. Outline a summary of the business processes such as through a flow chart. See if you can figure out how to make the business process more efficient and/or effective. Finally, if possible, see if the use of technology could contribute to an

Copyright © 2006, Idea Group Inc. Copying or distributing in print or electronic forms without written permission of Idea Group Inc. is prohibited.

improved process. (Note: do not choose this option if you did the BPR for your exercise last week).

6.   Read at least three e-government plans (or e-government section of IT plans) and write a critique of them. What are their positive aspects? What are weaknesses and limitations? How could they be improved?

7.   Seek access to the data that your government's Web site maintains concerning visits to the site. Analyze the data and seek to determine answers to questions such as the following: (a) What is the breakdown of what domains the visitors are coming from? Are there any unexpected findings here such as higher or lower percentages from domains than would be expected?; (b) What Web pages are visited the most often? Are there any surprises or disappointments concerning the popularity of individual pages? Also, what does the data say about the sequence of visits to the Web site?; and (c) Overall, does analysis of the data suggest any changes that might be needed to the Web site?

Copyright © 2006, Idea Group Inc. Copying or distributing in print or electronic forms without written permission of Idea Group Inc. is prohibited.

Chapter VI

Politics, Leadership, and Information Technology

Introduction

The underlying premise of this chapter is that information is power and consequently information management is inherently political. Information asymmetries give an advantage of one actor over others (Bellamy, 2000). Maintaining control over information can allow an individuals, departments, or organizations to control how successful they appear to others and thus may protect autonomy, job security, and funding. Therefore, in order to provide effective leadership for IT, the generalist and head IT manager will need to actively engage themselves in both internal and external politics. An excellent case illustrating the importance of political issues in managing IT occurred in California. The California Department of Information Technology (DOIT) was eliminated in June of 2002 (Peterson, 2002). The Department had been created in 1995 in order to solve the problem of several disastrous contracts in the IT area including a DMV project that cost over $50 million but never functioned as planned (Peterson, 2002). Peterson (2002) cites accounts from observers to support the argument that a major reason for the failure was due to the other major agencies that viewed the new department as a threat to their power and lobbied to reduce the authority of the agency in the legislation creating it. In particular, the opponents lobbied to deny the new DOIT control over operations in the legislation creating DOIT. Those with interests that were opposed to the new DOIT included existing departments that had major authority in the IT field and/or those with large data centers. The opposition was successful so that the legislation limited DOIT's role mainly to authority over the budget. Consequently, the

Copyright © 2006, Idea Group Inc. Copying or distributing in print or electronic forms without written permission of Idea Group Inc. is prohibited.

DOIT did not have control over data centers and was not able to achieve one of its major goals to centralize and consolidate these data centers (Peterson, 2002). This lack of operational authority limited its ability to influence other departments as Peterson (2002) summarizes:

Without controlling data centers or California's telecommunications network, DOIT simply had no juice, some sources argued. Because DOIT didn't add value to other state agencies, it couldn't exert any leverage on those agencies. DOIT could present ideas, but it couldn't make any real contribution to making those ideas happen. In other words, with the Department of Finance controlling IT budget processes, the Department of General Services controlling IT procurement and the state data centers handling computing needs, what was the DOI's responsibility?

Also, according to observers, the head of DOIT was not allowed to sit in on Cabinet meetings and there were reported cases of other departments doing "end arounds" concerning the formal requirement for DOIT to approve all major new projects. Another symbol of the weakness of the DOIT was that the governor appointed a new head of e-government who was independent of the DOIT, again lending credence to the perception that the DOIT lacked respect and power. The precipitating event in the death of DOIT was the quick approval by DOIT of a controversial project with the Oracle Corporation that resulted in an investigation and the resignation of several of the state's top IT officials. The California case illustrates how IT can become enmeshed in both internal and external political issues that I will analyze in this chapter.

In some cases such as those previously discussed, politics appears to refer to actions that tend to be viewed by outside observers as narrow-minded and self-serving. However, it is important to note that I use the term "politics" in a non-judgmental manner. Politics can be about money and the "mobilization of bias" as Schattschneider (1983) described it as different forces struggle to prevail. But politics can also be thought of as the attempt to mobilize the resources to achieve public objectives and thus is a necessary part of implementing any major project. I agree with Dickerson (2002) that politics need not be a "lot of nasty back-stabbing and infighting" but is most often about "working and negotiating with others...to get things done." It can be as simple as practicing good communication skills to keep others informed.

Although information management involves many technical issues, it is important to understand that it is involves major political challenges. A large portion of governmental information managers come from technical backgrounds such as computer science and business. They usually have excellent technical skills and they can quickly rise to leadership positions such as Chief Information Officer (CIO). However, decision-making concerning the management of information technology (IT) requires more than technical knowledge as Towns (2004) notes:

There's increasing talk that CIO's don't need to be technologists because the position's nature is changing. Project management skills and people skills now mean more to a CIO than IT skills, the argument goes.... (p. 15)

Copyright © 2006, Idea Group Inc. Copying or distributing in print or electronic forms without written permission of Idea Group Inc. is prohibited.

The most important critical success factors involve organizational and political skills that the technologically skilled often lack but these skills can be learned. In this chapter, I identify some of the key political problems that are likely to be faced. Many technical staff dislike politics and try to avoid dealing with political dilemmas. Molta (1999, p. 23) says "engineers and programmers frequently appear oblivious to the strategic issues that keep management awake at night." He goes on to state that managing information technology is "the most politicized issue of the modern organization" and that technical staff "need to get in the game." Refraining from politics will lead to more serious problems and result in ineffective management of information technology.

Before the days of the World Wide Web and electronic government, managers and user departments often deferred computing decisions to technical staff because information management was not central to organizations (Lucas, 1984) and generalist managers had little knowledge to contest decisions made by technicians. Now, since the information system has become a central concern, user departments often have their own technical staff and generalist managers may become "technical junkies" (Molta, 1999, p. 24) and keep abreast of technological trends. The result is that information management is a much more prominent issue and the potential to become the source of disagreement. Consequently, technical skills themselves are not sufficient to be effective for information managers to achieve their goals. A study (Overton, Frolick & Wilkes, 1996) of the implementation of executive information systems found that political concerns were perceived as the biggest obstacles to success. Many people felt threatened by the installation of such systems for a variety of reasons including fears of loss of their jobs and increased "executive scrutiny" (Overton, Frolick & Wilkes, p. 50). Feldman (2002) also sees politics as one of the biggest challenges for technical managers. Feldman (2002) observed that technicians often adopt a "bunker mentality" on important technology decisions and fail to take effective steps to achieve their goals. Peled (2000) also argues that information technology leaders need to bolster their "politicking" skills to boost the rate of their success. Noll & Wilkins (2002) did a survey of 67 employers who recruit IS professionals and asked them to rate the importance of skills they considered to be most important. They (Noll & Wilkins, 2002, p. 151-152) found that employers ranked "soft skills" such as knowledge of the specific business, ability to plan, organize, and to work collaboratively higher than technical skills. A survey (Anonymous, 1994) of over 500 British managers revealed that the majority believe that information flows were constrained by politics and that individuals use information politics for their "own advancement." In short, the effective use of political skills is an important component of effective information management.

Over the past decade, computing has become much more important in governmental as well as private organizations. Major decisions about computing have always involved politics. Detailed studies of cities in the 1970's (Laudon, 1974) & 1980's (Danziger et al., 1982) demonstrate several cases involving computing and politics. But computing was less central to public organizations then. Most employees had minimal contact with computing but now routinely employ computer technology in many of their day-to-day practices. They use e-mail, the Internet, and a variety of computer applications to accomplish their tasks. Computing is a central part of their jobs and they care about technology. The development of e-government and the Internet has greatly broadened the end users of governmental information systems so that now they include citizens and

Copyright © 2006, Idea Group Inc. Copying or distributing in print or electronic forms without written permission of Idea Group Inc. is prohibited.

groups such as contractors. Information technology now is employed to provide greater forms of accountability to the public, such as using computers to derive sophisticated assessments of performance and posting performance measures on the Internet. Many elected chief executives, such as governors, wanted to be associated with information technology. Coursey (forthcoming) points out, for example, that Jeb Bush wants to be known as an "e-governor." As a result, information technology decisions are more complex and subject to the influence of external politics.

I analytically differentiate the politics of information management into two major different categories: (1) Internal, organizational politics concerning issues involving organizational members; and (2) External politics concerning how the governmental organization relates to its councils or boards, other organizations, external groups, and general citizenry. However, these two forms of politics frequently overlap and influence each other as they did in the California case. I will not be providing many prescriptions to managers on how to behave politically, not only because research about politics is sketchy, but also due to the fact that politics is highly contextual. The course of action that should be pursued depends on the complex interplay of political resources of the actors involved, ethical concerns, legal issues, as well as economic and technical factors. My purpose is to sensitize information managers and generalist administrators to major political issues that are likely to affect IT decisions. I outline examples of both successful and unsuccessful strategies that managers have employed to deal with information politics.

Sources

This chapter makes use of my own experiences as well as drawing on literature concerning public information management. I found very little formal research in recent years that explicitly focuses on the politics of internal information management. By way of contrast, there is a rapidly growing literature on the use of external issues such as the use of the Internet to spur political involvement among citizens. But, my experience shows that internal political issues are pervasive and important for IT managers, most of the major and rigorous academic studies that have focused on the politics of computing date back to the mainframe era (e.g., Danziger, 1977; Dutton & Kraemer, 1985). Before IT became pervasive, these early studies by the "Irvine group" demonstrated that political and social factors generally affected how technology was structured and used (e.g., Northrop et al., 1990). Due to its lack of coverage in traditional academic journals, I make use of periodicals such as computer magazines and newspaper articles concerning computing. Also, many of my examples are based more than 20 years of experience in the IT field and also my study of public organizations at the municipal, state, and federal levels.

Copyright © 2006, Idea Group Inc. Copying or distributing in print or electronic forms without written permission of Idea Group Inc. is prohibited.

Information Systems and Internal Organizational Politics

Although almost any decision about computing can become embroiled in politics, my experience is that the most prominent and most important political issues involve questions of control and power over the following kinds of decisions:

1. **Information Management Structures:** How should information management be structured? Where should control over information be placed in the organizational structure? A related issue concerns what kind of backgrounds are the most effective preparation for technology department heads—technological or political?

2. **Hardware and Software Acquisitions:** What should be the nature of the process? How centralized should it be? Who should be involved? Should outsourcing be used?

3. **Information Management, Sharing Information, and Interdepartmental Relations:** What process should be used to determine information sharing and exchange? How will computing influence and be influenced by other aspects of interdepartmental and inter-organizational IT issues? How can obstacles to sharing information be overcome?

4. **Managing Personnel and Communication Flows:** How does computing influence employee relations and communication flows? What, if any, rules and procedures should be established? How do e-mail and other forms of computer-mediated communication (CMC) influence communication and organizational politics? How does information technology influence the careers of organizational members?

Although each of these issues has technical aspects, non-technical issues such as concerns about autonomy and power often prevail. Next, I outline how each of these decision areas involves important political aspects. Many information managers prefer to avoid these political aspects. Likewise, generalist managers, such as city managers, have often ignored direct involvement in these decisions due to their lack of expertise concerning computers. As a consequence, it has been my experience that persons other than information system or generalist managers often dominate these decisions. Consequently, these issues are often decided without adequate attention from those with the most expertise or broadest perspective.

Information Management Structures

In the days of the mainframe, there was often little interest on the part of most employees as to how computing was structured. Due to the fact that computing was used to perform routine tasks such as water bills and routine accounting reports, the computing function

Copyright © 2006, Idea Group Inc. Copying or distributing in print or electronic forms without written permission of Idea Group Inc. is prohibited.

was placed originally under the control of the Budget/Finance department in many municipalities and other levels of government. Computing was often done on a mainframe machine and data processing departments controlled the development of applications. End users tended to have little involvement in computing decisions. As the importance of computing has grown and spread along with decentralization due to microcomputers and distributed computing, the original structures have become outmoded. Now that virtually all employees actively employ computer technology and end-user departments care about how computing is organized.

But there is no consensus as to the best method of organizing computing. How centralized or decentralized should computing be? There are advantages and disadvantages to centralization of computing so that one major review of the centralization-decentralization debate (King, 1983) concluded that "political factors" are paramount in decisions on how to structure computing. Business organizations have encountered the same dilemma. Markus (1983) has described how business departments have resisted efforts at integration of information systems. Davenport et al. (1992) found several reasons behind information politics including: (1) Units that share information fully may lose their reason for existence; and (2) Weak divisions may be reluctant to share information when they are sensitive about their performance. Overall, in recent years, there has been an emphasis on centralization of authority as organizations move towards an enterprise-wide approach in which databases are centrally organized and standards govern the hardware and software systems of organizations.

Where should computing be placed in the organizational structure of a public organization such as a city? Should it be a separate, line department, a sub-unit of another department (e.g., budgeting/finance), or a staff unit to the manager/mayor? Should mayors/managers require that the head of computing report directly to themselves or should they place a staff member in charge? There is no universal answer to these questions. Small organizations may still rely primarily on generalist managers supplemented by assistance from consultants and contractors. For larger organizations, the centrality of today's computing to all departments would suggest that information management should be in a separate unit and not be structurally placed under another department such as budget/finance. There has been a strong movement at the federal and state levels to establish a CIO to deal with problems of technological issues that cut "cross departmental" boundaries and to head efforts at building corporate-wide e-government and intranet systems (Fabris, 1998). But managers, both computing and generalist, need to think carefully about the implications of these different arrangements and which structure is most likely to meet the needs of the organization. In the past, many local government executives have complained about the feeling that the information they need to run a city exists somewhere but that they can't seem to access it effectively (Danziger, 1977). Ackoff (1967) argued that managers who took a hands-off approach to computing would suffer from "management misinformation systems." Decisions concerning the structure of the system will be based on a number of factors including the degree of interest of the generalist managers in computing as well as what goals managers have for IT.

Molta (1999, p. 23) defines politics as the "allocation of resources within an organization." Some departments will want to control their own computing as much as possible through hiring their own information technology (IT) staff. Eiring (1999, p. 17) defines

Copyright © 2006, Idea Group Inc. Copying or distributing in print or electronic forms without written permission of Idea Group Inc. is prohibited.

politics as the "art of negotiation, compromise, and satisfaction" and urges information management staff to form strategic alliances that are beneficial to the IT cause and "nurture them as one would a good lasting friendship" (Eiring, 1999, p. 19). Feldman (2002, p. 46) warns that "when departments are doing their own thing—namely hiring their own IT staff—a central IT department is in political trouble." He goes on to point out that hiring their own staff implies unhappiness with the services of the central IT unit. However, in many organizations, it has been common and perhaps necessary for line departments to have staff dedicated to IT. For example, police departments often have their own dedicated systems and staff because of the early development of police information systems, the centrality of computer searches to their function, and the need to have secure and easy exchange with other police departments. When non-IT department information technology staff exist, one political issue is how they should relate to the central IT staff. Feldman (2002, p. 48) argues that the smart strategy is for the central IT staff to offer "to exchange information and support" with non-IT department staff." By taking these steps, Feldman (2002) argues that they can at least establish "*dotted line relationships.*" Feldman argues further that these non-IT technological staff are often isolated and appreciate the support from the central IT department. Anderson et al. (2003, p. 23) found examples of dotted line relationships in states like Pennsylvania where the formal authority of the state IT head over state agencies was weak: "Additionally, all agency CIOs have a 'dotted line' relationship to the state CIO even though they formally report to their own agency heads, they meet quarterly with him." The only alternative is to try to control all computing from the central IT department but this strategy can either work very well or turn out to be a disaster (Feldman, 2002, p. 48).

A major rationale for the existence of a CIO (as opposed to a traditional data processing manager) is that (s)he will not be restricted to technical issues but act as a change agent, politician, proactivist, and integrator as well (Pitkin, 1993). The federal government (Koskinen, 1996; Pastore, 1995) has firmly established the use of CIOs in order to improve information management. Will it have a positive impact? Should the CIO model be followed in municipalities and other public organizations? Merely assigning the CIO title does not ensure that these functions will be performed. For example, a study (Pitkin, 1993) of CIOs in universities found that, despite their title, they did not view themselves as executives and often do not perform these non-technical roles. Without a push from a CIO, public organizations may fail to make good use of information technology. For example, one study found that police regularly used their database systems for reports to external agencies but rarely for internal management purposes (Rocheleau, 1993). CIOs and centralized information structures help to fix responsibility and that can mean that they themselves become targets of unhappiness with technological decisions. There are many cases in which CIOs in the private sector have not been viewed favorably by their fellow managers (Freedman, 1994) and CIOs in both the public and private sector are blamed for failures (Newcombe, 1995; Cone, 1996).

As I discuss in my chapters on e-government and planning, there have been some secular trends that tend to push organizations towards certain structures. First, during the early days of computing, control over IT decisions was vested in the Finance/Budgeting department. With the growth and importance of IT, organizations of moderate to larger size now tend to have an independent IT department (Gurwitt, 1996) because IT is now viewed as infrastructure serving everyone and should not be under control of any single

Copyright © 2006, Idea Group Inc. Copying or distributing in print or electronic forms without written permission of Idea Group Inc. is prohibited.

department. Also, because there is now a strong acceptance of the need to have as much standardization of hardware and software as possible, the IT unit is often vested with final approval over major purchasing decisions and the heads of IT departments in federal, state and large local governments are often designated with the title of CIO (Gurwitt, 1996). But the California case shows that this centralizing trend can be reversed. According to Peterson (2002), the structure recommended to replace the State Department of Information Technology was to decentralize with the authority of the extinguished department being reassigned to the Finance and General Services departments. By way of contrast, a study by Rand Institute researchers (Anderson et al., 2003) recommended a more powerful and centralized department to replace California's deposed DOIT. However, it is interesting to note that the Rand Institute (Anderson et al., 2003) researchers studied the governance structures of four other states and found that some of the states (e.g., Illinois) had IT structures that were weak in formal authority but nevertheless worked effectively due to the fact that the IT leadership worked through brokering relationships. Likewise, according to the Rand study, Pennsylvania's system does not vest strong authority in the state CIO (Anderson et al., 2003, p. 23) but it depends on successful "dotted-line" relationships. Their conclusion is that there is no one best way to organize and that CIOs who have weak formal authority can use their negotiating and brokering skills to be successful. They also argue that management style is important. Successful state IT managers have a style that is "participative, collaborative," and emphasizes positive "carrots" rather than "sticks" in seeking change (Anderson et al., 2003, p. ix). In the California case, the politics of IT involved the legislature and also key vendors so IT leaders have to practice their communication and political skills on key external as well as internal constituencies.

In my experience, there is a wide variety in the amount of attention devoted by generalist managers to structural issues concerning computing. In one city, a city manager was very much focused on information management and devoted a great deal of attention to decisions made concerning computing by the city, in effect acting as the municipality's CIO. His focus on information technology enabled him to establish a positive reputation for innovation that helped to secure his next job. When this manager left for another city, he was replaced by another manager who was not especially interested in computing. Devoting great attention to computing can be both productive and counterproductive. The first manager who was heavily involved in computing decisions became embroiled in severe struggles with his new board and organization over IT issues that contributed to his resignation from his new job.

Although there is no single right way of organizing computing, each manager needs to ensure that the structure will provide relevant, timely and reliable information. Kraemer and King (1976, p. 25) argue that public executives spend too much of their time on decisions concerning the purchase of equipment and too little on other important information management issues that have less visibility but are equally important. Kraemer & King (1976) emphasize the need for generalist managers to take personal responsibility for computing and to be engaged in the following decisions: how to structure computing, the purposes to be served by computing, and implementation issues such as the goals of computing and the structures used to achieve them.

Some experts (e.g., Severin, 1993) argue that the Chief Executive Officer (CEO) of an organization should also be the true CIO. The former mayor of Indianapolis, Stephen

Copyright © 2006, Idea Group Inc. Copying or distributing in print or electronic forms without written permission of Idea Group Inc. is prohibited.

Goldsmith, is an example of a CEO who took charge of the information technology function and instituted a number of important policy changes such as privatizing many IT functions as well as encouraging e-mail from any employees directly to himself (Poulos, 1998). A related issue concerns the question of to what extent the head of IT needs to have a technical background. John Kost (1996) was appointed to be CIO of the State of Michigan by Governor Engler and instituted several policy goals of Engler's such as consolidation of state data centers, establishment of statewide standards, and reengineering of IT including its procurement process. It is notable that Kost did not have any IT background at all (Kost, 1996). Kost maintains that it is more important that the CIO understand the business of government than have a strong technology background (Kost, 1996, p. 30). Kost proceeded to do a major reengineering of IT in Michigan and claims that they successfully achieved many of the goals set by Engler. However, if the CIO does not possess strong technological skills as well as institutional knowledge about the IT system, (s)he will need to have trusted and reliable staff who do have such skills in order to have the trust and respect of client agencies. One of the problems with the California DOIT was that it had little operational authority and was primarily an oversight agency. Thus, one of the recommendations of Anderson et al. (2003, p. 53) is to "transfer the majority of people with technical skills" from Finance and other departments to the new IT department so that it would be "properly staffed and positioned to provide technical approval."

Paul Strassmann served as director of defense information at the Defense Department from 1991 to 1993 where he was in charge of a $10 billion annual budget for IT and instituted major changes in the procurement process. Strassmann subsequently published a book entitled, *The Politics of Information Management* (Strassmann, 1995, p. xxv) in which he argues that managing IT is "primarily a matter of politics and only secondarily a matter of technology." Strassmann goes on to hold that only the technical aspects of information can be safely delegated to computer specialists. Strassmann (1995, p. xxix) supports a "federalist approach to information management, delegating maximum authority to those who actually need to use the information." Strassmann (1994, p. 10) believes that it is the duty of the CEO to establish general principles: "Without a general consensus about the principles and policies of who does what, when, and how, you cannot create a foundation on which to construct information superiority." Strassman says that the CEO should never delegate the responsibility for information management to a CIO because it is the CEO who must decide how to apply information systems.

In a majority of organizations of a large size, there tends to be one or more advisory committee or groups set to assist the IT head in making decisions. In my experience, these advisory groups tend to fall into three categories: (1) End user groups involving end users who are especially engaged with IT; (2) Representatives of departments served by the IT department—they may or may not be heavy end users; or (3) External people who have substantial experience in IT. In Anderson et al.'s (2003) study of four states regarded as having successful IT departments (New York, Pennsylvania, Virginia, and Illinois), the state IT units generally had both internal groups made up of the line departments who represent the end-users of IT and an external group consisting of private sector IT heads who provided their expertise. I have known municipalities to use the same approach and one municipal IT head told me of how the private sector committee saved their community money with their advice about telecommunications strategy to

Copyright © 2006, Idea Group Inc. Copying or distributing in print or electronic forms without written permission of Idea Group Inc. is prohibited.

obtain low-cost services from vendors. A politically adept CIO can make good use of these committees to build her/his political base.

Comparison of Politically-Appointed vs. Career Administrators

As I have documented earlier, political skills are a necessary component of IT management. This has been documented at the federal level in studies of the jobs of federal CIOs carried out by the GAO (2004). Given the importance of politics, would we expect politically-appointed or career administrators to be more effective? The GAO study has some support for both positions. The GAO publication outlined what most CIOs considered to be major challenges and they all involve the use of political skills: (1) Implementing effective IT management; (2) Obtaining sufficient and relevant resources; (3) Communicating and collaborating internally and externally; and (4) Managing change.

According to the GAO (2004, p. 23) report, many thought that politically-appointed CIOs would be more successful because they have more clout and access. However, others thought that skilled career administrators would be more successful because "they would be more likely to understand the agency and its culture." Another variable is that politically-appointed CIOs (in federal agencies) had a shorter tenure of 19 months versus 33 months for the career administrator. The career administrators thought that this gave them a significant advantage because it can take a good deal of time to accomplish major tasks. Concerning their communication and collaboration skills, the GAO report (2004, p. 30) concluded that it is critical for CIOs to employs these abilities to form alliances and build friendships including with external organizations:

Our prior work has shown the importance of communication and collaboration, both within an agency and with its external partners. For example, one of the critical success factors we identified in our CIO guide focuses on the CIO's ability to establish his or her organization as a central player in the enterprise. Specifically, effective CIOs—and their supporting organizations—seek to bridge the gap between technology and business by networking informally, forming alliances, and building friendships that help ensure support for information and technology management. In addition, earlier this year we reported that to be a high-performing organization, a federal agency must effectively manage and influence relationships with organizations outside of its direct control.

Concerning the management of change, the GAO Report (2004, p. 31) found six CIOs (from the private sector) who said that dealing with government culture and bureaucracy was a major challenge and that they had to marshal resources to overcome resistance.

The Federal Computer Week Magazine (Hasson, 2004) conducted a survey that obtained responses from 129 CIOs concerning the career vs. political issue and it found similar results. Two-thirds of the CIOs agreed that the political appointee would have better

Copyright © 2006, Idea Group Inc. Copying or distributing in print or electronic forms without written permission of Idea Group Inc. is prohibited.

access and one-third agreed that they would be able to raise the profile of the IT department. One former CIO argued that the political appointee could be more aggressive while the career administrator "had to find a champion" to push projects through the legislature. But two-thirds also thought that the career CIO would have a bigger impact because of their longer tenure. In 2004, there were a number of prominent CIOs who left high-profile public positions including changes in Virginia and Florida's top IT officer (Towns, 2004). It is safe to say that in order to be effective, regardless of whether they are political appointees or career administrators, they will need to exercise effective political skills.

Peled (2000) presents two case studies involving information technology leaders in Israel. In one case, a prestigious scientist with outstanding technical skills was called in to solve transportation problems by employing computing technology. This technologist viewed his job in technical terms and attempted to develop a project without communicating with and building support from other key actors (Peled, 2000, p. 26). He refused to share information with other departments working on related projects and consequently encountered resistance leading to his resignation and the end of the project (Peled, 2000, p. 27). His failure was largely due to deficiencies in communication and lack of knowledge of organizational politics such as the need to obtain support from others in order to develop a project. Peled (2000) provides a second case study in which a leader without any major technical skills was able to solve serious problems of building a land-registry database. He used a training system to develop a core of users and people committed to the new database and negotiated with unions about wage demands for using the new system. This leader viewed his project in political terms from the very beginning and this approach helped him to achieve success. The importance of political skills in managing e-government has been confirmed by a study by Corbitt (2000) of the eight factors associated with the failure of e-government projects—only one of these concerned technical problems. The others (Corbitt, 2000) included the absence of a champion of change, lack of managerial support and attention, poor attitudes towards the IT department, lack of education and training, and a discrepancy between IT staff and the end users of the system. I am not saying that IT skills are not important. Indeed, in the numerous small governments that have only a tiny number of staff, they cannot afford to hire a non-technical IT manager. Nevertheless, even in these small organizations, political skills are also an essential component to IT leadership.

Politics and the Purchasing Process

As we saw in the California DOIT case, the failure of a large IT system can often embroil an organization in politics. It is crucial that generalist managers take measures to avoid such disasters. An underlying assumption of the current information resources management theory is that an organization's information system should be aligned with its business goals. A related assumption is that generalist managers must be involved in procurement and other important decisions. They need to specify what goals and functions should be achieved by the purchasing of new software and hardware. Sandlin (1996, p. 11) argues that managers need to be on guard for "technological infatuation." Sandlin (1996) points out that generalist managers would never let the transportation

Copyright © 2006, Idea Group Inc. Copying or distributing in print or electronic forms without written permission of Idea Group Inc. is prohibited.

departments buy a line of expensive cars but they often allow the equivalent purchases in the IT area. Managers sometimes purchase expensive systems (e.g., corporate-wide geographic information systems) because everyone else is getting them without thinking enough about whether the benefits from applications will justify the enormous costs involved.

The failure of expensive new computer systems is likely to expose governmental managers to political attacks. Even if knowledge of the failure remains internal, unsuccessful systems can undermine central management, IT and other departments involved. The problem often begins with the failure of internal management of the projects. For example, the Federal Retirement Thrift Investment Board fired and sued its contractor, American Management Systems (AMS) of Fairfax, Virginia (Friel, 2001), for breach of contract. The contractor defended itself by stating that the board had not determined system needs even three years after the beginning of the contract (Friel, 2000). The determination of system needs is primarily a managerial issue. The pervasiveness of contract failures has led to what some refer to as a "contract crisis" (Dizard, 2001) with political consequences:

Thanks to new project management techniques, improved oversight, employee training, and contract controls, several state CIOs reported that project failures are decreasing. But they agreed that the political cost of bungled projects remains high *[emphasis added].*

The U.S. General Accounting Office (2002) studied the Department of Defense Standard Purchasing System and found that 60% of the user population surveyed were dissatisfied with its functionality and performance. If a failed project has high visibility, then often external political issues also develop. But even if not visible to outsiders, failed purchases weaken the credibility of IT staff and thus the purchasing process is one of the most critical areas for managers and IT staff to negotiate.

When direct use of computing was restricted to computer programmers, there was little interest in other departments concerning decisions about hardware and software. But as end-user computing has grown, end users have enjoyed the freedom to innovate and strong centrifugal forces have resulted. Employees often have strong personal preferences and feelings concerning software and hardware purchases. Part of the ethos of end-user computing is the ability to make your own decisions about software and hardware. Allowing each end user (or end-user department) to make decisions about software is likely to lead to multiple hardware and software platforms. In some cases, the case for a separate standard is based on strong technical reasons. For example, Unix workstations have often been used by engineering departments in cities while the rest of the city is likely to use PCs. Until recently, only these Unix workstations had the power and software to perform the graphics required for the engineering jobs. Consequently, engineers often used Unix-based machines while the rest of the municipality usually employed microcomputers and this multiplicity of platforms was justified by technical considerations. Today, there is brewing a competition between open-source and Microsoft Windows technologies that could precipitate a similar struggle in the future.

Copyright © 2006, Idea Group Inc. Copying or distributing in print or electronic forms without written permission of Idea Group Inc. is prohibited.

There are other tradeoffs between allowing each department to use its preferred software and hardware versus centralization. Multiple platforms complicate training, backup, and maintenance, too. The existence of "platform zealots" is not unusual and can lead to conflict (Hayes, 1996). In my experience, these problems with multiple platforms have led certain managers toward establishing a single platform and also centralized control over hardware and software acquisitions. In some cases, this author has seen an interdepartmental committee established to make purchasing decisions that exceed some threshold of expenditure. In other cases, the review process is done alone by the person heading the information management function. Barrett and Greene (2001) make the point that leaders need to convince the end users of the strong advantages and rationale for standardization of hardware and software. If they fail to take this step, they are likely to encounter directly or indirectly, passive resistance to their policies. In some cases, formal control of IT purchases by the IT department is impossible if the funding source for hardware and software is from another level of government (e.g., state or federal funding). Regardless of what approach is taken, information management and generalist administrators need to provide the *centripetal force* needed to integrate information management in public organizations. If they don't do it, no one else will. But this integrating role often runs into stiff resistance and it requires that the manager use powers of persuasion, negotiation, bargaining, and sometimes authority and threats.

Many generalist managers may want to establish standard policies that influence purchasing choices of departments such as the following: (1) Some governments take a position that data processing functions should be privatized as much as possible; (2) Many governments have instituted online purchasing and forms of purchasing pools which departments may be required to adhere to; and (3) Some governments are establishing special arrangements with a small number of computer vendors with the idea of achieving advantageous pricing arrangements. Both the federal and many state governments have been revamping the purchasing process with more emphasis on speed and emphasizing best value rather than lowest cost (Rocheleau, 2000). Kost (1996) believes that the CIO and CEO need to take charge of the purchasing process if they are to achieve goals such as privatization and "value purchasing":

For example, a policy advocating privatization is doomed unless the purchasing process allows privatization to occur.... An intransigent purchasing director can often do more to thwart the direction of the administration than a policy-maker from the opposite political party. (p. 8)

At the federal level, Strassmann implemented a corporate information management (CIM) initiative that was aimed at streamlining the military's information system purchases, such as the use of the same systems across the different services. Strassmann enunciated the following principle that the technicians were expected to follow: enhance existing information systems rather than "opt for new systems development as the preferred choice" (Strassmann, 1995, p. 94). In one case, this CIM approach killed an $800 million Air Force system and replaced it with a similar one that was used by the Army (Caldwell, 1992). The Air Force had already spent $28 million on their system and resisted the move. Observers of the process noted that it was a "turf issue" and a GAO report concluded

Copyright © 2006, Idea Group Inc. Copying or distributing in print or electronic forms without written permission of Idea Group Inc. is prohibited.

that CIM required centralization and a "cultural change" that was difficult for the Defense Department (Caldwell, 1992, pp. 12-13).

The acquisition and implementation of new systems often engender resistance. One of the basic principles of planning for new computer systems is to involve the people who will be using the system in its design, testing, and implementation phases. Indeed, there are entire books written concerning the principles of participatory design (Kello, 1996). An apparent example of user resistance occurred in Chicago when a new computer system was introduced to speed the building permit process. After the system was implemented, lengthy delays drew widespread criticism (Washburn, 1998) and the delays caused a bottleneck during a time of booming construction. The new system tracked permit applications, allowed scanning of plumbing, electrical and other plans so that the plans could be viewed simultaneously on several screens. There were some technical problems acknowledged by city officials. For example, some staff had trouble seeing plan details on their screens and on-the-spot corrections were not possible due to the fact that applicants were not present when reviews were done. But officials argue that many of the complaints were due to the fact that the system had changed the process of handling permits. Permits are now done on a first-in-first-out basis compared to the previous situation where expediters used to "butt into line" and consequently they feared loss of influence under the new system (Washburn, 1998). The contention was that the expediters deliberately spread false rumors about extensive delays in an attempt to "torpedo the new system."

The desire to standardize can create political resistance. For example, vendors who target their products to municipal governments begin with a basic general ledger and finance product and then expand to develop modules for other functions, such as permitting and other processes. Managers see advantages to using the same vendor for all of their different modules, such as ensuring interoperability among them as well as gaining favorable financial terms. However, in this author's experience, vendors who have strong financial modules often are weak in other areas and thus the desire to standardize on one vendor's software can lead to problems with end users who do not like these other modules of the vendor. In such cases, it is clear that generalist and information system managers will have to be sensitive to organizational politics and either accept the need for diversity in vendors or employ their personal and political resources to achieve change.

Computing, Sharing Information, and the Politics of Interdepartmental Relations

In addition to purchasing issues, there are many other interdepartmental issues that need to be dealt with by CIOs and generalist managers in order to establish an effective information system. For example, computing creates the possibility of free and easy exchange of information among governmental organizations. But information is power and organizations tend to be sensitive about giving out information to outsiders, especially if it reflects on the quality of the organization's operations. Many agencies prefer to maintain autonomy over their data. For example, the author worked on a project with the job-training agency of a state agency in a project that was to employ databases

Copyright © 2006, Idea Group Inc. Copying or distributing in print or electronic forms without written permission of Idea Group Inc. is prohibited.

drawn from several state agencies to evaluate the state's job training programs. However, despite obtaining verbal agreements from the top managers of the agency, the lower-level programming staff delayed the sharing of data for months. It became clear that they saw our requests as an additional burden on them that would make their job more difficult if such requests were to become routinized.

Building e-commerce systems usually requires the cooperation and sharing of information among a number of different departments. Corbitt (2000, p. 128) conducted a case study of an organization that developed an e-commerce system and found that there were "important political and interest differences" among the departments as well as "differences in perceptions" that caused problems. In particular, Corbitt (2000, p. 125) found competition between the data division and the e-commerce group about what needed to be done and who should exert leadership over it. Corbitt (2000, p. 128) concludes that power is a "very substantial issue affecting implementation success."

Some new technologies such as geographic information systems (GIS) are forcing changes in computing structures and procedures among departments. Generalist managers may need to act to ensure that appropriate new structures are established. For example, although many geographic information systems are initiated by a single department, the systems are expensive and the software is relevant to many different departments. When Kansas City decided to build a GIS (Murphy, 1995), they found it necessary to form a GIS committee (made up of representatives of four participating departments: Public Works, Water, City Development, and Finance) to conduct an interdepartmental needs assessment and resolve problems such as how to resolve conflicts in databases and how to minimize database development costs. Although such developments do force structural changes, there is still wide latitude in regard to the nature of the structure. Sharing data can lead to conflict. In a study of exchange of information between municipal departments such as fire and police, this author (Rocheleau, 1995) found that a large percentage fail to exchange information despite overlaps in their job responsibilities concerning problems like arson and emergencies. I studied one city where the fire department, clerk's office, and building department all shared information responsibility for entering information about buildings, but each department tended to point their finger at others when mistakes in the data were discovered. A major task of generalist and information managers is to deal with departmental concerns with autonomy over the databases. If they defer to the status quo, information management will be less effective. Bringing about change required to achieve integration may aggravate such conflicts. Overcoming these obstacles requires negotiating, political and organizational skills.

Top managers may force the exchange of information via command. However, employees often find ways to resist change. For example, they may provide poor quality information that renders the exchange useless. Markus and Keil (1994) provide a case study of a new and improved decision support system designed to help sales persons that failed because it worked counter to underlying organizational incentives. The system was aimed at producing more accurate price quotes but it hampered the sales staff's ability to sell systems, their most important goal, so the new system was used little.

The relationship between technology and individual career ambitions can lead to political aspects of information management. Knights and Murray (1994) have conducted one of the few detailed studies of the politics of information technology. In their case

Copyright © 2006, Idea Group Inc. Copying or distributing in print or electronic forms without written permission of Idea Group Inc. is prohibited.

study of IT in an insurance company, they concluded that the success and failure of the systems was closely tied to the careers of mangers. Consequently, these managers often attempted to control the perception of the success of these systems because perception is reality (Knights & Murray, 1994):

The secret of success lies in the fact that if enough people believe something is a success then it really is a success…it was vital for the company and for managerial careers that the pensions project was a success." (p. 172)

One of the key points made by Knights and Murray is that computing decisions become inextricably entangled with career ambitions and fears of individual employees and become embroiled in a very personal form of politics. Another detailed case study (Brown, 1998) of the implementation of a new computer system in a hospital found that different groups (the hematology ward, hematology laboratory, and information technology team) had very different perspectives on the reason for the failure of a new computer system. Moreover, each of the three groups used the common goal of patient care to legitimate their view of the system. Brown (1998) concludes that the study shows that participants were influenced by "attributional egotism" in which each person and group involved attributes favorable results to their own efforts and unfavorable results to external factors. Similar to Knights and Murray (1994), Brown concludes that many of the actions are taken to protect individual autonomy and discretion.

Grover, Lederer and Sabherwal (1988) borrowed from the work and Bardach (1977) and Keen (1981) to outline 12 different "games" that are played by those involved in developing new systems. They tested their framework by in depth interviews with 18 IT professionals who confirmed that these games were played in their organizations. Most of their games involve interorganizational or interpersonal struggles similar to those I discussed previously. For example, they discuss how in the "up for grabs" game, control over a new IT system involves struggles between the IT and other departments. They illustrate what they call the "reputational" game with a story about an IT manager who projected "a rough exterior" (Grover, Lederer & Sabherwal, 1988, p. 153) in order to reduce demands on the IT department but this approach led to a coalition against him and the IT department and resulted in the eventual demise of the IT manager.

The lesson of these cases is that, prior to implementing new systems, information managers need to assess the organizational context and determine how proposed systems will be affected by incentives, informal norms, resistance to change and sharing, as well as other forms of organizational politics. A broad stakeholder analysis needs to be done (see our chapters on planning and purchasing for discussion of these analyses). Many of these factors may be addressed by including end users in the planning process. Managers will often have to be involved in exerting political influence and engage systems outside their direct control in order to assure a successful outcome. For example, Kost (1996) describes how the Michigan Department of Transportation decided to change from a mainframe to a client-server environment and this change endangered the jobs of a dozen mainframe technicians. The logical step was to retrain the mainframe technicians to do the new tasks, but the civil service rules and regulations required that the mainframe workers be laid off and new employees be recruited to fill the client server

Copyright © 2006, Idea Group Inc. Copying or distributing in print or electronic forms without written permission of Idea Group Inc. is prohibited.

positions (Kost, 1996). Thus, in order to have an effective information system, generalist and information managers will often have to seek to change rules, procedures and structures and, at the same time, alleviate as much as possible any perceived negative impacts of change. Still, change may bring information managers inevitably into conflict with other departments.

Computing and Communication Patterns

Information technology such as e-mail can affect organizational communication patterns. Changes in communication flows can be extremely political. For example, if a subordinate communicates sensitive information to others without clearing it with her/his immediate supervisor, strife is likely to result. While he was Mayor of Indianapolis, Stephen Goldsmith encouraged every police officer and other public employees to contact him directly via e-mail (Miller, 1995a). He claims to have read 400 e-mail messages a day. Should mayors/managers encourage such use of direct contacts from employees? Although such communication can and does occur via phone and face-to-face communication, e-mail communications are different from face-to-face communications—there is less rich information and many people act differently in e-mail than they do in person.

E-mail has become the dominant form of communication in many organizations and it has implications for organizational politics (Markus, 1994; Rocheleau, 2002b). Markus (1994) has shown that e-mail is routinely used as a device to protect employees in games in which they feel it is necessary to "cover your anatomy." E-mail now provides a digitized trail that can be used to support employees concerning their reasons for doing that they did. Employees often copy e-mail messages to their own or other superiors to let them know what they think is necessary, thus attempting to bring more pressure on the recipient of the e-mail (Phillips & Eisenberg, 1996). E-mail is now used for communicating bad news and even conducting negotiations. Many people (McKinnon and Bruns, 1992) are scornful of those who use e-mail for purposes such as reprimands and firings. But some research now shows that e-mail may work better in communications that involve "dislike or intimidation" (Markus, 1994a, p. 136).

The establishment of e-mail and other communication policies involves sensitive organizational issues. For example, if one employee sends a printed memo to an employee in another department concerning a matter of interest to his/her bosses, it is often expected that the sending employee will send a copy of the memo to the bosses. Should the same policy hold for e-mail exchanges? Is e-mail more like a formal memo where such a procedure is expected or more like an informal phone call where copying is not done? Such policies will likely lead to debate and perhaps conflict. Generalist and information managers need to be actively involved in making these decisions.

Technical leaders need to realize that keeping others informed in the organization is a crucial task and devoting time to such communication needs often to take precedence over more technical issues as the following IT director for a local government described:

With the manager—I don't want any surprises and I don't want my manager to have any surprises. So if I see it [some problem] coming, I am up there communicating with him.

Copyright © 2006, Idea Group Inc. Copying or distributing in print or electronic forms without written permission of Idea Group Inc. is prohibited.

This morning before you got here, I went to give a heads up to purchasing and to the manager's office to let them know, 'Hey, this is going to be coming to you' [an unexpected expenditure]. I spend a lot of time doing things like that ....The complaints that I hear a lot about are that people send things in and the manager's office doesn't know what is about.... So communicating those things to grease the skids, and letting people know that what I would like to have happen—I spend a lot of time on it. And I think it pays big dividends in getting things done.

In short, good political skills concerns the ability to communicate effectively with all of the key actors in the IT process from the end users to the top managers.

The External Politics of Information Management

There are several ways in which computing can become involved with external politics. Here are some examples:

1.   Information technology is being used to determine the performance of governmental organizations as well as the presentation of these performance measures on Web sites. These online evaluative reports (e.g., report cards for school systems) can have much greater visibility and accessibility than previous evaluations and thus e-government can lead to greater citizen involvement. Access of the public to information about the performance of governments and other organizations (e.g., hospitals, health professionals) can often lead to controversy.

2.   Legislatures, councils and boards of public agencies may contest the purchasing decisions of public organizations. Likewise, the award of computer contracts may involve political rewards. In the California case (Anderson et al., 2003), the legislature stepped into weaken the amount of authority given the new Department of Information Technology created in 1995—thus ensuring that the General Services Administration and Department of Finance would continue to dominate IT decision-making.

3.   It is possible that public computer records could be used for political purposes. The information could be used to schedule campaigns or find information that brings candidates into disfavor.

4.   Information systems often involve sharing amongst different levels of government as well as private organizations. Often there is conflict among these organizations over basic issues, such as how the information system should be structured and what data they should gather.

5.   The rise of the World Wide Web and e-government have created the potential for politics. Political issues have erupted over the use of Web sites and other forms

Copyright © 2006, Idea Group Inc. Copying or distributing in print or electronic forms without written permission of Idea Group Inc. is prohibited.

of CMC. A wide range of issues have developed such as the use of Web sites to attack governmental officials or their use for advertising purposes.

6. Major computer disasters or failures can bring negative attention to public organizations. These failures both hurt organizational performance and also threaten the jobs of staff.

7. A variety of computing technologies are viewed as a way of increasing citizen participation in government. These include interactive Web sites that allow citizens to easily post comments on proposed rules and other public issues. Public participation GIS (PPGIS) and Web logs could also be used to achieve enhanced participation but at the same time can lead to controversy and increased conflict.

As I discuss in depth in my chapter on accountability, the development of computing technology has had an important impact on measuring accountability and presenting this information to the public. One of the major obstacles to the use of accountability efforts has been the argument that comparisons of performance are invalid—no two situations are the same. Consequently, organizations with poorer results have been able to point to factors that differentiate them from better-performing organizations (Rocheleau, 2002a). The posting of information on the Internet makes this kind of information much more accessible than in the past when it would likely reside in obscure, hard-to-obtain governmental publications. These increased external forces often lead organizations to adopt strategies for resisting information or manipulating it so that negative information is not available to the public or oversight agencies (Rocheleau, 2002a). For example, a recent U.S. General Accounting Office (GAO) report (March 2002) found that abuse of nursing home patients was rarely reported. Indeed, colleges, universities, health maintenance organizations, and perhaps most organizations take steps to ensure that only positive information is reported via a number of strategies, especially if the information will affect high-stakes decisions (Bohte & Meier, 2001; Rocheleau, 2002a). Information is power and the demand for more external access to performance information makes the job of information management even more political. Now that this information is so accessible, organizations have to deal with demands for access to more information while other units may resist such demands and power struggles over information ensue. For example, the Tennessee teacher unions successfully resisted efforts to make public the scores of individual teachers based on a value-added system developed by the state (Gormely & Weiner, 1999). Other consequences include the likelihood that the data may be "cooked" in order to demonstrate high performance (Rocheleau, 2002a) and the IT managers may face ethical issues concerning how to handle such situations.

The External Politics of Purchasing and Privatization

Many city managers attempt to defuse controversies over the purchasing process by involving council/board members in developing the proposals. Thus decisions will not be brought up for decision until strong council/board support exists. Achieving such a consensus may be more difficult these days because board members are more likely to be involved with computing in their own organizations (e.g., Pevtzow, 1989). When

Copyright © 2006, Idea Group Inc. Copying or distributing in print or electronic forms without written permission of Idea Group Inc. is prohibited.

computing was restricted to mainframes and data processing departments, council/board members were less likely to feel knowledgeable and able to challenge purchases. Rocheleau (1994) found that there could be conflicts over purchasing, even if there is a consensus on what type of technology to use. Major contracts can be especially controversial during periods of budget strain and expensive IT contracts may be viewed as taking away from services. For example, some state legislators argued that $52 million of a $90 million contract that California State University had awarded to Peoplesoft should be redirected to educational programs to compensate for cutbacks made by Governor Gray Davis (Foster, 2004). There also may be tensions about whether to purchase from local vendors versus outside vendors. We saw earlier (Peterson, 2002) that major failures of large IT project led to the creation of a state IT department but controversies over another contract (with the Oracle Corporation) led to the denouement of the department after only seven years of existence. Major failures in procurement can turn a project that begins as primarily an internal matter into a political football and such failures have led several IT directors to lose their jobs.

The move to privatize information systems can create external conflicts with legislative bodies as well as unions. For example, the state of Connecticut's administration decided to sell the state's entire system from mainframes to the desktop and hire an external vendor to handle every aspect of the information function (Daniels, 1997). Later, they decided against the outsourcing because of a number of factors such as disputes with the state legislature and the union representing the IT employees, as well as reappraisals of the proposed contracts. Several other states have considered privatization including Indiana, Iowa, and Tennessee. In order to implement such plans, the managers will have to negotiate with legislatures and unions in order to negotiate agreements. For example, the Connecticut administration (Daniels, 1997) moved to assure jobs of the state IT workers for a period of two years at the same salary and benefits in order to have the privatization move approved. In more recent times, the cities of Memphis and San Diego have moved to outsource their entire information services function. The absence of unions has facilitated the privatization of the Memphis operation (Feldman, 2000). However, as we have seen earlier, effective communication and political skills are required for an effective IT system and the turning over the entire operation to a private vendor could disrupt the communication patterns and power relationships necessary for the system to work smoothly. That is why in many cases, the selected vendor often is an organization consisting of former employees or, as in the Memphis case, the winning vendor is expected to hire employees of the former municipal IT department (Feldman, 2002). One of the principles that Anderson et al. (2003, p. 31) found in their study of state IT structures was that "states with successful IT initiatives demonstrate commitment to employees during major changes." In some recent cases (Kahaner, 2004), state governments (e.g., New Jersey and Massachusetts) have passed laws that have outlawed outsourcing of call centers for services such as answering questions concerning electronic benefits such as food stamps. The outsourcing would have saved money directly in lower contract costs but some point to unemployment and other benefits that would have to be paid to the workers who would lose their jobs. In 2004, Florida technology officials became embroiled in a controversial outsourcing (that includes e-government) in which losing bidders complained about the bidding process (Towns, 2004), leading later to the resignation of the Florida CIO. The era of budgetary shortfalls

Copyright © 2006, Idea Group Inc. Copying or distributing in print or electronic forms without written permission of Idea Group Inc. is prohibited.

leads to demands that CIOs cut budgets and save money (Hoffman, 2004). This situation can lead to failure and resignations when CIOs are unable to meet these cutback expectations as occurred to the CIO of New Hampshire who resigned (Hoffman, 2004). Dealing with the implications or even expectations of personnel cutbacks due to IT decisions is one of the most sensitive and important tasks for IT leaders and the generalist administrators of governmental organizations.

Although privatization may be used to achieve positive goals, it can also be used for political rewards and result in problems. One such example occurred when a computer vendor, Management Services of Illinois, Inc. (MSI), was found guilty of fraud and bribery connected with Illinois awarding a very favorable contract to them (Pearson & Parsons, 1997). MSI had legally donated more than $270,000 in computer services and cash to Illinois Governor Edgar's campaign. The jury found that the revised contract had cheated taxpayers of more than $7 million. Campaign donations as well as the flow of governmental and political staff between government and private vendors can influence the awarding of contracts. More recently, there have been some suspicions that politics has been involved in the selection of no-bid contractors for "e-rate" contracts aimed at putting computers and other IT systems in Chicago's school system. Among the winners of no bid contracts were SBC (then headed by Chicago Mayor Richard Daley's brother) and another company (JDL Technologies) headed by a friend of Reverend Jesse Jackson (Lighty & Rado, 2004).

At the same time that many states and municipalities are exploring privatization of their information management function, there are several municipalities that are moving to become telecommunication owners and that leads to political controversy. For example, Tacoma's (Washington) municipal power company is aiming to build and provide cable services to homes and thus put it in competition with the local phone and cable companies (Healey, 1997). Many other cities including several small communities such as Fort Wright (Kentucky) are also planning to build telecommunication networks (Newcombe, 1997) in the U.S. and are also providing telecommunication services for businesses and private homes in their communities. The rationale behind these moves is that the private cable and local phone companies have a poor record of providing up-to-date service (Healey, 1997). These moves have often been labeled as "socialism" and opposed by the local cable and/or phone companies. But, in the Tacoma case, most local business leaders were backing the municipality because of the desire to have better technology (Healey, 1997). Some states (e.g., Texas, Arkansas, and Missouri) have prohibited municipal organizations from becoming telecommunication providers (Healey, 1997). The state of California is in the process of privatizing its state telecom system (Harris, 1998). But, in Iowa, many municipalities have been laying fiber to deliver cable in competition with cities and the first suit brought by a phone company was found in favor of the municipality (Harris, 1998). More recently, the Supreme Court (Peterson, 2004, p. 27) "upheld the right of states to ban municipalities entering the broadband market." The Missouri Municipal League had argued that the Federal Telecommunications Act prevented states from passing laws to limit entry into providing services but the Court said that this provision of the law did not apply to governmental units. Thus politics and the law are integrally related but there are few fixed principles about the law as it affects emerging computer technology.

Copyright © 2006, Idea Group Inc. Copying or distributing in print or electronic forms without written permission of Idea Group Inc. is prohibited.

When local governments decide to pursue broadband, they must be ready to be involved in a whole array of politics and will need to market their position to the public. One strategy of small local governments is to increase the viability of their position by collaboration with other municipalities. In Utah (Perlman, July 2003), several municipalities joined together to form UTOPIA (Utah Telecommunications Open Infrastructure Agency) to provide high-speed fiber optic network to their communities. But telephone and cable companies have allied with taxpayer groups to oppose the efforts. Eight of the 18 local governments that supported the initial feasibility study have withdrawn from UTOPIA and the remainder have committed themselves to taxpayer-backed bonds to finance the required infrastructure. The feasibility issue depends heavily on assumptions about take-up rates—what percent of the targeted business and residents buy into the service, the project will finance itself and, according to Perlman (2003), the take-up rate has averaged 40% in those local governments that have put "fiber to the home," and that only a 30% take-up rate is required for the project to "pay for itself."

A study by a conservative think tank researcher (Lenard, 2004) found that none of the municipal entrants into the broadband market had been able to cover their costs and argues that they are not likely to do so in the future either. Defenders of municipal entry see it as a movement to bring services and competition to areas that telecommunication companies have poorly served or totally ignored and that broadband is now infrastructure needed to attract businesses to the community and thus equivalent to building roads. Brookings researcher, Charles Ferguson (2004), has labeled the broadband situation an example of "market failure" due to a lack of real competition. Defenders would argue that, by entering the market, municipalities will provide the competition to obtain the quality services that have been denied them. Lenard (2004) argues that the competitiveness of the telcom industry makes it likely that the private sector will meet these needs without governmental involvement. In short, the debate over local governmental provision of Internet services goes to the very heart of what government should be doing.

More recently, a similar controversy has erupted over the desire on the part of some local governments to provide "hotspots" or "WI-FI" zones in the downtown areas. These local governments view the provision of WI-FI capability as a service to their citizens as well as a way of assisting economic development. Opponents of municipal provision of hotspots view it as inappropriate public sector competition with a service that is available from the private sector. In short, it is becoming clear that, although many information managers prefer to avoid controversy, telecommunications issues such as cable and access to the Internet have become so central to legislatures, councils, and the public that it will be difficult to avoid making politically sensitive decisions.

Computer Disasters and Information Management

It is likely that the majority of computer problems and disasters remain unknown to the public and even legislative bodies. However, certain disasters have so much impact on key operations that they do become public and create crises for generalist and information managers. For example, the delay in the opening of the new Denver Airport was due to software problems controlling the baggage system for the new airport. Likewise, the

Copyright © 2006, Idea Group Inc. Copying or distributing in print or electronic forms without written permission of Idea Group Inc. is prohibited.

state of Illinois' Medicaid program encountered many failures of the computer system with the system assigning patients to inappropriate health care providers (Krol, 1994).

Many disasters are beyond the control of managers and there is little they can do other than plan for emergencies. However, in many cases, disasters appear to result from overly high expectations for new computer systems and a lack of understanding on how difficult it is to implement a new system. This author has reviewed a large number of computer problems and failures (Rocheleau, 1997). Both the Federal Aviation Administration (FAA) and Internal Revenue Service (IRS) have experienced major failures that have led to threats from Congress to defund systems (Cone, 1998). Another example is Florida's new human services system that encountered much higher-than-projected costs and slower-than-expected implementation (Kidd, 1995). The perceived disaster led to the loss of job of the state official in charge of the new system along with threatened legal action. But over the long run, it appears that the system actually worked and has helped to reduce costs. Information management officials need to ensure that executives and the public have realistic expectations of system costs and performance. Computer problems and disasters are likely to occur more often as computing becomes central to governmental performance and communication with its constituents. In these situations, managers cannot avoid dealing with computing even if they have removed themselves from any decisions concerning it.

In contrast to the disaster cases, some politicians and managers make use of notable achievements in computing to boost their reputation for innovation and effectiveness. However, it can be dangerous for politicians or managers to claim success for large-scale new systems until the systems have been fully implemented and tested. For example, a former Illinois Comptroller introduced a powerful new computer system that was aimed at speeding the issuance of checks as well as improving access to online information during June of 1997 (Manier, 1997). But soon afterwards, there were complaints that checks were arriving behind schedule and that matters had not improved (Ziegler, 1997). The agency stated that it was just taking time for workers to get used to the new system. This is one case where there does appear to be a clear prescriptive lesson for managers: new computer systems that are large-scale and introduce major changes usually experience significant startup problems and claims of success should be muted until success can be proven.

Information Management and Interorganizational Struggles

Many of our largest governmental programs involve complex arrangements where administration and funding are shared by federal, state, and local governments. These governments are often at odds over how they view information systems. For example, the welfare reform legislation passed in 1996 led to needed changes in how state and local governments gathered and analyzed data. Since welfare recipients move from state to state, the new welfare time limits require states to share and redesign their systems so they can calculate time periods on welfare and whether a recipient has exceeded state or federal limits (five years total and two years consecutively for federal limits). Prior

Copyright © 2006, Idea Group Inc. Copying or distributing in print or electronic forms without written permission of Idea Group Inc. is prohibited.

systems were oriented to yearly information and were concerned only with welfare activities in their own state. The federal government has established data reporting requirements that many states view as burdensome and unnecessary (Newcombe, 1998). For example, they have to monitor the school attendance of teen-age mothers and that requires sharing of information with independent local school districts. The quality of the data submitted by the states is also an issue (Newcombe, 1998). The very purposes of the federal and state systems can be somewhat at odds. The federal government wants to use the system to determine the overall success of the program and to be able to compare the performance of states. The state governments often are opposed to the increase in the number of data elements required from 68 to 178 and the costs of gathering so much new information (Newcombe, 1998). Similar disagreements can occur between state and local governments with the latter often feeling that states are too autocratic in how they implement information systems. The resolution of such disagreements will involve conflict and bargaining with creative solutions that meet the primary needs of all involved.

Schoech et al. (1998) provide a case study of a volunteer group in Arlington, Texas who tried to create a databank aimed at helping reduce alcohol and drug abuse. This volunteer group "discovered the politics of information" (Schoech et al., 1998). Hospitals opposed the identification of drug-affected births by hospitals. When agency personnel changed, permission for access to the data had to be obtained all over again. Changes in the structure of government and functions of office also led to the need to start again. They found that data gathering was not a high priority for other agencies involved and access to data was often delayed or not forthcoming.

The Center for Technology (CTG) in government has conducted several case studies concerning the development of information systems that require the cooperation of several organizations. One case study involved the development of an information system for the homeless. First, several different actors needed to be involved in the development of the system, including the New York State Office of Temporary and Disability Assistance, the Bureau of Shelter Assistance, the New York City Department of Homeless, the Office of Children and Family Services, the Department of Health, the Department of Labor, the Office of Alcohol and Substance Abuse Services, and the Division of Parole, and many independent non-profit organizations that contribute to and use information on the system. The huge number of actors meant that the development of the system had to be very deliberate and the first priority was to develop a sense of trust amongst them first before getting into technical design (CTG, 2000). The new information system was to be used to help set goals and thus affect evaluation. Consequently, there were issues that had to be settled about how ambitious to make goals. Consensus had to be forged on key definitions such as "date of admittance" into the system because these definitions were important to funding of the end users of the system (CTG, 2000). Some agencies wanted a more detailed listing of ethnic options than others due to their federal funding requirements (CTG, 2000) so this detail needed to be negotiated, too. The basic points of this case study are that negotiation and trust are essential to creation of interorganizational and intergovernmental systems. Organizations that believe that their financial interests and viability will be threatened by a new system will resist it regardless of how rational and sensible the policy looks "on paper."

Copyright © 2006, Idea Group Inc. Copying or distributing in print or electronic forms without written permission of Idea Group Inc. is prohibited.

Another CTG (1999) study of attempts to build integrated criminal justice systems. They found many conflicts over budgets, organizational relationships, and procedures. CTG (1999) concluded that these problems were not technical in nature but due to "conflicting visions" related to organizational and political interests. They also found that trust, participation, and understanding of the business were among those elements required for success. To achieve buy-in, they had to pay much more attention to "interests and incentives" and use marketing and selling techniques. Political pressures played an important role in some cases. They found that "turf is the biggest killer of integration" (Center for Technology in Government, 1999):

Protecting turf can be particularly important when the potential loss of autonomy or control could benefit other agencies that are political or institutional adversaries. (p. 11)

There was also a need for a champion of the system who had major organizational or political influence that allowed this person to overcome the political barriers to integration. Bellamy (2000) found very similar results in a review of attempts to create criminal justice systems in England. Although technical skills are always useful and sometimes essential, the development of successful interorganizational systems necessitates major use of political skills and resources. The Anderson et al. (2003) study of four states found that it was important to have general executive leaders who are champions of IT:

States with exemplary IT practices have executive leadership (governor and state CIO) who are champions of IT initiatives. All four of the states we visited exemplify this characteristic. These leaders emphasize the value of IT for the state in performing its missions. They view IT as an investment, rather than a cost.... (p. 33)

These studies and other literature on IT have two important implications: (1) Generalist administrators who want to have successful IT programs need to be engaged in IT; and (2) IT heads need to cultivate support from generalist administrators.

In some cases, use of computing may help to reduce the amount of ad hominem politics and give more attention to the underlying facts of cases in development decisions (Dutton & Kraemer, 1985). They found that computing models did not eliminate politics. Developers and anti-developers employed competing models with different assumptions. But the focus on the computer models helped to direct attention to facts of the case and away from personalities and unverifiable assumptions, thus facilitating compromise and agreement.

Information Management and the Politics of Databases

Most information managers prefer to avoid the release of information with political implications. But often they cannot avoid releasing such information and need to have

Copyright © 2006, Idea Group Inc. Copying or distributing in print or electronic forms without written permission of Idea Group Inc. is prohibited.

a defensible policy in this regard. The New York State Attorney General's Office (Yates, 2001) plan to track flows of donations to victims of the September 11th tragedy was resisted by organizations such as the Red Cross due to privacy and confidentiality issues. Freedom of Information Act (FOIA) requests cover computer records in most states. Issues of privacy and public interest often collide and managers are often forced to make difficult choices. Although these problems existed prior to computers, the existence of computing has made it possible for outsiders to conduct very detailed critiques of the practices of public agencies with emphasis on pointing out the failures and questionable decisions on the part of public agencies. For example, the Chicago *Tribune* did a re-analysis of computerized information from the Illinois Department of Public Aid to do an expose of fraud and waste in its Medicaid system (Brodt, Possley & Jones, 1993). The extent, magnitude, and speed of their analysis would have been impossible without access to computerized records. Consequently it is not surprising that many governmental agencies resist FOIA requests. A series of articles (e.g., Mitchell, 1999) by the *News-Gazette* newspaper in Illinois revealed that many resist FOIA using a variety of reasons such as the fact that they don't have to create a new document. The existence of a good computerized system can serve to weaken the argument that the obtaining of records would pose too great a burden on the governmental agency.

Generalist and information managers picture technology as a way to better services but they should be aware that the same technologies and databases can be employed for political purposes. For example, many municipal and state governments are now constructing powerful geographic information systems (GIS) that are aimed at improving services to citizens through the mapping of integrated databases. However, GIS systems and their data are now being used for "cyber-ward-heeling" in the 1990s and facilitate such traditional functions like the mapping of volunteers, canvassing of voters, and location of rally sites (Novotny & Jacobs, 1997). Politicians are likely to seek data from these public information systems to conduct their political campaigns. For example, databases allow the targeting of campaigns so that candidates can use several different messages and conduct "stealth campaigns" without alerting their opponents. Thus, the more powerful and information rich that local GIS systems become, the more attractive they will be as data bases for political activities which could lead to controversy.

Online Computer Mediated Communication

The impact of the World Wide Web has especially important implications for politics. Researchers such as Robert Putnam (1995) point out to a substantial decrease in some forms of civic participation on the part of the public. Many people are frightened to speak at public hearings. The Web offers a way of increasing public participation in community decisions (Alexander & Grubbs, 1998). Many people see us entering a new age of cyber-democracy (Stahlman, 1995). Shy people and stutterers would be able to provide testimony electronically and their arguments would be judged based on content rather than their appearance or public speaking skills (Conte, 1995). Municipalities may help to develop useful networks such as senior citizen discussions. Parents can use the system to update themselves on student homework assignments. But, as noted earlier, there are

Copyright © 2006, Idea Group Inc. Copying or distributing in print or electronic forms without written permission of Idea Group Inc. is prohibited.

several drawbacks to teledemocracy and development of interactive Internet applications:

- There is less inhibition in telecommunications than in-person communications against intemperate statements. Consequently, electronic forums often degenerate into "flaming" wars. The originator of the Santa Monica (California) online discussion system argued that, if he were to do it over again, he would like to have a moderator for the system and charge user fees (Schuler, 1995; Conte, 1995).

- Some people lack the computing technology and/or skills to participate in these electronic discussions (Wilhelm, 1997).

- It is feared by some that easing access to public testimony and input to public officials may result in such a massive and discordant amount of input that democracy would be stymied and that gridlock would increase.

- The Internet raises fears about privacy. Efforts to improve access can often lead to resistance. For example, the Social Security Administration (SSA) made interactive benefits estimates available over the Internet but was forced to withdraw the service due to privacy issues (United States General Accounting Office, 1997; James, 1997). Social security numbers are not very private and all someone needed was the number plus the recipient's state of birth and mother's maiden name to gain access to earnings and benefits information.

- Public online systems may become campaign vehicles for certain politicians.

A detailed account (Schmitz, 1997) of a discussion group concerning homelessness on Santa Monica's PEN system made the following points about the successes and failures of online groups: (1) The discussion group was successful in bringing people together on an equal basis for discussion purposes who would never have engaged in face-to-face meetings; and (2) But electronic media demand keyboarding and writing skills. Thus there are many obstacles to the successful participation of the poor. One recent study by Gregson (1997) found that even politically active citizens were not able to transfer their activism to a community network without substantial training and experience. Hale (2004) did a study of the use of neighborhood Web pages and his overall assessment was that the overall usage rates were low and that consequently these pages were not meeting the hope that they might help to "revitalize democracy."

Both generalists and information management staff need to give careful consideration to the possibilities and drawbacks of tele-democracy. If they decide to support electronic discussion groups, should they employ a moderator and, if so, who should act as a moderator? Would a moderator's censoring of input be a violation of the right to free speech? Fernback (1997) argues that most people accept moderation not as "prior restraint but as a concession" for the good of the collectivity. How can the argument that tele-democracy is elitist be handled? Is the provision of public places (e.g., in libraries) for electronic input sufficient to deal with this objection? In this author's experience, I have found strong resistance to the establishment of online discussion groups. Many local governmental officials believe that such communication is likely to result in

Copyright © 2006, Idea Group Inc. Copying or distributing in print or electronic forms without written permission of Idea Group Inc. is prohibited.

contentious and strident behavior. Some also feel that increased participation would slow down and make governmental decision-making more difficult. Thus West's (2001) finding that few governmental agencies allowed interactivity such as the posting of online messages much less online discussion groups may not be merely the result of their lack of technological sophistication but may also be due to a calculated reluctance to sponsor CMC.

The Politics of Web Sites and Other Online Information

The creation of Web sites has created a whole new set of opportunities for politics to occur. What kinds of information should be online? Who should decide what information should be online? These are issues that have been highlighted by the Web. Before, most public information resided in reports that few had access to or even knew existed. The ease of online access has changed that situation and can lead to controversies that would not have existed when information was restricted to paper reports. As a result of the events of September 11th, some U.S. agencies have pulled data from their Web sites on hazardous waste sites. To many these actions make good sense but others have pointed out that the chemical industry has tried to keep such information private and that public access to this information can help to save lives (OMB Watch, 2002). The New York Attorney General's office began to develop a database to track the distribution of money donated to victims of the attack but the Red Cross raised privacy concerns (Yates, 2001). Web sites are sometimes used to attack government officials. A U.S. Geological Survey contract employee was allegedly fired for posting a map on the U.S. Government Web site that identified areas of the Arctic National Wildlife as moose calving areas that the Bush Administration would like to open to oil exploration (Wiggins, 2000). Recently, the American Education Association and American Library Association (Monastersky, 2004) have accused the Bush Administration of politics in deleting information from their Web site and they cited an internal memo that it was policy to remove information that was outdated or did not "reflect the priorities of the Administration." Thus putting up certain information or omitting information from Web sites can become a controversial and political issue.

A related issue is to what extent should Web sites of governments act as, in effect, a campaign Web site for elected officials? There is great variability in state and local governments but some governmental home pages appear to be campaign sites with photos of the top-level officials and their personal positions and accomplishments dominating much of the page. Such activities can stimulate opposition to political uses and Franzel & Coursey (2004) report that Florida banned the placement of almost any information other than basic personal and legal information on their Web sites. Coursey (forthcoming) cites an interesting example in which Governor Jeb Bush ordered an e-mail link be placed at the top of all of the state's Web pages but that led to thousands of responses that could not be answered in a timely fashion and the policy was eventually reversed.

Other battles occur over issues such as advertising, as I discuss in the chapters on e-government and privacy and ethics. Should advertising by private businesses be

Copyright © 2006, Idea Group Inc. Copying or distributing in print or electronic forms without written permission of Idea Group Inc. is prohibited.

allowed on governmental sites? Many governments are resisting advertising but some of the most successful, such as Honolulu (Peterson, 2000), have used advertising to fund advanced electronic governmental systems but few others have followed. Honolulu put out a banner for a bank on its Web site. Peterson (2000) cites other governments as either being interested in advertising or not depending on whether they see it as necessary for funding. Decisions about opening government sites to advertising will involve ethical and practical issues.

Even decisions about what links to have on Web sites can become involved in political and legal controversy. As I discuss in the chapter on Privacy and Ethical Issues, a court case was brought by an online newsletter (The Putnam Pit) against the City of Cookville, Tennessee due to their failure to provide a link to the newsletter despite the fact that several other for-profit and non-profit organizations were linked to the city's Web site (Anonymous, 2001). Many governments avoid making such links. The consensus is that if governments do make links, they need to have a carefully thought-out (non-arbitrary) policy for doing so.

E-Governance Issues

The focus of this book is primarily on administrative issues as they relate to computing. I will note that there is a large and rapidly growing literature about how IT will affect and change the nature of political decision-making as well as partisan politics. I will note some significant aspects of how e-governance can affect those who manage IT. *E-governance* is defined by Carlitz & Gunn (2002, p. 389) as the "use of computer networks to permit expanded public involvement in policy deliberations." One particular form of e-governance is to create an "e-docket" that is aimed at increasing participation in the creation of administrative rules so that they will be less likely to be challenged in courts. Coglianese (2004, p. 2) has defined *e-rulemaking* as "the use of digital technologies in the development and implementation of regulations." He argues that IT may help streamline and allow agency staff to "retrieve and analyze vast quantities of information from diverse sources." He cites early examples of rule-making such as the Bureau of Land Management's use of scanning of 30,000 comments concerning a proposed rangelands rule. Coglianese (2004) describes how the Department of Transportation and Environmental Protection Administration (EPA) created entire "e-docket systems" that provide "access to all comments, studies, and documents that are available to the public." Indeed, as I note in the chapter on e-government, the EPA has been designated the "managing partner" in an interagency project to establish a common Internet site for all federal regulatory issues to help the public find and comment on proposed regulations. There is a governmental Web site that describes this initiative at *http://www.regulations.gov/images/eRuleFactSheet.pdf* and has links to all of the federal agency e-rulemaking sites.

Carlitz and Gunn (2002) described how the e-rulemaking process ideally would work:

An online dialogue takes place over a several week period. The dialogue is asynchronous, so participants can take part at their convenience, with ample time to reflect on

Copyright © 2006, Idea Group Inc. Copying or distributing in print or electronic forms without written permission of Idea Group Inc. is prohibited.

background materials and the postings of other participants. Although in our experience a properly structured event is typically very civil, the dialogue is moderated to deal with the rare cases in which the discussion becomes too heated and to help keep the conversation focused. (p. 396)

But they go on to acknowledge that there are many legal concerns about abridgement of First Amendment rights through attempts to moderate discussions and make them more civil. Carlitz and Gunn (2002, p. 398) said they were advised by the EPA's Office of General Counsel not to use their "usual prerogatives" as moderators because of these legal concerns, though they note that other departments have taken different positions.

Concerning the local government level, Chen (2004) studied the involvement of local officials with e-mail and the Internet in the Silicon Valley area. She surveyed city and county officials. Her findings were somewhat surprising to me in that they found that these officials rated e-mail ahead of traditional "snail" mail in importance to their office, though the absolute differences were small. It is surprising to me because I would think that the act of writing and mailing a letter takes considerably more effort than sending an e-mail message, so that letters would be assigned a higher priority by officials. But she (Chen, 2004, p. 8) also found that only 9% of the officials checked their own e-mail, leaving this to their assistants. The burden of incoming e-mail was relatively small compared to the huge amount that goes to members of Congress—just over 50% said they got more than 50 e-mails per day (Chen, 2004, p. 11). Although they used e-mail to communicate with the public, they were careful about using "*broadcast*" features of e-mail that would allow them to send mass mailings to the public because of the resentment that spam can cause in citizens. Many governmental sites now do provide the voluntary opportunity for residents to sign up for various forms of electronic communication. In Chen's (2004) study, some local officials had suffered from "spoofing" in which opponents sent offensive messages to the public that appeared to embarrass them. The overall assessment of e-mail contact by most local officials was that e-mail is useful once a good relationship had been established via in-person or phone contact.

There are a number of other developments in which IT is being used to encourage greater participation on the part of the public. For example, "public participation geographic information systems" are now being designed to enhance citizen participation, for example, by allowing members of the public to be able to visualize consequences of development decisions by studying maps and accompanying images (Krygier, 1998). Likewise, blogs (logs of individual opinions on issues recorded on the Internet) are being employed by some managers and could be used by governments to provide an additional method for citizens to express their viewpoints about public issues. Use of blogs in government is still rare. The State of Utah CIO (Harris, 2005) offered blogs to employees in order to encourage more open communication. Use of the Internet is now viewed by some as a way of reorganizing government according to the views of certain ideologies. For example, some conservatives view the Internet and Web sites as a way of increasing "choice-based policies" (Eggers, 2005) in areas such as education. For example, information would be presented about the efficacy of providers of education (both public and private schools) so that citizens could make an informed and voluntary choice.

Copyright © 2006, Idea Group Inc. Copying or distributing in print or electronic forms without written permission of Idea Group Inc. is prohibited.

Conclusion

Failure to become engaged and knowledgeable about internal politics can undermine the efficacy of information managers. I know of cases where managers with good technical skills lost their jobs due to their failure to master organizational politics. Information managers need to negotiate, bargain, dicker, and haggle with other departments. They may need to form coalitions and engage in log rolling in order to achieve their goals. A good information manager needs good political skills to be effective. I have drawn from a number of resources to illustrate the politics of information management but there exists little systematic research concerning the topic as Strassmann (1995) has pointed out. We need more research concerning the crucial issue, both in-depth qualitative case studies and as well as surveys, concerning how managers employ politics in their dealings with information technology.

The lessons of our review are clear. As Fountain (2001) has pointed out, generalist managers can no longer afford to ignore IT. Fountain (2001) sees the urgency for generalist administrator involvement:

Public executives and managers in a networked environment can no longer afford the luxury of relegating technology matters to technical staff. Many issues that appear to be exclusively technical are also deeply political and strategic in nature. In some cases, new use of technology furthers an existing agency or program mission. But in others, using the Internet can play a transformative role and lead to expansion or rethinking of mission and change in internal and external boundaries, accountability, and jurisdiction. (p. 249)

Likewise, IT managers can no longer afford to ignore politics. Internal political issues such as those I have discussed (structures, purchasing, sharing information, and electronic communication) have become so central that managers will find questions about these issues that demand attention and decision. External political issues will continue to grow in number and importance as the Web and cyber-politics become more prominent. For better or worse, information managers have to possess effective political skills.

References

Ackoff, R. (1967). Management misinformation systems. *Management Science, 14*(4), 319-331.

Alexander, J. H., & Grubbs, J.W. (1998). Wired government: Information technology, external public organizations, and cyberdemocracy. *Public Administration and Management: An Interactive Journal* (online), *3*(1). Retrieved from http://www.hbg.psu.edu/Faculty/jxr11/alex.html

Copyright © 2006, Idea Group Inc. Copying or distributing in print or electronic forms without written permission of Idea Group Inc. is prohibited.

Anderson, R., Bikson, T. K., Lewis, R., Moini, J., & Strauss, S. (2003). *Effective use of information technology: Lessons about state governance structures and processes.* Rand Corporation. Retrieved July 30, 2004, from http://www.rand.org/publications/MR/MR1704/index.html

Anonymous. (1994). The politics of information. *Logistic Information Management*, 7(2), 42-44.

Anonymous. (2001). Court rules that Web publisher may contest denial of link to city's Website. *3CMA: News of the city-county communications & marketing association*, 1.

Bardach, E. (1977). The *implementation game: What happens after a bill becomes a law.* Cambridge, MA: MIT.

Bellamy, C. (2000). The politics of public information systems. In G.D. Garson (Ed.), *Handbook of public information systems* (pp. 85-98). New York: Marcel Dekker.

Brodt, B., Possley, M., & Jones, T. (1993, November 4). One step ahead of the computer. *Chicago Tribune*, 6-7.

Brown, A. (1998). Narrative politics and legitimacy in an IT implementation. *Journal of Management Studies*, 35(1), 1-22.

Caldwell, B. (1992, November 30). Battleground: An attempt to streamline the Pentagon's operations has triggered a fight for control. *Informationweek*, 12-13.

Center for Technology in Government. (1999). *Reconnaissance study: Developing a business base for the integration of criminal justice systems.* Retrieved July 30, 2004, from http://www.ctg.albany.edu/resources/pdfrpwp/recon_studyrpt.pdf

Center for Technology in Government. (2000). *Building trust before building a system: The making of the homeless information management system.* Retrieved July 30, 2004, from http://www.ctg.albany.edu/guides/usinginfo/Cases/bss_case.htm

Chen, E. (2004, April 15-18). *You've got politics: E-mail and political communication in Silicon Valley.* Paper prepared for presentation at the Midwest Political Science Association, Chicago.

Cone, E. (1996, August 12). Do you really want this job? *Informationweek*, 63-70.

Cone, E. (1998, January 12). Crash-Landing ahead? *Informationweek*, 38-52.

Conte, C. R. (1995, June). Teledemocracy: For better or worse. *Governing*, 33-41.

Corbitt, B. (2000). Developing intraorganizational electronic commerce strategy: an ethnographic study. *Journal of Information Technology*, 15, 119-130.

Corbitt, B., & Thanasankit, T. (2002). Acceptance and leadership-hegemonies of e-commerce policy perspectives. *Journal of Information Technology*, (1), 39-57.

Coursey, D. (forthcoming). Strategically managing information technology: Challenges in the e-gov era. In J. Rabin (Ed.), *Handbook of public administration* (3rd ed.). New York: Marcel Dekker.

Daniels, A. (1997, November). The billion-dollar privatization gambit. *Governing*, 28-31.

Danziger, J. N. (1977, June). Computers and the frustrated chief executive. *MIS Quarterly*, 1, 43-53.

Copyright © 2006, Idea Group Inc. Copying or distributing in print or electronic forms without written permission of Idea Group Inc. is prohibited.

Danziger, J. N., Dutton, W.H., Kling, R., & Kraemer, K.L. (1982). *Computers and politics: High technology in American local governments.* New York: Columbia University.

Davenport, T., Eccles, R.G., & Prusak, L. (1992, Fall). Information politics. *Sloan Management Review,* 53-65.

Dizard, W.P. (2001, November). CIOs labor over contracting crisis. *Government Computer News.* Retrieved November 21, 2004, from www.gcn.com

Dutton, W. H., & Kraemer, K.L. (1985). *Modeling as negotiating: The political dynamics of computer models in the policy process.* Norwood, NJ: Ablex.

Eggers, W.D. (2005, February). Made to order. *Government Technology.* Retrieved February 11, 2005, from http://www.govtech.net/magazine/story.php?id=92875

Eiring, H. L. (1999, January). Dynamic office politics: Powering up for program success. *The Information Management Journal,* 17-25.

Feldman, J. (2002, March 4). Politics as usual. *Networking computing,* 13(Part 5).

Ferguson, C. (2004). *The Broadband problem: Anatomy of a market failure and a policy dilemma.* Washington, DC: Brookings Institution.

Fernback, J. (1997). The individual within the collective: Virtual ideology and the realization of collective principles. In S.G. Jones (Ed.), *Virtual culture: Identity and communication in cybersociety* (pp. 36-54). London: Sage.

Foster, A. L. (2004, May 18). Faculty petition criticizes Cal Poly campus's plan to install PeopleSoft software. *Chronicle of Higher Education.* Retrieved May 18, 2004, http://chronicle.com/daily/2004/05/2004051801n.htm

Franzel, J. M., & Coursey, D. H. (2004). Chapter V. Government Web portals: Management issues and the approaches of five states. In A. Pavlichev, & G.D. Garson (Eds.), *Digital government: Principles and best practices* (pp. 63-77). Hershey, PA: Idea Group Inc.

Freedman, D. H. (1994, March 1). A difference of opinion. *CIO,* 53-58.

Friel, B. (2001, July 18). TSP board fires, sues computer modernization Firm. *GovExec.com.*

Gregson, K. (1997). Community networks and political participation–developing goals for system developers. *Proceedings of the ASIS Annual Meeting,* 34 (pp. 263-270).

Grover, V, Lederer, A. L., & Sabherwal, R. (1988). Recognizing the politics of mis. *Information & Management, 14,* 145-156.

Gurwitt, R. (1996). CIOs: The new data czars. *Governing Magazine.* Retrieved February 3, 2003, from www.governing.com

Hale, M. (2004, April 15). *Neighborhoods on-line: A content analysis of neighborhood Web pages.* Paper prepared for delivery at the Annual Meeting of the Midwest Political Science Association, Chicago.

Harris, B. (1998, March). Telcom wars. *Government Technology, 11,* 1 & 38-40.

Harris, B. (2005, February). The coming of blog.gov. *Government Technology.* Retrieved February 25, 2005, from http://www.govtech.net/

Hasson, J. (2004, May 17). No easy answer to career vs. political standing. *Federal Computer Week.*

Copyright © 2006, Idea Group Inc. Copying or distributing in print or electronic forms without written permission of Idea Group Inc. is prohibited.

Hayes, M. (1996, August 19). Platform Zealots. *Informationweek*, 44-52.

Healey, J. (1997, August). The people's wires. *Governing*, 34-38.

Hoffman, T. (2004, February 16). Turnover increase hits the ranks of state CIOs. *Computer World*. Retrieved January 10, 2004, from http://www.computerworld.com/governmenttopics/government/story/0,10801,90236,00.html

James, F. (1997, April 10) Social Security ends Web access to records. *Chicago Tribune*, 1 & 12.

Kahaner, L. (2004, September). A costly debate. *Government Enterprise*, 8-14.

Keen, P.G.W. (1981). Information systems and organizational change. *Communications of the ACM, 24*(1), 24-33.

Kello, C. T. (1996). Participatory design: A not so democratic treatment. *American Journal of Psychology, 109*(4), 630-635.

Kidd, R. (1995, March). How vendors influence the quality of human services systems. *Government Technology*, 42-43.

King, J. L. (1983). Centralized versus decentralized computing: Organizational considerations and management options. *Computing Survey, 15*(4), 319-349.

Knights, D., & Murray, F. (1994). *Managers divided: Organisation politics and information technology management.* Chichester, UK: John Wiley.

Koskinen, J. A. (1996, July 15). Koskinen: What CIO act means to you. *Government Computer News, 22.*

Kost, J. M. (1996). *New approaches to public management: The case of Michigan.* Washington, D.C.: The Brookings Institution, CPM Report 96-1.

Kraemer, K. L., & King, J. L. (1976). *Computers, power, and urban management: What every local executive should know.* Beverly Hills, CA: Sage.

Krol, E. (1994, June 24). State's health plan for poor comes up short. *Chicago Tribune*, 1, 15.

Krygier, J.B. (1998). *The praxis of public participation gis and visualization.* Retrieved April 2, 2005, from http://www.ncgia.ucsb.edu/varenius/ppgis/papers/krygier.html

Laudon, K.C. (1974). *Computers and bureaucratic reform: The political functions of urban information systems.* New York: Wiley.

Lenard, T. M. (2004). *Government Entry into the Telecom Business: Are the benefits commensurate with the costs?* The Progress Freedom Foundation. Progress on Point 11.4. Retrieved July 24, 2004, from http://www.pff.org/publications/

Lighty, T., & Rado, D. (2004, September 12). Schools' Internet bungle. *Chicago Tribune*.

Lucas, H. C. (1984, January). Organizational power and the information services department. *Communications of the ACM, 127*, 58-65.

Manier, J. (1997, June 27). State endorses powerful machine. *Chicago Tribune*, 1, 5.

Markus, M. L. (1983, June). Power, politics, and MIS implementation. *Communications of the ACM, 26*, 430-444.

Markus, M.L. (1994). Electronic mail as the medium of managerial choice. *Organizational Science, 5*(4), 502-527.

Copyright © 2006, Idea Group Inc. Copying or distributing in print or electronic forms without written permission of Idea Group Inc. is prohibited.

Markus, M. L., & Keil, M. (1994, Summer). If we build it, they will come: Designing information systems that people want to use. *Sloan Management Review*, *35*, 11-25.

McKinnon, S. M., & Bruns, Jr., W. J. (1992). *The information mosaic*. Boston: Harvard Business School.

Miller, B. (1995a, April). Interview with Indianapolis mayor, Stephen Goldsmith. *Government Technology*, 24-25.

Miller, B. (1995b, February). Should agencies archive e-mail? *Government Technology*, 22.

Mitchell, T. (1999, July 26). Stiff-armed, but not by law. *The News Gazette*. Retrieved October 2, 2004, from http://news-gazette.com/OpenRecords/monmains.htm

Molta, D. (1999, January 25). The power of knowledge and information. *Network Computing*, *33*(1), 23-24.

Monastersky, R. (2004, November 25). Research groups accuse education department of using ideology in decisions about data. *The Chronicle of Higher Education*.

Murphy, S. (1995, June). Kansas city builds GIS to defray costs of clean water act. *Geo Info Systems*, 39-42.

Newcombe, T. (1995, October). The CIO-Lightning rod for IT troubles? *Government Technology*, *58*.

Newcombe, T. (1997, March). Cities become telecomm owners. *Government Technology*, Retrieved from http://www.govtech.net/

Newcombe, T. (1998). Welfare's new burden: Feds tie down states with data reporting requirements. *Government Technology*, *11*(4), 1 & 14-15.

Noll, C. L., & Wilkins, M. (2002). Critical skills of IS professionals: A model for curriculum development. *Journal of Information Technology Education*, *1*(3), 143-154.

Northrop, A., Kraemer, K.L., Dunkle, D.E, & King, J.L. (1990). Payoffs from computerization: Lessons over time. *Public Administration Review*, *50*(5), 505-514.

Novotny, P., & Jacobs, R.H. (1997). Geographical information systems and the new landscape of political technologies. *Social Science Computer Review*, 15(3), 264-285.

OMB Watch. (2002, February 1). Access to government information post September 11th Retrieved April 2, 2005, http://www.ombwatch.org/article/articleview/213/1/104/

Overton, K., Frolick, M.N., & Wilkes, R.B. (1996). Politics of implementing EISs. *Information Systems Management*, *13*(3), 50-57.

Pastore, R. (1995, December 1). CIO search and rescue. *CIO*, 54-64.

Pearson, R., & Parsons, C. (1997, August 17). MSI verdicts jolt Springfield. *Chicago Tribune*, *1*, 12.

Peled, A. (2000, February 14). Politicking for success: The missing skill. *Leadership & Organization Development Journal*, *21*, 20-29.

Perlman, E. (2000, August). Moving IT out. *Governing*, 58.

Copyright © 2006, Idea Group Inc. Copying or distributing in print or electronic forms without written permission of Idea Group Inc. is prohibited.

Peterson, S. (2000, September). This space for rent. *Government Technology, 14,* 140-141.

Peterson, S. (2002, October). End of the line. *Government Technology,* 18-24.

Pevtzow, L. (1989, July 8). Bitterly divided Naperville leaders decide computer strategy. *Chicago Tribune, 5.*

Pitkin, G. M. (1993). Leadership and the changing role of the chief information officer in higher education. *Proceedings of the 1993 CAUSE Annual Conference* (pp. 55-66). Boulder, CO: CAUSE.

Poulos, C. (1998, May). Mayor Stephen Goldsmith: Reinventing Indianapolis' local government. *Government Technology,* Special ed., 31-33.

Putnam, R. D. (1995, Spring). Bowling alone revisited. *Responsive Community, 5*(2), 18-37.

Quindlen, T. H. (1993, June 7). When is e-mail an official record? Answers continue to elude feds. *Government Computer News, 1,* 8.

Rickert, C. (2002, April 7). Web site look-alike causes concerns. *Daily Chronicle, 1.*

Rocheleau, B. (1993). Evaluating public sector information systems: Satisfaction versus impact. *Evaluation and Program Planning, 16,* 119-129.

Rocheleau, B. (1994). The software selection process in local governments. *American Review of Public Administration, 24*(3), 317-330.

Rocheleau, B. (1995). Computers and horizontal information sharing in the public sector. In H. J. Onsrud & G. Rushton (Eds.), *Sharing geographic information* (pp. 207-229). New Brunswick, NJ: Rutgers University.

Rocheleau, B. (1997). Governmental information system problems and failures: A preliminary review. *Public Administration and Management: An Interactive Journal* (online), *2*(3). Retrieved from the World Wide Web at: *http://www.pamij.com/roche.html*

Rocheleau, B. (2000). Guidelines for public sector system acquisition. In C. D. Garson (Ed.), *Handbook of public information systems* (pp. 277-390). New York: Marcel Dekker.

Rocheleau, B. (2002a, March 25). *Accountability mechanisms, information systems, and responsiveness to external values.* Paper presented at the 2002 meeting of the American society for public administration, Phoenix, AZ.

Rocheleau, B. (2002b). E-mail: Does it need to be managed? Can it be managed? *Public Administration and Management: An Interactive Journal, 7*(2). Retrieved from http://pamij.com/7_2/v7n2_rocheleau.html

Ruppe, D. (2001). *Some US agencies pull data from Web.* Retrieved from http://dailynews.yahoo.colm/h/abc/20011005/pl/wtc_internetsecurity_011004_1.html

Schattschneider, E.E. (1983). *The semisovereign people: A realist's view of democracy in America.* Fort Worth, TX: Holt, Rhinehart, and Winston.

Schmitz, J. (1997). Structural relations, electronic media, and social change: The public electronic network and the homeless. In S. G. Jones (Ed.), *Virtual culture: Identity and communication in cybersociety* (pp. 80-101). London: Sage.

Copyright © 2006, Idea Group Inc. Copying or distributing in print or electronic forms without written permission of Idea Group Inc. is prohibited.

Schoech, D., Jensen, C., Fulks, J., & Smith, K.K. (1998). Developing and using a community databank. *Computers in Human Services, 15*(1), 35-53.

Schuler, D. (1995, December). Public space in cyberspace. *Internet World,* 89-95.

Severin, C.S. (1993, October 11). The CEO should be the CIO. *Informationweek, 76.*

Stahlman, M. (1995, December 25). Internet democracy hoax. *Informationweek, 90.*

Standing, C., & Standing, S. (1998). The politics and ethics of career progression in IS: a systems perspective. *Logistics Information Management, 11*(5), 309-316.

Strassmann, P.A. (1995). *The politics of information management.* New Canaan: Information Economics.

Towns, S. (2004, December). Year in review: People. *Government Technology Magazine, 13.*

United States General Accounting Office. (1997). *Social Security Administration: Internet access to personal earnings benefits information* (GAO/T-AIMD/HEHS-97-123).

United States General Accounting Office. (2002, February 7). *DOD's standard procurement system.* Washington, DC: GAO-02-392T.

United States General Accounting Office. (2004, July). *Federal Chief Information Officers' Responsibilities, Reporting Relationships, Tenures, and Challenges.* GAO-04-823.

Vittachi, I. (2005, March 25). Western Springs set to welcome wi-fi zone. *Chicago Tribune.*

Washburn, G. (1998, May 18). Building-permit delays spur city shakeup. *Chicago Tribune,* 1 & 10.

West, D. (2001, August 30-September 2). *E-government and the transformation of public sector service delivery.* Paper prepared for delivery at the meeting of the American political science association, San Francisco.

Wiggins, L. (2001, March/April). Caribou and the census. *URISA News, 5.*

Wilhelm, A.G. (1997). A resource model of computer-mediated political life. *Policy Studies Journal, 25*(4), 519-534.

Yates, J. (2001, September 29). NY plans to track flow of donations: Red Cross raises privacy concerns. *Chicago Tribune.*

Additional Reading

There has not been much research on the politics of IT outside of the work of Kenneth Kraemer and his associates. The Markus (1983) article is a classic about the politics of IT in the private sector. Strassmann's work focuses on structural issues. The lack of research does not signify that the topic is unimportant. Rather, it reflects the difficulty of trying to gather systematic information about such a sensitive topic.

Copyright © 2006, Idea Group Inc. Copying or distributing in print or electronic forms without written permission of Idea Group Inc. is prohibited.

Key Concepts

- Broadcast [function of e-mail]
- Dotted-line relationships
- E-governance
- E-rulemaking
- Political skills in managing it

Discussion Questions

1. If you had to pick a head of the IT organization unit for an organization with which you are familiar and you had to choose between two individuals, one with excellent technical skills but weak politics skills and another with little technical knowledge but excellent political skills, which would you choose? Why?

2. What do you think about the advisability of setting up online discussion systems for citizens similar to that of the PEN system of Santa Monica described in this chapter? If you were in charge, would you support or oppose the establishment of such a system? Why? Would you make it a moderated list? If so, who should moderate it?

3. What do you think of the e-governance and e-rulemaking systems being set up by organizations like the Environmental Protection Administration described in this chapter and in the publications by Coglianese? Do you think they will have any major impact on the outcomes of agency rule-making?

4. Read the account of the California DOIT going out of business by Peterson and the reports by Anderson et al. of Rand. What lessons can be learned about political skills needed for IT in the governmental sector based on this case?

5. Study the organizational structures of some governmental/nonprofit organizations and note the location and authorities of those units that pertain to information and communication technology. Be ready to discuss questions such as: (A) What is the most common structure for IT? Does the IT unit tend to be a "line" or "staff" agency? What is the title of the head of the unit—is the person headed referred to as a CIO?; (B) What positions, departmental or other units or persons participate in making ICT policy other than the formal IT unit?; and (C) Does the department have any inside and/or outside body that plays a role in policymaking for IT?

Copyright © 2006, Idea Group Inc. Copying or distributing in print or electronic forms without written permission of Idea Group Inc. is prohibited.

Exercises

1. Read Peterson's account of the broadband battle and Lenard's study of municipal involvement in broadband. Then write an opinion piece in which you argue for or against municipal involvement in broadband development.

2. Describe politics as it relates to IT in an organization with you are familiar. Have you observed any examples of the types of politics that we describe in this chapter?

3. Study the IT structure of some organization and find out how its current structure evolved historically. Do they have any formal structures to advise top managers such as an IT-policy or end-users groups? How involved are the generalist administrators in IT? How effective with respect to communication are the IT staff? What changes would you recommend to the existing IT structure? Why? Write a paper summarizing these points.

4. Check out the existing job description of the CIO/IT head of a governmental/non-profit organization. Does the description cover all of the areas that you believe should be dealt with? Rewrite the job description or justify why the existing job description is accurate and complete.

Copyright © 2006, Idea Group Inc. Copying or distributing in print or electronic forms without written permission of Idea Group Inc. is prohibited.

Chapter VII

Information Technology, Training, and Organizational Learning

Introduction

The development of information technology creates many new opportunities for organizations to acquire and disseminate knowledge and skills among its employees. Due to the crucial importance of knowledge and skills related to IT, human resource issues have arisen that need to be dealt with. A recent in-depth study (Nelson & Todd, 2004) of several organizations identified the following issues as being important to the management of IT personnel (Adapted from Nelson & Todd, 2004, p. 4):

1. How can the organization recruit employees with the needed skills?
2. How can IT staff work together with the human resources department?
3. How can the organization develop the right mix of skills?
4. How can the organization support career development programs that meet the needs of the organization and the staff?
5. How can the organization keep up with new technologies?
6. How can employees be compensated fairly?
7. How can an effective work environment be developed and maintained?
8. How can personnel balance work and personal life?
9. How can key personnel be retained?

Copyright © 2006, Idea Group Inc. Copying or distributing in print or electronic forms without written permission of Idea Group Inc. is prohibited.

This is not an exhaustive list. For example, one major issue for governmental organizations concerns the relationship between IT and public sector unions when it comes to outsourcing.

Coursey and McCreary (2005) discuss some examples of organizations employing online efforts at recruitment. These online recruitment systems have some very positive aspects such as the ability of applicants to track the status of their applications and the ability of the organization to use the computer's power to match up applicants for one position with other jobs that are available. Automated responses can inform applicants about the other positions. The functions may help save substantial personnel time. However, Coursey and McCreary (2005) also point out that paper applications must be maintained due to issues such as the digital divide.

The rapid speed of change in IT creates a need for continual learning for all levels or employees in government. Think about the changes that have occurred in the past decade. The Internet and related technologies such as e-mail have gone from being techniques exploited by relatively few public organizations to pervasive technologies that play a major role in everyday activities of public administrators. E-government is a fairly new development and as recently as two or three years ago, interactive Web applications existed in few organizations and they were regarded as innovative. Now most public organizations, even those with few IT resources, are likely support at least some interactive applications on their Web sites. Likewise, complex technologies such as geographic information systems (GIS) have emerged from a rarity to a commonplace at all levels of governments. There is a continual stream of promising new software applications aimed at governments. It seems that each day brings new IT-related concepts that public organizations need to consider implementing if they are to keep up with the best practices of leading organizations. The rapidity of these developments makes it virtually impossible for personnel to keep up with the pace of change (Lee, 2004, p. 114).

New information systems often have many costs that are hidden (Anderson & Dawes, 1991). Workers lose productivity as they need time to learn the new system. Currid (1995) describes a typical process for introducing a new system:

When a new system is introduced, it rocks day-to-day activity so much that some people don't adjust quickly. They stay less productive than they were without the new computer. And, if this situation goes unchecked, they may never recover. (p. 63)

In order to make up for this loss in productivity, users will require substantial training to improve their productivity through the new system. One report concluded that system benefits are obtained in local government only if technically qualified people are trained to operate the system (Schwartzrock & Jones, 1986). According to the Government Finance Officer Association (Miranda et al., 2002, p. 62), training for complex systems such as Enterprise Resource Planning systems is "often overlooked," but is crucial and should be budgeted for up to 20% of the implementation costs of the system. These rapid changes in hardware and software create the need for continuous learning. The problem is exacerbated by the fact that the turnover rate for IT employees is twice

Copyright © 2006, Idea Group Inc. Copying or distributing in print or electronic forms without written permission of Idea Group Inc. is prohibited.

that of business and other professionals (Magid & Shayo, 2004, p. 25). Other human resource issues also result such as the need to attract and retain personnel with the required IT skills and to revise position descriptions that have technical content. Moreover, changes in the IT field have altered the nature of the skills needed by IT leadership and staff. According to the Working Council for Chief Information officers, two major trends have changed the nature of IT work: (1) The growth and domination of packaged (rather than customized) applications, and (2) The use of outsourcing. For example, Riper and Durham describe the work of the project manager in charge of implementing an ERP program as involving the use of "numerous project management tools" including the construction of a Gantt chart that "contained 220 separate tasks." The importance of project management and other managerial skills is noted in the District of Columbia's 2002-2004 IT Strategic Plan:

District agencies need training to help fill numerous gaps in IT skills. Many agencies lack important IT management skills, such as business analysis, project management, and package implementation experience.

In an e-mail to me, an IT director echoed the point that IT managers often most need "soft" skills:

(IT Director) –My perspective is that people management skills far outweigh technical skills even in relatively small organizations. My reasoning is that the former skills are harder to inculcate than the technical skills, and that a technically limited manager with the right people skills can draw more value from his/her subordinates than a manager with godlike technical abilities. Secondarily, the ability to articulate the value of an effective IT infrastructure to management has more value for an IT team leader than technical understanding of the tradeoffs between IPSec and SSL. To put my perspective into perspective, I was a software engineer…. And I drifted into system administration and then into IT management. I had to invent the softer skills along the way in order to be effective, and I'm grateful to my supervisory mentors.

Darais et al. (2004, p. 93) echo this point: "the implication is that the IT professional is not simply writing code, but is also expected to understand and translate business processes into a technical solution." Soft skills is a category that, according to Schwarkopf et al. (2004, p. 54), includes several characteristics and traits including the individual's fit with the organization's culture, her/his communication and interpersonal skills, their leadership and project management capacities, their general industry knowledge, and their general problem-solving ability.

Another major change is the enormous growth in the service role of IT. These trends mean that, in addition to traditional technical skills, IT leadership and staff as well as generalist administrators with IT responsibilities need to be well trained in project management skills, negotiating, monitoring of contracts, management of long-term relationships with vendors, and learn how to provide effective support services to end users. At the same

Copyright © 2006, Idea Group Inc. Copying or distributing in print or electronic forms without written permission of Idea Group Inc. is prohibited.

time, both IT staff and end users will need to regularly upgrade their technical skills in order to support new systems and software.

There is empirical research (Guimares, Staples & McKeen, 2004, p. 313) that shows that end-user training is one of the important contributors to the success of IT systems. The importance and size of the effort required for training is reflected in the Strategic IT Plans of many governments. For example, the City of Honolulu, Hawaii (2000) discussed the importance of IT training in their plan:

Staff and staff training are critical issues for the effective and efficient use of technology. Users of technology must be adequately trained to use IT tools. As reflected in many TCO studies, the approximate $1,500 cost of a personal computer is trivial compared to the cost of the labor of the worker using that PC, or of the staff making sure that the PC works. More than 70% of the total cost of running distributed systems is associated with support. According to The Gartner Group, untrained users consume three to six times more support than trained users. The city must have a technically competent workforce in order to effectively and efficiently operate. Clear expectations for technical proficiency must be identified and high-quality training programs provided for end users and managers to meet those expectations. The city must form a partnership with employees to develop IT skills, with each taking part of the responsibility for skill acquisition.

Likewise, the City of Tampa, Florida (2002, p. 23) described the importance of training as follows:

- As noted throughout...there are critical training needs in each of the technical support groups. When this training is not provided, MIS staff spends time "learning on the job." This can be a painful learning process for our users. When MIS staff does not receive adequate training:
  - o Projects take longer to implement
  - o Staff "ignorance" causes major problems and "downtime"
  - o Routine maintenance has to be "outsourced" because in-house staff do not have the appropriate skill level
  - o Base level skills such as project management are missing as a core "competency"
  - o Transitions to new technical platforms are difficult and resistance to "change" is increased

Often expensive software is purchased because of their advanced capabilities but these capabilities are not used by their end users due to a lack of learning. The District of Columbia's Strategic 2002-2004 IT Plan emphasizes this point (Section 3):

Copyright © 2006, Idea Group Inc. Copying or distributing in print or electronic forms without written permission of Idea Group Inc. is prohibited.

Agency managers observe that many existing systems capabilities go unused because agency staff lack the training needed to fully utilize system capabilities. User training needs are especially urgent in customer applications, where employees must master both systems and information content to answer questions and deliver city services. (p. 13)

And the City of Sunnyvale's (California) 1999 IT Strategic plan put it as follows: "Information Technology is not an extra or specialized skill any longer but rather a key component of everyone's routine working responsibilities." Moreover, training of end users is crucial in dealing with huge and complex tasks such as controlling spam and viruses (Paul, 2001).

Some new systems require an especially large amount of training. For example, in order to implement an ERP system in Multnomah County, Oregon (Boyer, 2001), the county developed 44 different courses and nearly 500 training sessions for its employees over a period of less than one year. Kavanagh and Targosz (2001) point to training as one of the three most important success factors to CRM success in their case study of its implementation in the Michigan Economic Development Corporation (MEDC). Learning to use IT does not require just technical training. For some kinds of technologies such as "virtual teams," research (e.g., DeMarie, 2000, p. 17) has found that training should emphasize "interpersonal communication skills and how to overcome the challenges that conferencing technologies pose for effective teamwork." DeMarie goes on to note that many governments "underestimate the value of training people" and as a consequence, team members "underestimate the value of their technology tools" because they are not aware of its full range of capabilities.

Despite these statements attesting to the importance of IT training, there is evidence that organizations do not devote enough resources to learning. A study by Fletcher et al. (1992) of county governments reported that IT training was the most neglected aspect of IT management and a study by Nelson and Cheney (1987) found that training budgets made up between 0% and 2% of the overall IT budget. Wu & Rocheleau (2001) studied IT training efforts by public and private organizations and discovered that, although private organizations spent more on training than public, neither set of organizations spent much in absolute terms on IT training. It appears that spending on training tends to be sacrificed to direct service needs when there are budget shortages. The following IT director discusses how he was directed by generalist managers to cut the trainer from the IT budget during a period when the municipality had to make budget cuts due to decreased revenues:

(IT Director) – They [city manager office] didn't even tell me—I looked at the budget and that is how I found out that position [IT trainer] was cut...but by cutting the training position, they cut the training program.

Indeed, the consistent lack of emphasis to learning efforts is the reason that the "Balanced Scorecard System" (Kaplan & Norton, 200) includes "innovation and learning perspective" as one of their four categories of measures. They argue that unless learning

Copyright © 2006, Idea Group Inc. Copying or distributing in print or electronic forms without written permission of Idea Group Inc. is prohibited.

efforts are made part of the "metrics" that the organization measures and rewards, learning efforts such as training will tend to be neglected.

Planning for Learning: Needs Assessment

IT learning needs to be viewed as a continual process and IT training requires significant planning and should not be regarded as one-time event or even annual events. Planning for IT learning should be part of the overall IT planning process. As we saw in the chapter on planning for IT, standardization of software is one of the major goals of most governmental organizations and this standardization helps reduce the learning demands on the organization. Secondly, the purchasing process for any hardware or software system should incorporate training as an integral part of the purchase or, if the application is being developed internally, the IT department needs to provide for adequate training, too. Shayo, Olfman and Teitelroit (1999) and others have pointed out that formal training requires three essential components: (1) The *pre-training* phase in which needs of the trainees are assessed; (2) The administration of the formal training program; and (3) The *post-training period* when learners try to integrate their training into their jobs.

The U.S. General Accounting Office (GAO) (2003) studied the practices of leading private-sector companies with respect to training for IT and concluded that organizations should "document the competencies/skills required for each job description" (U.S. General Accounting Office, 2003, p. 13) and develop a "*gap analysis*" to determine what training was needed. Since training demands exceed supply, the organization will need to prioritize training needs to ensure they mesh well with organizational needs. The GAO study identified the need to plan for both long-term career development issues as well as short-term, "*Just-in-Time" (JIT) training* needs. The need for both long- and short-term learning and training is emphasized in some governmental IT plans. For example, the technology plan for Prince Williams County (Virginia) emphasized the need for longer term planning and gap analysis in its 1998 IT plan.

They encourage the establishment of formal "learning boards" and/or councils to develop training strategies and they note (GAO, 2004, p. 30) that software applications entitled "Learning Management Systems" are now used to register, track, and administer training" for employees. GAO argues that the organization should maintain an "*inventory of skills*" and that *individual development plans (IDPs)* should be developed for each employee. GAO argues that employees should be given responsibility for assessing their own needs (GAO, 2003, p. 21). This needs assessment process is outlined in GAO's (2003, p. 27) diagram in Figure 1.

However, it is important to note that the GAO study focused on large private-sector organizations and small-sized (or even moderately-sized) government agencies are unlikely to have special formal structures to make training decisions. Indeed, Schwarkopf et al.'s (2004) research on businesses found the same situation—small businesses cannot afford nor do they feel the need for formal systems:

Copyright © 2006, Idea Group Inc. Copying or distributing in print or electronic forms without written permission of Idea Group Inc. is prohibited.

Figure 1. Formal needs assessment for IT training

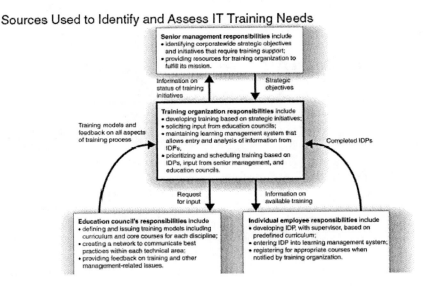

Source: U.S. General Accounting Office. (2003, January). Information *Technology Training: Practices of Leading Private-Sector Companies*. Washington, D.C.: GAO-03-390, p. 27.

Formal IT inventory systems were often integrated with org promotion and review processes which allowed employees to record any newly acquired skills. Smaller companies in our study found it difficult to justify the cost of a formal IT-skills-tracking system. Senior management of these companies stated that they were fully aware of their organization's skill inventory and did not need a formal skills-tracking system. (p. 61)

Thus training decisions for most government agencies will be based on balancing demands for training among IT, HR (Human Resource), and end-user departments. IT staff tend to come from technical backgrounds and may not be very interested or knowledgeable about training while HR staff often lack strong IT backgrounds. Indeed, Ryan and Todd argue that the development of a partnership between the IT and HR departments is a critical success factor in attracting and retaining IT staff. A team approach is often employed in hiring and, in some cases, HR staff are actually assigned to the IT department in large organizations (Schwarkopf et al., 2005, p. 56). Adding even greater complexity to the situation is the fact that it is the end-user departments that may best know their IT training needs of their staff so the development of an adequate training program requires collaboration among IT, end-user, and HR departments. Consequently, generalist managers need to step in and play an active role in the establishment and implementation of IT training and to prioritize training needs. The GAO model implies a

Copyright © 2006, Idea Group Inc. Copying or distributing in print or electronic forms without written permission of Idea Group Inc. is prohibited.

centralized approach to training and development which can be good in terms of taking advantage of standardization and economy of scale in meeting training needs. But training needs emerge quickly at the end-user level and it may not be feasible to wait for formal structures to respond in a timely matter. Indeed, another GAO publication (2004, p. 34) acknowledges the need to combine decentralized and centralized approaches to training and development.

A critical question that governments need to ask themselves about every application and hardware system is the degree to which they want to rely on outside training. The City of Houston's Strategic Technology Plan (2001, pp. 18-19) states that research shows that the "main reason for failure in technology implementation projects is lack of transfer of knowledge from the consultants to the client IT and department staff." The government's role can range from using the consultant for "quality advice" at strategic times to heavy dependence on consultants over the long term. The latter case represents a high-risk situation. Thus, in order to avoid dependence and risky situations, the organization has to train its staff adequately.

Sources for IT Training

There are a wide variety of sources for IT learning and training today. Traditional sources include formal training done within the organization by staff or external trainers for training within the organization. When new software and hardware systems are purchased, it is important that that the provision of adequate training be written into the contract. Staff may be sent to training provided by outside vendors and/or colleges. Employees differ as to the optimum approach to learning. For example, Compeau and Higgins (1995) have explored the use of modeling behavior to perform effective computer training. The theory is that by viewing a videotape of a "model" learning to do computing, learners will be able to better their own learning efforts, especially if the model is shown making common types of errors that most end users do. Another theory in training is that learning (Simon, Grover, Teng & Whitcomb, 1996) that is entirely passive is less effective than that which encourages exploration. Compeau and Higgins report evidence that there is an inverse relationship between the level of organizational support and end user's sense of self-efficacy. In my experience, this situation could be explained by the case where an expert solves problems for the end users but does not teach (and thus empower) employees to solve the problem themselves later. A study by Gist, Schwoerer and Wilson (1989) showed that end users with a weak sense of self-efficacy learned better through modeling approaches than tutorials. The amount of research on IT learning is limited but, overall, it suggests the need for the employment of multiple methods because users vary in what method works best with them.

My interviews with IT staff confirmed the difficulty and complexity of building an adequate IT training program. For example, the following manager expressed his frustration:

Copyright © 2006, Idea Group Inc. Copying or distributing in print or electronic forms without written permission of Idea Group Inc. is prohibited.

(Assistant City Manager) – "That is probably one of the most frustrating things we have to accomplish. Our training is very minimal and it is.... We don't have a formalized training process. That is one of the goals of the HR and IT depts., to work together to get a formal training program. The way it works now is that we set a new person down in front of the computer and each department handles its own internal training just enough so they can do the tasks necessary for that dept. We did implement skills testing just for applicants. Because we had the problem that if we asked if they could run Microsoft Office, they would say yes, but we had no basis to compare to find out if they actually could or not. So we have a system we are developing to test individual skills. Beginning, intermediate and advanced and then put together a curriculum to move them through. So when we are ready to forward with the new building, we have the plan. We [will] have a new computer training room in the new hall. That is one of the problems, we have no central computing training area. We don't even have the expertise to do the training.

(You prefer to do it in house?)

We have done both (send to junior colleges and hire vendors to train). ...I participated in some of those training sessions. We have found that it is hard to expect somebody to spend a day or afternoon going through a workbook and then retain it when they come back here. What we have found is that if somebody has a project or issue they are working on themselves on their job, if you challenge them and work with them, they are going to retain a lot more than the rote learning they do in one of these sessions. So we decided that is how we will do the training in the future but we just haven't developed the curriculum to date. We learned the hard way. We did bring some people in to do training and it was marginally successful. Very expensive. We just feel that in the long run, we can do it cheaper in-house. And more directed to our people.

According to my interviews, most employees are aware of the importance of IT training and say they want more of it. However, they often skip training when it is offered due to short-term job pressures. For example, Multnomah County (Oregon) found it very difficult to implement the training because of inadequate attendance at training sessions as well as the fact that the roles of key personnel changed during the project (Boyer, 2001). Organizations try to adapt training efforts so that they are less burdensome and disruptive. One organization's approach employed integrating training into short "bag lunch" sessions as a way to deal with these issues:

[Administrator] – "We had an initiative about two years ago, where [IT director] was coordinating what he called Lunch-and-Learn programs. They were done in-house so it saved a lot of money rather than having to send people to Word or PowerPoint classes. Everyone would pay a dollar and over lunch you would get a class on whatever you wanted it to be—Lotus Notes or spreadsheet or document. Those were well received and the in-house training was excellent. And [IT director] took the lead so we didn't have to pay an outside consultant to come in and do the training. And we have an MIS committee...help us find out what the needs of the department are."

Copyright © 2006, Idea Group Inc. Copying or distributing in print or electronic forms without written permission of Idea Group Inc. is prohibited.

This organization uses a nominal charge (e.g., one dollar per session) for its training efforts and has found that the small charge does seem to make a difference in attendance.

Traditional sources of training are now being supplemented by many "e-learning" sources as the GAO (January 2003, p. 46) outlined in the diagram in Figure 2.

Coursey and McCreary (2005) describe some e-learning efforts that governments are employing such as to obtain certifications but they also point out that these "on-demand" approaches are not as good as classroom training at handling difficult questions and tailoring the material to the unique needs of the user.

There is a complementary method to training and learning that organizations use to increase the organization's overall level of technology skill: recruit personnel with excellent IT skills. In the organizations I interviewed, new personnel may bring with them skills that they have learned on their own, in school, or via previous jobs. Many local governments with which I am familiar, use interns and entry-level people to deal with emerging IT needs such as managing and maintaining departmental Web sites. It is the general expectation that new junior level employees will have good IT skills. Thus recruitment can, like the informal training noted earlier, make up to some degree for weak formal training. However, if recruitment is to fulfill this function, it would suggest that IT skills should be considered as part of the evaluation process of new employees. It may be useful if not important to formalize expectations about the levels of IT skills needed for these new positions in the job descriptions. My own informal analysis suggests that IT skills are often ignored in most job descriptions, even though many jobs assume that the employees have at least good skills. Likewise, to assess IT skills, some organizations administer some kind of test of skills. There are computerized tests available or the organization may present the individual with, for example, a worksheet or database-related problem and ask the individual to develop the worksheet/data base application. New employees may be expected to bring with them electronic portfolios with examples

Figure 2. E-learning sources

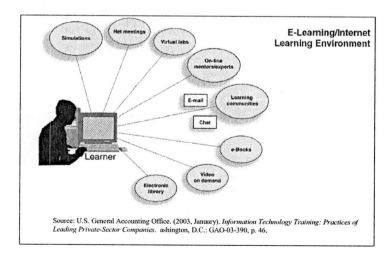

Source: U.S. General Accounting Office. (2003, January). *Information Technology Training: Practices of Leading Private-Sector Companies.* ashington, D.C.: GAO-03-390, p. 46.

Copyright © 2006, Idea Group Inc. Copying or distributing in print or electronic forms without written permission of Idea Group Inc. is prohibited.

of their best examples of applications which they should be ready to explain. Of course, if a person comes to an organization with good IT skills, it is still important for these skills to be regularly upgraded through training opportunities.

E-Learning and Online Communication

E-learning has become an important source of training and one of its key aspects is that, although it is possible to formally plan and encourage such learning, much of this e-learning is initiated by employees themselves. Such e-learning has major advantages that it can be scheduled at the convenience of the learner and they also tend to be inexpensive compared to formal classes (whether internal or external). These e-learning methods are likely to be very effective for those individuals who are capable of learning on their own. There are numerous online learning opportunities, especially in the information technology area, that can be employed by organizations that lack the staff or resources to do their own training. Of course, these online courses often are expensive and can necessitate extensive commitment of time so that management will have to be willing to provide the time and money to support this activity.

Another aspect of learning concerns information derived from the Internet and other communication technologies. There exist listservs and other forms of electronic communication that provide great opportunities for public and non-profit employees to gain invaluable information for free. The importance of this informal learning from such networks cannot be overestimated. For example, this author belongs to several online communities where I observe daily cases of useful sharing of technology-related information including the listservs of Government Information Management Science Association, the Innovation Groups (www.ig.org), City Webmasters (citywebmasters@listserv.ci.irving.tx.us), and the Information Systems Forum that is aimed at non-profit IT administrators (http://docs.yahoo.com/info/terms/). In the chapter on sharing IT systems, I discuss the importance of communities of interest like these in more detail. I believe that such communities have enabled extensive sharing of information and hence learning that helps to enhance the IT-related knowledge of their employees.

Informal Learning

In addition to e-learning, there is another major source of training that is often ignored by IT staff and generalist managers: peer-to-peer help. Such help is crucial for two reasons: (1) The resources devoted to formal training are often inadequate; and (2) Formal training must be integrated into specific on-the-job tasks and this integration is often difficult for many employees. Shayo et al. (1999) found that the post-training period is essential. If computing skills learned at formal training sessions are not supported when

Copyright © 2006, Idea Group Inc. Copying or distributing in print or electronic forms without written permission of Idea Group Inc. is prohibited.

they return to work, they can be lost and many supervisors did not encourage follow-up learning. This is illustrated by the experience of the Michigan Economic Development Corporation (MEDC) (Kavanagh & Targosz, 2001). It identified training as the weakest area of their CRM implementation because the training was consumed with learning the software basics and did not get into how staff could use the software to achieve specific job-related tasks. They concluded that they should have used a *"train-the-trainer"* approach and learned the software before the implementation of the project (Kavanagh & Targosz, 2001).

In short, many employees have problems translating learning done in classes to their jobs. Thus employees often turn to other employees for help. Often there are certain *"gurus"* or *"super users"* in organizations who take on important roles in providing the kind of specific task-related guidance that is missing from formal training sources. In one study (Wu & Rocheleau, 2001), we asked users in governments (and private organizations too) to identify their sources of IT learning and informal sources were far more commonly reported (92%) than formal sources (outside and internal classes were reported by only 38% and 29% respectively). Moreover, we asked the end users to evaluate the assistance they received from various sources and they rated assistance from peers as the most effective method (Wu & Rocheleau, 2001, p. 318). Overall, the vast majority (78% and 80% respectively) of public and private-sector employees said that their IT training came from informal sources. Indeed, the GAO's study of the practices of leading private-sector organizations concerning IT training (U.S. GAO, 2003, p. 30) emphasized the limitations of formal training:

The company provides formal training through a corporate university, online courses, and courses at local colleges, but it also uses on-the-job training since company staff believe that formal training provides only a small part of what an employee needs to know to perform effectively.

The importance of informal training is recognized in the plans of some public organizations. For example, the City of Bellevue's (Washington) 2001 Strategic IT Plan noted the importance of *"shadow staff"* as essential to supplementing central IT staff:

The growth in departmental shadow staff performing help-desk and PC support functions impacts service consistency and efficiency. At the same time, remote sites and alternative shift employees have a strong need for these services which central IT staff cannot easily meet. The situation is compounded by the tendency for the role of departmental application support staff to blur, with many co-workers seeing these individuals as PC support resources as well. This plans calls for formalizing shadow help desk support on a case-by-case basis. These employees must utilize the city's defined help-desk software —and will require appropriate training. Departments will need to actively encourage employees to use designated help-desk resources. Calls will first go to ITD's help desk (during normal business hours) and will be routed to ITD defined or defined shadow staff, as appropriate.

Copyright © 2006, Idea Group Inc. Copying or distributing in print or electronic forms without written permission of Idea Group Inc. is prohibited.

Note: When shadow staff are removed from the calculation, the city's help desk and PC support staffing ratios do not meet industry standards. If shadow staff are removed from providing this service investments in online help support options and/or additional staff in this function should be further evaluated. (pp. 2-16)

Likewise, the City of Boulder (2002, p. 28), Colorado's Strategic Technology Plan states the intention "to take advantage of both formal and informal opportunities for IT and user department employees to meet each other and develop positive working relationships." There have been cases where super users have taken over the implementation of enterprise software (Anderson, 1997). Reliance on informal assistance can cause problems. In a study of municipalities, I found that these gurus sometimes experienced conflicts between their regular duties and the informal role that they took on as "gurus" or super users (Rocheleau, 1985). In such cases, the guru may have to seek to have formal recognition of her/his informal guru role and an accommodation made and recognized by the organization or his/her performance ratings could suffer. Given the importance of informal training and learning, it is important that organizations reward, not penalize, these efforts. This may require that such efforts be recognized in the personnel evaluations and informal assistance may be written into the job descriptions and planning of the organization if it is judged to contribute to the overall productivity of the organization. Of course, to some extent, this means that "informal learning" becomes routinized and part of the formal system.

According to some IT department heads, certain IT learning can only be done by the end-user departments themselves. They are the ones who have the expertise and time to learn programs involving complex substantive operations and the training needs of a large municipality, which are too great for IT staff to master. The following IT head noted that they told some end-user staff they were responsible themselves for learning utility billing:

A lot of times they call us and say, 'I am having trouble with the utility billing function' and it took a lot of years meeting with them to say that we don't know utility billing, we are not going to be able to help you guys, you are going to need to develop your own internal expertise. And finally what it took was us reiterating it for several years and finally making it the culture where departments are responsible for understanding their own software. What we do is we load it, we troubleshoot it, make sure it operates correctly, we act as a liaison between [name of government software vendor] and our users, but what we can't do is be the people to operate it. I know in some governments that there are people who know that. They know the apps and how they work but in [name of city] that just doesn't work. It's too big for us to know.

One of the approaches to expanding the learning capacity of organizations is a *"train-the-trainers"* approach in which departmental staff, so-called *"super users,"* who show an interest and capability are given training first and then they take on the responsibility for training peers. For example, Naperville's 2001 Five Year Plan (Illinois) discussed how a major new proposed software package could be implemented by emphasizing super users:

Copyright © 2006, Idea Group Inc. Copying or distributing in print or electronic forms without written permission of Idea Group Inc. is prohibited.

To successfully integrate the proposed new technologies into the workplace, the departments should commit selected staff as 'Super Users.' These individuals will work from within the core departments to assist, train, and act as the expert liaisons to the IT department.... 'Super Users' form the foundation for on-going end-user training and support. These individuals should understand the technology and its use within the specific department. It can be accomplished through the use of external and vendor training, in-house tailored training programs, and self-taught training using a technology test/training 'lab' to encourage experimentation in a non-live environment.

The use of a "train-the-trainer approach" is common in implementation of major systems. RFPs for new computer systems should require vendors to specify their approach to development of trainers as is done in an RFP by theSeattle (WA) Police Department:

Please describe the process the vendor will use to develop the trainer training. List all coursework required to fully train the trainers that will in turn train the end users (SPD civilian and sworn personnel). For each course, please state the prerequisite requirements, size of class, and duration.

In another example, Des Moines (Iowa) picked one IT employee as "training coordinator" for the implementation of their ERP system and he was made responsible for sending other employees to receive "train-the-trainer" skills so that knowledge could be passed on (Riper & Durham, 1999, p. 4). Harris (1999) has summarized the advantages of the train-the-trainers approach as being its low cost and the fact that it encourages "knowledge transfer" from consultants to end users. But he also points out that the approach assumes that "trainers have the teaching skills, the proficiency, and the time necessary to train end users." Harris (1999), for example, points out that Alameda County's implementation of ERP had to hire external vendors to do training due to the lack of time and inability to juggle schedules by the in-house-trained "trainers."

The overall message from practitioners is that no single approach to training will be sufficient. For example, Prince Williams County's (Virginia) (1998) plan emphasizes the need to not rely too much on "just-in-time training" (JITT) because they need a combination of JITT, e-learning, classroom, and informal "mentoring." Formal training is expensive and governments try to take advantage of low-cost or no-cost training opportunities offered by associations and conferences they attend. *Cross-training* is called for in many IT plans of governments. The author has seen resistance to cross-training efforts on the part of some staff because they view their skills as "job insurance" and are reluctant to give up this insurance. The sharing of costs and responsibilities is an issue for the organization to decide. In many cases, the cost of training comes out of the budget of the end-user departments as is the case in Colorado Springs (2000):

Training must be an integral part of the purchase or implementation of new desktop software... IT and the operating units should continue to share responsibility for user training. IT's role should be to identify and make available training resources, including online distance learning and local classroom training provided by the

Copyright © 2006, Idea Group Inc. Copying or distributing in print or electronic forms without written permission of Idea Group Inc. is prohibited.

private sector. The operating units are responsible for identifying what their training needs are, matching up the appropriate training resources with these needs, and paying for this user training. (p. 38)

The IT training needs of IT staff are even greater than those of end users. Lee (2004) has pointed out that young IT employees experience a "shock" when they enter the IT work world. They expect to receive thorough training but they are disappointed because the training they receive only provides an overview and they are left to learn on their own at work and thus need to rely on their supervisors and colleagues for most of their learning (Lee, 2004, p. 125). Moreover, there is a strong ethic among IT workers that they should be able to solve problems independently (Lee, 2004, p. 126). This ethic makes learning difficult and it is the task of IT employees to find individuals with whom they are comfortable seeking information (Lee, 2004, p. 127).

Although formal training is not sufficient, nevertheless there is a great need for it. Some staff will need to go through formal programs such as certifications and recertifications for certain types of hardware and software support. In addition to technical training, there is also agreement (e.g., District of Columbia 2002-2004 Information Technology Strategic Plan, p. 13) that IT staff need a great deal of training in non-technical training such as "business analysis" and "project management" skills. Although some fear that well-trained IT employees may use their training to find better-paying jobs elsewhere, training for IT staff is universally seen as an important step to take in order to retain good quality staff (Dash, 2002). One Chief Technology Officer (Dickerson, 2004, p. 22) prefers the self-learning approach for IT staff such as through books because formal "classes tend to focus on the least common denominator." But he notes that book training can be frustrating and needs to be supplemented by mentoring done by in-house experts.

One major human resource issue concerns outsourcing in general and outsourcing of IT work in particular. Due to budget pressures, many states are turning to outsourcing arrangements to save money (Wreden, 2004). These moves are controversial and some outsourcing arrangements such as those of the State of Indiana have been canceled. The City of Chicago has outsourced its network, desktop support, and data center and, according to a study by Gartner (Wreden, 2004, p. 24), the customer satisfaction levels improved. However, the movement to outsourcing is not easy, as Chicago's CIO O'Brien acknowledges. In Chicago, the vendor hired most of the IT staff that were to lose their jobs and the City of Minneapolis required that the vendor offer jobs to personnel for at least three years (Wreden, 2004). Thus great emphasis on communication and "cultural" issues is necessary according to the leadership in those cases that have been viewed as successes for outsourcing.

How does one evaluate the training and education efforts of governments? Studies of private-sector organizations (Sircar, Turnbow & Bordoloi, 2000) found high correlations between IT staff training and sales and market share. Mecklenburg County (2003, p. 32) uses a number of indicators. It conducts a training survey to identify the percent of IT employees who self-report participation in training, the average training days per employee, and the percent that report that training "helped them in their jobs." David Molchany, CIO of Fairfax County (Virginia), plans to have trainees use their new knowledge soon after the class (Dash, 2002). Of course, the ultimate evaluation of the

Copyright © 2006, Idea Group Inc. Copying or distributing in print or electronic forms without written permission of Idea Group Inc. is prohibited.

efficacy of the training efforts may be whether they improve the results obtained when the IT function is evaluated by the organization.

References

Anderson, D. (1997, November 1). Super users speed to the rescue. *CIO, 11*(3), Section 1, 28-30.

Anderson, D. F., & Dawes, S.S. (1991). *Government information management: A primer and casebook*. Englewood Cliffs, NJ: Prentice-Hall.

Boyer, D. (2001). Erp implementation: Managing the final preparation and go-live stages. *Government Finance Review, 17*(6), 41-44.

City of Bellevue (Washington). (2001, November 7). *Enterprise strategic IT plan*. Retrieved December 22, 2003, from http://www.cityofbellevue.org/departments/ IT/pdf/Bellevue%20Enterprise%20Final%20Strategic%20IT%20Plan.pdf

City of Colorado Spring. (2000, October 1). *Information technology strategic plan: Digital direction*. Retrieved May 13, 2003, from http://www.springsgov.com/ units/IT/ITSP_2000_StrategicPlan.pdf

City of Honolulu, Hawaii. (2000, September). *Information technology master plan*. Retrieved February 12, 2003, from http://www.co.honolulu.hi.us/it/itplan.htm

City of Houston. (2001). *Strategic technology plan for the city of Houston*, Friday, July 20, 2001. Houston, TX: Arthur Andersen. Retrieved February 14, 2003, from http:/ /www.ci.houston.tx.us/it/strategics.htm

City of Naperville, Illinois. (2001, April). *Five-year strategic technology plan*. Schaumburg, IL: Actoras Consulting Group.

City of Seattle Police. (2003). *CAD rfp. Volume one-general specifications*. Retrieved February 17, 2003, from http://www.pan.ci.seattle.wa.us/

City of Sunnyvale, California. (1999). *Information technology strategic plan*. Retrieved February 14, 2003, from http://www.ci.sunnyvale.ca.us/info-tech/strategic-plan/ itdocume.pdf

City of Tampa. (2002). *FY 2002 technical infrastructure maintenance plan*. Retrieved January 15, 2004, from http://www.tampagov.net/dept_MIS/files/Infrastructure_ Plan_Master_2002.pdf

Coursey, D., & McCreary, S. (2005). Information technology challenges and opportunities for human resource managers. In S. Condrey (Ed.), *Handbook of human resource management in government* (2nd ed.) (pp. 189-214). San Francisco: Jossey-Bass.

Currid, C. (1995, February 6). Fighting 'technology shock.' *InformationWeek, 63*.

Darais, K., Nelson, K. M., Rice, S. C., & Buche, M.W. (2004). Chapter V: Identifying the enablers and barriers of IT personnel transition. In M. Igbaria, & C. Shayo (Eds.), *Strategies for managing IS/IT personnel* (pp. 92-112). Hershey, PA: Idea Group Inc.

Copyright © 2006, Idea Group Inc. Copying or distributing in print or electronic forms without written permission of Idea Group Inc. is prohibited.

Dash, J. (2002, March 18). The roi of Training. *Computerworld, 36*(12).

DeMarie, S. M. (2000, August). *Using virtual teams to manage complex projects: A case study of the radioactive waste management project.* The PriceWaterhouseCoopers Endowment for The Business of Government.

Dickerson, C. (2004, March 15). Hitting the books. *Infoworld.com, 22.*

District of Columbia. (n.d.). *Information technology strategic plan for the District of Columbia, 2002-2004.* Retrieved April 16, 2004, from http://octo.dc.gov/octo/cwp/view,a,1301,q,579939,octoNav,%7C32782%7C,.asp

Fletcher, P. T., Bretschneider, S. I., & Marchand, D. A. (1992). *Managing information technology: Transforming county governments in the 1990s.* Syracuse, NY: Syracuse University, School of Information Studies.

Guimaraes, T., Staples, D. S., & McKeen, J. D. (2004). Chapter XIV: Important human factors for systems development success: A user Focus. In M. Igbaria, & C. Shayo (Eds.), *Strategies for managing IS/IT personnel* (pp. 300-320). Hershey, PA: Idea Group Inc.

Harris, J. (1999). Designing change management strategies for ERP systems: observations from Alameda County, California. *Government Finance Review, 15*(4), 29-31.

Igbaria, M., & Shayo, C. (2004). *Strategies for managing IS/IT personnel.* Hershey, PA: Idea Group Inc.

Igbaria, M., & Shayo, C. (Eds.). (n.d.). Strategies for staffing the information systems department. In *Strategies for managing IS/IT personnel* (pp. 18-36). Hershey, PA: Idea Group Inc.

Kaplan, R.S., & Norton, D.P. (2001a). *The strategy-focused organization: How balanced scorecard companies thrive in the new business environment.* Boston: Harvard Business School.

Kavanagh, S., & Targosz, D. (2001). Power to the people: Implementing constituent relationship management in the public sector. *Government Finance Review, 17*(6), 26-31.

Lee, D.M.S. (2004). Organizational entry and transition from academic study: Examining a critical step in the professional development of young IS workers. In M. Igbaria, & C. Shayo (Eds.), *Strategies for managing IS/IT personnel* (pp. 113- 141). Hershey, PA: Idea Group Inc.

Nelson, R., & Todd, P. A. (2004). Chapter 1: Peopleware: The hiring and retention of IT personnel. In M. Igbaria, & C. Shayo (Eds.), *Strategies for managing IS/IT Personnel* (pp. 1-17). Hershey, PA: Idea Group Inc.

Nelson, R.R., & Cheney, P.H. (1987). Educating the CBIS user: A case analysis. *Data Base, 18*(3), 11-16.

Mecklenburg County. (2003, August). *2003 Report and 2004 Plan.* Retrieved December 17, 2003, from http://www.charmeck.org/Departments/IST/

Miranda, R., Kavanagh, S., & Roque, R. (2002). *Technology needs assessments: Evaluating the business case for ERP and financial management systems.* Chicago: Government Finance Officers Association.

Copyright © 2006, Idea Group Inc. Copying or distributing in print or electronic forms without written permission of Idea Group Inc. is prohibited.

Prince William County. (1998). *Strategic IT plan*. Retrieved May 12, 2003, from http://www.pwcgov.org/oit/strategic_plan/default.htm

Riper, K., & Durham, M. J. (1999). Phased ERP implementation: the city of Des Moines experience. *Government Finance Review, 15*(4), 37-42.

Rocheleau, B. (1985, Summer/Fall). Microcomputers and information management: Some emerging issues. *Public Productivity Review,* IX, 260-270.

Rocheleau, B., & Wu, L. (2002, September). Public versus private information systems: Do they differ in important ways? *American Review of Public Administration. 32*(3), 379-397.

Schwartzrock, K. D., & Jones, L.R. (1986). Computers and systems development for state and local government financial management. *Social Science Microcomputer Review, 4*(3), 310-324.

Schwarzkopf, A.B., Saunders, C., Jasperson, J., & Croes, H. (2004). Strategies for managing IS personnel: IT skills staffing. In M. Igbaria, & C. Shayo (Eds.), *Strategies for managing IS/IT personnel* (pp. 37-63). Hershey, PA: Idea Group Inc.

Shayo, C., Olfman, L., & Teitelroit, R. (1999). An exploratory study of the value of pretraining end-user participation. *Information Systems Journal, 9*, 55-79.

Sircar, S., Turnbow, J. L., & Bordoloi, B. (2000, Spring). A framework for assessing the relationship between information technology investments and firm performance. *Journal of Management Information Systems, 16*(4), 69-97.

Snyder, W. M., & Briggs, X.D.S. (2003, November). *Communities of interest: A new general tool for government managers*. IBM Center for the Business of Government. Retrieved July 8, 2004, from http://www.businessofgovernment.org/

U.S. General Accounting Office. (2003, January). *Information technology training: Practices of leading private-sector companies*. Washington, DC: GAO-03-390.

U.S. General Accounting Office. (2004, March). *Human capital: A guide for assessing strategic training and development efforts in the federal government*. Washington, DC: GAO-04-546G.

Wreden, N. (2004, Spring). Economy fuels debate on Outsourcing. *CDW-G State Tech*, 23-25. Retrieved April 3, 2005, from http://statetech.texterity.com/article/200403/17/

Wu, L., & Rocheleau, B. (2001). Formal versus informal end user training in public and private sector organizations. *Public Performance and Management Review, 24*(4), 312-321.

Additional Reading

The article by Shayo (1999) is important for illustrating the complexity of the training process including the facts that it is composed of several phases and that different approaches are needed for different kinds of end users. My article (with Dr. Liangfu Wu)

Copyright © 2006, Idea Group Inc. Copying or distributing in print or electronic forms without written permission of Idea Group Inc. is prohibited.

is useful for demonstrating the importance of informal learning in governmental organizations. Guimares and Shayo's (2004) book contains several chapters based on empirical studies (albeit private organizations) to support many of the generalizations we make in this chapter.

Key Concepts

- Cross-training
- E-learning
- Gap Analysis
- Gurus or Super users
- Informal or peer-to-peer training
- Individual development plans
- Inventory of skills
- Just-in-Time training
- Pre-training phase
- Post-training phase
- Shadow staff
- Train-the-trainer

Discussion Questions

1. How have you gained your knowledge of information technology? What sources and methods have been most important? About what percent of your knowledge has come from self-learning, help by peers, and formal learning such as classes? Which method of learning do you prefer the most? Why?

2. How important a role does e-learning play in learning on the part of employees in this organization? How much does the organization emphasize e-learning efforts? How would you evaluate these efforts?

3. How important a role does informal, peer-to-peer training play in learning in this organization? Are there certain key super users or gurus who dominate this process? If so, do these training efforts detract from their regular job?

4. Do you belong to any "communities of interest" that provide you with important information relevant to your job? Are these internal or external to your organization? Have you searched for relevant communities (e.g., listservs, newsgroups, etc.) on the Internet that could assist you with your job? If so, discuss the kinds of information they have provided you. Search and provide a list of listservs and

Copyright © 2006, Idea Group Inc. Copying or distributing in print or electronic forms without written permission of Idea Group Inc. is prohibited.

other forms of electronic learning that you have or could employ to assist you in your professional career.

5. How important are job skills in the assessment of job applicants for new positions in an organization with which you are familiar? To what extent does the organization formally assess the skills of applicants for jobs? If they do formally assess their skills, what method do they use? Are IT skills included in the job descriptions for any positions in the organization? If so, what is the nature of the IT skills that are noted?

Exercises

1. Analyze the learning and training with respect to ICT (Information and Communication Technologies) that take place in some organization with which you are familiar. Do they formally plan for training and learning? How many resources (money and staff) do they devote to IT learning? Then develop a training and learning strategy to improve the training for ICT for some organization with which you are familiar. The plan should address the types of training to be done, its timing, and the level and types of resources that should be devoted to it.

2. If you have not already, join some sort of interactive community on the Internet that is potentially relevant to your job or internship (or the job you would eventually like to obtain). This could be a listserv, a news group, or some other form of interactive communication. Keep a record of your experiences with this community. Write a critique of this experience concerning its utility and limitations.

Copyright © 2006, Idea Group Inc. Copying or distributing in print or electronic forms without written permission of Idea Group Inc. is prohibited.

Chapter VIII

Information Management and Ethical Issues in Government

Introduction

There are many ethical and legal issues raised by the growing of electronic information management and there is a growing literature on the development of "cyber-ethics." There is consensus among experts that organizations need to be proactive in addressing cyber-ethics. A U.S. Treasury Department study showed that 60% of computer security failures come from within the organization (Stone & Henry, 2003). That fact suggests a failure of organizations to instill a sense of ethics in its employees. The turnover rate of IT professionals has been relatively high compared to other professions and this may make them more problematic when it comes to ethical issues (Oz, 2001). Oz's comparative study of IT and other professionals found them somewhat less ethical with respect to software piracy and hacking but comparable to other professionals in their attitudes toward privacy. One of the problems is that ethics is not a part of the standard IT curriculum (Wilder & Soat, 2001), which is one reason that organizations may need to conduct active training about ethics. IT professional societies have codes of ethics such as that of the Association for Computing Machinery that is available online. However, Linderman and Schiano (2001) argue that IT "is not a profession" because it lacks important characteristics of a professional, such as certification standards and "sanctions for unprofessional behavior." They also point out that only 8% of IT professionals belong to the ACM.

Copyright © 2006, Idea Group Inc. Copying or distributing in print or electronic forms without written permission of Idea Group Inc. is prohibited.

Factors That Influence Ethical Behavior

One of the few empirical studies of computer abuse in organizations (Straub & Carlson, 1990), found *preventive approaches* such as "policy statements" and training on ethics increased awareness and were found to be effective. Proactive "detective" steps that organizations employed involved scanning of files and studying "unusual activities" (Straub & Carlson, 1990, p. 46). They also found "*deterrent*" approaches to be effective such as disciplinary actions. These actions ranged from fines and reprimands to suspension and dismissal. Straub & Carlson found that 41% of abuses were discovered accidentally and about 50% by normal controls. Few actual prosecutions occurred in the incidents studied but the authors claim that prosecution can act as a good deterrent. Larger organizations tended to be more rigorous with respect to disciplinary actions taken and "privileged" users were "less severely disciplined" (Straub & Carlson, 1990, p. 52). More recent research has looked at the influences on IT decision-making and identified three major factors that influence ethical behavior (Stone & Henry, 2003):

1. **Personal:** the individual's personal code of ethics.
2. **Informal:** The influence of co-workers' expectations.
3. **Formal company policies:** The company's formal code of ethics.

Pierce & Henry (2000) studied the impact of these three factors through the use of scenarios that forced a sample of over 2,500 IT professionals to choose which of these influences would dominate for a particular type of decision. Overall, the most important factor was personal ethics (49%) compared to 34% for informal and only 17% for formal codes. However, Pierce and Henry found that many employees in their study worked in smaller organizations that did not have any formal codes at all and the percent identifying formal codes as the most important factor was higher (30%) for IT professionals working in organizations with existing formal codes.

It is impossible to write ethical codes that pertain to all cyber-ethical situations. Thus scholars of ethics have identified general philosophical principles that can be used to guide decisions applied to specific IT situations. For example, Laudon (1995) notes that the Internet has spawned a strong libertarian, "*individual consequentialist*" ethic that individuals should be able "to do what they want" and the collective social good works best because pursuit of self-interest ultimately leads to positive consequences. Laudon argues that such an approach can lead to an "amoral free-for-all." Grupe, Garcia-Jay and Kuechler (2002) point out that most of the ethical frameworks mentioned for cyber-ethics are based on the tenets of individual ethics such as *utilitarianism* (maximize the good for the public), *risk aversion* (minimize costs and harm), *professionalism* (does it conform to the ethics of professional societies?), *impartiality* (are decisions biased?), and *compassion* (assist the most vulnerable) among others. They (Grupe, Garcia-Jay & Kuechler, 2002) suggest that organizations need to establish an *IT ethics committee* to establish communications to improve IT ethics. They propose that this committee should educate IT staff about ethical issues, make recommendations and provide for the

Copyright © 2006, Idea Group Inc. Copying or distributing in print or electronic forms without written permission of Idea Group Inc. is prohibited.

oversight of computer systems, and the general support for ethics standards. Such a committee may want to "adopt" a code of ethics such as that of the Association for Computing Machinery to guide the ethics of their own IT staff.

But, according to Mason, Mason and Culnan (1995), neither law nor codes of ethics provide clear solutions to dilemmas involving conflicting values. Thus the resolution of ethical issues involves going through a process that helps to clarify issues including the following steps (Mason, Mason & Culhan, 1995, pp. 103-105): (1) Determine the facts; (2) Determine what ethical standards should be applied; (3) Determine who should decide the issue; (4) Determine who should "benefit" from the decision; (5) Determine how the decision should be made; and (6) Determine what steps should be taken to prevent a reoccurrence of the issue. In their book, Mason, Mason and Culnan (1995, p. 14) point out that there is a *"moment of truth"* when an individual is faced with a choice of acting on emotions, out of habit, or giving a "reasoned consideration" of alternative courses of action. Faulty ethical decisions may lead to a *"slippery slope"* (Mason, Mason & Culnan, 1995, p. 99) where apparently small concessions to ethical principles lead later on to a descent into major violations of ethical rules and may create "worse problems than the ones it solves" (Mason, 1995).

Ethical and Legal Issues Concerning Computer-Mediated Communication

Private companies are also now facing ethical issues with respect to computer-mediated communication. For example, in the fall of 2000, an employee at Lockheed Martin inadvertently received an e-mail that contained information on figures used by one of their competitors on a bid to the Federal government (Wilder & Soat, 2001). The Lockheed employee responded in a very ethical manner, immediately notifying their company's legal counsel and taking action to delete the e-mail message from the company's server before anyone else could access it (Wilder & Soat, 2001). As the article point out, because of the changing communication patterns with e-mail supplanting other forms of communication, information technology departments now have to take on major ethical and legal issues concerning communication. For example, the communication of jokes has led to some notable court cases. For example, an employee (BNA Employment & Discrimination Report, 1995) of Microsoft was able to use e-mail messages from her boss in a discrimination case despite the organization's contention that the messages were irrelevant to the case. A lawsuit was brought against the Chevron Corporation because employees were offended by an e-mail joke about "reasons why beer is better than women" (Cohen, 2001). Governmental e-mail faces greater scrutiny than that of private organizations because it may be subject to Freedom of Information Act (FOIA) and sunshine laws that mandate public access to public records. The results of an antitrust suit against the Microsoft Corporation would seem to indicate that even private organizations cannot expect such protections. Indeed, both the governmental prosecution and the Microsoft defense were based on electronic messages to a great extent and many of these messages appeared to be of the "thinking out loud" variety. The government was able to contrast

Copyright © 2006, Idea Group Inc. Copying or distributing in print or electronic forms without written permission of Idea Group Inc. is prohibited.

Mr. Gates' taped remarks with his e-mail messages. Likewise, the Microsoft defense counsel cited e-mail correspondence from many corporate witnesses testifying against Microsoft to show that their own companies did exactly the same thing as Microsoft (Lohr, 1998). Lohr states that Microsoft handed over to the government an estimated 30 million documents, mostly e-mail, and concludes that "e-mail has supplanted the telephone as the most common instrument of communication." As Rosen (2000) has noted, e-mail has "blurred the distinction between written and oral communication" and become the repository of information that used to be "exchanged around the water cooler." Gotcher & Kanervo (1997) cite studies that show that users tend to view their e-mail as similar to phone messages despite the fact that, unlike the phone messages, they can be retrieved as legal evidence. As a result of the Microsoft case, organizations such as the Amoco Corporation have a policy of limiting e-mail communication to topics that are "not mission critical" (Sipior, 1998). However, this raises the question of whether this policy is relevant to public organizations which are supposed to be open?

The Difference Between Digital and Non-Digital Communication

Much of the early research hypothesized that individuals using e-mail or other forms of CMC would be more likely to use rude, uncivil language than if they used face-to-face (FTF) communication due to its remoteness and anonymity of CMC and hence the lack of social constraints that exist in FTF meetings (e.g., Bordia, 1997). These conditions are hypothesized to create a sense of "*de-individuation.*" There is some empirical evidence to support this position (see, e.g., Spears & Lea, 1994). However, a 2002 survey of "Netiquette" found that aggressive comments were not mentioned as among the most "aggravating issues" of annoying online behavior (Preece, 2004, p. 58), though they can be "devastating when they occur." There is also the belief that many FTF communication is better able to build trust (Jarvenpaa & Leidner, 1998). However, CMC among individuals who know each other either through belonging to the same organization or professionally does have constraints and later research has found a convergence among FTF, phone, and e-mail communications (Weisband, Schneider & Connolly, 1995).

There is another theory referred to as *Media Richness Theory* (MRT) which holds that CMC is a less rich form of communication than FTF communication. MRT posits that CMC lacks the immediacy and sensory feedbacks (e.g., facial expressions and signs of tenseness and voice intonations) that provide additional information to people necessary to understand fully the nature of the communication. Hence, MRT theory (e.g., Daft and Lengel, 1984; Adams, Morris & Scotter, 1998) suggests that richer forms of communication should be employed when dealing with complex issues involving *equivocality* characterized by their subjectivity and ambiguity (see, e.g., Menneke, 2000; Barkhi, 1999; Hightower & Sayeed, 1995). In addition, Phillips and Eisenberg (1996, p. 89) also note that managers may use face-to-face meetings even though not technically necessary for "symbolic reasons" associated with "warmth and openness."

Copyright © 2006, Idea Group Inc. Copying or distributing in print or electronic forms without written permission of Idea Group Inc. is prohibited.

However, in some situations, a lean medium like CMC may help to reduce tension where emotions such as when "fear, insecurity and excitement" or negative emotions are very strong (Adams, Morris & Van Scotter, 1998, p. 23; Moore, 1999, p. 24).

Despite these arguments that e-mail should not be used for important issues that involve equivocality, nevertheless it is clear that managers are now using e-mail to deal with all kinds of issues including strategic, political, and sensitive personnel issues. An article (Kelly, 1999) in the *New York Times* stated that, "E-mail is supplanting to a large extent face-to-face communication among all sorts of people." Another expert (Worthen, 2005) states that e-mail "has become the primary medium for how we communicate." Thus, although MRT provides some guidelines for when to use and not use e-mail, in practice, it appears that managers and employees are violating many of the prescriptions of MRT. The question is whether violation of MRT results in impaired organizational communication and there is little evidence on that.

As the legal case against Microsoft showed, e-mail is essentially different from (unrecorded) FTF and phone communication in one very important sense: *it presents an explicit, detailed, retrievable record* and thus does not provide the employee with the refuge of deniability or disagreement over what has been said that is available in normal FTF or phone communications. As Lohr (1998) points out in his coverage of the Microsoft trial, e-mail is essentially different because people communicate with it "more frankly and informally than when writing a memo," but the e-mail constitutes documentary evidence:

It [e-mail] can be a sharp contrast to formal oral testimony, so often coached by lawyers and influenced by selective memory. 'The E-mail record certainly makes the I-don't-recall line of response harder to sustain,' said Robert Litan, a former senior official in the Justice Department's Antitrust Division....

Harmon (2000) in an article entitled "E-mail is treacherous, So Why Do We Keep Trusting It?" points out that many companies have strict policies governing use of e-mail but that people "continue to send...messages that they would never commit to a written document – and save them." As a result of the Microsoft case, executives are "sanitizing their own e-mail" even if there are no formal policies requiring them to do so" and they are changing their use of language away from "warfare language" that frequently were used (Harmon, 1998). It appears to be the case that the many e-mail policies are given lip service and exist to protect the organization in case a problem occurs. Physicians worry about malpractice in all sorts of cases but, despite the attractiveness of using e-mail to communicate with patients, see CMC as increasing their vulnerability (Kassirer, 2000):

Not only could physicians be sued for diagnosing and prescribing without examining the patient, but (in contrast to telephone exchanges), the record of the electronic encounter is permanent. (p. 117)

Copyright © 2006, Idea Group Inc. Copying or distributing in print or electronic forms without written permission of Idea Group Inc. is prohibited.

Organizational Computer-Mediated Communication Policies

Ethical and legal issues with the most impact involve e-mail because e-mail has become such a pervasive aspect of organizational life and is perhaps the most common form of communication. There is substantial literature on the most common problems such as the development of rules and guidelines for e-mail use. As Rosen (2000) points out, postal mail has been protected since 1877 by a Supreme Court ruling that inspectors need a search warrant to open first class mail but such protection does not exist for e-mail.

Two chapters by Prysby and Prysby (1999, 2003) provide an excellent overview of the issues with respect to e-mail. They (Prysby & Prysby, 2003) point out that there are four different legal bases for the protection of the privacy of e-mail. First is the Fourth Amendment protection against unreasonable searches, but Prysby and Prysby (2003, pp. 278-279) emphasize that searches have not generally been viewed as unreasonable since the messages usually reside on equipment owned by the organization and the organization knows the password of the employee. Secondly, although the Electronic Communications Act (ECA) of 1986 provides for the same protections concerning the use of electronic communication as are afforded to protection against wiretapping of phone calls, nevertheless Prysby and Prysby (2003, pp. 280-282) state that ECA allows an exemption for "legitimate" business purposes and that the legislative record of the ECA was not aimed at restrictions on employer's right to monitor e-mail of employees. The third possible set of protections are state laws but Prysby and Prysby (2003, pp. 276-277) show that most state statutes (e.g., they provide examples from Nebraska, Virginia, and Idaho) give employers the right to monitor messages and provide no expectation of the right to privacy of these messages. The final legal base for e-mail privacy protection concerns tort law, but torts are made difficult if not impossible by the existence of a formal organizational policy that has been effectively communicated to employees that their messages may be monitored. The USA Patriot Act (P.L. No. 107-56) expanded the Federal government's authority to monitor electronic communications. According to Worthen (2005), both the Health Insurance Portability and Accountability Act (HIPAA) and Medicare "require health-care companies to save e-mails."

Despite the strong legal basis for organizational monitoring of employee e-mail, Prysby and Prysby (2003, p. 281) argue that it is to the advantage of most organizations *not* to monitor individual messages in order to have good morale and they cite universities in particular as organizations that tend to "stress the privacy of individual e-mail." However, a case occurred recently at Southern Mississippi University where two professors were proposed to be fired in part on the basis of information gathered by the monitoring of their e-mail messages (Smallwood, 2004). Two professors "investigated" the background of the University's Vice President for Research and the President of their University ordered the e-mail of these two professors to be monitored. The president accused the professors of "misusing state property." This case further demonstrates the fragility of the expectation that informal conventions will protect e-mail privacy even in organizations such as universities.

Copyright © 2006, Idea Group Inc. Copying or distributing in print or electronic forms without written permission of Idea Group Inc. is prohibited.

Figure 1. Key elements of computer use policy according to the U.S. General Accounting Office

Policy element	Type of statement
Monitoring use of proprietary assets	Statements that company computing systems are provided as tools for business and all information created, accessed, or stored using these systems are the property of the company and subject to monitoring, auditing, or review.
Establishing no expectation of privacy	Statements about the extent or limitations of privacy protections for employee use of e-mail, the Internet, and computer files.
Improper employee use	Statements that some uses of company computers are inappropriate - including specific notice banning offensive material (e.g., obscenity, sexual content, racial slurs, derogatio of people's personal characteristics), and language relating e-mail and Internet use to general prohibitions of harassment.
Allowable employee uses	Statements explaining proper or acceptable uses of the company systems, including whether or not personal use is permitted.
Protecting sensitive company information	Statements providing instructions for handling proprietary information on company systems.
Disciplinary action	Statements that there are penalties and disciplinary actions for violations of company usage policy.
Employee acknowledgement of policy	A statement requiring that employees demonstrate they understand the company policy and acknowledge their responsibility to adhere to the policy.

Source: Source: United States General Accounting Office. (2002a). Employee Privacy: Computer-Use Monitoring Practices and Policies of Selected Companies. September. GAO-02-717, p.10.

The U. S. General Accounting Office (GAO) (2002, pp. 9-10) studied organizational policies and identified common elements that were included in leading private company computer-use policies (see Figure 1).

However, there are differences between public and private policies in the latter's emphasis on protection of proprietary and sensitive information. Most governmental information by default is expected to be open to the public and there needs to be a justification for keeping it private. Other aspects of computer-use policy are similar in both public and private organizations.

Most public organizations now warn their employees that their e-mail is subject to being reviewed and that there should be no presumption of privacy concerning it. One prominent issue concerns whether e-mail for personal purposes should be allowed or banished completely. Menzel (1998, p. 447) summarizes the conditions under which some public organizations allow such e-mail: (1) Provided it is done on the employee's personal time; (2) Does not interfere with his or her job; and (3) Does not result in incremental expense for the organization. Mecklenburg County's (North Carolina) policy on Electronic Mail Usage allows "incidental" personal usage but goes on to warn that personal e-mail should not be forwarded to interdepartmental lists. The Cities of Marietta (GA) and Tampa Bay (Florida), and the Village of Streamwood (IL) are examples of organizations that have an explicit policy against the personal use of e-mail.

Menzel (1998) categorizes e-mail policies into three major types: (1) Generic approach in which e-mail is considered similar to other forms of communication and employees are reminded as to what types are impermissible; (2) Formalistic approach in which a long list of acceptable principles are stated but fewer specific "do's" and "don'ts" thus relying on the employee to use their common sense and discretion; and (3) A guidelines approach in which more emphasis is placed on guidelines than specific "do's and don'ts." In my review of governmental e-mail policies, I found that many governments combine elements of all three approaches. Specific do's and don'ts are often added to general

Copyright © 2006, Idea Group Inc. Copying or distributing in print or electronic forms without written permission of Idea Group Inc. is prohibited.

guidelines in an apparent attempt to make it clearer to employees what the implications of the guidelines are. Some examples of activities that are viewed as abuse of e-mail and Internet privileges include use for personal gain, making political statements, negative comments about groups, gambling, accessing pornographic materials, and revealing confidential information.

Legal advisors now warn organizations that it is not enough to simply have a policy but organizations need to ensure that employees are aware of and understand the policy. Now many systems (including my University's) have a statement that requires the system user to acknowledge and accept organizational policies concerning the use of electronic media before they can complete login to the organizational network every single time. However, organizations may need to go beyond this acknowledgement. The GAO study (2002) found that all companies included computer-use policies in their employee handbooks and eight out of the 14 required new employees to undergo training on computer-use policies and others had periodic training for all employees including some with online training sessions. Nancy Flynn, head of the e-Policy Institute that provides assistance to organizations in developing e-mail guidelines, advises employees "never to use company e-mail to send a really personal message" (Taylor, 2001). Flynn goes on to state that if an employee should receive an e-mail message that they think is "inappropriate" that they should report the message to the company in order to protect themselves (Taylor, 2001, p. 7).

The guideline approach appears to be much more realistic than the explicit outlawing of all personal mail although many public (and private) organizations have adopted the latter policy. As noted earlier, Prysby and Prysby (1999) argue that employees should be given the right to have personal e-mail and a degree of privacy concerning it because such a policy will not only encourage better morale but also more open discussion. They also note that business and personal items are often juxtaposed in the same messages just as they can be in phone calls and FTF meetings so that banning personal e-mail would make normal communication difficult. *Chicago Tribune* columnist Mary Schmich (Schmich and Zorn, 1999) summarizes the view that personal e-mail should be allowed and not monitored:

...I might think that because so many employees spend so many waking hours at work or getting there, they might be able to conduct some personal e-mail business without fear they were being spied on by a company peeping Tom. I might even argue that employees work better when they feel trusted.

This author is under the impression that many public organizations have established these rigorous e-mail policies as a legal protective device available if real abuse should occur but that most don't monitor to see if such policies are being implemented unless a problem is indicated with a specific employee. Lewis Maltby, President of the National Work Rights Institute, has stated that most notifications of the right to monitor e-mail are written by lawyers and that "it seems clear that companies are not reading each and every message" because "there are not enough hours in the day" (Taylor, 2001, p. 7). A recent GAO study (2002) of computer-use monitoring practices and policies of 14 selected companies found that all stored and kept their e-mail messages and other

Copyright © 2006, Idea Group Inc. Copying or distributing in print or electronic forms without written permission of Idea Group Inc. is prohibited.

electronic information such as Internet sites visited. Eight of the 14 said that they would review electronic transactions *"if they receive other information that an individual may have violated company policies"* [emphasis added] (U.S. General Accounting Office, 2002, p. 3). Six of the 14 *routinely* analyze their employee's electronic activities and this includes e-mail message titles, contents, and addresses for information that might be proprietary or offensive in nature (U.S. General Accounting Office, 2002, p. 6). The length of time that companies keep e-mail and Internet data varied with nine keeping them for 90 days or less. One organization that did not routinely monitor messages said that their policy was intended to "establish an atmosphere of trust" and one said they did not have enough resources to do such monitoring.

Software to Monitor Electronic Media

Despite the GAO study, other information indicates there appears to be a substantial degree of monitoring going on in the private sector. It is reported that a survey by the American Management Association (Rosen, 2000, p. 50) of 1,000 large companies found that "45% monitored e-mail files or phone calls" and that the percentage had increased significantly from a study done just two years before. There exist computer programs that will perform such monitoring (Guernsey, 2000) such as xVmail that allows managers to view and search the text of messages. As I noted earlier, one of the emerging problems of organizations concerns end users activities that burden organizational systems. One manager who uses such a program to protect against e-mail that will bog down networks estimated that *50% of the company's e-mail is not work-related* [emphasis added] (Guernsy, 2000). A major use of such monitoring is to avoid cases where personal misuse of e-mail may bog down servers such as forwarding of e-mail with large attachments. Lockheed Martin got rid of an employee who had sent "thousands of co-workers a personal e-mail message that requested an electronic receipt" (Taylor, 2001, p. 1 & 7). This action caused their e-mail system to crash. But monitoring software is becoming more sophisticated so that now it can read the actual text and make decisions based on rules as to whether e-mail should be allowed to be sent or redirected. For example, e-mail monitoring software is used by movie studios to protect against the loss of "intellectual property rights" (Cohen, 2001) and detects whether the message should be monitored or automatically be redirected. If an employee mistakenly tries to e-mail a confidential document outside the company, the software will redirect the e-mail (Cohen, 2001).

E-Mail, Open Meetings, and Public Records Laws

The Microsoft case emerged due to competition and struggle among private corporations. But e-mail is a potentially major issue for public organizations, too. In 1996, e-mail was officially labeled as an official record that is subject to the Federal Freedom of Information Act requests (Kelley, 1999). The Electronic Freedom of Information Act (EFOIA) required federal agencies to create "electronic reading rooms" (Sadagopan et al., 2000, p. 30). In Spokane, Washington, two county commissioners discussed public business via e-mail and could have been considered to have violated the state's open

Copyright © 2006, Idea Group Inc. Copying or distributing in print or electronic forms without written permission of Idea Group Inc. is prohibited.

public meetings act since there is only a total of three commissioners and thus an e-mail discussion among two of them constituted a quorum. The response of the county was to change the way they dealt with e-mail (Kelley, 1999). According to one County Commissioner:

'We eliminate all e-mails, delete them instantly from our mailbox, which in one respect cleans up our hard drive, but on the other side of the coin, we do not have a history of what goes on. I just chose to eliminate them rather than have someone else go through my e-mails. The county's server keeps e-mail messages for just a week,' he said.

As the County Commissioner himself notes, the deletion of such e-mail can lead to a loss of historical record concerning policies. One solution, according to Kelly (1999) is to place all e-mail between city council members in a public folder.

It is not yet clear whether and to what extent municipalities need to retain and make available such e-mail records. A discussion of "Open Meetings and Public Records Laws Regarding E-mail" in the Innovation Groups (March 5, 2001) revealed a range in approaches on the parts of various governments with some but not all of the differences being due to differences in their state statutes. The following is a summary of the some of the different policies expressed at the time of the discussion:

1.   Berkeley, California: Electronic mail is to be purged on a regular basis and may be purged automatically by the City. If employees wish to maintain any electronic mail as a permanent record, they must save that mail in a disk file or print a copy for permanent filing.

2.   Bellevue, Washington: E-mails are public records and subject to retention just as any other type of record. The City Council does not generally have discussions online and is part-time and thus the records retention had "been worked around this issue." The retention time period is based on the nature of the content and they distinguish between "informational" e-mails and "significant" e-mails that concern "the public's business" and the latter should be copied to an appropriate file.

3.   Grand Junction, Colorado: The open records law in Colorado does apply to e-mail and are furnished to citizens if they are willing to pay costs of locating and producing copies. Users are required to delete e-mail that is over 30 days old but if they receive an e-mail that is by "nature" a document they need to print it and file it like any other document.

4.   Hickory, North Carolina: The North Carolina Public Records Law states that e-mail is subject to public inspection and must be kept based on type of correspondence but "routine communications" can be kept only as long as they are relevant and can be deleted if they are not "public documents."

5.   Lenexa, Kansas: They strongly discourage e-mail conversations between Governing Body members due to the open meeting issue.

6.   Melbourne, Florida: The State Legislature put e-mail into the category of public record during 1995. There is differentiation made between e-mail that is *"transi-*

Copyright © 2006, Idea Group Inc. Copying or distributing in print or electronic forms without written permission of Idea Group Inc. is prohibited.

tory" and that which formalizes knowledge, establishes policies, guidelines, or procedures, or certifies a transaction. If the e-mail involves the establishment a policy, it will have to be kept permanently.

7.   Naperville, Illinois: They state that unilateral e-mailing would not constitute a gathering under the definition of the Illinois Open Meetings Act though a chat room discussion of a quorum would and thus would require 48 hours advance notice. They state that the Illinois Freedom of Information Act does not specifically address e-mail messages but does define all "electronic data processing records" as public records and thus theoretically e-mail should be stored for public access. But they point out that the reality is that most Illinois local governments do not save or archive e-mail messages and the Illinois legislature has been unwilling to address the issue in legislation.

The State of Nevada in its "Policy on Defining Information Transmitted via E-Mail" (Issue Date: October 1, 2003) states that some e-mail may be determined to be "public records" such as records with legal, administrative, or historical value and that agencies need to take steps to make the e-mail accessible, including procedures that make it efficient to locate specific files such as "meta-data" and "headers, forward headers, and transmission data."

The Washington Municipal Clerks Association (2002) has issued a memorandum based on a ruling by the Washington State Court of Appeals (July 27, 2001) that e-mails between members of a governing body can constitute a meeting even if e-mails initially constitute less than a majority of the governing body because subsequent exchanges can "relay the content to a majority of members," though "one-sided" informational e-mails to a majority may be acceptable. One of the key points in this case (Woods vs. Battle Ground School District) is that the term "meeting" needs to be construed broadly or the restrictions of the Open Meetings Act law can be easily circumvented by using a series of phone calls or e-mails in place of face-to-face discussions (Dowling-Sendor, 2002). One of the conclusions of the memorandum is "never decide at an open meeting that a majority of the governing body will complete an agenda item by e-mail" (Washington Municipal Clerks Association, 2002).

The gist of my review of policies (and the previously discussed are only a fraction of the sample that I reviewed) is that e-mail retention and accessibility policies vary greatly from government to government. Clearly, state law has a major impact on local governmental policies. But local governments and individuals retain significant discretion even in states where e-mail that is explicitly made accessible to the public. Many governments attempt to differentiate between "transitory" messages and those which have a more permanent value and require that only the latter has to be saved. Even if a discussion does involve a public policy matter, it may not necessarily be open to public disclosure. Prysby and Prysby (2003) note that the courts have made a distinction between communications that are *prior* to the adoption of a policy and those that concern a policy that has been adopted. They cite, for example, the Michigan Freedom of Information Act that "preliminary or advisory discussions should be exempt" in order to encourage the kind of "frank discussions" that are in the "public interest" (Prysby & Prysby, 1999, p. 241). Overall, there appears to be an emerging expectation that the organization and its employees need

Copyright © 2006, Idea Group Inc. Copying or distributing in print or electronic forms without written permission of Idea Group Inc. is prohibited.

to differentiate between e-mails that need to be saved and those that may be deleted quickly. However, the policies that I reviewed did not make it clear how these policies would be implemented and whether there was any attempt to check on compliance with this expectation.

As the Microsoft case and some other cases illustrate, top-level managers may be the biggest problem for revealing sensitive policies. It appears to be difficult to control their tendency to write about policies and politics via e-mail because it has become their preferred method of communication. One possible aid is software that deletes e-mail automatically. For example, Disappearing Inc. has developed an e-mail program that allows its users to set a time period after which a message can't be read (Scott, 2000). Once the time limit is reached, the message is deleted from the server. Other e-mail has been constructed that would enable senders to control whether their e-mail can be forwarded by the recipient (Harmon, 2000). But these software solutions may be useless if state and local governments may be required to archive e-mail that pertains to substantive policy as some have advocated (Miller, 1995).

The legal issue raises some important issues for public organizations that want to convert key operations to e-government. Neu, Anderson and Bikson (1999) explored e-government possibilities for the Rand Corporation among a variety of governmental agencies. For example, one possible application is to have the Health Care Financing Administration (HCFA) divert many of their phone calls to Web-based queries concerning potential beneficiaries that would be answered via e-mail. This could save substantial resources and might be more convenient for many potential customers. But Neu, Anderson and Bikson (1999) point out the potential danger of such a policy:

Representatives are not chosen for their ability to write clear, concise prose that will stand up to close (perhaps even legal) scrutiny. A written response to a query leaves a different kind of trail than does an oral explanation over the telephone and additional training may be required for representatives if written responses become commonplace. (p. 43)

In short, while the use of e-mail is becoming so pervasive that people view it similar to talking on the phone or in person conversation, there exists a crucial legal difference that managers need to give heed to. Committing messages to e-mail compromises their security and privacy in ways that are quite different from phone and FTF exchanges. Ideally, no message should be committed to e-mail that would harm the organization if it were subject to media exposure or legal scrutiny. Software programs may be able to control the most obvious types of problems such as forwarding attachments and chain letters that will bog down servers. But the much more difficult issues involve its use to discuss such matters as politics and policies. E-mail is so pervasive that it may be the case that the best managers can do is to encourage self-discipline on the part of employees (including the managers themselves).

Copyright © 2006, Idea Group Inc. Copying or distributing in print or electronic forms without written permission of Idea Group Inc. is prohibited.

Unions and E-Mail

Unions are beginning to use e-mail and the Web to disseminate information and help in organizing. In one case, a company (Pratt & Whitney) acknowledged that employees should be able to use e-mail to discuss "terms and conditions of employment" as long as the use was infrequent. In other cases, organizations have successfully opposed union use of e-mail. For example, one union sent e-mail to all of the factory's 2,000 engineers at their company e-mail addresses (Cohen, 1999). The company objected after a few such e-mailings. Unions have found it to be a very potent tool because it can combine "efficiency of the mass-produced leaflet" with intimacy of conversation (Cohen, 1999). However, some companies view union e-mail as "trespassing" on their system and contest it. Intel took legal action to stop the sending of e-mail from a former employee to current employees using this very argument (Cohen, 1999). Of course, if companies shut down the use of company e-mail systems for union efforts, unions can—and do—turn to online bulletin boards on the Web as a replacement (Cohen, 1999). However, the legal issues are still unresolved. Since public employee unions are often strong and have been the one growth sector in union organizing, it is quite possible that public organizations will be faced with making decisions about the use of organizational e-mail for such purposes.

Other Issues Related to Computer-Mediated Communication

In addition to the issues that I have discussed earlier, computer-use policies contain a variety of other specific concerns such as "style of communication" in which employees are expected to use "respectful and courteous" language. Some municipalities require that a "disclaimer" be included by users when they participate in discussions in external boards and listservs. There are emerging concerns about electronic communications such as the downloading and dissemination of large files that may slow the network system and needlessly fill storage space. Some organizations have stipulations about these such as City of Marietta (Georgia) in its Internet-Electronic Mail Acceptable Use Policy (Issue Date, November 2001):

Large File Transfers and Internet Capacity: *The Internet connection is a shared resource. While routine e-mail and file transfer activities won't impact other users much, large file transfers and intensive multimedia activities will impact the service levels of other users. Users contemplating file transfers of over ten megabytes per transfer or interactive video activities shall, to be considerate of other users, schedule these activities early or late in the day or, better, after business hours.*

Indeed, in today's environment, the major difficulties with respect to electronic communication involve the problems of viruses and spam. Organizations attempt to control as many problems as possible through technological fixes such as the use of firewalls,

Copyright © 2006, Idea Group Inc. Copying or distributing in print or electronic forms without written permission of Idea Group Inc. is prohibited.

Figure 2. Examples of end user issues that require education & training

Taking preventive actions against viruses.

Taking steps to prevent the unnecessary burdening of the organization's systems.

Identify and retain e-mail that should be regarded as public records.

Use of proper etiquette in CMC.

Proper back-up, documentation, and structuring of important end-user created data bases

and spreadsheets.

packet sniffing, spam filtering and proxy servers, among others that do not require the cooperation of end users. However, there are limitations to all of these technological solutions. Areas where end users participate present challenges to IT staff. Public organizations need the active cooperation of end users for a variety of issues (see Figure 1) such as to avoid opening attachments or downloading files without screening them for viruses. Proactive training is needed to deal with these issues (see Figure 2).

Information Overload and E-Mail

Although e-mail can be a great time-saver, there is also evidence that e-mail can produce information overload in which employees feel overwhelmed by the volume of information received. First, junk mail has become a major problem as it fills e-mail boxes and servers (Crowley, 1999). Use of filters and other devises may assist in keeping out such messages. A bigger problem (Crowley, 1999) can be internal e-mail such as jokes, chain letters, personal messages, and poorly written or useless organizational e-mail. Chain letters with sizeable attached files or headers can bring servers to a halt (Crowley, 1999). Monitoring may be useful for controlling these kinds of problems, too. Likewise, limits on the size of messages may be useful. Some organizations create Web sites and shared databases in order to eliminate wasteful sending of large attachments.

Nevertheless, as Barnes and Greller (1994) note, many employees have become "overwhelmed by the number of messages they receive." Although e-mail brings in valuable information to organizations, there is an indication that it may be driving out other forms of communication (FTF and phone) and activities (time to read, think, write, get outside the organization, etc.) Mackay (1988) noted more than a decade ago that e-mail is "seductive" and that most people read their e-mail as soon as it arrived even though it is not necessary to do so. Lantz (1998) surveyed employees of high-tech organizations and found that 51% of the users open their e-mail immediately. I cited previously a case where employees ignored visitors to their office in order to attend to the e-mail. Maltz (2000) did a study of managers in companies that manufacture high-tech equipment and found that some received 100 messages per day and the study suggested that "random

Copyright © 2006, Idea Group Inc. Copying or distributing in print or electronic forms without written permission of Idea Group Inc. is prohibited.

e-mail" had created a problem of information overload. Managers need to pay attention to the possibility that e-mail and other forms of CMC could drive out other activities that are important to the efficacy of the organization.

It is also clear that many employees are not able to manage their e-mail effectively. Mackay (1988) did a study of a research laboratory within a major corporation and found different categories of e-mail users. One category she labels as "prioritizers" as exemplified by one scientist who organizes her e-mail so that she only sees and reads what is important to her by reading her e-mail only once a day (Mackay, 1988). Moreover, she was willing to miss messages that could be important to her once in a while with the assumption that people will contact her by phone if it is really important. By way of contrast, the "archivers" organize their life around their e-mail that they view as essential. One archiver had over 600 messages in his inbox and over 40 mail folders. Mackay (1988, p. 388) notes that people differ greatly in their "feelings of control over" e-mail. Prioritizers don't read all of their mail, limit the number of times they read it, stay or get off e-mail lists, and keep few messages in their inbox. Archivers read most or all of their e-mail and belong to many lists but have difficulty finding their e-mail that they have put into folders (Mackay, 1988, p. 393).

Employee Feedback via E-Mail

While the loose use of e-mail has caused legal problems for organizations, at the same time it can perform the very useful function of obtaining honest feedback and increased communication among those in the organization including those at the top and bottom of the hierarchy. Thus there can be a trade-off between allowing openness in e-mail and protection for the organization against the legal challenges. Richtel (1998) pointed out that in many computer companies, the most honest criticism comes from employee e-mail forums. These exchanges are welcomed by many of the companies and viewed as a "form of catharsis" (Richtel, 1998). For example, one Netscape e-mail list is called "Bad Attitude." But Netscape shut down another, more elite and even more virulent e-mail-list name "Really Bad Attitude" due to fears about potential liability (Richtel, 1998). Schrage (2004) more recently has argued that blogs (short for Web log) that are personal journals intended for public reading can be employed effectively to obtain feedback on important IT issues such as the implementation of complex projects. Schrage refers to blogs devoted to a discussion of projects as "plogs."

Bishop (1999) conducted an in-depth case study of one company (again, a high-tech company with a skilled labor force) that allowed and, indeed, encouraged CMC among its employees. One listserv known as "Café" was moderated but allowed anonymous postings that made up about 25% of the messages. The system operator maintained confidentiality and resisted management pressure to divulge the name of people who submitted anonymous messages critical of the company (Bishop, 1999, p. 221). Management announced a revision of a profit-sharing plan that was less generous than the previous plan. The action led to a great deal of criticism on the "Café" – one of the most active employee bulletin boards. Subsequently, management changed the announced policy to one that was more generous to employees and this change was ascribed by

Copyright © 2006, Idea Group Inc. Copying or distributing in print or electronic forms without written permission of Idea Group Inc. is prohibited.

many to the impact of the bulletin board discussions (Bishop, 1999, p. 220). Later on, employees formed other "interest groups" such as one to raise general issues about employer-employee relations and another to support gay and lesbians in the company (Bishop, 1999, pp. 224-225). West and Berman (2001, p. 241), based on surveys from more than 200 cities with a population greater than 50000, found that 50% had bulletin board systems as part of their intranet. However, it is not clear whether these bulletin boards were used for critical feedback similar to that encouraged by private sector companies. A preliminary analysis of small to moderately sized municipalities by this author in the Chicago area revealed no such bulletin boards or listservs being employed. Such feedback could have both positive effects of bringing to the fore issues that otherwise would be neglected. At the same time, they would potentially be subject to FOIA and other forms of exposure that could embarrass the organization.

E-mail and other forms of CMC do not inevitably lead to greater sharing of information. Vandenbosh and Ginzberg (1996; 1997) reported that software such as Lotus Notes did not result in greater collaboration according to their study. They note that cultural change such as overcoming interdepartmental obstacles may need to precede new software programs.

Strategic Uses of E-Mail: Are They Ethical?

During the past, managers used to look down upon managers who used e-mail for negative actions such as reprimands and believed that managers should use FTF meetings for such important actions including negotiations (e.g., McKinnon & Bruns, 1992). But there is some qualitative evidence that many managers and other employees are employing e-mail for sensitive and even negative feedback purposes. Landry (2000, p. 134) reports evidence that e-mail is used "routinely" in order to "make unpopular requests" and conduct "performance reviews, work assessments, and decisions about resource allocation." Sussman and Sproul (1999) conducted a laboratory experiment and found that negative information was less distorted when done via computer. They point out that there is evidence in a number of areas that people are more honest in interacting with computers than in person. Sussman and Sproul (1999) also found that people were more satisfied delivering bad news via CMC. Of course, this finding could be evidence of the problem of using e-mail for such purposes because, if people do not "cushion" bad news in CMC, then the communication is likely to be received in an even more negative manner. Interestingly, Sussman and Sproul (1999) found that people, contrary to their hypothesis, also experienced more satisfaction in delivering good news via CMC than FTF communication.

There have been several examples in academia where e-mails have influenced personnel decisions. For example, a tenure-candidate at Yale sent "two incendiary e-mails" that criticized senior members of his department to all members of the Yale History Department prior to his tenure decision (Leatherman, 2000). Although the e-mails were ruled as "out-of-bounds" in the review of the professor's tenure case, nevertheless Leatherman (2000, p. A13) reports that "many in the department say the decision eventually turned on those e-mails." Listservs that contain information that is often critical of administration are common in many academic organizations but whether this will carry over to other

Copyright © 2006, Idea Group Inc. Copying or distributing in print or electronic forms without written permission of Idea Group Inc. is prohibited.

organizations where employees have less independence and are less protected by tenure is not clear.

Up until now, there is no clear evidence that managerial use of e-mail is harmful. Indeed, Markus (1994b) found that higher-level managers made greater use of e-mail. In her study, she found examples of the strategic and political use of e-mail. For example, one manager learned "the hard way" not to put politically sensitive information into a request because the person to whom she sent the information forwarded it to the person she had been "intriguing against" (Markus, 1994b, p. 522). Markus' (1994a, 1994b) studies of one private organization are seminal works in which she identified a number of other interesting patterns of e-mail use that need to be studied to see how prevalent they are in public organizations including the following:

1.   E-mail was viewed as by far the best medium for when communication "involved dislike or intimidation" and also when people were angry or fearful about how others would receive their messages (Markus, 1994a, p. 136). It appears that a large number of employees prefer to use e-mail when dealing with situations with which they feel uncomfortable. The lack of body language and voice inflection may be a positive aspect of e-mail communication in these situations.

2.   About 50% of her respondents (Markus, 1994a, p. 135) felt that too many people used e-mail in "accountability games" such as to "cover your anatomy."

3.   E-mail dominated communications in the organization so much so that many managers found it necessary to resort to the telephone from time to time in order to boost the quality of their relationships that they felt might be harmed to over-reliance on e-mail (Markus, 1994b, p. 139). Indeed, Markus found some employees gave curt attention to people who actually visited their offices in order to return to their e-mail (Markus, 1994a, p. 141).

4.   Markus found a "*documentation mania*" in which people put even simple requests into e-mail. She goes on to show that employees would often forward e-mail to upper level managers to point out the wrongdoing of those whom they believed had behaved incorrectly (Markus, 1994a, p. 142).

Phillips and Eisenberg (1996) employed qualitative methods to study the use of e-mail by employees of a not-for-profit research firm affiliated with a West Coast University and found the following findings that overlap those of Markus significantly:

1.   The organizational members copied their own boss when contacting others frequently in order to "let their boss know what they were requesting" (Phillips & Eisenberg, 1996, p. 74);

2.   They sometimes copied someone else's superior or peers in order to convey the "force" of a "manager looking over" the shoulders, though they admitted that such a practice as "rude" (Phillips & Eisenberg, 1996, p. 74);

3.   They copied their e-mail messages to others in order to "broaden the base" of people aware of the situation. For example, they cited the case where an employee

Copyright © 2006, Idea Group Inc. Copying or distributing in print or electronic forms without written permission of Idea Group Inc. is prohibited.

sent a supervisor a message expressing disagreement and the supervisor copied his reply to the employee's supervisor (Phillips & Eisenberg, 1996).

4.   They kept e-mails that ask someone else to do something as a record in case it is not done. When it is still not done a significant period later, they then ask for the same action again attaching the earlier request and, if necessary, copy the second request to higher-ups (Phillips & Eisenberg, 1996, p.74).

To summarize, e-mail is now being used as a device for creating a paper trail (e.g., over who is at fault for the failure of some project) and altering the context of the communication by bringing third parties into the situation. Of course, the same strategic purposes could possibly be achieved by other forms of communication but only with great difficulty as Phillips and Eisenberg (1996, p. 75) point out:

Obviously, these actions could be carried out face-to-face or via the telephone.... Imagine marching in to speak to Person A, asking Person A to do something, and letting them know you are also going to tell Person B (A's boss) that you asked them to do some task and then marching to Person B's office.... When the same task could have been accomplished via e-mail simply by hitting 5 to 10 extra strokes on the keyboard.

The existing qualitative studies reveal differences among organizations and employees in their approach to the privacy of e-mail. Coyne et al.'s (1996) study of an architectural firm's use of e-mail found that some users are conscientious about not forwarding personal messages to others unless they "seek permission to make them public." Many employees agree that e-mails should not be sent via "blind copy" so that the recipient is not aware of the fact that the message is being copied to one or more third parties. Markus (1994a, p. 140) cites one employee as saying that blind copying and forwarding of e-mails should be "outlawed."

Despite reservations about use of forwarding messages, managers can employ e-mail effectively for achieving goals they deem important. For example, Ngwenyama and Lee (1997, p. 154) draw on Habermas's critical social theory to identify four types of communicative actions: instrumental (to obtain objectives), communicative (to maintain mutual understanding), discursive (to achieve agreement), and strategic (to transform the behavior of others). They employ these concepts to analyze a case study that shows how one private sector manager (Ted) was able to use e-mail strategically to achieve conformance with the law by another manager (Sheila) who initially stated that she was in conformance with the law (Ngwenyama & Lee, 1997, pp. 159-163). Ted was able to send copies of memos by a third-party (Mike) to provide evidence that Sheila was not in conformance that helped to convince Sheila to admit that there was a problem that needed attention. Of course, such activities could also possibly be done via FTF meetings or via phone calls but the ease, speed and available of concrete evidence (the e-mail evidence suggesting non-conformance) makes e-mail the ideal medium to achieve desired change.

It was originally thought that e-mail would level status differences among communicants because communication styles frequently used by high-status persons in FTF meetings such as interruptions are no longer available to them in e-mail. However, David Owens

Copyright © 2006, Idea Group Inc. Copying or distributing in print or electronic forms without written permission of Idea Group Inc. is prohibited.

(Owens, Neale & Suton, 2000) has done empirical research that shows that e-mail is also used for status moves in organizations. He notes that the common use of a "signature" for e-mail communications often communicates status. Owens & Sutton (1999) developed a model that predicts different styles of e-mail communication based on the status of organizational employees. They hypothesize that low-status employees are likely to focus on enhancing the "social-emotional" climate of communication and use emoticons and other e-mail techniques that improve the "climate" of the group. High-status individuals are likely to appear busy, "say more with less," and thus message length will be inversely proportional to the status of the sender (Owens, Neale & Sutton, 2000). They note that listservs can have the impact of opening up communication because they can serve as a "perpetual open-door meeting" and that members can try "status moves" 24 hours a day, seven days a week (Owens, Neale & Sutton, 2000, p. 227). However, they note that often high-status individuals will form a smaller, more elite discussion list with marginal members left out. Owens studied 30,000 e-mail messages sent over four years and confirmed some of these hypotheses. He found that senior managers took the longest to respond and used curt messages while mid-status employees used long, contentious e-mails that were overkill for the simple questions involved (Headlam, 2001).

Unfortunately, there are very few studies available which have examined these very important and subtle uses of e-mail in the public sector. Consequently, there are few generalizations we can make to managers other than the following: (1) All employees need to be aware of these strategic uses of e-mail including their potential negative consequences; (2) They may want to consider the banning of practices such as blind copying and/or forwarding of e-mail without the knowledge of permission of the original sender; and (3) They need to be aware that e-mail can have positive as well as negative consequences for organizations and such policies would be hard to enforce. Indeed, it is not clear whether the effects of these strategic uses of e-mail are positive or negative. The documentation mania could lead to a great deal of time spent composing and reading e-mails that could be spent more productively. On the other hand, it may provide for greater accountability for actions to a greater degree in the past. Rules that clamp down on communication via e-mail may lead to less honest and open communication.

E-mail influences the personnel process and the workings of the organization in a variety of ways. For example, Barnes and Greller (1994, p. 132) point out that e-mail can often "bypass the traditional information gatekeepers such as secretaries." Likewise, some public executives such as Stephen Goldsmith, during his tenure as Mayor of Indianapolis, encouraged police officers and other street level employees to directly contact him via e-mail (Miller, 1995). Goldsmith reported receiving and reading as many as 400 e-mail messages a day. How does such activity on the part of the CEO of a public organization affect its performance? It can provide the CEO with a direct line of information about problems that otherwise might be squelched by going through the hierarchy and thus have positive effects. It could undermine middle-level managers and their relationships with their employees. Likewise, it could divert high-level executives from spending enough time on other activities (e.g., external activities) that are important to the success of the organization. We very much need case studies and other research to inquire into the impact of such use of e-mail. We have drawn heavily on the few cases that exist, such as Markus, but her study is based on a single private organization. We need more research into the extent and use of e-mail for such purposes. Nevertheless, in Figures 3A

Copyright © 2006, Idea Group Inc. Copying or distributing in print or electronic forms without written permission of Idea Group Inc. is prohibited.

Figure 3A. Summary of computer-mediated communication (CMC) characteristics & managerial strategies

CMC Characteristics	Advantages of CMC	Disadvantages of CMC	Possible Management Strategies
Asynchronous	Fit workers' schedules better— does not interrupt work. Especially helpful to coordinating work between shifts, in ad hoc groups, & in remote locations.	Not as immediate a response and thus less rich.	Policy on what kinds of messages are inappropriate for e-mail.
Breadth of Dissemination	Obtain feedback from persons otherwise would not take place, both inside & outside organization.	Spread potentially embarrassing & damaging messages that could be used against organization.	Policy & education of managers & employees on the legal & organizational impacts of e-mail. Monitor for inappropriate messages
Anonymity and/or lack of physical presence of those to whom sending the messages	More honest & accurate feedback. Greater participation of those lower in the hierarchy.	Flaming or extreme responses due to less sense of personal communication.	Etiquette policy for e-mail. Encourage use of FTF and/or Phone to personalize communications. Decide on legality & desirability of use by employees for increased participation.

Source: Adapted from Rocheleau, B. (1997). E-mail: Does it need to be managed? Can it be managed? *Public Administration and Management: An Interactive Journal*, 7(2), http://pamij.com/7_2/v7n2_rocheleau.html

and 3B, I have outlined a strategy for how managers can deal with e-mail and other forms of CMC.

Freedom of Information Acts and Electronic Records

There are significant variations in state Freedom of Information Acts (FOIA) but there appears to be a consensus among states on most points. Generally, electronic records are subject to FOIA. There are exemptions in many state acts such as for copyrighted material, trade secrets, and confidential material (Reporters Committee for Freedom of the Press, 1994). However, states such as Illinois did not consider it especially burdensome

Copyright © 2006, Idea Group Inc. Copying or distributing in print or electronic forms without written permission of Idea Group Inc. is prohibited.

Figure 3B. Computer-mediated communication characteristics & Freedom of Information Acts and electronic records

CMC Characteristics	Advantages of CMC	Disadvantages of CMC	Possible Management Strategies
Creates written record & not legally protected	Text allows more precise examination and preserves documentation of problems that may serve the organization. May open up policy heretofore-secret discussions to more public involvement.	Over-documentation by employees. May open the organization to damage if e-mails are inappropriate or poorly thought out. E-mail may violate FOIA and other statutes such as sunshine laws.	Policy on what types of communications should not be communicated via e-mail at all. Etiquette and/or rules on strategic uses of e-mail. Teach & remind employees about FOIA, sunshine, & other laws that affect e-mail. Establish publicly available record to which such exchanges are automatically copied
Volume of Communication	Allows much greater amount and variety of communication with diverse sources that can improve organizational productivity	Information overload & much of it may not be relevant to tasks. Employees don't delete and/or save messages into folders & are not able to make effective use of e-mail. Employees spend too much time on e-mail relative to other important activities	Filtering of spam and other irrelevant information that may degrade server. Set policy on situations where sending or forwarding of e-mail may disrupt server. Teach and remind employees on how to manage e-mail loads by saving important messages into folders & deletion of others. Emphasize importance of not allowing e-mail to divert employees from other important activities.

"to delete names and other identifying information" and scramble previously alphabetized records to protect identities (Reporters Committee for Freedom of the Press, 1994, p. 4). As far as charging for information, the tendency has been to charge for the cost of reproduction though additional costs may be necessary if the request requires specialized programming. Many FOIA laws contained exemptions if the request would create a huge burden and require the creation of "new records" but, if the electronic records reside in a well-designed computerized database, it may be difficult to argue that meeting requests is burdensome. One of the problems with responding to FOIA requests

Copyright © 2006, Idea Group Inc. Copying or distributing in print or electronic forms without written permission of Idea Group Inc. is prohibited.

Figure 4. RAND Institute's initial framework for assessing the Homeland Security sensitivity of publicly available geospatial information

Filter	Key Questions
Usefulness	Is information useful for target selection or location purposes?
	Is information useful for attack planning purposes?
Uniqueness	Is information available from other geospatial sources?
	Is information available from direct observation or other non-geospatial information types?
Societal benefits/costs	What are the expected benefits of public access to this geospatial information?
	What are the expected societal costs of restricting public access to this geospatial information?
Source: Adapted from RAND Institute. (2004). America's Publicly Available Geospatial Information: Does It Pose a Homeland Security Risk? Santa Monica: RB-9045-NGA, p. 3. Retrieved May 24, 2004 from www.rand.org	

concerning FOIA is that the major e-mail systems (Microsoft Exchange & Lotus Notes) were "not designed with today's management needs in mind" (Worthen, 2005). This limitation led the CIO of the Florida Department of Health (Worthen, 2005) to create a copy of every e-mail that is placed in a storage device in case they need to be retrieved. This takes the responsibility from individual workers to make decisions about whether a particular e-mail should be saved. Laws such as HIPAA and FOIA are creating the need for software that can effectively classify e-mail and make it easily retrievable through "context-based analysis" (Worthen, 2005).

Many local governments have placed FOIA request forms on their Web sites. FOIA requests can raise ethical dilemmas for governmental administrators. Many FOIA requests are made by commercial companies with profit in mind and may seem obtrusive and objectionable. For example, one local administrator receives requests from a publishing company for the names and addresses of everyone involved in traffic accidents in the local government's jurisdiction. The administrator consulted two attorneys. One attorney told him that the government would have to provide the data to the publishing company while another attorney told him that there were "two grounds for denying the claim." There is also the concern (Strickland, 2003) that once the re-seller obtains records, the records may be corrupted and/or may contain incorrect data but what would be the right of the public to access and correct information in the re-seller's database? From the perspective of governmental officials, FOIA claims, especially involving electronic records such as e-mail, seem obtrusive and working for the government is like "living in a fishbowl" and that there are few protections for privacy. However, groups representing reporters such as The Reporters Committee for Freedom of the Press see the post 9/11 era and developments such as privacy rights for medical data as restraining their legitimate access to information that affect public policy.

The 9/11 attack changed the assumptions about the right to access about infrastructure information. During the Clinton Administration, a policy was developed (Strickland, 2003) that encouraged discretionary release of information such as environmental information put on the Internet by the Environmental Protection Administration (EPA).

Copyright © 2006, Idea Group Inc. Copying or distributing in print or electronic forms without written permission of Idea Group Inc. is prohibited.

The terrorist attack led to the Homeland Security Act that included a "broad new FOIA exemption" (Strickland, 2003) that preempted state open records laws concerning "infrastructure." There is concern that such changes may lead to the use of this exemption to prevent public access to information that could pertain to public health concerns. Due to concerns about attacks on infrastructure, much information was removed from the governmental Internet sites, although a subsequent RAND (2004) study showed that little sensitive information was available on such sites that could not be obtained elsewhere. In addition, the RAND Institute (2004) developed a framework for weighing the benefits versus the threats of online geospatial information (See Figure 4).

There is concern that such changes may lead to the use of this exemption to prevent public access to information that could pertain to public health concerns. The RAND (2004) study provides a framework to guide decision-making about removal issues.

Privacy and Ownership of Data

Garson (1995, p. 75) argues that there needs to be a "balance" between the public's right to know and the "individual's right to privacy." He goes on to state that the "solution" to this tension must "emerge from a political rationality" (Garson, 1995, p. 76). Many governments wrestle with what information to put should be placed on the Internet such as ownership and tax data concerning properties that might make it easy for a stalker to locate their victims. Public officials point out that such data is publicly available anyway although one may argue that there is, in effect, a qualitative difference when it is made so much easier to access via the Internet, as a 1996 New Jersey Report stated (Harris, 2003, p. 36):

Practical barriers to information use and dissemination imposed by traditional paper documents disappear when information is stored in electronic bits and bytes...susceptible of being easily transferred around the globe.... This qualitative difference between paper and electronic records gives rise to an argument that the dissemination of public records in computer readable form should be restricted.

For example, the computerization of all court documents would include personal information on "those found innocent and even witnesses called to testify" (Harris, 2003, p 36). Some states such as Arizona have created rules to protect personal financial information such as Social Security and credit card numbers (Harris, 2003). The State of Washington made address and identity information confidential (Harris, 2003). But the overall trend has been to make all information available in paper format also accessible on Internet. For example, the National Center for State Courts developed guidelines for public access and concluded that the "presumption of openness is constitutionally based" and requires a "compelling interest" to void that presumption (Harris, 2003, p. 38).

Copyright © 2006, Idea Group Inc. Copying or distributing in print or electronic forms without written permission of Idea Group Inc. is prohibited.

Figure 5. Analysis of how agencies handle personal information data flow

Routine use with other government agencies

Agency	Agriculture	Education	Labor	State
Courts	x	x	x	
Defense Manpower Data Center	x		x	
Department of Justice	x	x	x	
Department of Labor	x			
Foreign governments				x[a]
HUD	x			
Internal Revenue Service	x			x
Law enforcement agencies (federal, state, local)	x	x	x	x
OMB		x	x	
OSHA			x	
Other governmental bodies			x	x
State agencies		x	x	
U.S. Postal Service	x		x	

[a] State shares information with foreign governments only on limited occasions.

Source: United State General Accounting Office. (2002). Information Management: Selected Agencies Handling of Personal Information. September. GAO-02-1058, p. 22.

Thus Grupe (1995, p. 236) argues that there is "no statutory basis" for the oft-stated aphorism that "a custodian must weigh the public's right to know versus the individual's right to privacy." Grupe (1995) points out that generally states do not even require that a requester provide a reason for seeking the information and may not even be required to "fill out a form to get the data." There is evidence that the public is concerned about the ease of access to personal information and the GAO (2002b) reported that a 2001 survey found that 81% were concerned that their personal information might be "misused." This concern with privacy issues was the reason why many Americans wanted to go slow with the implementation of e-government. However, the same GAO Report (2000b) studied the personal information submitted by individuals on a few forms by selected agencies. Their results showed that there exists a wide-range of sharing of personal information among agencies and other parties based on the "routine exception" principle (see Figure 5). There is evidence that the public's attitude towards privacy is complex and they like the advantages of access and sharing in some cases but not others. For example, Location-Based Services (LBS) are able to identify the location of wireless customers. These customers would like to have that done for emergency services but be able to turn off LBS in other situations (Elber, 2001). In short, people sometimes find accessibility invaluable and other times they find it intrusive.

Copyright © 2006, Idea Group Inc. Copying or distributing in print or electronic forms without written permission of Idea Group Inc. is prohibited.

Ethical and Legal Policies
for E-Government

When governments attempt to transform their service delivery to provide e-payment and other e-government services, it is necessary for them to examine privacy and other ethical and legal issues. A good example is the State of Texas, which convened an Electronic Government Task Force (2000) to study privacy issues. They found that the State had nearly 600 statutes that pertained to privacy but that the statutes were not consistent and could create problems for the state in implementing e-government. One of the major issues was the selling of personal information and the task force believes it is necessary to assure citizens about this issue because surveys showed that 60% found such sales to be "objectionable" but that not much data is protected from public sale. Assuring citizens of privacy should help to improve the use of e-government. Their review of the situation in Texas found that data on Texans turned up on Web sites like publicdata.com.

The State of Texas Task Force (2000) identified four issues that should be addressed in comprehensive legislation to assure privacy and confidentiality to people using e-government sites. First, governments need to make clear what their policy is for retention of data. Is the information gathered really necessary? How long will it be kept and will it be destroyed after it is no longer needed? Secondly, "uneven-ness" in data protection needs to be reconciled because what is considered private and protected by one agency could be made public by another. When confidential information is transferred from one unit to another, the confidential information must be made impossible (e.g., by scrambling the data) to breach the confidentiality assured. Third, the same assurances of confidentiality must be respected when data is shared with other levels of government. The fourth issue concerns data correction: citizens should have the same rights of inspection and correction of data that as given to information maintained by credit card companies. The State of Texas Task Force (2000) takes a strong position in favor of OPT-IN policies in which citizens must give specific permission for data about them to be released rather than OPT-OUT policies where the burden is on the citizen to request their data not to be shared.

Accuracy of Government Data
and Legal Liability

Some governments sell data. For example, the cost of developing GIS systems can be very expensive and governments may wish to recoup some if not all of the costs of developing the systems. Grupe (1995) reports that state departments of motor vehicles can make more than $10 million in one year from such sales. The federal government cannot copyright its data, but states such as Colorado copyright all of their data. However, the overall tendency has been for governments (e.g., Onsrud, 1995) to provide data and information for the "total costs of duplication." When governments sell or provide data such as GIS data, they provide a disclaimer that provides warnings that the data may be inaccurate

Copyright © 2006, Idea Group Inc. Copying or distributing in print or electronic forms without written permission of Idea Group Inc. is prohibited.

and that it is up to the user to determine its accuracy. Suppliers don't "assume responsibility for inconsistent, inaccurate, or out-of-date datasets" and reliability would only be guaranteed by a special contract (Videnic, 2003, p. 43). Onsrud (1999) discusses the situations of tort law under which the providers of GIS data can be sued.

Web Site Advertising and Links to Government Web Sites

In constructing governmental Web sites, officials are often faced with ethical and legal issues of what kinds of information and links should be placed on Web sites. One issue concerns the selling of advertisements on Web sites and a related issue is whether to have links to private enterprises at all. Advertising is potentially attractive as a source of funds to support the development of e-government functions. This issue was discussed with three municipalities in response to a query on the IG Knowledge Center (Innovations Group Knowledge Center Report, 2003) and none of the three favored the use of advertising. One saw it as likely to generate requests for advertising by businesses that would embarrass government (e.g., strip joints) and requests for ads by opponents of the administration. Another saw even links to non-profits that the city "does not support" as inappropriate and that such links belonged on other sites such as those of the "Chamber of Commerce."

There is one fairly well-known legal case concerning linkages: the case of "Putnam Pit, Inc. v. City of Cookeville, Tennessee" in the United States Court of Appeals, Sixth Circuit, that was decided on July 19, 2000. The plaintiff, Geoffrey Davidian, sued the City of Cookeville (TN) because he alleged it had violated his First Amendment rights by denying a link to his paper on the municipal Web site. The decision denied one of Davidian's claims that the Web site constituted a "public forum" because it was not structured for "free and open discussion," but the Court did hold that the city was open to "viewpoint discrimination" because it did not have a clear, neutral policy for deciding what sites should be linked. The conclusion of Horwood, Hopkins and Stein (2001) is that municipalities should have "well-defined" and "documented" policies concerning the use of their Web sites.

Another emerging trend is for public agencies to use Web site advertising to achieve their goals. For example, Melchior's (2004) study shows that public health agencies used Web site ads to promote campaigns for hotlines and smoking cessation and public works departments used Web ads to publicize recycling programs. However, normally, these ads do not appear on governmental Web sites, but are targeted at Web sites where they are most likely to reach their target audiences.

As governmental Web sites become more sophisticated, they open many other issues. For example, some governmental Web sites now feature customizability so that citizens can focus on those aspects of the sites that they find useful. The customization of governmental Web sites may involve the use of "cookies" but state laws such as the "Illinois State Agency Web Site Act" prohibit the use of "permanent cookies" unless the

Copyright © 2006, Idea Group Inc. Copying or distributing in print or electronic forms without written permission of Idea Group Inc. is prohibited.

cookies are used to add value to the users and are disclosed through a comprehensive Web site policy. There are countless other potential legal and ethical issues that crop up. For example, due to spamming, many governmental Web sites employ software to block e-mail that is likely to be spam but these controls may result in "false positives" in which legitimate communications are blocked. For example, this author belonged to a listserv (ISWORLD) for several years when suddenly I stopped receiving its messages. Upon inquiry, I learned that my university's e-mail sever had added a filter that treated the listserv messages as if they were spam. Upon request, my access to the listserv was restored. The major point of this chapter is that generalist and data-processing managers need to think carefully and systematically about the ethical and legal implications of their policies.

Computer-Matching and Privacy Laws

The history of computer-matching is illustrative of the complex issues of data privacy and the limitations of laws enacted to protect individual privacy. *Computer matching* originally referred to the computerized comparison of databases to identify individuals who were common to two or more of the record systems (Rocheleau, 1991). When a person turns up in two or more of the databases, it is referred to as a "hit." But the concept of computer-matching has extended to related procedures such as "*computer profiling*" in which a profile of characteristics of individuals (often who are suspected of some illegal activity such as welfare fraud or terrorism) are matched against databases to identify individuals for closer inspection. Finally, there is also an approach referred to as "*front-end verification*" in which computer databases are matched for specific individuals such as when a person applies for benefits (e.g., welfare or unemployment) or perhaps employment in a governmental agency.

Federal computer-matching began in 1977 during the Carter Administration and expanded rapidly during the Reagan Administration. States began conducting their own routine matching efforts (Rocheleau, 1991). In 1974, the Federal Privacy Act was passed to protect against abuses of privacy but the Act contained a "*routine use*" *exception* that permitted matching if the use was "compatible with the original purpose of the program." The identification of fraud and abuse in government programs has been deemed a legitimate government purpose compatible with most legislation (Rocheleau, 1991). States are free to match because the Federal Privacy Act does not cover them. Civil libertarians have argued that computer-matching violates Constitutional protections such as the Fourth Amendment since records are effectively being "searched" even though there is no evidence to begin the search and might be considered illegal "fishing expeditions." But courts have ruled that records maintained by "third parties for administrative purposes" are not protected (Rocheleau, 1991). Much of the original matching involved efforts to identify abuse and fraud of programs, especially those involved with welfare. Proactive matching could potentially be used for positive purposes such as to help, for example, patients to know when they have exceeded their deductibles for drugs or dangerous interactions among drugs. But the positive proactive

Copyright © 2006, Idea Group Inc. Copying or distributing in print or electronic forms without written permission of Idea Group Inc. is prohibited.

purpose could quickly be turned into criminal searches such as, for example, excessive use of drugs. Such searches could be applied to programs such as Medicare, which is a "social insurance" program and thus is not generally regarded as a "welfare program" since the recipients contribute directly towards the cost of the program. There is the fear that the government can employ its huge databases to become Big Brother. Ironically, one of the best protections that people have against the invasion of privacy has been the inefficiency of government (Keisling, 1984). The rapidly increasing ability of governmental organizations to exchange data easily could result in "virtual databases" that are very comprehensive. The protections against abuse of privacy in matching cases have been mainly procedural in nature that force governments to follow due process, but there is little in the way of substantive protections (Rocheleau, 1991). Of course, private sector companies such as those involved with credit card companies have huge and very personal data on people. The Right to Financial Privacy Act of 1978 forced the government to have a subpoena or court order to get that data (Scalet, 2003), but the Patriot Act did away with those requirements (Scalet, 2003). The Homeland Security Act allows any federal entity (before this law, it used to be restricted to law enforcement agencies) to look thorough an individual's private or business e-mail as long as long as the ISP has "good faith" that it constitutes some risk of death or injury (Tillman, 2003). Before this law, there had to be the "reasonable belief" that the communication represented an "immediate danger" (Tillman, 2003). The E-Government Act of 2002 requires that federal agencies do "privacy impact assessments" (PIAs) to consider how new or upgraded systems could affect the privacy of citizens (Miller, 2004). The assessments appear to be process-oriented. For example, the Department of Interior's (2002) assessment consists of a set of questions that agencies must address when they propose to gather new information. The questions appear to be useful in making agency personnel think about the relevance and accuracy requirements under privacy statutes but do not appear to provide any new substantive protections.

The definition of "ownership of data" has become complex. According to Chris Hoffnagle (Berinato, 2002), a member of the Electronic Privacy Information Center, many view the ability to acquire data as giving you "ownership of data," but that there exists no "theory of property that says that's OK." The concept of the *technological imperative* states that what "can be done will be done." Many of the major concerns about abuses of the ownership of data pertain to private sector organizations such as credit reporting agencies that sell data for profit (Berinato, 2002). Some states such as California have taken action to protect certain aspects of privacy such as Social Security numbers (SSNs). California (U.S. General Accounting Office, 2004, p. 20) prohibits the display of SSNs and well as affording other protections to the SSNs. California's rules have been widely adopted by the private sector and several other states (U.S. General Accounting Office, 2004). However, Grupe, Kuechler and Sweeney (2002, p. 64) state that the United States does not have the "general privacy protection safeguards" common to the countries of the European Union and that U.S. policy is characterized by a "market-driven view" in which information is a "saleable commodity" that belongs to corporations. Privacy legislation tends to be related to specific aspects of privacy and does not provide general protections.

Copyright © 2006, Idea Group Inc. Copying or distributing in print or electronic forms without written permission of Idea Group Inc. is prohibited.

Purchasing and Legal Issues

As we discuss in our chapter on procurement, there are a myriad of potential legal issues that can arise in information technology purchases. In this chapter, I am focusing on legal issues that are more closely related to ethical dilemmas but it is important to note again the huge importance of legal liability issues related to IT purchases. A good case study discussing the willingness of governments to spend large amounts of money to avoid legal problems is given by Brown (2002) in her case study of a municipality trying to upgrade their police-computer-aided dispatch (CAD) system prior to Year 2000. The manager was happy to commit $2 million to a vendor to make changes despite the fact that the police thought that the system would run without the changes and that the changes would be difficult to make and might very well disrupt the system. The explanation was that the city wanted to transfer legal liability for any Y2K problems to the vendor. In short, legal considerations can play a dominant role in crisis situations such as Y2K.

Conclusion

I have only scratched the surface in this chapter concerning the potential ethical and legal issues involved with IT. Ethical and legal issues are common in the IT area. Public organizations may use their corporate lawyers for advice on legal issues involved in this chapter but they are not a final solution either. First, few lawyers are expert in the area of cyber-law. Secondly, legal principles concerning many important issues have not been clearly established and, given the rapidity of change in technology, there will always be legal issues that do not have precedents. Thus the legally correct course of action may not be clear.

Ethical and legal issues are not an area in which IT specialists have been trained. Consequently, it is important for the leadership of public organizations to establish clear policies with respect to ethical and legal issues related to information technology. In addition, proactive efforts need to be made to ensure that employees understand and practice the application of these policies to specific situations. The growth of comput-erized communication and the Internet have raised challenging issues with respect to accessibility and privacy. In general, electronic information is treated similarly to written communication with respect to accessibility laws, such as state freedom of information acts, although electronic communication has fewer legal protections than, for example, personal letters or phone conversations. There exist a number of laws intended to protect the privacy of information residing in governmental databases, but these laws have proven generally to be tenuous in their protections. Given the weakness of the privacy laws and the growing demand for "transparency" of governmental data, the establish-ment of strong ethical guidelines is a key step in any information management program.

E-mail and other forms of CMC have important implications for management and personnel processes in organizations. CMC can foster important feedback albeit with the

Copyright © 2006, Idea Group Inc. Copying or distributing in print or electronic forms without written permission of Idea Group Inc. is prohibited.

risk of creating records that can embarrass organizations and sometimes open them to legal scrutiny. E-mail is now used by many employees, both supervisors and line workers, in strategic ways that may raise ethical questions. Organizations may want to consider prohibiting use of certain features such as "blind carbon copy" in setting their ethical guidelines for computer use. E-mail is an essential communication tool within and between public organizations. There is an indication that e-mail communication is converging with FTF and voice mail and many of the patterns of use and cautions that apply to them also hold for e-mail. Kettinger and Grover (1997) found that interorganizational e-mail allowed e-mailers to capitalize on the experience and knowledge of dozens of fellow e-mailers across the world and also found that more experienced users of interorganizational e-mail concentrated on task rather than social use of e-mail. Certainly, the constructive uses of e-mail can greatly increase the productivity of organizational members. Managers can support the positive uses of e-mail and other CMC by implementing and communicating thoughtful ethical policies.

References

Adams, H. L., Morris, M. G., & Van Scotter, J.R. (1998, Fall). Examining e-mail use in the context of virtual organizations: Implications for theory and practice. *International Journal of Electronic Commerce, 3*, 8-26.

Barkhi, R., Jacob, V. S., & Pirkus, H. (1999). An experimental analysis of face to face versus computer mediated communication channels. *Group Decision and Negotiation, 8*, 325-347.

Barnes, S., & Greller, L.M. (1994, April). Computer-mediated communication in the organization. *Communication Education, 43*, 129-142.

Berinato, S. (2002, July 1). Take the pledge. *CIO Magazine*, 56-63.

Bishop, L., & Levine, D. I. (1999). Computer-mediated communication as employee voice: A case study. *Industrial and Labor Relations Review, 52*(2), 213-233.

BNA Employment Discrimination Report. (1995, June 21). 786.

Bordia, P. (1997). Face-to-face versus cmc: A synthesis of the experimental literature. *Journal of Business Communication, 34*(1), 99-120.

Brown, M. (2002). Emergency management at the millennium: The role of information systems. In T. L. Rhodes (Ed.), *The public manager case book: Making decisions in a complex world* (pp. 13-36). Thousand Oaks, CA: Sage.

Cohen, N.S. (1999, August 23). Corporations battling to bar use of e-mail for unions. *New York Times*.

Cohen, S. (2001, February 26). Thought cop: Policing e-mail and internet usage is cultural and legal balancing act for many IT managers. *Infoworld, 26*, 39-40.

Coyne, R.D., Sudweeks, F., & Haynes, D. (1996). Who needs the internet? Computer-mediated communication in design firms. *Environment and Planning B: Planning and Design, 23*, 749-770.

Copyright © 2006, Idea Group Inc. Copying or distributing in print or electronic forms without written permission of Idea Group Inc. is prohibited.

Crowley, A. (1999, July 5). E-mail's got you. *PC Week Online*.

Daft, R.L., & Lengel, R.H. (1984). Information richness: A new approach to managerial information processing and organization design. *Management Science, 32*(5), 554-571.

D'Ambra, J. D., Rice, R. E., & O'Connor, M. (1998). Computer-mediated communication and media preference: An investigation of the dimensionality of perceived task equivocality and media richness. *Behaviour & Information Technology, 17*(3), 164-174.

Dimmick, J., Kline, S., & Stafford, L. (2000). The gratification of personal e-mail and the telephone. *Communication Research, 27*(2), 227-248.

Dowling-Sendor, B. (2002, February). A turf war over open meetings. *American School Board Journal, 189*(2). Retrieved May 18, 2004, from http://www.asbj.com/2002/02/0202schoollaw.html

Elber, G. (2001, October). Defending location privacy. *Geospatial Solutions*, 19-21.

Garson, G. D. (1995). *Computer technology and social issues*. Hershey, PA: Idea Group Inc.

Garton, L., & Wellman, B. (1995). Social impacts of electronic mail in organizations: A review of the research literature. In B. R. Burlseon (Ed.), *Communication yearbook* (pp. 434-453). Newbury Park, CA: Sage.

Goldsmith, S. (1995, April). Interview with Stephen Goldsmith. *Government Technology*, 24-25.

Gotcher, J. M., & Kanervo, E. W. (1997). Perceptions and uses of electronic mail: A function of rhetorical style. *Social Science Computer Review, 15*(2), 145-158.

Grupe, F. H. (1995). Commercializing public information: A critical issue for governmental IS professionals. *Information & Management , 28*, 229-241.

Grupe, F.H., & Kuechler, W. (2002, Summer). Is it time for an IT ethics program? *Information Systems Management, 19*(3), 51-57.

Guernsey, L. (2000, April 5). Management: You've got inappropriate mail: Monitoring of office e-mail is increasing. *New York Times*.

Harmon, A. (1998, November 11). Corporate delete keys busy as e-mail turns up in court. *New York Times,*.

Harmon, A. (2000, March 26). E-mail is treacherous. So why do we keep trusting it? *New York Times*.

Harris, B. (2003, April). Hung jury. *Government Technology*, 36-38.

Healam, B. (2001, April 8). How to e-mail like a CEO. *New York Times Magazine*, 7-8.

Hightower, R., & Sayeed, L. (1995). The impact of cmc systems on biased group discussion. *Computers in Human Behavior, 11*(1), 33-44.

Horwood, J. N., Hopkins, P. J., & Stein, A. N. (2001). Municipal web site liability under the first amendment. Reprinted from The Municipal Lawyer, January/February. Retrieved May 15, 2004, from http://www.spiegelmcd.com/pubs/municipal_web_liability.htm

Copyright © 2006, Idea Group Inc. Copying or distributing in print or electronic forms without written permission of Idea Group Inc. is prohibited.

Huff, C., Sproull, L., & Kiesler, S. (1989). Computer communication and organizational commitment: Tracing the relationship in a city government. *Journal of Applied Social Psychology*, 1371-1391.

Innovations Group (IG) Knowledge Center Report. (2001). Open meetings and public records Law regarding email. March 5. Retrieved May 10, 2004, from http://www.ig.org/

Ives, B., Hamilton, S., & Davis, G. B. (1980). A framework for research in computer-based management systems. *Management Science*, (9), 910-934.

Jarvenpaa, S. L., & Leidner, D. E. (1998). Communication and trust in global virtual teams. *Journal of Computer-Mediated Communication*, 3(4).

Kassirer, J. (2000). Patients, physicians, & the Internet. *Health Affairs*, 19(6), 115-123.

Keisling, P. (1984, May). The case against privacy. *Washington Monthly*, 12-28.

Kelley, T. (1999, April 1). Behind closed e-mail. *New York Times*.

Kettinger, W. J., & Grover, V. (1997). The use of cmc in an interorganizational context. *Decision Sciences*, 28(1), 513-555.

Kraut, R., Steinfeld, C., Chan, A., Butler, B., & Hoag, A. (1998). The role of electronic networks and personal relationships: Coordination and virtualization. *Journal of Computer-Mediated Communication*, 3(4).

Lantz, A. (1998). Heavy users of electronic mail. *International Journal of Human-Computer Interaction*, 10(4), 361-379.

Laudon, K. C. (1995, December). Ethical concepts and information technology. *Communications of the ACM*, 38(12), 33-39.

Lea, M., O'Shea, R., Fund, P., & Spears, R. (1992). "Flaming" in computer-mediated communication: Observations, explanations, implications. In M. Lea (Ed.), *Contexts of computer-mediated communication* (pp. 3-65). Hemel Hempstead, UK: Harvester Wheatsheaf.

Leatherman, C. (2000, July 7). A crusade against cryonism of a breach of collegiality. *The Chronicle of Higher Education*, A12-A14.

Linderman, J. L., & Schiano, W. T. (2001, Winter). Information ethics in a responsibility vacuum. *Database for advances in information systems*, 32(1), 70-74.

Lohr, S. (1998, November 2). Antitrust case is highlighting the role of e-mail. *New York Times*.

Mackay, W.E. (1988, October). Diversity in the use of electronic mail: A preliminary inquiry. *ACM Transactions on Office Information Systems*, 6(4), 380-397.

Maltz, E. (2000). Is all communication created equal? An investigation into the effects of communication mode on perceived information quality. *Journal of Product Innovation Management*, 17, 110-127.

Markus, M. L. (1994a). Finding a happy medium: Explaining the negative effects of electronic communication on social life at work. *ACM Transactions on Information Systems*, 12(2), 119-149.

Markus, M. L. (1994b). Electronic mail as the medium of managerial choice. *Organizational Science*, 5(4), 502-527.

Copyright © 2006, Idea Group Inc. Copying or distributing in print or electronic forms without written permission of Idea Group Inc. is prohibited.

Mason, R. O. (1995). Applying ethics to information technology issues. *Communications of the ACM, 38*(12), 55-57.

Mason, R. O., Mason, F. M., & Culnan, M. J. (1995). *Ethics of information management.* Thousand Oaks, CA: Sage.

McKinnon, S. M., & Bruns, W., Jr. (1992). *The information mosaic.* Boston: Harvard Business School.

Melchior, A. (2004). *Pioneers in cyberspace: Emerging public sector trends in Web site advertising.* Paper presented at the 2004 Annual Meeting of the American Political Science Association, New Orleans. Retrieved June 3, 2004, from http://archive.allacademic.com/

Mennecke, B. E., Valacich, J. S., & Wheeler, B. C. (2000). The effects of media and task on user performance: A test of the task-media fit hypothesis. *Group Decision and Negotiation, 9,* 507-529.

Miller, B. (1995, February). Should agencies archive e-mail? *Government Technology, 8,* 22.

Miller, J. (2004, May 17). Serious about privacy? *Government Computer News,* 1 & 12.

Moore, D. A., Kurtzber, T. R., Thompson, L. L., & Morris, M. W. (1999). Long and short routes to success in electronically mediated negotiations: Group affiliations and good vibrations. *Organizational Behavior & Human Decision Processes, 77*(1), 22-43.

Moyer, C. A., Stern, D. T., Katz, S. J., & Fendrick, A. M. (1999). We got mail: Electronic communication between physicians and patients. *American Journal of Managed Care, 5*(12), 1513-1522.

Neu, C. R., Anderson, R. H., & Bikson, T. K. (1999). *Sending your government a message: E-mail communication between citizens and government.* Santa Monica, CA: Rand.

Ngwenyama, O. K., & Lee, A. S. (1997). Communication richness in electronic mail: Critical social theory and the contextuality of meaning. *MIS Quarterly, 21*(2), 145-168.

Onsrud, H. J. (1999). Liability in the use of geographic information systems and geographic data sets. Retrieved May 18, 2004, from http://www.spatial.maine.edu/~onsrud/pubs/liability40.pdf

Overly, M. R. (1999). *E-policy: How to develop computer e-policy, and internet guidelines to protect your company and its assets.* New York: AMACOM.

Owens, D. A., Neale, M. A., & Sutton, R. I. (2000). Technologies of status management: Status dynamics in e-mail communications. *Research on Managing Groups and Teams, 3,* 205-230.

Owens, D. A., & Sutton, R. I. (1999). Status contents in meetings: Negotiating the informal order. In M.E. Turner (Ed.), *Groups at work: Advances in theory and research.* Mahway, NJ: Lawrence Erlbaum.

Oz, E. (2001, November). Organizational commitment and ethical behavior: An empirical study of information system professionals. *Journal of Business Ethics, 34*(2), 123-136.

Copyright © 2006, Idea Group Inc. Copying or distributing in print or electronic forms without written permission of Idea Group Inc. is prohibited.

Phillips, S. R., & Eisenberg, E. M. (1996). Strategic uses of electronic mail in organizations. *Javnost, 3*(4), 67-81.

Pierce, M. A., & Henry, J. W. (1996). The role of personal, informal, and formal codes. *Journal of Business Ethics, 15*(4), 425-427.

Postmes, T., Spears, R., & Lea, M. (1998). Breaching or building social boundaries? Side-effects of computer-mediated communication. *Communication Research, 25*(6), 689-715.

Preece, J. (2004, April). Etiquette online: From nice to necessary. *Communications of the ACM, 47*(4), 56-61.

Prysby, C., & Prysby, N. (1999). Legal aspects of electronic mail in public organizations. In G. D. Garson (Ed.), *Information technology and computer applications in public administration: Issues and trends* (pp. 231-245). Hershey, PA: Idea Group Inc.

Prysby, C. L., & Prysby, N. D. (2003). Electronic mail in the public workplace: Issues of privacy and public disclosure. In G. D. Garson (Ed.), *Public information technology: Policy and management issues* (pp. 271-298). Hershey, PA: Idea Group Inc.

Rand Institute. (2004). *America's publicly available geospatial information: Does it pose a homeland security risk?* Santa Monica, CA: RB-9045-NGA.

Reporters Committee for Freedom of the Press. (1994). *Access to electronic records: A guide to reporting on state and local government in the computer age.* Washington, DC: Reporters Committee for Freedom of the Press.

Richtel, M. (1998, September 7). Technology: At many companies, the most candid criticism emerges from company e-mail forums. *New York Times.*

Rocheleau, B. (1991). Human services and the ethics of computer matching. *Computers in Human Services, 8*(2), 37-56.

Rocheleau, B. (2002). E-mail: Does it need to be managed? Can it be managed? *Public Administration and Management: An Interactive Journal, 7*(2). Retrieved from http://pamij.com/7_2/v7n2_rocheleau.html

Rosen, J. (2000, April 30). The eroded self. *New York Times Magazine,* 46-53, 66-68 & 129.

Rudy, I. A. (1996). A critical review of research on electronic mail. *European Journal of Information Systems, 4,* 198-213.

Sadogapan, G. D., Richardson, Jr., J. J., & Skngh, R. (2000, January). Access issues: Complying with the freedom of information act. *Geo Info Systems,* 28-32.

Scalet, S. D. (2003, June 15). Balancing act: Q & A: Alan Westin on privacy. *CIO Magazine.* Retrieved July 1, 2003, from http://www.cio.com/archive/061503/balancing.html?printversion=yes

Schmich, M., & Zorn, E. (1999, October 18). Computer mischief has firms looking over our shoulders. *Chicago Tribune,* Metro-Chicago Section.

Schopler, J. H., Abell, M. D., & Galinsky, M .J. (1998). Technology-based groups – A review and conceptual framework for practice. *Social Work,* 254-267.

Schrage, M. (2004, May 15). The virtues of chit chat. *CIO Magazine.* Retrieved May 9, 2004, from *http://www.cio.com/archive/051504/work.html?printversion=yes*

Copyright © 2006, Idea Group Inc. Copying or distributing in print or electronic forms without written permission of Idea Group Inc. is prohibited.

Sipior, J. C., Ward, B. T., & Rainone, S. R. (1998, Winter). Ethical management of employee e-mail privacy. *Information Systems Management*, 41-47.

Spears, R., & Lea, M. (1994). Panacea or panopticon? The hidden power in computer-mediated communication. *Communications Research*, *31*(4), 427-459.

State of Texas. Department of Information Resources (2000, August). *Privacy issues involved in electronic government*. Prepared for the Electronic Government Task Force: Strategic Issues Subcommittee By the Department of Information Resources. Austin, Texas. Retrieved October 18, 2004, from http://www.dir.state.tx.us/taskforce/report/privacy.htm

Straub, D., & Carlson, C. L. (1990). Discovering and disciplining computer abuse in organizations: A field study. *MIS Quarterly*, 45-55.

Strickland, L. S. (2003, August/September). Records and information management perspectives: Part 2: Access to public information. *Bulletin of the American Society for Information Science & Technology, 29*(6), 7-9.

Sussman, S. W., & Sproull, L. (1999). Straight talk: Delivering bad news through electronic communication. *Information Systems Research*, *10*(2), 150-166.

Taylor, T. S. (2001, February 14). E-lessons. *Chicago Tribune*, Working Section, 1 & 7.

Tillman, B. (2003). More information could mean less privacy. *Information Management Journal*, *37*(2), 20-23.

United States Department of the Interior. (2002, September 16). *Privacy impact assessment and guide. Office of the Chief Information Officer*.

United States General Accounting Office (U.S.G.A.O.). (2002a, September). *Employee privacy: Computer-use monitoring practices and policies of selected companies*. GAO-02-717.

United State General Accounting Office (U.S.G.A.O.). (2002b, September). *Information management: Selected agencies handling of personal information*. GAO-02-1058.

United States General Accounting Office (U.S.G.A.O.). (2004, January). *Social security numbers: Private Sector Entities Routinely Obtain and Use SSNS, and Laws Limit the Disclosure of This Information*. GAO-04-11.

Vandenbosch, B., & Ginzberg, M. J. (1996-1997). Lotus notes and collaboration: Plus ca change..." *Journal of Management Information Systems*, *13*(3), 65-81.

Videnic, M. (2003, February). Legal issues abound regarding spatial data. *GeoWorld*, 42-43.

Weisband, S. P., Schneider, S. K., & Connolly, T. (1995). Computer-mediated communication: status, salience, and state differences. *Academy of Management Journal*. *38*(4), 1124-1151.

Western Municipal Clerks Association. (2002, April 2). *Memorandum: Applicability of the Washington state open public meetings act to e-mail exchanges*. Retrieved May 18, 2004, from http://www.wmcaclerks.org/Open%20Meetings%20Act%20and%20Email.htm

Copyright © 2006, Idea Group Inc. Copying or distributing in print or electronic forms without written permission of Idea Group Inc. is prohibited.

Worthen, B. (2005, January 15). Message Therapy. *CIO Magazine*. Retrieved January 18, 2005, from http://www.cio.com/archive/011505/compliance.html

E-Mail Policies of Selected Governmental Organizations Mentioned in Chapter

City of Marietta, GA: Internet-Electronic Mail Acceptable Use Policy. Issue Date: 11/01. Retrieved May 10, 2004, from http://www.lgov.org/

City of Tampa Bay, FL: Personnel Manual. B. Directives and Benefits. B39A. Computer Use. Issue Date: 04/06/99. Retrieved May 10, 2004, from http://www.lgov.org/

Mecklenburg County, NC: Electronic Mail Usage Policy. Date Effective: 5/20/96 Date, Revised: 2/02/98. Retrieved May 11, 2004, from http://www.lgov.org

State of Nevada. Policy on Defining Information Transmitted via E-M. Issue Date: 10/10/03. Retrieved May 10, 2004, fromhttp://www.lgov.org/

Streamwood, Village of, IL: Computer Systems Policies Manual. Issue Date: 03/01/03. Retrieved May 10, 2004, from http://www.lgov.org/

Additional Reading

There is an extensive and rapidly growing literature on privacy, freedom of information, and cyber-ethics. In terms of applying general ethical principles to practical governmental information management, the chapters by Prysby and Prysby are very useful concerning e-mail. Garson's (1995) book provides an excellent overview of the laws and dilemmas concerning privacy and freedom of information acts. It is useful to study the actual guidelines of individual governments such as those provided on Web sites such as WWW.LGOV.ORG and the Innovation Group "IG Knowledge Reports" concerning cyber-ethics. There are many online sources that provide excellent information on various legal and ethical issues. For example, The Reporters Committee for Freedom of the Press has a Web site (www.rcfp.org) that covers issues such as FOIA laws (by state), the Electronic FOIA, and other topics relevant to the press. The Center for Democracy and Technology has a Web site that includes a useful table organized by type of information and its relationship to specific laws and rules that govern matters such as notice, standards for access, data quality, security, among others at: http://www.cdt.org/security/guidelines/final_government_matrix.shtml

Copyright © 2006, Idea Group Inc. Copying or distributing in print or electronic forms without written permission of Idea Group Inc. is prohibited.

Key Concepts

- Broaden the base
- Compassion
- Computer matching
- Computer profiling
- Deterrent
- Documentation mania
- Electronic Freedom of Information Act
- Front end verification
- Impartiality
- Individualist consequentialist ethic
- IT ethics committee
- Media Richness Theory
- Moment of truth
- Open Meetings Laws
- Opt-In and Opt-Out policies
- Preventive and deterrent approaches to computer abuse
- Risk aversion
- Routine use exception
- Slippery slope
- Technological imperative
- Transitory e-mail
- Utilitarianism

Discussion Questions

1. Based on your own perspective as well as the reading for this class, what elements do you think should go into an organization's ethical guidelines?

2. What do you think are the consequences of putting up all printed records (e.g., property ownership, taxes, etc.) on the Internet? Do you think there are any printed records that should not be placed on the Internet?

3. What length of time do you think e-mail should be retained? Does your organization distinguish between "transitory" e-mails that can be erased quickly and those that should be saved?

Copyright © 2006, Idea Group Inc. Copying or distributing in print or electronic forms without written permission of Idea Group Inc. is prohibited.

4. What linkages, if any, to private sector organizations do you think should exist on a government's Web site? Do you think it is acceptable for governments to accept advertising on their Web site?

5. Do you think private uses of governmental e-mail should be allowed? If so, what constraints should be placed on private uses?

6. What factors most influence your treatment of cyber-ethical issues: organizational, peer, or individual? What ethical principles guide your treatment of computerized communication and data?

7. Have you (or anyone with whom you have exchanged e-mails) employed e-mail for strategic purposes as described in this chapter? For example, have you or anyone with whom you work in the organization used e-mail to "broaden the base" or establish a paper trail in case there are problems? Do you think these uses are ethical? Have you used the "blind carbon copy" (Bcc) option in sending e-mail? Do you think this is ethical?

8. Do you think it is ethical and/or effective to employ e-mail for sensitive personnel processes such as to discipline or fire an employee?

9. Do you think advertisements should be used to raise revenue on governmental Web sites? What kind of policies should be established in deciding what links to include on a government's Web site?

10. How important is your participation in CMC (internal or external) to your job? Do you ever encounter the problems of "flaming" and unethical uses of CMC in your CMC? Are there any actions that you would never use e-mail for? Why?

Exercises

1. Write a paper in which you analyze the ethical-legal policies of a governmental organization and compare these with the guidelines and recommendations stated by experts in this chapter. Are they lacking any elements that experts say are important? Do they include important components that we have not discussed? Suggest how you would alter or rewrite (or write if one does not exist) your organization's ethical guidelines.

2. Study and analyze the information provided by a governmental organization on its Web site. Does the site have a privacy policy? Do you think there exists other information that should be made accessible through the site? Are there any data on the site that you don't believe should be there? How does the accessibility provided by this site compare with other, comparable organizations? Does the site contain information concerning reliability issues? Construct a plan for revising the Web site so that it maximizes accessibility but does not violate privacy laws.

3. Has an organization with which you are familiar ever discovered any significant violation of ethical principles in regards to computer use? If so, analyze how your organization dealt with these issues and compare its handling of the cases with those recommended by Mason, Mason and Culhan.

Copyright © 2006, Idea Group Inc. Copying or distributing in print or electronic forms without written permission of Idea Group Inc. is prohibited.

Chapter IX

Evaluation and Information Technology

Introduction

It is important to evaluate information technology because if you don't assess results from IT, research (e.g., Markus et al., 2000, p. 255) shows that you will not achieve the goals you are pursuing. Moreover, investments in information technology hardware, software, and personnel have become a larger portion of the budgets of governments at every level so it makes sense to determine whether these expenditures are paying off. More importantly, a well-designed evaluation program can provide feedback on how to improve IT services. In this chapter, I review basic concepts of evaluation and apply them to the evaluation of information technology. I draw from research literature to identify models and approaches that have been employed in assessing the value and performance of information technology. Finally I look at some actual evaluation measures used by various governments to assess their information technology function.

What is Evaluation?

When I talk about evaluating information technology, I am referring to "systematic evaluation" in contrast to contrast to the informal, ad hoc evaluation that goes on all of the time in governments. Generalist managers are continuously assessing their perceptions of the performance of various aspects of their organizations including information technology (Farbey, 1993, p. 12). As I pointed out in the Preface, managers construct their own "personal information systems" in which they make use of their own observations

Copyright © 2006, Idea Group Inc. Copying or distributing in print or electronic forms without written permission of Idea Group Inc. is prohibited.

as well as informal comments of inside staff and key external people such as legislative and political leaders to determine if IT systems and support services are working well. If they see problems based on their own experiences or hear many complaints from these groups, they may act on this informal information or they may decide to inquire more formally into the problems. If they hear positive comments or fail to hear complaints, they may assume that the IT function is working well and not pursue additional evaluation information. In short, most of the evaluation that is done of IT is informal, ad hoc, and based on qualitative observations by managers and informal comments from end users.

If a manager is perceptive and has a good informal network of key internal and external sources of information about the organization, the manager may be able to operate much of the time without relying on formal evaluations. However, because of the growing importance and expense devoted to IT, many managers now want to institute a more systematic and rigorous evaluation of IT. The common characteristics that define evaluation that is more systematic and less subjective including the following characteristics:

1. **Public:** A purely subjective evaluation of IT is "owned" by the individual. A scientific evaluation of IT is open to being tested by someone other than the original evaluator. So there must be some measures that can be gathered and are open to public scrutiny and replication by persons other than the original evaluator.

2. **Comparison:** Evaluations are inherently comparative. When we say that IT is performing well, some standard is implied where there is a range of performance from excellent to poor. There are several types of comparisons such as comparing this year's IT performance with that of previous years. Another approach is to compare your organization's results with similar organizations or benchmarks that have been established by studying data from other organizations. Comparisons may also be constructed artificially such as by setting goals and targets and comparing actual performance with these goals. These goals may be derived by looking at the levels achieved by similar organizations or be constructed based on what managers believe to be desirable and achievable goals. This approach is often used as part of the IT planning process. Thus there are many different types of comparisons to judge IT but essentially all IT evaluation involves comparisons and managers have to decide which comparisons are most valid and useful.

3. **Values and priorities and the control of subjectivity:** Evaluations do not eliminate subjectivity (see, e.g., Posavac & Carey, 1997, p. 225). Every evaluation involves values because managers must select criteria and prioritize these criteria in order to evaluate IT. These criteria represent the goals or values that the organization is seeking to achieve. The determination of which goals to pursue is subjective. For example, should IT be judged primarily by how low it keeps costs or by how well it achieves high rates of citizen satisfaction? If we want to achieve both of these goals, what should be the trade-off between them—how much lowered satisfaction would we accept in order to save on costs? Such questions are political and there is no scientific way to set goals and priorities—that is a matter for the policymakers. However, scientific evaluation helps to control the subjectivity by making explicit

Copyright © 2006, Idea Group Inc. Copying or distributing in print or electronic forms without written permission of Idea Group Inc. is prohibited.

the measures so that once goals have been set, the measurement of the achievement of these goals is open to public scrutiny and replication.

4. **Applied Research Relevant to Decision-making:** Evaluation is intended to be applied research useful for making decisions. The information should be relevant to helping to understand IT. It may help to identify areas of strength and weaknesses and may help to point the way to improved services. Thus evaluation is intended to be practical and is not the same as "basic research." The implication is that evaluations need to focus on issues that management can do something about. For example, in evaluating the performance of educational systems, we know that the backgrounds that students bring with them to schools have major effects on outcomes, but (at least for public schools) there is little that can be done to affect the student backgrounds so evaluators will focus on variables that government can influence such as class size, teacher training, etc. In the IT area, many IT organizations have small resources and cannot afford new personnel or expensive hardware and software systems so evaluation takes place in a context and attention is focused on those factors that can be directly influenced by the organization.

5. **Causality:** Rigorous, scientific evaluations seek to determine whether IT caused the positive changes that are ascribed to it. In other words, did IT lead to the organization's improved productivity or was this due to other factors such as personnel changes or changes in the general economy? Rigorous determination of causality may require use of quasi-experimental designs and multivariate statistical analysis (see, e.g., Shadish, Cook, & Campbell, 2002) in order to control for the impacts of these non-IT variables. Most managers do not require or invest in evaluations that concentrate on the rigorous determination of causality and thus they do not use experimental or quasi-experimental methods. Causality issues have been more the concern of the academic researchers.

However, many of the current management techniques such as the Balanced Scorecard rely upon assumptions about the causal relationship between what the organization refers to as "*drivers*" (usually important internal processes that affect important aspects of services to customers) and outcomes and some business and public organizations are now rigorously studying the relationship between drivers and outcomes. For example, the City of Charlotte (North Carolina) police department analyzed their data on 911 calls and found that rapid response was a key issue in less than 1% of their calls for service and thus they de-emphasized rapid response time and concentrated more on preventing crimes (Kaplan & Norton, 2001a, p. 180). This also points to the fact that an organization's IT system is central to the conduct of evaluation in general because performance measures need to be built into the organization's information system.

There is a demand for more scientific and public evaluation than the purely subjective assessments relied upon by many organizations in the past and in this chapter I will present a variety of approaches that have been used to gather systematic evaluation data for assessing the IT function in public organizations. Next, I discuss 13 questions that need to be addressed in planning for an evaluation of IT in a public organization.

Copyright © 2006, Idea Group Inc. Copying or distributing in print or electronic forms without written permission of Idea Group Inc. is prohibited.

Figure 1. Key questions to address in planning for evaluation of IT

1: When should formal evaluation be done?
2: What kind of evaluation should be done?
3: From whose perspective is effectiveness being assessed?
4: On what domain of activity is the assessment focused?
5: What level of analysis should be studied?
6: What is the purpose of assessing effectiveness?
7: What time frame is being employed?
8: What type of data should be used in evaluations—qualitative or quantitative?
9: What is the basis of the comparison against which effectiveness is to be judged
10: Should formal evaluation be done by insiders or outsiders?
11: What is the relationship between the formal evaluation and politics?
12: What are the differences in evaluating the information systems of public versus private organizations?
13. Is the evaluation likely to be worthwhile?

Questions to Ask in Planning for Evaluation of IT

#1: When Should Formal Evaluation of IT be Done?

As noted earlier, many organizations do little or no systematic evaluation of IT because evaluating IT is difficult and also because many managers have great faith in their ability to do assessments through informal methods. What situations lead to a demand for more rigorous assessment of IT? Seddon, Graeser & Willcocks (2002, p. 24) studied the conditions that led to formal evaluation in organizations and identified the following situations as being most common: (1) When a new senior manager wants to get a handle on what is happening; (2) When senior managers are introduced to a new evaluation tool that seems relevant; (3) When the organization is experiencing a crisis and wants to figure out what is wrong; (4) When the IT department faces pressure to justify its rising costs; and (5) When organizations engage in large outsourcing contracts. Thus, in many cases, the demand for evaluation involves a short-term situation and evaluation may be ended when the conditions that brought it about no longer exist.

But there is a growing movement (see, e.g., Hatry, 1999) to develop ongoing performance measures to assure accountability in government including IT. In general, formal evaluations should be conducted when some significant stakeholder wants formal data about IT. These stakeholders could be members of the IT department itself, end-user departments, generalist managers, or the political leadership (executive and/or legislative). IT managers themselves often want formal evaluation data as a means of achieving feedback on how well their department is doing and to be proactive so as to improve services and also be ready if they are questioned about the results of IT.

There is one form of evaluation referred to as *"ex ante" evaluation* that takes place when the organization is deciding whether to invest in a new IT system. In this chapter, I concentrate on evaluations that are being done after the system has been implemented

Copyright © 2006, Idea Group Inc. Copying or distributing in print or electronic forms without written permission of Idea Group Inc. is prohibited.

and installed. I discuss "ex ante" evaluation in the chapter on procuring IT. I will point out there that the estimation in advance of costs and benefits of system is very difficult because, as Farbey et al. (1993, p. 62) have shown, many of the most important benefits are unexpected and the variance between estimated costs and actual costs can easily reach 100% (Farbey et al., 1993, p. 97). Indeed, the most accurate ex ante estimates are likely to take place where the evaluators have had experience in implementing similar systems in the past and, preferably, have conducted *"ex post" evaluations* of these systems so they have reasonably accurate estimates of the costs and benefits of the systems.

#2: What Kind of Evaluation Should be Done?

There are a wide variety of different types of formal evaluations that can be conducted of IT (Posavac & Carey, 1997, pp. 7-10). A *needs assessment* is often depicted as the first step of an evaluation in which baseline information is gathered about the most pressing IT needs of the organization. This is actually part of the planning process that helps to establish the goals for IT in an organization. Thus the planning and evaluation processes are intimately related and represent different steps in an overall policy cycle. If you examine the long-term strategic plans of many public organizations, they often include assessments of the strengths and weaknesses of the organization's IT. Needs assessments can create the baseline data for comparing the achievements of progress made on outcome and efficiency goals noted next. The needs assessment can focus on data such as the speed and reliability of the organization's network as well as on the perceptions of the support services offered by IT to its end users. Needs assessments thus help to paint a picture of the strengths and weaknesses of the IT system.

Process evaluations form an important component of overall programs and focus on questions such as whether the methods and processes used by the IT department conform with the approaches used by organizations recognized as excellent—the so-called *"best practices"* approach. There may be professional and industry standards set for the best way to accomplish various tasks ranging from networking to support of end-user computing and evaluators can compare the organization's IT department's methods with these standards. Process evaluation may include the tracking of the processes used by organizations to perform IT-related functions (e.g., the processing of permits for new developments) that can allow the organization to look for ways to speed and improve these processes through business process reengineering (BPR*)*. Process evaluation is often viewed by workers as the most useful form of evaluation by those being evaluated because process evaluations are often able to provide information as to what the organization can do to improve its performance.

The validity of process evaluation depends upon the assumption that the favored processes do indeed lead to better outcomes such as those discussed in the following. It is possible that some processes may be viewed as superior, but in reality do not produce superior outcomes. Thus it is useful to conduct both process and outcome evaluations when there are questions about the efficacy of certain processes. For example, there are numerous guidelines about the best approaches to designing Web sites and e-govern-

Copyright © 2006, Idea Group Inc. Copying or distributing in print or electronic forms without written permission of Idea Group Inc. is prohibited.

ment portals. A process evaluation would compare the organization's Web sites with these standards and allow us to identify cases where the Web site or portal deviates from these standards. But, an outcome study would focus on whether these changes actually result in the improved results such as increased usage and greater user satisfaction of visitors due to the design changes.

A category of evaluations that may be viewed as related to the process evaluations concerns *workload measures*. The basic purpose of workload measures is to indicate whether the IT department is working hard and performing many activities. For example, information may be presented concerning the number of end users and applications supported as well as network servers, and the number of work orders processed. If the measures are limited to quantitative measures of workload, then workload measures, like other process measures, do not indicate the qualitative aspects and outcomes of this workload and thus depend on assumptions about the quality and impact of the work. For example, an organization's IT department may be supporting a large number of users and servers but their qualitative performance of these tasks may be open to question. However, in many cases, organizations have implemented "customer evaluations" in which they ask end users to evaluate their performance of these IT support functions, but in that case the measure is more akin to outcome evaluations described next.

Outcome evaluations measure the extent to which the end goals of IT are achieved. These goals depend on the ends that organizations seek to achieve, but can range from satisfying internal customers and citizens to improving specific services and cutting costs of government. Outcome evaluation is often viewed as being superior to process evaluation in that it measures the end results and does not depend on assumptions like process evaluation. However, if only outcomes are measured, then an organization may result in a *"black box"* evaluation in which the end result is known (i.e., did the organization perform well or not?) but not the reasons *why* the outcome occurred or what can be done improve the results. If the outcome evaluation is negative, then there will likely be great frustration with the inability of outcome-oriented evaluations to inform the organization as to why the organization performed poorly and its inability to point to ways to improve outcomes. Consequently, it is good to combine process and qualitative measures to be able to provide a more complete analysis that can point the way to how to improve results.

Efficiency evaluations measure the relationship between costs and workload and outcome measures. For example, cost outcome measures may be used such as cost per-end-user or PC supported. Such measures would not necessarily speak to the qualitative dimension so outcome measures related to quality would need to be employed if there are issues concerning the quality as opposed to just the efficiency of the results.

To summarize, there are several major different kinds of evaluative information that can be gathered about an organization's IT and each type of information helps to provide part of an overall profile of its IT performance. Over time, organizations will need to gather different types of measures in order to provide a complete perspective on how well they are performing.

Copyright © 2006, Idea Group Inc. Copying or distributing in print or electronic forms without written permission of Idea Group Inc. is prohibited.

#3: From Whose Perspective is Effectiveness being Assessed?

In addition to the different categories of evaluation noted earlier, there are many other considerations that make the selection of IT evaluation all the more complex. I am adopting (with some additions) Cameron's (1986, p. 542) "critical questions" to identifying some key issues that need to be addressed in determining the nature of the evaluation that should be conducted of IT, as well as some of my own points: IT evaluations may be done from many perspectives including generalist management, political or legislative leadership's perspectives, end-user departments, and the IT department's own perspective. The perspective employed is important because different users tend to focus on different issues. For example, the IT department's perspective is likely to be concerned more with technical issues of IT while political leaders will tend to be more interested in evaluations that focus on budgetary implications and visible impacts of IT on citizenry. When governmental program evaluation first became popular, evaluations were often designed without systematic input from the stakeholders (other than perhaps top executives who often had only remote interest in the evaluation) with the unfortunate result that the results of most program evaluations were not used (Patton, 1986). Willcocks (1992) found that 44% of organizations did not include the user department in the evaluation process at the feasibility stage. In order to improve utilization, Patton (1986) developed the concept of "*utilization-focused*" evaluation in which the first step of the evaluation process is to identify the stakeholders who have an interest in the evaluation and to involve them on a continuous basis in the design, implementation, and utilization of the evaluation. In cases where there are a wide variety of persons and organizational units involved in evaluation, Farbey et al. (1993) argue that it is a good idea to develop a "stakeholder" map identifying all of these key interests. The logic behind utilization-focused evaluation is to be sure that there are one or more stakeholders who have an investment in using the evaluation results (Patton, 1986).

#4: On What Aspects of Activity is the Assessment Focused?

Today, IT departments' activities are wide-ranging including infrastructure and network services as well as IT support services for end users. A major part of the activities may be outsourced in which case it is the IT department's responsibility to evaluate the performance of the contractor. Given the great breadth of their activity, there are several different domains that IT evaluations may examine and the organization will need to decide which is likely to be most fruitful. Some important aspects of IT services may be overlooked. Farbey, Target & Land (1994) hold that the process of listing the potential IT benefits is because many of IT benefits attained are not the benefits that were originally expected. Years ago, IT services were fairly limited in number, but now they cover such a broad range that organizations may want to develop a long-range plan for evaluation so that different aspects of IT services are assessed periodically.

Copyright © 2006, Idea Group Inc. Copying or distributing in print or electronic forms without written permission of Idea Group Inc. is prohibited.

#5: What Level of Analysis Should be Analyzed?

Evaluations may be done of the entire IT function and its overall portfolio of investments as a whole down to a very specific evaluation of one component of one application (e.g., the performance of the accounts payable function of a governmental financial package). For example, recently, Carr (2003) has initiated a debate concerning the utility of the entire IT function taken as a whole, arguing that over time, IT is not of strategic importance to success in the marketplace and that IT applications eventually are similar to that of a utility in which the goals of managing IT should be to minimize costs and risks. Gurbaxani (2003) and others responded to Carr's analysis by pointing out that the impacts of information management do not result merely from mechanical operations like electricity. These analyses discuss IT at a very general level that academics (and some practitioners) find interesting. However, managers need much more specific and detailed analyses of particular systems and/or problems due to specific applications or even specific functions with a single application. For example, in my interviews with governmental officials, they often found modules of governmental ERP applications uneven with some aspects excellent and others mediocre or even poor so that, in order to be useful, evaluations need to assess specific functions of individual applications.

#6: What is the Purpose of Assessing Effectiveness?

Evaluations may be done to support summary judgments about the success of the IT and use these judgments to make major changes in IT policy such as outsourcing most of the IT function. Evaluations aimed at using the results to make major changes in policy and to hold public agencies and their personnel to account are referred to as "*summative evaluations*." Alternatively, evaluations may be done to gather feedback to improve IT services—such evaluations are referred to as "*formative*" evaluations. Summative evaluations are most threatening to staff and evaluations need to be sensitive and attempt to deal with these responses.

#7: What Time Frame is being Employed?

Differences in time frames can range from a few months to several years and the selection of the time frame for which benefits will be calculated can be an extremely important consideration. There are some major types of complex software systems such as Enterprise Resource Programs (ERP) and Geographic Information Systems (GIS) that are very expensive to implement and can take years to produce the results that recover the costs of their investments. For example, the results of an Accenture study reported in CIO Magazine (November 1, 2003) found that it took most companies two years to achieve major paybacks for ERP systems and even then, revenue goals were not met. Similarly, Markus et al. (2000) found that organizations were unlikely to find positive outcomes for ERP systems in the early phases unless the organization specifically pursues a strategy of "quick wins." In my interviews with the heads of IT departments, some thought that

Copyright © 2006, Idea Group Inc. Copying or distributing in print or electronic forms without written permission of Idea Group Inc. is prohibited.

they were unlikely to ever recover in hard dollar terms the costs of expensive GIS systems and that the point of such systems was more to improve services and the quality of information to citizens rather than produce cost savings. In some cases, legislative leaders became frustrated at spending large sums on IT and not seeing visible results in short order. Thus several of my interviews emphasized the need to identify "quick successes" and "low hanging fruit" when implementing expensive new software programs as the following IT director noted in discussing the implementation of their GIS system:

You know...I give him [person in charge of GIS project] a lot of credit.... He forced the city to build a really good foundation. A lot of people give him a lot of flak, saying 'When am I going to see stuff, when is the fruit coming?' We kept saying you have to wait, you have to build a good foundation.

One of the terms used in cost-benefit analysis is "*payback period*" which is the amount of time that it takes for benefits to catch up to the costs of IT projects. Major infrastructure investment costs occur before benefits occur and thus both benefits and costs need to be discounted to present value to rigorously calculate benefits of long-term projects. Thus expensive projects like GIS may take years, if ever, for financial benefits to catch-up to costs. Consequently the selection of the time frame for evaluation is an important and potentially controversial decision. A theme of my interviews with both generalist managers and IT department officials is the necessity to design the project so that it is able to demonstrate some concrete short-term benefits even with complex projects such as ERP and GIS systems.

#8: What Type of Data Should be used in Evaluations— Qualitative or Quantitative?

Both quantitative and qualitative data may be used in evaluations. Qualitative data refers to "rich information" gathering techniques such as open-ended and semi-structured interviews that are useful for obtaining the perspectives of the interviewees concerning IT and for obtaining insights into issues that evaluators may not be aware of prior to the interviews. Focused interviews are now conducted by some cities with selected citizens to obtain feedback about issues with which the organization is concerned. Thus qualitative data are useful for gaining insights into issues and understanding the perspective and context of IT in organization. It is generally difficult to reduce qualitative data into numeric form.

Formal evaluations tend to concentrate on gathering quantitative indicators because they can give more precise measures of success and thus determine degrees of success. Quantitative IT measures often include measures such as *Return on Investment (ROI)* in which the cash benefits of the system are compared with the costs to provide a net measure of outcome. Quantitative indicators also include survey data in which IT customers' responses are forced-choice options rather than open-ended responses such

Copyright © 2006, Idea Group Inc. Copying or distributing in print or electronic forms without written permission of Idea Group Inc. is prohibited.

as when they rate their satisfaction with IT services on a scale from very satisfied to very dissatisfied.

Quantitative measures have problems and limitations, especially for evaluation of public IT systems. First of all, much of IT spending is for infrastructure kinds of support (e.g., network servers). Consequently it is hard to connect specific IT expenditures with specific outcomes because IT is a general tool used to support other department's activities. Thus IT is only one of many factors that contributes to outcomes (Farbey, Land & Targett, 1999). For some very specific software or hardware applications, there may be clear connections and commonly used measures of outcome so that ROI can be reasonably calculated. For example, the ROI of new software systems to assist in pursuing parking ticket scofflaws may allow us to compare the increased revenues with the total costs of the system (including hidden costs due to disruption and training due to the new system) and thus calculate a fairly precise ROI. Likewise, we may be able to calculate the money saved by new e-government services such as having citizens downloading forms versus coming to the governmental office to pick up paper documents. In such cases, we can draw a clear cause-effect relationship between the IT system and some cash flow impacts. Structured surveys can be used to gather end-user and citizen perceptions of the quality of services. Organizations may use *time series* of the same metric over a period of years (e.g., comparing trends in the percent very satisfied with services) and inquire further as to why there are any major improvements or deteriorations. Gathering quantitative data such as these to measure the success of specific applications is very appropriate and useful assuming that the data are valid and reliable.

Many systems are aimed at providing managers with better information and the impact of IT depends in part on how the manager uses the information and thus the impact is indirect (Farbey, Land and Targett, 1992, p. 116). Also, for many issues and problems, there are important intangibles that are difficult to quantify. Farbey et al. (1993, p. 49) studied 16 IT projects and found that only three of them attempted to evaluate intangible benefits. The reason for the failure was that they did not believe that the qualitative data would be acceptable to decision-makers to "justify" the investment. Qualitative data can be made more rigorous by taking simple steps such as, for example, using systematic sampling methods to select end users or citizens to provide the qualitative feedback. Likewise, by converting qualitative data such as opinions and experiences with IT performance into written format, the data can be presented to the IT department and they can have a chance to assess its validity. This author (Rocheleau, 1982) has found that the collection of qualitative data such as detailed case accounts of how people were helped or hindered by systems can have a greater impact than abstract, quantitative data alone. Keen (2003) likewise points out the importance of "storytelling" in the establishment of business cases. An example of the use of qualitative data is contained in an article by Maholland & Muetz (2002) about the use of balanced scorecard system in St. Charles, Illinois. Their balanced scorecard system employed a variety of data including numerical data based on structured surveys and performance data from their IT system. But their major example of the success of the balanced scorecard system concerned their discovery that the City had a reputation among contractors for being "difficult to work with" and this finding was based on qualitative data from site visits and use of focus groups (Maholland & Muetz, 2002, p. 15). The advantage of such qualitative data is that they

Copyright © 2006, Idea Group Inc. Copying or distributing in print or electronic forms without written permission of Idea Group Inc. is prohibited.

are rich data and can yield unanticipated insights and often point to the direction to go to improve services. In a 1984 study, Daft & Lengel cite the strong preference of managers for qualitative data over that of information from management information systems. Deciphering the reasons for deterioration or improvement in services through quantitative indicators alone is difficult. To summarize, a comprehensive evaluation will employ both quantitative and qualitative methods because they complement each other and provide a stronger degree of confidence in the results.

#9: What is the Basis of the Comparison Against Which Effectiveness is Judged?

As I noted earlier, evaluations inevitably involve comparisons. Organizations may use time series data to compare their performance on how well they do in comparison with their own performance in previous years. Organizations may also compare their results with similar organizations elsewhere, often neighboring organizations with similar characteristics and constituencies. The advantage of comparing their current performance with their own performance in the past is that this comparison holds the intangibles and unique characteristics of the public organization constant and thus appears more valid and acceptable to IT staff. Another big advantage is that this approach is less threatening than comparisons with other organizations.

Another approach is to compare the results achieved versus goals for improvement set by management. These "constructed" goal-setting measures require judgments on what goals are ambitious enough to achieve real performance improvements when needed, but not too ambitious so as to be unrealistic. The difficulty of assessing artificial comparisons is a problem in any case where evaluations are tied into employee compensations. Kaplan & Norton (2001a, p. 257) discuss how the construction of goals for their balanced scorecards opens the possibility of "sandbagging of goals" to be too easy and the need to encourage "stretch" targets that are ambitious and reward employees even if they fail to meet these more ambitious goals. Thus the setting of artificial goals requires judgment.

#10: Should Formal Evaluation be Done by Insiders or Outsiders?

Evaluations can be conducted by insiders or outsiders. Internal evaluations of IT are often conducted by the IT staff themselves or though the central management of the organization. Many organizations hire outside consultants to conduct assessments of IT often as part of their strategic planning process. These may be local consultants or nationally known organizations such as the Gartner Group. There are advantages to both approaches. Insider evaluation will tend to be less expensive and the insiders already know the important contextual information about the organization that will take external consultants a good deal of interviewing to acquire. Insiders will be around to help to implement changes that may be recommended as a result of the evaluation. On the other hand, it is easier for outsiders to be more objective about IT and to bring in extensive

Copyright © 2006, Idea Group Inc. Copying or distributing in print or electronic forms without written permission of Idea Group Inc. is prohibited.

knowledge of other organizations' IT systems and thus be able to bring new perspectives that insider evaluators lack. Of course, organizations do not have to choose only one approach—many governments conduct ongoing performance measurement of IT while bringing in outside consultants when some key stakeholder feels the need to gain an independent perspective.

#11: What is the Relationship Between the Formal Evaluation and Politics?

Evaluation inherently involves sensitive issues because evaluation is making a statement about the value or worth of organizational staff and it is natural for people to be concerned and wary about such assessments. The implementation of a program evaluation system, as Kaplan & Norton (2001a, p. 16) note, is not merely a system of metrics but a "change project." Even if the evaluation information is not supposed to be related to compensation and other key decisions, employees will be concerned about how they and their departments look on these measures and speculate about how these measures could be used in the future.

Consequently, evaluation is affected by political issues. Serafeimidis (2001, p. 99) reviewed work on the institutional dimensions of evaluation and concludes that there is often a gap between the evaluative methodologies available and recommended by academics and the actual methods of evaluation employed because of pressures from major stakeholders:

"Meanwhile, the actual use of such methodologies in practice is often largely determined by the subjective views of individual stakeholders facing a combination of business, organizational and technical pressures."

Seddon, Graeser & Willcocks (2002, p. 24) found decreased demand for evaluation due to the risk of offending people if the assessments are negative. Farbey, Land and Target (1993) argue that evaluation is always a political process because it affects the interests of different groups. Lacity & Willcocks (1997) note that evaluation of IT tends to be a political process in both the public and private sectors because evaluation is often used as the basis for deciding to outsource IT, thus threatening jobs. Indeed, the evaluation literature shows that in addition to using evaluation to improve services, evaluation can have latent goals such as to kill programs that management view with disfavor or exonerate programs that managers favor. If an evaluation is viewed as being used to make a summative judgment that may lead to major programmatic and personnel changes, then the evaluation situation is likely to be especially difficult and political. Evaluations that are intended mainly as providing formative feedback to improve the program will still be sensitive, but are likely to be somewhat less threatening and hence tend to be less political.

Thus conducting any evaluation involves sensitive political and ethical issues that evaluators need to give attention to. Sensitive evaluations can lead to passive or active resistance on the part of staff whose cooperation is needed to successfully complete the evaluation. As I will discuss in much more detail in the chapter on accountability, when

Copyright © 2006, Idea Group Inc. Copying or distributing in print or electronic forms without written permission of Idea Group Inc. is prohibited.

evaluation data are used for important programmatic and personnel decisions, goal displacement is likely to occur in which IT personnel over-emphasize activities that help to maximize their performance and ignore important tasks that are not part of the evaluation system. Ward (1996, pp. 60-61) emphasizes this point when he states that "what you measure is what you get." Consequently Ward (1996) argues that productivity measures tend to be "dangerous" because they can lead to unproductive behavior and that measures should focus on "quality," rather than productivity.

#12: What are the Differences in Evaluating the Information Systems of Public and Private Organizations?

There has not been much research on what, if any, systematic differences should exist between evaluating a governmental and private sector information systems. Bozeman and Bretschneider (1986) outlined differences between public and private management information systems in a seminal 1986 article that has implications for evaluation. They point out that public management information systems (PMIS) of necessity give more attention to accountability, openness, and representativeness. These characteristics may have implications for the evaluation of PMIS because, for example, Bozeman and Bretschneider (1986) expect public organizations to be more focused on external issues and vertical linkages than private organizations. Newcomer & Caudle (1991) argue that there are "no generic, readily standardized procedures for systems evaluation" in government and thus evaluation of a PMIS is even more complex than that of private systems. Private organizations have profit as a generic outcome measure that cuts across all of its units while such a global measure with legitimacy is lacking in government. It is difficult to employ measures popular in private sector evaluations such as Return On Investment (ROI) as outcome indicators for governments except for specific systems that are aimed at increasing revenues. Indeed, a study of "best practice" systems in the federal government found that ROI was often not used and, if it was, there were difficulties in its application (DeSeve et al., 1997). In measuring ROI, governments tend to focus on decreasing costs as the key measure of return (Eickelman, 2001) as opposed to increased revenues and profit. Perlman's (2003a) review found that several state and local governments employ ROI but most agree that estimates are "rough approximations" and focus on decreased costs. For example, the City of Baltimore employed "CityStat" and "CityTrak" software systems that helped reduce overtime costs and achieve other efficiencies that justified the cost of the systems. But the Baltimore CIO, Elliot Schlanger, acknowledged that ROI is difficult to apply in governments because systems are often aimed at improving responsiveness to service calls and complaints that do not result in increased revenues that are reflected in an ROI (Perlman, 2003a). The State of New Mexico demands "hard" measures for ROI for projects that are supposed to lower the costs of government or IT operations, but allows "soft" measures for projects that are aimed at "constituent services" and economic development (Perlman, 2003a).

Kaplan (2001) points out that it can be difficult to identify the "customer" in the evaluation of non-profit organizations. In particular, he raises the question of whether

Copyright © 2006, Idea Group Inc. Copying or distributing in print or electronic forms without written permission of Idea Group Inc. is prohibited.

the customer is the person donating funds or the people receiving charitable goods and services. Bannister (2002) has developed a model of information systems value for government IT and points out that certain key concepts in the private sector such as "enhancing customer value" may not be meaningful because some governmental customers such as welfare recipients do not pay for their services and that customer retention is "largely irrelevant" because (for general purpose governments) they may have little choice. Likewise, Bannister argues that enhanced profitability has no meaning in the public sector. Bannister (2002) says that the key purposes of government such as assuring equality of treatment, inclusiveness, and democratic values have little or no equivalence in the private sector.

Consequently, in theory, the evaluation of PMIS would appear to be quite different from that of the private sector. In reality, evaluation of IT is difficult to assess even in private organizations because much of IT spending is done for support services and much of IT use is indirect and affects intangibles (Lim, 2001). Thus IT organizations in the private sector also find it difficult to relate many of their systems directly to profit and ROI measures. Much of the practical evaluation that I have come across in government appears to be similar to that done by many private organization in that they both tend to focus on customer satisfaction and other measures of the adequacy of support services as well as the availability of infrastructure resources such as servers. One potential area where there may be differences between the two sectors would be the use of e-government in such matters as encouraging political access and participation, but these goals have been addressed by relatively few governmental organizations so far (West, 2003).

#13: Are the Costs of Systematic Evaluation Efforts Justified?

Systematic evaluations require formal data collection and, if the information does not already reside in the organization's information system, evaluation will add to the costs of the organization and thus will only be useful if the use of the information justifies the cost of collecting it. For example, Rosenman (2001) makes the point that Balanced Score Card (BSC) evaluation is costly and only cost effective when it is applied to important and complex IT investments such as ERP systems. Kaplan & Norton (2001a) admit that BSC can involve a heavy investment but point out that the BSC approach can often lead to a reduction in the number of indicators used compared with systems that are not focused on strategy. For example, they point to the example of Charlotte (NC) that had been using 1,000 performance indicators and the switch to BSC helped reduced the burden (Kaplan & Norton, 2001a, p. 325). Their general rules for individual scorecards are that they should not exceed 15 measures and should include a "mix" of leading and lagging indicators (Kaplan & Norton, 2001a, p. 246). Measuring too many metrics can weaken the purpose of BSC to focus on certain strategic goals.

Any system of data collection should be judged periodically on its utility. The BSC and other approaches are promising, but it is possible that much of their benefit derives from the enthusiasm that derives from trying something new. In program evaluation terms, this

Copyright © 2006, Idea Group Inc. Copying or distributing in print or electronic forms without written permission of Idea Group Inc. is prohibited.

is known as the "Hawthorne effect" and suggests that much if not all of the positive impact of the system may vanish under conditions where this sense of newness and enthusiasm no longer exists. This is true of any evaluation system. Wholey (1994) has emphasized the importance of doing an *evaluability assessment* prior to conducting an evaluation. He argues that evaluations are not worth doing if any of the following conditions exist: (1) If the intended users and evaluators cannot agree on how to measure the success of the program; (2) The goals of the program are unrealistic given its resources; (3) Information needed to assess the program is not available; and (4) Program heads are not willing to make changes on the basis of the evaluation study. In short, evaluation consumes resources, especially the time of individuals, and the evaluators and decision-makers need to be sure that this expenditure of effort is likely to be used.

Evaluation Approaches and Models

How Do We Measure Quality of IT: The Research Perspective

There is a substantial research literature on evaluation of IT. Over the past generation, much of this literature has been stimulated by the desire of researchers to inquire into issues such as whether end-user involvement in the design of IT systems leads to greater success of the application. In order to answer such questions, researchers have developed a variety of measures to assess the outcomes of IT. Over the years, it became apparent among researchers that certain measures appeared to be most heavily used and to have a good degree of validity and reliability. DeLone & McLean (2003) developed the model of information system success that has been most heavily used by researchers and thus I will summarize the variables and measures that they employ. Their revised 2003 model employs three major categories of variables (DeLone & McLean, 2003) as leading to greater use and user satisfaction with IT systems. The first major category concerns measures of information quality such as (DeLone & McLean, 2003, p. 13-14) "accuracy, timeliness, completeness, relevance, and consistency." They propose measuring the impacts of information quality by studying effects on job performance—for example, does the data allow them to improve their decision-making and work effectiveness? The second major category of variables concern system quality that includes (DeLone & McLean, 2004, p. 13-14) indicators such as "ease of use, functionality, reliability, flexibility, data quality, portability, integration, and importance." In order to measure the effects of system quality, DeLone & McLean (2003, p. 13) propose to measure their impacts on the quality of work and job performance issues. The third category concerns service quality because with the emergence of End User Computing (EUC), IT departments took on the job of not just producing information but the support of end users as a major part of their job. Measures of IT service quality (known as "SERVQUAL") developed by Pitt, Watson, and Kavan (1995) include the following items: how up-to-date is the hardware and software of the organization, how dependable is the IT support, how

Copyright © 2006, Idea Group Inc. Copying or distributing in print or electronic forms without written permission of Idea Group Inc. is prohibited.

quick is service, how knowledgeable are IT staff, and to what extent are IT staff able to relate empathically to end users (DeLone & McLean, 2003)?

DeLone & McLean (2003) go on to discuss their key measures of system success: use of IT and satisfaction with IT. They note that system use can be complex in its relationship to system success. In earlier days of research, greater use of systems was often assumed to be associated with greater success. Later, researchers pointed out that use may be mandated and thus system use does not necessarily mean success. Or a difficult-to-use system may require more hours of use than a more successful system. Use can also be indirect. Still, they point out that if a system is not used, then it is a failure and so it is a relevant measure to assess outcomes.

The IT success measures used by DeLone and McLean and many other researchers have definite advantages from the point of view of the research community. They are generic measures that can be used across a wide variety of organizations to evaluate a broad set of systems and have proven to have reasonable validity and reliability. Some of the governmental IT evaluation instruments that I will review employ indicators similar if not identical to the measures outlined previously including the SERVQUAL (Pitt, Watson & Kavan, 1995) instrument aimed at assessing the quality of IT services. Moreover, researchers in many cases have tested the reliability and validity of the measures and steps that practitioners do not have the time, nor the inclination to do. So these measures are a useful pool to search for evaluators to select from. Often they will need to be modified or supplemented because they do not provide specific information that meets the needs of the stakeholders conducting evaluations.

The Balanced Scorecard System as an Evaluation Approach to IT

In recent years, the Balanced Scorecard (BSC) system has emerged as the most discussed and one of the most frequently adopted formal approaches to assessing overall organizational performance. Seddon, Graser & Willcocks found that nine out of the 90 organizations that responded to their survey about evaluation approaches were employing the BSC system. The Balanced Scorecard system began (Kaplan & Norton, 2001a; Berghout & Renkema, 2001) with the goal of making organizations realize that the traditional financial indicators were inadequate measures of organizations. Kaplan & Norton (2001a, p. 212) found that despite the fact that most organizations give lip service to the position that their "most important assets are their employees," in reality they don't gather any measures of employee attitudes and skills. Thus the BSC approach forces organizations to look at important non-financial indicators by including the following four categories of measures:

1.   Financial perspective;
2.   Customer perspective;
3.   Internal perspective; and
4.   Innovation and learning perspective.

Copyright © 2006, Idea Group Inc. Copying or distributing in print or electronic forms without written permission of Idea Group Inc. is prohibited.

Research by Ho & Chan (2002) shows that most (more than 80%) municipal governments have already been collecting financial, customer satisfaction (about 72%), and employee performance (about 66%) measures. Municipalities are gathering these indicators in response to calls by the Governmental Accounting and Standard Board (GASB) for more information on Service Efforts and Accomplishments (SEA) (Ho & Chan, 2002). This part of GASB mandates the ongoing and systematic collection of outcome measures of government services. One set of measures where BSC is likely to bring about change in evaluation concerns the innovation and change category where only 40% of the municipalities claimed to have developed such measures (Ho & Chan, 2002). Thus the BSC movement has encouraged municipal officials to gather more non-financial measures (Ho & Chan, 2002), such as measures of education and training efforts.

BSC has evolved into a strategic management system (Ho & Chan, 2002). Kaplan & Norton (2001a) now see the BSC as a way to measure strategy and to make sure the different parts of the organization are aligned with that strategy. Thus the BSC system follows a top-down approach in which decision-makers (the political decision-makers and top managers) decide on what the key strategies should be for the organization. For private organizations, these strategies are often aimed at improving internal processes that are related to achieving financial goals by providing a unique set of cost, access, price, and quality combination (what Kaplan & Norton refer to as the "value proposition"). According to Kaplan & Norton, there are generally crucial internal processes that are often referred to as the "drivers" and are similar in meaning to what others have referred to as "critical success factors." Kaplan & Norton (2001a) identify these drivers as "*leading indicators*" because they are key to determining whether the organization succeeds in its longer term goals measured by the "*lagging*" or financial indicators. Now that they have tied the BSC system into measuring strategies, they see BSC as superior to performance measurement systems (e.g., Key Performance Indicators or KPI) that develop "stand-alone" measures that don't relate to one another or to the organization's strategic goals (Kaplan & Norton, 2001a, p. 103). Remenyi (1999) views KPIs as critical success factors (CSFs) that have been quantified so that they can be measured.

Kaplan & Norton (2001b) discuss the situation where other approaches such as ABC (Activity-Based Costing) may be preferable to BSC. They admit that if the "biggest problems facing the organization" involve "inefficient processes" and "indirect and support expenses" that ABC should be employed first to get these under control. But if the organization wants to institute or make a major modification in its strategy, then they claim that BSC is the best system to use.

How does BSC relate to the evaluation of information systems? According to Kaplan & Norton (2001a, pp. 46-47), the IT department of most organizations would be viewed as a "*shared service unit*" *(SSU)* or staff function in which the primary function of these units is to support other "business units" that produce the products and services for customers. Of course, some aspects of IT, such as e-government interactive bill-paying and other services, have direct business-unit kinds of activities but the majority of IT work is to provide infrastructure and support for other units. Thus its customers tend primarily to be internal to the organization.

In order to construct scorecards for these units, Kaplan & Norton describe how the Mobil Corporation had their business units form "buyers' committees" who worked out an

Copyright © 2006, Idea Group Inc. Copying or distributing in print or electronic forms without written permission of Idea Group Inc. is prohibited.

annual contract between these *"natural business units" (NBUs)* and the SSUs. In the Mobil case, they found that the NBUs often came up with services that were top priority for them and had not even been considered by the SSUs. The customer part of the BSC for SSUs such as the IT department concerned the satisfaction of the business departments with IT services (Kaplan & Norton, 2001a, p. 47).

Kaplan & Norton (2001a, pp. 163-165) point out that the information system is the key to recording and distributing information about the scorecards and success. In a study of health care organizations use of BSC (Inamdar et al., 2002), successful use of the BSC system required heavy expenditures on IT. In particular, data on customer preferences were lacking and customer data is important to the BSCs and the data needs to be integrated and timely so it required heavy investments in data repositories (Inamdar et al., 2002). Kaplan & Norton (2001a) point out one instructive example of a Balanced Scorecard system that failed due in large part to the IT unit. The case involved a bank that wanted to develop innovative financial services that could be accessed from anywhere in the world. The bank's IT department constructed their scorecard by *benchmarking* their performance against the best IS departments and their results showed they were performing at a very high level. But Kaplan & Norton (2001a) discovered that this IT department had failed to deliver the strategic services needed by the NBUs. This example serves to support Kaplan & Norton's argument that the BSC method is superior to benchmarking and other traditional performance measurement systems because it focuses metrics on the strategic goals and hence the "drivers" that are needed to achieve success. Seddon et al. (2002) found that organizations using the BSC reported certain problems including that some organizations found it difficult to implement the full range of measures and that the results were sometime not adequately used.

Customer Satisfaction as a Measure of IT Success

Customer satisfaction has become one of the most popular methods of measuring the success of information systems and is often employed as one of the "drivers" in BSC scorecards. A *CIO Magazine* study (Working Council for Chief Information Officers, 2003) of 539 IT executives found that 36% of the organizations did not conduct any customer satisfaction evaluations, 42% did surveys of internal customers, 4% surveyed only external customers, and 17% did surveys of both internal and external customers. Iivari & Ervasti (1994) found that user information satisfaction was related to the quantity and quality of the output of IS applications in Finnish cities. Many people don't realize that measuring IT customer satisfaction (both internal customers of other governmental departments and external citizenry) can be a complex issue. It seems simple because it can be done very simply by asking customers or citizens to rate IT services. However, the complexity is due to the fact that satisfaction depends in part on expectations (Wilkin, Carr & Hewitt, 2001). For example, it is possible for two IT departments offering the same services to obtain different customer satisfaction ratings if the customers have differences in expectations of what kind of service should be provided. In my conversations with end users in some municipal organizations, they often tempered their assessments of the IT departmental performance because of their awareness of the daunting workload

Copyright © 2006, Idea Group Inc. Copying or distributing in print or electronic forms without written permission of Idea Group Inc. is prohibited.

faced by their small IT staffs. Likewise, some IT managers tried to manage expectations such as warning staff not to over promise what new systems would be able to accomplish.

There are three limitations of relying too much on satisfaction measures. First, most satisfaction studies of public services find well over 50% satisfaction. This speaks well to the quality of municipal services, but the universality of the outcome means that a gross satisfaction measure is not a very sensitive outcome for detecting need for improvement in services. For example, in the mental health field, a dissatisfaction rate of more than 10% is rare and can be a bad sign (Lebow, 1983). One alternative is to distinguish between those users who are very satisfied versus those who are just somewhat satisfied. In most studies, these two categories are lumped together but it can be argued that when someone says they are "somewhat satisfied," they have some significant reservation about services. Thus, in a study I conducted of consumer satisfaction with human services (Rocheleau, 1980), I used this approach to identify which variables predicted whether customers would rate their satisfaction as "very satisfied" or one of the remaining categories (ranging from somewhat satisfied to very dissatisfied). This analysis turned up some useful variables that could be controlled by management (e.g., active involvement of the customers in the planning for services) that did predict fairly accurately whether users of services were more or less satisfied.

In study of police information systems, I (Rocheleau, 1993) found that satisfaction is dynamic with more than 47% of the respondents reporting that their satisfaction with police information systems had changed through time (25% reported improved satisfaction and 22% declining satisfaction) (see Figure 2). This finding may be due to the fact that what is regarded as a high level of performance at one point in time will eventually become the expected level of performance.

Thus IT organizations need to pay attention to the dynamics of change with respect to customer attitudes toward their IT systems. I combined the answers to the overall satisfaction measure with the question concerning whether it had changed to identify three major groups of users: (1) The clearly positive group; (2) The clearly negative group; (3) The unclear or unsure group (See Figure 3).

Another issue of concern to business organizations about customer satisfaction and non-financial indicators in general is whether they are related to organizational success measures such as retention of customers, profit, and stock value. Iitner and Larcker (1998) studied the impact of customer satisfaction measures and found that they had a

Figure 2. Change in satisfaction: Has your satisfaction with your information system changed with time?

Nature of Change	Percent
Yes, improved through time	25.4
No, stayed the same	52.3
Yes, declined	22.3
N=130	

Source: Adapted from Rocheleau, B. (1993). Evaluating public sector information systems: Satisfaction versus impact, *Evaluation and Program Planning.* 16, p. 124.

Copyright © 2006, Idea Group Inc. Copying or distributing in print or electronic forms without written permission of Idea Group Inc. is prohibited.

Figure 3. The dynamics of customer satisfaction

Positive Group	Percent
Very satisfied & Improving	13.8
Very satisfied & Steady	27.7
Very satisfied & declining	2.3
Somewhat satisfied & improving	8.5
Somewhat satisfied & steady	15.4
Totals: Positive Group	67.7
Unclear Group	
Somewhat dissatisfied & improving	3.1
Somewhat satisfied & declining	11.5
Totals: Unclear Group	14.6
Negative Group	
Dissatisfied & Steady	9.2
Dissatisfied & Declining	11.5
Totals: Negative Group	17.7

Adapted from Rocheleau, B. (1993). Evaluating public sector information systems: Satisfaction versus impact, *Evaluation and Program Planning*, 16 , p. 124.

significant impact on customer retention—a 10% increase in their customer satisfaction index resulted in a 2% improvement in customer retention and also had a positive impact on revenue changes. Customer satisfaction also improved the stock's book value after controlling for other variables (Iitner & Larcker, 1998, p. 24). However, the findings were tempered by the fact that the impacts were small—customer satisfaction explained only 2% of the variation (Lambert, 1998, p. 39) and the impact varied across industries and did not occur in some such as manufacturing. Moreover, there were thresholds—raising customer satisfaction above the 80% level did not produce greater revenue (Iitner & Larcker, 1998, p. 11).

How valid and useful is citizen (customer) satisfaction as an evaluation measure for governments? This is an issue that has to be decided by the political and managerial leadership of organizations. For governmental organizations, it is doubtful that citizen satisfaction is directly related to financial health but most governmental organizations consider the satisfaction of citizens as a core part of their missions and thus citizen satisfaction has inherent validity as an important goal. The satisfaction of certain key categories of government customers such as their business community could be related to positive or negative changes if, for example, they decided to move elsewhere due to unhappiness with their service but this is likely to happen only over a long time period. However, many of the satisfaction measures employed by evaluators of IT are aimed at internal customers because, as I noted earlier, most of the activity of IT departments can be categorized as providing for infrastructure and support for departments that deal directly with citizens.

Lambert (1998) points out that the business community is uncomfortable in dealing with "soft" indicators like customer satisfaction compared to financial indicators because ratings may not be comparable from user to user. Ho and Chan's (2002, p. 12) research shows that most governmental officials are also loathe to trust measures of customer satisfaction and other non-financial measures at face value. In their survey of municipal officials, they asked if the officials were "willing to bet [their] job on the quality of information" and low percentages stated confidence in customer satisfaction (36%),

Copyright © 2006, Idea Group Inc. Copying or distributing in print or electronic forms without written permission of Idea Group Inc. is prohibited.

efficiency measures (26%), innovation and change measures (18%), and employee performance measures (19%). By way of contrast, 80% were willing to bet their jobs on the quality of financial measures (Ho & Chan, 2002, p. 12). Moreover, the skepticism about the non-financial indicators was also present in the 11 governments that had implemented a BSC system.

Examples of Governmental Evaluation Measures

Next, we explore the evaluation measures that governments actually use. I did not find much research on how governments assess their IT function. There are some chapters on how governments *should* evaluate their IT services such as through the use of a Balanced Scorecard system (e.g., Eickelmann, 2001). Perlman (2003b) describes the metric used by the Kentucky Information Technology Department that tracks the percent of time that its network is available to its users and has a goal of 99%. But, Perlman (2003b) also cites the need to change goals once they are consistently met. Lim (2001) developed and implemented a complex evaluation matrix that he applied to Korean cities but there is little information on how governments evaluate themselves. Thus the information next is useful because there is often a big difference between how academic evaluation theorists posit that evaluation should be done and what practitioners do. In order to find IT evaluations conducted by practitioners, I did online searches and conducted queries concerning evaluation of IT from practitioner organizations such as The Innovations Group and the Governmental Management Information Sciences organization (GMIS). I also searched through the Web sites of the top-rated e-government municipalities as judged by Daryl West (2003) and attempted to search for evaluation documents that were available online. When I did not find such documents, I sent e-mails to the IT director requesting any such documents.

I did not find many documents online or through these requests devoted to the evaluation of IT. In part, this may be due to the fact that not much formal evaluation is being done, although it is also likely due to the fact that evaluation documents are viewed as sensitive material by many organizations. Thus they are not made available online or through requests such as those that I made. There is a fair amount of evaluation information in comprehensive planning documents of some governmental organizations and these are the primary sources of the examples I have next. The examples that I use next do not represent a random sample of the state of evaluation in governments such as municipalities. I suspect that organizations willing to present their evaluative information on the Internet tend to be high-performers and confident of the quality of their achievements. However, my contacts and interviews with governmental IT staff lead me to believe that the measures and approaches next tend to be fairly typical of ongoing evaluation efforts.

I found that the majority of evaluation measures used by governments fell into a few categories: (1) Customer satisfaction; (2) Performance measures with a major emphasis on the percentage of time that systems were available; (3) Performance measures that

Copyright © 2006, Idea Group Inc. Copying or distributing in print or electronic forms without written permission of Idea Group Inc. is prohibited.

focused on cost efficiency measures concerning the cost per support of service with industry and/or other governmental systems; (4) Other miscellaneous quantitative measures; and (5) Qualitative assessments based on interviews and discussions with customers such as end users and department heads.

In Figure 4, I have reproduced part of the customer satisfaction survey employed by Contra Costa County (California). As you can see, the survey covers a wide variety of

Figure 4. Contra Costa (California) customer satisfaction survey

Source: Retrieved February 13, 2004 from http://www.lgov.org/library_frames.html

Copyright © 2006, Idea Group Inc. Copying or distributing in print or electronic forms without written permission of Idea Group Inc. is prohibited.

issues—it is not just a summary measure of overall satisfaction. It is also broken up into sections based on the different teams that constitute the IT department: (1) Administration Team; (2) Information Security Team; (3) Operations Team; (4) Systems & Programming Team; (5) Telecommunications Team; and (6) Desktop/Network Services Team. This instrument shows that IT departments are involved in a wide range of activities and that a simple overall assessment satisfaction measure could hide exceptional or poor performance in individual activities. All of the items are phrased in a positive manner where agreement is satisfaction with the service on a 5 (highest quality) to 1 (lowest quality) scale. Finally at the end of the survey are three "overall ratings" of satisfaction that ask the customer whether the IT department is worth the monthly cost, whether they would like to use more IT services, and if they would keep the IT department as "their vendor of choice." There are many other approaches to measuring customer satisfaction. For example, the City of Vacaville (CA) used a 15-question instrument in which most of the questions asked the customer to rate both the importance (on a 1 to 6 scale) and the effectiveness (on a 1 to 6 scale) of selected IT services ranging from help desk support to assessment of in-house and online training (see Figure 5).

Most of the evaluation results obtained high percentages expressing satisfaction with IT services. The City of Bellevue (Washington) posted the results of evaluations including consumer satisfaction over a three-year period (2000-2002) (see Figure 6). It reveals that the repetition of the survey each year creates a time series in which over the long-run, it may be possible to determine if there are significant changes in the levels of satisfaction even though all of the percentages are well over 50% and thus make the measure a more useful indicator of success. In Bellevue's case, satisfaction with the applications increased from about 70% in 2001 to about 80% in 2002 (see Figure 6). The Bellevue performance measures also illustrate the fact that many organizations use speed of response to assess the help-desk function. Likewise, the percent of time that the servers are available is used as a measure of network and system support and is usually (as in this case) very close to 100%. Such indicators are useful as management by exception indicators to indicate when a problem exists with services.

One challenge in customer satisfaction surveys is to determine, "What do the evaluation results mean?" How do we know whether the evaluation results are positive or negative? As I discussed previously, the persons involved in the evaluation will have to determine the standards they use. One well-known approach by The Gartner Group is to break down performance ratings into certain "color-coded categories" of success. These levels of performance are determined by a series of statements about the performance of the IT department so that agreement with each statement expresses satisfaction with the performance of that particular function. The ratio of the "agrees" (i.e., satisfaction) to "disagrees" (dissatisfaction) is calculated and the results are classified into color coded categories with green representing a satisfactory performance if the ratio of agrees to disagrees with the following categories:

Copyright © 2006, Idea Group Inc. Copying or distributing in print or electronic forms without written permission of Idea Group Inc. is prohibited.

Figure 5. City of Vacaville: information technology baseline survey

Please rate the following categories according to two scales: **Importance** and **Effectiveness**. The scales are rated from **1-6**, ranging from **1** "least" to **6** "most", circle **0** if the service does not apply to you.

Importance	- Level of importance for the specific service.
Effectiveness	- Effectiveness in addressing the specific service *(skill, knowledge & ability to resolve your computing need/problem).*

Service	N/A	Importance	Effectiveness
1. Helpdesk via phone *(x 5489)*	0	1 2 3 4 5 6	1 2 3 4 5 6
2. Helpdesk via email *(IT Support)*	0	1 2 3 4 5 6	1 2 3 4 5 6
3. After-hour support (emergency calls)	0	1 2 3 4 5 6	1 2 3 4 5 6
4. Solve problem via phone support	0	1 2 3 4 5 6	1 2 3 4 5 6
5. Telecommunications daily maintenance services *(phones, radios, pagers, etc.)*	0	1 2 3 4 5 6	1 2 3 4 5 6
6. Request for application support *(e.g., CAD, CCS, ESCOM, etc)*	0	1 2 3 4 5 6	1 2 3 4 5 6
7. Request for IT assistance in setting up technology in conference rooms	0	1 2 3 4 5 6	1 2 3 4 5 6
8. Acknowledge user's problem within a one-hour response time	0	1 2 3 4 5 6	1 2 3 4 5 6
9. Solve technical support question within a four-hour response time	0	1 2 3 4 5 6	1 2 3 4 5 6
10. Conduct follow-up to closed call ticket	0	1 2 3 4 5 6	1 2 3 4 5 6
11. Communicating when there is scheduled down time *(server down, power outages)*	0	1 2 3 4 5 6	1 2 3 4 5 6
12. Current method of in-house PC training	0	1 2 3 4 5 6	1 2 3 4 5 6
13. Opportunity for on-line training, accessible from your desktop, through the Internet	0	1 2 3 4 5 6	1 2 3 4 5 6

14. How do the current range in offering of PC courses meet your needs?

☐ **1.** Does not meet my needs   ☐ **2.** Sometimes meets my needs   ☐ **3.** Meets my needs

15. Overall, during the last 6 months, the level of IT Support Service has:

☐ **1.** Not met my expectations   ☐ **2.** Met my expectations☐ **3.** Exceeded my expectations

Source: Retrieved January 30, 2004 from http://www.misac.org/state_library.htm

Green: Ratio of Agrees to Disagrees: 80% or higher.

Yellow: Ratio of Agrees to Disagrees 60% to 79%.

Red: Ratio of Agrees to disagrees less than 60%.

Copyright © 2006, Idea Group Inc. Copying or distributing in print or electronic forms without written permission of Idea Group Inc. is prohibited.

Figure 6. City of Bellevue (Washington) performance measures

Key Performance Measures	2000 Actual	2001 Actual	2002 Actual	2002 Target	2002 Target Met or Exceeded
Program: Applications Services					
Effectiveness					
1. Percent of customers rating level of consulting services for business analysis and system design as good to excellent (a)	70.0%	69.0%	78.0%	76.0%	✔
2. Percent of customers rating the maintenance and support provided for their application(s) as good to excellent (a)	71.0%	77.0%	80.0%	76.0%	✔
Workload					
3. Number of Applications (b)	NA	NA	110	NA	
Program: Desktop Support Services					
Effectiveness					
4. Percentage of Help Desk repair calls resolved the next business day (b)	NA	39.0%	14.0%	NA	
5. Percentage of Help Desk repair calls resolved within 4 hours (b)	NA	9.0%	9.0%	NA	
6. Percentage of Help Desk calls resolved at the time of the call (b)	NA	48.0%	65.0%	NA	
7. Percentage of customers rating satisfaction with Desktop Support Services as good to excellent	84.0%	83.0%	85.0%	89.0%	
Workload					
8. Number of PCs supported/number of technicians	1011/5	1150/4.5	1250/4	1200/5	✔
Program: Network & Systems Support Services					
Effectiveness					
9. Percent of time phone system fully functional during business hours	99.8%	99.9%	99.9%	99.5%	✔
10. Percentage of time servers are fully functional during business hours	99.0%	99.7%	99.9%	99.5%	✔
Efficiency					
11. Cost of city phone line vs. phone company business line (City phone cost per month/phone company business line per month)	$15/$35	$18/$38	$17/38	$23/$45	✔
Workload					
12. Number of servers supported (c)	NA	43	61	NA	
13. Number of phone line/number of technicians	1,570/1.0	1,548/.65	1,575/1.0	1,480/1.0	✔

Information Technology Department

Annual Scorecard of Performance Measures

(a) Normal problems encountered in the implementation of new systems are expected to impact overall customer satisfaction;
(b) New Performance Measure, Historicals reported;
(c) New Performance Measure. Replaces 'Number of servers/technicians', which was deleted in 2001. Servers are now maintained and supported by outside contractor.

J:\ADMIN\BUD\PerfMeas\02PerfMeas\02scor-6.doc   09/17/03   City of Bellevue 2002 Performance Measures

Source: Retrieved December 22, 2003 from http://www.cityofbellevue.org/page.asp?view=2606

For example, in their assessment of the Nashville-Davidson County IT department, the areas assessed included several statements that the customers either agree or disagree with concerning their performance in each of the following areas: (1) Vision: the extent to which the IT vision is clear and appropriate; (2) Governance issues such as whether the IT department does a good job of prioritizing changes; (3) Planning issues such as whether the IT department does effective planning; (4) Standards and policies issues concerning whether applications meet the department's business standards; (5) Infrastructure issues such as whether the hardware is adequate to satisfy business requirements; (6) Staffing issues such as whether the IT department has adequate staff to meet the customer's needs; (7) Training issues such as whether the IT staff have the skills needed to support the customers; and (8) Funding issues such as whether the IT funding is adequate. An aggregate summary measure for each area is then produced by averaging

Copyright © 2006, Idea Group Inc. Copying or distributing in print or electronic forms without written permission of Idea Group Inc. is prohibited.

Figure 7. Information on the City of Portland's (Oregon) efficiency of IT services

Number of Desktops Supported by IT FTE
☐ IDC Average ■ City of Portland
100.00
50.00
0.00

Number of Servers Supported by IT FTE
☐ IDC Average ■ City of Portland
4.00
2.00
0.00

Number of Server Locations per IT FTE
☐ IDC Average ■ City of Portland
0.40
0.20
0.00

With 76 IT professionals (25% higher than the IDC average numbers), BIT Operations provide services for approximately 4500 desktops and laptops (33% higher than in IDC average), approximately 250 mail, file and print, data and other servers (89% higher than IDC average) located at 28 different locations (sites). To make the comparison meaningful, we calculated the number of different elements (desktops, servers, and site locations) per FTE; the results of the comparison are illustrated in the charts.

The data indicates that City of Portland IT professionals support higher numbers of IT equipment in more locations not only in absolute numbers, but also per FTE. While it immediately suggests excellent management and high efficiency by City technical staff, actual levels of service provided cannot be validated. There is a possibility that the technical services and support in the companies included in IDC survey are higher than in the City of Portland. At the same time, there is no doubt that the City staff are stretched and that server/site consolidation will be required to gain additional efficiencies.

Without proper consolidation of servers and their locations, and IT operations (Help Desk, Desktop Support, Network Management) we will eventually need to increase the FTE count to provide needed service levels.

IT Strategic Business Plan	- Page 23 of 69 -	January 2002

Source: City of Portland, IT Strategic Business Plan (January 2002). Retrieved December 11, 2003 from http://www.portlandonline.com/shared/cfm/image.cfm?id=10759

the "agree to disagree" ratio of responses for each area and the color code indicates the overall status for that particular area.

The percentages employed by the Gartner Group (e.g., 80% for "green" status) are arbitrary and in many cases, a significant portion of respondents refused to reply positively or negatively and thus the ratio of results could be misleading. The Gartner questions are all framed so that agreement is equivalent to satisfaction with the particular aspect of IT performance and this positive framing is likely to encourage positive responses. Although the Gartner criteria are arbitrary, the color-coded schema does help to capture the attention of stakeholders better than purely unadorned tabular data.

The City of Portland assessed the efficiency of their IT services by comparing the number of desktops, servers, and service locations per-IT-FTE with data from the International Data Center (IDC) and found that Portland's workload was higher on all three indicators of efficiency (see Figure 7). However, they acknowledge that "the technical services and support" provided by the companies in the survey could be "higher than in the City of Portland" and part of the purpose of these comparisons is to support the eventual increase in IT FTEs. Similarly, the City of Tampa's (2002) Technical Infrastructure Plan compared its level of IT investment with those of similar-sized cities (St. Petersburg, Orlando, and Tallahassee) and found that the level of investment in IT in Tampa was smaller. They also compared the level of expenditures in Tampa with the expenditures on the IS budget per user as reported by a Gartner study of local government IT expenditures and found that their current IT budget would have to increase by nearly $4 million to reach the average level reported by the Gartner survey.

Copyright © 2006, Idea Group Inc. Copying or distributing in print or electronic forms without written permission of Idea Group Inc. is prohibited.

The City of Austin (Texas) gathers a great deal of performance information for its Department of Communications and Information Technology Management (see http://www.ci.austin.tx.us/budget/eperf/index.cfm?fuseaction=home. Program&DEPT=560& PROGRAM=3SNO). This department has several different program units and most of the performance measures concern quantitative indicators such as the percent of time that various computer systems are available that tend to be well over 99%. There are some cost efficiency measures such as the cost of the data center divided by the number of hours that computer systems are available. For training, they provide an outcome indicator measuring the percentage of employees reporting improvements in their ability to use applications as well as the number of hours of training provided and the cost of training per hour. In addition, the Austin City Auditor (May 2002) conducted an audit of the project management of IT in the city and used a customer satisfaction survey to assess performance based on answers concerning the performance of 12 systems. The survey consisted of statements so that agreement indicated satisfaction with the performance of essential functions of a system, its ease of use, and how smoothly the system integrated into work process (1= Strongly Agree; 5=Strongly Disagree). The overall rating was 2.45 with only one project representing a majority of dissatisfied users.

This same Audit Report (City of Austin, May 2002) illustrates the use of a *best practices approach to evaluation of IT* in government. The Report identifies some governmental organizations similar to Austin that are regarded as leaders in information technology and identified their ("best") practices and these practices are compared with the City of Austin's. By following this procedure, the Auditor identified the following "best practices" for project management such as: (1) The existence of an IT strategic plan that aligns with the organization's business objectives; (2) An inventory of major IT projects; and (3) A common project management methodology. These best practices are compared with the practices of the municipality being evaluated in order to find ways that the city (Austin in this case) can improve its IT management. This best practices approach is an example of a process evaluation. Process evaluations can be very useful because they point to how the organizations being evaluated can improve their performance. The best practices approach to evaluations assumes that the procedures are related to outcomes. Choosing organizations of similar size and resources for best practices is important since many small organizations view many of the written documentation and plans as superfluous and not cost effective for them given their tiny staffs.

The Mecklenburg County (August 2003) Information Services & Technology (IST) department has conducted a Balanced Scorecard evaluation that serves to illustrate how this methodology can be applied to a governmental agency. Among the measures they used were "increased employee motivation and satisfaction." They employed the Gartner approach and found that they had achieved "18 green lights (63%), 3 yellow, and 6 red lights" in their questions from an "Employee Climate Survey." Another goal concerned decreased turnover but they found that one of their measures (average number of days that vacant IST positions remained open) had to be discarded because the Human Resources department was unable to provide it. Their FY2004 scorecard includes the following goals and selected measures illustrated in Figure 8. The overall amount of data being gathered to assess their attainment of scorecard goals appears to be substantial. The real value of the Balanced Scorecard approach is that, if it works as it is supposed

Copyright © 2006, Idea Group Inc. Copying or distributing in print or electronic forms without written permission of Idea Group Inc. is prohibited.

Figure 8. FY 2004 scorecard of Mecklenburg County Information Services & Technology: selected measures

Increased Service Value	One measure is specific questions from the IST Customer Survey
Improved Communication & Information Management	Measures are draw from customer and employee satisfaction survey questions about "effective communication"
Improved Productivity	One measure is implementation of at least one process improvement per business unit
Preserved Financial Stability & Maintain Organizational Integrity	One measure is IST costs compared to industry costs
Improved Funding/Resource Allocation Decisions	One measure is the percent of IST controllable scorecard results achieved
Increased Employee Motivation & Satisfaction	Measures include the use of employee perception ratings concerning the value of innovative ideas and job enhancement opportunities
Enhanced Workforce Retention & Recruitment	One measure is the perception of flexible work scheduling
Increased Employee Knowledge Skills & Abilities	One measure is the percent of IST employees who report that training helped them in their jobs
Improved Technology-Related Capacities	One measure is employee perception concerning the availability of Technological Resources

Source: Adapted from the 2003 Report and 2004 Plan of the Information Services & Technology Department of Mecklenburg County (North Carolina). Retrieved February 3, 2004 from http://www.charmeck.org/Departments/IST/2003+Annual+Report+and+2004+Plan/Home.htm

to, the measures will be related to the strategic goals and also force attention to matters such as learning and innovation that were previously ignored by many performance reporting systems.

The City of Jacksonville (Florida) employs a "process control system" for system development projects that developed a flow chart (Levriett, 2004) that shows how the program is supposed to work and what evaluation measures are collected at each stage. The flow chart shows what evaluation measures are taken at each step of the process and who is responsible for the measures. As with many of these local government cases, customer satisfaction and speed of resolving issues are key measures. In systems development, changes in the scope and deviations from the original plan are added evaluation measures.

There is one area in which a great deal of evaluation has been done and it concerns the evaluation of governmental Web sites. There are some obvious reasons why e-government and Web sites have drawn so much evaluative attention. First and foremost, the Web sites are easily accessible and evaluations can be done by external evaluators without any permissions required by the organization. Secondly, e-government is one area where IT has a direct role in serving customers in contrast to other aspects of IT that contribute only indirectly to serving external customers, so a governmental Web site draws more attention. There have been numerous evaluations done by researchers such as West (2003) employing a wide range of indicators to assess governmental Web sites

Copyright © 2006, Idea Group Inc. Copying or distributing in print or electronic forms without written permission of Idea Group Inc. is prohibited.

in terms of criteria such as ease of use, extent of interactivity, readability, and so forth. I explore these issues in the chapter on e-government.

Conclusion

In the early years, much of the evaluative research focused on utilization of systems. In more recent years, measures of satisfaction with the quality of services have become common. The best practices approach has been employed by several state and local governments. Although much discussion is devoted to measuring Return on Investment (ROI), I found only a few examples of governments that conducted such analyses. Benchmarking is commonly used to compare workloads and efficiency measures of IT organizations. Many organizations collect numerous indicators of IT workloads and efficiency measures on a regular basis. Many of their indicators pertain to the availability of systems and speed of response to requests for services. Other than customer satisfaction measures, there do not appear to be many attempts at documenting the outcomes of IT systems other than through qualitative discussions that include verbal descriptions of how new or changed systems have improved services. This latter finding points to the need to use qualitative as well as quantitative assessments of IT.

References

Bannister, F. (2002, December). Citizen centricity: A model of IS value in public administration. *Electronic Journal of Information Systems Evaluation, 5.* Retrieved November 10, 2003, from http://www.iteva.rug.nl/ejise/vol5/Issue%202/paper3/citize~1.htm

Berghout, E., & Renkema, T. (2001). Methodologies for IT investment evaluation: A review and assessment. In W. Van Grembergen (Ed.), *Information technology evaluation: Methods and nanagement* (pp. 78-98). Hershey, PA: Idea Group Inc.

Bozeman, B., & Bretschneider, S. (1986). Public management information systems: Theory and prescription. *Public Administration Review, 46,* 475-487.

Cameron, K. S. (1986, May). Effectiveness as paradox: Consensus and conflict in the conceptions of organizational effectiveness. *Management Science, 32*(5), 539-553.

Carr, N. G. (2003, May). IT doesn't matter. *Harvard Business Review,* 41-49.

City of Austin. (2002, May) Office of the City Auditor. Citywide information technology management. Retrieved February 13, 2004, from http://www.ci.austin.tx.us/auditor/sup_au01301.htm

City of Tampa. (2002). FY 2002 Technical infrastructure plan. Retrieved January 15, 2004, from http://www.tampagov.net/dept_MIS/files/Infrastructure_Plan_Master_2002.pdf

Copyright © 2006, Idea Group Inc. Copying or distributing in print or electronic forms without written permission of Idea Group Inc. is prohibited.

Daft, R. L., & Lengel, R. H. (1984). Information richness: A new approach to managerial behavior and organizational design. In B. M. Staw, & L. L. Cummings (Eds.), *Research in organizational behavior* (Vol. 6, pp. 191-223). Greenwich, CT: JAIU.

Danziger, J. N., & Kraemer, K. L. (1986). *People and computers: The impacts of computing on end users in organizations.*

DeLone, W. H., & McLean, E. R. (2003, Spring). The DeLone and McLean model of information systems success: A ten-year update. *Journal of Management Information Systems, 19*(4), 9-30.

DeSeve, E., Pesachowitz, A. M., & Johnson, L. K. (1997). *Best IT practices in the federal government.* Washington, DC: Chief Information Officers/Industry Advisory Council.

Eickelmann, N. (2001). Chapter XVII: A comparative analysis of the balanced scorecard as applied in government and industry organizations. In W. Van Grembergen (Ed.), *Information technology evaluation methods and management* (pp. 263-268). Hershey, PA: Idea Group Inc.

Farbey, B., Land, F., & Targett, D. (1992). Evaluating investments in IT. *Journal of Information Technology, 7,* 109-122.

Farbey, B., Land, F., & Targett, D. (1993). *How to assess your IT investment.* Oxford: Butterworth-Heinemann.

Farbey, B., Land, F., & Targett, D. (1999). The moving staircase – Problems of appraisal and evaluation in a turbulent environment. *Information Technology & People, 12*(3), 238-252.

Farbey, B., Targett, D., & Land, F. (1994). The great IT benefit hunt. *European Management Journal, 12*(3), 270-279.

Gurbaxani, V. (2003, June). Letter from Vijay Gurbaxani in response to "does IT matter." *Harvard Business Review, 14.*

Hatry, H. (1999). *Performance measurement: Getting results.* Washington, DC: The Urban Institute.

Ho, S. K., & Chan, Y. L. (2002, Winter). Performance measurement and the implementation of balanced scorecards in municipal governments. *Journal of Government Financial Management, 51*(4), 8-19.

Iitner, C. D., & Larcker, D. F. (1998). Are nonfinancial measures leading indicators of financial performance? An analysis of customer satisfaction. *Journal of Accounting Research, 36* (Supplement), 1-35.

Iivari, J., & Ervasti, I. (1994). User information satisfaction: IS implementability and effectiveness. *Information & Management, 27,* 205-220.

Inamdar, N., Kaplan, R.S.B., Bower, M., & Reynolds, K. (2002, May/June). Applying the balanced scorecard in healthcare provider organizations. *Journal of Healthcare Management, 47*(3), 179-196.

Kaplan, R. S. (2001). Strategic performance measurement & management in nonprofit organizations. *Nonprofit Management & Leadership, 11*(3), 353-370.

Copyright © 2006, Idea Group Inc. Copying or distributing in print or electronic forms without written permission of Idea Group Inc. is prohibited.

Kaplan, R.S., & Norton, D.P. (2001a). *The strategy-focused organization: How balanced scorecard companies thrive in the new business environment.* Boston: Harvard Business School.

Kaplan, R. S., & Norton, D. P. (2001b). Transforming the balanced scorecard from performance measurement to strategic management: Part II. *Accounting Horizons, 15*(2), 147-160.

Keen, J. (2003, June 15). ROI's secret ingredient. *CIO Magazine.* Retrieved June 17, 2003, from http://www.cio.com/archive/061503/value.html?printversion=yes

Lacity, M. C., & Willcocks, L. (1997). Information systems sourcing: Examining the privatization option in USA public administration. *Information Systems Journal, 7*, 85-108.

Lambert, R. A. (1998). Customer satisfaction and future financial performance: Discussion of are nonfinancial measures leading indicators of financial performance? An analysis of customer satisfaction. *Journal of Accounting Research, 36*, 37-46.

Levriett, W. (2004, January 20). Phone discussion and e-mail concerning the city of Jacksonville's process control system.

Lim, S. K. (2001). A framework to evaluate informatization level. In W. Van Grembergen (Ed.), *Information technology evaluation methods and management* (pp. 2-24). Hershey, PA: Idea Group Inc.

Maholland, L., & Muetz, P. (2002, April). A balanced scorecard approach to performance measurement. *Government Finance Review*, 12-16.

Markus, M. L., Axline, S., Petrie, D., & Tanis, C. (2000). Learning from adopters' experiences with ERP: Problems encountered and success achieved. *Journal of Information* Technology, *15*, 245-265.

Mecklenburg County. (2003, August). Information services & technology department. 2003 Report and 2004 Plan. Retrieved February 13, 2004, from http://www.charmeck.org/Departments/IST/2003+Annual+Report+and+2004+Plan/Home.htm

Nashville (City of) & Davidson County, Tennessee. (2001, May 15). Gartner/Metro information technology services strategic plan. Retrieved December 10, 2003, from http://www.nashville.gov/isd/gartner.htm

Newcomer, K. E., & Caudle, S. L. (1993, September/October). Evaluating public sector information systems: More than meets the eye. *Public Administration Review, 51*(5), 377-384.

Patton, M.Q. (1986). *Utilization-focused evaluation* (2nd ed.). Beverly Hills, CA: Sage.

Perlman, E. (2003a, December). Technology: Line-item value. *Governing Magazine.* Retrieved December 9, 2003, from http://www.governing.com/archive/2003/dec/roi.txt

Perlman, E. (2003b, July). *Measure for measuring.* Retrieved June 30, 2003, from http://www.governing.com/archive/2003/jul/techtalk.txt

Pitt, L.F., Watson, R.T., & Kavan, C.B. (1995). Service quality: A measure of information systems effectiveness. *MIS Quarterly, 19*(2), 173-188.

Copyright © 2006, Idea Group Inc. Copying or distributing in print or electronic forms without written permission of Idea Group Inc. is prohibited.

Posavac, E. J., & Carey, R.G. (1997). *Program evaluation: Methods and case studies* (5th ed.). Upper Saddle River, NJ: Prentice Hall.

Remenyi, D., & Serwood-Smith, M. (1999). Maximize information systems value by continuous participative evaluation. *Logistic Information Management, 12*(1/2), 14-31.

Rocheleau, B. (1982). Qualitative methods of evaluation research: Major applications for mental health program evaluation. In G. J. Stahler, & W. R. Tash (Eds.), *Innovative approaches to mental health evaluation* (pp. 305-328). New York: Academic.

Rocheleau, B. (1993). Evaluating public sector information systems: Satisfaction versus impact. *Evaluation and Program Planning, 16*(4), 119-129.

Rocheleau, B., & MacKesey, T. (1980, December). What, consumer feedback surveys again? A guide to improving the utility of consumer evaluations. *Evaluation and the Health Professions, 3*(4), 405-419.

Rosenman, M. (2001). Evaluating the management of enterprise systems with the balanced scorecard. In W. Van Grembergen (Ed.), *Information technology evaluation methods and management* (pp. 171-184). Hershey, PA: Idea Group Inc.

Seddon, P. B., Graeser, V., & Willcocks, L. P. (2002, Spring). Measuring organizational effectiveness: An overview and update of senior management perspectives. *The DATA BASE for Advances in Information Systems, 33*(2), 11-28.

Serafeimidis, V. (2001). The institutional dimensions of information systems evaluation. In W. Van Grembergen (Ed.), *Information technology evaluation methods and management* (pp. 99-110). Hershey, PA: Idea Group Inc.

Shadish, W. R., Cook, T. D., & Campbell, D.T. (2002). *Experimental and quasi-experimental designs for generalized causal inference.* Boston: Hougton Mifflin.

Van Grembergen, W. (Ed.). (2001). *Information technology evaluation: Methods and management.* Hershey, PA: Idea Group Inc.

Ward, J. A. (1996, Winter). Measurement management: What you measure is what you get. *Information Systems Management, 13*(1), 59-61.

West, D. (2003). Urban e-government. Retrieved January 30, 2004, from http://www.inside politics.org/egovt03city.pdf

Wholey, J. (1994). Assessing the evaluability and likely usefulness of evaluation. In J. Wholey et al. (Eds.), *Handbook of practical program evaluation* (pp. 15-39). San Francisco: Jossey-Bass.

Wilkin, C., Carr, R., & Hewett, B. (2001). Evaluating IS quality: Exploration of the role of expectations on stakeholders' evaluation. In W. Van Grembergen (Ed.), *Information technology evaluation: Methods and management* (pp. 111-129). Hershey, PA: Idea Group Inc.

Willcocks, L. (1992, June). IT evaluation: Managing the catch 22. *European Management Journal, 10*(2), 220-229.

Working Council for Chief Information Officers. (2003). *IT balanced scorecards: End to end performance measurement for corporate IT performance.* Retrieved November 11, 2003, from http://www.cio.executiveboard.com/Images/CIO/PDF/CIO73748.pdf

Copyright © 2006, Idea Group Inc. Copying or distributing in print or electronic forms without written permission of Idea Group Inc. is prohibited.

Additional Reading

In order to have a broad overview of evaluation, a textbook like that of Posavac and Carey (2003) is useful. The various works of Kenneth Kraemer and associates explored the impacts of IT on governments in a wide variety of publications such as Danziger and Kraemer's (1986) book entitled, *People and Computers: The Impacts of Computing on End Users in Organizations*. The Van Grembergen (2001) book contains a broad variety of chapters on the evaluation of IT including a few that have a significant amount of material concerning the evaluation of governmental IT. For those interested in the balanced scorecard approach, the Kaplan & Norton (2001a) is the most in depth treatment though it has only a few parts that deal directly with IT.

Key Concepts

- Balanced Scorecard
- Benchmarking
- Black Box Evaluation
- Business Process Reengineering
- Efficiency Evaluation
- Evaluability Assessment
- Formative Evaluation
- Lagging Indicators
- Leading Indicators
- Needs Assessment
- Natural Business Unit (NBU)
- Outcome Measures
- Payback periods
- Return on Investment (ROI)
- Time Series
- Summative evaluation
- Utilization-Focused Evaluation
- Workload Measures

Copyright © 2006, Idea Group Inc. Copying or distributing in print or electronic forms without written permission of Idea Group Inc. is prohibited.

Discussion Questions

1. Discuss the timing of formal evaluations in a governmental or non-profit organization with which you are familiar. When should formal evaluations be done? Do you think that systematic evaluation should be done on a regular basis?

2. Give examples of process and outcome measures that could be used to evaluate the IT system for some governmental or non-profit organization (hypothetical or real). Which evaluative measures do you think are best to use? Why?

3. How much faith do you have in non-financial measures such as customer satisfaction? Is there any alternative to using such measures?

4. What role should qualitative data play in the evaluation of governmental IT? How would you weigh or "mesh" qualitative data with quantitative metrics?

5. Can you calculate an ROI for some governmental system? Give an example of how you would go about calculating it.

6. Critique the evaluations done by governments that we have outlined in this chapter. What are the strengths, weaknesses, and limitations?

Exercises

1. Design an evaluation plan to assess information and communication technologies for some public or nonprofit organization (hypothetical or real). How would you develop such a plan? What steps would you use? Why? What would be the major steps that are necessary for implementing the evaluations you propose?

2. Develop a plan for conducting a Balanced Scorecard evaluation of the IT unit in some organization (real or hypothetical). What steps would be necessary to do a BSC evaluation and how would they differ from a typical outcome evaluation?

3. Develop an interview guide for semi-structured interviews with the customers of a governmental or non-profit IT organization that is to be aimed at identifying the strengths, weaknesses, and limitations of its IT services. Let us assume that there have been numerous informal complaints about the IT service both from the top leadership and end-users.

Copyright © 2006, Idea Group Inc. Copying or distributing in print or electronic forms without written permission of Idea Group Inc. is prohibited.

Chapter X

Governments and IT Sharing

Introduction

There are many reasons why today's computerized information systems can achieve more sharing in government than ever before. Over the last decade, an increasing emphasis has been placed on taking an enterprise-wide view of governments in order to replace "stovepipe" systems that focus on one department's needs with integrated systems that would allow users from any department to access to information they need to achieve their jobs. This ability to share information across departmental boundaries has become accepted as one of the basic goals of modern information management in government. One of its key precepts is that data should only be input once into a system and any user (with a valid need) can use that information from anywhere at any time in a variety of forms.

The implications of this enterprise-wide approach are visible when one studies the requirements to establish standards that facilitate sharing within and between governmental organizations. IT standards generally require that each department's new applications be compatible with the organizational network and its major platforms and these requirements are aimed at ensuring compatibility as well as saving money on IT support.

There are other developments that facilitate sharing between organizations including the development of data warehousing, the World Wide Web, and software developments such as *XML* (Extensible Markup Language). The purpose (Weinman, 2002, p.10) of XML is to enable better interactivity between Web sites and databases. Data warehousing refers to the combination of hardware and software that allows an organization to set up a database that can integrate information from a wide variety of sources such as legacy applications on mainframes and allow for sophisticated analyses. Governments have

Copyright © 2006, Idea Group Inc. Copying or distributing in print or electronic forms without written permission of Idea Group Inc. is prohibited.

made use of data warehouses and data marts to integrate data to meet the demands of the new welfare reform (Newcombe, 2000a). The World Wide Web allows easy sharing of information and the development of XML standard enhances this capability even further. For example, XML has been used as the approach for sharing of park data in an experimental project entitled Government Without Boundaries (2003). A major advantage of XML-based sharing is that it does not necessarily require major changes to legacy and mainframe-based systems and thus is affordable in times of budget stress (Peterson, 2003; National Electronic Commerce Coordinating Council, 2001). It enables governments with disparate and even antiquated information systems to successfully exchange information in a manner that is minimally intrusive and least disruptive.

In addition to the GWoB project, there are efforts by other organizations to encourage shared systems and shared data. For example, the NASCIO (National Association of State Chief Information Officers) has focused many of its efforts on achieving integration. In the human services, the U.S. General Accounting Office (GAO) has encouraged efforts to integrate human services to recipients through integration of information systems of the agencies that provide services for them (U.S. General Accounting Office, 2002a). The criminal justice area has long emphasized sharing. The online National Crime Information Center Computerized Criminal History (NCIC-CCH) was proposed in 1968 and the number and size of CCH record systems in criminal justice continue to grow (Laudon, 1986a; O'Shea, 1998). There are numerous other efforts at sharing criminal justice information such as the Regional Information Sharing Systems (RISS) Program that has been funded by U.S. Department of Justice to share intelligence across jurisdictional boundaries (http://www.iir.com/riss/).

The growth of geographic information systems (GIS) also helps to spur sharing of information. Federal, state, and local governments have established numerous onsite sharing systems that organizations can use due to the existence of common geographic identifiers that serve as the "*foreign keys*" (common identifiers that allow the joining of two separate tables of data) to integrate all kinds of information from governmental organizations and the private sector. There is now an Open GIS Consortium (OGC) that is aimed at making sharing more effective. There are several examples of long-standing multi-organizational sharing of GIS data (e.g., Bamberger, 1995). The growth of "open standards" makes sharing much easier. But the sharing that is done may be of a limited nature or, as one critic said, "low-level, stripped-out, dumbed-down conversion" (Robinson, 2003). Indeed, the most promising sharing is enabled by agreements between major private vendors due to commercial reasons (Robinson, 2003). The GIS movement has also spurred some of the most advanced examples of metadata (information that describes key characteristics of data such as its source, date of creation, etc.) that assists users in finding data that meets their needs (Douglas, 2003) such as a "Geospatial One-Stop" where agencies can access data from other organizations throughout the U.S.

In short, the last few years have made the vision of almost universal, seamless, integrated information systems appear to be imminent. However, despite these strong forces that enable shared systems and data, there remain many forces that make sharing difficult. In this chapter, I review research on sharing of information technology in government. Then I study examples of sharing by organizing them into categories by types of organizations involved and/or the type of sharing. Finally, I propose a framework on sharing in

Copyright © 2006, Idea Group Inc. Copying or distributing in print or electronic forms without written permission of Idea Group Inc. is prohibited.

government IT to guide future research. In studying sharing, I define the term broadly to include all significant forms of sharing related to IT, whether formal or informal in nature.

Previous Research

There is relatively little theoretical research that has focused on sharing of information between governmental organizations outside of the GIS area. The Onsrud & Rushton (1995) volume has several analytical chapters proposing frameworks concerning the sharing of GIS data. One major set of studies has been conducted by researchers at the Center for Technology in Government (CTG) at Albany, New York. These researchers have published a number of reports that we employ in our analysis next with most of them focusing on sharing between state and local governments. The CTG researchers have developed a framework that identifies the obstacles to sharing as well as several prescriptions on how sharing can be enhanced. They identify key environmental factors that constrain effective state-local systems such as variation in state-local relations and local conditions (Dawes et al., 1997, p.2). They point out that these factors can lead to inconsistent local participation, a tendency to create stand-alone systems and uneven participation in efforts to share. Their work (Dawes et al., 1997, p. 10) identifies the following set of barriers to state-local sharing: (1) A general lack of education and information about both technology and programs; (2) Lack of a shared, reliable computing and network infrastructure; (3) Goals that are too ambitious for the resources available to achieve them; (4) Human and organizational resistance to change; (5) Unrealistic time frames; (6) Organizational, programmatic, technological, and legal complexity; (7) Changing priorities; and (8) Overlapping or conflicting missions among the participating organizations.

The CTG researchers (Dawes et al., 1997, p. 21) have developed a number of "best practice" recommendations on how to facilitate sharing relationships between state and local governments including the following: (1) The system is designed to integrate with the related systems and business processes of the affected organizations; (2) Standard definitions of key data need to be used by all participants; (3) Built-in safeguards assure system security and the confidentiality of sensitive or personal information; (4) The design adheres to commonly accepted industry standards and does not rely on proprietary technologies; and (5) The design takes into account the current technical capabilities of the participating organizations. They go on to identify user support features that would characterize the "ideal system," such as continuing user training and support as well as provision for local modification of the systems based on local needs (Dawes et al., 1997, p. 21). They identify a number of other "best practices" such as identifying existing models, use of a prototype approach to test out possible solutions, and frequent communication with stakeholders (Dawes et al., 1997, pp. 11-12).

Brown & O'Toole (1998) compared the success of geographic information systems (GISs) in government including single-unit operations with multi-departmental and inter-institutional arrangements at the local level. Their research was aimed at testing

Copyright © 2006, Idea Group Inc. Copying or distributing in print or electronic forms without written permission of Idea Group Inc. is prohibited.

hypotheses as to whether shared systems were more expensive and less successful than single-unit operations. Their findings showed that the shared arrangements were not more expensive than single-unit GIS systems, but that the inter-institutional systems did not achieve as high a level of success.

Laudon (1974, p. 143) conducted case studies that emphasized the importance of political obstacles to sharing such as the fact that organizations seek to control information in order to serve "as an important boundary-maintaining device against potentially disruptive external inquiries." The author (Rocheleau, 1995; 1996) reviewed the literature on interorganizational and interdepartmental information sharing. Based on this review, I identified facilitating forces that encourage sharing such as common goals and functions, legal mandates to share, political pressures to share, funding, and individual-reward incentives. I identified obstacles to sharing including technological incompatibilities, privacy and other legal restrictions, and asymmetry of benefits. If there is perceived to be a substantial asymmetry in which one unit benefits and another unit does not, then the less enthusiastic organization may resist or sabotage (e.g., by poor quality of data entry) the shared effort (see examples in Rocheleau, 1996). This review turned up examples of organizations that desire to maintain autonomy over their information due to "survival" and other political reasons similar to those discovered by Laudon (1974). In an empirical study of sharing of municipal data (Rocheleau, 1995) between the police department and other municipal departments, I found that sharing took place less often than expected among departments that shared functions and common goals such as police and fire. The research discovered that police shared most frequently with those departments that had the most formal authority and influence over them such as the central manager office and the finance department.

What can the public sector learn about sharing from research that has been conducted in the private sector? The work of Michael Porter (e.g., Porter & Millar, 1985) encouraged the view that information and information systems can help an organization to achieve a strategic advantage over competitors. This view would support a reluctance of organizations to share, at least with organizations which they view as competitors. Indeed, there are examples of companies in which their IT systems have been integral to their success (e.g., Amazon) and consequently they refuse to share details about their information system. By way of contrast, governments do not have the same incentives to keep information about their successes private. Thus this is one reason why the willingness to share information among governments may be greater than that of the private sector (Rocheleau & Wu, 2002). In addition, government information is subject to Freedom of Information Act and other laws (e.g., sunshine laws) that create a sense of living in a "fishbowl." Bozeman & Bretschneider (1986) noted the fishbowl quality of government information as being one of its key contrasts with private sector information management in their model of public management information systems.

However, there is research to show that even competitive private organizations can and do share information and systems under certain circumstances. Carr (2003) has recently argued that, although technologies have been used to provide a competitive advantage at first, later on the technology (e.g., electricity) became more valuable when it is shared than used in isolation. Meier and Sprague (1991) point to several areas where sharing of information has become a strategic necessity, such as in the health care and travel

Copyright © 2006, Idea Group Inc. Copying or distributing in print or electronic forms without written permission of Idea Group Inc. is prohibited.

industries. Likewise, Clemens and Knez (1988) point to the ATM (Automated Teller Machines) area as an example where it is more advantageous for private for-profit organizations to share than to compete. However, research on private sector interorganizational systems shows that they too encounter many obstacles (e.g., Boddy, 2000) and that in areas like community health (Payton, 2000), competition can be an important obstacle in some cases, although it varied from situation to situation. Kumar & Dissel (1996) identify different kinds of interorganizational systems (pooled information resources, value-supply-chain, and networked) that are related to the kind of interdependency relationship that exists among the organizations. They also point out that the successes of interorganizational systems are affected by the quest for dominance and clash of personalities and organizational cultures (Kumar & Dissel, 1996, p. 289). The term interoperability has been used (Institute of Electrical and Electronics Engineers, 1990; Landsbergen & Wolken, 2001) to describe the "engineering and technical requirements" used to design systems so they can work together effectively. However, the previous research shows that neither in the public nor private sector are technological advancements and the emphasis on interoperability sufficient conditions to establish interorganizational sharing. Personal and organizational priorities often take precedence.

I will return to the research issues at the conclusion as I attempt to synthesize the results of the literature and identify the most promising research and theoretical approaches to sharing government IT.

Sources

I conducted a broad literature review employing both traditional library searches as well as the use of Internet search engines to identify examples of interorganizational and intergovernmental information sharing. In addition to these literature searches, I also put out queries to an association whose membership includes a variety of government information technology executives: The Governmental Management Information Sciences (GMIS) organization. This query resulted in several communications about sharing relationships in which they were involved and I have included these in the analysis next. I have also used some material based on semi-structured discussions with governmental employees who were guaranteed anonymity in order to encourage candor.

Sharing Among Local Governments

The ultimate form of sharing occurs when the IT systems of two separate organizations merge to become one. One example is the City of Auburn (Alabama) where the City provides all IT services for the school system (Buston, 2003). James C. Buston, Director of Information Technology for Auburn, puts the case for integration as follows:

Whenever I talk about shared infrastructure, I use the following analogy. If you were

Copyright © 2006, Idea Group Inc. Copying or distributing in print or electronic forms without written permission of Idea Group Inc. is prohibited.

the city and if I were to come to you and tell you that I needed separate roads: one road to go to schools only and one road to the city facilities only, you would tell me I was crazy. If I were to further request separate water systems and separate electrical system for schools and city buildings, you would know I was crazy. However, if I come to you and tell you that we need to provide separate data infrastructures, one for the city and one for the schools, you would hardly raise an eyebrow.

One of the few detailed descriptions of a governmental integration effort is provided by Hall (2001) concerning the intergovernmental agreement in which the City of Douglas, Douglas County, and the Omaha/Douglas Public Building Commission contracted to purchase a shared ERP (Enterprise Resource Planning) system. The initiating forces were the need to upgrade the financial systems in view of the upcoming Y2K crisis and the fact that ERP systems are very expensive and require substantial resources so that sharing could lighten the burden. The case study acknowledges conflict due to the fact that the County IT director opposed any sort of outsourcing. Hall describes the "politics" as being "intense" but the steering committee (made up of the heads of the different governments) decided to proceed anyway. In a note to me, Hall (2003) states that the two IT shops "formally merged under the umbrella of a non-profit corporation whose governing board reports to the County Board, City Council and Mayor."

Another model of integration is exemplified by the LOGIS (Local Government Information Systems Association) system that has served a number (24 in 1995) of municipalities and certain other organizations in Minnesota. The cities and other agencies signed a "joint powers agreement" in which it is controlled by a board of directors containing one representative (a non-elected official) from each organization (Norton, 1995, p. 43). An executive committee elected by the board has overview responsibility for the system while an executive director manages the organization on a daily basis (Norton, 1995, p. 43). LOGIS has a wide range of software applications that it offers including financial, GIS, utility billing, and human resources, among others. Members can choose which applications they want to use and they only pay for those they employ. Hardware, support, and training support are provided by the organization. What effect does LOGIS have on the need to have local IT staff? In a communication with this author (Garris, 2003), Mike Garris, the executive director of LOGIS, said that typically cities with a population of over 50,000 have three IT staff, those with 25,000 to 50,000 have two IT staff, and one IT coordinator suffices for those from 10,000 to 25,000. The role of the local IT staff is to support their local pcs and troubleshoot office applications, deal with printer problems, and do some of the city service administration tasks. LOGIS staff do the work that requires network (e.g., Microsoft and Cisco) certified training and help to maintain the LOGIS WAN (wide area network) as well as the city servers. LOGIS application specialists provide help for financial, utility billing, public safety and other applications. LOGIS allows a great deal of flexibility for participating organizations. LOGIS members can share via the use of a central-site or distributed processing. In 1995, the smallest municipality in LOGIS was Farmington with a population of 8,000 and the largest government represented was Coon Rapids (59,945).

These arrangements involved major forms of integration in which the IT unit gives up a substantial degree of its autonomy over applications. Another approach is sharing that is restricted to specific functions, applications and/or hardware systems. For example,

Copyright © 2006, Idea Group Inc. Copying or distributing in print or electronic forms without written permission of Idea Group Inc. is prohibited.

a group of northwest suburbs of Chicago have formed a GIS Consortium (http://www.giscon.org/). The key purposes of the consortium are to reduce risk and costs (Thomey, 2003). The initial set up of the organization (GIS Consortium) heavily involved top administrators and it was definitely a "top down" solution. But they now have heavy involvement of a "second tier" staff such as program directors or coordinators (Thomey, 2003). The consortium has contracted with a private IT consulting firm that provides GIS technical staff to the participating municipalities. The cost sharing is based on a formula related to population size and density. The municipalities involved are generally small in size and most could not afford GIS staff on their own.

Indeed, the growth of GIS systems has spurred many data sharing arrangements among state and local governments. Sharing of GIS information is not new by any means. Bamberger (1995) reports on the San Diego Regional Urban Information System (RUIS) that was established in 1984 to share costs among the city, county, and other governments and also private organizations that had overlapping interests in GIS data. For example, instead of spending large amounts of money to build their base map, RUIS contracted to obtain the data from the San Diego Gas and Electric Company (SDG&E) in exchange for providing SDG&E with all updates and enhancements as well as a share in any sales of base map products to the private sector (Bamberger, 1995, p. 129). Bamberger points out that this agreement and other aspects of the sharing occurred only after substantial degree of politics and pressure took place. RUIS initially adopted a decentralized approach to base map maintenance because it was the "path of least resistance" and would not upset "existing organizational structures" (Bamberger, 1995, p. 130). A more recent example is the Minneapolis-St. Paul's MetroGIS that is a geo-data collaborative (Landkamer, 2003). The Metropolitan Council, a regional agency responsible for collecting and treating wastewater and for oversight of land use planning, spurred the effort to develop a regional GIS that includes public, nonprofit, and private sector organizations. The MetroGIS has a 12-member Policy Board made up of officials from key local governments and a policy board whose 25 members come from a variety of organizations (Landkamer, 2003). Landkamer (2003) points out that the structure of the agency is unusual in that it has "no formal legal standing" and participation is voluntary, but that options to move towards a more formal setup have been rejected in favor of the ad hoc arrangement.

In some cases, local governments can use their combined market to develop more favorable contracts with IT consulting firms than otherwise would be possible. For example, in one case, several small municipalities have developed a contract with a consulting firm in which the firm gives it a favorable price for IT consultants. Several of these municipalities lack any IT staff at all and the joint contract has provided better access to needed expertise. This is an example of the sharing of resources to leverage a better contract but the local IT systems remain independent of one another.

There are many examples of sharing arrangements limited to specific functional areas such as Computer-Aided Dispatch systems where local governments provide funding for shared operations. In many cases, the IT department of one unit of government will provide Computer-Aided Dispatch and other systems to other units of government. For example, the City of Reno provides a computer-aided dispatch and other systems (e.g., police records management) to other units of government such as Washoe County

Copyright © 2006, Idea Group Inc. Copying or distributing in print or electronic forms without written permission of Idea Group Inc. is prohibited.

(Vandenberg, 2003). In the GIS area, in addition to the City of Reno and Washoe County, a private sector company, the Sierra Pacific Power Company, cooperates in obtaining ortho-photos and parcel database maintenance. There are many examples of sharing of data centers such as has occurred in Mecklenberg County (North Carolina) and the City of Charlotte. Their partnership began with the co-location of a common facility in 1988, progressed to a shared mainframe in 1993, a consolidated mainframe data center under the County in 1996, and then progressed to competitive bidding in 1999 as forced by the City (Pinkard, 2003). Perlman (2001) describes how Palo Alto (California) performs six services for East Palo Alto, a smaller city with fewer resources. Palo Alto has hired additional staff and is interested in becoming a "Government Service Provider" and developing contracts with other agencies. Of course, this sharing is voluntary and I know of cases where small local governments have approached larger governments and been refused. We lack longitudinal studies of these types of arrangements. It would be interesting to compare such "governmental service provider" arrangements with the success of private vendor services to local government.

Criminal Justice Sharing Efforts: Local-Local and State-Local Efforts

Criminal justice agencies have been sharing information for decades in a variety of intergovernmental arrangements. A NASCIO report (July 2003, p. 22) has classified different categories of sharing that take place among criminal justice agencies:

1. Query (and receive a response) from local, regional, state, and national databases.

2. Push operational information from one agency to another based upon actions taken regarding subjects or cases by the sending agency.

3. Pull operational information from another agency based upon actions the other agency has taken regarding subjects or cases.

4. Publish operational information on key transactions and events regarding subjects, events, and cases in traditional (e.g., paper) and electronic media.

5. Subscription/Notification of key transactions and events regarding subjects, events, and cases.

Thus *push-and-pull technologies* are useful ways for governments to share information with other as well as with their customers without engaging in spam. In the push technology approach, an agency or individual will register to receive certain types of information either through e-mail or by phone (Poulakos, 2002; Hibbard, 1997).

Sharing in the criminal justice area appears to take time to develop and formal sharing is generally preceded by much informal sharing. For example, sharing in Harris County, Texas (includes the City of Houston) began in 1977 by creating the Harris County Justice

Copyright © 2006, Idea Group Inc. Copying or distributing in print or electronic forms without written permission of Idea Group Inc. is prohibited.

Information System. It grew incrementally and now has a board that includes members of all county agencies and courts. The conclusion of the Center for Technology in Government's (1999) study of criminal justice information systems is as follows:

In many cases, informal networking forms a key component of integration. There are many potential interested parties in any integration initiative. Their collaboration requires much communication and ongoing opportunity for interaction. Informal networks and other opportunities for joint effort are often necessary and effective in moving integration forward.

A study by O'Shea (1998) examined sharing of information between police officers of the Chicago Police Department and the communities they police. The report echoes the CTG study's conclusions in regard to the importance of trust. In regard to community policing, O'Shea cites one officer who said that some police officers tried to develop a trusting relationship with community residents while other police officers tried to maintain a distance. This officer (O'Shea, 1998) found that trust was the key to gaining information from community residents:

I know people on my post by their first name and they know me. I'm not out there looking for information from them. I sit and visit.... They're looking for someone they can trust to help. Once they see you as a person who cares and isn't just passing through you get more information than you can use. (pp. 91-92)

As for sharing among police officers themselves, the willingness to share depends on whether the officers who share information will get credit in the official personnel system for sharing. If they don't, then no more information will be shared as one officer described it (O'Shea, 1998):

They are not going to tell us anything that might screw up their pinch. The only way to get anything is to get it from someone that trusts you and you make sure his name goes on the arrest report. But screw him once and that's the last you'll get from him. (p. 91)

Laudon (1986b) found that police had more confidence in local than state or federal systems and he emphasizes the importance of the human element in communications. Laudon also points out that the justice information systems lacked the "self-correcting" nature of financial systems in which outside auditors as well as customers studying their bills provide mechanisms to identifying and correcting poor quality data.

Copyright © 2006, Idea Group Inc. Copying or distributing in print or electronic forms without written permission of Idea Group Inc. is prohibited.

State-Local (Including Private Providers) Systems

The Center for Technology in Government studied the attempt to build a homeless information system in New York City that included a variety of state and local governmental agencies as well as many private non-profit organizations who delivered the actual services to the homeless. The original plan had been to use a "canned commercial system" but that plan was abandoned because the information from such as system would not be useful to the case managers (Center for Technology in Government, 2000). The non-profit providers were concerned that the Bureau of Shelter Services would set performance goals unrealistically high. Indeed, it was found that agreement had to be negotiated even on key concepts such as "admit date" of the client because these basic terms were open to different interpretations and different actors had an interest in how they were defined. CTG researchers concluded that contextual knowledge was crucial and that the system designers needed to understand how data were collected, again implying the sharing of informal, qualitative information in order to understand how the system "really works." The CTG researchers major conclusion is reflected in the title of their publication, "Building trust before building a system: the making of the Homeless Information Systems." It is necessary for the organizations engaged in sharing the information to "trust" one another if the system is to work. Thus technical issues such as whether to use an "SQL server or data warehouse" were set aside for the time being in order to achieve this trust.

Dawes et al. (1997) outline several sharing arrangements that exist between the State of New York and its local governments concerning state-local information systems. Based on the description of Dawes et al., it appears that in several of their cases, such as the Aging Network Client Based Service Management System, the Probation Automation Project and the Real Property System, the systems are essentially state systems with active efforts to solicit input from local governments at the start of the projects and to provide for ongoing communications thereafter. The state IT officials realized in cases such as the Local Social Services Imaging Project that their system needed to integrate with the local systems and they attempted to accomplish this task by making sure that the system was compatible with "as many mainstream hardware and software standards as possible" (Dawes et al., 1997, p. 62). Thus this form of sharing involves giving input opportunities as to the goals and needs of local organizations so that the state system may be more responsive as well as attempting to facilitate sharing by the establishment of standard platforms. It is undoubtedly the case that much sharing of informal information (e.g., about organizational and political issues and obstacles) takes place as a result of these consultation efforts. For example, Dawes et al. (1997, p. 52) discuss the automation by the State of probation information. County Probation Directors provided guidance for the design of the State system but these local officials had problems finding money in their own budgets to travel to the meetings so the state paid travel expenses and received the benefits of the expertise of these officials and also undoubtedly helped to cement local support for the state project and spur the kinds of informal communication necessary to build trust and the willingness to share crucial information.

Copyright © 2006, Idea Group Inc. Copying or distributing in print or electronic forms without written permission of Idea Group Inc. is prohibited.

State-to-State and Interdepartmental Sharing Within States

Many states are attempting to build more integrated systems that avoid information silos among their departments. Information silos refer to the situation in which each department organizes its information for its internal use and does not give attention to other, outside users thus making sharing of information difficult. Utah has developed an e-government council to set priorities for major IT projects and one of the goals is to encourage cross-agency projects (Perlman, 2003). Governor Leavitt's approach was to use his power to push a top-down solution. One of their first major projects involved the creation of unified systems for dealing with eligibility determinations concerning TANF (Temporary Assistance to Needy Families), Medicaid, child care, and food stamps. The three state agencies involved established a written agreement on what resources they will contribute as well as staff (Perlman, 2003). The initial funding of the system was simple because it used TANF funds, which is a block grant that the state is able to use in a flexible manner. But the article notes that agreement from other federal agencies is difficult when monies from different programs (e.g., Food Stamps) are mixed together because it makes it necessary to trace whether funds have been spent as intended by that particular program. Such interagency systems also may require the approval of several legislative committees and the project must be sold to all of these committees that it makes business sense (Perlman, 2003).

Perlman (2003) also points to *"shallow solutions"* employed by presenting Web pages of information to users that give the impression of integrated information while the data actually reside on separate backend servers. Pennsylvania uses this approach in their Web site to allow businesses to fill out one form to register with three different agencies (Perlman, 2003). The U. S. General Accounting Office (2002a) likewise found states using *integration by "screens"* to assist in integration efforts:

To enhance service integration, the state initiatives are making data from different programs available to case managers and, in some cases, to program applicants using a single computer screen. For example, New Jersey's One Ease-E Link initiative provides hardware and software to counties so they can create county-level networks comprised of a multitude of public and private service providers, including non-profit agencies. The Internet-based system enables these providers to share recipient information using case management software and assess applicants' program eligibility by using an eligibility-screening tool". (pp. 2-3)

The shallow solution appears to avoid many difficult organizational problems because the IT systems do not actually have to be merged (hence the term "shallow" integration) and these shallow approaches may become more prevalent with the development of XML.

Some states (and other governments) are sharing applications and code. Swope (2003) describes a case in which Kansas used a program to manage grants to school districts

Copyright © 2006, Idea Group Inc. Copying or distributing in print or electronic forms without written permission of Idea Group Inc. is prohibited.

by using code that Missouri had given them. In this particular case, the Missouri application did virtually everything that was needed by Kansas with only a few gaps (Swope, 2003). Kansas hired the same vendor that had developed the Missouri system to fill in these few gaps (Swope, 2003). According to Perlman (2001), Arizona is now running Hawaii's Medicaid information system with the Hawaii data residing on the computers in Arizona. Hawaii paid Arizona $11 million for the initial system and will also pay for processing time. Hawaii will share in the cost for modifications of the system as well (Perlman, 2001). There is a proposal to create a nation-wide software component sharing system for governments (Perlman, 2001).

There are also examples of where the borrowing of systems has led to problems. There are examples from the child support mandate by the federal government that states replicate systems created by other states. Perlman (1998) cites an example of North Carolina modeling its system on Virginia's but discovering that the processes underlying the system differed. These differences led to basic problems such as the inability to reconcile bank records with the state database (Perlman, 1998). Likewise, a study of children's information systems by U.S. GAO (2003, p. 40) found that Iowa did not save any money by borrowing because the maintenance of the borrowed systems "takes just as much money as building them."

Federal-State Intergovernmental Sharing

Human services is an area where a potentially large number of organizations are often involved in serving one consumer or a family unit. Consequently, the potential for information systems sharing among various human services systems (e.g., Medicaid, Food Stamps, TANF, and Job Training) is great. These programs are intergovernmental in nature with the federal government providing funding and setting certain rules and guidelines while state governments administer the programs on a day-to-day basis. The realization of the potential for information sharing is not new. Indeed, the idea to use information systems to help integrate human services dates back to the 1970's when the movement for integrated human services first developed and there were attempts to make the information system a key force for integrating these services so that consumers of human service programs would receive better services through integrated intake processing. But a recent assessment of integration efforts by Ragan (2003a, p. 62) concluded that "human service information systems are more often viewed by local staff as a barrier" to integration.

It is instructive to look at some selected areas of human services to identify the reasons why the growth of successful sharing has been so difficult. Each state has a unique human services system. Indeed, over the past generation, the general movement of intergovernmental programs has been to devolve more authority to the states so states can have unique programs and thus it is impossible for the federal government to set up a single system for any of these programs. Consequently, it is impossible to implement

Copyright © 2006, Idea Group Inc. Copying or distributing in print or electronic forms without written permission of Idea Group Inc. is prohibited.

a single system that "fits all sizes" for complex intergovernmental programs like TANF. Nevertheless, the federal government does need to gather aggregate data including the monitoring of program success and failures in order to report to Congress and the President. Thus the federal government must create a hybrid system at the federal level by integrating data from the 50 states. How does the federal government design a system that will meet its own needs when there is so much state-to-state variation in both the programs and information systems? The approach of the federal government is to require that the states provide data and meet standards and requirements set by the federal government. As a part of the 1996 Welfare Reform Act, the federal government set rules and guidelines for the program but the program remains decentralized and run by state governments on a day-to-day basis. There are general federal rules that must be adhered to such as the five-year time limit that individuals can be on welfare total and the requirement that TANF recipients cannot be in the program for more than two years consecutively, though states can implement more rigorous time limits if they wish. The predecessor program, AFDC (Aid to Families with Dependent Children) had no such time limitations and the focus of the previous information system was structured around a yearly time frame. Thus the change-over to the TANF system requires that state systems now be able to provide a longitudinal analysis of clients to ensure that they do not violate these time limits. Likewise, the federal requirements necessitate that states gather information on clients who have moved from other states to learn how much total time and consecutive months they have been receiving TANF benefits. Thus the reform led to a major change in the structure of the information system and interstate sharing is necessary.

The federal government also sets goals for the hours of work and the percent of recipients who will be engaged in work-related activities. The federal government requires that the states provide information on state compliance with these rules. The federal government also provides incentives to states that excel on certain performance indicators and states must report to the federal government their success on these measures. The TANF program also has complex relationships with other programs such as Medicaid, Food Stamps, and "support services" for TANF clients such as transportation and child care. Indeed, the relationship between the TANF program and these other programs proved problematic because there was concern that many citizens incorrectly lost both Medicaid and Food Stamp benefits as a result of initial implementation of the reform and the inadequacies of the state information systems (U.S. General Accounting Office, 2002a, p. 7).

The limitations of the older IT state systems are revealed by the fact that many states had to revert to "manual processes to prevent eligibles from losing Medicaid coverage" (Ragan, 2003b). The persistence of this problem, as Ragan (2003b) notes, is indicated by the fact that five years after the reform, the federal government is still sending states guidance on this issue. In such an intergovernmental system, what ability does the primary funding agency (the federal government) have over the recipient of funding (the state governments) to ensure that they take corrective actions? Basically, there are three methods (Ragan, 2003b): (1) They can provide positive enticements to the states by enhanced funding for the development of better systems; (2) The federal government can employ on-site reviews that can identify weaknesses and require improvements; or (3) The federal government can rely on legal cases brought by advocates against the state

Copyright © 2006, Idea Group Inc. Copying or distributing in print or electronic forms without written permission of Idea Group Inc. is prohibited.

government handling of cases. But, as Ragan and others (e.g., Derthick, 1975) have noted, the federal government is generally very reluctant to cut off funding for such programs so threats are used sparingly and are not often enforced.

Although the picture painted by GAO and Ragan suggests that the federal government is lax in its implementation of federal standards for information systems, some view the states as being unfairly penalized by inflexible federal standards. For example, the federal government denied funding to the North Carolina system because it was not *"statewide,"* but North Carolina argued against the federal definition of statewide because some wealthy counties did much more than the minimum required by the state or federal government. Bill Cox (2001) of North Carolina argues that the federal role should be oversight in setting strategic objectives but letting the states decide how to meet these.

An interesting point made by another GAO report is that systems developed at the state level often do not meet the needs of local officials (Nathan & Ragan, 2001; U.S. General Accounting Office, 2000). Similarly, the attempt to build a statewide child welfare system in California was resisted by the local governments and many argued that it was not "feasible" to build a centralized system but rather they needed "a variety of systems that" could "interface with one another" (Daniels, 1997). A study by Hahm et al. (1995) of a Texas state property inventory system found similarly that the system was designed for a particular set of end users and tends to ignore the needs of other uses. A study of 15 states conducted by the U.S. GAO of welfare systems (Sherrill, 2001) asked to what extent state and local managers were able to obtain information needed to perform their jobs. Sixty-seven percent (10 of 15) of state managers versus only 40% (six of 15) of local managers agreed that the system provided most or all of the information required. The general implication based on this appears to be that the level of government that controls the design of the system fashions it to meet its own needs and pays less attention to the needs of other organizations involved. This is supported by a U.S. GAO (2003b) study of GIS sharing that explains why local governments have little interest in spending money and effort to share with the federal government:

Existing commercial products using a variety of formats are already meeting the needs of states and localities in providing...information. Hence these organizations are likely to have little incentive to adopt potentially incompatible federal standards that could require substantial new investments. According to Arizona's state cartographer, many local governments currently do not comply with FGDC [Federal Geographic Data Committee] standards because most of their GIS applications were created primarily to meet their internal [emphasis added] needs, with little concern for data sharing with federal systems. (p. 11)

A related finding of Sherrill's (2001) is that different data needs exist among different categories of users. Case managers need information on individual clients and it has to be "real time" if it is to be effective (Sherrill, 2001, pp. 8-10). Program oversight officials need aggregate data on program performance. So sharing may be successful in meeting one group of users but fail to meet others' needs. Although the terms intergovernmental and interorganizational information systems would seem to imply that at least some of the needs of all parties are met to some degree, the actual degree to which information systems fulfill needs of users is an open question. Often important needs may not met.

Copyright © 2006, Idea Group Inc. Copying or distributing in print or electronic forms without written permission of Idea Group Inc. is prohibited.

The job training programs initiated by the Workforce Investment Act (WIA) illustrate another attempt by the federal government to use information systems to integrate services and spur better performance by state and local agencies. A primary vehicle used to achieve better performance is to provide "one stop shopping" for consumers that state information systems gather and report performance to the federal government (Department of Labor in this case). In order to be successful, this popular one stop shopping approach requires service coordination and sharing of information. But the General Accounting Office in a review of WIA found that the gathering and reporting information had the opposite effect on the program (U.S. GAO, 2002c):

The system's narrow focus on program outcomes for a limited number of participants misses a key requirement of WIA to support the movement toward a coordinated system. In fact, the measures may focus the opposite—a siloed approach that encourages competition and limits their cooperation. (p. 28)

Consequently the shared accountability information had some undesirable goal displacement effects, leading some programs to ignore certain groups of consumers (e.g., those that would result in poor performance results) and also led to competition among local programs for desirable recipients and less willingness to refer consumers to other more appropriate programs. Thus the sharing of information between levels of government may or may not lead to the achievement of better integrated services depending on how the key actors (usually the local service providers) react to these information requirements.

Federal government monitoring of nursing homes provides another example of intergovernmental human services information systems. The states collect data on nursing homes but this data is fed into federal Medicaid case-mix reimbursement system that determines the amount of funding that will be received by the states and nursing homes (U.S. General Accounting Office, 2002b). The GAO found that the states were not accurately recording harm done to patients and that one of the reasons was the lack of clear definition of harm that federal guidance on this key definition contributed to the problem (U.S. General Accounting Office, 2002b). The GAO found that separate onsite interviews were important to assuring accuracy of data and that interviews with nursing home personnel familiar with the resident provided valuable information. But most states did not conduct such reviews but relied on "off-site" data provided by the nursing homes. GAO also reported that the timing of the nursing home reviews was crucial (U.S. General Accounting Office, 2002b). If state reviews were too predictable, the facilities were able to hide problems. Finally, GAO reports that the Health Care Finance Administration (HCFA) rarely sanctioned the homes that harmed patients and thus the reporting system did not have its intended effect of protecting patients from harm. In general, it appears difficult for the federal government to effectively monitor the quality of the data provided to them by states in the human services area where there is a lack of a "self-correcting" mechanism (e.g., a customer who protests an inaccurate bill). Also, this example shows that that qualitative information such as face-to-face interviews and in person visits to facilities is crucial to checking the validity of quantitative measures concerning important and sensitive measures of outcomes.

Copyright © 2006, Idea Group Inc. Copying or distributing in print or electronic forms without written permission of Idea Group Inc. is prohibited.

The implementation of Statewide Child Welfare Automation provides still another example of the difficulties of designing and implementing federal-state intergovernmental information systems. The development of these systems has taken well over a decade (U.S. GAO, 2003) and remains problematic and thus is instructive for our purposes. States had the option of developing their own systems or to receive federal matching funds. If states took federal funds, it was expected that they would utilize models of other states that had already developed systems in order to save time and resources. The state systems were required to meet standards established by the federal government. As with the nursing home case, the states did not believe that they received clear guidance from the federal government on issues related to data quality. Some states such as Vermont did not join the federal matching effort because they viewed the federal requirements as too restrictive and not relevant to their efforts (GAO, 2003). Cuddy (2001) argues that the federal approach to intergovernmental systems is outdated because its approach is linear and sequential and imposes heavy paperwork and reporting requirements whenever changes need to be made to the original plan while, in contrast, new system development approaches are "fast-moving and flexible" and constantly changing to meet user needs.

The borrowing of other state systems proved to be problematic for some states such as New York and Colorado because their own systems and problems did not match up with the borrowed systems and the system-sharing led to more problems than would have been the case if they had developed systems on their own. The quality of the data, as with all systems, is dependent on the street level "bureaucrats," in this case, the caseworkers who input the data. The states want the system to mirror their own processes and processes vary from state to state. For example, Iowa divides child welfare work between child abuse neglect investigations and ongoing case management processes. Thus, system development is a difficult task because it requires that the developers have a deep understanding of the work processes of the end users but there was high turnover among the private vendor staff that developed many of the state systems. One lesson learned is that a relatively successful approach to the development of systems was the encouragement of user groups. These groups freely exchanged a great deal of information that facilitated success. The reporting needs of states differ from those of the federal government and these differences affect the reliability of the data (GAO, 2003, p. 24):

...36 of the 50 states...reported that technical challenges, such as matching their state data element definitions to HHS's [Department of Health and Human Service's] data categories, affected the quality of the data that they report to the federal government.... In cases where state policy differs from federal policy, state officials must carefully reformat their data in order to meet federal reporting requirements.

Agreement on basic definitions is also a problem. For example, how does one count the number of times a child moves while in foster care? This can be a crucial number because it is often assumed that a large number of moves is undesirable and reflects negatively on the agency. But there is variation in how states reported the number of movements. For example, the states claim that the federal government in some places instructs them to count as a move "anytime a child sleeps in a different place" and in other cases, the federal government excludes "runaways" and "trial home visits" from contributing to the number of movements (GAO, 2003, p. 29).

Copyright © 2006, Idea Group Inc. Copying or distributing in print or electronic forms without written permission of Idea Group Inc. is prohibited.

Another point raised by the federal-state intergovernmental systems is the crucial role played by software vendors and private agencies that deliver the services. Much of the software development at all levels of government is done by private vendors and their strengths and limitations affect the quality of the systems they develop and thus they must be considered, in effect, as part of the intergovernmental system. Likewise, many of the services delivered by federal and state programs are provided by private service organizations (both non-profit and for-profit) and they in effect become the end users of intergovernmental information systems and part of the information system even though they are not government employees.

Informal Sharing

There is a tremendous amount of informal sharing of information among IT professionals in governments. In the IT listservs that are aimed at governments, such as that of Governmental Information Management Sciences (GMIS) and Innovations Group, members share their experiences with hardware, software, and a variety of issues. RFPs and other documents are also freely shared. Indeed, informal sharing may even include code of applications written by one government that another government can use. Finn (2004) has described how The Information Systems Forum listserv began that is made up of 2700 IT professionals serving the technology needs of nonprofit organizations.

This informal sharing may remain entirely informal. The informal sharing but it can be organized into more formal groups whose purpose is, in effect, to share their expertise. Examples of attempts to build these *"communities of practice"* include special-interest groups formed by the federal CIO Council. A community of practice refers to people who share an interest in a topic, issue or problem. The community can be within a single organization or could exist across organizational boundaries. It could be based entirely on face-to-face and/or phone conversations but it is now customary to "digitize their exchanges" via listservs, online discussion boards, or other forms of digital communication (Schwen & Noriko, 2003; Newcombe, 2000b). It is difficult to overestimate the importance of informal sharing as IT professionals and others are able to obtain valuable information that would be likely to be expensive, time-consuming and perhaps even impossible to get through formal channels or contracts with consultants.

Framework for Studying Sharing Relationships

In attempting to define sharing relationships, I begin with two ideal type situations to identify the extremes of sharing and lack of sharing among systems. In one case, let us imagine two organizations that are legally separate entities but that have completely merged their information systems so that hardware, software, and data are totally shared including even informal information that is not available on the computerized systems.

Copyright © 2006, Idea Group Inc. Copying or distributing in print or electronic forms without written permission of Idea Group Inc. is prohibited.

In the second case, let us conceive of two organizations that exist in the same environment but for whatever reasons do not share any hardware, software or even swap information of any kind, whether formal or informal. We can use these two extremes to conceive of sharing as representing points on a continuum between total sharing and total non-sharing.

This is a useful mechanism because it allows us to study degrees of sharing as a variable—it is not an "all or nothing" kind of phenomenon. IT sharing can involve a number of different elements. First, organizations can share hardware including computers, servers, networks, fiber, etc. I have pointed out a number of such cases with hardware sharing being particularly common among local governments who jurisdictions overlap or are geographically close. Secondly, they can share software applications. We saw examples of this where the sharing was voluntary and involuntary such as in child welfare development case where the federal government established requirements for sharing. Thirdly, they may share IT personnel as illustrated in the GIS Consortium in Illinois. Fourth, they may share funding. The sharing of funding can take on complexities as in the Illinois case where several small municipalities banded together to achieve a favorable contract with a private vendor for IT services, and thus their systems remained separate. Fifth, organizations can share the formal information that resides in their IT systems such as reports and databases. As we saw in several of the federal-state intergovernmental systems, it is difficult for there to be a single system and thus the approach of the federal government is to establish information requirements and standards (e.g., concerning data reliability and privacy) to which the states are supposed to adhere. Sixth, they can share informal information that is non-digitized that can include information about matters such as values, procedures, political and organizational issues that they may be reluctant to commit to print or digital form. I pointed to listservs aimed at government IT professionals such as GMIS and Innovations Group but informal sharing among governments is, I believe, very important but has been largely ignored as a research topic.

Sharing then is complex and can take many forms and can help to achieve a degree of integration among information systems. In order to assess the state of sharing and/or integration among two or more systems, the dimensions shown in Figure 1 should be assessed.

Figure 1. Sharing and integration of IT resources between organizations

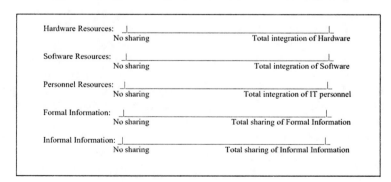

Copyright © 2006, Idea Group Inc. Copying or distributing in print or electronic forms without written permission of Idea Group Inc. is prohibited.

When I first began this research, when I used the terms interorganizational and intergovernmental information sharing, I conceived of sharing as referring to cases where hardware and/or software systems were involved. In seemed to me that such sharing was needed to constitute a true interorganizational information *system*. However, as I progressed in my research on sharing, I realized that much of the sharing that exists does not involve formal systems at all but that these other forms of sharing can nevertheless be extremely important to the organizations involved and in my view need to be incorporated into an overall model of sharing.

Three other dimensions that appears to me to be important is the extent to which sharing is voluntary, the degree to which power over sharing is equal among the organizations involved, and the sensitivity of the information to be shared (see Figure 2). To what extent does one organization dominate? If one organization dominates, it may speed formal integration and make sharing easier, though it also may create resentment and passive resistance among the other organizations. Much of the literature on interorganizational systems has focused on voluntary efforts where it is extremely important that each organization be given its due and treated equally. Agranoff & Lindsay (1983, p. 236) studied several successful intergovernmental bodies and conclude that it is important that the autonomy of each is respected, that each have a feeling of joint ownership and stake, and that the relationships needs to be "non-hierarchic, non-systematic, and non-superior-subordinate in nature." In some of these cases (e.g., the Illinois GIS case), it appears that such a non-hierarchical relationship is practiced. But in several of cases cited earlier such as the federal-state and state-local examples, there is a clear dominance of one actor over others due to factors such as legal authority, control over funding, control over expertise and other resources. The degree of symmetry in costs and benefits is a related issue and most likely overlaps the autonomy issue. Asymmetry of benefits may engender active or passive resistance on the part of the weaker units if they believe they are not getting a worthwhile return for their efforts.

Another implication of our analysis is that some data are especially sensitive because they affect funding and/or may be perceived as reflecting on the quality, effectiveness, and efficiency of services rendered. The development of sharing concerning sensitive data will be especially difficult. Agranoff and Lindsay (1983) in their study of intergovernmental management noted that these organizations often "avoided the most sensitive issues" such as program evaluations and threats of elimination of services. It appears that successful sharing is much easier when it does not involve information that could be perceived to have a big impact on issues such as funding and evaluation. Many of the successful case studies described by Dawes et al. appear to be of a non-threatening nature while the cases where sensitive data were involved (e.g., the CTG homeless case and the GAO studies of child welfare and nursing home abuse) concern very sensitive issues and thus the difficulties are much greater. Legal mandates and funding incentives may be needed to force sharing of sensitive information. For example, Sherrill (2001, p. 9) reports that most of the linkages established between TANF (the new welfare program) and other programs existed where there was either a federal mandate and/or funding incentives and that desirable linkages that did not have mandates or funding incentives had not been established. The movement to put performance data such as "organizational report cards" on the Internet for accountability purposes is becoming common and required in some situations such as concerning school performance (Gormely & Weimer,

Copyright © 2006, Idea Group Inc. Copying or distributing in print or electronic forms without written permission of Idea Group Inc. is prohibited.

Figure 2. Key factors that influence sharing relationships

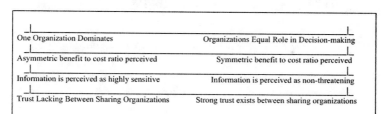

1999). Organizations are likely to want to exert more control over how such sensitive information is presented (Rocheleau, 2002).

The cases discussed in this chapter show that the development of successful voluntary sharing relationships usually takes a long period of development and necessitates a good degree of trust among the sharing organizations. Often the sharing develops incrementally from informal and limited types of sharing to more extensive efforts and formalized efforts. Trust appears to be strongly influenced by face-to-face contact and the opportunity for informal sharing prior to formal sharing. Undoubtedly, e-mail exchanges, even though they are digital, over time may now substitute for some of the old phone or face-to-face contact. Many intergovernmental systems such as those involved in human services are mandated and thus tend to be developed without the time or effort made to develop the informal knowledge, trust, and recognition of the other actor's needs that characterizes voluntary sharing efforts. As a consequence, mandated intergovernmental systems have encountered many problems.

Conclusion

Overall, the degree of sharing has greatly improved over the last decade due to the development of hardware and software standards as well as the development of the Internet and other forms of networking such as intranets. Moreover, organizations now view information as a strategic asset and are attempting to create enterprise-wide systems that make sharing easy. These same developments also create the possibility for easier sharing between organizations.

Nevertheless, our review shows that technological developments are not sufficient to assure successful sharing. Interorganizational and intergovernmental sharing of IT resources are important and complex phenomena that have received little attention by researchers. Successful sharing requires that each organization understand the other's organization, its culture, and its procedures. The system developers need to understand the processes of the system's end users and this takes deep knowledge that can only be obtained by open sharing by the end users and/or participant observation. The importance of understanding processes is true whether system development is

Copyright © 2006, Idea Group Inc. Copying or distributing in print or electronic forms without written permission of Idea Group Inc. is prohibited.

intraorganizational as well as interorganizational and this point has emphasized by organizations such as Wal-Mart according to a recent story (Schrage, 2003):

He [Wal-Mart's then-CIO] told me that before Wal-Mart's people actually write and deploy an app, they make the developers work in the job the app is being written to support. If Wal-Mart devices a new point-of-sale system, for example, software members have to spend time working the cash registers first.

The same need to achieve deep understanding of the processes exists in governmental interorganizational systems but the complexity is far greater given the fact that the developers are "outsiders" and will not be trusted to the same extent as organizational members. There are additional problems such as the fact that the vendor IT employees who actually develop the systems often have high turnover rates. Likewise, the end users at the bottom of the human services system are often private sector employees such as employees of nursing homes funded by the Medicaid program or child welfare workers in nonprofit human service organizations who minister to abused children. In short, both the designers and end users in today's "intergovernmental information systems" in the human services area are often private sector employees! The governmental role in human services is to provide funding and oversight, and to integrate the information in order to evaluate services and provide for accountability to the public.

The federal-state nursing home, child welfare, and work training cases suggest that in order to be effective in achieving its goals, an intergovernmental information system needs to have clear definitions of key concepts and measures understood by all parties. Secondly, the sharing must mesh well with the personnel and funding systems and rewards of the organization. Examples like the Chicago police department and WIA cases suggest that the personnel systems and funding of the organizations involved must reward sharing or, no matter how advanced the hardware and software involved, the system is likely to be ineffective due to overt or passive resistance (e.g., the provision of missing or poor quality data).

Most importantly, governments need to gather a variety of types of information and not rely on one source (particularly if this single source is likely to have a bias). In many of the examples cited previously, it is clear that qualitative information such as through interviews with direct service providers is key to detecting problems concerning sensitive issues such as harm to patients. Despite the tremendous growth in digitized information systems, qualitative data is absolutely essential to obtaining deep knowledge about important issues but the role of qualitative data has been largely neglected by information researchers whose enthusiasm for digital systems has blinded them to need for other types of information. In my view, the gathering and use of qualitative data should be an integral part of information management if it is to be effective.

In the last decade, sharing of IT resources among governments has become a common goal but there is little serious empirical research concerning this phenomenon in the public sector. In attempting to identify sources for this article, I relied heavily on a few sources such as studies done by the Center for Technology in Government, the U.S. General Accounting Office, and news articles from Governing Magazine, and Govern-

Copyright © 2006, Idea Group Inc. Copying or distributing in print or electronic forms without written permission of Idea Group Inc. is prohibited.

ment Technology. We need in-depth research that follows sharing relationships through time. We need to develop some common measures to determine the degree of sharing and integration. We also need in-depth comparative qualitative studies to examine the impact of variation in key aspects of sharing such as the degree of symmetry of costs and benefits. Much of the literature such as that of the CTG (e.g., Dawes and Prefontaine, 2003) has focused on "collaborative efforts" that are voluntary in nature and often do not involve highly sensitive information. The most challenging and important sharing is often that which is mandatory and related to highly sensitive information such as performance evaluation. In short, the exploration of IT sharing needs a great deal of development.

References

Agranoff, R., & Lindsay, V. A. (1983). Intergovernmental management: Perspectives from human services problem-solving at the local level. *Public Administration Review, 43*(3), 227-237.

Bamberger, W. J. (1995). Sharing geographic information among local government agencies in the San Diego region. In H. J. Onsrud, & G. Rushton (Eds.), *Sharing geographic information* (pp. 119-137). New Brunswick, NJ: Center for Urban Policy Research, Rutgers University.

Boddy, D. (2000). Implementing interorganizational IT systems: Lessons from a call centre project. *Journal of Information Technology, 15*, Part 1, 29-38.

Bozeman, B., & Bretschneider, S. (1986). Public management information systems: Theory and prescription. *Public Administration Review, 46*, 475-487.

Brown, M. M., & O'Toole, L.J. (1998, October). Implementing information technology in government: An empirical assessment of the role of local partnerships. *Journal of Public Administration Research and Theory, 8*(4), 499-525.

Buston. J. C. (2003, September 9). Personal communication (e-mail).

Carr, N. G. (2003). IT doesn't matter. *Harvard Business Review, 81*(5), 41-49.

Center for Technology in Government. (1999). *Reconnaissance study: Developing a business case for the integration of criminal justice information.* Retrieved January 6, 2002, from http://www.ctg.albany.edu/projects/doj

Center for Technology in Government. (2000). *Building trust before building a system: The making of the homeless information systems.* Albany, NY: Center for Technology in Government. Retrieved December 7, 2000, from http://www.ctg.albany.edu/projects/hims

Clemons, E.K., & Knez, M. (1988). Competition and cooperation in information systems innovation. *Information & Management, 15*(1), 25-35.

Cox, B. (2001, June 28-29). *Reengineering business process to integrate the delivery of human services in North Carolina.* Prepared for the Conference on Modernizing Information Systems for Human Services, Reston, VA.

Copyright © 2006, Idea Group Inc. Copying or distributing in print or electronic forms without written permission of Idea Group Inc. is prohibited.

Cuddy, J. (2001, June 28-29). *Re-engineering the approach by which the federal government approves and monitors the creation of state human services information systems.* Paper prepared for the Conference on Modernizing Human Information Systems for Human Services, Reston, VA. Retrieved October 10, 2003, from http://www.gao.gov/special.pubs/GAO-02-121/ap4.pdf

Daniels, A. (1997, September). The child support computer meltdown. *Governing Magazine.* Retrieved August 7, 2003, from http://www.governing.com/archive/1997/sep/child.txt

Dawes, S. S., Pardo, T. A., Green, D. E., McInemey, C. R., Connelly, D. R., & DiCaterino, A. (1997). *Tying a sensible knot: A practical guide to state-local information systems.* Albany, NY: Center for Technology in Government. Retrieved August 12, 2003, from http://www.ctg.albany.edu/publications/guides/tying

Dawes, S. S., & Prefontaine, L. (2003). Understanding new models of collaboration for delivering government services. *Communications of ACM, 46*(1), 40-42.

Derthick, M. (1975). *Uncontrollable spending for social services.* Washington, DC: The Brookings Institution.

Douglass, M. (2003, August). One-stop shopping. *Government Technology.* Retrieved August 6, 2003, from http://www.govtech.net/magazine/story.php?id=62033

Finn, D. E. (2004, December 9). *The information systems forum: Or, how to find 2,699 co-conspirators and learn a lot without really trying.* Retrieved January 20, 2005, from http://blog.deborah.elizabeth.finn.com/blog/_archives/2004/12/9/267365.html

Garris, M. (2003, September 19). Personal communication (e-mail).

Gormely, Jr., W. T., & Weimer, D. L. (1999). *Organizational report cards.* Cambridge, MA: Harvard University.

Government Without Boundaries. (2003). *Government without boundaries: A management approach to intergovernmental programs. Executive Summary.* Retrieved September 7, 2003, from http:www.gwob.gov/report/executivesummary.html

Hahm, S. D., Szczypula, J., & Plein, L. C. (1995). Barriers to information sharing in state agencies: The case of the Texas General Land Office. *International Journal of Public Administration, 18*(8), 1243-1267.

Hall, K. A. (2001, December). Intergovernmental cooperation on erp systems. *Government Finance Review, 17,* 6-13.

Hall, K.A. (2003, September 5). Personal communication (via e-mail).

Hibbard, J. (1997). Pull technology fights back. *Computerworld, 31*(21), 25-35. Retrieved November 3, 2003, from http://firstsearch.oclc.org/WebZ/FTFETCH?sessionid=sp01sw07-34329-dmkspdt3-zc43m7:entitypagenum=32:0:rule=990:fetchtype=fulltext:dbname=ABI_INFORM_FT:recno=8:resultset=7:ftformat=ASCII:format=T:isbillable=TRUE:numrecs=1:isdirectarticle=FALSE:entityemailfullrecno=8:entityemailfull resultset=7:entityemailftfrom=ABI_INFORM_FT

Institute of Electrical and Electronics Engineers. (1990). *IEEE standard computer dictionary: A compilation of IEEE Standard computer glossaries.* New York: .

Copyright © 2006, Idea Group Inc. Copying or distributing in print or electronic forms without written permission of Idea Group Inc. is prohibited.

Kumar, K, & Dissel, H. G. (1996). Sustainable collaboration: Managing conflict and cooperation in interorganizational systems. *Management Information Systems Quarterly, 20*(3), 279-300.

Landkamer, J. (2003). Minneapolis-St. Paul's metro gis: A collaborative effort overcomes obstacles to data sharing. *GeoWorld, 16*. Retrieved August 1, 2003, from http://www.geoplace.com/gw/2003/0303/0303.mnn.asp

Landsbergen, D., Jr., & Woken, G., Jr. (2001). Realizing the promise: Government information systems and the fourth generation of information technology. *Public Administration Review, 61*(2), 206-220.

Laudon, K. C. (1974). *Computers and bureaucratic reform: The political functions of urban information Systems*. New York: John Wiley.

Laudon, K. C. (1986a). *Dossier society*. New York: Columbia University.

Laudon, K.C. (1986b, January). Data quality and due process in large interorganizational record systems. *Communications of the ACM, 29*, 4-11.

Meier, J., & Sprague, Jr., R. H. (1991). The evolution of interorganizational systems. *Journal of Information Technology, 6*, 184-191.

Nathan, R., & Ragan, M. (2001, June 28-29). *Federalism and its challenges*. Albany, NY: The Nelson A. Rockefeller Institute of Government. Prepared for the Conference on Modernizing Information Systems for Human Services, Reston, VA. Revised October 9. Retrieved August 19, 2003, from http://www.rockinst.org/publications/general_institute/NathanRaganInfSys.pdf

National Association of State Chief Information Officers (NASCIO). (2003, July). *Concepts for integrated justice information sharing*. Version 1.0. Retrieved October 28, 2003, from https://www.nascio.org/hotIssues/EA/ConOps2003.pdf

National Electronic Commerce Coordinating Council. (2001, December). *Interoperable, practical and remarkable e-government: When, why and how to put reusable xml components to work with Web services*. Retrieved December 16, 2004, from http://www.ec3.org/

Newcombe, T. (2000a, April). Technology helps states transform welfare. *Government Technology*. Retrieved October 1, 2003, from http://www.govtech.net/magazine/gt/2000/apr/feature/feature.phtml

Newcombe, T. (2000b, June). The art of knowledge sharing. *Government Technology*, 19-20 & 49.

Norton, P. (1995, June). A Minnesota consortium finds benefits in sharing. *Government Finance Review, 11*, 43-45.

Onsrud, H. J., & Rushton, G. (1995). *Sharing geographic information*. New Brunswick, NJ: Center for Urban Policy Research, Rutgers University.

O'Shea, T. C. (1998). Analyzing police department data: How and how well police officers and police departments manage the data they collect. In L. J. Moriarty, & D. L. Carter (Eds.), *Criminal justice in the 21st century* (pp. 83-98). Springfield, IL: Charles C. Thomas.

Copyright © 2006, Idea Group Inc. Copying or distributing in print or electronic forms without written permission of Idea Group Inc. is prohibited.

Payton, F. C. (2000). Lessons learned from three interorganizational health care information systems. *Information & Management, 37*, 311-321.

Perlman, E. (1998, September). TechnoTrouble. *Governing Magazine*. Retrieved September 23, 2003, from http://www.governing.com/archive/1998/sep/tech.txt

Perlman, E. (2001, August). Playing together. *Governing Magazine*. Retrieved October 1, 2003, from http://www.governing.com/archive/2001/aug/egshare.txt

Perlman, E. (2003, January). The anti-silo solution. *Governing Magazine*. Retrieved October 28, 2003, from http://www.governing.com/archive/2003/jan/it.txt

Peterson, S. (2003, April). The XML factor. *Government and Technology*. Retrieved October 20, 2003, from *http://www.govtech.net/magazine/sup_story.php?magid=8&id=42782&issue=4:2003*

Pinkard, J. (2003, September 5). Director of Information Technology, Mecklenberg County, North Carolina. E-mail communication.

Porter, M., & Millar, V.E. (1985). How information gives you competitive advantage. *Harvard Business Review, 63*(4), 149-160.

Poulakos, J. (2002). Giving communication a push. *American City & County, 117*(17), 12.

Ragan, M. (2003a). Building comprehensive human service systems. *Focus, 22*(3), 58-60.

Ragan, M. (2003b, January). Managing medicaid take-up. State University of New York. Federalism Research Group. Retrieved April 7, 2005, from http://www.rockinst.org/publications/general_institute/NathanRaganInfSys.pdf

Robinson, B. (2003, August). Mapping users plot new ways to share. *Federal Communication Week, 11*, 34-36.

Rocheleau, B. (1995). Computers and horizontal information sharing in the public sector. In H.J. Onsrud, & G. Rushton (Eds.), *Sharing geographic information* (pp. 207-229). New Brunswick, NJ: Center for Urban Policy Research, Rutgers University.

Rocheleau, B. (1996). Interorganizational and interdepartmental information sharing. In S.S. Nagel, & G. D. Garson (Eds.), *Advances in social science and computers* (Volume 4) (pp. 183-203). Greenwich, CT: JAI.

Rocheleau, B. (2002, March 25). *Information systems and accountability*. Paper presented at the 2002 Conference of the American Society for Public Administration, Phoenix, Arizona.

Rocheleau, B., & Wu, L. (2002). Public vs. private information systems: Do they differ in important ways: A review and empirical Test. *American Review of Public Administration, 32*(4), 379-397.

Schrage, M. (2003, September 15). Don't trust your code to strangers. *CIO Magazine*. Retrieved on September 24, 2003, from http://www.cio.com/archive/091503/work.html

Schwen, T. M., & Noriko, H. (2003). Community of practice: A metaphor for online design. *Information Society, 19*(3), 257-270.

Sherrill, A. (2001, June 28-29). *The capabilities of state automated systems to meet information needs in the changing landscape of human services*. Paper prepared

Copyright © 2006, Idea Group Inc. Copying or distributing in print or electronic forms without written permission of Idea Group Inc. is prohibited.

for the Conference on Modernizing Information Systems for Human Services, Reston, VA.

Swope, C. (2003, August). Common code. *Governing, 18*, 36-38.

Thomey, T. (2003). Senior Manager with Municipal GIS Partners, Inc. Interview (via telephone), August 14.

United States General Accounting Office. (2000, April). *Welfare reform: Improving state automated systems requires coordinated effort*. Washington, DC: GAO/HEHS-00-48.

United States General Accounting Office. (2002a, January). *Human services integration: Results of a GAO cosponsored conference on modernizing information systems*. Washington, DC: GAO-02-121.

United States General Accounting Office. (2002b, February). *Nursing homes: Federal efforts to monitor resident assessment data should complement state activities*. Washington, DC: GAO-02-279.

United States General Accounting Office. (2002c, February). *Workforce investment act: Improvements needed in performance measure to provide a more accurate picture of WIA's effectiveness*. Washington, DC: GAO-02-275.

United States General Accounting Office. (2003a, July). *Child welfare: Most states are developing information systems but the reliability of the data could be improved*. Washington, DC: GAO-03-089.

United States General Accounting Office. (2003b). *Geographic information systems: Challenges to effective data sharing*. Washington, DC: GAO-03-874T.

Vandenberg, R. (2003, September 5). Director of Communications Technology, City of Reno, Nevada. Personal communication (e-mail).

Weinman, L. (2002). *Dreamweaver 4: Hands-On Training*. Berkeley, CA: Peachpit.

Key Concepts

- Communities of practice
- Foreign keys
- Information silos
- Interoperability
- Metadata
- Push-and-pull technologies
- Shallow solutions (to sharing)
- XML

Copyright © 2006, Idea Group Inc. Copying or distributing in print or electronic forms without written permission of Idea Group Inc. is prohibited.

Discussion Questions

1. What do you believe are the most important obstacles to information sharing? How would you overcome these obstacles? Are there legitimate reasons why organizations refuse to share information? Discuss.

2. What do the terms "push" and "pull" systems refer to? Are you aware of any organizations that employ these mechanisms to share information with other governmental or non-profit agencies?

3. If you were designing a new system to serve citizens of a particular entity (you may specify the entity), what steps could you take to maximize sharing of information with other units both within the organization and external to the organization?

4. What are some of the causes of data quality problems with intergovernmental systems? What steps can be taken to deal with these issues?

Exercises

1. Select an organization (or a department within the organization) with which you are familiar and inventory the sharing of information they do with other organizations. Analyze this information. How much of the sharing is voluntary sharing and how much is mandated by law or necessary due to funding imperatives?

2. One of the goals of modern IT management is to abolish information silos in organizations and, in some cases, between organizations. Analyze either an organization (or a subunit within an organization such as a department) or a policy area (e.g., criminal justice) and try to identify whether there remain interoperability and silo problems. To what extent has the development of modern IT solved these problems?

3. Read the case study of the homeless information system by the Center for Technology in Government and do a stakeholder analysis of the needs and wants of the major actors. The Case study is available at Center for Technology in Government: Building Trust Before Building a System: The Making of the Homeless Management Information System (http://www3.ctg.albany.edu/static/usinginfo/Cases/bss_case.htm). What factors are most likely to cause resistance to sharing?

Copyright © 2006, Idea Group Inc. Copying or distributing in print or electronic forms without written permission of Idea Group Inc. is prohibited.

Chapter XI

Information Technology, Accountability, and Information Stewardship

Introduction

Over the past two decades, there has been an unabated demand for more accountability from public organizations. The term "*accountability*" is employed with a variety of different meanings. I view the purpose of these assessments as responsiveness to public or external values. As Meijer (2001, p. 234) points out, accountability is a practice rather than an outcome. The essence of accountability is the idea that an individual or organization "is held to answer for performance" and public organizations should be responsive to the values of their customers (Meijer, 2001, p. 259). For example, we do not want to allow professors to over-concentrate on research and ignore teaching, so new many states require that institutions prove that students are achieving their goals, such as obtaining jobs and passing professional examinations. In other words, the purpose of accountability mechanisms is to achieve responsiveness to external values held by the public and the constituencies served by public agencies. Although most accountability reports tend to emphasize quantitative performance measures, qualitative assessments of the adequacy of performance may also be used to achieve responsiveness.

Copyright © 2006, Idea Group Inc. Copying or distributing in print or electronic forms without written permission of Idea Group Inc. is prohibited.

Public organizations of all kinds are being asked to prove that they are achieving their goals. There is a consensus that measurements that emphasize inputs and processes are inadequate to ensure that governmental organizations are being responsive to public values. The underlying assumption behind this consensus is that employees will tend to act in their own self-interest and not be responsive to public values, unless their performance is monitored. The focus on measurement of outcomes may provide public organizations with information they need to improve services as well as to provide positive information to the public about their accomplishments.

Information systems now play a central role in the movement to achieve the desired responsiveness. Many data elements that are aimed at measuring outcomes are being added to information systems so that the public and oversight bodies can determine if governmental organizations are doing a good job. The increasing sophistication and power of computerized information systems allows the tracking of hundreds or even thousands of indicators that would have been difficult or impossible in previous eras. Information systems now enable the general public to view these outcome measures on the World Wide Web. Thus performance indicators are easier for the public to access than earlier attempts at providing accountability. Information technology is also being employed to provide ways of holding agencies accountable by attempting to control for contextual factors that have often made it difficult to measure success in the past. Likewise, information technology is also beginning to be used to detect both fraud and errors in information provided by agencies that may frustrate efforts to achieve respon- siveness to public values. Wholey (1994, p. 16) states that programs need "relevant" and "feasible measures" that can be obtained at "reasonable cost" in order to correct weaknesses and perform better. Gormely & Weimer (1999, p. 143) found that organiza- tional report cards, though initially resisted, brought about positive change in the performance of certain health organizations. Quantitative assessments may help to provide guidance to public employees on what works and what does not work and thus allow them to focus on superior methods and better allocation of time (Gormely & Weimer, 1999). They may also prevent self-serving behaviors such as over-concentration on personal goals, laziness, and waste of resources.

E-Reporting

The new element in accountability is the ability to increase access via the posting of governmental information on the World Wide Web. This movement has been referred to as "e-reporting" by Lee (2004). Prior to the World Wide Web, there was probably a very small percentage of the population who would be willing to go to local governments or their libraries to access publications that provided information on governmental perfor- mance, if that information even existed. Since people can now access accountability reports from the convenience of their own homes, the existence of e-reporting increases the likelihood that they will access this information.

There have been several other interrelated forces that are pushing governments to gather and report more performance information. The Federal Government Performance Results

Copyright © 2006, Idea Group Inc. Copying or distributing in print or electronic forms without written permission of Idea Group Inc. is prohibited.

Act (GPRA) was passed in 1993 and requires that every Federal agency prepare and submit annual reports with performance information (Lee, 2004, p. 13). The movement has extended to other levels of government because the Governmental Accounting Standards Board (GASB) has encouraged all levels of government to gather and report performance data. The GASB began to call for *Service Efforts and Accomplishments* (SEA) reporting in the 1980's (Fountain et al., 2003). Another force that influenced this movement, according to Fountain et al., was the emphasis on managing for "results" spurred by the works of Drucker, Hatry, and Osbourne and Gabler. In recent years, there have been rating systems, such as those published by Governing Magazine, that assess states and local governments on their management practices, and these publicly disseminated grades have created an incentive on the part of many professional managers to do well.

The e-government movement has created the expectation and imperative that virtually all significant accountability information be provided online in easily accessible form on governmental Web sites. The hope is that making this information available online will have some important and very desirable effects and the Cyberspace Policy Research Group (CPRG) has formulated hypotheses concerning them (Wong & Welch, 2004):

- Web technology diffusion into public organizations increases organizational openness, which exists to the extent that organizations provide comprehensive information about their attributes and maintain timely communications directly to key public audiences.

- Openness in public organizations produces an expansion of Web-oriented "new knowledge management" practices likely to result in consolidation of managerial authority.

The term *transparency* has become a popular way to describe governments that provide accountability information online. The 5th Annual Mercatus Report assesses how well government agencies "inform the public" using the following criteria (McTigue et al., 2003, p. 3):

Reports should be accessible, readable, and useable by a wide variety of audiences, including Congress, the administration, the public, news media, and stakeholders. If a report fails to make significant achievements and problems apparent, benefits to the community arising from agency activities will remain secret to all but a few insiders, and citizens will have no real opportunity to indicate their approval or disapproval.

By making performance information accessible, it is expected that over the long haul the performance of governments will improve. Thus the responsiveness of governments to the values of the public will increase and the goals of "e-democracy" will be furthered.

Putting evaluative information on the Internet has become fairly common as we saw in the chapter on e-government. Indeed, e-reporting has become so common that there have arisen systematic analyses to rate the quality of the reporting systems of governments.

Copyright © 2006, Idea Group Inc. Copying or distributing in print or electronic forms without written permission of Idea Group Inc. is prohibited.

Figure 1. Mercatus Center report criteria

Transparency
1.   Is the report easily accessible via the Internet and easily identified as the agency's Annual Performance and Accountability Report?
2.   Is the report easy for a layperson to read and understand?
3.   Are the performance data valid, verifiable, and timely?
4.   Did the agency provide baseline and trend data to put its performance measures in context?

Public Benefits
5.   Are the goals and objectives stated as outcomes?
6.   Are the performance measures valid indicators of the agency's impact on its outcome goals?
7.   Does the agency demonstrate that its actions have actually made a significant contribution toward its stated goals?
8.   Did the agency link its goals and results to costs?

Leadership
9.   Does the report show how the agency's results will make this country a better place to live?
10. Does the agency explain failures to achieve its goals?
11. Does the report adequately address major management challenges?
12. Does it describe changes in policies or procedures to do better next year?

Source: Adapted from McTigue, M., Wray, H., & Ellig, J. (2004). Mercatus Report. 5th Annual report scorecard: Which Federal agencies best inform the public? Mercatus Center, George Mason University, April. Retrieved July 14, 2004 from http://www.mercatus.org/governmentaccountability/category.php/45.html

The Mercatus Report (McTigue et al., 2003, p. 5) is the best known of these efforts and uses the major criteria listed in Figure 1 in assessing openness of governments.

The concept of accessibility also pertains (Mctigue et al., 2004, p. 15) to other desirable characteristics such as breaking the report into downloadable sections (and multiple formats) if it is large, as well as the inclusion of contact information if anyone has questions concerning the report. It is instructive to look at the Mercatus Report's comments on specific government agencies concerning transparency to observe in more depth what kinds of actions the authors regard as providing for good transparency. The U.S. Department of Labor scored highly and the positive comments include the fact that the accountability report is linked to the home page and is downloadable in "multiple PDF documents" (Mctigue et al., 2004, p. 30), and they praise the report for being "clearly written" and providing trend data since 2000, although it notes that more trend data concerning key problems would have improved it. By way of contrast, the report critiques the Department of Health and Human Services (DHHS) for the obscurity of its report, stating that they could only find the report on the department's Web site via a "circuitous trip." They also down rated the report for not providing information about the quality of the data of any of the 600 measures it uses. The Mercatus Report acknowledges that an agency's actual performance may not be correlated directly with the Mercatus score. This brings up the issue of the quality of the data, and the Mercatus Report states that the agency should indicate how confident it is in the quality of the data and, to ensure transparency, it should make the data available for independent verification.

The National Center on Educational Outcomes (NCEO) assesses the reports done by state education agencies and has been assessing their Web sites for outcome informa-

Copyright © 2006, Idea Group Inc. Copying or distributing in print or electronic forms without written permission of Idea Group Inc. is prohibited.

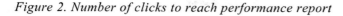

Figure 2. Number of clicks to reach performance report

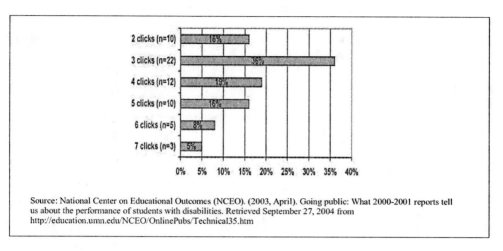

Source: National Center on Educational Outcomes (NCEO). (2003, April). Going public: What 2000-2001 reports tell us about the performance of students with disabilities. Retrieved September 27, 2004 from http://education.umn.edu/NCEO/OnlinePubs/Technical35.htm

tion since 2001. Some of their evaluative criteria refer to the organization of the information on the Web site. Among the criteria they used to assess a state Web site were the following: (1) Are there clear "words" or links to get to the report on the agency Web site?; (2) How many clicks did it take to get from the agency's home page to the disaggregated results?; and (3) What is the proximity of data on special education to the data for all students? Although the outcome information was within three clicks for a slight majority of Web sites, there was substantial variation (NCEO, 2003):

NCEO found that most states did have the outcome data on students with disabilities within two clicks of the data for all students. The attention given to clear and quick linkages to reports such as these emphasizes the importance of structuring Web sites as I discuss in the chapter on e-government. In terms of substance, much of the NCEO focus is on the needs of students with disabilities and their report analyzes how states report on the percentage of students with disabilities participating in the general assessments. This is a key issue, as it is well-known that the scores of states can be substantially improved by excluding a large percentage of these students (NCEO, 2003). They found substantial variation in the percentage of students excluded in this way, ranging from 30% in West Virginia to over 97% in Kansas. A major point that NCEO's analysis raises is that performance reports should allow users to look at disaggregated results for particular groups, such as the disabled.

Lee (2004) has reviewed a wide range of federal, state, and local e-reporting efforts. He distinguishes between public reports aimed at informing the public and others aimed at such purposes as marketing and internally-focused reports. Lee developed a set of 29 questions to assess the quality of the reports. His criteria overlap those of the Mercatus reports quite a bit including easy accessibility to information from the Web site as well as the presence of a full, complete, and timely set of performance indicators. However, he includes a special section on the use of "e-government technology" that includes the

Copyright © 2006, Idea Group Inc. Copying or distributing in print or electronic forms without written permission of Idea Group Inc. is prohibited.

following questions (Lee, 2004, p. 15): (1) Does it include two-way, interactive features that allow people to obtain "self-directed, more in-depth information?; (2) Are the contents of the Web site searchable?; (3) Is it easy or hard to share the report with another interested person?; (4) Is there an "electronic tear-off coupon" to encourage readers to share their opinion of the report?; and (5) Does it include options for public involvement of the citizen and/or option to be informed of similar reports in the future? Lee's (2004, p. 23) empirical study of reports found that federal agencies were far more likely to have online reports (70%), compared to state (2%), county (8%), and city (22%) governments, and he notes the reason is due to the existence of the Federal Government Performance Review Act law. Other pertinent findings include the fact that the reports on average required a 10th grade reading level.

The City of Chicago (Welch, 2004) has implemented a system called ICAM (Information Collection for Automated Mapping) which divides the city into 279 beats and provides detailed statistics and maps for meetings between a police department representative and residents interested in reducing crime in their areas. The Web site associated with the system also allows residents to send e-mail to the police concerning crime in their area, leading to arrests. The system was supported by a centralized technology unit and the beat officers, and as it became more heavily used, it required more interaction between these two different groups of officers. The system shows the possibilities of disaggregating information down to specific neighborhoods in an easily understandable format of maps combined with real life meetings with officers that could bring more responsiveness to the public.

The possibilities of e-reporting appear to be exciting in terms of their potential for increasing public knowledge of governmental performance. However, this author has come across little data on how heavily such e-reports are being accessed or used by the public. The lists of most heavily used or desired governmental pages generally have not included e-reports on governmental performance. For example, Dykhouse (1997) reports that for the San Diego Web site, the police department auction, the tel-net access to the local public library, and photos of the San Diego lifeguards were among the most popular pages. General reports on governmental performance are fairly abstract and are likely to have limited interest to the public. It would seem to me that the most heavily used reports would be those that tell about the performance of organizations and programs that directly influence their own and their children's well-being, such as the quality and outcome measures for schools and health organizations. I will explore the use of these in depth below.

Information Stewardship and Assessing Data Quality

The value of e-reports depends on the quality of the data. The accepted position of information management professionals is to view information as an asset (or public good) that has to be taken care of just as any other asset. *Information stewardship* has been defined by the Center for Technology in Government (CTG, 1998) as the focus on the quality, integrity, security, reliability, documentation, and maintenance of information. CTG (1998) holds that information has to be protected and "nurtured."

Copyright © 2006, Idea Group Inc. Copying or distributing in print or electronic forms without written permission of Idea Group Inc. is prohibited.

The importance of quality is central to e-reporting. Everyone knows the meaning of the phrase "Garbage In-Garbage Out" but there is evidence that governmental organizations do not give much systematic attention to ensuring the quality and integrity of their non-financial data. According to Williams (2002), a study by the National Association of State Auditors, Comptrollers, and Treasurers found that only eight out of 50 states had some form of performance measurement verification. Williams (2002) goes on to note that only six out of nearly 250 local government auditors were planning to verify performance measures. Likewise, the Texas State Auditor Department (2001) found large percentages (over 50%) of the measures used by departments were unreliable. Moreover, they found that the trend was for increasing unreliability. They found a lack of documentation to show that the indicators had been collected consistently and accurately. They found that sometimes agencies substituted their own measures for ones that were supposed to be collected without obtaining approval for the change.

There are numerous other examples of inaccurate data in governmental systems that report on program performance. The U.S. General Accounting Office (GAO) (2000) found that in fully 20 out of 24 agencies studied, the Chief Financial Officers expressed only "limited" confidence in their performance data. A 2001 GAO audit of the annual costs of the Forest Service's Time Sales Program found that it was impossible to determine costs, because the Forest Service's data were "totally unreliable." One of the major causes of the unreliability was the fact that Forest Service employees made changes to previously reported cost information without creating any audit trail of the changes. Likewise, GAO (2001) found that staff time was charged based on the amount budgeted rather than actual time spent and that this practice made it impossible for the Forest Service to provide useful and reliable data. Indeed, a study of data quality (Divorski & Scheirer, 2001) across a wide variety of federal agencies "concluded that they provided limited confidence in their data" and that most agencies were not undertaking actions to "compensate for the lack of quality data."

Data quality problems appear to be especially troublesome in intergovernmental programs. For example, the GAO found that data measuring the success of the JOBS (Job Opportunities and Basic Skills) program for welfare recipients was inaccurate (U.S. General Accounting Office, 1993b). GAO studied four states and concluded that they had little incentive to improve the data due to the costs that would be involved. Moreover, the states questioned the need for change. Their reasoning was as follows: since the Department of Health and Human Services (DHHS) had been accepting the data that was reported, there was no need to make any changes (U.S. General Accounting Office, 1993b). DHHS stated that they did not have the resources, such as travel funds, to give close scrutiny to the state data.

Medicaid data has also been shown to be extremely inaccurate and many DHHS personnel did "not believe the data states were submitting" (U.S. General Accounting Office, 1993a, p. 4). The study found that states submitted Medicaid data that were inconsistent with information in other federal reports. For example, Medicaid data for Hawaii in 1990 reported fewer than 200 aged or disabled enrollees, compared to more than 13,000 such enrollees according to Social Security Administration data. There are also discrepancies of billions of dollars between different HCFA reports and the discrepancies have been worsening through time. The GAO reported that HCFA officials could not

Copyright © 2006, Idea Group Inc. Copying or distributing in print or electronic forms without written permission of Idea Group Inc. is prohibited.

explain why these differences existed, nor were officials from the states involved even aware of these differences. GAO found that HCFA did not use error tolerance standards and had not penalized states if they did not report complete and accurate information (U.S. General Accounting Office, 1993a, p. 7).

What is to be done? Williams (2002) outlines a *program for verification* of performance information. He suggests that it begin with an identification of the most important indicators (e.g., those that receive the most public scrutiny). Every step in the collection and calculation of the indicators should be documented and checked to see if the numbers provided in reports can be recreated. Conformance with formal definitions of measures is necessary and it should be determined if adequate controls exist to ensure consistent reporting. Acceptable error rates may be established—for example, the State of Texas employs a plus or minus 5% error allowance. Sampling should be used and the source documents checked for accuracy.

The Center for Government in Technology (1998) discusses tools used to assure data quality. In addition to the auditing tools are *data cleansing* tools. One technique is parsing—the breaking up of data into the smaller units so they are more useful. A very simple example is that you do not want to combine two fields that are more useful to separate (e.g., first and last name) into one field. Another step is computerized checking of data against other "known" databases. As I discuss in the chapter on ethical issues, computer-matching is heavily used by human services to verify data for people receiving governmental benefits. Computers can also be employed to ensure consistency of items within the same record and to check against rules for the database such as searching for data that does not conform to valid data ranges. Data should only be captured once to ensure the consistency of information. High quality data are essential if e-reports are to achieve the goal of making government more responsive.

Cleansing of data is also important for *data warehousing,* which has become an important tool for the detection of fraud and abuse in Medicaid payments (Newcome, 1999). Newcome describes data warehousing as follows:

The typical warehouse consists of data stores, which are databases containing the operational data; data conversion and extraction procedures that translate and convert disparate data into a standardized format; the warehouse itself, which is a powerful database optimized for online analytical processing; business-intelligence tools, which provide the interface for users to query data-warehouse information; and warehouse-administration tools for monitoring and support.

The Medicaid program generates such a large amount of data that computer analyses not only help it to detect fraud and abuse but also help make better informed decisions about reimbursement rates. Cleansing of data is essential especially when several different units are involved in its collection (Faden, 2000) because the data often turn out to be inconsistent. Miner (2000) reports that one insurance company discovered that an unexpectedly large percentage of claims were being assigned to "broken legs" and, upon investigation, it was found to be due to the fact that the broken leg code was the default code used by the company.

Copyright © 2006, Idea Group Inc. Copying or distributing in print or electronic forms without written permission of Idea Group Inc. is prohibited.

Meta-data, "data about data," are important to e-reporting. When data are put on the Internet, readers should be provided with as complete a description of the information contained in reports as possible. For example, government should provide meta-data that includes the source of the information, the date(s) when the data were collected, the accuracy of the data, information about the characteristics of specific data fields, accessibility, copyright issues, and contact information in case of questions about the data. Geographic information system (GIS) data have a number of specific fields that are expected to be a part of their meta-data, such as the geographic area covered and the projection system employed.

Data inventories are now maintained by some organizations as part of their strategy to manage data. Levitin & Reynolds (1998) state "most corporations have no idea what data they have, which data are most critical," and "the sources of critical data." The situation is similar in many governments as end users create data sets in programs such as Excel, Access, and Word that are not well-documented and are unknown to others in the organization. The movement to enterprise-wide view of information systems is leading to the centralization of many shared data items, but it is likely that end users will continue to create shadow data sets.

Although the use of formal techniques such data cleansing, meta-data, and data inventories may help achieve and maintain quality data, Orr (1998) posits the hypothesis based on open systems theory that use is the key to achieving and maintaining data quality. Orr argues that in order to correct incorrect data, someone has to spot the inconsistency between the data and "the real world," report the inconsistency, and then the organization has to take steps to ensure the inconsistency is corrected. Of course, as I noted above, some inconsistencies can be caught by the computer through logic checks. But more subtle biases and problems will not be caught by these mechanical methods. Orr's insights have some important implications. Data that are not used will "atrophy" and tend to have serious problems. An anecdote about the mental health department of one state illustrates the principle of atrophy. A social worker at a local community mental health center looked at all of the data that their agency sent the state and federal governments and decided that much of it was not worthwhile and was not being used so (s)he stopped sending the data. It took the higher levels of government more than two years to notice that anything was missing.

Orr (1998) supports a *"use-based" audit* in which attention is given to what data are being used and compare that with the information being collected. Such an audit would raise useful questions such as "if data are not being used and are not viewed as useful, then should the data be gathered?" Yoon, Aiken, & Guimares (2000) also found that the "most fundamental aspect of data quality" concerns whether the information is "useful to the user community." The atrophy theme was raised long ago by Ackoff (1967) in a classic article entitled "Management Misinformation Systems" in which he argues that the less we understand something, the more information is gathered about it. Ackoff emphasizes the tendency to gather too much information and states that key functions of information managers are evaluation, filtration, and condensation of information. Orr, too, notes the problem of information overload is real today. If too much data is gathered that is not used, then it is not surprising that organizations such as the Texas Audit Office would find increasing unreliability of data.

Copyright © 2006, Idea Group Inc. Copying or distributing in print or electronic forms without written permission of Idea Group Inc. is prohibited.

Figure 3. Agency approaches for verifying and validating performance information

Fostering Organizational Commitment and Capacity for Data Quality
1. Communicate support for quality data.
2. Review organizational capacities and procedures for data collection and use.
3. Facilitate agencywide coordination and cooperation.
4. Assign clear responsibilities for various aspects of the data.
5. Adopt mechanisms that encourage objectivity and independence in collecting and managing data.
6. Provide responsible staff with training and guidance for needed skills and knowledge.

Assessing the Quality of Existing Data
1. Build data quality assessment into normal work processes, including ongoing reviews or inspections.
2. Use software checks and edits of data on computer systems and review their implementation.
3. Use feedback from data users and other stakeholders.
4. Compare with other sources of similar data or program evaluations.
5. Obtain verification by independent parties, including the Office of the Inspector General.

Responding to Data Limitations
1. Report data limitations and their implications for assessing performance.
2. Adjust or supplement problematic data.
3. Use multiple data sources, with offsetting strengths and limitations.
4. Improve the measure by using another source or new methods of measurement.

Building Quality Into the Development of Performance Data
1. Use prior research or analysis to identify data elements that adequately represent the performance to be measured.
2. Gain agreement among internal and external stakeholders about a set of measures that are valid for their intended uses.
3. Plan, document, and implement the details of the data collection and reporting systems.
4. Provide training and quality control supervision for all staff who collect and enter data, especially at local levels.
5. Provide feedback to data collectors on types of error found by data checks.
6. Use analytic methods and transformations appropriate for the data type and measure being reported.

Source: Adapted from U.S. General Accounting Office. (1999, July). Performance plans: Selected approaches for verification and validation of agency performance information. Washington, D.C.: GAO/GGD-00-139, p. 6.

Divorski & Scheirer (2001, p. 86) outline a broad four-pronged strategy for producing quality data: (1) The organization must demonstrate a commitment and develop a capacity to assure data quality; (2) An organization must assess the quality of its existing data; (3) The organization must respond to data integrity problems; and (4) The organization must build quality into any new data-gathering efforts. A summary of the approaches used by the GAO and other federal agencies is contained (U.S. G.A.O., 1999) in Figure 3.

The GAO study's first point is the key one—does the organization demonstrate a commitment to gathering quality data? This point agrees with empirical research by Klein (2000) who states that there must be strong formal and informal incentives, such as pay increases and promotions related to detection of errors. The GAO study also makes the point that reports should provide information on the limitations of the data as well as what verification procedures have been employed. Klein, Goodhue, & Davis (1997) did an

Copyright © 2006, Idea Group Inc. Copying or distributing in print or electronic forms without written permission of Idea Group Inc. is prohibited.

experimental study that showed that when error detection is made a goal with incentive rewards, they improve their ability to detect problem data. However, Klein (2000) found that there was "little evidence that organizations were using formal incentives" to improve user error detection.

Accountability and Empirical Studies of Performance Measurement

In the previous pages, I have outlined some of the key concepts that I have found in the IT and e-government literature about accountability and information stewardship. However, the IT field has given little attention or even shown awareness of crucial organizational and political factors that affect the validity and reliability of information. As I will show, there is substantial reason to expect that performance measures that draw attention and affect decision-making will be subject to manipulation and corruption. Moreover, it is not clear that typical data cleansing mechanisms will be able to recognize or deal with these problems. Therefore, it is important for both IT people and generalist managers to be aware of these errors and biases in data due to organizational processes such as goal displacement, manipulation, and cheating. These insights are based on a synthesis of literature concerning the use of quantitatively-oriented accountability measures including the following areas where performance measurement has been extensively applied and sometimes used to make important "high-stakes" decisions concerning budgets and personnel rewards:

1. School Testing for K-12 grades: School testing has been the subject of numerous accountability efforts including many of the most sophisticated in terms of measurement instruments used. It is common for these test results to be made available on the Internet.

2. Higher Education Performance Measurement and Budgeting: States have implemented performance measurement and performance budgeting systems in the higher education area that, in some cases, have been used for many years.

3. Performance budgeting at the state and local government levels. The Governmental Accounting Standards Board (GASB) has sponsored in-depth case studies of performance measurement that have given attention to the validity and reliability of the data as well as problems encountered in the implementation effort.

4. Other areas where quantitative assessments were used and efforts were made to assess the impact of these measures on the organization and attention is given to the possibility of dysfunctional consequences.

Copyright © 2006, Idea Group Inc. Copying or distributing in print or electronic forms without written permission of Idea Group Inc. is prohibited.

Accountability Systems and the Informal Organization

There have been some important predecessor works that establish the importance of the informal systems and other organizational variables that influence the success of performance measurement systems. Roethlisberger and Dickson's (1939) work revealed the existence of informal group norms that inhibit attempts to achieve greater productivity. Workers were afraid that achievement of very high performance levels for a period of time would lead to the institution of higher expectations that would result in a never-ending "ratcheting" up of work demands. The message of the Roethlisberger and Dickson's study is that organizations need to assess the impact of measurement and reporting systems on the behaviors of agencies being assessed. How are they responding to the assessment? Blau's *The Dynamics of Bureaucracy* (1963, p. 44) brought attention to the dysfunctional consequences of statistical records. He detailed several examples of *goal displacement* including employment officers focusing on getting jobs for those clients who were most likely to be successful (creaming). Goal displacement refers to the phenomenon in which employees become focused on doing well on the performance measures rather than the ultimate goals and thus the measures may be unexpected and often negative consequences. Blau also found outright cheating and falsification of records. The difficulty of developing performance measures is reflected by the fact that Blau (1963, p. 287) admits that after observing the problems of statistical record keeping systems, he attempted to develop "a measure of performance quality" but found that he "could not construct a valid one." The works of Roethlisberger-Dickson and Blau pose serious questions to all those who would develop measurement systems as to how they would deal with problems of goal displacement and cheating. Yet very few measurement systems give serious attention to these behaviors.

Ginsberg's (1984, p. 3) article entitled "The Dysfunctional Side Effects of Quantitative Indicator Production" argues that the use of quantitative indicators produces "insidious side effects" that "distort the data" and make it difficult to benefit from the information at all. She provides examples from mental health to show how program staff and administrators often manipulate the system in order to help clients but confound those trying to assess performance by placing too much confidence on statistics. For example, mental health organizations charged patients for a partial hour by a psychiatrist at a high rate so that they could actually see a social worker at a much cheaper rate with the psychiatrist retaining a small fee for supervising the case. She gives other examples of how mental health staff manipulated administrative rules, both for idealistic and self-serving reasons. These steps include staff altering their time reporting. Staff assumed that outside monitors wanted them to spend lots of time in direct service to clients and so therapists scheduled longer appointments (Ginsberg, 1984, p. 5).

Ginsberg presents several hypotheses concerning these dysfunctional consequences including one borrowed from Campbell (1979, p. 85) which states that "the more often a quantitative social indicator is used for decision making, the more subject it will be to corruption pressures" and likewise "the more likely the indicator will be to corrupt the processes it is intended to monitor." Ginsberg (1984, p. 9) concludes by stating that these manipulations are often well intentioned but result in a "cumulative white lie effect" that distorts information systems data especially as "data are aggregated." Ginsberg's article elicited several responding articles in the same journal issue and they all concurred about

Copyright © 2006, Idea Group Inc. Copying or distributing in print or electronic forms without written permission of Idea Group Inc. is prohibited.

the ubiquity of the manipulation of data. For example, Smith (1984) relates how special education staff manipulated the use of tests and other data in order to provide services to youths in need even if they did not meet the formal criteria for special education. One of the important points of Ginsberg's and these other studies is that manipulation and fudging may sometimes be aimed at the achievement of positive purposes such as citizen- or consumer-oriented goals and are not necessarily selfish in nature. Thus formal computerized data often cannot be trusted and informal perceptions sometimes need to be employed to detect and correct for these deficiencies. Fisher and Kingma (2001) studied two disasters, the Challenger explosion and mistaken shooting down of the Iranian Airbus to emphasize the importance of using "intuition" to compensate for problems in the data.

Goal-Setting for Performance Indicators: How are Goals Set and What Impact Does This Have?

There are major differences in how quantitative assessments are initiated, developed and implemented. Who selects the measures to be used? What is the process for setting goals? And what impact do these processes have on outcomes? Based on my review of the literature, there is a tendency for measures to be initiated, developed, and implemented by top executives (e.g., the governor or city manager), by legislators, and oversight staff. For example, the case studies conducted by General Accounting Standards Board (GASB) researchers of various state and local governments consistently reveals a top-down development effort dominated by high-level officials in the initiation and implementation phases. Often there is little involvement of middle and lower staff at these stages. Examples include the State of Texas in which development of performance measures was led by the governor's office and agencies had "little input into the development of them" (Tucker, 1999, p. 4). In the City of Tucson, the city manager established an extensive number of workload measures in 1993 but Bernstein's interviews (2002a, p. 4) found that there had been little "buy-in from middle and lower levels of management." Bernstein (2002a) points out that involvement of lower levels is critical because they generate the data. In Oregon, the governor established benchmarks as the basis for setting budgeting priorities but they had not been developed "to reflect the programs of the state agencies" (Fountain, 1999, p. 6). In school testing, the Tennessee system was developed due to a court case and was aimed at helping poor schools but also to avoid "the redistribution of existing resources" (Ceperly & Reel, 1997, p. 134). When the Tennessee implementation threatened probation to schools doing poorly and the state also proposed that tests be used in teacher evaluations, the organization representing teachers took actions to keep teachers' records "closed to the public" (Ceperly & Reel, 1997, p. 136). These examples show that involvement of those low in the hierarchy tends to occur after the system has been developed. In Kentucky, the governor offered a "blunt bargain" to the heads of colleges and universities that they would have to support his performance funding or he would cut budgets (Burke & Serban, 1988, p. 32). Tennessee's higher educational performance measurement system began in 1979 at the initiative of the governor, but through the years adjustments have been made that reflect some of the objections of the universities and colleges (Banta et al., 1996, p. 24).

Copyright © 2006, Idea Group Inc. Copying or distributing in print or electronic forms without written permission of Idea Group Inc. is prohibited.

In Missouri, the legislature initiated the effort towards developing assessment and accountability measures and the Coordinating Board for Higher Education led the effort (Burke & Serban, 1998). In addition to achieving responsiveness to the values of the board, one of their rationales was to head off a legislative-mandated system so that colleges and universities would have quantitative measures that would be more to their liking (Burke & Serban, 1998, p. 38). In a recent conference on financing of higher education, Missouri was cited as the state that has had the most successful performance funding system and its relative success has been attributed to the fact that it was developed by the state higher education board with consultation with colleges and universities in "the least threatening way" (Schmidt, 2002a, p. A21).

To summarize, most initiations and implementations of quantitative assessments tend to be dominated by legislatures, executives and their staffs. When planning for the purchase of new IT systems, one of the general rules for achieving a successful implementation is to do a stakeholder analysis to be sure that end users are buying into the new system. However, in making decisions about what data to collect, many organizations do not seek the input of the employees who will be most affected by these decisions. I hypothesize that the greater the degree of participation there is on the part of those to be assessed in the initiation and implementation of quantitative measurement systems, the less resistance employees are likely to take against the system once it is in effect.

High Stakes Performance Measures

Quantitative assessments can have many types of links to decision-making. They can be tightly linked to high stake decisions that affect both the overall organization's survival (e.g., put on probation lists with potential threat of cutbacks or even shutdown) and individual reward systems with direct links to pay increases. On the other hand, performance systems can be used strictly for feedback purposes with no direct link at all to decisions. Governments using the latter approach may argue that employees desire to do an effective job and feedback of relevant information is sufficient to provide them the incentive and means to achieve improvement.

The most prominent area of *high stakes* linkage of quantitative measurement has been K-12 educational testing that is being used by many states (and soon, the federal government) to make important decisions about students, teachers, and schools (Barksdale & Thomas, 2000). In Illinois, schools whose students fail to pass the tests can be put on a warning list and the state has had "the authority to close schools" since 1991. But the State "has been slow to put any teeth into its accountability system" (Banchero, Olzewski & Dougherty, 2001). In Prince Williams County, Virginia it is reported by Bernstein (2002B) that information from performance measures has been used to make important budgetary decisions. The County's general rule is that programs "with low strategic importance and poor performance" are to be cutback but those with great strategic importance and poor performance may get increased funding. In the Prince Williams' case, police received budget increases despite poor performance on the measures because they effectively argued that they had lower levels of staffing than

Copyright © 2006, Idea Group Inc. Copying or distributing in print or electronic forms without written permission of Idea Group Inc. is prohibited.

comparable local governments while a substance abuse program with poor results had its funding cut (Bernstein, 2002b).

In most of the other policy areas I have studied, there has been reluctance to use quantitative measures for making decisions with major impacts on organizations and individuals. For example, a recent review of state higher education performance budgeting found that in most states, it had affected less than "3% of the state's funds for public colleges" (Schmidt, 2002). Indeed, in many states, the initiation of performance budgeting for higher education is tied into positive reward systems in which institutions compete only with their own past performance for positive incentive funds. For example, in Tennessee performance funding was used successfully in 1979 to attract new funding for higher education from the Tennessee legislature (Banta et al., 1996, p. 42). Banta et al. (1996) note that if performance funding were to be withdrawn, then it is likely that the funding supplement would also disappear, so there is an incentive to keep the performance system. However, the degree of impact of such systems may lessen through time. In Kentucky, the original plan was to have "two-thirds of any new state appropriation" go for current activities while the remaining percent would be split with 60% for equity and 40% for performance (Burke and Serban, 1998, p. 33). But the amount of budget contingent on performance totaled only $3.3 million in 1996 and even less in later years (Burke and Serban, 1998, p. 33). The most striking case is South Carolina, which originally planned to directly link budget increases to performance measures, but has "as a practical manner" allocated just "3% of state funds based on performance" (Schmidt, 2002, pp. A20-A21). Asworth (1994, p. 4) notes in his study of performance-based funding in Texas higher education that massive redistributions of money would take away from the "predictability" needed to do institutional planning.

Streib and Poister (1999) used a mail survey to senior officials in municipalities to study the functionality of performance measurement systems and these officials reported positive impacts in terms of employee focus on organizational goals as well as service improvements. However, in the GASB studies of state and local governments, the immediate and apparent impacts of performance measurement were generally indirect and subtle. For example, Fountain (1999, p. 13) reports that the State of Oregon sometimes used the measures to raise questions but they played only a small part in the decisions-making process:

There is also the knowledge that performance measures are only one input or tool in the decision process and that they may even make the decision-making process more complex.

In the City of Portland, Oregon, performance indicators were used to "raise questions" and improve the dialog among managers and staff about city programs and what they should accomplish but again appeared to have little budgetary impact (Bernstein, 2002c, p. 2). In the City of Austin, Epstein & Campbell (2002a, p. 9) report that "performance measures are seen as supplementing the political process" and did not make the process less political.

The expectation that performance budgeting or other quantitative measures can or should be linked in a mechanical way to have a large impact on budgeting and personnel

Copyright © 2006, Idea Group Inc. Copying or distributing in print or electronic forms without written permission of Idea Group Inc. is prohibited.

matters appears to be naïve. In the program evaluation literature, a similar expectation existed during the 1960's but evaluators found that their evaluations usually had little immediate impact on budgeting decisions for programs. Patton (1978, p. 265) wrote that decision makers receive "multiple sources [of information] all the time" and thus evaluation represents only one small piece of the picture. Patton (1978, p. 268) goes on to say that the key factor is whether evaluation can produce information that "reduces uncertainty and provides direction" for positive change. Indeed, as noted above concerning police services in Prince Williams County (Virginia), poor performance led to increased funding because of the crucial nature of the service and the fact that the police chief was able to show that they had fewer resources than comparable agencies.

An alternative approach to the direct link to budgeting is to put primary emphasis on reporting the information so that the public, legislators, as well as agency staff can see the results but not to have any direct link to high stakes decisions. This approach is one that has been characterized as the "*shine the light approach.*" The assumption of the approach is that universities and colleges will want to look good (or at least not bad) on these measures and will take actions to improve their performance even if there are no direct sanctions to force them to do so. In Illinois currently, the overseeing agency requires that each department in colleges and universities set expected student learning outcomes and measure these on the basis of an "end of program assessment." They are then to report on how well they are doing on attainment of these goals and what measures they are taking to rectify any problems. The shine the light process attempts to get those being assessed to make their own changes. The proposed process in Illinois would encourage universities themselves to take difficult steps such as setting up a "watch list" and suspending enrollment for programs that are not doing well.

If one assumes that organizations and their employees want to do a good job, then measurement may have very positive impacts if the information is useful. Gormley & Weiner (1999, p. 159) cite examples of where systems with no direct links to decisions have had an impact. They give an example that occurred in one school in Tennessee with the desire to improve performance led to high-performing teachers sharing information so the low-scorers could improve. Geron (1991, pp. 142-143) studied the use of a positive incentive program in Illinois nursing homes and found that staff cared more about how many "stars" (the index to represent quality in the report card system used by the state) received than the small monetary reward incentives provided. Gormely & Weimer cite research that "surgery report cards" on mortality rates for surgeons used by New York State led to a decrease in "risk-adjusted" mortality rates, partly due to shift of surgeries to less risky surgeons but also due to the fact that poorly-rated surgeons examined their procedures and compared them to more effective surgeons.

The shining the light approach may be more likely to work quickly when there is competition among those providing services. For example, in the hospital case, the information on mortality rates is likely to filter down to potential patients, and physicians who do poorly are likely to lose patients. But Bohte & Meier (2001, p. 181) argue that private sector contractors are likely to have even weaker norms against cheating than they found in the public sector. Hatry (1999, p. 162) suggests that there are non-monetary

Copyright © 2006, Idea Group Inc. Copying or distributing in print or electronic forms without written permission of Idea Group Inc. is prohibited.

Figure 4. Nature of link to decisions

		Direct Link	Indirect Link
Nature of Stakes	**High Stakes**	Much manipulation	Moderate manipulation
	Low Stakes	Moderate manipulation	Little Manipulation

incentives that can be used to reward good performance including recognition awards and giving managers flexibility in exchange for more accountability.

I propose that the nature of the link to decisions and the degree of impact that these links have on tangible rewards for the organization and its employees will be correlated with the amount of manipulation that can be expected to occur. Thus high stakes performance measures are most likely to result in manipulation and need the most attention.

Accountability and Time Factors

In studying the impact of quantitative measurement systems, one of the most striking factors involves the time perspective. The Mercatus Report encourages public organizations to maintain the same measures over a period of time because that allows us to observe trends in performance. Moreover, it is likely that an accountability system will have to be in effect for several years in order to have a marked impact on organizational processes. However, change of leadership and administration is frequent and often leads to an abandonment of the accountability mechanism. For example, Burke & Modarresi (2000, p. 432) found that by 1999, 16 states had adopted performance funding for higher education but four states "had already abandoned their efforts." In some cases, this abandonment was due to a change in administrations but in other cases, as in Kentucky, the governor changed from funding higher education by results to funding by incentives (Burke & Serban, 1998, p. 33). Gaither (1998, pp. 89-90) cites research on higher education that finds that "externally imposed quality assurance measures encourage a short-termism" that can harm quality and lead to "cynicism and resistance" on the part of those being measured.

Lee and Burns (2000, pp. 48-49) studied performance measurement in state budgeting from 1990 to 1995 and found that more than half of the states "backslid." They conclude that use of performance measurement is not achieved in a "straight line of progression." Gabris (1986, p. 13) provides several examples of use of quantitative measures in state and local government to show that top officials often call a mechanism a failure if it does not produce quick results. It is not surprising that workers opposed to a performance measurement system will pursue a "Wait Strategy" as described by Epstein & Campbell (2000b, p. 31) from one of their interviews in their study of performance measurement in Louisiana:

Copyright © 2006, Idea Group Inc. Copying or distributing in print or electronic forms without written permission of Idea Group Inc. is prohibited.

One of the things that we had a problem with is that everybody thought that it would go away. 'Hold your breath, make a book, and put it on the shelf and that will be the end of it'.

Halachmi (1998) has also emphasized the importance of providing sufficient time for performance measurement efforts to succeed. Glaser (1991, p. 315) argues that performance measurement in local government needs to show that it is "more than an exercise" and has real impact on budgeting and resource allocation. Otherwise, he argues that employees will play a "waiting game" for the performance measurement effort to fade.

Ginsberg (1984, p. 7) argues that the dysfunctional consequences are more likely in situations where change is rapid and major. She argues that low-level personnel affected by change need time to adapt but decision makers are "unaware of the street-level world of adaptations" that occur in response to their quantitative controls. In order to survive and to have impact on organizational processes, the measures will likely have to develop a constituency beyond those initiating the effort. The mere fact that measures are gathered for a long period of time does not necessarily guarantee that they will have impact. Organizational information systems are replete with data that are not used. Collection of data elements is often initiated by some stimulus but they continue to be collected long after interest in them ceases.

Performance Reporting and the Nature of the Comparisons

All performance measures require that some form of comparison be made in order to judge how good performance is. The nature of the comparisons can have an impact on the response of those being assessed. If they accept both the indicator(s) used and the comparison(s) as valid, then resistance to use of the measures is likely to be less.

There are many possible kinds of standards for comparison. One common practice is for the oversight organization to establish targets and standards for judgment of performance. For example, Kentucky (Koretz et al., 1996, p. 3) has set a long-term goal that "each school should be able to have all of its students" at the "proficient level"—a goal that many teachers and administrators view as unobtainable. Illinois' law requires that each school must have half of its students reach certain standards or they will be put on a warning list if they fail two years in a row (Banchero, 2001). Such standards are a result of aspirations to high performance but nevertheless they can be unrealistic and may be unfair. For example, McCorkel Fine Arts Academy in Chicago four years ago had only 7% of its students meet national norms on the Iowa Tests (Olszewski, 2001). Today 27% are meeting these norms and 35% are meeting Illinois test standards. By way of contrast, other schools beginning at the same low level have not made equivalent progress but they are all lumped together in the same category. Thus their principal argues that they have made significant improvements and that the goals cannot be met so quickly (Olszewski, 2001).

In higher education, performance is often compared against national or statewide norms (Serban & Burke, 1998, p. 166). Any comparison with other state institutions that is

Copyright © 2006, Idea Group Inc. Copying or distributing in print or electronic forms without written permission of Idea Group Inc. is prohibited.

unfavorable can be challenged on the grounds that the comparison is unfair. In Illinois, it has been the practice to do program reviews on similar programs during the same year in order to facilitate inter-institutional comparisons. However, institutions that do poorly on these comparisons can point to potentially valid reasons as to why their scores should be lower such as differences in the nature of the programs that may require higher costs for one than the other. For example, institutions with large number of urban students who are part-time point out that their students will take longer to graduate than the time provided for by the standards. Institutional researchers at universities are adept at discovering and pointing out what they view as inequitable comparisons. This might be referred to as the "*apples and oranges*" problem in accountability efforts.

As a consequence, there is a clear preference in higher education for non-competitive approach to performance budgeting (Serban and Burke, 1998). Rather, institutions and programs are compared against their own previous performance and such comparisons are more difficult to refute, though factors outside the control of colleges/universities may still be blamed. This contrasts with the willingness of states to compare all K-12 performances by the same standards. This difference between the treatment of the K-12 and higher education may be due to the perceived greater complexity of higher education.

Although states are willing to compare different schools throughout the state to each other, many states prefer to use their own state tests for determining performance in K-12 rather than use national tests. The use of their own tests is often justified by the argument that it enables them to tie the test more directly to the curriculum and goals they are pursuing. However, use of their own state test also gives the state control over determining what performance is acceptable and reduces the likelihood that their performance will be compared directly with other states and reflect unfavorably on them. In general, organizations prefer to retain as much control as possible over how their own success is defined.

In areas such as health and K-12 education, there exists a substantial body of research that can help determine what would constitute high-level performance for a particular area. However, research can often result in conflicting results that make reliance on empirical research difficult because it can shift so quickly. Statistical techniques can be used to control for factors that make each program and individuals' performance unique. Thus the existence of sophisticated multivariate statistical techniques combined with the power of today's computer systems may overcome objections about comparing "apples with oranges." If the research is consistent and demonstrates that it is controlling for contextual factors, it may exert a strong impact on organizations and their personnel. The health area is a good example of where empirical research on mortality rates for certain types of surgery has achieved some acceptance and impact (Gormely & Weiner, 1999).

One approach that appears to have interesting possibilities is the calculation of the amount of "value added" by systems, organizations, and individual employees. The value-added approach in assessing K-12 education in Tennessee is complex and based upon a "mixed model methodology" (Sanders, Saxton & Horn, 1997). It employs a "repeated measures, multivariate response analysis" (Sanders, Saxton & Horn, 1997, pp. 137-139) in which each student serves as his/her "own control." The method, according to its authors, allows for calculation of the amount of *value added* by schools and teachers while controlling for socioeconomic factors and overcomes problems such as

Copyright © 2006, Idea Group Inc. Copying or distributing in print or electronic forms without written permission of Idea Group Inc. is prohibited.

missing data that frustrates more traditional statistical approaches (Sanders, Sexton & Horn, 1997, p. 138). The focus on gains in the method has raised criticism that the standards may be set too low but the system developers argue that if each school provides gains at least equal to the national norms every year, then the level of performance should be good (Sanders, Sexton & Horn, 1997, p. 161). The authors admit that the system provides summative information only and is based on a standardized test (the Tennessee Comprehensive Assessment program) that assesses only five subjects. They argue that it can be used as the basis for developing formative information (Sanders, Sexton & Horn, 1997). The statistical explanation of the value-added approach is complex but its authors claim that school officials have accepted the results and found them useful. They note that some objections have been raised by some "affluent schools" that showed relatively small gains (Gormely & Weiner, 1999, p. 85). Sanders, Sexton & Horn (1997, p. 161) argue that the value-added methodology can "shrink the variability" in performance among schools by lifting up those schools that have been lower in the past.

One study ranked business schools using a value-added approach and found big differences from rankings by other methods such as those employed by Business Week and U.S. News & World Report (Gormely & Weiner, 1999, p. 69). The top ten in value-added terms included institutions such as Wake Forrest and the University of New Mexico that did not make the top 20 in the more traditional rankings (Gormely & Weiner, 1999, p. 69.) A major advantage of the value-added approach is that it gives "equal opportunity" to organizations at any existing level of performance to perform very well. In most performance systems, organizations whose level of performance has been high in the past continue to dominate. However, the long-term success of value-added approaches depends on whether the employees and organizations can make use of the information and have enough impact on the level of performance. Since many key factors that affect performance are outside the control of schools and teachers, the performance of organizations that begin at a very low level may be limited even if there is good value-added progress.

To summarize, the nature of the comparisons is one of the crucial decisions that organizations must make in developing reporting systems. Without comparisons, it is impossible to judge the meaning of performance information. The most common approach appears to be to compare governments to their own past performance. The advantage of this approach is that it has obvious face validity for practitioners and the public alike and it is easily understandable. Other approaches primarily involve using statistical techniques to develop systems of assessment that make for fair comparisons that are accepted by those to be monitored. These statistical approaches rely heavily on computerized analysis.

How Many Performance Indicators Should be Gathered?

Performance measurement systems vary greatly in the degree to which they attempt to develop a comprehensive set of measures that cover all-important aspects of organizational goals. There are some assessments that focus on just a small number of indicators, sometimes a single measure. Coe (2001, p. 29) summarizes the position against using a

Copyright © 2006, Idea Group Inc. Copying or distributing in print or electronic forms without written permission of Idea Group Inc. is prohibited.

single indicator, stating that it is a "dubious position" and that "governmental services are far too complex for such simplistic analysis." I hypothesize that goal displacement and other forms of "manipulating" the system are more likely when concentration is focused on a very small (e.g., 1 or 2) number of indicators. Recently, Van Thiel & Leeuw (2002, p. 272) argue that "the fewer the number of indicators used, the more difficult it becomes to get an accurate measure of performance."

However, there are also problems with using a large number of indicators. First of all, gathering and analyzing such a large amount of information contributes to high costs and time burdens on staff. Also, when a large number of indicators are used, they need to be weighted or by default, they will all be equal in weight and no single indicator will be worth much. Coe (2000) criticizes systems that fail to employ weights and also those that use weights but fail to provide a rationale for them.

Moreover, use of multiple indicators that pull employees in different directions can cause strains on employees. Ridgeway (1956) cites an air force study that showed that when only one indicator was emphasized that the squadrons were able to concentrate on that indicator and respond to the demand for improved performance albeit with some slacking off on other areas. Consequently, a composite performance indicator system was introduced that combined measures emphasizing very different aspects of performance without giving the squadrons greater means to achieve them. The result was that the squadrons suffered from tension, morale problems, and apathy. Ridgeway (1956) argues that it is in these kinds of situations involving a "ratcheting up" of expectations that informal norms restricting efforts are likely to develop as a survival device among workers when they consider the measurement system unfair and unrealistic.

In K-12 school testing, emphasis is placed on standardized tests that usually cover a small number of areas and neglect some significant curriculum components. Critics charge that such standardized tests ignore more creative and higher-level forms of education and skills. Some standardized tests such as those employed by the State of Kentucky do include open-ended components such as "performance events," and portfolios that represent an attempt to get at these higher-level skills (Koretz et al., 1996, pp. 2-3).

State governments are large and complex and many states are collecting numerous indicators of performance. For example, Tucker (2002a, p. 12) reports that the State of Texas collects 10,000 measures "of which 3,000 are labeled "key performance indicators." It is not surprising that barriers to the use of the Texas indicators mentioned by interviewees included concerns about "narrowing the number of measures," "finding the correct number of units of measures," and "the cost of collecting the data" (Tucker, 2002a, p. 22). Epstein and Campbell's (2002c, p. 27) study of the State of Iowa reports that one agency began with 32 indicators for 11 programs but "wound up with 100 measures." Epstein & Campbell go on to say that this agency has not been able to identify "the key measures" and that the information system limitations have affected their development. In Iowa, as in most states, the emphasis (mandated by the Department of Management in the Iowa case) is on results-oriented, not process, measures. The State of Louisiana, according to Epstein & Campbell (2000b, p. 23), has more than 6,000 indicators but hopes the number will drop down to 5,000.

In higher education, many performance-based systems began with a fairly large number of indicators but there has been a secular trend to reduce these down to a small number. For example, South Carolina (Schmidt, 2002) began with 37 measures to assess colleges

Copyright © 2006, Idea Group Inc. Copying or distributing in print or electronic forms without written permission of Idea Group Inc. is prohibited.

and universities but plans to reduce these to a set of 14 measures. Burke and Modarresi (2000) argue for an intermediate number of indicators because too few ignore important priorities while too many "trivialize" important goals. Layzell (1998, pp. 105-106) outlines some of the key reasons for keeping the number of indicators small: (1) If many indicators are used, the value of them as a means of setting priorities is lost; and (2) Use of multiple indicators such as improved access to colleges and higher graduation rates are in conflict with one another.

Layzell's analysis points to an important alternative in development performance measures. Performance systems may be aimed at emphasizing specific strategic priorities rather than a comprehensive assessment of all areas of performance. In higher education, the use of a smaller number of indicators to set priorities is the trend. This method aims to ensure that those being monitored are responsive to external values. In higher education, performance measures have concentrated on matters such as graduation rates, access, retention, and undergraduate education but have given little or no emphasis to research. Since it is clear that most universities and colleges already give high priority to research, the narrowness of the higher education indicators can be interpreted as an attempt to intentionally use goal displacement by emphasizing teaching-related measures to offset what is perceived to be an informal bias towards research. In effect, they may assume that any new goal displacement caused these performance measures is merely offsetting existing goal displacement towards research.

One of the suggestions that Divorski & Scheirer (2001, p. 86) make to deal with data limitations is to use multiple data sources with offsetting strengths and limitations. This is, in essence, the idea of triangulation—a well-known concept in social science data-gathering. However, the tendency in most accountability movements is to desire a clear and specific numerical index that can be used to distinguish in a clear manner between successful and unsuccessful organizations. The use of multiple sources and acknowledgement of data limitations would create ambiguity and discretion in the making of judgments and may not please those seeking decisive judgments for accountability purposes.

In short, there is no easy "best practice" that can be used to decide how many or what performance indicators to choose. Such decisions will need to be based on the priorities of the decision-makers, an assessment of the costs and benefits of gathering the information, and assumptions on how government employees will respond to these measures.

Perceived Validity, Reliability and Legitimacy

It is not an easy task to develop a valid measure of performance. Coe (2001) recently graded report cards used by various governmental organizations with respect to their validity and comparability. Coe (2001, p. 2) assessed validity based on how well the measures "measured what they claimed to," whether weights were assigned, and whether measures were factor analyzed. He gave about 18% of the report cards a grade of A, 38% B, and the remaining 44%. Coe (2001, p. 29) concluded that most report cards do not "explain the rationale for how they weight the items." Coe also argues that report cards need to remain stable in order to maintain comparability for measuring change over time.

Copyright © 2006, Idea Group Inc. Copying or distributing in print or electronic forms without written permission of Idea Group Inc. is prohibited.

It appears that many performance measures are not formally tested for validity and reliability. In certain areas such as K-12 education, there exists a substantial amount of research that allows for checking new instruments against those that have been found to be valid. For example, Rand Institute researchers compared performance on the Texas Assessment of Skills (TAAS) used by the State of Texas and found that gains on the TAAS diverged greatly from the measures obtained when compared to scores on the National Assessment of Educational Progress (NAEP). The NAEP is usually considered the "gold standard" (Klein et al., 2000, p. 3) for the quality of its measurement of educational attainment.

The case studies by the GASB researchers found varying confidence levels in the validity and accuracy of the information used in their performance measures. There did not appear to be any formal attempts to determine validity, though many of the state and local governments did have audits for checking data quality. Epstein & Campbell (2000b, p. 24) in their case study of performance measures in Louisiana found several people who questioned the quality of the information and one respondent described the measures in a skeptical manner:

Executive planning staff said: 'We have indicators, and we try to do this with humor, that fall into categories like Greasy Pigs: These are indicators that change every year; perhaps the method of calculation changes. You can't get a real handle on it.' Orphans: that is the indicator where people say, 'I don't know where that information came from'.

In the City of Austin, Texas there were complaints from several staff about the practice of some departments changing indicators before enough time series was available to evaluate performance (Epstein & Campbell, 2002a, p. 22). In some cases such as Iowa, Epstein & Campbell (2002c, p. 26) found that central management staff are comfortable about the quality of most departments' data but certain departments (not named) "have serious concerns about data quality." In the State of Texas, Tucker (2000a, p. 20) reports that the Auditor's Office claims that 80% of their information is accurate. The GASB case study interviews were primarily conducted with top-level administrators and staff so they may not be obtaining the views of those lower in the organizational hierarchy. Also, accuracy is not the same as validity. We can accurately measure items but they may not be valid measures of organizational output from the perspective of those being assessed.

Most validity discussions focus on technical ways of determining validity such as whether an instrument predicts behavior or is correlated with existing instruments that have been determined to be valid. However, Patton (1978, p. 244) argues that practical program evaluation measures must have *face validity* so that "users can look at the items and understand what is being measured." This can also be equated with "legitimacy"— do those being assessed accept the measures? If instruments have face validity and legitimacy, they are less likely to encounter resistance. Gormely & Weiner (1999, p. 107) give an excellent example of what of the difference between technical and face validity for parents of school children. They cite a study that parents in certain school systems in North Carolina and California regarded information on staff, services, programs offered, graduation rates, number of advanced placements, and school environment as more important than standardized test grades. Their conclusion was that school admin-

Copyright © 2006, Idea Group Inc. Copying or distributing in print or electronic forms without written permission of Idea Group Inc. is prohibited.

istrators and journalists very much overrated parental interest in standardized test scores. This finding points out the importance of doing a careful needs assessment of the stakeholders and customers of a government rather than relying on assumptions.

In the higher education field, there is a preference by educators for qualitative measures (e.g., ratings by accreditation teams) over quantitative measures. Banta et al. (1996, p. 29) asked the persons chiefly responsible for compiling performance data in the Tennessee higher educational system to rate the performance indicators in terms of their overall quality and peer–judgment-related measures including accreditation were consistently rated the highest. Measures based on college student testing and other quantitative indicators such as retention and graduation goals were rated near the bottom. Similarly, these same quality and peer-oriented measures were also rated as higher in terms of effectiveness in "promoting improvement" (Banta et al., 1996, p. 29). According to Burke and Serban (1998), one of the problems with college-level tests for accountability is that students have low motivation to do well on these tests because they are not related to course grades or other individual incentives.

The Costs of Performance Measurement Systems

Hood et al. (1999, p. 27) point out that governments have made almost no attempt to measure the costs of performance monitoring systems and they cite evidence that (for Great Britain) more resources are spent on regulating government than privatized utilities. The formal costs of quantitative assessments are greatest in the early stages of development. Once they are developed, the cost of instruments may be low. For example, Gormely & Weiner (1999) cite the cost of the Tennessee K-12 assessment tool as less than 1/10 of 1% of the per-pupil expenditure and they argue that the costs are very reasonable. The issue of costs of gathering the information surfaced in several of the state and local government GASB case studies. For example, in the City of Tucson, Arizona, the "most frequent barrier" mentioned in interviews was the lack of "time to collect performance information" (Bernstein, 2002a, p. 4). In the same case study, one interviewee stated that the city had created many measures "but they had no value" and thus the burden of tracking performance became salient (Bernstein, 2002a, p. 6).

The calculation of costs of the systems is very difficult. For school testing, the cost per test may be low to purchase and process the test as in the Tennessee case but the amount of time spent by staff in preparing for tests and responding to their results can be enormous. For example, the surveys done by Koretz et al. in Kentucky found that 74% of school principals rated it as being "more than a minor burden" and 39% of middle school principals rated it as a "great burden" (Koretz, 1996, p. 9). Smith & Rottenberg (1991, p. 8) studied the impacts of external tests on elementary schools and found that the "most glaring impact is on instructional time"—that for every hour of testing, the teachers spent three hours in preparation and very little time was spent on "ordinary instruction." They also point out that "time is a fixed resource" and consequently schools "neglect material that external tests exclude" (Smith & Rottenberg, 1991, p. 9).

Copyright © 2006, Idea Group Inc. Copying or distributing in print or electronic forms without written permission of Idea Group Inc. is prohibited.

Does the Performance Information Provide Help Needed to Improve?

The current accountability systems focus on gathering outcome information since the achievement of good outcomes represents the bottom line of what agencies are trying to accomplish. However, it is crucial that the intended users of the measures be provided useful information that will enable them to improve and meet expectations. Bouckaert (1993) argues that functionality, validity, and legitimacy are all necessary if measurements are to be effective. As I have already described, there are few detailed examples of the use of performance data for improving services in the cases that we studied. Although Gormley & Weiner as well as Sanders, Saxton & Horn (1993) cite a couple of anecdotes about the efficacy and functionality of the TVAAS system, they don't provide empirical evidence that proves the positive impacts. Koretz et al. (1996) used surveys of teachers and principals to determine the impact of the Kentucky test system and reported that it was the "open response items" that were perceived as having the most positive impact (Koretz et al., 1996, p. 56). Koretz et al. (1996, p. 40) found that 58% of the teachers reported having spent a "great deal of time" improving instruction due to the test and 29% said they "focused a great deal on requiring more and harder work." And almost all teachers said they allocated more time to writing. These impacts certainly can be considered positive impacts. However, teachers also reported spending less time on art, social science, sciences, and reading (Koretz et al., 1996, p. 25). Moreover, Koretz et al. (1996, p. 41) found that 46% of the teachers reported that they focused their teaching "a great deal" on the material on the test. Indeed, schools and teachers have learned that the most effective way to improve performance is to "*teach to the test.*"

In the city and state studies by GASB, many of the impacts cited were general statements that the performance measures had been used directly or indirectly to make decisions. There are some cases cited in which information from the measures was used to make changes that were regarded as positive developments. For example, Prince Williams County (Bernstein, 2000b, pp. 16-17) found that their library costs were higher than other comparison counties so they cut costs in the library area and succeeded in reducing overall governmental costs. The County also reported that they shifted toward more spending to strategic areas. The satisfaction rate with services of the County's citizens increased from 65.5% in 1993 to 93.3% in 1998 but then fell back to 89.9% in 1999. Bernstein (2002b) said that there was no explanation provided as to why the statistically significant increases or decreases occurred. In many of the other case studies, reports of improved services as a result of performance measures tend to be vague. In some case, such as in Tucson, performance measures were found wanting (Bernstein, 2002a, p. 11):

Another interviewee said that during the...budget process, none of the Council's decisions were related to performance measures. Yet another interviewee said that he/she had not seen performance measures used for decision-making because performance measures do not indicate why things are happening *[emphasis added].*

Copyright © 2006, Idea Group Inc. Copying or distributing in print or electronic forms without written permission of Idea Group Inc. is prohibited.

In higher education, the use of performance indicators appears to have had modest effects at best. Missouri is the state in which performance measurement has had its longest sustained implementation. A recent assessment (Schmidt, 2002b) found some small discernible impacts such as increased monitoring of student progress but otherwise the impact has been minimal as Schmidt (2000b, p. A21) states:

...public colleges have made only marginal improvements, or even lost ground. And where public colleges have made progress, it is difficult to say with certainty that the existence of performance incentives brought about the improvements.

Employees fear the focus on the negative. In the Illinois case study, Tucker (2000c, p. 11) found that fear existed concerning the negative uses that would be made of performance measures:

There is a fear among some that performance measures illustrating deficiencies will result in punitive action against a department or program.

Sometimes the negative external publicity is justified as in the case in which the Illinois Department of Children and Family Services failed to correct problems in child abuse investigations revealed by its own performance measurement system (Tucker, 2000, p. 11). However, most organizations prefer to hide "their dirty laundry" and attempt to fix problems internally before any negative information is allowed outside. This fear of negative effects is likely to stimulate resistance and manipulation in response to accountability mechanisms.

The link between performance measure and improvement in services is not direct. It requires that employees take the information seriously and attempt to identify and then implement strategies that improve performance rather than finding ways to resist, manipulate, and "game" the performance measures. Performance measurement systems that only focus on results are referred to as "*black box*" evaluations. Over the past two decades, program evaluation has emphasized the need to gather information on inputs and processes as well as outcomes in order to provide useful feedback to organizations on how to improve their programs (Posavac & Carey, 1997, pp. 14-15 & p. 27). Consequently, if program personnel are to make use of the quantitative assessments, they have to do so through gathering their own process information and try to relate it to outcomes such as through contacts with those who are more successful.

Forms of Manipulating the System

There are many ways in which monitored employees respond that can frustrate and prevent the achievement of responsiveness to the values of the public. The best-known problems are goal displacement and creaming. Goal displacement refers to situations in which organizations overemphasize what is being measured in a way that is not responsive to the ultimate external goals. Creaming refers to the situation in which

Copyright © 2006, Idea Group Inc. Copying or distributing in print or electronic forms without written permission of Idea Group Inc. is prohibited.

organizations are selective in accepting customers who are most likely to make them look good on performance measures. In program evaluation literature, creaming constitutes the "selection threat" to validity (Campbell, 1968).

Since problems with goal displacement and creaming are so well known, one might assume that organizations would design performance measurement systems to avoid goal displacement. Indeed, the large number of indicators used by many state governments reflects in part the desire to avoid over-attention to any single measure. But new measurement systems appear regularly that neglect goal displacement and other forms of manipulation. For example, the Workforce Investment Act (WIA) is a program that Congress passed to unify the employment and training system and better serve job seekers and employers. WIA replaced the Job Training and Partnership Act (JTPA). But the manner in which the performance measures were developed created goal displacement, creaming and other problems. A study by the United States General Accounting Office (2002b, p. 15) found that many states were not registering many WIA participants due to concerns by local staff that they not "provide WIA-funded services to job seekers who may be less likely to get and keep jobs." Since the performance measures include the rate at which they gain and retain employment, the concern is legitimate. One of the performance measures is "earnings replacement rate" for dislocated workers who have lost jobs due to the movement of factories to other locations. GAO (2002b, p. 15) found many dislocated workers had earned high wages before losing their jobs and it would be hard to achieve a high replacement rate. Consequently, WIA agencies may be reluctant to serve them.

Although WIA was supposed to improve coordination, the performance measures concentrated on the assessment of individual programs and one of the consequences was that it caused competition among these programs and a reluctance to refer workers elsewhere (U.S. General Accounting Office, 2002b, p. 25). Furthermore, WIA performance measures only assess WIA-funded services but the so-called one-stop system is supposed to coordinate services for programs provided by other agencies. The U.S. General Accounting Office (2002b, p. 28) summarized its findings as follows:

The system's narrow focuses on program outcomes for a limited number of participants misses a key requirement of WIA to support the movement toward a coordinated system. In fact, the measures may focus the opposite—a siloed approach that encourages competition and limits their cooperation.

Some states are taking action on their own such as using regression analysis and using indicators of difficulty to compensate for the incentive to "cream" those most likely to succeed. Underlying the problems of the system is that WIA is a "high stakes game" and the state's future funding depends on its performance on these measures. The above case is an excellent example of how a performance measurement system could worsen performance.

The use of tests in K-12 for high stakes decisions clearly causes goal displacement in the form of teaching to the test. There is little disagreement about this fact and Gormely and Weiner (1999), who strongly support testing, admit its occurrence. However, Gormely and Weiner (1999, p. 144) argue that teaching to the test represents what they

Copyright © 2006, Idea Group Inc. Copying or distributing in print or electronic forms without written permission of Idea Group Inc. is prohibited.

call "honest cheating" in which organizations respond rationally to how they are being assessed and they argue that whether teaching to the test is good or bad "depends on whether the measure is a good surrogate for quality." For example, in schools that performed at low levels and have little discipline, the focus and incentive to pass tests may have a very beneficial impact. However, the magnitude of the teaching to the test effort in Kentucky was very large as Koretz et al. (1996, p. xiv) point out in their findings:

Despite educators' reports of reliance on broad improvements in instruction as a method for improving scores, relatively few expressed confidence that their own school's increases on KIRIS were largely the results of improved learning. About half of he teachers reported that increased familiarity and test-preparation materials had contributed a great deal to their score increases, while only 16% said that broad improvements in knowledge and skills had contributed a great deal.

If teaching to the test results in learning that could be generalized to other areas, then it could have a positive effect. However, the evidence is not promising. Koretz & Barron (1998, pp. xiv-xv) in a later study of the validity of the gains in scores in Kentucky found that the gains in KIRIS far exceeded Kentucky student performance on the NAEP test and Kentucky students' improvements on NAEP were similar to increases in the national average. They conclude that sponsors of new test assessments should "discount gains over the first years of the program" as likely to be due to what evaluators would call the testing effect in which students become familiar with test materials (Koretz et al., 1998, p. xvii). However, Koretz & Barron point out that they are not aware of any instances where sponsors of testing have taken such a step.

One of the other side effects of testing is that it leads to more testing in poorer schools than in better schools that generally exceed the state requirements. Both Herman & Abedi (1994) and McNeil & Valenzuela (2000, pp. 3-6) conclude that good schools don't have to modify their curriculum much while schools that start off low are more pressured to improve and consequently spend time on consultant and test-preparation materials that they can ill afford. Smith & Rottenberg (1991, p. 10) found that teachers expressed relief rather than pride when their students scored high. They also argue that teachers often repeated drills to prepare for tests because they mistook student errors due to lack of mastery but it was boredom that actually caused the errors (Smith & Rottenberg, 1991, p. 10). Koretz et al. (1996) also report that writing became emphasized so much in the curriculum in Kentucky that "some students became tired of writing" (Koretz, 1996, p. 28).

I found relatively few explicit examples of goal displacement in the state-local case studies but this lack may reflect the fact that the link between performance indicators and organizational incentives was tenuous at best. This supports my hypothesis that goal displacement is less prominent when little or no stakes are involved.

In addition to goal displacement and creaming, organizations are able to find other mechanisms to improve performance. Some are legal and may be referred to as manipulation while others are clearly cheating. In Kentucky, 37% of the principals and 52% of the teachers agreed that "improvements in performance were misleading because some schools aimed for poor performance in the baseline years" (Koretz et al., 1996, p. 17). In Kentucky, the test was administered in certain grades so there were reports of transfers

Copyright © 2006, Idea Group Inc. Copying or distributing in print or electronic forms without written permission of Idea Group Inc. is prohibited.

of good teachers to the fourth and eight grades because those were the grades in which testing was done (Koretz et al., 1996, p. 19).

Bohte and Meier (2000, pp. 176-177) found that students' exemptions from the tests in Texas K-12 tests were correlated with increases in test scores and that "only 30% of the variance" in the percent of students tested was due to legitimate reasons. Koretz (1998, p. 17) found that some schools retain students in the "non-accountability grades" in order to improve scores. Haney (2000) also reports that the number of students in Texas classified as taking special education doubled between 1994 and 1998 and there was also an upturn of people taking GED tests to avoid the TAAS.

Outright cheating where teachers helped students with answering the questions also appears to have occurred to a significant degree. In Kentucky, surveys (Koretz, 1996, p. xiii & pp. 46-48) found that more than one-third of the teachers reported that "questions had been rephrased during test administration" and 43% said that certain items were occasionally read and 15% stated that "answers were occasionally written by the teacher."

Jacob & Levitt (2002) have used multivariate techniques to detect cheating in Chicago schools on standardized tests and found that cheating occurs in 4% to 5% of elementary schools annually and this cheating was done when only mild incentives existed to cheat. Moreover, Jacob & Levitt's analysis of cheating primarily focuses on instances where teachers suggested or filled in answers for students and did not measure other forms of cheating such as giving students extra time so their estimate is likely to be low compared to the overall amount of manipulation that is involved.

Goal displacement refers to the case in which employees change their behavior in order in order to perform better on success measures. Another approach is for organizations and their individual workers to change their reporting of their behaviors to improve their scores on measures but not necessarily change their actual behaviors. In program evaluation literature, this is known as an "instrumentation" problem. For example, discretion can be employed in reporting important time indicators such as police response time. Response time is often used as a performance indicator but there are alternative ways in which response time is reported. In some cases, the response time may be reported when police initially respond to the call while in other cases, it will be calculated for when police arrive at the scene and take some action. In one case study of Las Vegas (Layne, 1990, p. 25), police "would arrive at the scene of high priority calls before being dispatched."

Inaccurate reporting, whether due to underreporting or over-reporting is common. Organizations are generally reluctant to make public sensitive information that reflects negatively on themselves and their employees. Consequently, underreporting of problems is common in all organizations, public and private. The implication is that many crucial indicators cannot be relied upon for assessing performance. Reporting procedures change through time and only through other sources of information such as participant observation and interviews or "whistle-blowing" does such information ever reach the public. For example, a federal program "to protect patients from incompetent doctors is failing because health maintenance organizations and hospitals rarely report doctors" to governmental agencies even though they are mandated to do so (U. S. General Accounting Office, March 2002). Moreover, comparison of the national data

Copyright © 2006, Idea Group Inc. Copying or distributing in print or electronic forms without written permission of Idea Group Inc. is prohibited.

bank with data from the states indicate that only about one-fifth of estimated actions against physicians were reported to the national practitioner data bank that is supposed to maintain data on such actions (Associated Press, 1995). There are ways to "game the system," according to one report (Sendrick, 1993, p. 45):

We know anecdotally...that there are many techniques that can be used to avoid reporting. For example, you only have to report adverse actions that last longer than 30 days; so some people may ask for a suspension that lasts only 30 days....

Three-fourths (75%) of hospitals have never reported a disciplinary action against physicians since government tracking abuses in the National Practitioner Databank began in 1990 (Associated Press, 1995b).

Patients and their relatives are often reluctant to report abuse in nursing homes, because the patients fear retribution and the relatives fear the patients will be told to leave. Nursing home managers are reluctant to report abuse because they fear that it will cause "adverse publicity" or that state regulators will impose fines and other penalties (U.S. General Accounting Office, 2002a). Nursing home employees fear losing their jobs or being alienated from co-workers if they report abuse. King & Hermodson (2000) have shown how strong the ethic is against reporting co-workers especially in cohesive organizations. In some states and in some nursing homes, it is difficult to learn the correct telephone number for reporting abuse. Nursing homes rarely incur any penalty for failing to report abuse (U.S. General Accounting Office, March 2002). Many other examples of failure to report negative information exist. Recent reports (e.g., Hamilton & Reich, 2002) show that the Catholic Church hid sexual abuse charges.

An annual survey is conducted that measures the degree of "student engagement" in their colleges and 470 institutions have participated and many feel the information is valuable. The results are reported in aggregate format but individual institutions are not identified in the report nor are most willing to give out such information (Bartlett, 2001). When they released the previous survey for 2000, the head of the survey also released the names of four colleges that had scored well and he was attacked for releasing these names. The director of the survey said that "most colleges would not participate if they knew the results would be made public" (Bartlett, 2001). The organizational norm of the priority of survival and silence about problems is strong and organizations frequently socialize new employees to be silent and "go along" (Roebuck & Barker, 1974, p. 427). Yakel (2001) studied radiologists and discovered that they adopted several techniques that served to reduce their accountability for mistakes. One was the use of "hedging language" (Yakel, 2001, p. 239) in which terms such as "appears to have progressed" and "consistent with" are repeatedly employed. Another tactic was to use the passive voice and phrases such as a certain disease "cannot be excluded" (Yakel, 2001, p. 241). She points out that it is the litigiousness of society that has caused the use of such defense mechanisms and the fact that the medical record is now open not only to other physicians but can become a public record in malpractice suits (Yakel, 2001, p. 242). Yakel (2001) implies that more direct and open communication is only likely in "oral presentations" that are "private affairs." She concludes that the only way to achieve the desired responsiveness is to have it "internalized" (Yakel, 2001, p. 244).

Copyright © 2006, Idea Group Inc. Copying or distributing in print or electronic forms without written permission of Idea Group Inc. is prohibited.

Another manipulative approach is to change reporting procedures so that time series comparisons cannot be made. For example, in the City of Austin GASB study, Epstein & Campbell (2002a, p. 22) said that certain departments changed indicators before there was enough time series data to evaluate and there was at least one suggestion that changes were made to avoid unfavorable results. Consequently, a policy was instituted that they had to keep measures for at least three years and could not change measures without permission.

Rubin (1977, p. 250) describes several procedures used by universities to protect "certain kinds of expenditures by obscuring them." Some non-academic and academic positions were lumped together and/or redefined as non-academic. Rubin found (1977, p. 25) that some administrative costs were categorized as "costs of teaching" so that the line disappeared "while the expense and function did not." She reports that faculty time reports with the apparent collaboration of the administration were rearranged for faculty. Departments hid vacancies. She summarizes by saying that existing models of organizations failed to account for the "systemic distortion of information" that occurred. It is useful to note that Rubin was describing universities during a period of retrenchment when the pressure they were under was especially great.

Verification and Other Incentives for Information Integrity

Discussions of verification play a small role in most discussions of performance measurement. Barata & Cain (2001, p. 249) describe traditional controls that are employed such as exception reports, reconciliation of subsystems with the general ledger (for financial transactions), audit trails for transactions and details to support account balances and the ability to link source documents to financial statements. Pollitt & Bouckaert (2000, pp. 69-70) identify three stages of auditing ranging from the traditional financial audit to performance auditing that concentrates on efficiency and effectiveness.

Some procedures for verification were discussed in the GASB case studies. Prince Williams County, Virginia uses one of the most common procedures of looking for outliers (Bernstein, 2000b, p. 22). They did periodic, but not annual audits and used benchmarking to compare their figures with those of other counties. But some questioned the objectivity of the internal measures (Bernstein, 2002b, p. 24). In the state and local governments, there generally exists some organization (e.g., state auditor) that presumably checks the data for consistency but no detailed discussion is provided. Some data are clearly harder to manipulate than others. For example, mortality rates are harder to manipulate than a school test, which in turn is likely to be more solid than self-reported time allocation figures. Gormely & Weiner (1999, p. 182) conclude their book on organizational report cards that "specification of verification procedures should go hand-in-hand with any reporting requirements set by government." They also push for penalties for failure to report accurate data. Indeed, universities are required to report crime rates and there is a $10,000 fine for false data (U.S. General Accounting Office, 1997). The importance of verification of data used in organizational report cards is demonstrated

Copyright © 2006, Idea Group Inc. Copying or distributing in print or electronic forms without written permission of Idea Group Inc. is prohibited.

by a GAO study (U.S. General Accounting Office, 1994d, p. 3) that found the following major obstacles to the use of report cards:

1.   Much of the information in medical records is inaccurate, misleading, or incomplete.

2.   The indicators [as currently measured] may not measure quality.

3.   There is little agreement on formulas for calculating performance results.

4.   No verification mechanisms are in place to ensure the accuracy of reported results.

Some studies show that much of the data provided by health care providers is poorly coded and either missing or inaccurate. For example, only 65% of reported admissions to hospitals in one study were actual admissions (U.S. General Accounting Office 1994d, p. 37). Hospitals and practitioners often have incentives such as insurance benefits to manipulate data they place in records. The social context also influences physician diagnoses including the desire to help the patient with insurance payments as well as to avoid stigmatizing diagnoses such as AIDS and mental illness. Another study (Jollis et al., 1993) found discordance between insurance and clinical databases with the indicator of agreement being as low as .09 for some problems. Some experts fear that organizations will over emphasize those measures that are contained in the report cards and ignore other important areas.

In the school testing area, the validity of the tests is checked for by administering other tests that have been accepted as valid and studying the correlation of the results for the two tests. Study of erasure patterns is a common form of detection of cheating on standardized tests to see, for example, whether they involve changes from incorrect to correct answers. Bohte and Meier (2001) studied student exemptions from tests to detect manipulation by school systems. Jacob and Levitt (2002, p. 4) developed an algorithm to detect errors in which they focused on "unexpected test score fluctuations" and "unusual patterns of answers for students within a classroom." They point out that the easiest way for a teacher to cheat is to alter the same block of consecutive questions for a substantial portion of students in the class and their algorithm focuses on such patterns (Jacob & Levitt, 2002). Koretz et al. (1996, p. xiii) found reports that teachers assisted students in a variety of ways, often clarifying questions or suggesting answers. Cheating such as extending time of the test or cheating that uses random procedures would escape their algorithm, Jacob & Levitt (2000) admit.

Wholey (1999) has provided one of the most extensive treatments of how to check for the accuracy of performance measurement systems. Wholey (1999, p. 226) points out that in addition to checking for the quality of data, organizations also need to audit the usefulness of the measurement system itself. Wholey argues that independent efforts are needed periodically to ensure the accuracy of data. One of the most consistently used mechanisms to verify data is to look for rapid or unusual changes in one of the measures. The private sector has been thought to have a much easier time of auditing due to the fact that they have common measurement instruments (e.g., focus on profit, financial transactions that are amenable to generally accepted auditing standards). Delaney (1994) has shown that many private corporations employ a strategic approach to "constructing the bottom line" so that they commonly present radically different information to

Copyright © 2006, Idea Group Inc. Copying or distributing in print or electronic forms without written permission of Idea Group Inc. is prohibited.

different audiences such as stockholders and the IRS. Recent events have reinforced the truth that measures such as "profit" can be difficult to pin down and subject to manipulation. Allen Greenspan has recently (Neikirk, 2002) complained about the way accounting rules "currently value stock options" so that profits have been "overstated since 1995." Greenspan concluded that "unless you change the incentive to game the accounting system, it will be gamed by corporations." The recent accounting scandals have shown that measures such as earnings, profit, and cash flow have been manipulated without discovery by certified public accountants (e.g., Collingswood, 2002; Kerber, 2002). Pay incentives that tie executive bonuses to private sector performance contributed to the tendency to overstate profits (Leonhardt, 2002). Thus, private sector accountability has many limitations and difficulties despite the fact that its concepts and measures are relatively well-defined, accepted, and formally audited. If the less well-audited performance measures of government are tied into high stakes decisions, should we not expect them to be "gamed" too?

Those initiating accountability systems, the political leadership, are likely to respond strongly to clear cases of cheating that are brought to light, but the lack of checking into other forms of goal displacement and manipulation raises questions about their willingness to address these more subtle forms of manipulation. They have a vested interest in these systems being viewed as effective. In other words, the sponsors of accountability mechanisms don't want to "look a gift horse in the mouth."

Conclusion and Implications

E-reporting is one of the most exciting aspects of e-government because it provides citizens with the tools to become more knowledgeable about agencies and could lead to better performance by government. But if e-reports increase the visibility and importance of these performance measures, they at the same time will create the incentive to manipulate these data. My review of the performance measurement systems shows that it is difficult to make these systems work as intended. Many performance measurement systems have been adopted and then abandoned. Works such as those of Hood et al. (1999) have shown that these systems can be enormously expensive in terms of the time spent by employees involved with them but the visible use of them appears to have been limited in most of the cases that we have studied. There has been little serious discussion of information overload in the IT field or guidance on how many indicators should be gathered.

The standard measures to cleanse data may not work for the kinds of problems that I have outlined where there are subtle and systematic biases operating. More promising avenues for assuring that data are valid concern organizational steps. In particular, all levels of employees as well as the public should be involved with decisions on what data to gather. There are difficult choices to make, such as how much information to gather and what kinds of measures (e.g., inputs, process, or outcome) should be studied. A theme that comes out of the auditing literature is that computerized checks and formal data cleansing methods are inadequate to detect many data integrity problems. Even in

Copyright © 2006, Idea Group Inc. Copying or distributing in print or electronic forms without written permission of Idea Group Inc. is prohibited.

traditional auditing, qualitative information is crucial. Hayes (1995, p. 10) states that "interviews are essential" for auditors to detect fraud and that auditors must have awareness of how personnel react to questions. Heeks (1998) states that "control of corruption" necessitates a "holistic view" including examination of motivations, the design of jobs, and work flows. He concludes that you "can't rely just on information technology." I would state further that qualitative data gathered through participant observation and open-ended interviews are valuable at not only identifying poor quality data but in understanding the context of performance measures. McKinnon and Bruins (1992) have described what they call the "management by walking around" approach, which involves gathering qualitative information and making contact with workers. Glaser also makes the point that qualitative measures are needed as well as quantitative but (Glaser, 1991, p. 313) points out that quantitative measures are often "considered" superior even "when the numbers assigned are meaningless." The movement to digitized information systems has obscured the value of qualitative data. For example, although police have sophisticated information technology, the most important information to solve cases often does not reside in information systems but requires that police concentrate more on "people issues" (Laudon, 1986). Wilson has pointed out that the most valuable information is gained by talking with suspects, their associates and visiting places where they are likely to be found but there are few incentives to do this (Wilson, 1984, p. 8):

Yet it is most unlikely that officers in many departments will make field contacts...because there is no immediate apparent benefit to the officer. On the contrary, getting such information often means leaving the squad car on a cold, unpleasant day and talking to people who are at best suspicious and at worst hostile and then writing down something the officer may never see again.

Time is a scarce resource and, in many cases, time currently devoted to information technology might be more productively spent in low-tech activities. Information system researchers have been so fixated on computerized information systems that they have forgotten that the important information usually does not reside in digitized information systems. Political information, personal information, and informal information about norms, values, and behaviors must largely be exchanged via face-to-face or by phone calls. It is true that much of informal information is now being shared via e-mail but such usage can be dangerous as I point out in the chapter on ethics. Qualitative information is crucial at all levels from the bottom to top of organizations and qualitative methods are often the only way to get at the sensitive information. Qualitative methods are often the best way to identify problems in processes and thus are necessary to improving services. Qualitative methods are also necessary to check on the validity and reliability of quantitative indicators. In my view, one of the major responsibilities and needs for managers is to develop knowledge gained from qualitative sources both within and outside the organization to supplement the formal and digital information residing in computers. As I outlined in Figure 2 in Chapter 1, a manager needs to develop a "personal information system" that makes use of both types of data and use each to offset the limitations and biases present in the other.

Copyright © 2006, Idea Group Inc. Copying or distributing in print or electronic forms without written permission of Idea Group Inc. is prohibited.

My final point returns to the fact that improvement is most likely to occur when the "street-level bureaucrats" are motivated to make changes themselves. Indeed, Brown & Pyers (1998, p. 110) point to the fact that, although the private sector places a great deal of emphasis on performance measurement, these measures remain internal and management does not generally provide this information to outsiders:

In the private sector such measures are usually placed in the larger context of an internal managerial accounting control system, rather than in the domains of external reporting.

Brown & Pyers (1998, p. 111) go on to note that the private sector example is "instructive" as to "who the real users are likely to be." E-reporting may spur public organizations to look good on the reported measures but it is difficult for e-reports or audits to force responsiveness to values. Thus personnel selection and socialization to external values are the most effective mechanisms to the desired responsiveness as Kaufman (1969) pointed out in his classic work, "The Forest Ranger." Information systems are important but remain only one element that can contribute to achieving change. Generalist and information technology managers need to understand how the informal system affects the success of information technology and that making accountability-related information more accessible on the Internet will bring about unintended consequences.

References

Ackoff, R. (1967, June). Management misinformation systems. *Management Science*, 319-331.

Asworth, K. H. (1994, November). Performance-based funding in higher education: The Texas case study. *Change, 26*(6), 8-15.

Banchero, S., Olszewski, L., & Dougherty, G. (2001, November 15). 75% of city's grade schools on warning list. *Chicago Tribune*.

Banta, T. W., Rudolph, L. B., Van Dyke, J., & Fisher, H. S. (1996, January/February). Performance funding comes of age in Tennessee. *Journal of Higher Education, 67*, 23-45.

Barata, K., & Cain, P. (2001). Information, No technology, is essential to accountability: Electronic records and public-sector financial management. *The Information Society, 17*, 247-258.

Barksdale-Ladd, M. A., & Thomas, K. F. (2000). What's at stake in high-stakes testing: Teachers and parents speak out. *Journal of Teachers Education, 51*(5), 384-397.

Bartlett, T. (2001, November 23). Colleges praise new source of data, as long as their scores stay secret. *Chronicle of Higher Education*, 13a.

Copyright © 2006, Idea Group Inc. Copying or distributing in print or electronic forms without written permission of Idea Group Inc. is prohibited.

Bernstein, D. J. (2002a, September). Portland, Oregon: Pioneering external accountability. *GASB Research Case Study*. Retrieved April 20, 2005, from http://www.seagov. org/sea_gasb_project/local_portland.pdf

Bernstein, D. J. (2002b). Prince William County, Virginia. *GASB SEA Research Case Study*. Retrieved from http://www.seagov.org/sea_gasb_project/local_prince.pdf

Bernstein, D. J. (2002c). Tucson, Arizona. Retrieved April 20, 2005, from http:// www.seagov.org/sea_gasb_project/local_tucson.pdf

Bernstein, D. (2002d). City of Winston Salem, Georgia. *GASB SEA Research Case Study*. Retrieved April 20, 2005, from http://www.seagov.org/sea_gasb_project/ local_winston.pdf

Bohte, J., & Meier, K. J. (2001). Goal displacement: Assessing the motivation for organizational cheating. *Public Administration Review, 60*(2), 173-182.

Bouckaert, G. (1993, Fall). Measurement and meaningful management. *Public Productivity & Management Review, XVII*(1), 31-43.

Brown, R. E., & Pyers, J. B. (1998, Winter). Service efforts and accomplishments reporting: Has its time really come? *Public Budgeting & Finance,* 101-113.

Burke, J. C., & Modarresi, S. (2000, July/August). To keep or not to keep performance funding: Signals from stakeholders. *Journal of Higher Education, 71*(4), 432-452.

Burke, J. C., & Serban, A. M. (1998). State synopses of performance funding programs. In J. C. Burke, & A. M. Serban (Eds.), *Performance funding for public higher education: Fad or trend?* (pp. 25-48). San Francisco: Jossey-Bass.

Campbell, D. T. (1969). Reforms as experiments. *American Psychologist, 24*(4), 409-429.

Center for Technology in Government. (1998). Data quality tools for data warehousing –A small sample survey.

Ceperly, P. E., & Reel, K. (1997). The impetus for the Tennessee value-added accountability system. In J. Millman (Ed.), *Grading teachers, grading schools: Is student achievement a valid evaluation measure?* (pp. 133-136). Thousand Oaks, CA: Corwin.

Coe, C. K. (2001, August 30-September 2). *Performance measurement: Grading report cards and single performance measures*. Paper prepared for delivery at the 2001 Conference of the American Political Science Association, San Francisco.

Collingwood, H. (2002, June 9). The earnings cult. *New York Times*.

Delaney, K. J. (1994). The organizational construction of the 'bottom line'. *Social Problems, 41*(4), 497-518.

Divorski, S., & Scheirer, M.A. (2001). Improving data quality for performance measures: results from a GAO study of verification and validation. *Evaluation and Program Planning, 24*, 83-94.

Dykhouse. C. (1997, August). First great city of the 21st century. *Government Technology*.

Epstein, P. D., & Campbell, W. (2002a). City of Austin. *GASB Research Case Study*. Retrieved April 20, 2005, from http://www.seagov.org/sea_gasb_project/ local_austin.pdf

Copyright © 2006, Idea Group Inc. Copying or distributing in print or electronic forms without written permission of Idea Group Inc. is prohibited.

Epstein, P. D., & Campbell, W. (2002b). State of Louisiana. *GASB Case Study.* Retrieved April 20, 2005, from http://www.seagov.org/sea_gasb_project/state_la.pdf

Epstein, P. D., & Campbell, W. (2002c). State of Iowa. *GASB Case Study.* Retrieved April 20, 2005, from http://www.seagov.org/sea_gasb_project/state_ia.pdf

Faden, M. (2000, April 10). Data cleansing helps e-businesses run more efficiently. 136-144.

Fisher, C. W., & Kingma, B. R. (2001). Criticality of data quality as exemplified in two disasters. *Information & Management, 39,* 109-116.

Fountain, J. (2002). State of Oregon: A performance system based on benchmarks. *GASB SEA Research Case Study.* Retrieved April 20, 2005, from http://www.seagov.org/sea_gasb_project/state_or.pdf

Fountain, J., Campbell, W., Patton, T., Epstein, P., & Cohn, M. (2003, August). Reporting performance information: Suggested criteria for effective communication. Governmental Accounting Standards Board. Retrieved April 20, 2005, from http://www.seagov.org/sea_gasb_project/suggested_criteria_report.pdf

Gabris, G. T. (1986, Winter). Recognizing management technique dysfunctions: How management tools often create more serious problems than they solve. *Public Productivity Review, 40,* 3-19.

Gaither, G. H. (1998, Fall). The future of quality assurance: Promises and pitfalls. *New Directions for Institutional Research, 99,* 87-91.

Geron, S. M. (1991). Regulating the behavior of nursing homes through positive incentives: An analysis of Illinois quality incentive program (QUIP). *Gerontologist, 31*(3), 292-301.

Ginsberg, P. E. (1984). The dysfunctional side effects of quantitative indicator production: illustrations from mental health care (A message from chicken little). *Evaluation & Program Planning, 7,* 1-12.

Glaser, M. (1991). Tailoring performance measurement to fit the organization: From generic to germane. *Public Productivity & Management Review, XIV*(3), 303-319.

Gormely, Jr., W. T., & Weimer, D. L. (1999). *Organizational report cards.* Cambridge, MA: Harvard University.

Halachmi, A. (1998, November). Performance measurement: Don't abuse it through GPRA. *Ninth Public Sector Productivity Conference: Performance Improvement Online Conference,* 9-20.

Hamilton, E., & Rich, E. (2002, March 17). Papers show Egan hid abuse charges. *Chicago Tribune, 8.*

Haney, W. (2000, August 19). The myth of the Texas miracle in education. *Education Policy Analysis Archives, 8*(41).

Hatry, H. P. (1999). *Performance measurement: Getting results.* Washington, DC: The Urban Institute.

Hayes, A. A., Jr. (1995, December). Fraud happens; A primer on lying, cheating, and stealing. *Government Finance Review,* 7-11.

Copyright © 2006, Idea Group Inc. Copying or distributing in print or electronic forms without written permission of Idea Group Inc. is prohibited.

Heeks, R. (1998). *Information technology and public sector corruption.* Working Paper Series, Working Paper No. 4.

Herman, J. L., & Abedi, J. (1994). Assessing the effects of standardized testing on schools. *Educational and Psychological Measurement, 54*(2), 471-482.

Hood, C., Scott, C., James, O., Jones, G., & Travers, T. (1999). *Regulation inside government.* Oxford: Oxford University.

Jacob, B.A., & Levitt, S.D. (2002, February). *Rotten apples: An investigation of the prevalence and predictors of teacher cheating.* Unpublished manuscript.

Jollis et al. (1993). Discordance of databases designed for claims payment versus clinical outcomes research. *Annals of Internal Medicine, 119*(8), 844-850.

Kaufman, H. (1969). *The forest ranger.* Baltimore: Johns Hopkins.

Kerber, R. (2002, July 2). Some tricks of the trade: Going beyond accounting 101. *The Boston Globe.*

King, G., III, & Hermodson, A. (2000, November). Peer reporting of coworker wrongdoing: A qualitative analysis of observer attitudes in the decision to report versus not report unethical behavior. *Journal of Applied communication Research, 28*(4), 309-329.

Klein, B. D. (1997, June). Can humans detect errors in data? Impact of base rates, incentives, and goals. *MIS Quarterly, 21*(2), 169-194.

Klein, B. D. (2000). Detecting data errors in organizational settings: Examining the generalizability of experimental findings. *Informing Science, 3*(3), 97-108.

Klein, S. P., Hamilton, L. S., McCaffrey, D. F., & Stecher, B. M. (2000). *What do test scores in Texas tell us?* Santa Monica, CA: Rand.

Koretz, D. M., Barron, S., Mitchell, K. J., & Stecher, B. M. (1996). *Perceived effects of the Kentucky instructional results information system (KIRIS).* Santa Monica, CA: Rand.

Laudon, K. C. (1986). *Dossier society.* New York: Columbia University.

Layne, K. (1990). Unanticipated consequences of the provision of information: The experience of the LVMPD. *Journal of Police Science and Administration, 17*, 20-31.

Layzell, D. T. (1998). Linking performance to funding outcomes for public institutions of higher education: The U.S. experience. *European Journal of Education, 33*(1), 103-111.

Lee, R. D., & Burns, R. C. (2000, Spring). Performance measurement in state budgeting: Advancement and backsliding from 1990 to 1995. *Public Budgeting & Finance,* 38-54.

Leonhardt, D. (2002, April 7). Did pay incentives cut both ways? *The New York Times.*

Levitin, A., & Redman, T. C. (1998, Fall). Data as a resource: Properties, implications, and prescriptions. *Data as a Resource, 40*(1), 89-101.

Massy, W. F., & Zemsky, R. (1994). Faculty discretionary time: Departments and the "academic ratchet." *Journal of Higher Education, 65*(1), 1-22.

Copyright © 2006, Idea Group Inc. Copying or distributing in print or electronic forms without written permission of Idea Group Inc. is prohibited.

McKinnon, S. M., & Bruns, W. J. (1992). *The information mosaic*. Boston: Harvard Business School.

McNeil, L., & Valenzuela, A. (2000). The harmful impact of testing in Texas: Beneath the accountability rhetoric. *The civil rights project*. Harvard University.

McTigue, M., Wray, H., & Ellig, J. (2004). Mercatus report. 5th Annual Report Scorecard: Which federal agencies best inform the public? Mercatus Center, George Mason University, April. Retrieved July 14, 2004, from http://www.mercatus.org/governmentaccountability/category.php/45.html

Meijer, A. (2001). Electronic records management and public accountability: Beyond an Instrumental Approach. *The Information Society, 17*, 259-270.

Milem, J. R., Berger, J. B., & Dey, E. L. (2000, July/August). Faculty time allocation. *The Journal of Higher Education, 71*(4), 454-475.

National Center on Educational Outcomes. (2003, April). Going public: What 2000-2001 reports tell us about the performance of students with disabilities. Retrieved September 27, 2004, from http://education.umn.edu/NCEO/OnlinePubs/Technical35.htm

Neikirk, W. (2002, February 28). Economy picks up pace. *Chicago Tribune,* Business Section, 1 & 4.

Newcome, T. (1999, November). Is there a doctor in the warehouse? *Government Technology.*

Olszewski, L. (2001, November 17). Test scores don't credit school gains. *Chicago Tribune.*

Orr, K. (1998, February). Data quality and systems theory. *Communications of the ACM, 41*(2), 66-71.

Patton, M. Q. (1978). *Utilization-focused evaluation*. Beverly Hills, CA: Sage.

Pear, R. (2001, May 29). Inept doctors escaping law requiring disclosure. *Chicago Tribune.*

Pollitt, C., & Bouckaert, G. (2000). *Public management reform: A comparative analysis*. Oxford: Oxford University.

Posavac, E. J., & Carey, R. G. (1997). *Program evaluation: Methods and case studies*. Fifth Edition. Upper Saddle River, NJ: Prentice-Hall.

Ridgeway, V.F. (1956, September). Dysfunctional consequences of performance measurements. *Administrative Science Quarterly, 1*(2), 240-247.

Roebuck, J. B., & Barker, T. (1974). A typology of police corruption. *Social Problems, 21*(3), 423-437.

Rubin, I. (1997, September). Universities in stress: Decision making under conditions of reduced resources. *Social Science Quarterly,* 242-254.

Sanders, W. L., Saxton, A. M., & Horn, S. P. (1997). The Tennessee value-added assessment systems: A quantitative, outcome-based approach to educational assessment. In J. Millman (Ed.), *Grading teachers, grading schools: Is student achievement a valid evaluation measure?* (pp. 137-162). Thousand Oaks, CA: Corwin.

Copyright © 2006, Idea Group Inc. Copying or distributing in print or electronic forms without written permission of Idea Group Inc. is prohibited.

Schmidt, P. (2002a, February 22). Missouri's financing system is praised but more for longevity than results. *Chronicle of Higher Education*, A21.

Schmidt, P. (2002b, February 22). Most states tie aid to performance, despite little proof that it works. *Chronicle of Higher Education*, A20-A21.

Sendrick, K. (1993, February 5). Two years and running: The national practitioner data bank begins to roll, but issues remain. *Hospitals, 67*, 44-45.

Serban, A., & Burke, J. C. (1998). Meeting the performance challenge: A nine state comparative analysis. *Public Productivity & Management Review, 22*(2), 157-176.

Smith, M. L. (1984). Distorted indicators in special education: A response to Ginsberg. *Evaluation and Program Planning, 7*, 13-14.

Smith, M. L., & Rottenberg, C. (1991). Unintended consequences of external testing in elementary schools. *Educational Measurement: Issues and Practices, 10*(4), 7-11.

Streib, G. D., & Poster, T. H. (1999). Assessing the validity, legitimacy, and functionality of performance measurement systems in municipal governments. *American Review of Public Administration, 29*(2), 107-123.

Tucker, L. (2002a). State of Texas. *GASB SEA Research Case Study*. Retrieved April 20, 2005, from http://www.seagov.org/sea_gasb_project/state_tx.pdf

Tucker, L. (2002b). State of Arizona. *GASB SEA Research Case Study*. Retrieved April 20, 2005, from http://www.seagov.org/sea_gasb_project/state_az.pdf

Tucker, L. (2002c). State of Illinois. *GASB SEA Research Case Study*. Retrieved April 20, 2005, from http://www.seagov.org/sea_gasb_project/state_il.pdf

U.S. General Accounting Office. (1993a, May). *Data improvements needed to help manage health care programs*. Washington, DC: U.S. General Accounting Office, GAO/IMTEC-93-18.

U.S. General Accounting Office. (1993b, May). *Welfare to work: JOBS participation rate data unreliable for assessing states' performance*. Washington, DC: U.S. General Accounting Office, GAO/HRD-93-73.

U.S. General Accounting Office. (1994d, September). *Health care reform: "report cards" are useful but significant issues need to be addressed*. Washington, DC: U.S. General Accounting Office, GAO/HEHS-94-219.

U. S. General Accounting Office. (1997). *Campus crime: Difficulties meeting federal reporting requirements*. Washington, DC: United States General Accounting Office, GAO/HEHS-97-52.

U. S. General Accounting Office. (1999, July). *Performance plans: Selected approaches for verification and validation of agency performance*. Washington, DC: GAO/GGD-99-139.

U. S. General Accounting Office. (2000, March). *Managing for results: Answers to hearing questions on program data quality*. GAO/GGD-00-108R Hearing Questions on Program Data Quality.

U. S. General Accounting Office. (2001, September 21). *Financial management: Annual costs of forest service's timber sales program are not determinable*. GAO-01-1101R Forest Service Timber Costs.

Copyright © 2006, Idea Group Inc. Copying or distributing in print or electronic forms without written permission of Idea Group Inc. is prohibited.

U. S. General Accounting Office. (2002a). *Nursing homes: More can be done to protect residents from abuse*. Washington, DC: GAO-02-312.

U. S. General Accounting Office. (2000b). Workforce Investment Act: Improvements Needed in Performance Measure to Provide a More Accurate Picture of WIA's Effectiveness. Washington, DC: GAO-02-275.

Van Thiel, S., & Leeuw, F. L. (2002). The performance paradox in the public sector. *Public Performance & Management Review, 25*(3), 267-281.

Welch, E., & Fulla, S. 2002. Framing virtual interactivity between government and citizen: A study of feedback systems in the Chicago police department. *Proceedings of the 35th Hawaii International Conference on System Sciences*. Retrieved June 4, 2004, from http://csdl.computer.org/comp/proceedings/hicss/2002/1435/05/14350125b.pdf

Wholey, J. S. (1994). Assessing the feasibility and likely usefulness of evaluation. In J. S. Wholey, H. P. Hatry, & K. E. Newcomer (Eds.), *Handbook of practical program evaluation* (pp. 40-68). San Francisco: Jossey-Bass.

Williams, W. A. (2002, April). Trusting the numbers: The power of data verification. *Government Finance Review,* 18-21.

Wilson, J. Q. (1984). Problems in the creation of adequate criminal justice information systems. In U.S. Department of Justice, Bureau of Justice Statistics. Information Policy and Crime Control Strategies (pp. 8-11). *Proceedings of a BIS/SEARCH Conference*. Washington, DC: U.S. Department of Justice, NCH 93926.

Yakel, E. (2001). The social construction of accountability: Radiologists and their record-keeping practices. *The Information Society, 17*, 233-245.

Yoon, V. Y., Aiken, P., & Guimaraes, T. (2000, July-September). Managing organizational data resources: Quality dimensions. *Information Resources Management, 13*(3), 5-13.

Key Concepts

- Accountability
- Corruption pressures
- Data atrophy
- Data cleaning
- Data inventory
- Data warehousing
- Goal displacement
- Information stewardship
- Metadata

Copyright © 2006, Idea Group Inc. Copying or distributing in print or electronic forms without written permission of Idea Group Inc. is prohibited.

- Service efforts and accomplishments
- Shine the light
- Teach to the test
- Used-based audit
- Value-added
- Verification program
- Transparency

Discussion Questions

1. In your view, what is the essence of accountability and does the existence of e-government and the World Wide Web affect accountability in important ways? Do you think e-reporting makes government more responsive?

2. What do you think of the rating criteria used by the Mercatus Report? Do you agree with their measures? What modifications or additional rating criteria would you employ?

3. Do you think your organization collects too little, too much information, or just about the right amount of information? What kinds of information are most heavily employed in making important budgeting and other decisions? What are examples of data collected by the organization that could be dropped with no negative effects? What role does qualitative information play in the decision-making process compared to formal data?

4. Do you know of any organizations that reward error detection or make it a high priority goal? Do you know of any examples where data quality problems and manipulation of data are ignored?

5. What measures of quality of performance are used in areas that you are familiar with? How valid and reliable do you think these data are? How could they be improved?

Exercises

1. Conduct a data inventory for some part of an organization (this could range from the entire organization, to a department, to a sub-unit, or even the information gathered by a single employee). List all of the data elements that are gathered for the formal information system. Try to identify how each data element is used and whether there are any data elements that appear to be unused. Are there any data needs that are unmet—that is, information that would be very useful to gather but isn't? Are these data reliable and valid? How do you know?

Copyright © 2006, Idea Group Inc. Copying or distributing in print or electronic forms without written permission of Idea Group Inc. is prohibited.

2.   Examine the data quality of some organization. What steps does the organization take to ensure that the data have integrity. To what extent does it conform with the recommendations cited in this chapter? What, if any, computerized procedures are employed? Are any audits done on information, particularly the non-financial data? Are there any problems of data manipulation or goal displacement that you can identify? Write a memo in which you assess the quality of the organization's data.

Copyright © 2006, Idea Group Inc. Copying or distributing in print or electronic forms without written permission of Idea Group Inc. is prohibited.

About the Author

Bruce Rocheleau is a professor of political science at Northern Illinois University, DeKalb (USA). He received a BA from the University of Pennsylvania, an MA from New York University, and a PhD from the University of Florida. Professor Rocheleau has extensive practitioner experience. He has worked for the Department of Health and Human Services and has consulted with state and local governments. He became interested in information management while working for the federal government in the late 1970s and published numerous articles and chapters as well as monographs related to information management and government. His work focused on the challenges of managing information technology in the public sector. The integrating theme of his work is that, despite the fact that information technology changes so rapidly, the same processes remain important and that managers can be effective by learning how to handle these tasks using knowledge gained from the best available research and practice.

Copyright © 2006, Idea Group Inc. Copying or distributing in print or electronic forms without written permission of Idea Group Inc. is prohibited.

Index

A

acceptance testing 80
accountability
    117, 180, 252, 285, 322, 335
acquisitions 181
acts of God   83
adoption 142
alignment 27, 87
analysis software 166
"any-any-any-any" goal 33
application server provider (ASP) 69
architectural standards 26
architecture 25, 38, 59
ASP (application server provider) 69
atrophy 343
autonomy 177

B

backfilling 89
balanced scorecard 276
baselining 59
benchmarking 291, 365
best of breed 72
best practice 3, 35, 62, 101, 140, 217,
    278, 310, 356

best value 56
black box 279
BPR (business process reengineering)
    34, 60, 129
broadcast 206
broaden the base 252
business cases 7, 23, 58, 112, 283
business plan 25
business process reengineering (BPR)
    34, 60, 129
business reference model 146

C

California 177
capability maturity model (CMM) 109
causality 276
Center for Digital Government 16
CFF (critical failure factors) 118
chief information officer (CIO) 178
CIO (chief information officer) 178
citizen-centric 129
CMM (capability maturity model) 109
commercial-off-the-shelf 34
communication 181, 226, 239
communication flow 181
communities of practice 324

Copyright © 2006, Idea Group Inc. Copying or distributing in print or electronic forms without written permission of Idea Group Inc. is prohibited.

community input 36
compassion 237
competition 5
computer matching 262
computer profiling 262
computer-mediated communication 238
continuing costs 80
corruption pressures 346
criminal justice 315
critical failure factors (CFFs) 118
cultural fit 84
customer 128
customize governmental Web sites 158
cyber-ethics 236

D

data cleansing 345
data inventory 376
data warehousing 342
decision making 1
defender organization 32
detailed specifications 80
deterrent 237
digital communication 239
digital divide 134
documentation mania 252
dotted line relationships 183

E

e-commerce (electronic commerce) 56, 129
e-democracy 129
e-governance 128, 205
e-government (electronic government)
    5, 57, 102, 128, 217
e-learning 225
e-mail 62, 218, 315
e-management 129
e-rulemaking 205
e-services 129
efficiency evaluation 279
electronic commerce (e-commerce) 56, 129
Electronic Freedom of Information Act 244
electronic government (e-government)
    5, 57, 102, 128, 217
electronic media 244, 315
employees 216

end user 11, 28
enterprise architecture 145
enterprise resource planning (ERP)
    22, 31, 60, 217
ERP (enterprise resource planning)
    22, 31, 60, 217
ethics 236
evaluability assessment 288
evaluation 274, 278
extensible markup language (XML) 308
external alignment 31

F

Fairfax County 44
fast followership 113
federal enterprise architecture 59, 145
force majeure 83
foreign keys 309
formative 281
front-end verification 262

G

G2 129
G2B 129
G2C 129
G2E 129
G2G 129
gap analysis 221
geographic information systems (GIS)
    217, 309
GIS (geographic information systems)
    217, 309
goal displacement 286, 345
government 31, 56, 100, 236, 274, 308
gurus 227

H

hacking 236
gardware acquisitions 181
human resources 216

I

i-bonds 135
ICT (information and communication
    technologies) 129

Copyright © 2006, Idea Group Inc. Copying or distributing in print or electronic forms without written permission of Idea Group Inc. is prohibited.

IDP (individual development plan) 221
IFB 76
impartiality 237
incentive 1
indemnification 84
individual 275
individual consequentialist 237
individual development plans (IDPs) 221
industry standard 26, 39, 88
informal learning 226
informal training 225
information and communication technologies (ICT) 129
information management 3, 181
information managers 1
information overload 249
information sharing 181
information silos 39, 318
information stewardship 340
information systems 1, 100, 308
information technology (IT) 2, 23, 56, 102, 177, 216, 274
interagency planning 48
intergovernmental planning 48
internal alignment 31
Internet 129
interoperability 120, 190, 312

J

job security 177
just-in-time (JIT) 221

L

lagging indicators 287
leadership 177

M

machine model 75
managers 1
managing partner 148
market share 7, 88, 113, 230
media richness theory (MRT) 239
Medicaid 5
metadata 309

most favored nation 85
MRT (media richness theory) 239
multi-modal 132

N

National Electronic Commerce Coordinating Council 140
natural business units 291
needs assessment 48, 56, 191, 221, 278
Netiquette 239
Nevada 246
non-digital communication 239

O

ongoing costs 66
open meetings 244
open standards 39
OPT-IN 260
OPT-OUT 262
organizational learning 216
organizational politics 181
outcome measures 279, 336

P

payback period 282
performance-based contracting 86
personnel flow 181
PMIS (public management information systems) 2
policy statements 237
political skills 120, 179
politics 177, 187
portals 129
post-training period 221
pre-training 221
preventive approaches 237
private (e-government) partner 138
private information systems 1
private organizations 1
professionalism 237
public information systems 1
public management information systems (PMIS) 2
public organizations 1
public records 244

Copyright © 2006, Idea Group Inc. Copying or distributing in print or electronic forms without written permission of Idea Group Inc. is prohibited.

purchasing 57, 187
push-and-pull technologies 315

R

replacement funds 39
requests for proposals (RFPs) 27, 60, 76,
    111
return on investment (ROI) 38, 102, 282
RFI 76
RFPs (requests for proposals) 27, 60, 76,
    111
RFQ 76
rich data 284
risk aversion 2, 144, 237
ROI (return on investment) 38, 102, 282
routine use exception 262

S

seat management 69
Section 508 162
security 177
selective outsourcing 74
service efforts 337
shadow staff 227
shallow solutions 318
shared service unit 290
shine the light approach 350
slippery slope 238
software acquisitions 181
software piracy 236
sole source 76
stakeholder analysis 26, 151, 192
stovepipe system 308
strategic plans 27
strategic weapons 10
subject matter experts 79
subjectivity 275
summative evaluations 281
sunk costs 57
super users 227
SWOT (strengths-weaknesses-opportuni-
    ties-threats) 156
systematic evaluation 274

T

take-up rate 142
TAM (technology acceptance model) 142
TCO (total cost of ownership) 39, 65
teach to the test 359
technological imperative 263
technology acceptance model (TAM) 142
technophilia 34
thin client 72
time series 283
total cost of ownership (TCO) 39, 65
train-the-trainer 229
transformational 130
transitory 245
transparency 264, 337
triangulate 29

U

unions 248
United Parcel Service (UPS) 9
universal design 160
UPS (United Parcel Service) 9
use-based audit 343
user fees 66, 135, 203
utilitarianism 237
utilization-focused 280

V

value added 353
vendor 56
verification 342
visioning analysis 28

W

waiver 82
weasel words 80
Web portal 129
Web server log 166
Web sites 158
workload measures 279, 347

X

XML (extensible markup language) 308

Copyright © 2006, Idea Group Inc. Copying or distributing in print or electronic forms without written
permission of Idea Group Inc. is prohibited.

Experience the latest full-text research in the fields
of Information Science, Technology & Management

InfoSci-Online

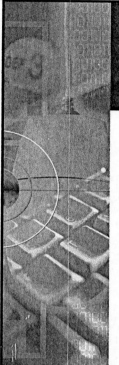

InfoSci-Online is available to libraries to help keep students,
faculty and researchers up-to-date with the latest research in
the ever-growing field of information science, technology, and
management.

The InfoSci-Online collection includes:
- Scholarly and scientific book chapters
- Peer-reviewed journal articles
- Comprehensive teaching cases
- Conference proceeding papers
- All entries have abstracts and citation information
- The full text of every entry is downloadable in .pdf format

Some topics covered:
- Business Management
- Computer Science
- Education Technologies
- Electronic Commerce
- Environmental IS
- Healthcare Information Systems
- Information Systems
- Library Science
- Multimedia Information Systems
- Public Information Systems
- Social Science and Technologies

**InfoSci-Online
features:**
- Easy-to-use
- 6,000+ full-text
  entries
- Aggregated
- Multi-user access

*"...The theoretical bent
of many of the titles
covered, and the ease
of adding chapters to
reading lists, makes it
particularly good for
institutions with strong
information science
curricula."*
— Issues in Science and
Technology Librarianship

To receive your free 30-day trial access subscription contact:
Andrew Bundy
Email: abundy@idea-group.com • Phone: 717/533-8845 x29
Web Address: www.infosci-online.com

InfoSci-Online
Full Text · Cutting Edge · Easy Access

A PRODUCT OF IDEA GROUP INC.
Publishers of Idea Group Publishing, Information Science Publishing, CyberTech Publishing, and IRM Press

infosci-online.com

Single Journal Articles and Case Studies Are Now Right at Your Fingertips!

Purchase any single journal article or teaching case for only $18.00!

Idea Group Publishing offers an extensive collection of research articles and teaching cases that are available for electronic purchase by visiting www.idea-group.com/articles. You will find over **980** journal articles and over **275** case studies from over 20 journals available for only $18.00. The website also offers a new capability of searching journal articles and case studies by category. To take advantage of this new feature, please use the link above to search within these available categories:

- ◆ Business Process Reengineering
- ◆ Distance Learning
- ◆ Emerging and Innovative Technologies
- ◆ Healthcare
- ◆ Information Resource Management
- ◆ IS/IT Planning
- ◆ IT Management
- ◆ Organization Politics and Culture
- ◆ Systems Planning
- ◆ Telecommunication and Networking
- ◆ Client Server Technology

- ◆ Data and Database Management
- ◆ E-commerce
- ◆ End User Computing
- ◆ Human Side of IT
- ◆ Internet-Based Technologies
- ◆ IT Education
- ◆ Knowledge Management
- ◆ Software Engineering Tools
- ◆ Decision Support Systems
- ◆ Virtual Offices
- ◆ Strategic Information Systems Design, Implementation

You can now view the table of contents for each journal so it is easier to locate and purchase one specific article from the journal of your choice.

Case studies are also available through XanEdu, to start building your perfect coursepack, please visit www.xanedu.com.

For more information, contact cust@idea-group.com or 717-533-8845 ext. 10.

www.idea-group.com

IDEA GROUP INC.

Library Use Only